W0080356

Enabling Flexibility in Process-Aware
Information Systems

Manfred Reichert • Barbara Weber

Enabling Flexibility in Process-Aware Information Systems

Challenges, Methods, Technologies

 Springer

Manfred Reichert
University of Ulm
Ulm
Germany

Barbara Weber
University of Innsbruck
Innsbruck
Austria

ISBN 978-3-642-30408-8   ISBN 978-3-642-30409-5 (eBook)
DOI 10.1007/978-3-642-30409-5
Springer Heidelberg New York Dordrecht London

Library of Congress Control Number: 2012946210

ACM Computing Classification (1998): H.4, J.1

© Springer-Verlag Berlin Heidelberg 2012
This work is subject to copyright. All rights are reserved by the Publisher, whether the whole or part of
the material is concerned, specifically the rights of translation, reprinting, reuse of illustrations, recitation,
broadcasting, reproduction on microfilms or in any other physical way, and transmission or information
storage and retrieval, electronic adaptation, computer software, or by similar or dissimilar methodology
now known or hereafter developed. Exempted from this legal reservation are brief excerpts in connection
with reviews or scholarly analysis or material supplied specifically for the purpose of being entered
and executed on a computer system, for exclusive use by the purchaser of the work. Duplication of
this publication or parts thereof is permitted only under the provisions of the Copyright Law of the
Publisher's location, in its current version, and permission for use must always be obtained from Springer.
Permissions for use may be obtained through RightsLink at the Copyright Clearance Center. Violations
are liable to prosecution under the respective Copyright Law.
The use of general descriptive names, registered names, trademarks, service marks, etc. in this publication
does not imply, even in the absence of a specific statement, that such names are exempt from the relevant
protective laws and regulations and therefore free for general use.
While the advice and information in this book are believed to be true and accurate at the date of
publication, neither the authors nor the editors nor the publisher can accept any legal responsibility for
any errors or omissions that may be made. The publisher makes no warranty, express or implied, with
respect to the material contained herein.

Printed on acid-free paper

Springer is part of Springer Science+Business Media (www.springer.com)

Foreword

"Not a company exists whose management doesn't say, at least for public consumption, that it wants an organization flexible enough to adjust quickly to changing market conditions." This is how Michael Hammer and James Champy opened their best-selling book *Reengineering the Corporation*, which was first published in 1993. It was a remarkable book in many respects. Firstly, it was groundbreaking in its emphasis on business processes as primary organizational assets. Secondly, Hammer and Champy were among the first to identify information technology as the enabler to reengineer such business processes towards higher levels of organizational performance.

When you consider the two concepts these management guru's talked about, business process and information technology, you will immediately understand what this other remarkable book is about, the one you are reading right now. It is about process-aware information systems. Such information systems are aware—let's credit the technology with a certain level of consciousness—of the business processes that companies execute to a considerable level of detail. A process-aware information system gives companies ultimate control over the way they do their business; it helps them to manage the activities, people, policies, data, and other technologies that are needed to produce and deliver the products and services their clients want from them.

A legitimate question now is whether process-aware systems have helped organizations to become more flexible in the way that Hammer and Champy envisioned that they all prefer to be. For quite some time, the answer seemed to be a plain "no". I am old enough to recall the terrifying first case studies on the industrial use of workflow management systems, the earliest types of process-aware information systems. These studies painted grim pictures of people forced to dance to the tunes of Orwellian conductors (automated or otherwise). Even while the workers knew what was good for their customers, the workflow management system simply wouldn't let them do it. O my! Still, that was also the time I started implementing such systems myself. In the projects I was involved in, I certainly noted the need to allow workers to occasionally deviate from perfectly good yet standardized procedure. However, when you would think a little about it, exploit all

the features of the system—both the documented and the non-documented ones—
you would be able to find a way to create those much-needed work-arounds. Also,
the workflow management system really helped to carry out a business process more
efficiently. The story, therefore, did not seem so grim after all.

This book is about lightening up the picture entirely. Its main subject is how
the flexibility of process-aware information systems has evolved over the past
two decades towards a very high level of sophistication. The book deals with
the whole spectrum of mechanisms that we are aware of now in the Business
Process Management research field. The authors of this book, Manfred Reichert
and Barbara Weber, have played an instrumental role in the development of many
of these mechanisms and can oversee the area as no one else can. It may seem
old-fashioned to write books in a time when researchers are credited for their
papers in top journals and the funding they acquire, but I am truly grateful to
them for investing their time in this project. I think that students, researchers, and
practitioners will agree with me after they have completed reading this book. And
my message to managers that are fond of reading books like *Reengineering the
corporation* is: Use a process-aware information system and your business processes
will be as flexible as you like them to be.

Rosmalen, April 2012   Dr.ir. Hajo Reijers

Preface

The idea for writing this book emerged in 2009 when Ralf Gerstner from Springer approached us after the *Seventh International Conference on Business Process Management* (BPM'09) in Ulm with the idea of writing a book on process flexibility. There we had given a tutorial on dynamic life cycle support for flexible processes.

Since both of us have been actively collaborating in this research area for many years and have been working on a variety of aspects related to flexible business processes, we were immediately enthusiastic about the idea of writing a book about the state of the art. In addition, we saw the opportunity to present our own work in an integrated and comprehensive manner.

However, we also wanted to write a book that provides a good overview of the area as a whole and as such also covers a considerable amount of new material recently contributed by other researchers. We tried our best to provide a comprehensive, representative, and fair account of relevant work on flexible business process and we hope that we succeeded with this at least to some degree.

Writing a book like this would not have been possible without the help of many others. First of all we would like to thank Ralf Gerstner for motivating us to write a book on flexible processes and for providing guidance throughout this process.

Moreover, special thanks goes to the members of our research teams who worked with us in the last years on many of the topics described in this book and supported us with their critical feedback during the writing process. In particular, we would like to express our appreciation to Carolina Chiao, Simon Forster, Gregor Grambow, David Knuplesch, Jens Kolb, Vera Künzle, Andreas Lanz, Matthias Lohrmann, Linh Thao Ly, Jakob Pinggera, Thomas Porcham, Rüdiger Pryss, and Stefan Zugal.

Furthermore, we would like to express our gratefulness to all our colleagues with whom we had many inspiring discussions over the last couple of years when collaborating on some of the topics described in this book: Wil van der Aalst, Clara Ayora, Irene Barba, Thomas Bauer, Ralph Bobrik, Malú Castellanos, Jan Claes, Peter Dadam, Andrea Delgado, Boudewijn van Dongen, Rik Eshuis, Dirk Fahland, Diogo R. Ferreira, Kathrin Figl, Christian W. Günther, Ignacio García Rodríguez de Guzmán, Christian Haisjackl, Alena Hallerbach, Clemens Hensinger, Joachim Herbst, Andrés Jiménez Ramírez,

Martin Jurisch, Ulrich Kreher, Markus Lauer, Richard Lenz, Chen Li, Ronald Maier, Ana Karla A. de Medeiros, Jan Mendling, Mirjam Minor, Dominic Müller, Bela Mutschler, Roy Oberhauser, Mor Peleg, Ricardo Pérez-Castillo, Maja Pesic, Mario Piattini, Paul Pichler, Stanislav Pokraev, Hajo A. Reijers, Stefanie Rinderle-Ma, Francisco Ruiz, Shazia Sadiq, Helen Schonenberg, Isabella Seeber, Pnina Soffer, Lucineia Thom, Victoria Torres, Carmelo Del Valle, Irene Vanderfeesten, Matthias Weidlich, Mathias Weske, Roel Wieringa, Werner Wild, and Andreas Wombacher.

Especially, we would like to thank Stefanie Rinderle-Ma and Peter Dadam for their intense collaboration as well as for their valuable contributions to the field of process flexibility.

In addition, we would like to especially thank Pnina Soffer as well as the anonymous reviewers, who helped us very much with their valuable feedback and their very detailed comments to improve our book.

Large parts of the exercises have been developed over the last couple of years as part of our teaching activities on business process management. We would like to thank our students for their valuable feedback which helped us to continuously improve the exercises and to spot inconsistencies.

Last but not least we would like to thank Robert Courland for the invaluable support he provided when proofreading this book.

Ulm, Innsbruck   Manfred Reichert
                                                                    Barbara Weber

Contents

Acronyms

ADEPT	Application development based on encapsulated process templates
AI	Artificial intelligence
API	Application programming interface
AST	Alaska simulator toolset
BPM	Business process management
BPMN	Business process model and notation
BNF	Backus-Naur form
CBR	Case-based reasoning
CCBR	Conversational case-based reasoning
C-EPC	Configurable event-driven process chain
CHS	Case-handling system
CRG	Compliance rule graph
DBMS	Database management system
ECA	Event-condition-action
ECF	Electronic circulation folder
EJB	Enterprise Java Beans
EPC	Event-driven process chain
ECF	Electronic circulation folder
HL7	Health level 7
ISO	International organization for standardization
IT	Information technology
ITIL	Information technology infrastructure library
LTL	Linear temporal logic
LTS	Labeled transition system
MRT	Magnetic resonance tomograph
MXML	Mining extensible markup language
OCL	Object constraint language
PAIS	Process-aware information system
PMS	Process model smell
PrMS	Process management system
QoS	Quality of service

SAL	Symbolic analysis laboratory
SE	Software engineering
SLA	Service level agreement
TDM	Test-driven modeling
TDMS	Test-driven modeling suite
UML	Unified modeling language
WS-BPEL	Web service business process execution language
WSM Nets	Well-structured marking nets
YAWL	Yet another workflow language

Part I
Basic Concepts and Flexibility Issues

Chapter 1
Introduction

Abstract During the last decade process-aware information systems (PAISs) have become increasingly popular to effectively support the business processes of a company at an operational level. However, to cope with the dynamic nature of business processes, PAISs not only need to be able to deal with exceptions, change the execution of single business cases on the fly, efficiently deal with uncertainty, and cope with variability, but must also support the evolution of business processes over time. The goal of this book is to address these flexibility needs and to provide an overview of PAIS flexibility issues including challenges, methods, and technologies. This chapter discusses the scope of the book in detail, describes its intended target audiences, and presents learning objectives.

1.1 Motivation

In today's dynamic business world the success of an enterprise increasingly depends on its ability to react to changes in its environment in a quick and flexible way. Examples of such changes include regulatory adaptations (e.g., the introduction of Sarbanes–Oxley or Basel II), market evolution, changes in customer behavior, process improvement, and strategic shifts. Companies have heretofore identified business agility as a competitive advantage to address business trends like increasing product and service variability or faster time-to-market, and to ensure business IT alignment. In particular, improving the efficiency and quality of their business processes and optimizing their interactions with partners and customers have become crucial success factors for companies [232, 273, 366].

In this context, a *business process* can be defined as a set of one or more connected *activities* which collectively realize a particular *business goal* [366, 367]. Usually, a business process is linked to an *organizational structure* defining functional roles and organizational relationships. Further, a business process may involve one department, but may also cross departmental borders or even involve different organizations. Examples of business processes include insurance claim

M. Reichert and B. Weber, *Enabling Flexibility in Process-Aware Information Systems*, DOI 10.1007/978-3-642-30409-5_1, © Springer-Verlag Berlin Heidelberg 2012

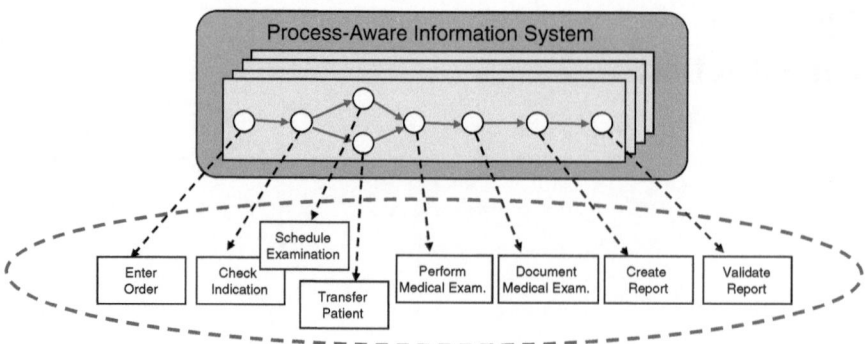

Fig. 1.1   Separation of process logic and application code

processing, order handling, personnel recruitment, product engineering, and patient treatment.

When using contemporary enterprise information systems, however, business agility is often hindered by a lack of flexibility. Often, companies choose to abandon new business initiatives rather than attempting to make modifications to their enterprise information systems. In order to improve their business processes and to manage them in a flexible manner, enterprises are increasingly interested in aligning their information systems in a process-centered way offering the right *business functions* to the right *users* at the right *point in time* along with the needed *information* and *application services* [71, 82].

Along this trend, a new generation of information systems—so-called process-aware information systems (PAISs)—has emerged [13, 24, 138, 178, 237, 349], which target at overcoming this inflexibility. Examples of PAISs include workflow management systems, case handling tools, and service orchestration engines. As opposed to data- or function-centered information systems, a PAIS separates process logic from application code and thus provides an additional architectural layer (cf. Fig. 1.1). In particular, most PAISs describe process logic explicitly in terms of a *process model* providing the schema for *process execution*. Usually, the core of the process layer is built by a *process management system*, which provides generic services for process modeling, process execution, process monitoring, and user interaction (e.g., worklist management). Furthermore, PAISs foster the splitting of monolithic applications into smaller components and services, which can then be orchestrated by the PAIS. Maintainability and traceability are significantly enhanced by this extended architecture. Changes to one layer often can be performed without affecting the other layers. For example, modifying the application service which implements a particular process step (i.e., activity) does usually not imply any change of the process layer as long as interfaces remain stable. In addition, changing the execution order of activities or adding new activities to the process model can, to a large degree, be accomplished without touching the implementation of any application service.

   Though separating process logic and application code makes PAISs more flexible in comparison to traditional information systems, this is not sufficient to meet today's need for greater system flexibility. The major reason for this is that most existing PAISs require a complete specification (i.e., process model) of a business process in advance, which is then used as the schema for process execution. However, dynamic processes demand a more agile approach recognizing the fact that in dynamic environments process models quickly become outdated and hence require closer interweaving of modeling and execution. PAISs not only need to be able to deal with exceptions, change the execution of single business cases on the fly, efficiently deal with uncertainty, and cope with variability, but must also support the evolution of business processes over time.

1.2   Goal and Intended Audience

The goal of this book is to address these flexibility needs and to provide an overview of flexibility issues in PAISs including challenges, methods, and technologies. The field of PAISs is a highly interdisciplinary area with the involvement of many different stakeholders like enterprise architects, enterprise system managers, business (process) analysts, process owners, change managers, risk managers, quality managers, software engineers, software architects, and chief technology officers. This book does not intend to cover all aspects of the field. Its focus is on technological and methodological issues, whereas managerial issues are outside its scope. Not only the involved stakeholders, but also the reasons for launching business process management (BPM) initiatives are manifold and may include process documentation, reorganization of processes, process monitoring and controlling, process improvement, process automation, quality management (e.g., ISO 9000), benchmarking, or knowledge management. The focus of this book is on the operational support for business processes using PAISs. In addition, this book puts emphasis on flexibility issues related to the different phases of the process life cycle (i.e., modeling, execution, and evolution), and it presents methods and technologies to address these challenges.
   The discussion of methods and technologies is not intended to be exhaustive, instead representative approaches will be presented. Most of the technologies described in this book are already available in open source software or commercial process management systems. Formal representations are used only where they are really necessary and helpful. To foster understandability, this book is complemented with numerous examples derived from different real-world case studies, which are partially simplified for the sake of accessibility. To further improve readability, examples are highlighted by gray boxes.
   Our primary target groups are

• Researchers, PhD students, and Master students who are working in the field of
   information systems in general and PAISs in particular. This book will help them

to better understand flexibility aspects of PAISs as well as related challenges, methods, and technologies.
• Professionals specialized in BPM who want to obtain a good understanding of flexibility challenges in BPM and their solutions (i.e., the state of the art).

Moreover, this book (or selected chapters thereof) is designed as a course book for graduate courses on BPM. To support this goal a series of exercises is provided at the end of each chapter. Teaching slides and solutions for most of the exercises are provided for teachers on the book's web site www.flexible-processes.com. Moreover, the book's companion web site provides pointers to further readings. Additional information regarding the described systems and technologies (e.g., screencasts), including download links for selected systems and screencasts, can be found on the web site as well.

This book is written to be self-contained in order to be attractive for our target groups. However, an understanding of basic concepts and principles of information systems is helpful.

1.3   Learning Objectives

This book covers challenges, methods, and technologies for addressing flexibility needs in PAISs. After completing this book, readers should

• Have a clear picture of the most relevant flexibility issues in PAISs.
• Have obtained an appreciation and understanding of the typical challenges that exist when targeting at flexible process support within information systems.
• Know the particular distinguishers concerning the flexible support of prespecified as well as loosely specified processes in all phases of the process life cycle.
• Know different paradigms for realizing flexible PAISs (e.g., prespecified processes, constraint-based processes, and data-driven processes).
• Be aware of gaps in industry needs and existing solutions for realizing flexible PAISs.
• Have obtained a better understanding of how to cope best with process changes and evolving business processes in information systems.

1.4   Outline and Organization of the Chapters

In response to the need for flexible and easily adaptable PAISs, different paradigms and technologies for realizing them have emerged. Typical representative examples discussed in this book include prespecified, constraint-based, and data-driven approaches. Using real-world cases from different application domains, this book will present a comprehensive review of the challenges that exist for flexible PAISs, and it will give detailed insights into concepts, paradigms, and technologies for realizing them. Our approach is to present real-world needs and then to deliberate on various developments from academia and industry that may address these needs, thus identifying open questions where relevant.

This book is organized in five parts. Part I starts with an introduction of fundamental PAIS concepts and establishes the context of process flexibility in the light of practical scenarios. This is followed by a discussion of the challenges, concepts, methods, and technologies around process flexibility. More precisely, we discuss flexibility requirements of both prespecified processes and loosely specified processes. In summary: Part I of this book introduces PAISs and elaborates on flexibility challenges relating to them.

Part II focuses on flexibility support for prespecified processes, the currently predominant paradigm in the field of BPM. First of all it discusses their modeling, verification, execution, adaptation, and evolution. Advanced topics covered in Part II include process modeling, process configuration, exception handling, ad hoc adaptations of running process instances, analysis of dynamic processes, process model evolution, and business process compliance along the process life cycle. Finally, realistic examples and exercises are provided for each chapter to illustrate the practical use of the different concepts and techniques.

Part III focuses on flexibility support for loosely specified processes. Unlike prespecified process models, they only partially specify the process model at build time, while decisions regarding the exact specification of certain parts are deferred to the run time. Part II introduces different decision deferral patterns for dealing with uncertainty and discusses constraint-based approaches to business process modeling and execution as well as data-driven processes. Part IV introduces existing technologies and systems for realizing a flexible PAIS. Finally, Part V summarizes the main ideas of this book and gives an outlook on advanced flexibility issues and topics.

In summary, the following topics are covered by this book:

- Challenges and requirements for flexible PAISs.
- Flexibility support for both prespecified processes and loosely specified processes.
- State-of-the-art concepts, methods, and technologies for enabling process flexibility, e.g., process configuration, exception handling, ad hoc process changes, process schema evolution, process model refactoring, and late modeling.

Chapter 2
Process-Aware Information Systems

Abstract The success of commercial enterprises increasingly depends on their ability to flexibly and quickly react to changes in their environment. Businesses are therefore interested in improving the efficiency and quality of their business processes and in aligning their information systems in a process-centered way. This chapter deals with basic concepts related to business process automation and process-aware information systems (PAISs). Characteristic properties, perspectives, and components of a PAIS are presented based on real-world process scenarios.

2.1 Introduction

As discussed in Chap. 1, businesses are increasingly interested in improving the quality and efficiency of their processes, and in aligning their information systems in a process-centered way; i.e., to offer the right *business functions* at the right *time* to the right *users* along with the *information* and the *application services* (e.g., user forms) for them. In this context, process-aware information systems (PAISs) have emerged to provide a more dynamic and flexible support for business processes [82].

To provide additional value for the business, however, any automation of its processes through PAISs should be preceded by process re-engineering and optimization efforts [130, 273]; i.e., business processes have to be (re-)designed to meet organizational goals in an economic and efficient manner. Frequent goals pursued in this context are shortening process cycle times, reducing process costs, increasing customer satisfaction by utilizing available resources in an efficient and effective manner, and decreasing error rates.

To discuss alternative process designs with stakeholders and to evaluate the designed processes in respect to these goals, process knowledge must be first captured in *business process models*. These models describe business processes at a rather high level of abstraction and serve as a basis for process analysis, simulation, and visualization. More precisely, a business process model should comprise all the activities of a business process and their attributes (e.g., cost and time) as well

M. Reichert and B. Weber, *Enabling Flexibility in Process-Aware Information Systems*,   9
DOI 10.1007/978-3-642-30409-5_2, © Springer-Verlag Berlin Heidelberg 2012

as the control and data flow between the activities. The activities in a business process, in turn, may be *manual* ones without the potential to be automated and hence lying outside the scope of a PAIS, or *system-supported* ones requiring human or machine resources for their execution [367]. Hence, a business process model does not always correspond to the part of the business process automated in a PAIS.

Accordingly, a distinction has to be made between business process models on one hand, and their executable counterparts (also denoted as *executable process models* or *workflow models*) on the other [240]. The latter can realize the automation of business processes and thus, in whole or part, the implementation of their models. When interpreting an executable process model, documents, data objects, or activities are passed from one process participant to another according to predefined procedural rules [367].

Modern PAISs describe process logic explicitly in terms of such executable process models which provide the schema for process enactment. This book focuses on executable process models and their flexible support through PAISs, whereas issues related to the modeling, analysis, and redesign of business processes are outside the scope of this book. When realizing a PAIS based on executable process models, however, one has to bear in mind that there is a variety of processes showing different characteristics and needs. On one hand, there exist well-structured and highly repetitive processes whose behavior can be fully *prespecified*. On the other hand, many processes are knowledge-intensive and highly dynamic. Typically, the latter cannot be fully prespecified, but require *loosely specified* process models. Using real-world process scenarios, this chapter gives insights into these different process categories. Furthermore, it presents properties, perspectives, and components of PAISs. Thereby, it abstracts from the subtle differences that exist between the different PAIS-enabling technologies and process modeling paradigms, focusing instead on core features.

The chapter is organized as follows: Section 2.2 presents examples of prespecified and repetitive processes, and discusses their basic properties, while Sect. 2.3 introduces examples of knowledge-intensive and dynamic processes to illustrate the broad spectrum of business processes to be supported by PAISs. Following this, Sect. 2.4 deals with the different perspectives on a PAIS, and Sect. 2.5 presents its build- and run-time components. Section 2.6 concludes this chapter with a short summary.

2.2 Prespecified and Repetitive Processes

This section deals with repetitive business processes whose logic is known *prior* to their execution and can therefore be prespecified in process models [178]. After emphasizing the need for the IT support of business processes, we provide two realistic examples of prespecified processes from the health care domain.

2.2.1 Motivation

To understand why IT support for repetitive business processes is needed, we first describe a medical scenario (cf. Example 2.1).

Example 2.1 (Need for Supporting Prespecified Processes). The work of a hospital's medical staff is significantly burdened by organizational tasks [172]. Medical procedures (e.g., lab tests and diagnostic imaging) have to be planned and prepared, appointments with different service providers (e.g., cardiology or radiology) scheduled, lab specimens or the patients themselves transported, visits of physicians from other departments arranged, and medical reports written, transmitted, and evaluated. Thus, cooperation between the medical staffs of different departments is a repetitive, but crucial task. Still, in many hospitals such organizational tasks have to be coordinated manually by staff members requiring, for example, time-consuming phone calls and documentation steps. In practice, this often leads to organizational problems and to high administrative loads for staff members resulting in numerous errors and undesired delays. Patients may have to wait because resources (e.g., physicians, rooms, technical equipment) are not available. Medical procedures may be impossible to perform if information is missing, or preparatory work is omitted, postponed, canceled, or requires latency time. Previously made appointments may then have to be rescheduled, again resulting in phone calls and a loss of time. Moreover, insufficient communication and missing process information are among the major factors contributing to adverse events in a medical environment (e.g., complications due to incorrect treatment). For these reasons hospital stays are often longer than required, and costs or invasive treatments unnecessarily high.

From this scenario, it becomes clear why the demand for effective IT support of repetitive processes for businesses is growing, especially in hospitals. In this context, a PAIS can foster the collaboration and communication among staff members and contribute reducing the number of errors by selectively providing accurate and timely information to process participants. To further illustrate this, Sect. 2.2.2 presents two examples of processes that are relevant in the context of the scenario described in Example 2.1.

2.2.2   Examples of Prespecified Processes

This section introduces two real-world examples of prespecified processes from the health care domain [172, 267]. The first one deals with medical order entries and the respective reports generated by them (cf. Example 2.2). This process is characteristic for many hospitals and enables the coordination of interdepartmental communication between a ward and a radiology department.

Example 2.2 (Medical Order Entry and Result Reporting). Consider Fig. 2.1. It shows the process of handling a medical order between a ward and the radiology department. First, the medical order is placed by the ward's nurse or a physician; this is accomplished by performing consecutively activities *Prepare Order* and *Enter Order*. Following this, the order is sent to the radiology department. When receiving the order, this department checks the medical indication to decide whether or not the order can be accepted (activity *Check Indication*). Depending on the outcome of this activity, either the order is rejected (activity *Reject Order*) or the requested X-ray is scheduled (activity *Schedule X-rays*). In both cases, the ward is informed accordingly. If the order is rejected, the process will be completed. Otherwise, at the scheduled date, the patient is sent to the radiology department (activity *Transfer Patient*), where the X-rays are performed by a radiographer (activity *Perform X-rays*), and the resulting images are diagnosed by the radiologist in the examination room (activity *Diagnose Images*). Afterward the radiology report is created (activity *Create Report*) and its validity is checked (*Check Validity*). If required, iterations for corrections may be performed before a senior radiologist validates the report (*Validate Report*). The final report is then printed (*Print Report*) and signed (*Sign Printed Report*), before it is sent to the ward. When the ward receives the report (*Receive Report*) the process is completed.

The *prespecified process model* from Fig. 2.1 reflects the activities to be performed and the control flow between them. For example, the process model comprises the two activities *Prepare Order* and *Enter Order* as well as the precedence relation between them (represented by the arc linking these two activities). The latter indicates that activity *Prepare Order* has to be completed before activity *Enter Order* may be started. Furthermore, the process model contains alternative execution paths; e.g., after completing activity *Check Indication* either *Reject Order* or *Schedule X-rays* is performed. Finally, the depicted process model also refers to different organizational units, i.e., a *ward* and the *radiology department*.

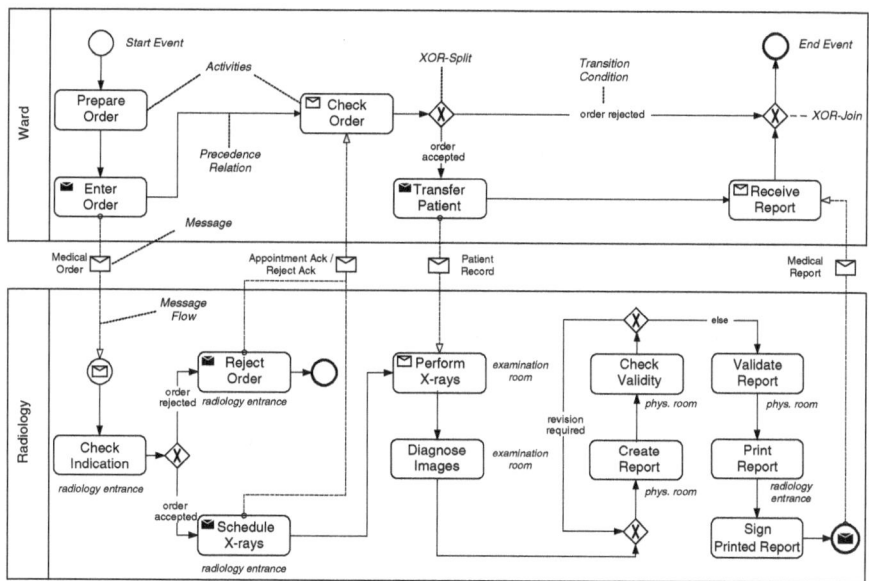

Fig. 2.1 Process for medical order handling and result reporting

Our second process example deals with laparoscopic surgery in a woman's hospital (cf. Example 2.3). This process is highly repetitive and provides routine medical services like cyst removal, dilation, or curettage. Furthermore, it is well structured and involves three organizational units: the outpatient department, the surgical ward, and the surgical suite.

Example 2.3 (Planning and Performing a Laparoscopic Surgery). Consider the prespecified process from Fig. 2.2. It starts with the referral of a patient to the hospital. The patient is first admitted to the outpatient department (1) where a medical checkup is performed (2), a medical examination takes place (3), and then anesthesia and its attending risks are discussed with the patient (4 and 5). Following this, a decision is made (6). If there are contraindications, a discharge letter will be written (7) and the process is completed. Otherwise a date for the surgery is scheduled (8), before the patient may return home. Before the day of the surgery, a physician from the surgical ward to which the patient will be admitted checks the patient's medical record (9). On the scheduled date, the patient is admitted to the surgical ward (10), prepared for the surgery (11), and sent to the surgical suite (12), where the surgery is then performed (13). Afterward, the patient is transferred back to the surgical ward (14), where postsurgical care is provided (15). Usually, the patient is discharged on the same day (18). Meanwhile, the doctor from the surgical

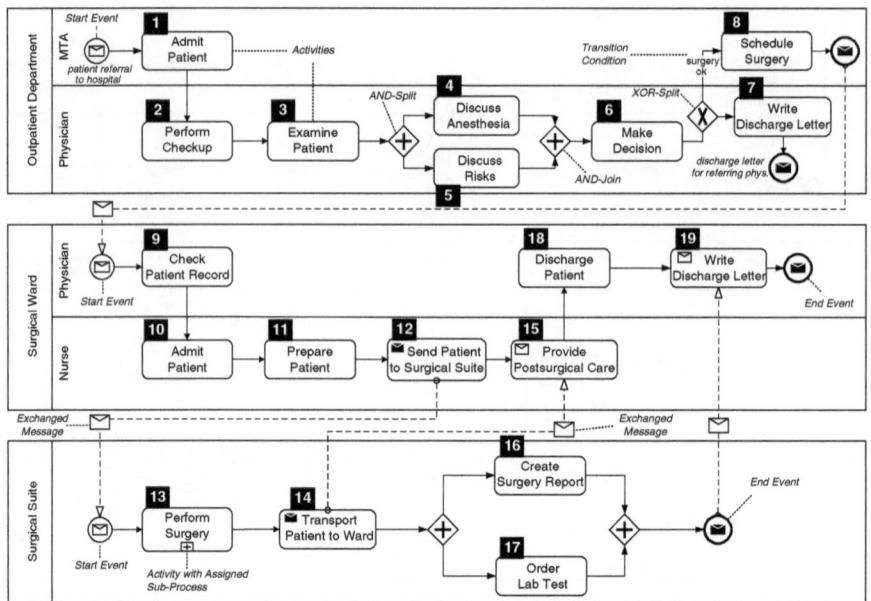

Fig. 2.2 Prespecified process for planning and performing a Laparoscopic surgery

suite orders a lab test (17) and creates a surgery report (16). Based on this, a discharge letter is created (19) and sent to the physician who referred the patient to the hospital.

The prespecified process model from Fig. 2.2 starts with an incoming message on the referral of a patient and ends with an outgoing message referring to the discharge letter. Furthermore, the process model includes activities that may be executed in parallel. For example, this applies to activities *Create Surgery Report (16)* and *Order Lab Test (17)*. Finally, for each human activity, the prespecified process model contains information about the potential actors performing this activity. In our example, this is accomplished by referring to entities from the *organizational model* of the hospital; e.g., activity *Examine Patient (3)* may be performed by any user designated *Physician* who belongs to the *Outpatient Department*.

2.2.3   Discussion

Processes as illustrated in Examples 2.2 and 2.3 can be found in every hospital. Particularly, they are highly repetitive and represent the organizational knowledge necessary to coordinate daily tasks among staff members and across organizational units. Although the described processes are long-running (up to several days, weeks, or months), they are well structured; i.e., process logic is known *prior* to the process execution and thus can be prespecified in *process models* like the ones depicted in Figs. 2.1 and 2.2. Generally, such a *prespecified process model* captures the activities to be executed, their control and data flow, the organizational entities performing the activities, and the data objects and documents accessed by them. Note that at this stage, it is not important to fully understand the notation used in Figs. 2.1 and 2.2 (cf. Chap. 4), but to recognize that there are existing processes whose logic is usually known prior to their execution and thus can be prespecified in the respective process models. Prespecified processes and their support, along the different phases of the process life cycle, will be discussed in *Part II (Flexibility Support for Prespecified Processes)* of the book, i.e., in Chaps. 4–10.

2.3   Knowledge-Intensive Processes

2.3.1   Motivation

In practice, many business processes are *knowledge-intensive* and highly *dynamic*; i.e., the process participants decide on the activities to be executed as well as their order. Typically, respective processes cannot be fully prespecified like the ones described in the previous section. Example 2.4 emphasizes this in a clinical scenario.

Example 2.4 (Complex Patient Treatment Scenario).   When being confronted with a complex patient treatment case, physicians have to dynamically decide which examinations or therapies are necessary (e.g., taking costs and invasiveness into account) or even dangerous due to contraindications and treatment-typical problems. Further, many procedures require a preparation; e.g., before a surgery can take place a patient has to undergo preliminary examinations, either of which requires additional preparation or excludes other interventions. While some of them are known in advance, others have to be scheduled dynamically. Generally, decisions about the next process steps have to be made during treatment by interpreting patient-specific data according to medical knowledge and by considering the current state of the patient. It is generally agreed that such knowledge-intensive processes cannot be fully automated [172]; i.e., physicians should not blindly obey any arbitrary step-by-step treatment plan (i.e., prespecified process model), but need to provide the best possible treatment for their patients after taking into account the given situation.

Supporting such complex scenarios requires loosely specified processes (e.g., medical guidelines providing assistance in the context of a particular medical problem) as the one described in Example 2.5. Furthermore, as will be shown in Example 2.6, in many scenarios it is even not possible to straightjacket a process into a set of activities, but to explicitly consider the role of business data as a driver for flexible process coordination.

2.3.2   Examples of Knowledge-Intensive Processes

We introduce two examples of knowledge-intensive processes. While the first one can be directly related to the scenario from Example 2.4 and corresponds to a loosely specified process, the second example emphasizes the role of data as a driver for process execution.

2.3.2.1   Loosely Specified Processes

Example 2.5 deals with a simplified medical guideline we adopted from [19]. It describes a constraint-based process of treating a patient admitted to the emergency room of a hospital suspected of having a fracture (cf. Fig. 2.3).

Example 2.5 (Fracture Treatment Process). Consider Fig. 2.3. Before any treatment may be chosen, activity *Examine Patient* has to be performed by a physician (constraint *init*). If required, additional medical diagnosis is done by executing activity *Perform X-rays*. Depending on the presence and type of fracture, four different treatments exist: *Prescribe Sling*, *Prescribe Fixation*, *Perform Surgery*, and *Apply Cast*. Except for *Apply Cast* and *Prescribe Fixation*, which are mutually exclusive (constraint *not co-existent*), the treatments can be applied in any combination and each patient receives at least one of them (*1-of-4 constraint*). Activity *Perform X-rays* is not required if the specialist diagnoses the absence of a fracture when performing activity *Examine Patient*. If activity *Perform X-rays* is omitted, only the treatment *Prescribe Sling* may be applied. All other treatments require *Perform X-rays* as preceding activity in order to rule out the presence of a fracture, or to decide how to treat it (constraint *precedence*). Simple fractures can be treated just by performing activity *Apply Cast*. For unstable fractures, in turn, activity *Prescribe Fixation* may be preferred over activity *Apply Cast*. When performing activity *Perform Surgery*, the physician is further advised to (optionally) execute activity *Prescribe Rehabilitation* afterward

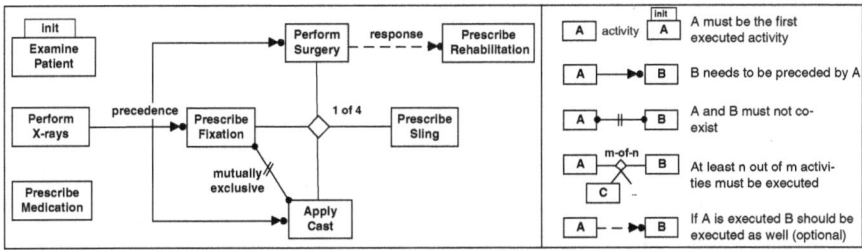

Fig. 2.3 Example of a constraint-based process (adopted from [19])

(optional constraint *response*). Moreover, the physician may execute activity *Prescribe Medication* (e.g., pain killers or anticoagulants) at any stage of the treatment. Note that activities *Examine Patient* and *Perform X-rays* may be also performed during treatment.

Figure 2.3 depicts the *loosely specified process model* corresponding to Example 2.5 when using a *constraint-based process modeling* approach. The boxes represent *activities* and the relations between them are different kinds of *constraints* for executing these activities. The depicted model contains *mandatory constraints* (solid lines) as well as one *optional constraint* (dashed line). As opposed to fully prespecified process models (cf. Figs. 2.1 and 2.2) that describe *how* things have to be done, constraint-based process models (cf. Fig. 2.3) only focus on the logic that governs the interplay of actions in the process by describing the *activities* that can be performed and those *constraints* prohibiting undesired behavior.

Note that in more complex cases, the physician in charge may have to choose from dozens or even hundreds of activities. While some of them may be executed any number of times and at any point in time during the treatment process, for others a number of constraints have to be obeyed; e.g., certain activities may have to be preceded or succeeded by other activities or may even exclude certain activities. Moreover, depending on the particular patient and his medical problems, certain activities might be contraindicated and should therefore not be chosen. The challenge is to provide PAIS support for such knowledge-intensive processes and to seamlessly integrate the described constraints within the physician's work practice. Generally, the structure of knowledge-intensive processes strongly depends on user decisions made during process execution; i.e., it *dynamically* evolves.

Loosely specified processes will be discussed in *Part III (Flexibility Support for Loosely Specified Processes)* of the book, i.e., in Chaps. 11–12.

2.3.2.2 Data-Driven Processes

Both prespecified and loosely specified processes are *activity-centric*; i.e., they are based on a set of activities that may be performed during process execution. In practice, however, many knowledge-intensive and dynamic processes exist that cannot be straightjacketed into a set of activities [24, 159]. Characteristic of these processes is the role of business data acting as a driver for process execution and coordination. Capturing the logic of respective processes in activity-centric process models like the ones depicted in Figs. 2.1–2.3, therefore, would lead to a "contradiction between the way processes can be modeled and preferred work practice" [315].

In the area of human resource management, for instance, recruitment constitutes an example of a knowledge-intensive, data-driven process [156, 160]. It starts with the human resource department receiving recruitment requisitions from a department of the organization, followed by steps like preparing the job description, identifying the employees to be involved (e.g., advertising and interviewing activities), finding the best candidates among the applicants, arranging and conducting the interviews with the selected candidates, and making the final decision. Example 2.6, which we adopted from [160], describes such a recruitment process.

Example 2.6 (Recruitment Process). Applicants may apply for *job vacancies* via an Internet form. The overall process goal is to decide which applicant shall get the job. Before an applicant can send her *application* to the respective company, specific information (e.g., name, e-mail address, birthday, residence) has to be provided. Once the *application* has been submitted, the responsible officer in the human resource department is notified. Since many applicants may apply for a *vacancy*, usually, a number of various personnel officers might be handling the *applications*. If an *application* is ineligible, the applicant is immediately rejected. Otherwise, personnel officers may request internal *reviews* for each applicant. Depending on the respective divisions of the company involved, the concrete number of *reviews* may vary from *application* to *application*.

Corresponding *review* forms have to be filled in by employees from the various company divisions before a stated deadline. Employees may either decline or accept performing the requested *review*. In the former case, they must provide a reason; otherwise, they propose how to proceed; i.e., they indicate whether the applicant shall be invited for an *interview* or be rejected. In the former case, an additional appraisal is needed. After the employee has filled in the *review* form, she submits it to the personnel officer. In the meanwhile, additional *applications* may have arrived; i.e., different *reviews* may be requested or submitted at different points in time. In this context, the personnel officer may flag already evaluated *reviews*. The processing

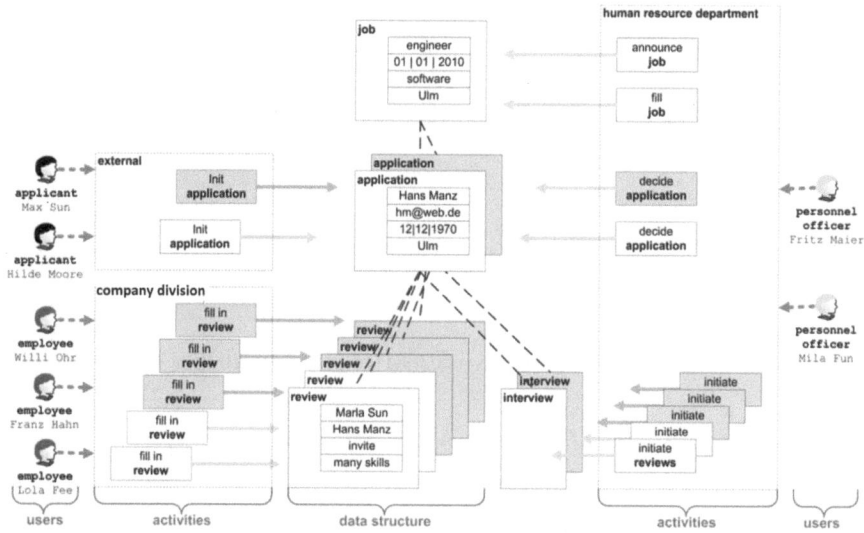

Fig. 2.4 Example of a data-driven process (adopted from [160])

of the *application* proceeds while corresponding *reviews* are created; e.g., the personnel officer may check the CV and study the cover letter of the *application*. Based on the incoming *reviews* he makes a decision about the *application* or initiates further steps (e.g., *interviews* or additional *reviews*). Finally, he does not have to wait for the arrival of all *reviews*; e.g., if a particular employee suggests hiring the applicant. An illustration of this example is provided by Fig. 2.4.

Example 2.6 describes a scenario in which *business data* acts as a driver for process execution; i.e., *objects* (e.g., applications and reviews), *object attributes*, and *object relations* play a fundamental role for process execution. Therefore, a tight synchronization between the object and process state is required; i.e., it is no longer sufficient to only model processes in terms of black-box activities. Instead, their execution is related to *objects* and *object states* [158]. Unlike activity-centric approaches, enabling a particular process step does not directly depend on the completion of preceding process steps, but rather the changes of certain object attribute values.

Data-driven processes will be discussed in *Part IV (User- and Data-Driven Processes)* of the book, i.e., in Chaps. 13–14.

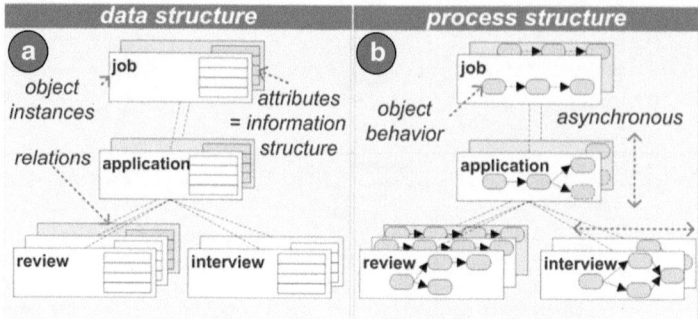

Fig. 2.5 Relation between data and process modeling (adopted from [160])

2.3.3 Discussion

Typically, knowledge-intensive processes are very dynamic. In particular, the concrete activities to be performed, as well as their exact course, may depend on decisions made by process participants during process execution; i.e., knowledge-intensive processes cannot be completely prespecified. Instead, more maneuvering room for process participants and looseness of process execution are required. In certain cases this can be achieved by using constraint-based process models focusing on *what* shall be done by describing the activities that may be performed as well as related constraints prohibiting undesired process behavior.

As further shown, there are scenarios in which an activity-centric approach is not suitable at all, but a tighter integration of process and data is required. In accordance to data models comprising object types and object relations (cf. Fig. 2.5a), the modeling and execution of processes have to be based on two levels of granularity: *object behavior* and *object interactions* (cf. Fig. 2.5b).

The scenarios presented in Examples 2.2–2.6 indicate that a variety of business processes exist for which PAIS support is needed. Effective IT support for this wide spectrum of business processes necessitates different approaches considering the specific properties of prespecified, loosely specified, and data-driven processes. Later chapters of this book will introduce dedicated approaches supporting processes of the different categories in a flexible manner. For the remainder of this chapter, however, we abstract from the subtle differences existing between the these process support paradigms and focus on basic commonalities and notions of PAISs.

2.4 Perspectives on a PAIS

Generally, different perspectives on a PAIS can be taken (see [138] for a corresponding framework). For example, relevant perspectives include function, behavior, information, organization, operation, and time. As illustrated by Fig. 2.6, operational

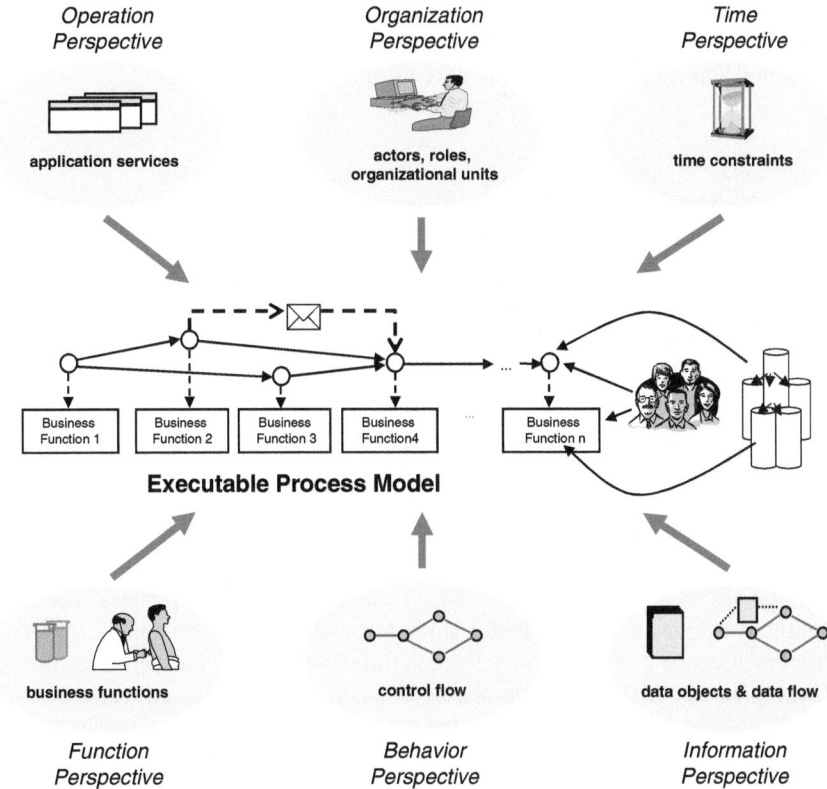

Fig. 2.6 Perspectives in a PAIS

support of these perspectives and their integration with executable process models are needed in order to offer the right business functions at the right time and to the right users along with the information and the application services needed. In the following, the different perspectives are presented in detail.

2.4.1   Function Perspective

The *function perspective* covers the functional building blocks from which activity-centric process models can be composed; i.e., *atomic activities* representing elementary business functions as well as *complex activities* representing subprocess models. To be more precise, an atomic activity constitutes the smallest unit of work, i.e., a description of a business function that forms one logical step within an executable process model. Usually, atomic activities require human or machine resources for their execution (cf. Example 2.7). In the former case, the activity is allocated to process participants during process execution. In the latter case, the activity is handled by the PAIS in an automated way by directly invoking an associated application service without requiring any user interaction.

Example 2.7 (Atomic Activity). Consider the prespecified process model from Fig. 2.2. *Perform Checkup* constitutes an atomic activity performed by a user with the role *Physician*, whereas the activity *Provide Postsurgical Care* has to be performed by a user with the role *Nurse*.

Activity *Print Report* from Fig. 2.1, in turn, constitutes an example of an atomic activity that can be handled in an automated way.

A *complex activity*, in turn, represents a step in a process model referring to a *subprocess model*. This signifies that the subprocess model implements the activity. Every time a complex activity gets enabled during process execution, its corresponding subprocess model is executed. Generally, a subprocess is described by its own process model and may have both input and output data containers to pass data between it and the subordinate process. Basically, subprocesses constitute a powerful concept for describing the common parts of different process models and so for enabling their reuse. Furthermore, the use of complex activities allows process designers to hierarchically structure the overall process (e.g., limit the number of activities contained in a (sub)process model).

Example 2.8 (Complex Activity). Consider again the prespecified process model from Fig. 2.2: *Perform Surgery* constitutes a complex activity which refers to a subprocess that aggregates a number of related activities not depicted in Fig. 2.2 (e.g., *Prepare Surgical Suite, Check Patient Record*, and *Perform Surgical Intervention*).

2.4.2   Behavior Perspective

The *behavior perspective* captures the *dynamic behavior* of an executable process model. For example, in activity-centric process models this corresponds to the *control flow* between the process activities. A control flow schema includes information about the order of the activities or the constraints for their execution. As we will see in later chapters of this book, depending on the process modeling language used and its underlying paradigm (prespecified, loosely specified, or data-driven process models), major differences can exist regarding the specification of the behavior perspective.

Example 2.9 (Behavior Perspective: Prespecified Process Models). Consider Fig. 2.2. Among others, it shows the behavior perspective of a prespecified process model. First, the depicted model contains activity sequences; e.g., activity *Admit Patient* (10) is followed by *Prepare Patient* (11), which, in turn, is followed by *Send Patient to Surgical Suite* (12). Second, the process model contains parallel splits of the control flow; e.g., *Create Surgery Report* (16) and *Order Lab Test* (17) may be performed in parallel. As another example, consider the process model from Fig. 2.1 that contains conditional branchings; e.g., either activity *Schedule X-rays* or *Reject Order* may be executed. Furthermore, this process model contains a loop structure embedding the two activities *Create Report* and *Check Validity*; i.e., these two activities may be repeated if a revision is required.

Existing languages for defining prespecified process models offer a variety of control flow elements [142], e.g., for defining sequential, conditional, parallel, and iterative activity executions. Chapter 4 presents these and other *control flow patterns* for prespecified process models and discusses how they can enable *flexibility-by-design*.

Prespecified process models prescribe how, and in which order, the activities of a process have to be executed. Opposed to this, the behavior of a constraint-based process model allows for loosely specified processes, and rather describes *what* shall be done by defining a set of activities and a set of constraints prohibiting undesired behavior [19, 243].

Example 2.10 (Behavior Perspective: Loosely specified Process Models). The constraint-based process model from Fig. 2.3 comprises activities *Examine Patient, Prescribe Medication, Perform X-rays, Prescribe Sling, Prescribe Fixation, Perform Surgery, Apply Cast,* and *Prescribe Rehabilitation*. Moreover, this process model comprises several constraints prohibiting undesired execution behavior. For example, each patient gets at least one out of four treatments (i.e., *Prescribe Sling, Prescribe Fixation, Perform Surgery*, or *Apply Cast*). Furthermore, activities *Apply Cast* and *Prescribe Fixation* are mutually exclusive. Finally, activity *Perform X-rays* needs to be executed before any treatment (except *Prescribe Sling*) may take place.

Note that Example 2.10 refers to a constraint-based process model. Generally, loosely specified processes may be partly prespecified, but contain unspecified parts which are detailed by end-users during process execution (cf. Chap. 11).

As discussed in the context of Example 2.6, there are processes which cannot be straightjacketed into activities. Instead, a tight integration of process and data is needed. In accordance to a data model comprising object types and object relations, the modeling and execution of processes can be based on two levels of granularity: *object behavior* and *object interactions*. First, *object behavior* determines in which order and by whom object attributes may be read or written, and what the valid attribute settings are. To achieve this end, a set of states may be defined for each data object type, each of them postulating the specific object attribute values to be set. More precisely, a state can be expressed in terms of a data condition referring to a number of attributes of the object type. The second level of process granularity concerns the *object interactions* between the instances of the same or of different object types. Note that whether the processing of a particular object instance may proceed also depends on the states of other object instances processed in parallel.

Example 2.11 (Behavior Perspective: Data-Driven Processes). We refer to the recruitment process from Example 2.6.

Object Behavior. Consider object type *Review* and its attributes (cf. Fig. 2.7a), the abstract states of this object type (cf. Fig. 2.7b), and its behavior expressed in terms of a state diagram (cf. Fig. 2.7c). The latter restricts possible state transitions; i.e., for each reachable state, possible successor states are defined. More precisely, a *review* must be first initiated by a *personnel officer*. The employee may then either decline or accept performing the *review*. In the latter case, he submits the review back to the personnel officer. Furthermore, states are linked to object attributes; i.e., once a state is entered, it may only be left if certain attribute values are set. For example, state *initiated* may only be left if values are assigned to attributes *applications* and *employee*.

Object Interactions. The behavior perspective of data-driven processes not only deals with the behavior of single objects, but also considers the interactions between them. Consider the scenario from Fig. 2.4. Assume that a *personnel officer* announces a *job*. Following this, *applicants* may submit their *applications*. After receiving an *application*, the *personnel officer* requests internal *reviews* for it. If an *employee* acting as referee proposes to invite the *applicant* to come in, the *personnel officer* will conduct an *interview*. Based on the results of *reviews* and *interviews*, the *personnel officer* makes a decision about the *application*. Finally, in the case of acceptance the *applicant* is hired. Obviously, whether one may continue with the processing of a particular object depends on the states of other objects as well (see Chap. 14 for details).

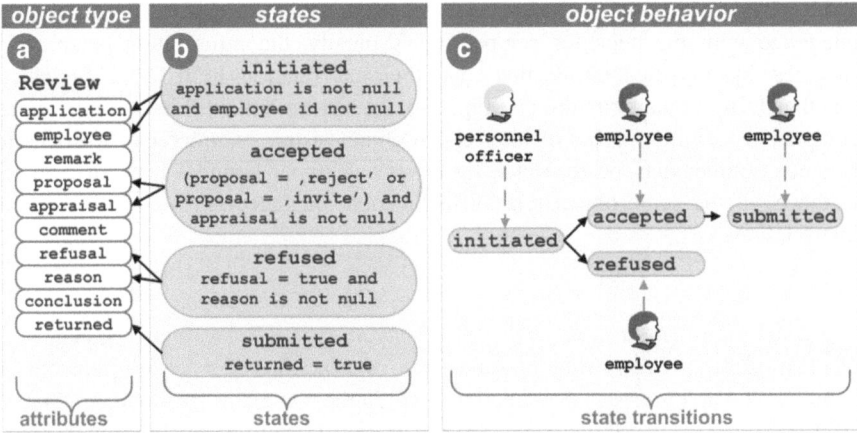

Fig. 2.7 Object behavior

2.4.3   Information Perspective

In activity-centric process models (i.e., prespecified or constraint-based process models), the *information perspective* usually comprises a set of *data objects* as well as the *data flow* between the activities. The latter describes which activities may read or write which data objects (including data mappings and data type conversions where required) [310]. Generally, in activity-centric PAISs, a distinction is made between *application data*, *process-relevant data*, and *process control data* [367]. *Application data* is specific to a particular application and is usually managed by the application services invoked in the context of an activity execution (i.e., it is outside the control of the PAIS). *Process-relevant data*, in turn, is used by the PAIS to evaluate state transitions within process instances, i.e., to decide which execution paths shall next be taken at respective split nodes. Finally, *process control data* comprises information about the current state of a process as well as its execution history.

Example 2.12 (Information Perspective: Activity-centric Processes). Consider the prespecified process model from Fig. 2.1. Its information perspective includes data objects (and exchanged messages respectively) like *Medical Order* and *Medical Report*. Usually, these objects are stored as application data in an application system, while the generic process support services of the PAIS only refer to them via object identifiers. An example of process-relevant data needed for evaluating transition conditions is the *order status* indicating whether an order is accepted. Finally, when executing a process instance, respective control data (e.g., the time at which activities are started or completed) is logged.

In data-driven process models, in turn, the information perspective is tightly integrated with the behavior perspective. Typically, the information perspective captures object types, their attributes, and their interrelations [156, 158, 225], which together form a data structure (cf. Fig. 2.4). At run-time the different object types comprise a varying number of interrelated object instances, whereby the concrete instance number may be restricted by lower and upper bounds. Typically, object instances of the same object type differ in their attribute values as well as their interrelations.

Example 2.13 (Information Perspective: Data-driven Processes). An example illustrating the information perspective of a data-driven process is depicted in Fig. 2.4 and has been explained in detail in the context of Example 2.6. For instance, for a particular *application* only two *reviews* might be requested, while for others three *reviews* are initiated.

2.4.4 Organization Perspective

The *organization perspective* deals with the assignment of human activities to organizational resources. To enable such an assignment, a process model usually contains references to an organizational model [298]. An organizational model, in turn, captures entities like *actors*, *roles*, or *organizational units* as well as their relationships (e.g., *is-manager* or *is sub-ordinate*). Furthermore, it may incorporate a variety of attributes associated with those entities (e.g., skill or role). Typically, an organizational model incorporates concepts such as hierarchy, authority, and substitution as well as attributes associated with organizational roles. The latter refer to a group of actors exhibiting a specific set of attributes, qualifications, or skills. Simply speaking, any actor having the role required by a particular activity may perform this activity. Example 2.14 illustrates the organization perspective.

Example 2.14 (Organization Perspective: Activity-centric Processes). Consider the process depicted in Fig. 2.2. It involves different organizational units (i.e., outpatient department, surgical ward, and surgical suite) as well as different user groups. For example, activities *Perform Checkup* and *Examine Patient* need to be carried out by a staff member of the *Outpatient Department* and possessing the role *Physician*. Further, there might be additional constraints concerning the execution of single activities; e.g., it might be required that the same physician who performs the medical checkup should also examine the patient; i.e., the concrete assignment of an actor to an activity at run-time may depend on the process execution history. Generally, information on user roles and organizational units is captured in the organizational model of the hospital.

Regarding data-driven processes, forms are usually used to enable access to selected attributes of an object instance (cf. Example 2.15).

Example 2.15 (Organization Perspective: Data-driven Process Models). Consider the scenario from Example 2.6. Here, a *review* form has to be filled by *employees* from various *company divisions*. Furthermore, undesired updates of these attribute values have to be prevented after reaching certain states; e.g., after an *employee* from a company division has submitted her *review*, she is no longer allowed to change the value of attribute *recommendation*.

2.4.5 Operation Perspective

The *operation perspective* of a PAIS that is based on activity-centric process models (i.e., prespecified or constraint-based process models) covers the implementation of the process activities; i.e., the business functions to be performed when executing these activities. Many PAISs treat activity implementations as a *black-box*; i.e., they coordinate the sequence of activities independent from their implementation [178]. More precisely, the application service invoked in the context of an activity expects that its input parameters are provided upon invocation by the run-time environment of the PAIS; then the service only has to take care that correct values for its output parameters are provided (cf. Fig. 2.8).

The application service linked to a particular activity may either be implemented from scratch or be reused from a service repository. Generally, a PAIS should be able to invoke arbitrary application services (e.g., Web Services, EJB Components, Office Applications) in the context of an activity execution. This heterogeneity, in turn, should be hidden from application developers, which necessitates appropriate service abstraction as well as service invocation mechanisms. As examples, consider an *Enterprise Service Bus* for invoking web services or an *Application Server* supporting EJB components.

Regarding Examples 2.2 and 2.3, most human activities can be implemented in terms of electronic forms. In addition, several connectors for integrating legacy applications (e.g., to document a surgery or access the electronic patient records in a

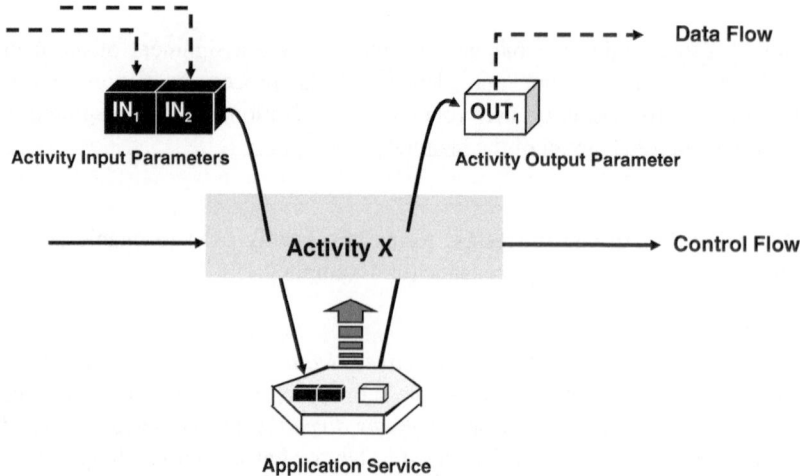

Fig. 2.8 Passing data between a PAIS and an invoked application service

hospital information system) are required. Generally, the IT support of prespecified processes is related to *enterprise application integration* [203] as illustrated by Example 2.16 (for more details on this topic we refer to [34]).

Example 2.16 (Hospital Application Integration). The architecture of a typical hospital information system is characterized by many different departmental systems that have usually been optimized for the support of different categories of business functions (i.e., services provided by different medical disciplines like radiology, cardiology, or pathology), but not for the support of cross-departmental business processes. The need to consolidate the data produced by these ancillary systems with a global (patient-centered) view and to support the cross-departmental processes has been a prime mover in the development of standards for data and message interchange in health care, as well as the enactment of similar standards in other application domains. These standards also play an important role, not only when cross-departmental processes are supported, but cross-organizational ones as well. Today, HL7 is the leading standard for systems integration in health care and may be also used to integrate health care application services with clinical PAISs [172].

In data-driven process models, the operation perspective is usually represented by *user forms* [24, 158]. When executing an electronic form related to a data-driven process, attributes of the corresponding object instance may be read, written, or updated using the respective form (e.g., the form an applicant may use for entering his application data). Generally, forms provide *input fields* (e.g., text-fields or check-boxes) for writing and *data fields* for reading selected attribute values of object instances, depending upon the object state and the process state.

2.4.6 Time Perspective

The *time perspective* captures temporal constraints that need to be obeyed during process execution. For example, consider an *activity deadline*; i.e., a time-based scheduling constraint requiring that a particular activity has to be completed by a certain date (i.e., the *activity deadline*). Typically, such a deadline is dynamically set during process execution. Generally, a PAIS should take care that activity deadlines are met or—if a deadline expires—that appropriate *escalation* and *notification* procedures are triggered (cf. Chap. 6); e.g., reminding a process participant to work on a particular activity or informing a process owner about the expiration of the deadline [21].

Note that in actual practice, many other temporal constraints exist (see [170] for a representative collection). For example, the *time patterns* described in [170] allow specifying activity durations as well as time lags between activities or—more generally—between process events (e.g. milestones). Furthermore, there exist patterns for expressing temporal constraints in connection with recurrent activities (e.g., cyclic flows and periodicity). Since the focus of this book is not on the time perspective, we will omit further details and instead refer interested readers to [170].

Example 2.17 (Time Perspective).

- In the context of Examples 2.2 and 2.3, a number of existing temporal constraints have not yet been touched upon; e.g., a surgery is usually scheduled for a particular date. Furthermore, a patient record has to be checked at least 1 day before the scheduled surgery takes place (minimum time distance). Finally, a checkup of a patient should not take longer than 30 min (activity duration).
- Regarding the data-driven process illustrated in Example 2.6, applications for a particular job vacancy have to be submitted by a certain date (deadline). Furthermore, a requested review has yet to be performed by an employee from a company division within the specified time frame (duration). Finally, job interviews must take place on a fixed date.

2.5 Components of a PAIS

This section summarizes basic components and artifacts of a PAIS.

2.5.1 Overview

As depicted in Fig. 2.9, a distinction is made between the *process type* and *process instance level*. While the former defines the schemes for executable process models, the latter refers to the execution of related process instances, i.e., single enactments of an executable process model referring to particular business cases. Accordingly, a PAIS distinguishes between build- and run-time components. While *build-time* components enable the creation and management of the type-level artifacts of the PAIS, *run-time* components refer to the process instance level and support the creation, execution, and management of process instances.

Figure 2.10 shows an overview of the build- and run-time environment of a PAIS. Regardless of the paradigm chosen (i.e., prespecified, constraint-based, or data-driven process), the *build-time environment* includes tools for defining, configuring, and verifying executable process models. The core of the *run-time* environment, in turn, is built by a *process engine*. The latter is a generic software service that allows creating, executing, and managing the instances of executable process models. This includes the creation of new process instances, the run-time interpretation of these process models according to the defined behavior, the execution of activity instances (including sub-process instances), the management of user worklists, and the invocation of application services (e.g., web services or user forms) in the context of activity executions. Furthermore, the run-time environment comprises *end-user tools* enabling access to worklists or status monitors.

2.5.2 Build-Time Environment

Before implementing a business process in a PAIS, it must first be decided which parts of the process are to be automated. Then, an executable process model covering these parts needs to be created. Usually, the latter task is accomplished using the *process model editor* of the PAIS (cf. Fig. 2.11). This build-time component allows process designers to define, configure, and verify the different perspectives of an executable process model. The latter includes the activities of the executable process model (i.e., function perspective) as well as the control and data flow between them (i.e., behavior and information perspectives). Furthermore, for each atomic activity an application service (e.g., a user form or web service) has to be provided either through implementation or reuse from a service repository (i.e., operation perspective). In turn, for complex activities, an executable subprocess model must be defined. Finally, for human activities, so-called actor expressions have to be

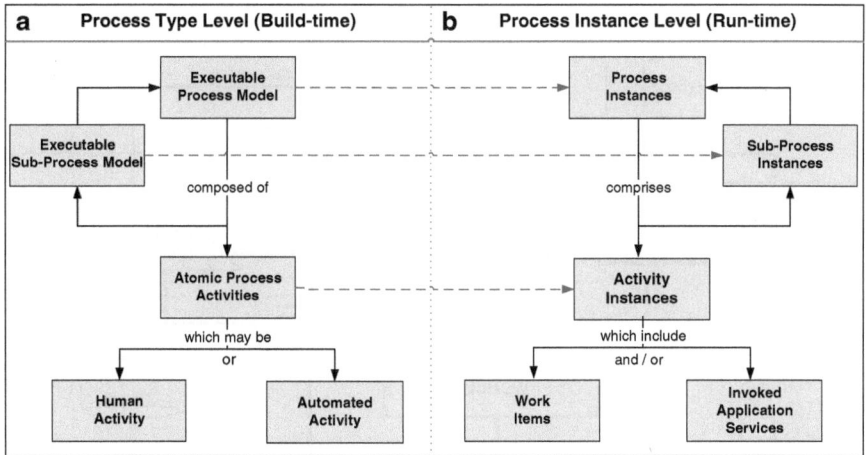

Fig. 2.9 Build-time and run-time artifacts of a PAIS (adopted from [367])

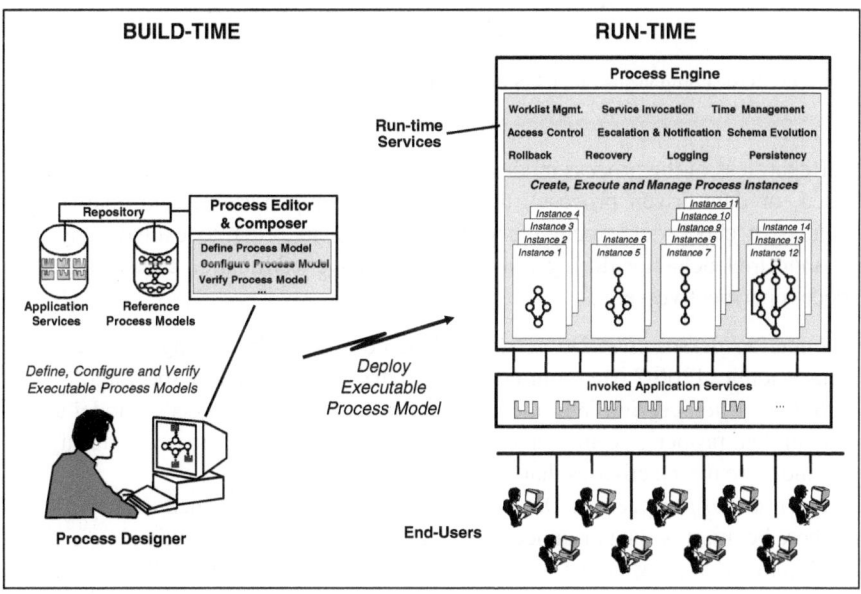

Fig. 2.10 Build-time and run-time environment of a PAIS

specified to enable the PAIS to assign these activities to potential actors during run-time (i.e., organization perspective). In turn, an actor expression refers to entities from the *organizational model* of the PAIS, such as roles or organizational units (cf. Fig. 2.11).

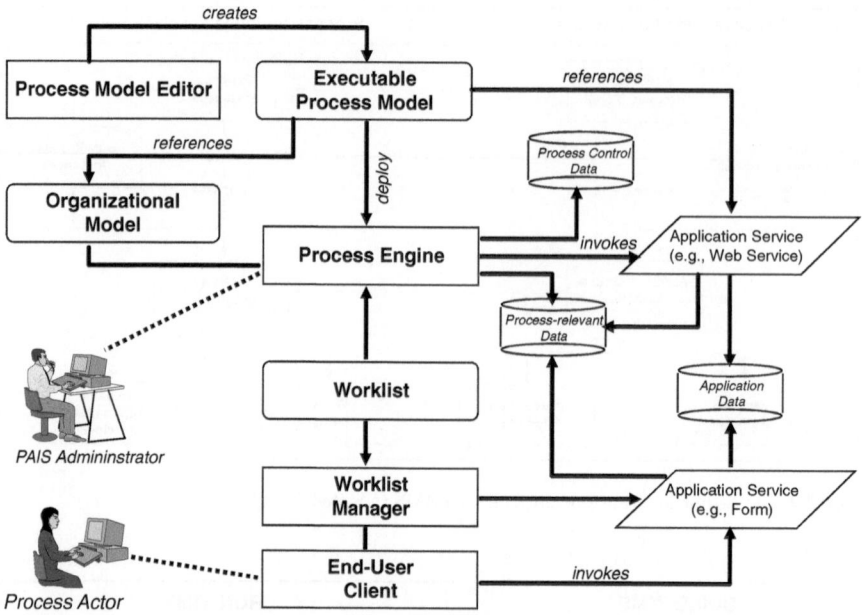

Fig. 2.11 Basic components of a PAIS (adopted from [367])

Regardless of the process modeling approach used (i.e., prespecified, constraint-based, or data-driven process), the build-time components should enable comprehensive checks of executable process models in order to exclude any error or undesired behavior during run-time. Respective verification tasks concern all process perspectives, e.g.:

- *Function perspective*: Do activity labels comply with existing guidelines and taxonomies [206]? Are required activity attributes completely specified?
- *Behavior perspective*: Will the instances of an executable process model always complete properly or may undefined states (e.g., deadlocks) occur during run-time? Are there activities that will never be executed?
- *Information perspective*: Does each data object have a defined data type? Will there be missing data or unnecessary data during process execution?
- *Organization perspective*: Do all organizational entities to which actor expressions of human activities refer exist in the organizational model? Can we ensure that there will be always at least one user authorized to execute a particular human activity?
- *Operation perspective*: Does each atomic activity have an assigned application service? Will there always be assigned values for the input parameters of an invoked application service at run-time?

Focusing on the behavior and information perspectives, later chapters of this book will show how modeling and verification tasks look like for prespecified, constraint-based, and data-driven process models.

2.5.3 Run-Time Environment

After releasing an executable process model, it can be deployed to the PAIS run-time environment whose core component is the *process engine*. A process engine allows creating, executing, and managing process instances related to the same or to different process models; i.e., a process engine constitutes a software service providing the run-time environment for executing a collection of process instances.

Figure 2.11 shows build-time and run-time components of a PAIS as well as their relationships. Core services provided by these PAIS components are as follows:

- Creating new instances of an executable process model.
- Executing process instances and related activities through interpretation of executable process models.
- Managing process instance data (i.e., control data and process-relevant data).
- Creating work items for instances of human activities and assigning these work items to the worklists of qualified actors.
- Orchestrating the application services and subprocesses linked to the activities of a process model according to the defined process logic.
- Invoking the right application service when starting the execution of an activity and exchanging parameter data with this service.
- Monitoring the progress of process instances and logging relevant execution events to ensure process traceability.

In the following, the notions of process instance, activity instance, and work item will be explained in detail.

2.5.3.1 Process Instances and Their Life Cycle

Once an executable process model has been deployed to a process engine, new *process instances* can be created and executed according to this model. Generally, several instances of the same process model may exist representing different *business cases* (e.g., treatments of different patients). The process engine employs a *state model* to control the concurrent execution of these process instances; i.e., each process instance exhibits an internal state representing its progress toward completion and its status with respect to its activities and data objects.

Process Instance Life Cycle. Figure 2.12 depicts the life cycle of a process instance. A newly created process instance has state Created. When starting its execution, this state changes to Running; i.e., the process model is then interpreted by a process engine, and activities whose preconditions are met become

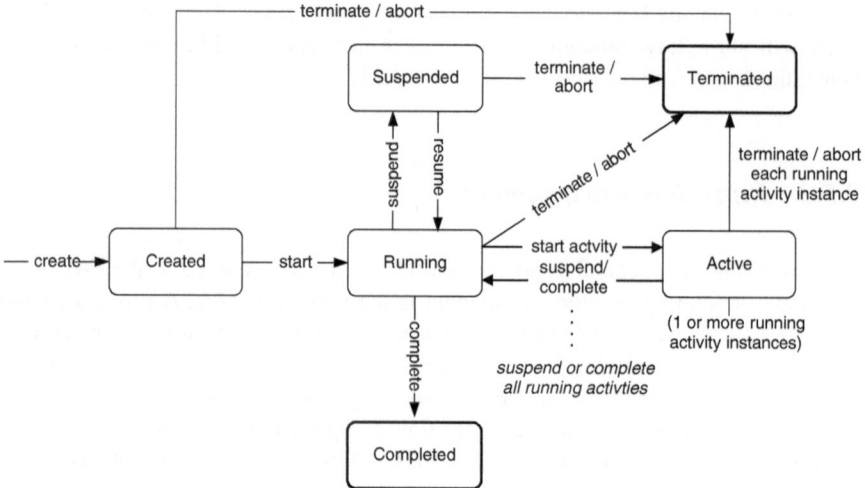

Fig. 2.12 Possible states and state transitions of a process instance

enabled. As soon as at least one of the enabled activities is running (i.e., it has been started), the process instance enters state `Active`. The distinction between the two states `Running` and `Active` is useful since different actions may be applied in these states. A process instance without currently running activities can be easily suspended or completed. Conversely, this is not immediately possible with a process instance with running activity instances. Furthermore, in the case a process instance is abnormally terminated or aborted (i.e., the instance enters state `Terminated`), different actions are required, depending on the concrete state of the process instance; e.g., for a process instance in state `Active`, each running activity instance needs to be terminated before the process instance itself may enter state `Terminated`.

Example 2.18 (Process Instance). Figure 2.13 shows an example of a process instance representing a *Request for Credit* by one particular customer. In detail, activities *Collect Credit Data* and *Assess Risk* have been completed, while activity *Accept Credit* is enabled. Activities *Request Approval* and *Refuse Credit*, in turn, have been skipped during the execution of the process instance. Furthermore, the instance state includes information about produced and consumed data objects, as well as about the actors who have worked on human activities (not depicted in Fig. 2.13).

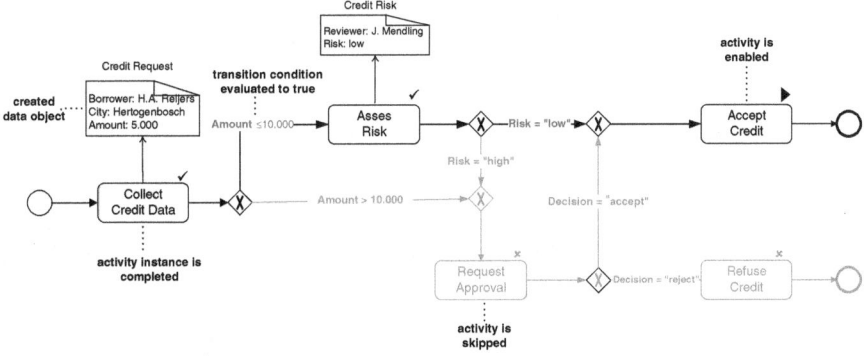

Fig. 2.13 Internal state of a process instance

Event Logs. Generally, all relevant events occurring during the execution of a process instance (e.g., start and completion of activities) are recorded in a an *event log* (also denoted as an *execution log* or *audit trail*). Respective event logs provide detailed information about the actual sequences of activities, key attributes of the performed activity instances (e.g., start and completion times), and the resources or human actors that performed these activities. Based on event logs, the PAIS additionally offers a run-time component for *monitoring* and *visualizing* the progress of its running process instances [53]. In particular, process monitoring relieves staff members from manually keeping track of their processes.

> *Example 2.19 (Process Monitoring).* Regarding the process dealing with order entry and result reporting from Example 2.2, a process monitoring component will allow hospital staff to answer questions like "Has an ordered X-ray already been made?" or "Why is there no medical report for a previously ordered X-ray?".

Note that in connection with data-driven processes, respective monitoring components usually do not only provide a *process-oriented view*, but also a *data-oriented view* for accessing business data at any point in time.

2.5.3.2 Activity Instances and Their Life Cycle

When the preconditions for executing a particular activity are met during run-time, a new instance of this activity is created. Hence, an *activity instance* represents a single invocation of an activity during the execution of a particular process instance. Furthermore, an activity instance utilizes data associated with its corresponding process instance and itself produces data utilized by succeeding activities.

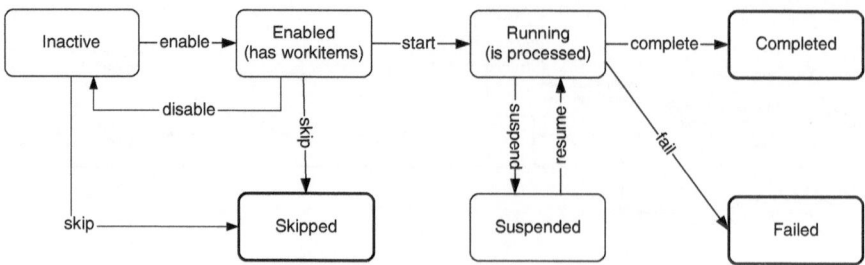

Fig. 2.14 States and state transitions of an activity instance

Activity Instance Life Cycle. Figure 2.14 illustrates the life cycle of a single
activity instance. When the preconditions for executing an activity are met during
process execution, the state of the activity instance changes from Inactive to
Enabled. If no human interaction is required, the activity instance immediately
enters state Running and its corresponding application service is invoked. In
this context, process-relevant data is passed from the process engine to the input
parameters of the invoked application service, which then processes these data (cf.
Fig. 2.15). When completing the execution of the application service, in turn, its
output parameters are mapped to process-relevant data, which may then be accessed
in subsequent activity executions of the same process instance. Otherwise (i.e.,
human interaction is required), corresponding *work items* are created for qualified
actors and added to their worklists. As soon as one of these actors starts processing
this work item, the activity instance switches to state Running (cf. Sect. 2.5.3.3).
Finally, when an activity instance completes, its state changes to Completed.
Usually, this is followed by an evaluation of the preconditions of subsequent
activities.

To cover more advanced scenarios, three states have to be added as indicated
in Fig. 2.14. First, an activity instance in state Inactive or Enabled may be
skipped (i.e., it enters state Skipped) if an alternative path is chosen for execution.
Second, a human activity (e.g., writing a medical report) in state Running may be
suspended (i.e., it enters state Suspended) and resumed later (i.e., it reenters state
Running). Finally, if a running activity instance fails due to technical or semantic
errors, it then switches to state Failed.

2.5.3.3   Worklists and Work Items

When a human activity becomes enabled during the execution of a process instance,
the PAIS first determines all actors qualifying for this *activity instance*. Basic to this
is the *actor expression* that is associated with the respective activity and can be used
for querying the organizational model of the PAIS.

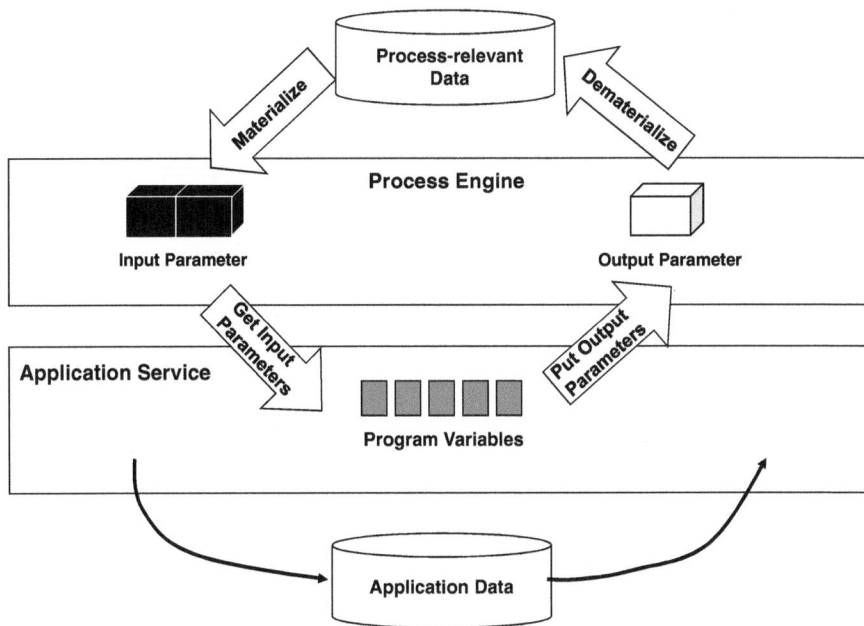

Fig. 2.15 Exchanging data between process engine and invoked application service

Example 2.20 (Actor Assignment for a Human Activity). Consider the process model from Fig. 2.2. Activity *Perform Checkup* will be offered to all actors with role *Physician* and who are also a member of the *outpatient department.*

For each potential actor, a *work item* referring to the activity instance is created and added to his *worklist*, i.e., work items related to a particular activity instance may be added to different user worklists. Generally, a worklist comprises all work items currently offered to, or processed by, a user. Example 2.21 illustrates the relationships that may exist between executable process models, process instances, and work items. Note that this example abstracts from those actor expressions that have led to the creation of respective work items.

Example 2.21 (Worklists and Work Items). Consider Fig. 2.16, which depicts two prespecified process models (i.e., *Biopsy* and *Medication*) and five related process instances I_1 to I_5. While instances I_1, I_2, and I_3 are running on process model *Biopsy*, instances I_4 and I_5 are based on process model

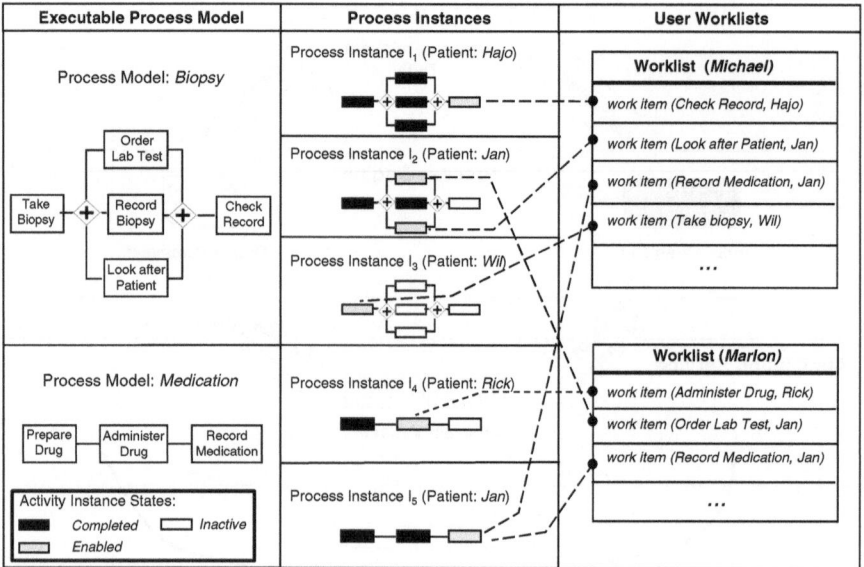

Fig. 2.16 Executable process models, process instances, and work items

Medication. Furthermore, the depicted worklists of users *Michael* and *Marlon* comprise work items relating to process instances I_1 to I_5.

- An instance of activity *Check Record* belonging to I_1 is enabled and a corresponding work item has been added to the worklist of user *Michael*.
- Regarding I_2, two work items exist belonging to different activity instances. One of them refers to an instance of activity *Order Lab Test*—a corresponding work item has been added to the worklist of user *Marlon*. The other one refers to an instance of activity *Look after Patient*. For this activity, a corresponding work item is added to the worklist of user *Michael*.
- For activity instance *Record Medication* of I_5 there are two work items assigned to the worklists of *Michael* and *Marlon*.

Generally, process participants interact with a PAIS via end-user clients and the worklists displayed by them. When an actor allocates a work item from his worklist, all work items related to the same activity instance are removed from the worklists of other users. Further, as illustrated by Fig. 2.17, the user to whom the work item is allocated may then trigger the start of the application service associated with the corresponding activity instance.

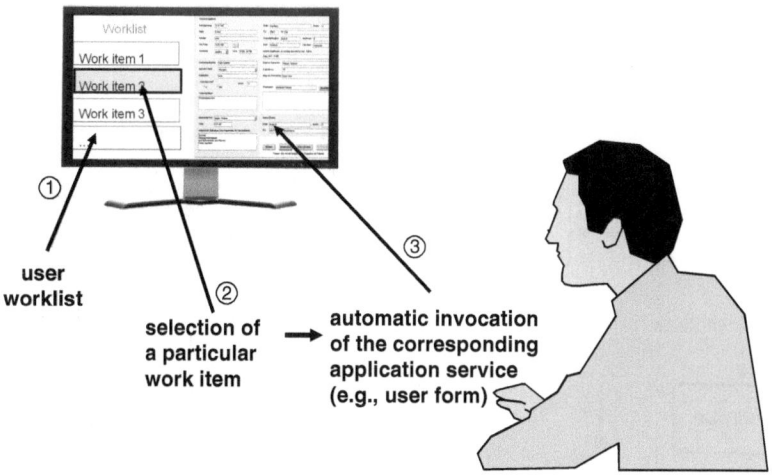

Fig. 2.17 Selecting a work item from a worklist

Work Item Life Cycle. As illustrated by Fig. 2.16, several work items may exist for a particular activity instance. In the following, the states of a single work item and its processing are discussed.

Figure 2.18 illustrates the *work item life cycle* from the perspective of one particular actor to whom this work item is assigned [311]: A work item typically progresses from state Offered to Allocated to Started, and finally to Completed. Initially, the work item has state Offered; i.e., it is offered to all qualified actors (e.g., all user possessing a particular role). If one of these actors wants to perform the task associated with the work item, he needs to issue an allocate request. The work item is then allocated to this actor. At the same time, all work items from other worklists referencing the same activity instance are removed. When the actor who allocated the work item wants to start its execution, he issues a start request, and the state of the work item changes to Started. Finally, once the work item is processed, the actor issues a complete request and the state of the work item changes to Completed. Three additional states need to be added to this life cycle as indicated by the dotted arcs in Fig. 2.18. First, a work item will immediately change from its initial state Offered to state Withdrawn if another work item belonging to the same activity instance, but being offered to a different actor, is allocated by that actor. Second, the processing of a started work item may be temporarily suspended (i.e., the state of the work item switches from Started to Suspended) and later be resumed. Third, if the execution of a work item fails, its state will change to Failed. The latter corresponds to a termination action in relation to the work item which is outside the control of the actor. We will extend the life cycle from Fig. 2.18 in Chap. 6 to show what additional support is needed to flexibly cope with exceptional situations during run time.

In principle, process participants do not need to know the exact logic of a process instance when working on a corresponding work item; i.e., they may solely interact

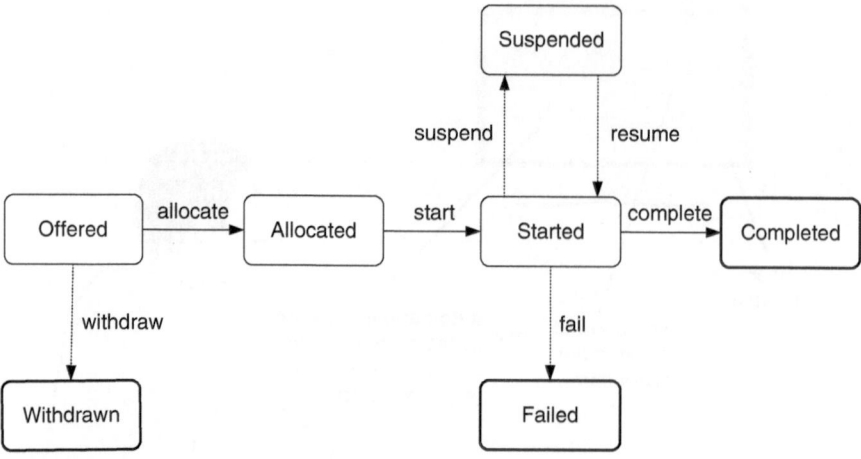

Fig. 2.18 Work item life cycle from the perspective of a particular actor

with the PAIS via their worklist (cf. Fig. 2.17). When completing the processing of a work item, new work items referring to subsequent activity instances are created and added to user worklists.

2.6 Summary

Turning away from hard-coded process logic toward explicitly specified process models significantly eases PAIS development and maintenance. In summary, a PAIS

- knows the logic of the supported processes; i.e., processes are explicitly described in terms of executable process models (e.g., comprising a set of activities and a number of constraints for their execution).
- ensures that activities are executed in the specified order or considering the specified constraints (i.e., the PAIS manages the flow of control during run-time).
- controls the flow of data between the activities; i.e., the output data of a particular activity can be consumed as input data by subsequent activities.
- knows the application service to be invoked when an atomic activity is started.
- assigns work items related to human activities to the worklists of authorized users and manages these worklists.
- provides reminders if users do not complete an activity instance before a certain deadline is reached.
- enables end-users to monitor the progress of process instances and to trace their previous execution.

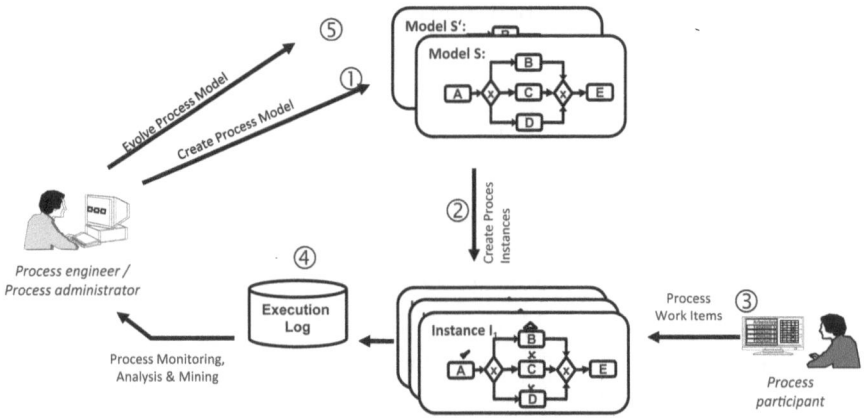

Fig. 2.19 Traditional process life cycle

Traditional PAISs enable process life cycle support as depicted in Fig. 2.19: At build-time, an initial representation of the business process to be supported is created either by explicitly modeling the process based on the result of a process analysis or by discovering the process model through the mining of execution logs [11, 133] (1). At run-time, new process instances can be created from the executable process model (2), each representing a concrete business case. In general, process instances are executed according to the process model they were originally derived from. While automated activities are immediately executed once they become enabled, nonautomated activities are assigned to the worklist of qualified actors who may perform the respective activities (3). Thereby, execution logs record information about the start and completion of activity instances as well as their chronological order (4). The analysis of respective logs by a process engineer and/or process intelligence tools allows discovering malfunctions or bottlenecks. In turn, this triggers the evolutionary change of the process model (5).

We will extend this life cycle in subsequent chapters to accommodate the different flexibility needs for PAISs as discussed in Chap. 3.

Exercises

2.1. Process Perspectives
Think of a business process you are familiar with that utilizes a PAIS (e.g., ordering goods in a Web shop or performing a financial transaction using Internet banking). Give examples of the different perspectives on a PAIS using this scenario.

2.2. Process Instances, Activity Instances and Work Items

(a) Consider the states of a process instance as illustrated in Fig. 2.12. Explain the difference between states Completed and Terminated.
(b) What is the relationship between the life cycle of an activity instance (cf. Fig. 2.14) and the one of a single work item (cf. Fig. 2.18)?
(c) Consider the life cycle of an activity instance from Fig. 2.14. What exactly is the difference between states Enabled and Running?
(d) Which of the following statements are true?

    – A worklist may contain more than one work item.
    – Each activity instance is associated with exactly one work item.
    – For a process instance in state Running multiple work items related to the same activity instance may exist at a certain point in time.
    – A work item switches from state Offered to state Withdrawn if another work item related to the same activity instance is allocated by a user.

2.3. Application Data, Process-Relevant Data, and Process Control Data

(a) Describe the differences between application data, process-relevant data, and process control data. Give examples.
(b) Explain how data may be exchanged between a started activity instance and the application service invoked during its execution.
(c) Describe how data is passed between the activities of a process instance.

2.4. Build-Time and Run-Time Components of a PAIS

Give examples of build- and run-time components of a PAIS. What services are offered by them?

Chapter 3
Flexibility Issues in Process-Aware Information Systems

Abstract Traditionally, process-aware information systems (PAISs) have focused on the support of predictable and repetitive business processes. Even though respective processes are suited to be fully prespecified in a process model, flexibility is required to support dynamic process adaptations in case of exceptions. Flexibility is also needed to accommodate the need for evolving business processes and to cope with business process variability. Furthermore, PAISs are increasingly used to support less structured processes which can often be characterized as knowledge intensive. Processes of this category are neither fully predictable nor repetitive, and therefore cannot be fully prespecified at build-time. The (partial) unpredictability of these processes also demands a certain amount of looseness. This chapter deals with the flexibility needs of both prespecified and loosely specified processes and elicitates requirements for flexible process support in a PAIS. In addition, the chapter discusses PAIS features needed to accommodate flexibility needs in practice like, for example, traceability, business compliance, and user support.

3.1 Motivation

Traditionally, process-aware information systems (PAISs) have focused on the support of predictable and repetitive business processes, which can be fully described prior to their execution in terms of formal process models [178]. Typical examples falling in this category include business processes in banking and insurance companies; e.g., opening a new bank account or granting a loan. Even though repetitive business processes are usually predictable, a certain degree of flexibility is needed to support dynamic process adaptations in case of exceptions; e.g., death of a policyholder or a marital divorce requiring a change of insurance and/or beneficiaries [336]. Moreover, flexibility is required to accommodate the need for evolving business processes. As an example consider process changes due to altered legal requirements. Finally, support for business process variability is needed. For example, different process variants may exist depending on the type of insurances.

M. Reichert and B. Weber, *Enabling Flexibility in Process-Aware Information Systems*, 43
DOI 10.1007/978-3-642-30409-5_3, © Springer-Verlag Berlin Heidelberg 2012

PAISs are increasingly used to support less structured business processes as well. The latter are often characterized as *knowledge intensive*. Processes of this category feature *non-repeatability*, i.e., the models of two process instances do not fully resemble one another. Generally, knowledge-intensive processes tend to be *unpredictable* since the exact course of action depends on situation-specific parameters [336]. The values of these parameters are usually not known a priori and may change during process execution. Moreover, knowledge-intensive processes can be characterized as *emergent*, i.e., knowledge gathered during the execution of the process determines its future course of action [140]. Consequently, respective processes cannot be prescribed at a fine-grained level at build-time. In addition to variability, adaptation, and evolution that is required for predictable processes, they require looseness. Typical examples of the latter process category include innovation processes (e.g., introducing a new product or service) and call center processes (e.g., handling of a computer problem by the helpdesk).

The vast majority of business processes, however, can be characterized by a combination of predictable and unpredictable elements falling in between these two extremes. Health care processes, for example, reflect the combination of predictable and unpredictable elements quite well. While procedures for handling single medical orders or examinations are relatively predictable, complex patient treatment processes are rather unpredictable and unfold during process execution [172]. Similar considerations hold for law enforcement processes (i.e., investigation of a crime) [336]. A criminal investigation constitutes an example of a knowledge-intensive process that can be characterized by non-repeatability, unpredictability, and emergence. However, this process has predictable elements as well; e.g., lab analysis or witness deposition.

Providing appropriate support for this wide range of business processes poses several challenges, which will be detailed in this chapter. In Sect. 3.2 we elaborate in detail on the different flexibility needs. Once these are identified, Sect. 3.3 elicitates fundamental requirements for flexible business process support by a PAIS. Finally, Sect. 3.4 discusses the organization of the remaining book chapters along the identified flexibility needs.

3.2   A Taxonomy of Flexibility Needs in Process-Aware Information Systems

Flexible process support by a PAIS can be characterized by four major flexibility needs, namely support for variability, looseness, adaptation, and evolution (cf. Fig. 3.1). Each of these flexibility needs may affect each of the process perspectives (i.e., behavior, organization, information, operation, function, and time) introduced in Chap. 2. In the subsequent sections of this chapter, we present a brief summary of each flexibility need and present real-world processes to illustrate it. A detailed discussion of concepts and methods satisfying these needs follows in the remaining chapters of this book.

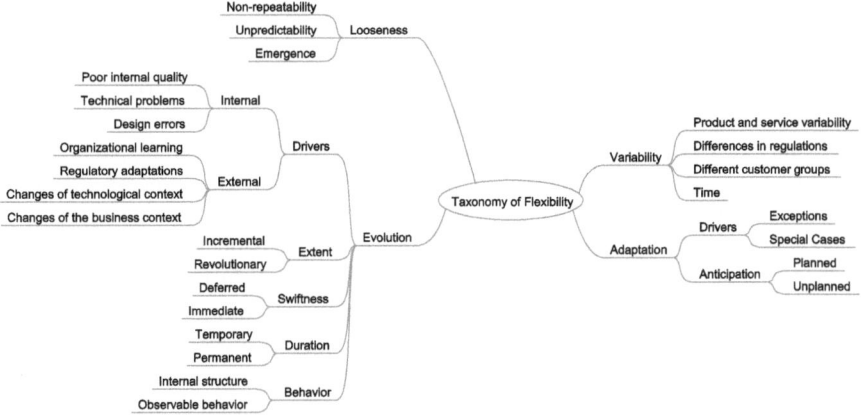

Fig. 3.1 A taxonomy of process flexibility needs

3.2.1   Variability

Process variability can be found in many domains and requires processes to be handled differently—resulting in different *process variants*—depending on the given context [106, 124, 129]. Process variants typically share the same core process whereas the concrete course of action fluctuates from variant to variant. *Product and service variability*, for example, often require support for different process variants depending on the concrete product variant [226]. Moreover, process variants might exist due to *differences in regulations* found in different countries and regions [128]. Variability might be also introduced due to different *groups of customers* (e.g., priority care for premium customers) or due to *temporal differences* (e.g., seasonal changes). The parameters causing process variability are mostly known a priori (e.g., country-specific regulations). Even though the concrete variant can often only be determined during process execution, the course of action for a particular context is well understood.

> *Example 3.1 (Vehicle Repair).*   The process for handling vehicle repair in a garage constitutes a good example of a process showing high variability. Depending on the process context, different variants of this process are required. While some parts of the process are shared by all variants, variability is introduced due to country-specific, garage-specific, and vehicle-specific differences. Overall, hundreds of variants may exist in such a context [128].

3.2.2 *Looseness*

As discussed, knowledge-intensive processes can be characterized as *non-repeatable* (i.e., every process instance looks slightly different), *unpredictable* (i.e., the exact course of action is unknown and is highly situation-specific), and *emergent* (i.e., the exact course of action only emerges during process execution when more information becomes available). For processes of this category, only their goal is known a priori (e.g., treating the rupture of a patient's cruciate ligament or the judical process in seeking a criminal conviction). In turn, the parameters determining the exact course of action are typically not known a priori and might change during process execution. As a consequence, these processes cannot be fully prespecified. In addition, it is not possible to establish a set of process variants for these processes, since the parameters causing differences between process instances are not known a priori (unlike with variability). Instead, processes of this category require a loose specification.

> *Example 3.2 (Patient Treatment Processes).* Patient treatment processes in a hospital typically comprise activities related to patient intake, admission, diagnosis, treatment, and discharge [172]. Typically, such processes comprise dozens up to hundreds of activities and are long-running (i.e., from a few days to several months). Furthermore, the treatments of two different patients are *rarely identical*; instead the course of action greatly depends on the specific situation; e.g., health status of the patient, allergies and chemical intolerances, decisions made by the physician, examination results, and clinical indications. This situation can change during the treatment process, i.e., the course of action is *unpredictable*. Moreover, treatment processes typically unfold during their execution, i.e., examination results yield information determining how to continue with the treatment. The overall treatment process thereby emerges through the arrangement of simple, well-structured processes (e.g., handling medical orders) often resulting in complex process structures.

3.2.3 *Adaptation*

Adaptation represents the ability of a PAIS to adapt the process and its structure (i.e., prespecified model) to emerging events. Respective events often lead to situations in which the PAIS does not adequately reflect the real-world process anymore. As a consequence, one or several process instances have to be adapted in order to realign the computerized processes with the real-world ones.

Drivers for Adaptation. Process adaptations are triggered by different drivers. Respective adaptations might be required to cope with *special situations* during process execution, which have not been foreseen in the process model [334], e.g., because they only occur very rarely. Moreover, *exceptions* occurring in the real-world (e.g., an allergic reaction of a patient) or processing errors (e.g., a failed activity) often require deviations from the standard process. A detailed discussion of sources for exceptions will follow in Chap. 6.

Anticipation of Adaptation. Usually, many exceptions can be anticipated and therefore be *planned* upfront by capturing them in the process model. Generally, a deviation can only be planned if both the context of its occurrence and measures to handle it are known. However, it is hardly possible to foresee all exceptions that may occur in the context of a particular process. Therefore, support for dealing with *unplanned* exceptions is additionally needed.

> *Example 3.3 (Examination Procedures in a Hospital).* A simple examination procedure in a hospital comprises activities like *Enter Order, Schedule X-rays, Inform Patient, Transfer Patient, Perform X-rays, Create Report,* and *Validate Report* (cf. Example 2.2 in Chap. 2). Even for such a simple process, exceptional situations might occur, which require deviations from the prespecified process. For example, in case of an emergency there is no time to follow the usual procedure. Instead the patient is immediately examined without making any appointment or preparing the examination facility. To cope with such situation, it should be possible to skip one or more activities. In exceptional situations it can further be required to perform additional (i.e., unplanned) activities for a particular patient (e.g., to carry out an additional preparation step for the examination). In addition, changes in appointments, cancelations, and failures in the execution of activities (e.g., omitted preparations, loss of a sample, or incorrect collection of diagnostic material) might lead to deviations from the standard procedure (e.g., by redoing activities). If an appointment is canceled, for example, the patient treatment process (including the previously made appointment) will have to be aborted.
>
> In the medical domain such deviations from the standard procedure are the norm and have to be flexibly addressed by physicians and nursing staff.

3.2.4 Evolution

Evolution represents the ability of the process implemented in a PAIS to change when the corresponding business process evolves [61, 290]. Since business processes can evolve over time, it is not sufficient to implement them once and then to never touch the PAIS again. In order to ensure that real-world processes and

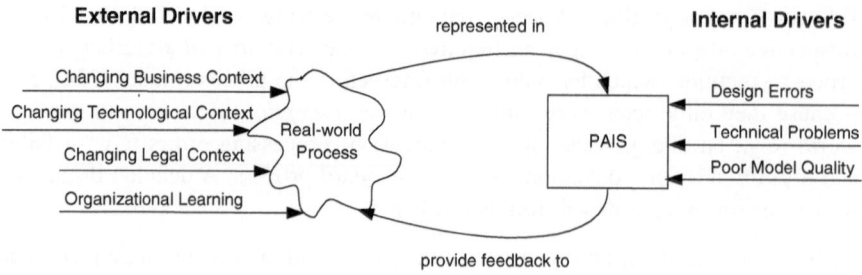

Fig. 3.2 Real-world versus computerized processes

the PAIS remain aligned, these changes have to be propagated to the PAIS as well. Typically, such evolutionary changes are planned changes at the process type level, which are conducted to accommodate evolving needs.

Drivers for Business Process Evolution. Process evolution is often driven by changes in the business, the technological environment, and the legal context [14]. Another driver is organizational learning. All these drivers are *external* to the PAIS (cf. Fig. 3.2). Evolution of real-world processes can be triggered by a changing *business context* like an evolving market (e.g., emergence of new competitors) or changing customer behavior. Changes in the *technological context* might have far reaching effects on the business processes of an organization. For example, the increasing popularity of mobile devices is revolutionizing the way how people are interacting with each other. Changes might further be triggered by *regulatory adaptations* like, for example, the introduction of Sarbanes–Oxley [338] or Basel II [42]. Finally, changes of business processes might be a result of *organizational learning* and be triggered by emerging optimization opportunities or misalignments between real-world processes and the ones supported by PAISs.

In addition to external triggers, changes of processes implemented in a PAIS might become necessary due to developments inside the PAIS, i.e., there exist *internal* drivers for changes as well [14]. For example, *design errors* might cause problems during the execution of process instances in the PAIS (e.g., deadlocks or missing data). Moreover, *technical problems* like performance degradation (e.g., due to an increasing amount of data) may require changes in the PAIS. Finally, *poor internal quality* of process models (e.g., non-intention revealing naming of activities or redundant process model fragments) may require changes [351].

Extent of Evolution. Process evolution may be *incremental* (i.e., only requiring small changes of the implemented process) as for continuous process improvements [137, 238, 241], or be *revolutionary* (i.e., requiring radical changes) as in the context of process innovation or process reengineering [130].

Swiftness of Evolution. Depending on the kind of evolutionary change, different requirements regarding the treatment of ongoing process instances exist [254]. In some scenarios, it is sufficient to apply the changes only to those process instances which will be newly created and to complete the ongoing ones according to the old version of the business process. This, in turn, would require *deferred evolution* and coexistence of different versions of a process model within the PAIS. In many practical scenarios, however, evolutionary changes have an effect on ongoing process instances as well. For example, regulatory changes often have a retroactive impact and require ongoing process instances (if they have not progressed too far) to be adapted. Such *immediate evolution* is mostly relevant for long-running processes instances, i.e., process instances with a duration up to several weeks or months.

Duration of Evolution. Evolutionary changes can be *permanent* or *temporary*. While *permanent changes* are valid from the time they are introduced (unless they are compensated by later permanent changes), *temporary changes* are only valid for a certain period of time, e.g., during a special promotion period.

Visibility of Evolution. Evolutionary changes may either be changes of the *observable process behavior* or the *internal structure* of the PAIS. While changes of the *observable behavior* are always reflected by the PAIS support of the real-world processes, changes of the *internal structure* are kept inside the PAIS (e.g., to address poor internal model quality) [351]. Adding or deleting activities from a process model are examples of changes concerning the observable behavior. A typical change only affecting the internal structure of the PAIS includes the removal of process model redundancies by extracting common parts to subprocess models.

Example 3.4 (Tender Preparation). A typical process for tender preparation comprises activities like *Enter Customer Request, Check Feasibility, Create Offer*, and *Submit Tender*. For *standard customers* the offer is usually created based on the latest price list, while for *gold customers* a special offer is prepared which has to be authorized by the department head. Since the creation of special offers (including checks of the special terms of the offer) turned out to be more expensive than estimated benefits (e.g., through increased customer loyalty), the management decided to evolve the process such that no special offers would be made in future.

In this example the evolution is triggered through organizational learning and economic concerns. The change is incremental and affects the external behavior of the process in a permanent manner. Moreover, the change is deferred; i.e., it only affects newly created offers (i.e., future process instances).

Example 3.5 (Introduction of New Medical Devices). The introduction of new medical imaging devices in a hospital sometimes has implications on the corresponding examination process. Assume that due to the high acquisition cost for the new device the hospital decides to use it for examining outpatients as well (in addition to inpatient examinations). This, in turn, implies changes in the registration procedure. These changes affect not only new patients but also ongoing examination processes.

In this example the evolution is triggered through economic concerns. As in Example 3.4 the change is incremental and affects the external behavior of the process in a permanent manner. Moreover, the change is immediate; i.e., it also affects ongoing examination processes.

Example 3.6 (Inconsistent Naming of Process Models). Large process model repositories that have evolved over many years often have significant inconsistencies regarding activity labels and labeling styles. For example, the repository described in [323] contained 16 process models all having activities dealing with the scheduling of medical procedures (e.g., surgeries, medical examinations, and drug administrations). Though all these activities had similar intentions, different labels and labeling styles were used (e.g., "Make Appointment", "Appointment", "Schedule Examination", "Fix Day", "Agree on Surgery Date", and "Plan"). This, in turn, required a huge effort when reusing the models later in the context of a large process model harmonization. In particular, activity labels had to be consolidated by refactoring respective process models [351].

3.3   Requirements for a Flexible PAIS

From the previously described flexibility needs (i.e., variability, looseness, adaptation, and evolution), technical requirements can be derived which have to be met by any PAIS supporting flexible processes (cf. Table 3.1). To enable process variability at a technical level, PAISs need to provide support for *configurable process models* and for the context-specific configuration of particular *process variants*. To accommodate the need for looseness, in turn, PAISs must provide support for *loosely specified process models*, which do not require a completely prespecified process model, but allow deferring modeling decisions to the run-time. Moreover, support for planned exceptions in terms of *exception handling support* as well as unplanned or unanticipated exceptions through the support of *ad hoc changes* allowing for deviations from a prespecified process model is needed. To adequately cope with business process evolution, PAISs require *versioning support for process models* (i.e., for deferred evolution) enabling the coexistence of different

Table 3.1 Mapping flexibility needs to technical requirements

Flexibility need	Dimension	Technical requirement
Variability		Configuration
Looseness		Loosely specified processes
Adaptation	Planned	Exception handling
	Unplanned	Ad hoc changes
Evolution	Deferred evolution,	Versioning
	Immediate evolution,	Process instance migration
	Poor model quality,	Refactoring
	Organizational learning	Monitoring, analysis, and mining

process model versions at the same time. Additionally, immediate evolution requires the *migration* of ongoing *process instances* to the new process model version. The problem of poor process model quality, in turn, requires adequate support for *process model refactoring*, which improves the quality of a process model without altering the observable behavior. Finally, to provide feedback regarding the execution of real-world processes and to foster organizational learning, IT support for *monitoring, analyzing, and mining* flexible processes becomes crucial.

In addition to the support for variability, looseness, adaptation, and evolution, flexible PAISs have to provide several other features to enable process flexibility in practice.

Accountability and Traceability. Even though PAISs become less prescriptive with increasing flexibility, both traceability and accountability still need to be guaranteed. Organizations are required to comply with a wide range of regulations like Sarbanes Oxley (SOX) [338] or Basel II [42]. In the context of SOX, for example, it is important to be able to trace back *who* made *which* changes *when* and *why*. For this, executed activities as well as applied process changes have to be logged. If users need to bypass the PAIS, because a change requirement cannot be implemented quickly enough in the PAIS, traceability is no longer guaranteed and a mismatch between the PAIS and the real-world processes it supports exists.

Business Compliance. In addition to accountability and traceability, compliance with existing rules and regulations is another fundamental issue. Despite the provided flexibility, it has to be ensured that (dynamic) process changes in PAIS do not lead to such violations, or that the reasons of such compliance violations are at least documented to ensure traceability as described above.

Access Control. With increasing flexibility, PAISs become more vulnerable to misuse [77, 354]. Therefore, the application of changes at the process type as well as the process instance level must be restricted to authorized users.

Correctness of Changes. When adapting or evolving business processes—potentially in the midst of their execution—it has to be ensured that changes are performed in a controlled manner and do not lead to run-time errors; e.g., crashed activity programs due to missing input data, deadlocks due to blocking activities, or data inconsistencies due to lost updates.

User Support. With increasing PAIS flexibility, the need for user support becomes more and more important [322]. While traditional PAISs provide little maneuvering room for their users, loosely specified processes require many decisions to be made along the way and therefore require significantly more user experience.

Need for Learning from Process Instance Changes. Regarding *instance-specific process adaptations*, same or similar exceptions might occur more than once, making the reuse of existing exception handling procedures desirable [217,359]. For example, the knowledge that a magnetic resonance tomography (MRT) could not be performed for a patient with cardiac pacemaker is highly relevant when treating other patients with the same or similar problems. Generally, when similar exceptions occur frequently, this often indicates a gap between the modeled processes and the corresponding real-world ones. This misalignment often stems from errors in the design of a process model or is the result of changing requirements. Therefore, flexible PAISs should continuously monitor deviations between a predefined process model and the actual process enactment in order to detect discrepancies between modeled and observed process behavior.

In the context of *loosely specified processes*, two process instances are rarely identical. However, similarities between process instances often exist. As a consequence, reuse of previously conducted process instances or the discovery of frequently occurring similar process fragments should be supported.

Concurrency of Changes. Any PAIS supporting instance-specific adaptations should be able to cope with *concurrent* changes. In particular, PAISs need to handle situations in which instance-specific adaptations (i.e., ad hoc changes) and evolutionary changes overlap. This is especially important when evolution has to be immediate and not deferred.

3.4 Summary

This chapter discussed the flexibility needs of both prespecified and loosely specified processes in detail; i.e., adaptation, evolution, looseness, and variability. Based on these flexibility needs characteristic requirements were derived that any PAIS, enabling flexible business process support, has to fulfill. PAISs and their process models do not only need to be configurable, be able to deal with exceptions, and allow for changing the execution of single business cases (i.e., process instances) on-the-fly, but must also support the evolution of business processes over time. Responsiveness to change is fundamental for any PAIS, and thus continuous process model refactorings are needed to ensure maintainability, especially when process model repositories become increasingly large. Moreover, monitoring, analysis, and mining of processes are fundamental. In addition, this chapter discussed fundamental PAIS features that are also needed to accommodate the described flexibility needs in practice. In particular, traceability and accountability must be ensured at all times and changes need to be performed in a controlled manner to guarantee correctness. Furthermore, security constraints as well as compliance with existing policies and regulations need to be ensured. Flexible PAISs should also assist their users through recommendations and learning from instance deviations.

3.5 Book Structure

Figure 3.3 depicts the overall organization of the remaining chapters of this book dealing with the four major needs for variability, looseness, adaptation, and evolution.

Part II of this book deals with flexibility support for prespecified processes. This part primarily considers predictable and repetitive processes. Chapter 5 addresses the need for variability in business processes and discusses techniques enabling process configuration support. Chapter 6 explores on the handling of planned adaptations through exception handling techniques, while Chap. 7 deals with unplanned exceptions and their support through ad hoc changes of individual process instances. Chapter 8 discusses monitoring, analysis, and mining support for flexible processes fostering the incremental evolution of business processes. Chapter 9 addresses the requirement for evolution and elaborates on versioning, instance migration, and refactoring support. Part II ends with Chap. 10, which discusses business compliance issues in the context of process changes.

Part III of this book focuses on less predictable processes with a comparably low degree of repetition and deals with the need for looseness. Chapter 11 first provides an overview of different approaches and techniques realizing loosely specified process models. With constraint-based processes, Chap. 12 then introduces one specific approach for realizing loosely specified processes in more detail.

Part IV deals with the integration of data and processes and discusses the potential for increasing flexibility through such an integrated approach. Chapter 13 introduces object-centric, artifact-based, and data-driven approaches, while Chap. 14 deals with a specific framework enabling flexible object-aware and data-driven processes.

Finally, Part V focuses on tool support. Chapter 15 introduces the Aristaflow BPM Suite process management technology as a representative for a system supporting prespecified processes including advanced support for adaptation and evolution. Chapter 16 describes Alaska, which provides support for different approaches enabling loosely specified processes. Additional tools are discussed in Chap. 17.

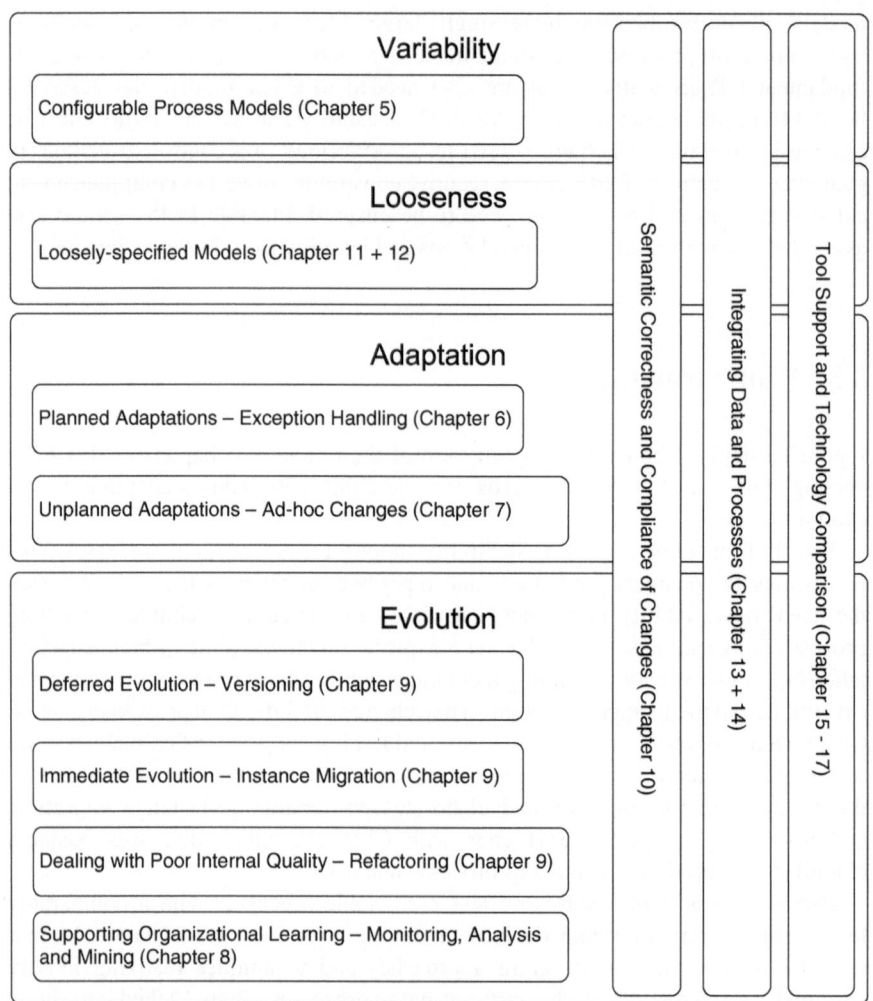

Fig. 3.3 Organization of the remaining chapters

Exercises

3.1. Flexibility Needs

In the following, the check-in and boarding procedures from the perspective of two hypothetical travelers, we will call Tom and Tina Traveler, are depicted.

Tom Traveler wants to spend the weekend in Barcelona to explore the city his friends are so enthusiastic about. Since the flight is departing in 90 min from the nearby airport in Innsbruck, Tom calls a taxi, which arrives a few minutes later and takes him to the airport which is just a few kilometers from his home. Tom arrives at the airport about an hour before departure. He then immediately goes to the check-in counter where he drops off his bag and gets the boarding pass. Since there is still enough time before boarding Tom decides to drink a quick coffee. Afterwards he gets through security, which is usually quite fast in Innsbruck and only requires a few minutes to complete. For this, Tom has to get his laptop out of his carry-on bag and puts it in the provided bin. He then places his bag as well as his jacket on the conveyor belt to be X-rayed. Having placed the laptop, his bag and the jacket on the conveyor belt, he waits for the signal to proceed through the metal detector. Once he has passed the metal detector, Tom is asked by the screener to take out his camera from the carry-on bag so that she can look through the lens. After this check he is allowed to repack. Tom then buys a newspaper and walks to the gate to wait for the boarding call. Five minutes later boarding starts and Tom enters the airplane.

Like Tom Traveler, Tina Traveler wants to spend the weekend in Barcelona. Tina takes the bus to get to the airport in Innsbruck and arrives about 20 min later at the airport. Having arrived at the airport she immediately goes to the check-in counter where she drops off her bag. Unlike Tom, Tina has already printed out her boarding pass at home. After baggage drop-off Tina immediately wants to get through security. Tina places her jacket as well as her carry-on-bag in the provided bin provided on the conveyor belt to be X-rayed. She then waits for the signal to proceed through the metal detector. After the check she gets her carry-on bag as well as her jacket. Tina then buys a newspaper and walks to the gate to wait for the boarding call. A few minutes later boarding starts and Tina enters the airplane.

(a) How would you classify this process in terms of predictability and repeatability?
(b) What kind of flexibility needs can you identify in this context?

3.2. Flexibility Needs

Give examples (others than the ones described in this book) for business processes requiring variability, looseness, adaptation, and evolution.

(a) Give examples where process variability is required. What are the driving forces behind variability in these examples?
(b) Think about processes that are characterized by non-repeatability, unpredictability, and emergence, and therefore require looseness.
(c) Give examples for both planned and unforeseen process adaptations.
(d) Think about situations where deferred evolution is sufficient. Give examples where immediate evolution is required. Use the taxonomy depicted in Fig. 3.1 to characterize the scenarios.

Part II
Flexibility Support for Prespecified Processes

Chapter 4
Process Modeling and Flexibility-by-Design

Abstract This chapter deals with process models whose behavior can be pre-specified at build-time and their run-time support in a PAIS. Usually, such a prespecified process model defines all activities to be executed, their control flow and data flow dependencies, organizational entities performing the activities, the data objects manipulated by them, and the application services invoked during their execution. The chapter gives insights into the modeling, execution, and verification of prespecified process models, and therefore serves as foundation of the subsequent chapters of this book. In particular, it introduces control flow patterns as major building blocks for creating process models and discusses how flexibility-by-design can be achieved using these patterns. Furthermore, the chapter explores the verification of process models and the assurance of their correct executability before deploying them to the PAIS run-time environment. Finally, it elaborates on the enactment of process instances and the coordination of corresponding activities at run-time as specified in the process model.

4.1 Motivation

This chapter deals with business processes whose behavior can be prespecified at build-time, as well as their run-time support in a PAIS. Compared to data- and function-centric information systems, a PAIS introduces an additional archi-tectural layer enabling a strict separation of process logic and application code (cf. Chap. 2). For this purpose, the logic of processes is explicitly represented in terms of *executable process models* maintained by the PAIS. Such a process model prespecifies all activities to be executed, their control and data flow dependencies, organizational entities performing the activities, the data objects manipulated by them, and the application services (e.g., electronic user forms) needed. Based on it, process instances can be created at run-time, each representing a concrete business case (e.g., an X-ray examination for patient Robben). At run-time, the PAIS is responsible for enacting these process instances and for coordinating their activities

M. Reichert and B. Weber, *Enabling Flexibility in Process-Aware Information Systems*, DOI 10.1007/978-3-642-30409-5_4, © Springer-Verlag Berlin Heidelberg 2012

as specified in the process model. The process model thereby serves as reliable schema for process execution. Prespecified process models are primarily suited for supporting predictable and repetitive business processes.

This chapter deals with the modeling, verification, and execution of prespecified processes and serves as foundation for Chaps. 5–10. Section 4.2 discusses how business processes can be formalized as process models and how *flexibility-by-design* can be achieved. Section 4.3 deals with their interpretation and execution by the PAIS at run-time, and Sect. 4.4 addresses the verification of process models. Finally, Sect. 4.5 closes the chapter with a summary.

4.2 Modeling Prespecified Processes

For each business process to be supported (e.g., handling a customer request or processing an insurance claim), a *process type T* represented by a *process model S* (also denoted as *process schema*) has to be defined. Generally, for one particular process type several process models may exist representing the different *versions* of this process type that emerged over time. For specifying process models, a variety of process modeling languages exist. Examples are Event-driven Process Chains [319], Business Process Model and Notation (BPMN) [117], Workflow Nets [2], and Well-Structured Marking Nets (WSM Nets) [260, 290]. These languages have distinct elements and sometimes display subtle differences in their expressiveness and operational semantics. In this book, we abstract from these differences to a large extent and focus on basic commonalities of the languages instead. Even though we will use BPMN (due to its widespread use in both academia and practice) for illustration purposes throughout the book, most of the discussed concepts are applicable irrespective of the process modeling language used.

4.2.1 Basic Concepts

In the following the *control flow schema* of a process model is represented as a directed (process) graph, which comprises a set of *nodes*—representing *start/end nodes*, *activities* or *control connectors*—and a set of *control edges* between them.

Activities. *Activities* can either be *atomic* or *complex*. An atomic activity refers to a human or automated task, and is associated with an invokable application service. While *automated* activities are automatically executed without human interaction (e.g., by invoking web services, Java applications, or database functions), *manual* activities (e.g., electronic forms) are made available as work items to authorized users (cf. Chap. 2). A complex activity, in turn, refers to a subprocess or, more precisely, a *subprocess model*. This allows for the modularization of a business process through *hierarchical* decomposition and the reuse of subprocess models within (different) process models.

Control Connectors, Control Edges, and Transition Conditions. *Control connectors* are used to express splits and joins in the control flow. An XOR-split, for example, allows choosing one out of several outgoing branches, whereas an OR-split allows choosing at least one out of several outgoing branches. *Control edges*, in turn, express precedence relationships between the nodes of a process model. They can be optionally associated with the aforementioned *transition conditions*, which are then evaluated during run-time in order to determine with which path(s) to continue the execution. Moreover, an outgoing control edge of an (X)OR-Split can also be flagged as *default path* which is chosen if for no other outgoing control edge of this node the associated transition condition evaluates to true.

Example 4.1 (Basic Notions–Control Flow). Figure 4.1 shows a process model of a car repair process (in BPMN notation). The depicted process model consists of a start node, an end node, eight activities, and eight control connectors: Activity *Enter Repair Order* is followed by activity *Determine Defect*, which, in turn, is followed by activity *Check Availability of Spare Parts* in the flow of control. Next, if the estimated duration of the repair is more than 1 day, activity *Provide Replacement Car* is performed. In parallel, if the preceding check shows that one or more spare parts required for the repair are missing, activity *Order Spare Parts* is executed. As soon as all spare parts are available, activity *Repair Car* can be performed. Finally, activities *Create Invoice* and *Notify Customer* are executed in parallel to each other.

Data Objects and Data Edges. Additionally, a process model comprises process-relevant *data objects* and *data edges*. A data edge links an activity with a data object and either represents a read or write data access of this activity to the respective data object. Not only may data objects be linked to activities, but they may also be referenced by *transition conditions* attached to outgoing control edges of (X)OR-splits.[1] Transition conditions are usually defined in terms of predicates based on the values of process data objects. Usually, the values of data objects read by an activity (indicated via a read data edge) are passed to the input parameters of the invoked application service or subprocess, and output parameters of an application service or subprocess are written to data objects associated with the activity via a write data edge (cf. Chap. 2). Moreover, some process modeling languages can differentiate between *mandatory* and *optional* read access to a particular data object. Before executing activities with mandatory read access, the respective data object has to be written, though this is no requirement for optional read access [260]. Further, data from the outside environment can be passed to the process (i.e., data

---

[1]Note that in BPMN (X)OR-splits can be expressed either explicitly using gateways or implicitly by allowing for activities with several outgoing control edges.

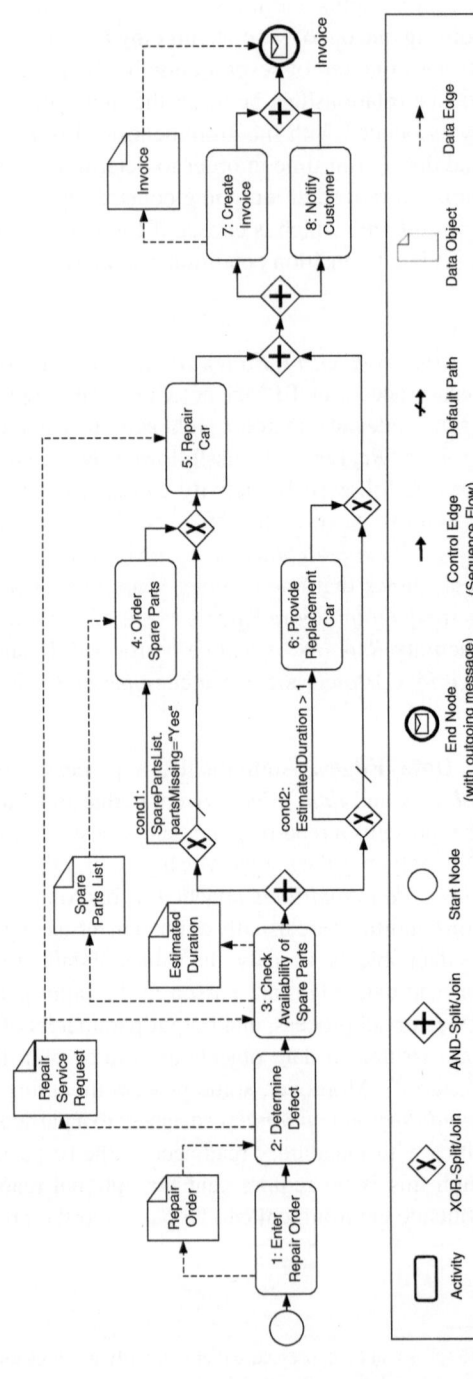

Fig. 4.1 Core modeling concepts

objects thereof) via *start messages* and from the process (i.e., data objects) to the environment via *end messages*.

> *Example 4.2 (Basic Notions–Data Flow).* Figure 4.1 shows the data flow schema of the car repair process as well. Data object *Repair Order* is written by activity *Enter Repair Order* and is read by activity *Determine Defect*. Activity *Determine Defect*, in turn, produces data object *Repair Service Request* which is read by activities *Check Availability of Spare Parts* and *Repair Car*. Data objects *Spare Parts List* and *Estimated Duration* are both written by activity *Check Availability of Spare Parts* and referenced in transition conditions cond1 and cond2 respectively. Moreover, data object *Spare Parts List* is read by activity *Order Spare Parts*. Finally, activity *Create Invoice* creates data object *Invoice*, which is then passed via an end message to the outside environment.

Process Fragments. When referring to specific parts of a process model (instead of the entire model), we use the notion of *process fragment*, which is closely related to single-entry, single-exit (SESE) regions [342]. Figure 4.2 shows process model S from Fig. 4.1 and its decomposition into SESE regions represented as *process structure tree* (for details on SESE decomposition see [342]). SESE regions can be single activities (e.g., R2, R3, R4) or can be nested (e.g., R2, R3, R4, R5, and R12 are contained in R1). Moreover, SESE regions can be sequentially composed (e.g., regions R8 and R10 build region R6), or be disjoint (e.g., regions R6 and R7). A *process fragment* refers to a SESE region (which might be nested) or a sequence of SESE regions, but not to disjoint SESE regions. For example, SESE region R5 constitutes a process fragment. Also the sequence of SESE regions R2, R3, and R4 constitutes a process fragment. The combination of SESE regions R6 and R7, in turn, does not constitute a process fragment, since these two SESE regions are disjoint.

4.2.2   Control Flow Patterns

To capture reusable process modeling knowledge, *control flow patterns* have been devised [23, 309]. In the vein of software design patterns, control flow patterns provide reusable solutions for common modeling problems. In this section some of the most widely used control flow patterns are described (cf. Figs. 4.3 and 4.4). For a complete account of these patterns we refer to [23, 309].

Control flow patterns provide means to describe typical control flow constructs in a language-independent manner and to enable a better understanding, as well as comparison of the expressiveness of existing process modeling languages. In the

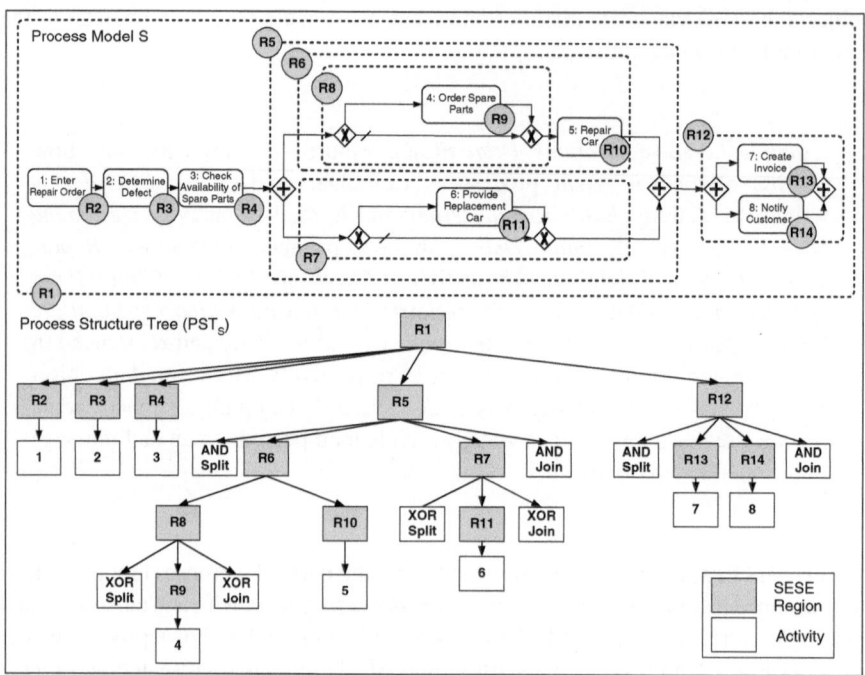

Fig. 4.2 Process model with SESE regions

following we use event diagrams (as proposed in [366]) to informally describe the semantics of selected control flow patterns.

Background: Event Diagrams and State Transition Events. Event diagrams refer to the state transitions of activity instances like `enable`, `start`, or `complete` (cf. Fig. 2.14). For example, `enable(A)` means that the state of activity A changes from `Inactive` to `Enabled`. Further, `start(A)` indicates that the state of activity A changes from `Enabled` to `Running`. Finally, `complete(A)` expresses that A changes from state `Running` to state `Completed`. Based on these activity instance states, event diagrams explain how the different control flow patterns restrict the occurrence of respective events during process execution.

The *sequence pattern* expresses that an activity B becomes enabled directly after an activity A has completed (cf. Fig. 4.3a). The *parallel split pattern* allows splitting the thread of control into multiple threads which are then concurrently executed. As

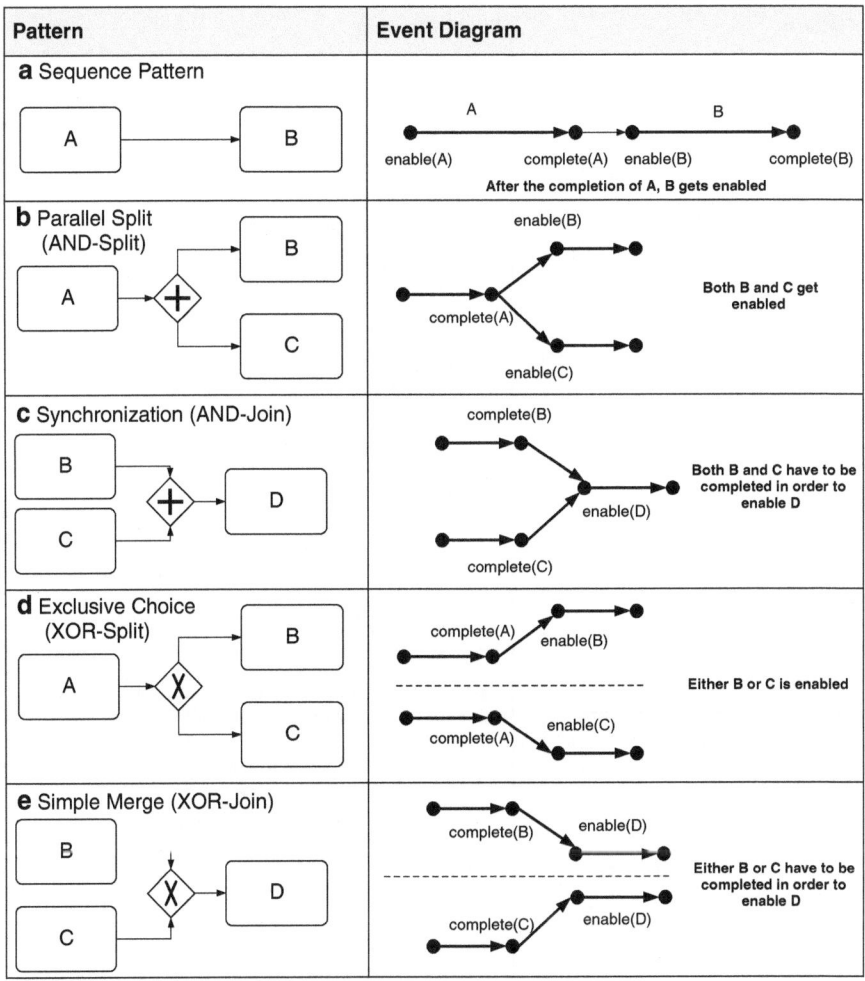

Fig. 4.3 Basic control flow patterns (adopted from [366])

illustrated in Fig. 4.3b, after completing activity A, both activity B and C become enabled. The *synchronization pattern*, in turn, merges multiple concurrent threads of control into a single one. As illustrated in Fig. 4.3c, activity D only becomes enabled, if there are completion events for activities B and C. The *exclusive choice pattern* (also denoted as XOR-split) allows choosing one out of several branches, e.g., by evaluating transition conditions linked to the outgoing edges of the XOR-split. After completing A, either B or C becomes enabled (cf. Fig. 4.3d). The *simple merge pattern* merges two or more branches without synchronization. To enable D, a completion event of either B or C is required (cf. Fig. 4.3e).

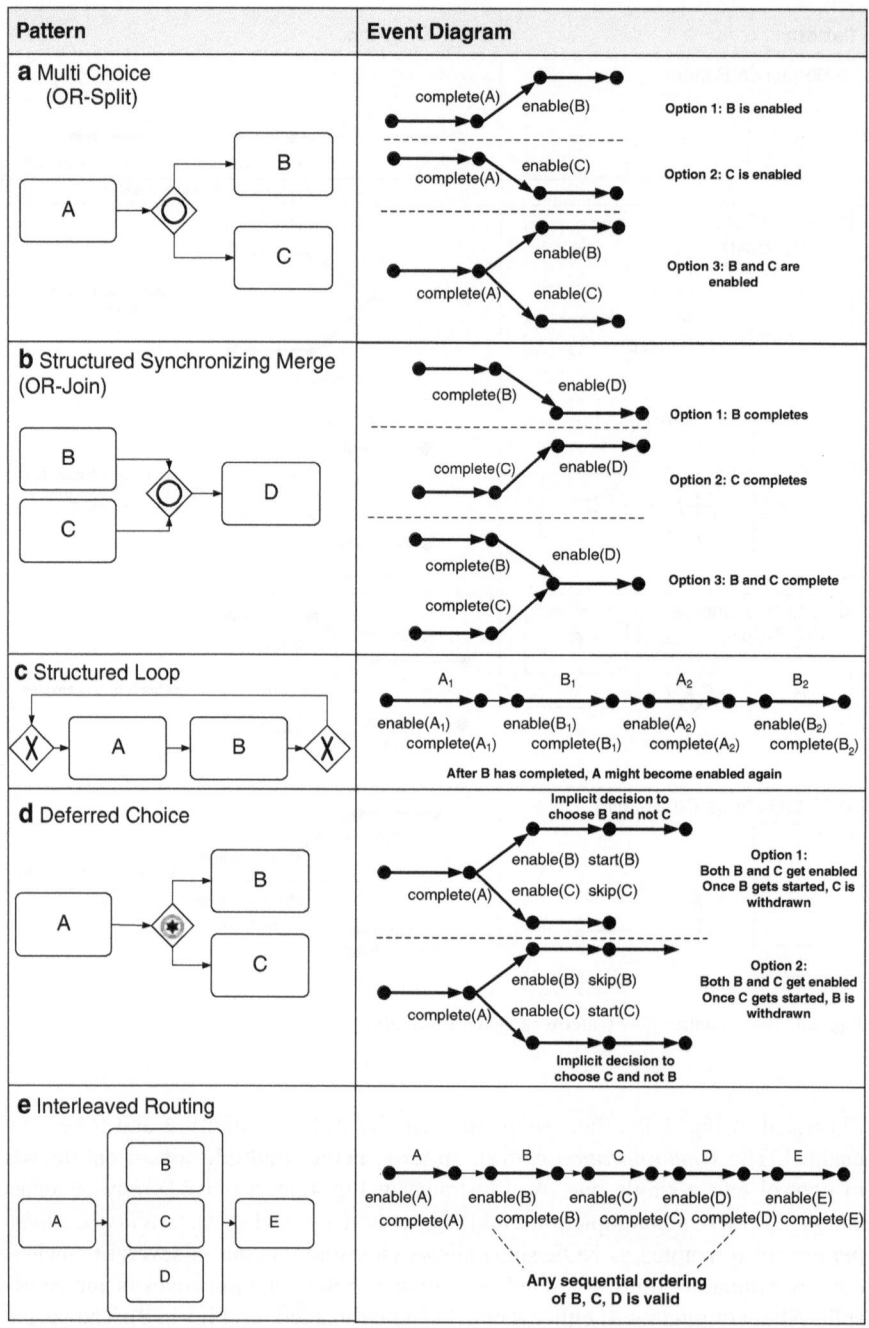

Fig. 4.4 Additional control flow patterns (adopted from [366])

The *multi-choice pattern* (also denoted as OR-split) allows selecting one or several out of multiple alternative branches, e.g., by evaluating transition conditions linked to the outgoing control edges of the OR-split. As illustrated in Fig. 4.4a, after completing activity A several options exist: activity B gets enabled, activity C gets enabled, or both activities B and C get enabled. The *structured synchronizing merge pattern* (also denoted as OR-join), in turn, allows merging several threads of control into a single one. As illustrated in Fig. 4.4b, activity D gets enabled when all preceding active branches are completed. If only B has been selected, activity D is enabled after its completion. If only C has been selected, activity B is enabled after completing C. If both activities B and C have been selected, D is only enabled after the occurrence of completion events for B and C. The *structured loop pattern* allows for the repeated execution of a particular activity or SESE fragment. Figure 4.4c illustrates an event diagram for two loop iterations. The *deferred choice pattern* allows for the selection of one out of several branches in an implicit way (in contrast to the exclusive choice pattern for which this decision is explicit). As illustrated in Fig. 4.4d, after terminating activity A, both activity B and C become enabled. More precisely, the choice between B and C is deferred to that moment at which either B or C is started by a user (e.g., activity B in Fig. 4.4d). Once one of the activities is started, all other branches are skipped (i.e., activity C in Fig. 4.4d). Finally, the *interleaved routing pattern* allows for the sequential execution of a set of activities, whereby the execution order is decided at run-time and each activity has to be executed exactly once. Activities B, C, and D in Fig. 4.4e can be executed in any sequential ordering. Typically, the execution order has to be determined before the first activity of the pattern can get started. An extended variant of the pattern, however, removes this restriction allowing for a deferred choice between activities B, C, and D.

Example 4.3—which has been adopted from [13]—illustrates the usage of the above-discussed control flow patterns.

Example 4.3 (Control Flow Patterns). Adventure Travel is a travel agency that is specializes in supporting their customers in planning their personal adventures. When a customer contacts Adventure Travel the customer request is first registered. Following this, the team of Adventure Travel prepares a proposal, which is then presented to the customer. If the customer likes the proposal, the journey is booked. Alternatively, the customer could ask for further proposals since he was not satisfied with the ones so far presented, or has lost interest. In the latter case, Adventure Travel cancels the customer request. In parallel to the booking of the journey, different insurance policies are offered to the customer, e.g., travel cancelation and delay insurance, baggage insurance, travel emergency insurance, and travel health insurance. Afterwards, a booking confirmation is sent to the customer. Shortly before the journey, the documents (including boarding passes) are sent to the customer who may cancel the journey at any time before starting the journey.

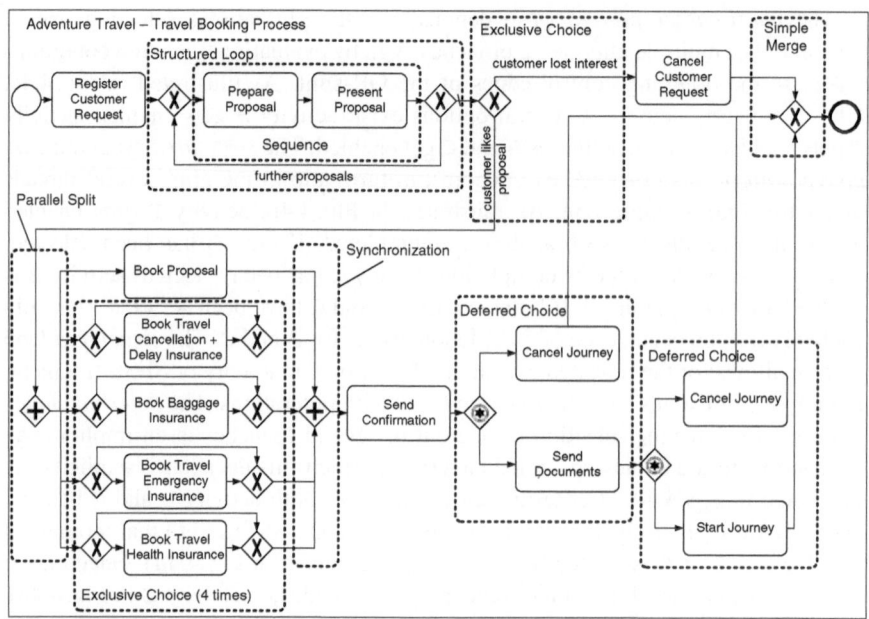

Fig. 4.5 Travel booking-process model and used control flow patterns

Figure 4.5 shows the travel booking process of Adventure Travel and highlights the control flow patterns used. Activities *Prepare Proposal* and *Present Proposal*, together with the precedence relations between them, constitute an example of the *sequence pattern*. In case the customer wants more proposals, activities *Prepare Proposal* and *Present Proposal* are repeated (i.e., *structured loop pattern*). If the customer looses interest, his request is canceled. Otherwise the process continues with the booking. Note that this constitutes an example of an *exclusive choice pattern*. Booking and preparation of insurances can be handled in parallel (i.e., *parallel split and synchronization*). For each insurance option, the customer can decide whether or not to take it (i.e., *exclusive choices*). The choices between activities *Cancel Journey* and *Send Documents* as well as *Start Journey* and *Cancel Journey* are modeled using two *deferred choice patterns*. Finally, the branches are merged using the *simple merge pattern*.

Note that several ways of representing a business process may exist. For example, the booking of the journey including the different insurances could be also modeled using a combination of the *multi-choice* and the *structured synchronizing merge patterns*.

There exist many other control flow patterns in addition to the ones discussed. Table 4.1 shows the catalog of control flow patterns and their categorization as

Table 4.1 Catalog of control flow patterns (for details see http://workflowpatterns.com)

Basic control flow patterns	Cancellation and force Completion patterns
• Sequence • Parallel split • Synchronization • Exclusive choice • Simple merge	• Cancel task • Cancel case • Cancel region • Cancel multiple instance activity • Complete multiple instance activity
Advanced branching and synchronization Patterns	**State-based patterns**
• Multi-choice • Structured synchronizing merge • Multi-merge • Structured discriminator • Structured partial join • Blocking partial join • Cancelling partial join • Generalised AND-join • Local synchronizing merge • General synchronizing merge • Thread merge • Thread split	• Deferred choice • Interleaved parallel routing • Milestone • Critical section • Interleaved routing **Iteration patterns** • Arbitrary cycles • Structured loop • Recursion
Multiple instance patterns	**Termination patterns**
• Multiple instances without synchronization • Multiple instances with a priori design-time knowledge • Multiple instances with a priori run-time knowledge • Multiple instances without a priori run-time knowledge • Static partial join for multiple instances • Canceling partial join for multiple instances • Dynamic partial join for multiple instances	• Implicit termination • Explicit termination **Trigger patterns** • Transient trigger • Persistent trigger

proposed in [309]. For a detailed discussion we refer to [23, 309]. Moreover, there exists a large set of patterns related to the data and resource perspectives [310, 311].

4.2.3 Flexibility-by-Design Through Control Flow Patterns

Most of the introduced control flow patterns foster *flexibility-by-design*, i.e., they enable process designers to build flexibility into the process model. Some forms of *flexibility-by-design* can be achieved using the basic control flow patterns introduced in Sect. 4.2.2; e.g., by enumerating different alternatives in the process model or by allowing activities to be executed in parallel [321]. While the basic control flow patterns are supported by most PAISs, the more advanced control flow patterns are only available in selected systems.[2] As illustrated in Example 4.4, expressiveness and *flexibility-by-design* are closely related. Missing expressiveness often requires workarounds, which potentially leads to unnecessarily large and complex process models (cf. Fig. 4.6b).

Example 4.4 (Expressiveness of Process Modeling Languages). Figure 4.6a shows the process for preparing spinach stuffed mushrooms. The process consists of 13 activities and contains two instances of the *interleaved routing pattern* (cf. Fig. 4.4e). Activities *Add Mushroom Stems*, *Add Onions*, *Add Salt*, and *Add Pepper* can all be executed exactly once in arbitrary sequential ordering. Assuming the extended variant of the *interleaved routing pattern*, the exact ordering of the activities is determined during run-time through deferred decisions (cf. Fig. 4.4d). The same holds for activities *Add Feta to Spinach Mixture*, *Add Salt to Spinach Mixture*, and *Add Pepper to Spinach Mixture*.

Without support for the extended variant of the *interleaved routing pattern*, the process designer is forced to enumerate all possible combinations of these activities leading to a very large and complex process model (cf. Fig. 4.6b). As illustrated in Fig. 4.6b, after having completed activity *Preheat Oven* and *Heat Oil*, there is a deferred choice between activities *Add Mushroom Stems*, *Add Onions*, *Add Salt*, and *Add Pepper*. When completing one of these four activities, another deferred choice between the remaining three activities has to be made. Then, after having executed one of these three activities, yet another deferred choice is needed. Without respective pattern support expressing that *Add Mushroom Stems*, *Add Onions*, *Add Salt*, and *Add Pepper* can be all executed at most once whereby every sequential ordering of these activities is possible, requires 4! (=24) different execution sequences in total. In addition to the unnecessary complexity coming with this task, missing expressiveness can hamper process model maintainability since changes might have to be conducted multiple times. Using the interleaved routing pattern, in turn, the required flexible behavior can be modeled in a much more elegant and compact way (cf. Fig. 4.6a).

Generally, increasing expressiveness also has its downsides. In particular, it makes it more difficult for domain specialists to understand the process models, since they have to know more patterns and their underlying semantics. As a consequence, for example, zur Muehlen and Recker [374] recommend the usage of a

---

[2]See http://workflowpatterns.com for an evaluation of PAISs based on control flow patterns.

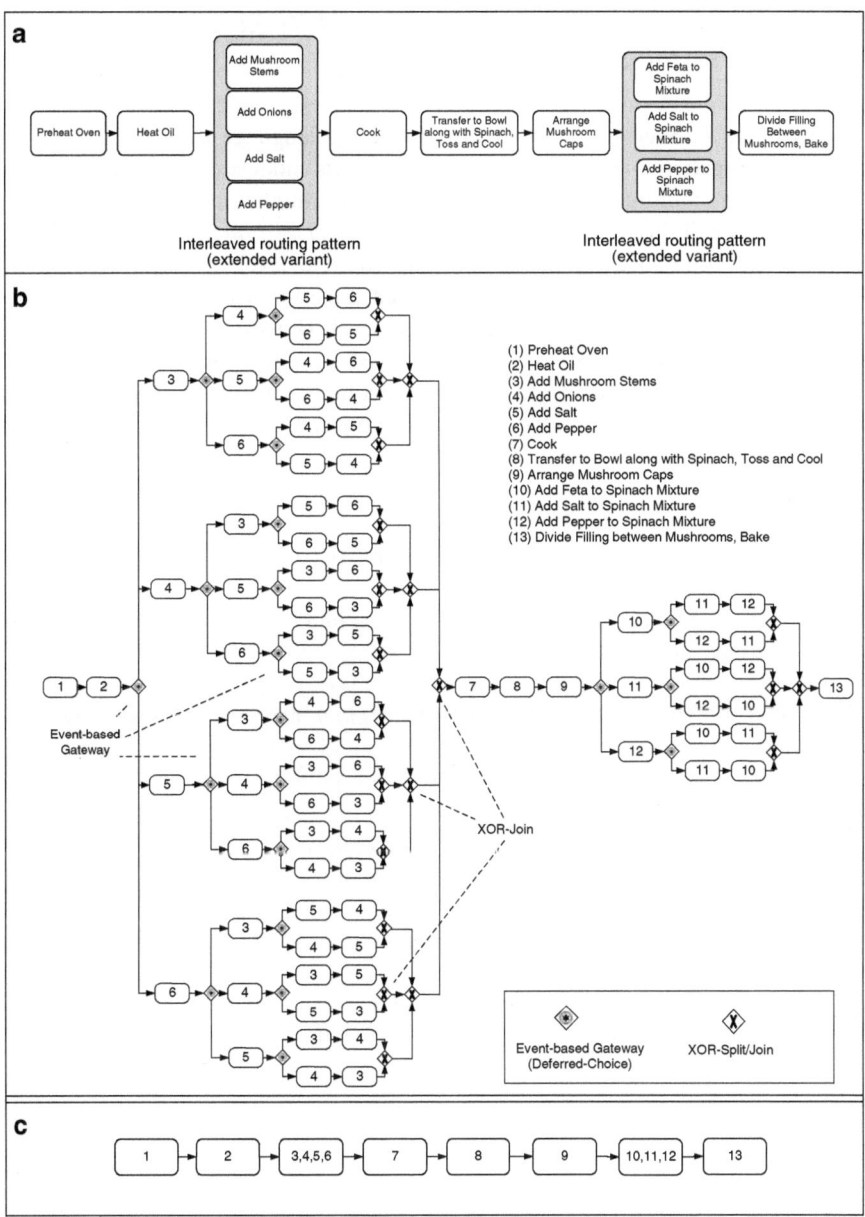

Fig. 4.6 Expressiveness, flexibility-by-design, and granularity

domain-specific subset of a process modeling language that is sufficiently expressive in the given context. Moreover, high expressiveness also leads to more complex run-time environments making it more difficult to provide PAIS support for run-time adaptability.

4.2.4   Granularity of Process Models and Its Relation to Flexibility

As discussed in Sect. 4.2.3, the process modeling language used determines the control flow patterns available for defining process models (i.e., expressiveness). Consequently, it influences flexibility-by-design. Another important factor that impacts the flexibility of a process model is the *level of granularity* applied during process modeling [302]. Generally, the appropriate level of detail depends on the context in which a process model is used. Fine-grained models enable more PAIS guidance and traceability at a detailed level. However, they tend to restrict flexibility, since more details will be prescribed if more control is shifted to the PAIS. Coarse-grained models, in turn, enable a higher degree of flexibility, but at the same time offer fewer guidance and enable traceability only at a coarse-grained level.

Example 4.5 (Granularity of Process Models). Figure 4.6b shows the process for preparing spinach stuffed mushrooms at a rather fine-grained level. Figure 4.6c, in turn, depicts the same process in a more coarse-grained way. By merging activities *Add Mushroom Stems*, *Add Onions*, *Add Salt*, and *Add Pepper* as well as activities *Add Feta to Spinach Mixture*, *Add Salt to Spinach Mixture*, and *Add Pepper to Spinach Mixture* into one activity, model size could be reduced from 85 to 8 activities. Even though the process model from Fig. 4.6b allows for some flexibility-by-design, it implies several restrictions on how activities *Add Mushroom Stems*, *Add Onions*, *Add Salt*, and *Add Pepper* are executed; i.e., each activity can be executed only once and activities have to be executed sequentially. The process model from Fig. 4.6c, in turn, is not making any assumption regarding the execution of these four activities anymore, but control is shifted to the application services implementing the merged activity (if it is an automated activity) or to the end-user (if it is a manual activity). Shifting control to application services or end-users, however, has implications for the traceability of business processes.

4.3   Executing Prespecified Processes

Traditional PAISs strictly separate between build- and run-time (cf. Chap. 2). As described in Sect. 4.2, at build-time a process model is created, based on which multiple process instances can be derived during run-time. To execute such a process instance, typically, its process model is interpreted by the PAIS. Depending on the process modeling language used, the operational semantics driving process execution differs. While certain formalisms (e.g., Workflow Nets [2], YAWL [22], or FunSoft Nets [73]) are based on token flows known from Petri Nets, other approaches like WSM Nets [272] or Activity Nets [178] explicitly mark skipped branches and preserve markings of completed or skipped activities when progressing with the flow of control. When using the latter approach in connection with loops, activities of the loop body have to be reset to state `Inactive` at the beginning of each loop iteration. Furthermore, techniques to skip activities of non-followed branches are required (e.g., *dead path elimination* [178]). In the following sections—to a large extent—we abstract from the concrete operational semantics driving the execution of the process models in a PAIS. Instead we present basic notions being independent of the operational semantics of the used process modeling language. For the sake of understandability we use activity markings to graphically illustrate the state of process instances.

4.3.1 Process Instance and Execution Trace

A process instance I is defined by its model S and a trace σ_I on S reflecting its previous execution events and thus its current execution state.

> **Definition 4.1 (Process Instance).** Let S be a process model. Then: A process instance $I = (S, \sigma_I)$ on S is defined by S together with an instance-specific trace σ_I. Trace σ_I logs events related to the execution of activities (e.g., start and completion events) or to the evaluation of transition conditions of S (cf. Definition 4.2).

Events related to the execution of the activities of a particular process instance are recorded in an *execution trace* (*trace* for short). In particular, a trace contains start and completion events of activities. Additionally, it may comprise other events related to the state transitions of activity instances (e.g., `suspend`, `resume` and `fail`; cf. activity instance lifecycle in Sect. 2.5). Generally, a large number of process instances being in different states may exist for a given process model at a particular point in time.

Depending on the concrete use of a trace only certain types of events are considered. For restoring the state of a running process instance, for example, information regarding start and completion events is needed. This includes information about the values of data objects written by completed activities during process execution. Moreover, to determine all enabled activities, information on how the transition conditions were evaluated is needed.

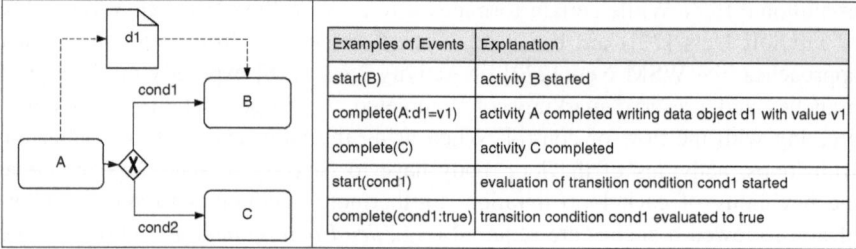

Fig. 4.7 Events related to the execution of activities/transition conditions

---

Definition 4.2 (Execution Trace). Let S be a process model and $Insts$ be
the set of all process instances running on S. Then:

(a) The *execution* trace σ_I of process instance $I \in Insts$ is given by $\sigma_I = {<}e_1, \ldots, e_k{>}$ where the order of e_i in σ_I reflects the temporal order in
    which events e_i related to the execution of activities or the evaluation of
    transition conditions occurred on S.
(b) The total set of traces on S capturing all instances $I \in Insts$ is denoted
    as *execution log*.

Figure 4.7 provides examples of events related to the execution of activities and
the evaluation of transition conditions as contained in a trace. First, events may refer
to the state transitions of activity instances (e.g., start(B) or complete(C);
see also the background box on event diagrams in Sect. 4.2.2). Second, events
may refer to the evaluation of transition conditions attached to outgoing control
edges of (X)OR-Splits (e.g., start(cond1), complete(cond1:true)).
Completion events of activities may be additionally annotated with information
about the data object values written by the respective activity instance, e.g.,
complete(A:d1=v1).

Traces may refer to running process instances as well as completed ones. Thus,
to emphasize that a particular process instance has not reached a final state yet (i.e.,
the process instance is not in state Completed), the notion of *partial trace* will be
used throughout the book. For traces related to completed process instances, in turn,
the notion of *completed trace* will be used. Finally, the notion *sub-trace* will be used
to refer to a sub-sequence of a trace.

Example 4.6 (Execution Traces). Figure 4.8 depicts a model S and four
traces with start and completion events corresponding to instances I_1–I_4.
Execution trace σ_1, for example, shows that activities *Enter Repair Order*,

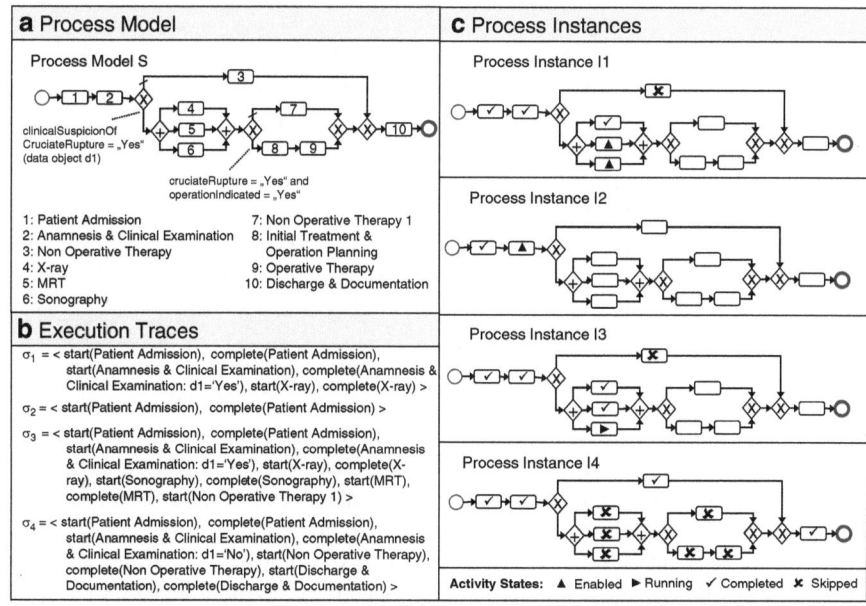

Fig. 4.8 Execution traces and process instance states

Determine Defect, and *Check Availability of Spare Parts* are completed for instance I_1. While traces σ_1, σ_2 and σ_4 are all *partial traces*, trace σ_3 constitutes a *completed trace*.

4.3.2 Enabled Activities and Instance Completion

Given process instance $I = (S, \sigma_I)$, the current execution states of its activities (i.e., the state of each activity of S and the current values of data objects) can be determined (cf. Chap. 8). Exact preconditions for activity enablement depend on the used control flow patterns (cf. Figs. 4.3 and 4.4 for examples).

Definition 4.3 (Enabled Activities). Let S be a process model with activity set A and let $I = (S, \sigma_I)$ be a corresponding process instance with partial trace σ_I. Then, an inactive activity $a \in A$ becomes enabled as soon as all completion events required for its enablement (as defined by the used control flow patterns) have occurred in trace σ_I.

Example 4.7 (Process Instance States). Figure 4.8 illustrates a process model *S* and the execution traces as well as execution states of four process instances I_1-I_4 on S. Regarding process instance I_4, for example, activities *Enter Repair Order, Determine Defect, Check Availability of Spare Parts*, and *Order Spare Parts* are completed. Activity *Provide Replacement Car*, in turn, has been skipped since the transition condition cond2 of the alternative branch was evaluated to false. Activity *Repair Car*, in turn, is enabled for I_3 since a completion event for activity *Order Spare Parts* is contained in σ_1, but no start event for activity *Repair Car*.

Depending on the process modeling language used, the completion semantics of a process instance might differ and either can be *implicit* or *explicit. Explicit completion* means that a process instance completes when it reaches a nominated state. Typically, this is the case when a designated end node is reached (e.g., Workflow Nets or BPMN when using a single end node only). *Implicit completion*, in turn, expresses that a process instance correctly completes (i.e., it reaches state Completed) if there is no enabled or running activity anymore. In certain process modeling languages, for example, state Completed implies that all activities are either completed or skipped. In contrast to the explicit completion of a process instance, implicit completion does not require the presence of a designated end node (like in Activity Nets [178] or in BPMN when using multiple end nodes).

Example 4.8 (Instance Completion). Consider again process model *S* and the corresponding four process instances I_1-I_4 from Fig. 4.8. While instances I_1, I_2 and I_4 are still running, instance I_3 has completed, i.e., after executing activity *Create Invoice* and *Notify Customer*, instance I_4 has reached state *Completed*.

4.4   Verifying Prespecified Process Models

Generally, correct and robust execution of a process model by the PAIS is fundamental. Consequently, the verification of process models constitutes a fundamental task during process implementation (and, as we will see in Chaps. 7 and 9, also in the context of dynamic process model changes during run-time). In particular, at build-time it has to be ensured that process models being deployed to the PAIS run-time environment can be properly executed; i.e., corresponding process instances will always complete in a well-defined and proper state. In particular, a business process executed by a PAIS must not be blocked due to modeling errors (e.g., non-satisfiable execution constraints) leading to deadlocks or other kinds of severe problems (e.g., missing initialization of data objects). By verifying process models at build-time, potential problems can be identified a priori and the model can be corrected before its deployment.

4.4.1 Process Model Soundness

First of all, a process model must be *syntactically correct*, i.e., conform to the grammar rules as defined by the process modeling language used. Examples of such rules include block-structuring, presence of explicit start/end nodes, and bipartite graph structuring (e.g., like in Petri Nets and Event Driven Process Chains) depending on the process modeling language used. However, syntactical correctness is not sufficient to guarantee for the correct executability of process instances. Typical problems that might occur when executing process models at run-time and therefore need to be prevented by applying respective checks on these models already at build-time include deadlocks and dead activities.

In general, there exists a number of properties every process model should exhibit. One fundamental property an executable process model has to fulfill is *soundness*. Informally, soundness can be described as the combination of three basic characteristics concerning the dynamic behavior of a process model [368]:

- *Option to complete*: A process instance, once started, can always complete.
- *Proper completion*: When a process instance completes, there exists no related activity of this instance which is still running or enabled.
- *No dead activities*: A process model does not contain any dead activity, i.e., for each activity there exists at least one completed trace producible on that model and containing this activity.

Subsequently, these characteristics are formally described based on the trace notion (cf. Definition 4.2), i.e., independent of a particular process modeling language. In the examples illustrated, however, we assume explicit termination.

Option to Complete. A process model S has the *option to complete* if for each partial trace (cf. Definition 4.2) producible on S a sequence of activity start and activity completion events can be added such that a completed trace on S results.

Definition 4.4 (Option to Complete). Let S be a process model with activity set A and let E be the set of events related to the execution of activities from A or the evaluation of transition conditions from S. Let further QS_S be the set of all completed traces producible on S. Then, for each partial trace $\sigma_I = \; < e_1, \ldots, e_k >, e_i \in E$ on S, representing a potential instance I running on S, there exist events $e_{k+1}, \ldots, e_n \in E$, related to the execution of

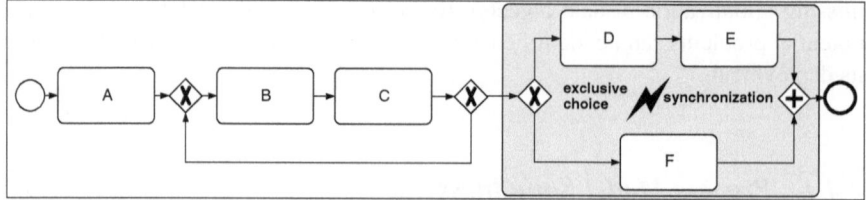

Fig. 4.9 Example of a process model containing a deadlock

activities from A such that $\sigma = <e_1, \ldots, e_k, e_{k+1} \ldots, e_n> \in QS_S$; i.e., I can complete.

Example 4.9 (Option to Complete). Figure 4.9 shows an example of a non-sound process model. More precisely, a deadlock occurs during process execution, i.e., the process model has no option to complete. The *deadlock* is caused by a connector mismatch in the highlighted process fragment. Due to the use of the *exclusive choice pattern* only one of the two branches is executed, i.e., either activities D and E or activity F. The *synchronization pattern* at the end of the fragment, however, requires completion events from E and F.

Proper Completion. *Proper completion* can be ensured if any process instance, reaching its final state Completed, has no enabled or running activities.

Definition 4.5 (Proper Completion). Let S be a process model with activity set A and QS_S be the set of all completed traces producible on S. Then: For any trace $\sigma = <e_1, \ldots, e_n> \in QS_S$ there is no activity being in state Enabled or Running after applying all events $e_i \in \sigma$, $i = 1, \ldots, n$ in the order of their occurrence to S (i.e., after replaying σ on S).

Example 4.10 (Proper Completion). Figure 4.10 illustrates a process model for which proper completion cannot be guaranteed. If, after the completion of A, transition condition cond1 evaluates to true and cond2 evaluates to false, proper completion cannot be ensured anymore. In particular, the process

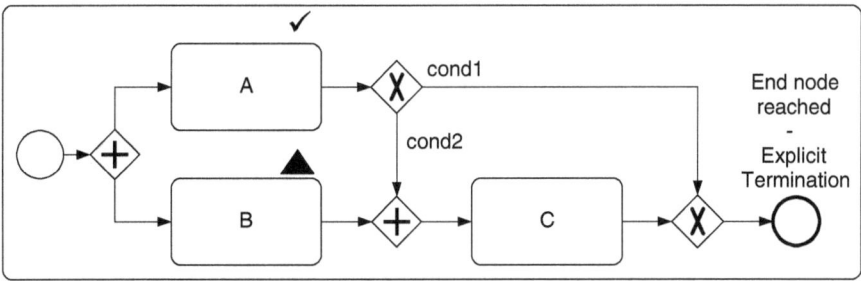

Execution Trace

σ₁= <start(A), start(B), complete(A), start(cond1), complete(cond1:true),
    start(cond2), complete(cond2:false)>

Fig. 4.10 Example of a process model for which proper completion cannot be achieved

might reach the end node and thus complete (assuming explicit completion),
while activity B is still in state Enabled or Running.

Dead Activity. An activity contained in a process model S is denoted as *dead* if
none of the traces producible on S contains that activity.

Definition 4.6 (Dead Activity). Let S be a process model with activity set A.
Let further QS_S be the set of completed traces producible on S. Then, an
activity $a \in A$ is called dead iff there is no trace $\sigma \in QS_S$ that contains a
completion event for activity a (i.e., $complete(a)$). Formally:
$$\nexists \sigma \in QS_S : complete(a) \in \sigma.$$

Example 4.11 (Dead Activity). Figure 4.11 illustrates a process model with
two dead activities. Since transition condition cond1: x < 0 AND x
> 1 always evaluates to false, there is no completed trace containing any
event related to activity B or C. Since completion events for B and C are not
contained in any of the producible traces, they both constitute dead activities
which will never be executed.

For checking soundness of a process model, different verification frameworks
and tools exist [1, 4, 79, 249, 327, 343, 344]. Techniques frequently applied to
verify soundness (cf. Definitions 4.4–4.6) include reachability analysis and model
checking depending on the process modeling language used.

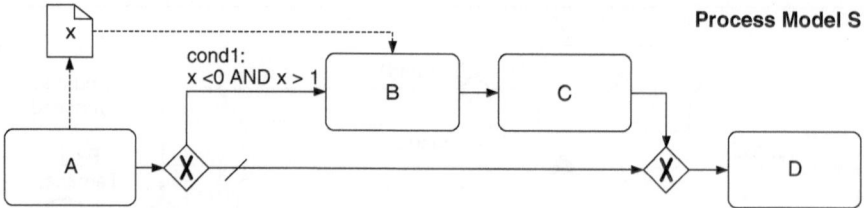

Traces Producible on S:
σ_1= <start(A), complete(A:x=5), start(cond1), complete(cond1:false), start (D), complete(D)>

Fig. 4.11 Example of a process model containing a dead activity

4.4.2   Correctness of Data Flow

Existing techniques mostly focus on control flow verification. To guarantee PAIS robustness, however, correctness of the data flow perspective is fundamental as well [327]. In particular, data flow errors like missing data, unnecessary data, or lost updates have to be avoided [318, 335, 337]. Note that this is particularly important in the context of dynamic process changes (cf. Chap. 7). Verification issues related to the data flow schema of a process model, for example, are addressed by [260, 337] and are considered in few existing PAISs like ADEPT [260] and Websphere Process Server [148]. In the following a set of important data flow errors is described in detail; for a discussion of other kinds of data flow errors we refer the interested reader to [337]. To reason about potential data flow errors, in the following, start messages (i.e., start nodes) and end messages (i.e., end nodes) are logically treated like activities with start and completion events captured in execution traces. More precisely, a start message is logically treated like an activity writing a data object and an end message like an activity reading data objects.

Missing Data. The data flow schema of a process model S might cause missing data at run-time if a data object exists which can be read during run-time without having been written by any preceding activity or provided by the outside environment (i.e., by a start message).

Definition 4.7 (No Missing Data). Let S be a process model with activity set A (including start and end nodes), set of transition conditions C, and set of data objects D. Let further QS_S be the set of all completed traces producible on S with start and completion events related to activities (including start and end messages) and transition conditions.

Then, the problem of missing data is not present in the data flow schema of S, iff: For every trace $\sigma \in QS_S$ containing the start event of an activity from $a \in A$ (including end nodes) or a transition condition from C reading

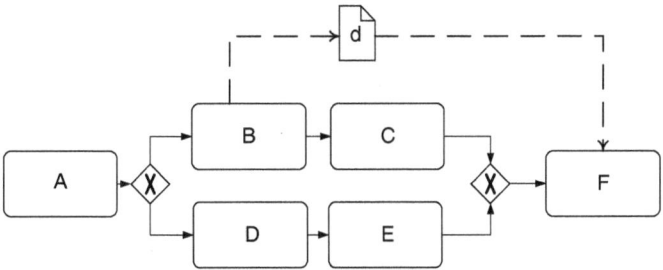

Fig. 4.12 Process model with missing data

a data object $d \in D$ mandatorily, there exists at least one completion event of an activity $y \in A$ (including start nodes) writing d and preceding the start event of activity a in σ. Formally:

$$\forall \sigma \in QS_S : (\exists\, x \in A \cup C \text{ with start(x) } \in \sigma \wedge [x \text{ reads } d \text{ mandatorily}])$$

$$\Rightarrow$$

$$(\exists\, y \in A \text{ with complete(y) } \in \sigma \wedge \text{ complete(y) } < \text{ start(x) } \wedge$$

$$[y \text{ writes } d])$$

Example 4.12 (Missing Data). Figure 4.12 illustrates a process model with an incorrect data flow schema due to potentially missing data. Activity F requires data object d as input. Since d is produced by activity B (which is part of an alternative branch), data supply cannot always be guaranteed. If the branch with activity B is skipped (i.e., the lower branch with activities D and E is chosen), d required by activity F will never be produced.

Note that missing data might cause severe problems during run-time; e.g., an invoked activity service might crash or produce wrong outputs.

Unnecessary Data. A data object written by an activity of process model S is called *unnecessary* if it is neither read by any subsequent activity or transition condition nor passed to the outside environment via an end message.

Definition 4.8 (No Unnecessary Data). Let S be a process model with activity set A (including start and end nodes), set of transition conditions C,

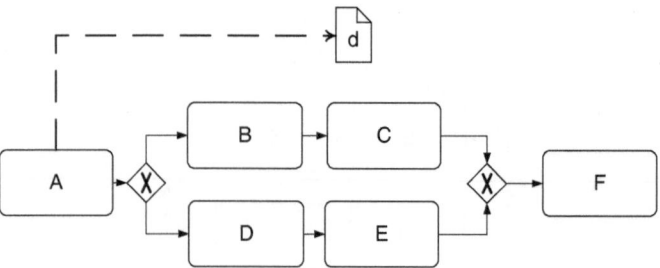

Fig. 4.13 Process model with unnecessary data

and set of data object D. Let further QS_S be the set of all completed traces producible on S. Then: a data object $d \in D$ is not *unnecessary* if (1) d can be written by at least one process instance on S and (2) if d is written by an activity (or start message) it is read by at least one subsequent activity, end message, or transition condition. Formally:

(1)$\forall d \in D : \exists \sigma \in QS_S, \exists x \in A$ with complete(x) $\in \sigma \wedge [x$ writes $d]$

(2)$\forall d \in D : \exists \sigma \in QS_S, \exists x \in A$ with complete(x) $\in \sigma \wedge [x$ writes $d], \Rightarrow$

$\quad\quad (\exists\, y \in A \cup C : $ start(y) $\in \sigma \wedge$ complete(x) $<$ start(y) $\wedge [y$ reads $d])$

Example 4.13 (Unnecessary Data). Figure 4.13 illustrates a very simple process model with an incorrect data flow schema due to the presence of an unnecessary data object. Activity A writes data object d which is never read.

Compared to missing data, the problem of unnecessary data is less severe since it usually does not prevent a process model from being correctly executed [148]. Nevertheless, unnecessary data objects should be avoided as they are not used anywhere in the process and thus decrease model comprehensibility.

Lost Data. Finally, the data flow schema of a process model S might cause *lost data* at run-time if a data object written by an activity is updated by a subsequent activity, but without reading the data object in between.

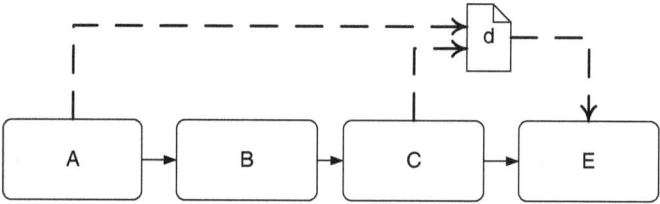

Fig. 4.14 Process model producing a lost update

Definition 4.9 (No Lost Updates). Let S be a process model with activity set A (including start and end nodes), set of transition conditions C, and data object set D. Let further QS_S be the set of all completed traces on S. Then, the data flow schema of S does not allow for any lost updates on data objects from D iff:

There exists no trace $\sigma \in QS_S$ containing a completion event of an activity $x \in A$ (including start messages) writing data object $d \in D$ which is followed by the completion event of another activity $y \in A$ writing the same data object d, without at least one activity or transition condition $z \in A \cup C$ reading d and being in between x and y. Formally:

$\forall \sigma \in QS_S$: $(\exists\, x, y \in A$ both writing data object $d \in D$ $\wedge$

         complete(x), complete(y) $\in \sigma$ with complete(x) $<$ complete(y))

         $\Rightarrow$

         $(\exists\, z \in A \cup C$ with [z reads d]$\wedge$

         (start(z) $\in \sigma$ $\wedge$ complete(x) $<$ start(z) $<$ complete(y))

Example 4.14 (Lost Updates). Figure 4.14 illustrates a process model with an incorrect data flow schema due to lost updates of a data object during runtime. Activity A writes data object d which is needed by activity D as input. Data object d is then overwritten by activity C without having read the data produced by activity A and thus resulting in lost data.

4.4.3   Well-Structured Versus Unstructured Process Models

In general, process models can either be classified as *well-structured* (also denoted as *block-structured*) or *unstructured*. A *well-structured* process model is composed of *blocks*, which may be nested, but must not overlap; i.e., their nesting must be regular [143, 260, 342]. Thereby, a *block* refers to a SESE region as described in Sect. 4.2. In general, a block can be a single activity, a sequence, a parallel branching, a conditional branching, a loop block, or *S* itself.

> *Example 4.15 (Blocks).* Figure 4.2 highlights the different blocks of the car repair process. Region R1, for instance, is an example for the nesting of blocks. It comprises regions R2, R3, R4, R5, and R12. Region R5, in turn, again comprises two blocks (i.e., regions R6 and R7). Further, region R2 constitutes a block comprising a single activity solely. Region R6 with region R9 and activity *Repair Car* is an example of a sequence block. Region R12, with activities *Create Invoice* and *Notify Customer*, is a parallel block. Finally, region R8 constitutes an example of a conditional block.

The concept of block-structuring is well known from structured programming languages [76], and can be found in process modeling and execution languages like BPEL, XLANG, and WSM Nets. While the modeling languages used by process management systems like ADEPT [70], CAKE2 [216, 217], and Work-Party [306] enforce block-structuring, other languages also allow for the modeling of unstructured process models (e.g., BPMN, YAWL [368], and Corepro [225]). For process models meeting certain structural constraints (e.g., block-structuring) soundness can be ensured or checked rather easily. For unstructured process models, in turn, advanced verification techniques need to be applied to ensure proper dynamic behavior of the modeled processes. Well-structured process models also offer integrated verification techniques for ensuring data flow correctness (e.g., ADEPT [260]). For unstructured models, however, ensuring data flow correctness is much more difficult and sometimes practically unfeasible [68].

In many cases, unstructured process models can be transformed into block-structured ones [15, 143, 246, 370]. Since this is not possible in general [143], it is recommended to avoid unstructured process models if possible, since they constitute a significant source of error [3, 171]. The well structurednesss of process models has been discussed as a guideline not only to reduce errors [68, 207], but also to facilitate model understandability [207].

Figure 4.15 illustrates an unstructured process model and its behavior-equivalent structured version. In the unstructured version of the process model not all blocks are regularly nested; i.e., this process model comprises two loop-backs (i.e., activities F and G) resembling two GOTO-statements known from some programming languages. In the structured version, in turn, these GOTO-statements have been removed by accepting two redundant activities (i.e., C and D).

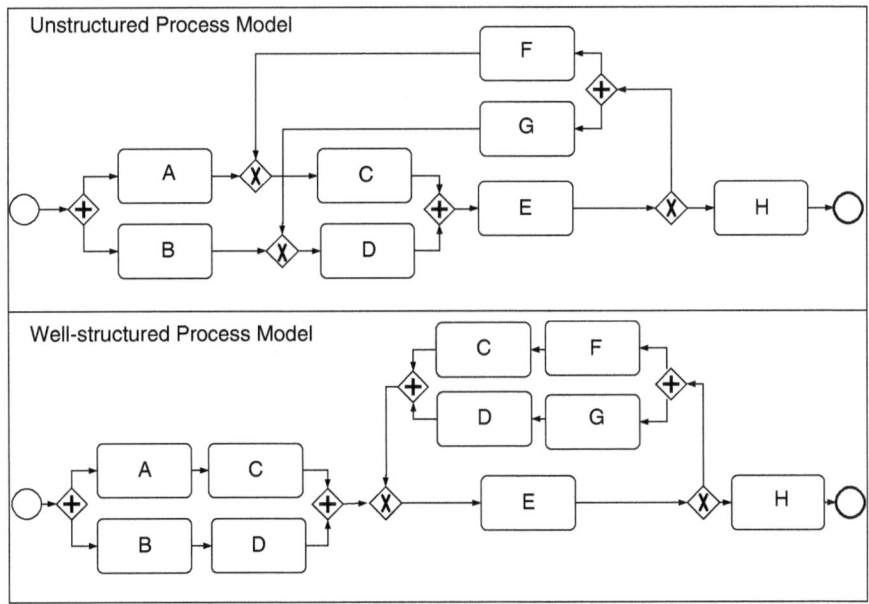

Fig. 4.15 Unstructured process model and behavior-equivalent structured process model

4.5 Summary

This chapter introduced basic concepts for the modeling, verification, and execution of prespecified processes as supported by traditional PAISs. Prespecified processes provide a reliable schema for process execution and are well suited for automating repetitive and predictable business processes. Even though prespecified processes allow for *flexibility-by-design* (especially if a high degree of expressiveness is provided by the PAIS), missing support for variability, adaptation, and evolution makes them unsuitable for addressing all flexibility needs introduced in Chap. 3. In the subsequent chapters, we will discuss advanced methods for supporting variability, adaptation, and evolution in the context of prespecified processes.

Exercises

4.1. Understanding Prespecified Process Models

Which of the following statements are true for the process model shown in Fig. 4.5?

(a) After activity *Send Confirmation* has completed, both activity *Cancel Journey* and activity *Send Documents* are enabled.

(b) *Present Proposal, Book Baggage Insurance, Book Proposal, Book Travel Health Insurance, Send Confirmation* is a valid sub-trace (assuming that traces only comprise activity completion events).
(c) After *Send Confirmation* has completed, the journey can be cancelled at any point; i.e., one of the two occurrences of activity *Cancel Journey* is always enabled until the process instance reaches state *Completed*.
(d) In every trace the number of occurrences for *Prepare Proposal* is larger or equal than the number of occurrences of activity *Book Proposal*.
(e) If a trace contains activity *Cancel Journey*, it never contains activity *Send Documents*.
(f) When activity *Cancel Journey* becomes enabled (immediately after activity *Send Confirmation* has completed), activity *Send Documents* is skipped.
(g) Activities *Book Proposal* and *Book Baggage Insurance* can be executed concurrently, i.e., both activities become enabled at the same time. Further, their completion can occur in arbitrary order.
(h) For any process instance with partial trace *<Register Customer Request, Prepare Proposal, Present Proposal>* at least one, and at most eight, activities need to be executed to complete the process instance.
(i) After completing activity *Present Proposal* one of the following activities must directly follow: *Book Proposal, Cancel Customer Request, Book Baggage Insurance, Book Travel Health Insurance, Book Travel Cancellation + Delay Insurance*, or *Book Travel Emergency Insurance*.

4.2. Understanding Prespecified Process Models

Which of the following statements are true for the process model of Fig. 4.16?

(a) After activity *Transport Patient to Ward* has completed, activities *Provide Postsurgical Care, Create Surgery Report*, and *Order Lab Test* become enabled.
(b) Activity *Schedule Surgery* and *Write Discharge Letter* never appear in the same trace.
(c) It is possible that activities *Discharge Patient, Create Surgery Report*, and *Order Lab Test* are all in state enabled.
(d) *<Admit Patient, Perform Checkup, Examine Patient, Discuss Anesthesia, Discuss Risks, Make Decision, Write Discharge Letter>* is a valid trace.
(e) To enable activity *Write Discharge Letter*, activities *Discharge Patient, Create Surgery Report*, and *Order Lab Test* need to be completed.

4.3. Process Modeling with BPMN

(a) Model the process of the scouting department of an American football team acquiring new players through the NFL draft using BPMN.

At the beginning of the process the scouting team watches tapes from college football games. Afterwards the scouting team attends games in which the player they are interested in is participating. If the scouting team is still interested in

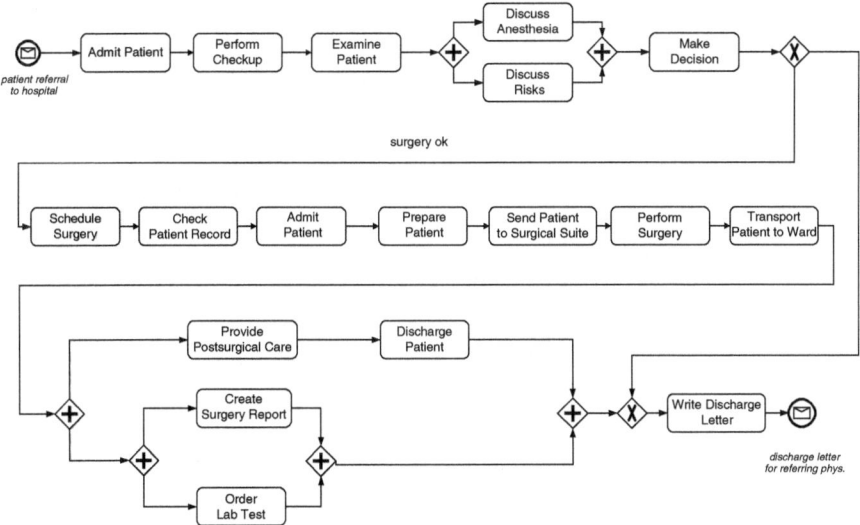

Fig. 4.16 Process for planning and performing a keyhole surgery

the player (after having attended his games), they attend the NFL Scouting Combine. Otherwise, the scouting team goes back to watching tapes. After attending the NFL Scouting Combine the scouting team talks to the player. If the scouting team is not interested in the player anymore, the process ends. Otherwise, the scouting team performs a background check to identify possible issues concerning the player's character. At the same time, the scouting team talks to the player's coaches as well as his family. If the scouting team is not interested in the player anymore the process is completed. Otherwise, if the player is still available, the scouting team drafts the player. If the player is no longer available, the process is completed.

Additional Information (Do not model this part)

NFL Draft. The NFL Draft is an annual event in which the 32 National Football League teams select newly eligible college football players. It is the NFL's most common source of player recruitment.
NFL Scouting Combine. The NFL Scouting Combine is a week-long showcase, occurring every February in Indianapolis, Indiana's Lucas Oil Stadium, where college football players perform physical and mental tests in front of National Football League coaches, general managers and scouts prior to the NFL Draft.

(b) Which workflow patterns can you identify in this scenario?

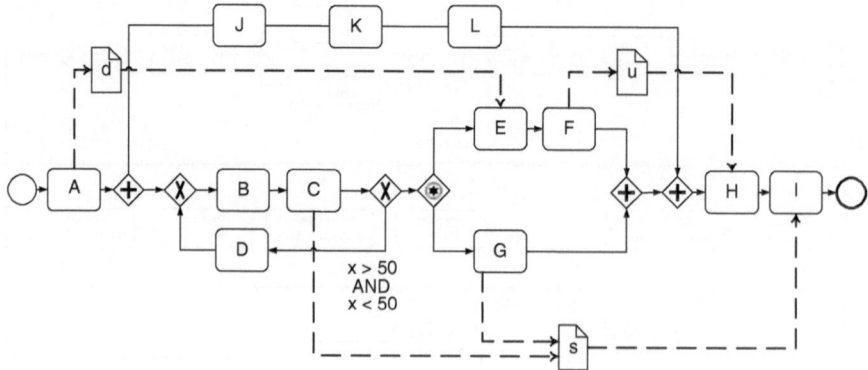

Fig. 4.17 Incorrect process model

4.4. Workflow Patterns

In this chapter only a small subset of the control flow patterns has been introduced.

(a) To learn about additional control flow patterns visit the workflow patterns web
     site at http://workflowpatterns.com/ and check out some of the flash animations.
(b) In addition, have a look at the resource and data patterns presented at the above
     web site.
(c) Have a look at the evaluation reports provided at the aforementioned web site.
     Which of the control flow patterns can be commonly found in existing PAISs?
     Are there any patterns which are almost never supported?

4.5. Process Model Verification

Which modeling errors can you detect in the process model depicted in Fig. 4.17?

Chapter 5
Process Configuration Support

Abstract In practice, process models are often reused in a different application context, resulting in a large number of related process model variants. Typically, these process variants pursue the same or similar business objectives and share several commonalities. However, they can also exhibit some variable attributes, depending on how they are used in different application environments. This chapter presents concepts for the configuration and management of business process variants. It introduces different approaches for capturing variability in business process models and for deriving process variants through configuration of these models. The latter is supported through a number of techniques that can be used by domain experts.

5.1 Motivation

As illustrated by Example 5.1, process models are often reused in a varying application context, e.g., different industries, enterprises, or projects [164].

Example 5.1 (Variants of Invoice Checking and Approval Processes). Consider the process of *Invoice Checking and Approval*, which is prevalent in almost all industries and companies. It deals with the receipt of a supplier invoice and its compliance with the corresponding purchase order. In practice, numerous variants of this business process exist, whereby variability is introduced by various industry-, company-, and supply-specific factors. For example, depending on whether incoming goods or provided services are charged, the process would look different. In the first case, the duly receipt of physical goods has to be checked and the invoice be compared with order and delivery documents, while in the latter case, specialists employed or hired by the company have to be contacted to approve that charged services were provided according to the agreements made. Moreover, terms of payment might differ in these two cases. While physical goods are usually charged once, the payment of long-running services is usually split into several invoices.

The reuse of a process model in different application environments often results in a large collection of related *process model variants* (*process variants* for short) belonging to the same *process family* [38]. In particular, respective process variants pursue the same or similar *business objective* and have certain activities (and their ordering constraints) in common, while at the same time differences due to their use in heterogeneous application context exist, e.g., certain activities may be relevant for only some of the process variants or different execution paths that need to be taken depending on the application environment.

Obviously, companies can learn a lot from the process knowledge characteristic of their domain [164, 172]. Hence, it would be too costly for them to design and implement standardized business processes as the one described in Example 5.1 from scratch. For these reasons, there is a great interest in capturing common process knowledge only once and using it in terms of *reference process models* (*reference processes* for short). Following this trend, a variety of reference processes have been suggested in the last few years. Examples include ITIL for IT service management [134], SAP reference models representing business processes as supported in SAP's enterprise resource planning system [209], or medical guidelines for patient treatment [172]. Typically, these reference processes are described in text using a narrative form or by using a conventional process modeling language (e.g., SAP reference processes are specified in terms of Event-driven Process Chains) [209]. Regarding theses examples, however, there is no comprehensive support for explicitly describing the *variation points* of a reference process. Instead, individual process variants have to be manually derived from such a reference process, which is a cumbersome and error-prone task.

Example 5.2 illustrates the process of handling medical examinations with several of its variants. Throughout this chapter we will refer to this example in order to illustrate different approaches for capturing variability in business process models.

Example 5.2 (Process Variants Handling Medical Examinations). Consider the four process variants in Fig. 5.1. These variants have several activities (e.g., *Order Medical Examination, Perform Medical Examination*, and *Create Medical Report*) in common. In Fig. 5.1, these common activities are gray-shaded. However, the variants also show differences, e.g., in respect to the kind of examination (i.e., standard vs. emergency medical examination), the way the examination is handled (e.g., scheduling an examination later by making an appointment with the examination unit or registering one for the

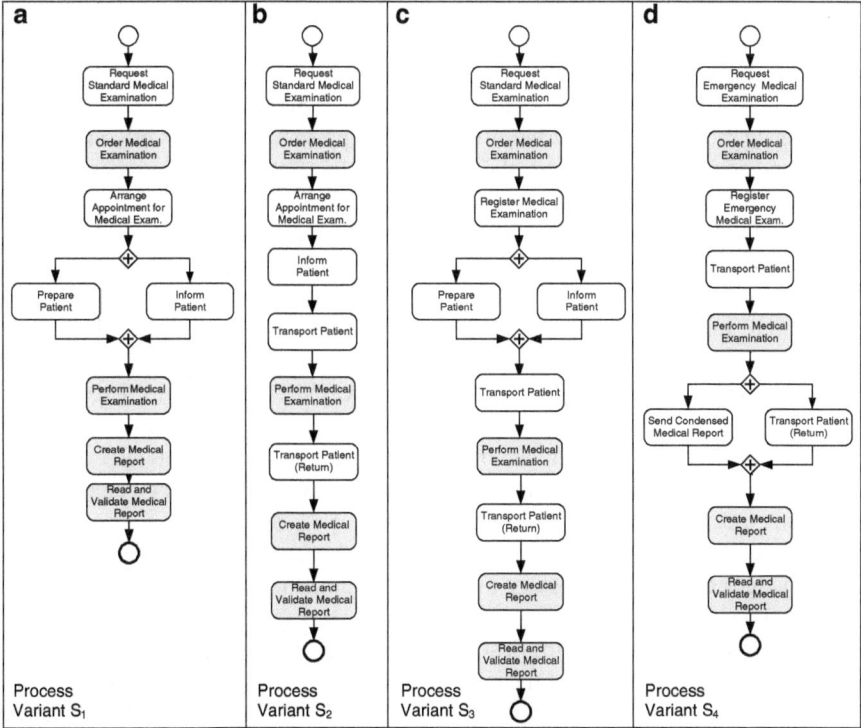

Fig. 5.1 Variants of a process for handling medical examinations

same day), or the need of specific activities depending on the given application environment (e.g., *Prepare Patient* or *Transport Patient*).

Many process modeling tools do not adequately support the handling of such process variants. These have to be prespecified either in terms of separate process models or by using one process model with conditional branchings. However, both approaches can result in model redundancies that significantly aggravate model maintenance, and thus turn it into a time-consuming and error-prone task. Hence, a modeling approach for explicitly capturing variability in process models is needed, i.e., for representing a family of related process variants in a compact, reusable, and maintainable manner. In particular, it should be possible to easily configure a process family to an individual process variant that best fits the requirements of the given application environment. This way, established practices and process knowledge can be reused, while affording companies the flexibility to individualize their business processes.

This chapter presents different approaches for modeling variability in business processes as well as for configuring respective models to individual process variants.

First, Sect. 5.2 introduces *behavior-based approaches* capturing the behavior of all process variants in the same artifact called *reference process model*; i.e., a reference process model merges a multitude of process variants into one configurable model capturing both the commonalities and the differences of the process variants. In such a reference process model, variation points are represented in terms of configurable nodes and edges. By configuring these, the behavior of the reference process model can be customized to the given context. *Second*, Sect. 5.3 presents a *structural approach* which allows adding, removing, or changing the process behavior by adjusting the structure of a configurable process model accordingly (e.g., by adding or deleting activities).

In both approaches the selection of the most suitable variant is denoted as *configuration*. Thereby, for each *configuration* option (e.g., *variation point*) it must be decided which of the available alternatives shall be chosen. After making these choices, the configured model can be transformed into an executable one by dropping those parts that are no longer required. The latter step is called *individualization*. Both the configuration and the individualization of a configurable process model constitute build-time activities; i.e., they can be accomplished without need for any run-time knowledge. In particular, they do not constitute run-time changes becoming necessary to deal with unplanned or exceptional situations (cf. Chap. 7).

In the described scenario, the design phase is split into two subphases: one during which the process family (i.e., the configurable process model and its configuration options) is designed, and one in which this model is configured and individualized for a particular process variant. In order to enable domain experts to accomplish the latter task, high-level configuration techniques exist, including questionnaire models, feature diagrams, and context-based approaches (cf. Sect. 5.4).

Finally, there are further aspects which need to be considered by any framework enabling business process configuration. For example, it has to be ensured that individualized process variants are sound (cf. Sect. 5.5).

5.2   Behavior-Based Configuration Approaches

This section introduces two behavior-based approaches for capturing variability in business processes. While the first one (cf. Sect. 5.2.1) allows configuring a process model based on the hiding and blocking of control edges and execution paths, the second approach (cf. Sect. 5.2.2) uses configurable nodes (i.e., configurable activities and control connectors) as variation points and additionally provides guidance and constraints regarding possible configuration options.

5.2.1 Hiding and Blocking

A language-independent approach for capturing variability in prespecified process models is described in [105]. In particular, the operators *hiding* and *blocking*, as known from the *inheritance of process behavior* [9], are applied to *labeled transition systems (LTSs)*. First, this section discusses how process behavior can be expressed in terms of an LTS, then it shows how hiding and blocking operators can be used for configuring an LTS-based reference process model.

5.2.1.1 Expressing Process Behavior Based on LTS

We abstract from the concrete elements of the process modeling language used and then apply LTSs to represent process behavior. An LTS constitutes a formal abstraction of a computing process. Hence, any process modeling language being equipped with operational semantics can be mapped onto an LTS. Basically, an LTS is a graph that comprises nodes representing *states*, and directed edges between these nodes representing *labeled transitions*, and thereby denoting some event or activity.

Definition 5.1 (Transition System). A labeled transition system is a tuple $TS = (S, E, T, s_i)$ where S is the set of states and E is the set of events. Further, $T \subseteq S \times E \times S$ is the transition relation and $s_i \in S$ is the initial state.

Example 5.3 (Transition System). Figure 5.2 depicts an example of a simple transition system $TS = (S, E, T, s_i)$ with $S = \{a, b, c\}$, $E = \{x, y, z\}$, $T = \{(a, x, a), (a, y, b), (b, z, a), (b, y, c), (c, z, b), (c, y, c)\}$, and $s_i = a$. The semantics of such a transition system is simple, i.e., starting from the initial state, any path through the transition system is possible. For example, $\langle x, x, x, y, z, x \rangle$, $\langle y, y, y, z, z, x \rangle$, and $\langle \rangle$ (the empty sequence) are possible behaviors of the transition system depicted in Fig. 5.2.

Based on Definition 5.1, any process model can be defined in terms of a labeled transition system with a designated final state.

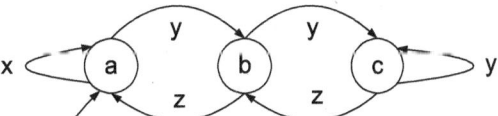

Fig. 5.2 Example of a labeled transition system

Definition 5.2 (Process Model Expressed as Transition System). A process model is a tuple $PS = (A, s_{start}, s_{end}, TS)$ where

- A is a set of activities,
- s_{start} is the initial state of the process,
- s_{end} is the final state of the process, and
- $TS = (S, E, T, s_i)$ is a labeled transition system where S is the set of states, $E = A \cup \{\tau\}$ is the set of events (i.e., all activities extended with the so-called "silent activity" τ), $T \subseteq S \times E \times S$ is the transition relation, $s_{start} = s_i$ is the initial state, and $s_{end} \in S$ is the final state of the process.

$\mathscr{P}$ is the set of all process models.

Generally, the behavior of any process model can be described in terms of a transition system TS with some initial state s_{start} and some final state s_{end}. Such a transition system does not only define the set of possible traces (i.e., execution orders), it also captures the moment of choice. Moreover, it allows for "silent steps" that are denoted by τ and constitute activities within the system changing the state of the process, but not observable in execution logs. Note that s_{end} denotes the *correct*, and, thus, final state of a process. If the process model is incorrectly specified or executed, there may be further possible final states. However, we take the correctness of process models as a precondition, and therefore the assumption of a single final state is valid. Note that this assumption can be made without loss of generality. If several final states shall be modeled for a process, these can be connected to one single final state with transitions labeled as τ.

5.2.1.2   Using Hiding and Blocking for Process Configuration

In the following, we assume that a reference process is modeled in terms of an LTS. The concepts of *hiding* and *blocking* can then be applied to configure the edges of this reference process model in order to restrict process behavior. According to the inheritance of a process behavior [9], *blocking* enables *encapsulation*, i.e., the execution (occurrence) of an atomic activity (event) is disabled. Regarding an LTS, this means that a blocked edge cannot be "fired" anymore, and hence the process will never reach a successor node unless respective nodes can be reached via another path from the start node of the LTS. Therefore, blocking an edge logically implies the removal of this edge, and all the nodes succeeding the blocked edge until a join node with other incoming edges is reached (see Fig. 5.3a for an example). *Hiding*, in turn, enables *abstraction*, i.e., the occurrence (execution) of an event (activity) becomes non-observable. With an LTS, a hidden edge is skipped, i.e., its associated activity is replaced by a silent activity not producing any trace entry. However, the corresponding path is still accessible (see Fig. 5.3b for an example).

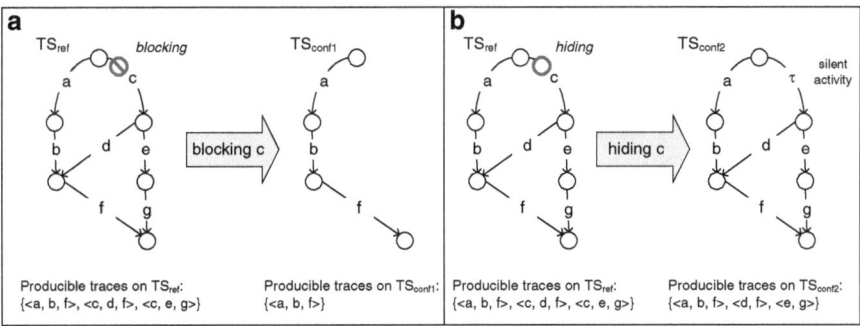

Fig. 5.3 Configuring an LTS through hiding and blocking

Example 5.4 illustrates how a reference process model expressed in terms of an LTS can be configured using hiding and blocking operators.

Example 5.4 (Configuring a Reference Process Model through Hiding and Blocking). Figure 5.4a depicts a simplified version of an LTS-based reference process model for handling medical examinations. Note that a traditional choice (i.e., the XOR) is modeled as a node with several outgoing edges; e.g., a choice between the edges labeled *Request Emergency Medical Examination* and *Request Standard Medical Examination* has to be made when leaving the start node. For the sake of simplicity, transitions capturing the parallel execution of activities have been omitted in this example. Figure 5.4b shows a possible configuration of this reference process model based on the sketched blocking and hiding operators. In this example, three edges are blocked and one is hidden. Note that on the left-hand side of the LTS, the edges *Order Medical Examination, Prepare Patient,* etc. have not been explicitly blocked. However, these edges as well as the nodes in-between are removed automatically due to the blocking of the edge labeled *Request Emergency Medical Examination.* The process variant model resulting from the application of the described hiding and blocking operations, as well as the removal of irrelevant parts, is depicted in Fig. 5.4c.

Generally, approaches capturing the behavior of all valid process variants in one and the same reference process model should allow specifying which control edges and labels respectively may be hidden or blocked. Corresponding concepts have been applied to extend existing process modeling languages (e.g., Petri Nets, YAWL, and WS-BPEL) with configuration facilities. For example, Gottschalk [103] extends the YAWL process modeling language to C-YAWL. In the latter, hiding and blocking operations are applied to the so-called input and output ports of activities. An input port may be configured as enabled to allow triggering the activity via this port, or blocked to prevent the triggering, or hidden to skip activity execution

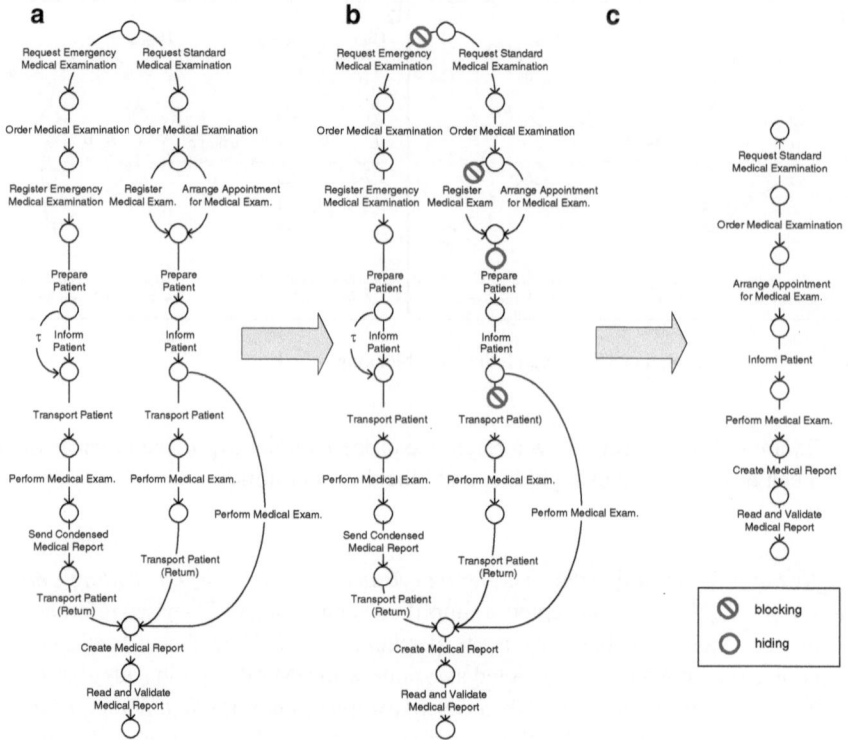

Fig. 5.4 Reference process model (**a**), configured process model (**b**), and resulting process variant (**c**)

without blocking the subsequent process part. An output port, in turn, can be enabled to allow for the triggering of paths leaving this port, or be blocked to prevent their triggering. In C-YAWL, by default, all ports are configurable and enabled.

In the following section, we present such a high-level configuration approach—*configurable nodes*—which can be based on the presented hiding and blocking operators. In addition, configurable nodes provide guidance and constraints for restricting possible configurations.

5.2.2 Configurable Nodes

A behavior-based approach for capturing process variability is provided by *configurable nodes* [164, 303]. Modeling languages supporting this approach include *Configurable Event-driven Process Chains (C-EPC)* and *C-YAWL* (see [103] for an overview). Both extend an existing process modeling language by adding *configurable elements* for explicitly representing *variability* in *reference process models*.

This section abstracts from a concrete language for modeling configurable reference processes and instead focuses on core concepts. In a reference process model, selected activities and control connectors may be flagged as configurable [164]. Such *configurable nodes* represent *variation points* of the reference process model and can be associated with a number of *configuration alternatives*. Furthermore, *configuration constraints* over the set of configurable nodes may be added to restrict possible combinations of configuration alternatives. By taking a configurable reference process model as input, and setting each of its configurable nodes to exactly one of the allowed alternatives, a particular *process variant* can be derived.

In principle, any activity or control connector of a reference process model may be flagged as *configurable*. In the reference process model depicted in Fig. 5.9, e.g., configurable nodes are highlighted with thicker border. This reference process model describes a family of process variants for managing medical examinations, i.e., for handling medical orders and reporting related results (see Fig. 5.1 for examples of corresponding process variants). The depicted reference process model comprises five configurable activities and eight configurable control connectors. Its non-configurable nodes, in turn, represent the parts common to all process variants. For example, activity *Perform Medical Examination* denotes such a commonality since it is not configurable. Hence, this activity will be contained in all process variants that may be derived from the reference process model. Before digging deeper into the modeling and configuration of this reference process (see Example 5.8), we introduce basic concepts of configurable nodes [164]; i.e., configurable activities, configurable control connectors, and configuration requirements.

Configurable Activities. There exist three configuration alternatives for a configurable activity: *included* (ON), *excluded* (OFF), and *conditional* (OPT). The first two alternatives allow process engineers to decide at configuration time whether or not to keep an activity in the derivable process variant. The last alternative allows deferring this decision to the run-time, i.e., the execution of the activity may be dynamically skipped by users depending on the instance-specific context. Semantically, switching off a configurable activity corresponds to hiding this activity (cf. Sect. 5.2.1), i.e., the path on which this activity is contained may still be chosen.

Example 5.5 (Configurable Activity). Consider the configurable process model from Fig. 5.5a. Here, B constitutes a configurable activity, which is indicated by its thicker border. If B shall be not contained in the resulting process variant, it needs to be configured to OFF. As a consequence, the respective activity node is deleted and its incoming and outgoing control edges are connected (cf. Fig. 5.5b). If B is configured to OPT, a conditional branching surrounding B is added to the resulting process variant in order to allow users to optionally skip this activity at run-time (cf. Fig. 5.5b).

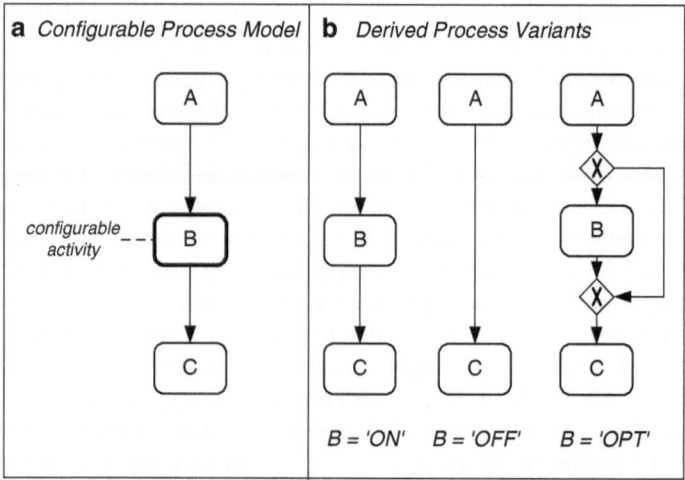

Fig. 5.5 Example of a configurable activity

ConnectorType Configurable Connector	OR	XOR	AND	SEQ
Configurable OR	X	X	X	X
Configurable XOR		X		X
Configurable AND			X	

Fig. 5.6 Configuration alternatives of configurable control connectors (adopted from [164])

Configurable Control Connectors. There exist three different kinds of configurable control connectors: *Configurable OR*, *Configurable XOR*, and *Configurable AND*. A configurable control connector may only be configured to a connector being equally or less restrictive, i.e., the derived process model should be able to produce the same or fewer execution traces (cf. Chap. 4) compared to the original reference process model. To be more precise, a *Configurable OR* may be configured to a regular OR, or be restricted to an XOR, AND, or just one outgoing/incoming branch (cf. Example 5.6). A *Configurable XOR*, in turn, may be set to a regular XOR or to just one outgoing/incoming branch. Finally, a *Configurable AND* may only be mapped to a regular AND, i.e., no particular configuration is allowed. These three configurable connectors are summarized in Fig. 5.6.

Example 5.6 (Configurable Control Connector). Figure 5.7 illustrates the configuration alternatives of a *Configurable OR*. Figure 5.7a depicts a part of a configurable reference process model with two configurable OR connectors.

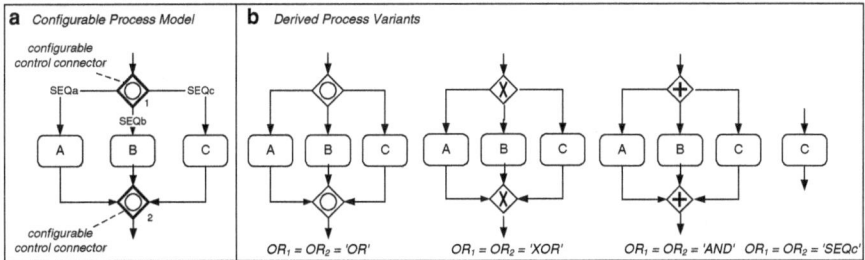

Fig. 5.7   Example of a configurable OR connector

Figure 5.7b shows four process variants that can be derived from this reference process model when making specific configuration choices for the two configurable OR connectors.

Configuration Requirements and Guidelines. *Configuration requirements* define constraints over all the configuration alternatives that may be chosen for the configurable nodes of a reference process model. Only if these constraints are met, the resulting process variant is considered as being *valid. Configuration guidelines*, in turn, do not prescribe mandatory constraints, but only serve as a kind of recommendation guiding users during the configuration. Both configuration requirements and configuration guidelines can be expressed in terms of simple predicates. Graphically, they are depicted as *post-it notes* attached to one or several configurable nodes.

Example 5.7 (Configuration Requirements). Consider the reference process model from Fig. 5.8a. Possible configurations of its configurable connectors are restricted by four requirements. According to Requirement 1, the configurable connector XOR_1 must be either set to SEQ_{1a} or SEQ_{1b}; i.e., XOR_1 is configured to one of its outgoing branches and must not be set to a regular XOR. Requirement 2, in turn, ensures that the configurable connector XOR_2 is configured in the same way as XOR_1 (i.e., the incoming branch of XOR_2 corresponds to the outgoing branch of XOR_1). Requirement 3 postulates that if XOR_1 is configured to its left (right)-hand side branch, XOR_3 has to be configured to its left (right)-hand side branch as well. Finally, Requirement 4 ensures that control connector XOR_4 is configured in the same way as XOR_3. When considering these four requirements, two valid process variants exist that can be configured out of the given reference process model (cf. Fig. 5.8b).

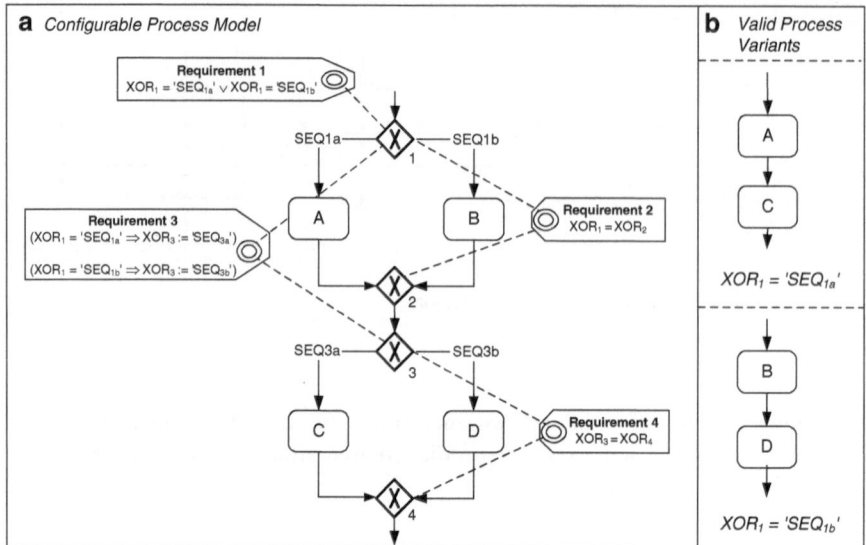

Fig. 5.8 Examples of configuration requirements

Based on the presented concepts, we will now take a closer look at the reference process model from Fig. 5.9 (cf. Example 5.8).

Example 5.8 (Reference Process Model for Handling Medical Examinations). Consider the reference process model in Fig. 5.9. It covers a family of process variants for handling medical examinations, including activities dealing with order handling, scheduling, transportation, and reporting. Examples of process variants that can be configured out of this reference process model are depicted in Fig. 5.1.

The gray-shaded activities in Fig. 5.9 reflect the common parts of the producible process variants; i.e., these activities are contained in each process variant (see Fig. 5.1 for examples). Process variability, in turn, is caused by varying factors like the kind of examination involved, the way examinations are scheduled, or the decision whether patient transportation is required. More precisely, emergency and standard medical examinations need to be distinguished from each other (Requirement 1). For standard medical examinations, either an appointment is scheduled or a simple registration is made (Requirement 2). (The latter means, the examination unit is informed about the later arrival of the patient, but does not appoint a date for the examination.) For emergency medical examinations, in turn, a specific registration is needed (Requirement 3). Furthermore, for a standard medical examination, activity *Inform Patient* is always required (Requirement 4). Patient transportation, in turn, is mandatory for emergency medical examinations (Requirement 5), while for standard medical examinations this depends on other domain facts (Guideline 1). A condensed medical report has to be sent in the context of emergency medical examinations to enable quick feedback (Requirement 6). Finally, if the configurable activity *Transport Patient* is switched on, its counterpart (i.e., activity *Transport Patient (Return)*) has to be switched on as well (Requirement 7). All requirements considered, there exist several activities that may be contained in some process variants, but which are not required for others (e.g., *Prepare Patient* and *Inform Patient*).

Overall, the reference process model from Fig. 5.9 comprises five configurable activities, eight configurable connectors, seven configuration requirements, and one configuration guideline. As discussed, configuration requirements constrain the configuration alternatives that may be chosen for the configurable nodes of the reference process model. For the sake of readability, we have omitted trivial requirements like the ones requiring that join connectors are configured in the same way as corresponding split connectors.

Using such a reference process model, the desired process variants can be derived by setting the configuration alternatives of its configurable nodes accordingly (cf. Example 5.9).

Example 5.9 (Configuring a Reference Process Model). Consider the four process variants from Fig. 5.1. The configuration settings needed for deriving the four variants from the given reference process model (cf. Fig. 5.9) are depicted in Fig. 5.10. Remember that switching off a configurable activity corresponds to hiding this activity, i.e., the path on which this activity is contained may still be chosen. For each process variant, its configuration settings comply with the given configuration requirements, i.e., all four process variants are valid. Note that, in principle, it is not necessary to explicitly specify a configuration alternative for all configurable nodes since these settings can be partially derived from other configuration settings. In Fig. 5.10, for example, the configuration settings in gray color do not have to be explicitly specified when exploiting the knowledge about the defined configuration requirements.

This section has focused on core concepts of configurable nodes. As previously mentioned, respective configuration features are supported in reference modeling languages like C-EPC and C-YAWL [103]. There are other approaches for configuring the behavior of a reference process model in a similar way. ADOM [278,279], for example, builds on software engineering principles and allows for specialization in addition to configuration. In particular, ADOM is capable of specifying guidelines

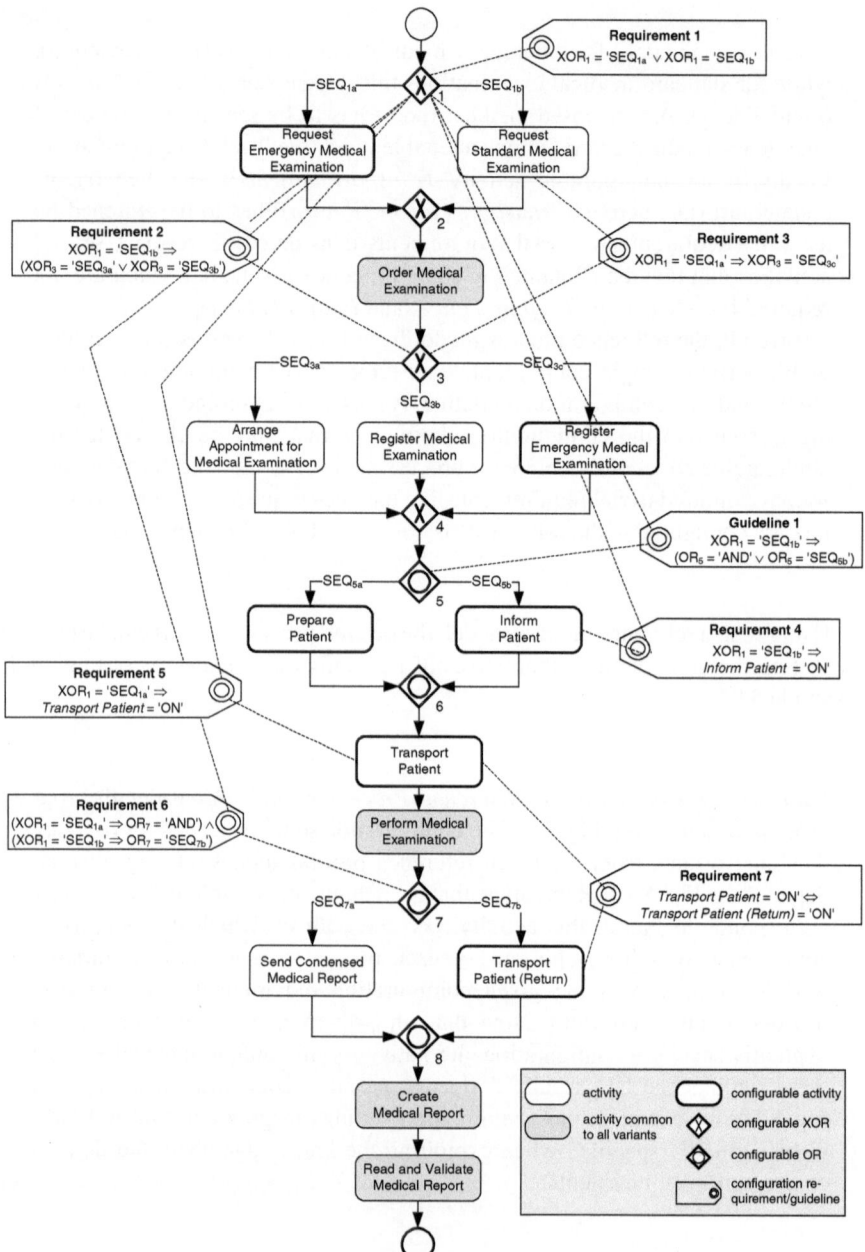

Fig. 5.9 A reference process model for handling medical examinations

	Settings of Configurable Connectors								Settings of Configurable Activities				
	XOR1	XOR2	XOR3	XOR4	OR5	OR6	OR7	OR8	Register Emergency Medical Examination	Prepare Patient	Inform Patient	Transport Patient	Transport Patient (Return)
Process variant S1	SEQ1b	SEQ1b	SEQ3a	SEQ3a	AND	AND	SEQ7b	SEQ7b	OFF	ON	ON	OFF	OFF
Process variant S2	SEQ1b	SEQ1b	SEQ3a	SEQ3a	SEQ5b	SEQ5b	SEQ7b	SEQ7b	OFF	OFF	ON	ON	ON
Process variant S3	SEQ1b	SEQ1b	SEQ3b	SEQ3b	AND	AND	SEQ7b	SEQ7b	OFF	ON	ON	ON	ON
Process variant S4	SEQ1a	SEQ1a	SEQ3c	SEQ3c	SEQ5b	SEQ5b	AND	AND	ON	OFF	OFF	ON	ON

Fig. 5.10 Configuration settings for deriving the process variants from Fig. 5.1

and constraints (similar to the configuration requirements and guidelines presented) as part of the reference process model and of validating a specific process variant against the reference model. An overview of other approaches enabling variability management in business process models can be found in [38].

5.3   Structural Configuration Approaches

This section presents another approach for modeling a process family and configuring process variants. It is based on the observation that, in practice, process variants are often created by cloning a prespecified process model and manually adapting it to the given application environment. For example, the process variants depicted in Fig. 5.1b–d could be derived from the prespecified process model from Fig. 5.1a by adding and removing activities.

Generally, every process model S' can be configured from a prespecified process model S by structurally adapting S accordingly, i.e., by applying a number of structural changes to S [179]. Based on this observation, the Provop approach provides a comprehensive framework for modeling process families and deriving process variants from a prespecified process model—called *base process model*—through structural model adaptations [124, 126, 128, 129]. In particular, process variants can be derived in a *context-driven* way by applying a number of context-dependent, prespecified changes to S (e.g., to insert, delete, or move activities or process fragments). Figure 5.11 illustrates the basic principle behind this approach by showing how different process variants can be derived from a base process model through structural adaptations.

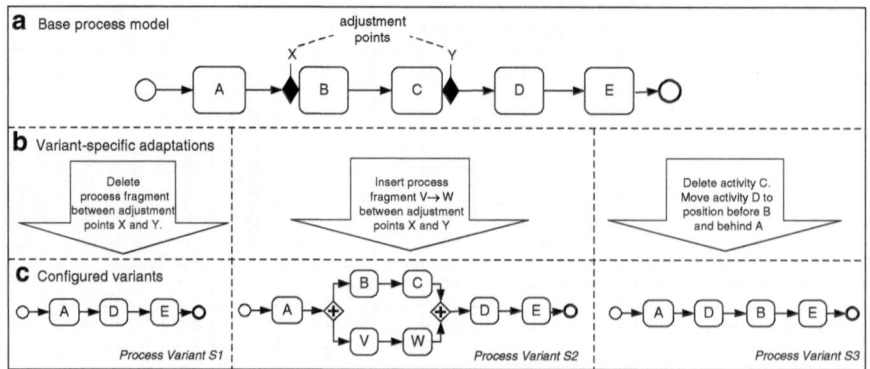

Fig. 5.11 Deriving process variants through structural changes of a base process model

5.3.1 Representing a Process Family Through a Base Process and Prespecified Changes

As emphasized, a process family can be represented in terms of a *base process model* and a set of *prespecified model changes* that may be applied individually or in combination to this base process model. As opposed to the reference process models described in Sect. 5.2, a base process model does not have to capture all possible process behavior. Hence, process engineers have more flexibility regarding the design of a configurable process model when compared to the approaches presented in Sect. 5.2.

5.3.1.1 Base Process Model

Structural configuration offers high flexibility in respect to the choice of the base process model and the prespecified model changes. Similar to the behavior-based configuration approaches presented in Sect. 5.2, for example, one may merge all process variants in the base process model. In this case, the prespecified changes needed for model configuration can be based solely on delete operations. At the other extreme, a base process model may only comprise the common parts of all process variants. Then, the prespecified changes for model configuration will not contain any delete operations. Hallerbach et al. [128] introduces five policies for defining a base process model and related changes:

- *Policy 1 (Reference process)*. The base process corresponds to a domain-specific reference process. A particular process variant can then be derived from the base process model by structurally adapting it using a subset of the prespecified changes.

- *Policy 2 (Most frequently used process).* If a particular process variant is used much more often than other variants, it may be chosen as base process to avoid configuration efforts for respective cases.
- *Policy 3 (Minimum adaptation efforts).* Given a collection of process variants, the base process model is chosen in such a way that the average number of changes needed to derive a process variant from this base process becomes minimal (see Chap. 8 for respective techniques).
- *Policy 4 (Superset of all process variants).* The base process model covers the behavior of all relevant process variants. Hence, every element (e.g., activity) belonging to at least one process variant model is part of the base process model as well (similar to configurable process models as described in Sect. 5.2). Consequently, prespecified changes for deriving process variants from the base process model can be based solely on delete operations (i.e., operations removing elements from the base process model).
- *Policy 5 (Intersection of all process variants).* The base process model exactly covers the commonalities shared by all relevant process variants; i.e., it comprises only those elements (e.g., activities) that are common to these variants. Consequently, the prespecified changes required for model configuration do not require delete operations.

Policies 1–5 differ in one fundamental aspect: When using Policy 1 or 2 the base process models covers only one specific use case; i.e., it represents a particular process variant valid in a specific context (and being directly executable in the PAIS). Policies 3–5, in turn, can efficiently derive variants from a base process model. Hence, for them the base process model does not necessarily represent a semantically valid process variant.

5.3.1.2 Prespecified Changes

As emphasized, a base process model can be structurally adapted in order to derive a particular process variant. In this context, the Provop framework supports the following adaptation patterns: INSERT, DELETE, and MOVE process fragment, and MODIFY process element attributes (see Chap. 7 for other adaptation patterns). To allow for a robust referencing of its process fragments and elements, a base process model may contain *adjustment points*, and link them to the entry or exit of an activity or control connector. Adjustment points have unique labels and serve as stable reference points for prespecified changes. For example, consider adjustment point X in Fig. 5.11 which corresponds to the entry of activity B. Figure 5.12 lists selected change operations as provided in the Provop framework.

As the number of change operations required to derive process variants from a prespecified base process model may become very large, the Provop framework allows *grouping change operations* into so-called *change options*. This is useful, for example, if certain change operations are always applied together with each other when deriving particular variants (cf. Example 5.10).

1. INSERT-Operation	
Symbol	
Purpose	Adding a *process fragment* (e.g., a single activity or an activity sequence).
Parameters	• Process fragment to be added • Target position of the process fragment to be added in the base process, specified in terms of adjustment points
2. DELETE-Operation	
Symbol	
Purpose	Removing a *process fragment*
Parameters	• Process fragment to be deleted with entries and exits being marked by adjustment points • Alternatively: deleting single activities by referring to their ID
3. MOVE-Operation	
Symbol	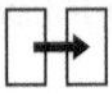
Purpose	Changing the execution order of activities
Parameters	• Process fragment to be moved with entries and exits being marked by adjustment points • Target position of the process fragment to be moved, specified in terms of adjustment points

Fig. 5.12 Examples of change operations (adopted from [128])

Example 5.10 (Grouping Changes in Change Options). Consider the handling of a medical examination in the radiology unit of a hospital. While no transport between a ward and the radiology department needs to be arranged for patients in ambulant care, in-patients may also have to be transported between these places. To capture the latter variant one might have to add two activities at different positions in the base process. This can be achieved by defining two respective insert operations and grouping them in one change option.

Example 5.11 illustrates how a base process and related prespecified changes might look like for our running example.

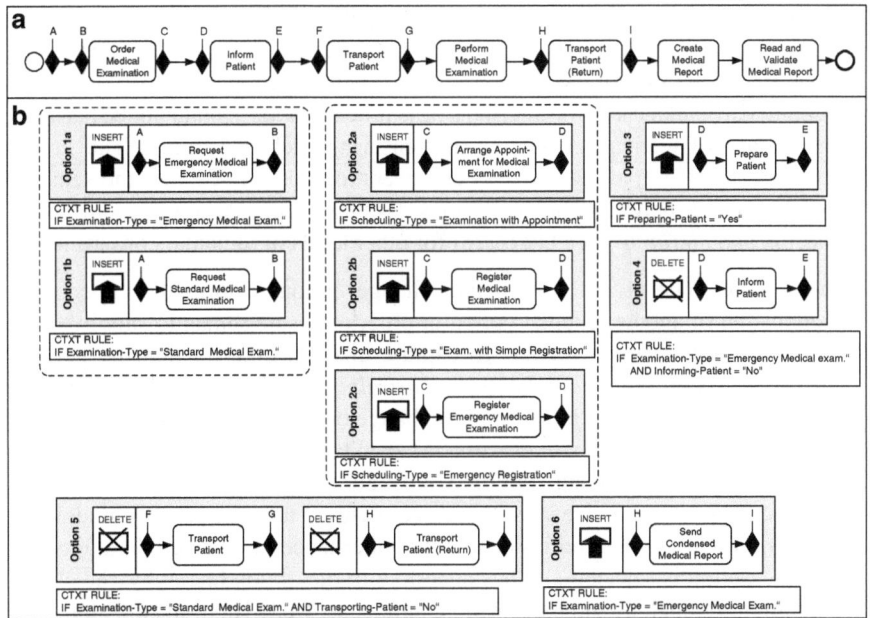

Fig. 5.13 Example of a configurable base process model and related change options

Example 5.11 (Base Process and Related Change Options). Figure 5.13 illustrates how the process family for handling medical examinations can be captured in Provop: Fig. 5.13a shows a base process model, from which the process variants can be derived (see Fig. 5.1 for selected examples). Note that this base process model contains several adjustment points to which change options and their change operations respectively may refer. The nine change options applicable to this base process are depicted in Fig. 5.13b. For example, *Option 3* inserts activity *Prepare Patient* between adjustment points D and E, whereas *Option 4* deletes activity *Inform Patient* from the base process. *Option 5* constitutes an example of a change option comprising two change operations. More precisely, *Option 5* deletes the two activities dealing with patient transportation in the base process model.

5.3.1.3 Constraining the Use of Change Options

Generally, several change options may be conjointly applied to a base process model in order to derive the desired process variant. However, this must not imply that arbitrary combinations of change options will be allowed.[1] For example, two change options may mutually exclude each other, while others may imply further change options in order to ensure syntactical and semantical correctness of the process variant. In particular, users configuring a base process model should not be burdened with the task of manually checking and ensuring such constraints. The Provop framework, therefore, allows process engineers to explicitly capture the semantic relations existing between change options. Examples include *implication, mutual exclusion*, and *hierarchy* (see [124, 128] for other kinds of semantic constraints):

- *Implication.* The use of a particular change option requires the concomitant application of another change option in order to ensure semantic validity of the derived process variant model. To capture this semantic relationship between two change options, an *implication constraint* must be defined for them. For example, if a change option A implies change option B, and A is applied during the configuration of the base process, B has to be applied as well.
- *Mutual exclusion.* A change option X must not be applied in conjunction with a change option Y (and vice versa) when configuring the base process model.
- *Hierarchy.* Option hierarchies enable the inheritance of change operations. If a change option is selected and has ancestors in the option hierarchy, the change operations defined by the latter will be applied as well. This way, the number of change operations to be defined for the different change options can be reduced and the option set structured. In particular, maintenance is improved.

For the change options of a process family, these and other relations may be defined. In the Provop framework this can be accomplished by using constraint graphs (cf. Fig. 5.14). Thereby, it is ensured that no contradictory relations are defined (e.g., a mutual exclusion between a change option and its parental option).

Example 5.12 (Option Constraints). Figure 5.14 shows the constraint graph for the change options introduced in Example 5.11 and Fig. 5.13 respectively. For example, *Option 1a* and *Option 1b* mutually exclude each other; i.e., they must not be both applied to the configurable base process from Fig. 5.13a. Similarly, *Option 1a* and *Option 5* mutually exclude each other; i.e., if activity *Request Emergency Medical Examination* is added to the base process, the two activities *Transport Patient* and *Transport Patient (Return)* must not be removed from the base process model (remember that patient transportation is always required in handling emergency cases). Furthermore, between *Option 1a* and *Option 6* an implication constraint exists. More precisely, if *Option 1a* is applied (i.e., activity *Request Emergency Medical Examination* is added), *Option 6* needs to be applied as well (i.e., activity *Send Condensed*

---

[1] Basically, this corresponds to the idea of *configuration requirements* as described in Sect. 5.2.2.

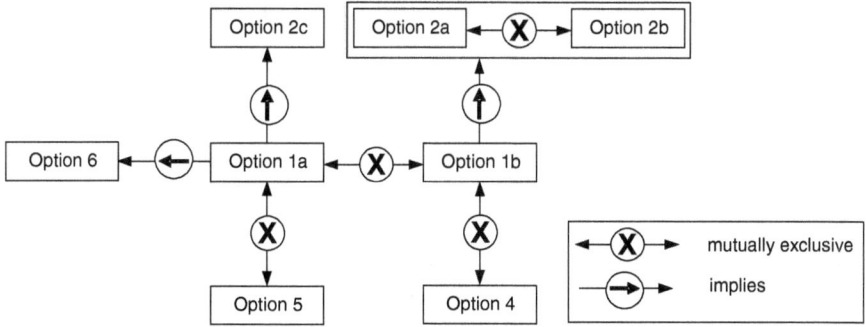

Fig. 5.14 Constraining allowed combinations of change options

Context Variable	Value Range
Examination-Type	Standard Medical Exam., Emergency Medical Exam
Scheduling-Type	Examination with Appointment, Examination with Simple Registration, Emergency Registration
Preparing-Patient	Yes, No
Informing-Patient	Yes, No
Transporting-Patient	Yes, No

Fig. 5.15 Context model of the process family for handling medical examinations

Medical Report needs to be added). Similarly, if *Option 1b* is applied (i.e., activity *Request Standard Medical Examination* is added) either *Option 2a* or *Option 2b* needs to be co-applied.

5.3.1.4 Context Model

Provop allows for the context-driven configuration of a base process model [125]; i.e., a process variant is derived by applying only those change options to the base process model relevant to the given application environment (and meeting the defined configuration constraints). This, in turn, requires an appropriate *context model*. In Provop, such a context model comprises a set of context variables. Each context variable then represents one specific dimension of the process context, and is defined in terms of its name and value range. Figure 5.15 shows the context model of the process family from Fig. 5.13.

5.3.2 Configuring a Process Variant Through Structural Changes

During the configuration phase, the base process model, the set of change options and their constraints, and the context model can be used to configure a particular process variant. The major steps for this are as follows:

Step 1. Select relevant options. Typically, to derive a particular process variant, only a subset of the available change options has to be applied. A first step in the configuration phase, therefore, is to identify relevant options. One approach is to ask users to manually accomplish this task. However, this would likely be error-prone and also require profound knowledge on available change options as well as on their effects and interdependencies. A more sophisticated approach is to automatically select relevant options by utilizing contextual knowledge. To enable this, options may be associated with *context rules*. These define Boolean expressions referring to selected variables from the context model. Consequently, in a given context, all change options whose associated context rule evaluates to *true* are selected.

Example 5.13 (Context Rules). Consider the base process model and its related change options as depicted in Fig. 5.13. As one can see, each change option has an associated context rule (cf. Fig. 5.13b). For example, *Option 5* has context rule *<IF Examination-Type = Standard Medical Exam. AND Transporting-Patient = No>*. In other words, *Option 5*, and hence the removal of the two transportation steps, will only be applied if context variable *Examination-Type* has value *Standard Medical Exam.* and *Transporting-Patient* is set to *No*.

Example 5.14 picks up the base process and change options from Fig. 5.13 and illustrates how the context-driven selection of change options looks like.

Example 5.14 (Configuration Phase—Selection of Relevant Options). Consider the context model from Fig. 5.15 and assume that context variables have the following values: *Examination-Type = Standard Medical Exam.*, *Scheduling-Type = Examination with Appointment, Preparing-Patient = Yes*, and *Transporting-Patient = No*. Consider further the base process model and the prespecified change options from Fig. 5.13. According to the given settings the context rules of the following options evaluate to *true*: *Option 1b*, *Option 2a*, *Option 3*, and *Option 5*; i.e., these options are considered as being relevant for the context-driven configuration of the base process model in the given scenario. Note that users may manually adapt this option set if required.

Step 2. Ensure compliance of the selected options with option constraints. In this step, compliance of the selected option set with defined option constraints has to be checked in order to ensure semantical correctness of the resulting process variant. For example, if a selected option implies another one not yet contained in the option set, this set will have to be extended accordingly. Generally, this can be achieved either by adding missing options or by removing the ones that caused the constraint violation. For example, a constraint violation will also occur if the option set contains mutually excluding options. In this case, at least one of the conflicting options has to be removed.

Example 5.15 (Configuration Phase—Ensure Compliance of Option Set with Option Constraints). Consider Example 5.14 where *Option 1b*, *Option 2a*, *Option 3*, and *Option 5* have been selected as candidate options to be applied to the base process model from Fig. 5.13a. Obviously, the option set complies with the option constraints defined by the constraint graph from Fig. 5.14. For example, due to the presence of *Option 1b*, neither *Option 1a* nor *Option 4* may be contained in the option set. Further, the presence of *Option 1b* implies the presence of either *Option 2a* or *Option 2b*. This constraint is met as well. Note that in more complex scenarios the candidate option set resulting from Step 1 will not always comply with the given option constraints, i.e., constraints need to be explicitly checked.

Step 3. Determine the order in which options shall be applied. Generally, the changes defined by an option set have to be applied in sequence; i.e., the order in which the change options shall be applied has to be specified when configuring the base process model. If the change options are commutative (i.e., independent from the order in which they are applied we obtain the *same* variant model) this order can be chosen arbitrarily. Note that this is the case for the change options used in Example 5.15. Generally, commutativity of change options cannot be ensured, particularly when also considering other model perspectives (e.g., data elements and data flow). However, when applying options in the wrong order, unintended or inconsistent variant models may result. To avoid such problems, Provop asks for an explicit definition of the order in which selected options shall be applied. Furthermore, wrong option sequences, resulting in erroneous variant models afterwards, are detected and excluded based on well defined correctness notions [124, 127].

Step 4. Configuring the base process model by applying the selected change options and their change operations to it. After selecting the change options and determining their order, corresponding change operations are applied to the base process model. This, in turn, results in the model of the context-specific process variant.

Example 5.16 (Configuration Phase—Configuring the Base Process). Figure
5.16 shows how the selected change options are sequentially applied to the
given base process model. Therefore, adjustment points of the base process
model (cf. Fig. 5.16a) serve as stable references for the change options and
their change operations. After applying the four options selected in the
preceding steps (cf. Fig. 5.16b), the adjustment points are removed, resulting
in the process variant model depicted in Fig. 5.16c. Note that this process
variant corresponds to the one from Fig. 5.1a.

The Provop framework also covers variability in the information and organization
perspectives of a business process [124]. Furthermore, it provides advanced tool
support for defining change options and for ensuring the syntactical and semantical
correctness of derived process variants as well as their soundness [127]. A proof-
of-concept implementation has been provided using the ARIS Business Architect as
basic platform (see [268] for details).

5.4   End-User Support in Configuring Process Variants

This section deals with the support of *domain experts* in configuring (reference)
process models. It is generally not a good idea to use low-level configuration tables
such as the one depicted in Fig. 5.10 for this purpose. End-users should not be
burdened with manually checking to see whether configuration constraints are met.
This is particularly important since constraint numbers might become very large in
real-world configuration scenarios [103, 124, 162].

The following subsections introduce three techniques for supporting end-users in
configuring a (reference) process model. In particular, these techniques complement
the fundamental approaches presented in the previous sections and are independent
of the process configuration and process modeling languages used.

5.4.1   Questionnaire-Driven Process Configuration

In [162, 163], a questionnaire-based framework for configuring reference process
models is introduced. In this framework, *questionnaires* serve as user interface
enabling a domain-specific representation of configuration decisions.

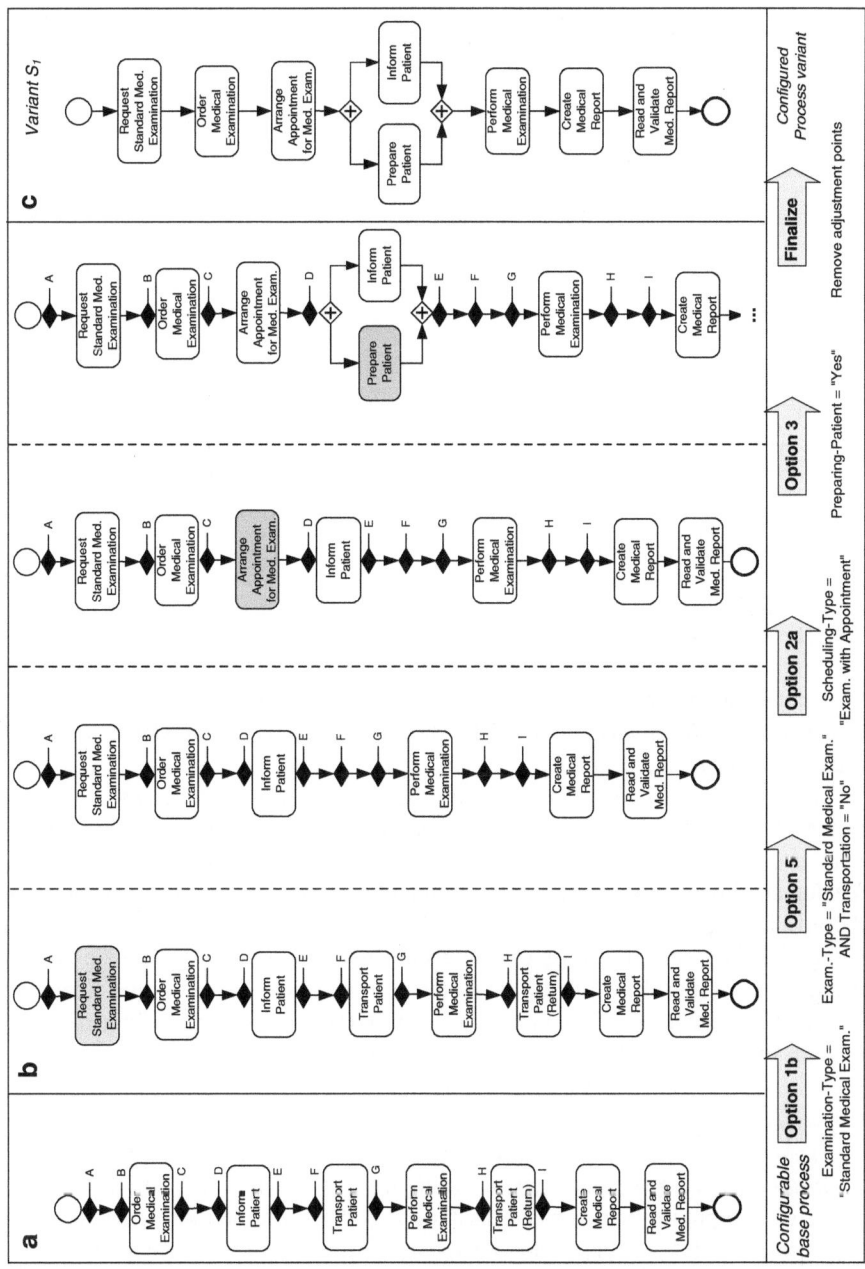

Fig. 5.16 Configuring a base process model through structural adaptations

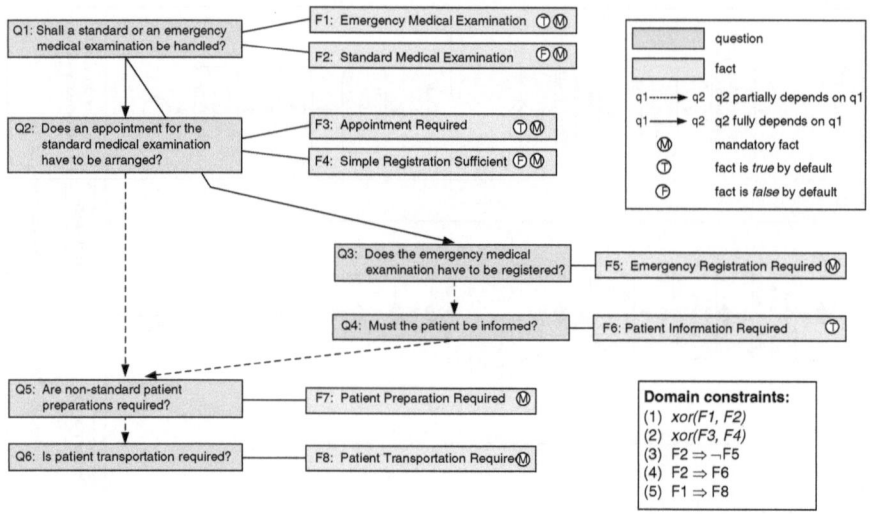

Fig. 5.17 Example of a questionnaire model

5.4.1.1 Questionnaire Models

The framework described in [162,163] captures the variability of a business process in a *questionnaire model*. Figure 5.17 shows a questionnaire model that can be related to our running example.

Basically, a questionnaire model comprises a set of *domain facts* corresponding to the answers of a set of *questions* that are expressed in natural language. Each domain fact corresponds to a Boolean variable representing a particular *feature* of the domain. Such a feature, in turn, may either be *enabled* or *disabled* depending on the given application context. Furthermore, each domain fact may have a *default value* characterizing the most common choice for it. Finally, a domain fact is *mandatory* if it must be explicitly set by the user when answering the questionnaire. If a non-mandatory domain fact is left unset (i.e., the corresponding question remains unanswered), its default value will be used instead.

> *Example 5.17 (Domain Fact).* Consider Fig. 5.17. Fact *F8:Patient Transportation Required* constitutes an example of a domain fact to be enabled for certain process variants and disabled for others. Furthermore, since most process variants dealing with order handling and result reporting refer to standard medical examinations, one can assign a default value of *true* to the domain fact *F2:Standard Medical Examination* and a default value of *false* to the domain fact *F1:Emergency Medical Examination*.

In a questionnaire model, related domain facts may be grouped and assigned to the same question. This way, they can be set all at once when answering the respective question.

> *Example 5.18 (Grouping Domain Facts in Questions).* Question *Q1:Shall a standard or an emergency medical examination be handled?* groups the domain facts *F1:Emergency Medical Examination* and *F2:Standard Medical Examination*, which therefore can be configured all at once when answering *Q1*.

Altogether, the questionnaire model of our running example (cf. Fig. 5.17) comprises six questions and eight domain facts. The domain facts refer to the kind of examination (i.e., standard vs. emergency medical examination), the way the examination shall be scheduled, and the decisions whether patient transportation, patient information, or patient preparation are required.

In principle, a questionnaire model may also contain questions referring to high-level business decisions (e.g., maximum costs or invasiveness of the medical examination under consideration), which then must be mapped to domain facts and hence to variation points in configurable process models.

The domain facts of the same or different questions may be related; i.e., their values must not be set independently of each other. Such dependencies between facts constitute constraints over the elements of the considered domain and can be modeled in terms of Boolean predicates and expressions.

> *Example 5.19 (Domain Constraints over Facts).* Consider the questionnaire model from Fig. 5.17. Regarding question $Q1$, either fact $F1$ (i.e., *Emergency Medical Examination*) or $F2$ (i.e., *Standard Medical Examination*) may be *true*, but not both (see *domain constraint 1* in Fig. 5.17). A similar constraint holds in respect to question $Q2$, and facts $F3$ and $F4$ (cf. *domain constraint 2*). Other domain constraints concern the relation between question $Q1$, on one hand, and questions $Q3$ and $Q4$, on the other. More precisely, if $F2$ is *true* and $F1$ is *false* (i.e., the variant describes the handling of a standard medical examination), $F5$ must be *false* (i.e., no emergency registration is required; cf. *domain constraint 3*) and $F6$ be *true* (i.e., patient information is required anyway; cf. *domain constraint 4*). Finally, if $F1$ is true, $F8$ must be true as well (i.e., for emergency medical examinations patient transportation is required; cf. *domain constraint 5*). As stated, domain constraints can be modeled in terms of Boolean predicates and expressions. The constraints mentioned above can be expressed by the following predicates and expressions: $xor(F1, F2)$, $xor(F3, F4)$, $(F2 \Rightarrow \neg F5 \wedge F6)$, and $(F1 \Rightarrow F8)$.

Any implementation of a questionnaire model should adequately consider domain constraints to guide users when filling out the questionnaire. To further optimize user guidance, questionnaire models may additionally comprise an *order relation* for asking questions. For this purpose, partial and full dependencies between questions can be defined. More precisely, a *partial dependency* describes an optional precedence between answering two questions, while a *full dependency* represents a mandatory precedence.

Example 5.20 (Order Dependencies). Consider again the questionnaire model from Fig. 5.17. There are two full dependencies (solid arrows) between question $Q1$ and questions $Q2$ and $Q3$, respectively; i.e., $Q2$ or $Q3$ may only be posed after $Q1$, since answering these questions depends on the settings of the domain facts produced by $Q1$. Furthermore, the questionnaire model contains four partial dependencies (dashed arrows); e.g., it is preferable that $Q3$ is answered before $Q4$, $Q4$ before $Q5$, and $Q5$ before $Q6$. However, these orders are not mandatory, e.g., users may answer $Q5$ before $Q4$.

Generally, the order dependencies set out by a questionnaire model should be designed in a way that the most discriminating questions are asked first—in our example, the most discriminating question is $Q1$. After answering it, subsequent questions can be partly answered by using the given domain constraints; e.g., when setting fact $F2$ to *true* when answering $Q1$, questions $Q3$ and $Q4$ can be automatically answered when taking into account the given domain constraints (cf. Fig. 5.17).

5.4.1.2 Questionnaire-Based Configuration of a Reference Process Model

Once a questionnaire model is defined, one still needs to establish the link between the questionnaire model, on one hand, and the variation points of a configurable (reference) process model, on the other hand. Based on this link, it should be possible to configure the reference process model by filling in the corresponding questionnaire. To establish such link, each variation point of a reference process model needs to be associated with a Boolean expression over the domain facts of its corresponding questionnaire model. Hence, a configuration alternative of a variation point (e.g., a configurable activity or connector) is chosen if the corresponding expression evaluates to *true*. Example 5.21 discusses how the variation points of the reference process model from Fig. 5.9 can be configured based on the domain facts from the questionnaire model shown in Fig. 5.17.

Configurable Activity	Configuration Alternative	Boolean Expression Over Facts
Register Emergency Medical Examination	ON	F1 $\wedge$ F5
Prepare Patient	ON	F7
Inform Patient	ON	F6
Transport Patient (...)	ON	F8

Fig. 5.18 Establishing a mapping between domain facts and configurable activities

Example 5.21 (Linking a Reference Process Model with a Questionnaire Model). Figures 5.18 and 5.19 show how the configurable nodes of the reference process model from Fig. 5.9 can be connected to the domain facts of the questionnaire model from Fig. 5.17. A configurable activity is set to ON if—and only if—the Boolean expressions over facts as depicted in Fig. 5.18 evaluate to *true*; e.g., *Inform Patient* is configured to ON if fact $F6$ is *true*.

In the same way, the configuration alternatives of a configurable connector are bound to the facts of a questionnaire model. For example, a direct mapping between question $Q1$ and the two alternatives of the configurable connector $XOR1$ can be established. More precisely, if fact $F1$ is *true*, this connector is configured to its left-hand side branch (i.e., SEQ_{1a}); otherwise (i.e., $F2$ is true) the right-hand side branch (i.e., SEQ_{1b}) is chosen as a configuration alternative (cf. Fig. 5.19). Consider now the configurable connector $OR5$ in Fig. 5.9. If both facts—$F6$ and $F7$—evaluate to *true*, $OR5$ is set to an AND split. If only one of the two facts is *true*, $OR5$ is set to either the left- or right-hand side branch. (Note that the chosen branch(es) may still become "empty" since the activities they contain may be both configured to OFF).

Based on the described mapping, the reference process model from Fig. 5.9 can be easily configured by filling out the corresponding questionnaire. Example 5.22 illustrates this.

Example 5.22 (Configuring a Reference Process Model by Filling out a Questionnaire). Consider the process variant from Fig. 5.1a. It can be configured out of the reference process model from Fig. 5.9 by answering four questions of the corresponding questionnaire model (cf. Fig. 5.17). First, question $Q1$ is answered by setting fact $F1$ to *false* and fact $F2$ to *true*, respectively. Due to the domain constraints defined by the given questionnaire model, $Q3$ and $Q5$ are then automatically answered by setting $F5$ to *false* and $F6$ to *true*. Second, question $Q2$, which mandatorily succeeds $Q1$, has to be

Configurable Connector	Configuration Alternative	Boolean Expression over Facts
XOR$_1$	SEQ$_{1a}$	F1
	SEQ$_{1b}$	F2
XOR$_3$	SEQ$_{3a}$	F2 $\wedge$ F3
	SEQ$_{3b}$	F2 $\wedge$ F4
	SEQ$_{3c}$	F1 $\wedge$ F5
OR$_5$	AND	F6 $\wedge$ F7
	SEQ$_{5a}$	F7 $\wedge \neg$ F6
	SEQ$_{5b}$	F6 $\wedge \neg$ F7
	OR	*false*
	XOR	*false*
OR$_7$	AND	F1
	SEQ$_{7a}$	*false*
	SEQ$_{7b}$	F2
	OR	*false*
	XOR	*false*

Fig. 5.19 Establishing a mapping between domain facts and configurable connectors

answered by setting $F3$ to *true* and $F4$ to *false* respectively. Third, $Q5$ and $Q6$ are answered setting $F7$ to *true* and $F8$ to *false*. Note that the suggested precedence relations between $Q2$, $Q5$, and $Q6$ are optional.

In summary, the questionnaire-based approach enables domain-specific user interfaces for configuring reference process models. This can be done using a configuration tool which poses natural-language questions in an order consistent with the order dependencies of the questionnaire model and preventing users from entering semantically invalid answers to subsequent questions by checking domain constraints on-the-fly. Furthermore, constraints on allowed combinations of configuration alternatives do not need to be checked manually. Once a questionnaire is completed, all facts can be collected and then be mapped to Boolean expressions of the variation points in the respective reference process model. This way, a reference process model can be automatically and correctly configured. Overall, the configuration of a reference process model can be significantly eased through the use of questionnaire models when compared to low-level configuration approaches (like the one depicted in Fig. 5.10). Finally, the questionnaire-based approach has been implemented in a tool called *Quaestio* [162] and be tested with reference process models expressed in terms of C-EPC and C-YAWL, respectively.

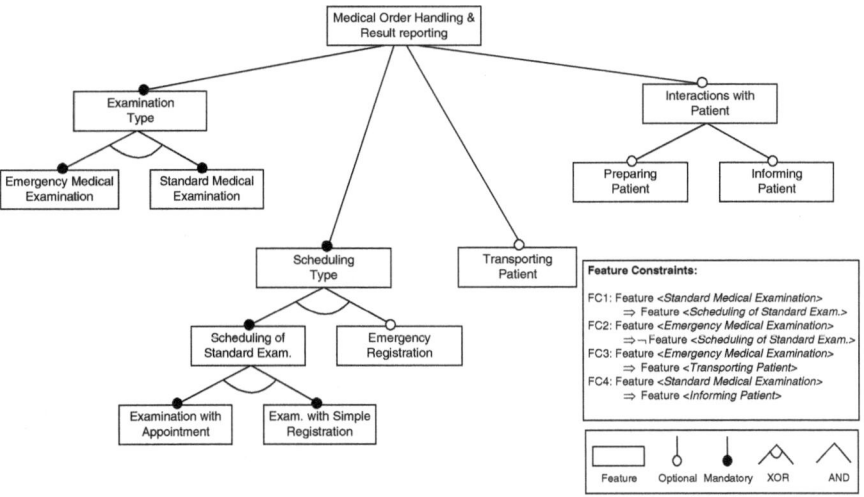

Fig. 5.20 Example of a feature diagram

5.4.2   Feature-Driven Process Configuration

A widespread notion for capturing variability at a high level of abstraction is provided by *feature diagrams* [320]. These were originally introduced to capture variability in software product lines, but can be applied in the context of process variability as well. Several *feature modeling languages* have been suggested [320]. Basically, they enable the specification of *feature models* representing the common and varying *features* of a product or process in a structured and comprehensible manner. A feature corresponds to a domain property of the described product or process. Typically, a feature model is visualized in terms of one or several *feature diagrams*. These constitute tree-like structures whose non-leaf nodes represent *higher-level features* that are broken down into *sub-features*, and whose leaf nodes correspond to *basic features*. Figure 5.20 depicts the feature diagram related to our running example (cf. Example 5.23) by using the notation suggested in [45].

Feature diagrams are usually enriched with *feature descriptions* and *feature constraints*. While the former may represent rather informal descriptions similar to questionnaire models, the latter are described in terms of logical expressions about feature values that constrain allowable feature combinations. Specifically, for higher-level features, the number of selectable sub-features can be restricted. This is graphically expressed through the relations AND, OR, and XOR. AND means that all sub-features are selected if the higher level feature is chosen, and XOR expresses that exactly one of the sub-features is chosen. When using the OR relation, one or more sub-features can be selected, whereby the minimum and maximum number of selectable sub-features can be explicitly expressed. Finally, features can be flagged as mandatory or optional. Mandatory means the feature is required unless it is excluded due to an OR/XOR relation or the non-selection of an optional ancestor.

Example 5.23 (Feature Diagrams). Consider Fig. 5.20. It contains different features related to the type of examination, the way it shall be scheduled, the decision whether patient transportation is required, and the potential interactions with the patient (i.e., features *<Preparing Patient>* and *<Inform-ing Patient>*). Furthermore, features are either flagged as mandatory or optional. For example, feature *<Examination Type>* and its two sub-features *<Emergency Medical Examination>* and *<Standard Medical Examination>* are mandatory. However, note that one of these two sub-features will be excluded due to the XOR relation to which these two sub-features are bound. Feature *<Transporting Patient>*, in turn, constitutes an example of an optional feature, i.e., its selection depends on other choices.

In addition to the relations between siblings, a number of feature con-straints restricting allowed feature combinations exists; e.g., constraint $FC3$ requires that feature *<Transporting Patient>* will always be selected if feature *<Emergency Medical Examination>* is chosen.

Similar to questionnaire models, feature diagrams can be used for configuring a reference process or base process model. In particular, direct mapping between the features chosen and the alternatives provided by configurable nodes (cf. Sect. 5.2.2) or change options (cf. Sect. 5.3.1) can be easily established.

5.4.3   Context-Driven Process Configuration

Another way of supporting end-users in configuring a reference or base process model is to utilize contextual knowledge. An example of such an approach has been already presented in Sect. 5.3 in conjunction with the configuration of a base process model through structural adaptations. Only those changes of a base process are suggested to the user that are relevant in the given context. Together with other information (e.g., constraints regarding allowed combinations of configuration changes), context-driven user guidance becomes possible.

5.5   Further Aspects

This section discusses further aspects that should be considered by any framework enabling configurable process models.

5.5.1   Capturing Variability of Multiple Process Perspectives

The previous sections have focused on the variability of activities and their control
flow, whereas the variability of other process perspectives (e.g., data and resources)
has yet to be considered. To overcome this limitation, La Rosa et al. [165, 166]
suggest a configurable process modeling notation, which incorporates features for
capturing resources, data, and physical objects involved in the performance of
activities. Similarly, the Provop approach (cf. Sect. 5.3) considers variability of the
information and organization perspective [124].

5.5.2   Ensuring Correctness of Configured Process Variants

A big challenge for any process configuration approach is to ensure that configured
process variants are *sound* (cf. Chap. 4). When considering the large number of
process variants that may be configured out of a (reference) process model, as well
as the many syntactical and semantical constraints these process variants have to
obey, this constitutes a nontrivial task. In particular, manually correcting potential
errors would hamper any process configuration approach. Instead, efficient and
automated techniques for ensuring the soundness of process variant models are
required.

The approach presented in [12] proposes a formal foundation for incrementally
deriving process variants from a configurable reference process model, while preserving correctness, in respect to both syntax and behavioral soundness. Specifically,
assuming the configurable reference process model itself is behaviorally sound, the
derived process variants are guaranteed to be sound as well. The underlying theory
was developed in the context of Petri nets and then extended to Event-driven Process
Chains.

To ensure soundness of process variants, [16] suggests a verification approach
inspired by the "operating guidelines" used in the context of partner synthesis [190].[2] For this purpose, the configuration process itself is viewed as external
service. Using partner synthesis, a *configuration guideline* is computed that constitutes a compact characterization of all feasible configurations. In particular, this
allows ruling out configurations that lead to soundness violations. The approach
is generic and imposes no constraints on the configurable process models to
which it may be applied. Moreover, all computations are done at design time
(i.e., when defining a configurable process model) and not at configuration time;
i.e., there is no need for repeatedly checking each individual configuration when
configuring a process variant model. Thus, once the configuration guideline has been

---

[2] Partner synthesis is a proven technique to evaluate the correctness of a service. A partner
of a service is another service such that their composition and hence interactions are sound.
Conceptually, a partner is synthesized by first overapproximating the service's behavior in any
possible composition and then removing undesired states yielding deadlocks or livelocks.

generated, the response time is instantaneous, thus encouraging the practical use of configurable process models. The approach is implemented in a checker integrated in the YAWL Editor.

While these two techniques deal with soundness issues related to behavior-based configuration approaches (cf. Sect. 5.2), Hallerbach et al. [127] discusses how the soundness of process variants can be ensured when applying a *structural configuration approach* (cf. Sect. 5.3). In particular, Hallerbach et al. [127] presents advanced concepts for the context- and constraint-based configuration of process variants, and shows how respective information can be utilized to ensure soundness of the configured process variants.

5.5.3   Merging Process Variants

Designing a configurable process model is usually not done from scratch, but rather by analyzing existing process variants. Hence, merging these variants constitutes an important task that is also particularly relevant in today's world of company mergers and organizational consolidations. Considering the large number of process variants that may exist in enterprises, however, manually merging process models would be a tedious, time consuming, and error-prone task. Instead, techniques are required for automatically merging process variants in order to derive a configurable process model.

The concrete techniques for merging process variants depend on whether a behavior-based or a structural approach shall be used for capturing process variability. Regarding *behavior-based approaches* (cf. Sect. 5.2) variant merging needs to meet the following requirements. First, the behavior of the produced process model should subsume that of the input variant models (via the union of these input models). Second, it should be possible to trace back from which process variants an element has originated (via annotations). Third, one should be able to derive each input process variant from the merged one (via variation points). La Rosa et al. [167] presents an algorithm producing a single configurable process model from a pair of process variant models. This algorithm works by extracting the common parts of the input process variants, creating a single copy of them, and then appending the differences as branches of configurable connectors. This way, the merged process model is kept as small as possible, while still capturing all the behavior of the two input models. Moreover, analysts are able to trace back from which model(s) a given element in the merged model originated. The algorithm has been prototypically implemented and tested based on process models from several application domains. A similar approach for merging Event-driven Process Chains is presented in [104].

Regarding *structural approaches* (cf. Sect. 5.3), a family of algorithms for merging process variants has been suggested in [186]. These algorithms discover a process model by mining a given collection of process variants. Thereby, the discovered process model has a minimum average weighted distance to the considered process variants (see Chap. 8 for more details). By adopting the discovered model as new reference process model, future process configurations become more efficient, since the efforts (in terms of changes to be applied) for deriving the variants will be reduced.

5.5.4 Adaptive Reference Process Modeling

Generally, the designer of a reference process model might not foresee all configuration options that are required in actual practice. Hence, additional model adaptations might become necessary when configuring a particular process variant. In order to assist domain experts in performing respective adaptations, appropriate methods minimizing user efforts are needed. In this context, Becker et al. [48] proposes to integrate generic model adaptation techniques with configurative reference modeling. Moreover, recommendations for constructing modeling languages integrating configurative and generic reference process modeling are presented.

5.6 Summary

Enhancing process-aware information systems with configurable (reference) process models, and the capability to derive syntactically and semantically sound process variants from them, fosters the reuse of process knowledge and increases process model quality in large process repositories [351]. Two basic approaches for configuring prespecified process models were presented: *Behavior-based* configuration approaches that capture the behavior of all relevant process variants in one and the same artifact called a *configurable (reference) process model*. When configuring such a reference process model, an individualized variant can be derived through the hiding and blocking of control edges. Alternatively, configurable activities and control connectors can be used in this context. Based on these techniques, higher-level languages for configuring process models can be realized. *Structural* configuration approaches, in turn, enable configurations of a given base process model through structural adaptations, i.e., through the application of a sequence of high-level change operations. In addition, advanced techniques fostering process model configuration by domain experts not being familiar with the configuration approach or language used were described: questionnaire models, feature diagrams, and context models. Finally, other relevant aspects enabling process configuration were discussed: variability of process perspectives (other than control flow), required correctness guarantees for configured process variants, merging of process variants, and adaptive reference process modeling.

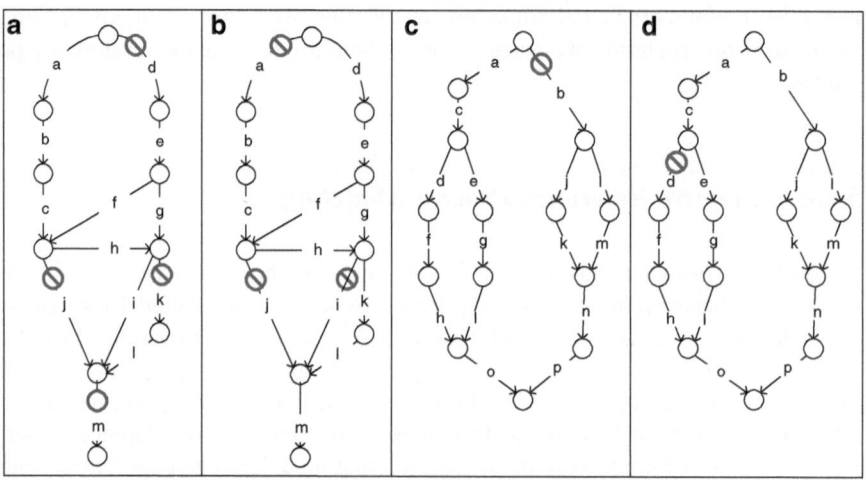

Fig. 5.21 Configuring transition systems through hiding and blocking

Exercises

5.1. Hiding and Blocking

Consider the configured process models (i.e., LTSs) from Fig. 5.21. Draw the process variants resulting from the application of the depicted hiding and blocking operations.

5.2. Configurable Nodes

Consider the reference process model from Fig. 5.22, which describes a family of process variants for handling a vehicle repair in a garage. (Assume that join connectors are configured in the same way as their corresponding split connectors.)

(a) What are the commonalities shared by all process variants that may be configured from this reference process model? What are the variation points of this reference model?
(b) Produce all process variants that may be configured from this reference process model.
(c) Design both a questionnaire model and a feature diagram for configuring this reference process model.

5.3. Configuration Through Structural Changes

Consider the base process model and the prespecified change options depicted in Fig. 5.13. Furthermore consider the three process variants from Fig. 5.1b–d.

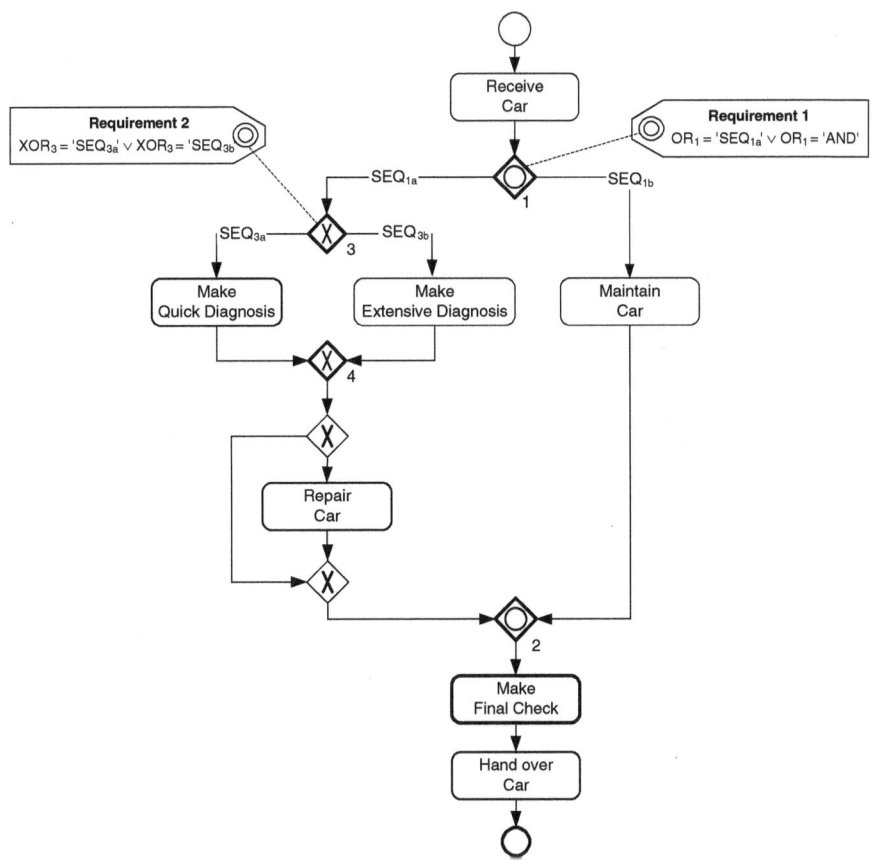

Fig. 5.22 Configurable reference process model of a vehicle repair process

(a) For each of the three process variant models, explain how it can be derived through the configuration of the given base process model; i.e., for each process variant model specify its process context as well as the change options required to derive this variant.

(b) Assume that during process configuration Option 1b is applied to the base process model from Fig. 5.13. Why is it then not allowed to apply Option 4 to this base process model as well?

5.4. Designing a Base Process Model and Related Change Options

Consider the reference process model from Fig. 5.22 and Exercise 5.2, respectively. Design a base process model and related change options based on which the same process variant models can be derived as for the configurable reference process model from Fig. 5.22. Provide a context model for this process family as well.

5.5. Questionnaire-Based Configuration of a Reference Process Model

Consider the three process models from Fig. 5.1b–d. These constitute variants of the reference process model depicted in Fig. 5.9. Discuss how each of these process variants can be derived when using the questionnaire model from Fig. 5.17.

5.6. Process Configuration Approaches

(a) What are the major benefits of configurable process models?

(b) Describe commonalities and differences of behavior-based and structural process configuration approaches.

(c) Why is it important to also consider the data flow perspective when configuring a process model?

Chapter 6
Exception Handling

Abstract Due to exceptional or special situations occurring in the real world, a business process cannot be always executed as desired. This chapter deals with anticipated exceptions occurring during the execution of prespecified process models. These range from activity failures to deadline expirations to unavailable resources. For coping with such anticipated exceptions, exception handlers are typically provided by process designers at build-time. These handlers are automatically invoked by the process-aware information system (PAIS) during run-time when corresponding exceptions occur. This chapter describes selected exception handing patterns frequently applied in PAISs to deal with anticipated exceptions. Moreover, the chapter gives insights into the semantic rollback of process instances, which is especially important when handling semantic activity failures during run-time.

6.1 Motivation

As discussed in Chap. 3, a prespecified process cannot always be executed as desired due to emerging exceptions or special situations. Regarding computerized processes such exceptions are common [242, 334]. Process-aware information systems (PAISs) are particularly vulnerable to exceptions when compared to data- or function-centered information systems.

Exceptions can either be anticipated or not. While *anticipated* exceptions can be *planned*, *unanticipated* ones typically have to be addressed in an ad hoc manner during process execution. In this chapter we focus on the handling of anticipated exceptions, whereas Chap. 7 addresses unanticipated exceptions and their handling through ad hoc process changes at run-time.

As illustrated in Fig. 6.1, exceptions may occur due to various reasons denoted as *exception sources* in this book. To deal with anticipated exceptions and special cases in a reliable and systematic way, PAISs require sophisticated exception handling mechanisms [242]. More precisely, at build-time process designers have to provide *exception handlers*, which are then invoked during run-time to cope

M. Reichert and B. Weber, *Enabling Flexibility in Process-Aware Information Systems*,   127
DOI 10.1007/978-3-642-30409-5_6, © Springer-Verlag Berlin Heidelberg 2012

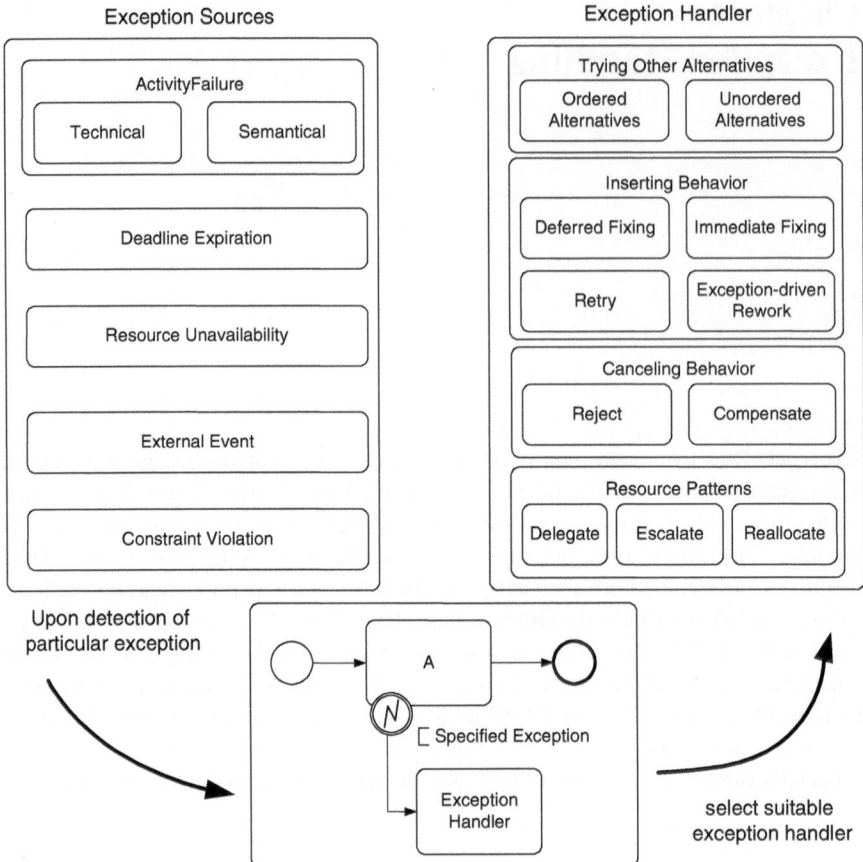

Fig. 6.1 Exception sources and exception handlers

with the anticipated exceptions; i.e., if a particular exception is detected by the PAIS during run-time, a suitable exception handler will be invoked by it. The occurrence of exceptions and their handling during run-time must not lead to poor process performance, process inconsistencies, or—even worse—process errors (e.g., blocked processes due to *deadlocks*). This is especially important since no PAIS will be accepted by its users if its use in exceptional situations is too complex or more cumbersome than just handling the exception by a phone call to the right person [86].

The remainder of this chapter is organized as follows. Section 6.2 discusses typical sources of exceptions in PAISs and their detection. Section 6.3 then introduces exception handling patterns which constitute frequently used strategies to address anticipated exceptions in PAISs. Section 6.4 picks up the topic of compensation handling in the context of activity and process failures. In Sect. 6.5

existing approaches for both exception and compensation handling are discussed. Finally, Sect. 6.6 concludes this chapter with a summary.

6.2 Exception Sources and Their Detection

Section 6.2.1 first describes typical sources of anticipated exceptions that might occur during process execution. Section 6.2.2 then discusses their detection within PAISs.

6.2.1 Sources of Exceptions

Potential sources of (anticipated) exceptions in a PAIS occurring during the execution of prespecified process models include activity failures, deadline expirations, resource unavailability, discrepancies between real-world business process and its computerized counterpart as executed in a PAIS, and constraint violations [311]. In this section these different sources of exceptions are examined in detail.

Activity Failures. From a process perspective, critical exceptions often occur during activity execution, i.e., the execution of single process steps [88]. Such activity failures can be divided into technical failures (i.e., system failures) and semantic failures [84]. *Technical failures* include IT infrastructure or system-related failures, i.e., the abnormal termination of an activity (e.g., activity crash) due to failures of the invoked application service, or hardware, software or network failures. *Semantic failures* (cf. Example 6.1), in turn, are caused by a negative, but not abnormal termination of an activity. Semantic failures usually occur during activity execution.

> *Example 6.1 (Semantic Activity Failure).* During the treatment of a particular patient, an unanticipated reaction occurs due to a previously unknown medical allergy. Emergency actions are required to stabilize the patient (i.e., administration of adrenaline) and the application of the medication causing the allergic reaction is stopped.

Deadline Expirations. Deadline expirations constitute another source of exceptions whose handling might require certain actions not covered by the normal flow of control. In a PAIS, work items can be associated with deadlines and upon deadline expiration an exception will be raised. As a consequence, corresponding *escalation* procedures (e.g., *notification* of selected users about the expiration) are invoked.

Example 6.2 (Deadline Expiration).

- Reviewers are asked to submit their reviews by a particular deadline. If the reviews have not been submitted yet when the deadline is reached, a notification e-mail is sent to the respective reviewers. If the reviews have still not been submitted after several more days have passed, the papers will be reassigned to other reviewers.
- A payment period of 10 days has been agreed upon with the customer. If no payment has been received after a period of 14 days, a payment reminder will be sent and a handling charge be raised (escalation mechanism).
- To perform chemotherapy for an inpatient the physician has to inform the pharmacy about the correct dosage of the cytostatic drug by 11:00. If the deadline is missed the pharmacy will check back by phone for the exact dosage (escalation mechanism).

Resource Unavailability. Another typical source of exceptions in PAISs is the unavailability of resources (e.g., human actors).

Example 6.3 (Resource Unavailability). If a particular user falls sick, his work (i.e., work item) may have to be reassigned to another user. In certain situations resource unavailability might even lead to the cancelation of activities (e.g., if no substitute can be found).

Discrepancies Between Real-World and Computerized Process. Exceptions often occur due to inconsistencies between the real-world process and its computerized counterpart as executed in the PAIS. These inconsistencies may be caused through incompleteness of the process model (i.e., uncovered special cases), or by temporary changes in the real-world process, but also by data inaccuracies (e.g., incorrect data values) [332]. To keep the real-world process and the prespecified process model running in the PAIS aligned with each other, respective changes have to be propagated to the PAIS. Typically, such exceptions cannot be automatically detected by the PAIS, but usually need to be triggered by the user. Moreover, discrepancies between real-world and computerized processes are often not anticipated (techniques for handling unanticipated exceptions will be discussed in Chap. 7).

Example 6.4 (Discrepancies between Real-world and Computerized Process).

- To diagnose disorders of a cervical spine, a magnetic resonance tomography is usually conducted. For patients with cardiac pacemaker, however, another imaging technique (e.g., computer tomography) has to be performed instead.
- To diagnose fructose malabsorption, typically, a hydrogen breath test is performed, which requires individuals to fast for at least 12 h prior to the test. Occasionally, it happens that a particular patient has not fasted long enough before the test. In such situations the test cannot be conducted and the patient has to be sent home.
- A traffic jam on the route between a container truck's departure and destination locations requires its driver to take an alternative route.

Constraint Violations. Violations of constraints over data, resources, or process model elements (e.g., activities) often raise exceptions; e.g., data required for activity execution might be missing.

Example 6.5 (Constraint Violations). Service Level Agreements (e.g., concerning response times) are typically monitored throughout process execution. If a particular process instance runs the risk of violating the Service Level Agreements agreed upon, a notification is sent to selected PAIS users.

6.2.2   Detecting Exceptions

Section 6.2.1 has described typical sources of exceptions. Whether or not these exceptions are *detectable* by the PAIS depends on its capability of noticing their occurrence [194]. To enable the detection of exceptions many existing PAISs allow process designers to define *events* representing triggers like, for example, timers, messages, and errors. Moreover, to notify the PAIS about inconsistencies between real-world and computerized processes (cf. Example 6.4), several PAISs allow users to explicitly throw an exception. Upon detection of a respective event, a suitable exception handler is selected and invoked by the PAIS (cf. Sect. 6.3).

6.3   Handling Exceptions

To be able to adequately deal with anticipated exceptions during run-time, process designers need to associate prespecified process models with *exception handlers* at build-time. These will then be invoked during run-time if a particular exception is

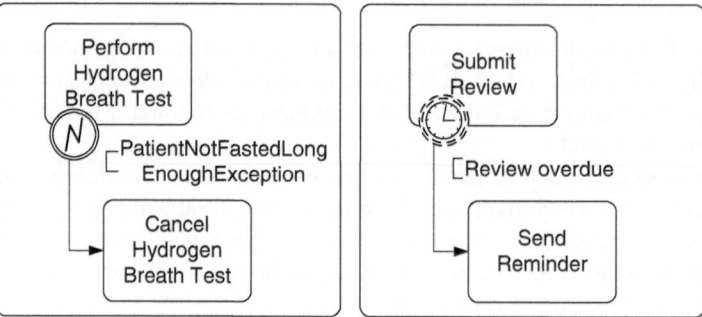

Fig. 6.2 Simple exception handler

raised (similar to exception handling in programming languages). If an exception occurs during run-time and disrupts the normal flow of control, it is passed to the run-time system of the PAIS; i.e., an *exception is thrown*. The PAIS then looks for a suitable, predefined *exception handler* being able to handle the respective exception. If such a handler is found, the exception is passed to it; i.e., the handler is said to *catch the exception*. Moreover, it includes actions to recover from the exception in order to continue with the normal flow of the prespecified process model afterwards or to cancel the process instance.

Depending on the concrete PAIS implementation, events like timers, messages, and errors might interrupt the normal flow of the prespecified process model, and trigger the execution of the exceptional flow defined by the corresponding exception handler. After handling the exception, the execution of the prespecified process model either resumes with the activity triggering the exception or continues at some other position in the process after canceling activity execution. Alternatively, the exceptional flow might run in parallel to the normal one.

Example 6.6 (Exception Handling). Figure 6.2 shows two simple exception handling scenarios:

- The first scenario is based on Example 6.4. If a particular patient has not fasted long enough before performing a hydrogen breath test, the test cannot be conducted and must therefore be canceled. In this scenario the exception interrupts activity *Perform Hydrogen Breath Test*.
- The second scenario is based on Example 6.2. If the review has not been submitted by the deadline, a reminder will be sent to the respective reviewer. Note that this deadline expiration does not interrupt activity *Submit Review*, since the review might still be submitted.

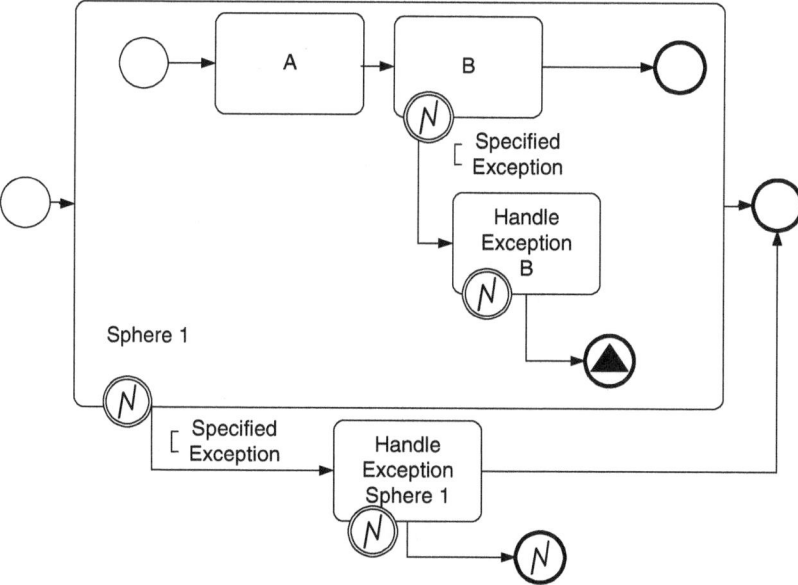

Fig. 6.3 Exception handling spheres

Exception handling can be applied to single activities, predefined regions of a process comprising multiple activities, or the entire process. Therefore, many PAISs allow process designers to group activities into *spheres*, which may be (regularly) nested with other spheres. If a particular exception cannot be handled within the current sphere several options exist: First, the exception may be propagated to a surrounding sphere, e.g., by throwing the same exception at the higher level sphere again. Second, an error message can be sent to the process owner, if the PAIS cannot properly respond to the exception. Third, a human task might be invoked to correct the exception. Fourth, if the issue cannot be resolved by the exception handler it may become necessary to roll back and compensate the process.

Example 6.7 (Exception Handling Spheres). Figure 6.3 provides a scenario with several exception handlers assigned to different spheres. First, activity B has an associated exception handler which is invoked when this activity throws an exception. Moreover, there is an exception handler for Sphere 1, i.e., the process region comprising activities A and B.

If the exception handler associated with activity B is unable to handle an exception thrown by B, the exception is passed to the exception handler surrounding Sphere 1 (indicated by the end signal). If this handler is also unable to deal with the exception, the process itself will terminate with an exception.

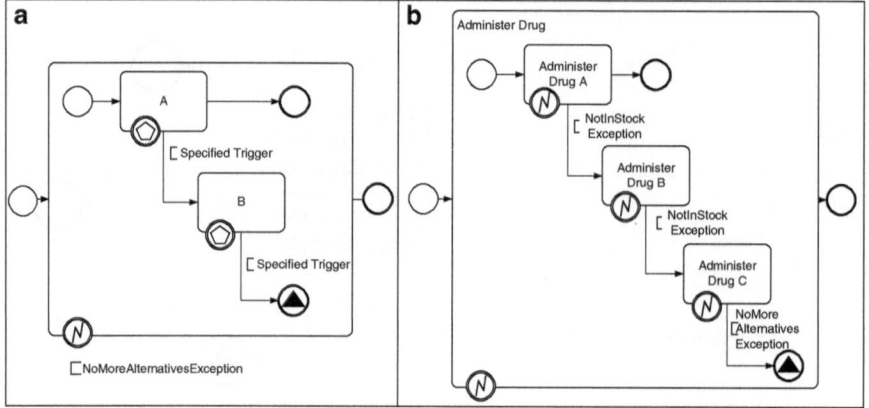

Fig. 6.4 Ordered alternatives (Part **a** adopted from [176])

6.3.1 Exception Handling Patterns

This section introduces *exception handling patterns* frequently applied in practice to deal with anticipated exceptions [176]. These patterns can be roughly divided into three categories: *trying alternatives* (cf. Sect. 6.3.1.1), *adding behavior* (cf. Sect. 6.3.1.2), and *canceling behavior* (cf. Sect. 6.3.1.3). Moreover, we discuss resource-related exception handlers (cf. Sect. 6.3.1.5) as well as strategies for flexible work item handling (cf. Sect. 6.3.1.4).

6.3.1.1 Trying Alternatives

One option to deal with occurring exceptions is to try alternatives in case an exception prohibits users to execute a process instance as planned. Alternatives may either be tried in a predefined order (i.e., *ordered alternatives pattern*) or in arbitrary order (i.e., *unordered alternatives pattern*). Figure 6.4a depicts the structure of the *ordered alternatives pattern*: By default, activity A is executed. If A fails, activity B will be alternatively executed. If B also fails no more alternatives exist and a *NoMoreAlternativesException* is thrown and then propagated to the higher level sphere.

Example 6.8 (Ordered Alternatives Pattern). To treat a patient with a particular disease, usually, *Drug A* is administered since it is the cheapest drug containing the desired active substance (cf. Fig. 6.4b). If *Drug A* is not available, alternatively, *Drug B* will be administered. If *Drug B*, in turn, is not available, *Drug C* will provide another slightly more expensive option. Finally, if this option also fails, a *NoMoreAlternativesException* will be raised.

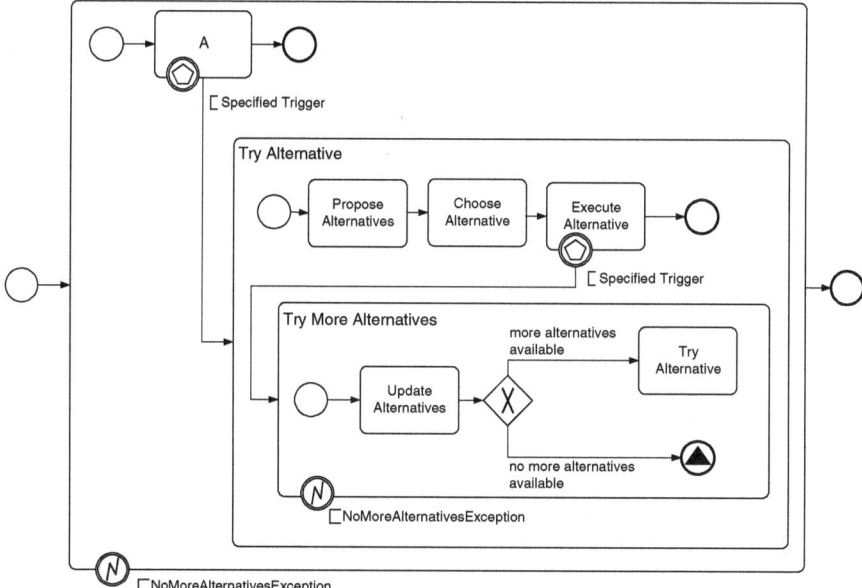

Fig. 6.5 Unordered alternatives [176]

While the *ordered alternatives pattern* assumes that the preferred order of the alternatives can be established a priori, the *unordered alternatives pattern* defers this decision to run-time. Factors that might influence the order in which the alternatives are tried include the state of the process, resource availability, or available knowledge of participating actors. Figure 6.5 illustrates the *unordered alternatives pattern*: by default, activity A is executed. If this activity fails, a set of alternatives will be proposed from which one alternative has to be chosen. If the execution of this alternative activity leads again to an exception, further alternatives will be explored. For this, the set of alternatives is updated; i.e., already discarded alternatives are no longer considered. If no more alternatives are available, the original activity will terminate with an exception, otherwise additional alternatives can be tried.

Example 6.9 (Unordered Alternatives Pattern). Consider the process of buying tickets for a musical. Unfortunately, tickets for your favorite musical are no longer available. Therefore, you try to get tickets for another musical which are also available for that particular day.

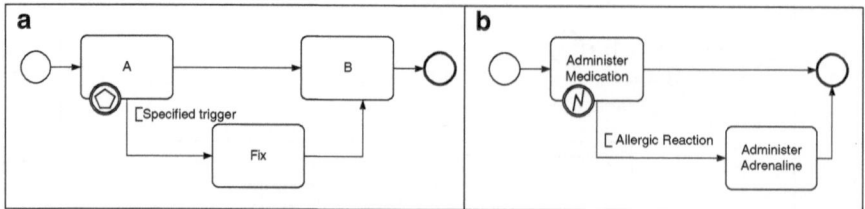

Fig. 6.6 Immediate fixing (Part **a** adopted from [176])

6.3.1.2   Adding Behavior

Frequently, exceptions occurring during process execution can be handled by executing additional activities, i.e., through *immediate fixing, deferred fixing, retrying*, or *rework*. Using the *immediate fixing pattern*, the exception is handled before continuing with process execution. Using the *deferred fixing pattern*, in turn, the problem is noted (e.g., in a trouble report) potentially allowing a work around that can be addressed later. Figure 6.6a illustrates the structure of the *immediate fixing* pattern. If, during the execution of activity A, an event with one of the specified triggers is detected, the normal flow will be interrupted and the process will continue with the exceptional flow. The latter includes an activity to handle an exception that needs to be completed before continuing with the normal flow.

Example 6.10 (Immediate Fixing). Figure 6.6b illustrates a potential complication when administrating a medication to a particular patient (i.e., an allergic reaction to a medication). This complication requires an immediate solution. To deal with this exception and to stabilize the patient, adrenaline is given. Note that this exception is caused by a *semantic activity failure*.

Figure 6.7a, in turn, illustrates the structure of the *deferred fixing* pattern.

Example 6.11 (Deferred Fixing). During a preflight inspection of an aircraft, a malfunction is detected (cf. Fig. 6.7b). Since the affected item is on the *Minimum Equipment List,* which lists all instruments and equipment that may be inoperative without jeopardizing the safety of the aircraft, the aircraft is allowed to take off. Before taking off, however, the pilot has to enter the defect into the open item list. The defect itself is fixed at a later stage.

Additionally, exceptions are often addressed by *retrying* the activities that caused the exception. Figure 6.8a illustrates the structure of the *retry pattern*. While executing activity A an exception is thrown. To handle it, first, activity *Update*

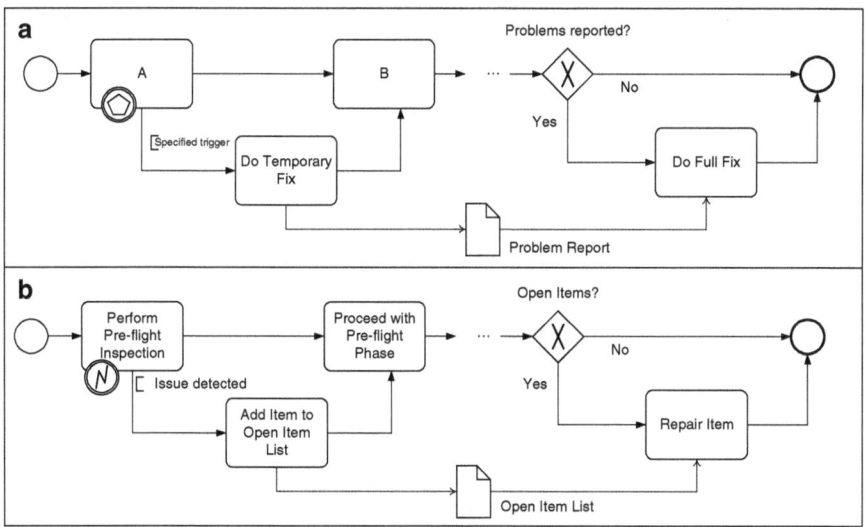

Fig. 6.7 Deferred fixing (Part **a** adopted from [176])

Context is performed before retrying A (e.g., to change parameter settings of activity A). To avoid that A is continuously retried, activity *Update Context* is responsible for determining whether to continue with retrying A or to throw an exception and handle it somewhere else (e.g., at a higher-level sphere).

> *Example 6.12 (Retrying).* Assume that for the duration of her vacation in Canada, Bettina buys a data plan for her mobile device with one of the Canadian phone providers (cf. Fig. 6.8b). When activating the data plan on her mobile device she is asked to enter her name, address, and phone number. The data is validated by the system and she is asked to enter a valid Canadian address. Since she has no Canadian residency, she tries to activate her account with the address of her Canadian friend Pam. This scenario constitutes an example of a *semantic activity failure*, i.e., activity *Activate Data Plan* fails due to an invalid address.

Frequently, occurring exceptions are not immediately detected and process execution proceeds. In such situations *rework* might become necessary (i.e., to re-execute the activity that caused the problem) in order to restore overall process consistency. As opposed to the *retry pattern*, which assumes that the exception is *immediately detected* and *handled*, the *rework pattern* is less restrictive and allows the problem to be fixed at *any time*.

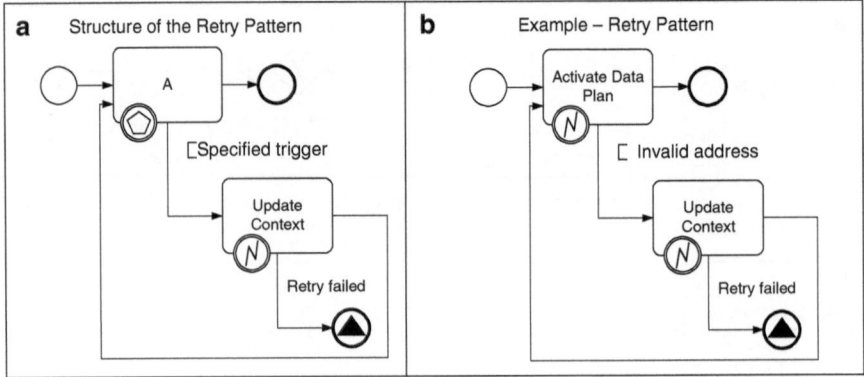

Fig. 6.8 Retry pattern (Part **a** adopted from [176])

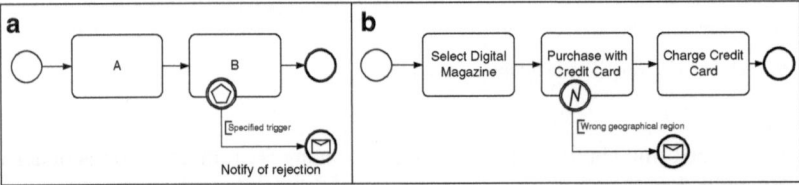

Fig. 6.9 Reject pattern (Part **a** adopted from [176])

Example 6.13 (Exception-driven Rework). As part of a medical treatment process the blood count of a particular patient has to be determined. For this, a blood sample is taken and sent to the lab to be analyzed. On the way to the lab, however, the blood sample gets lost. The problem is detected only a few days later, since the diagnostic findings of the lab are still missing. To handle this situation a new sample has to be taken and sent to the lab for analysis.

6.3.1.3 Canceling Behavior

Certain exceptions require canceling process behavior. This might include the cancelation of the entire process or of process parts (*reject pattern*), but also undoing already completed work (*compensate pattern*).

Figure 6.9a illustrates the *reject pattern*. It includes two final states, one for the normal flow and another one for the exceptional flow.

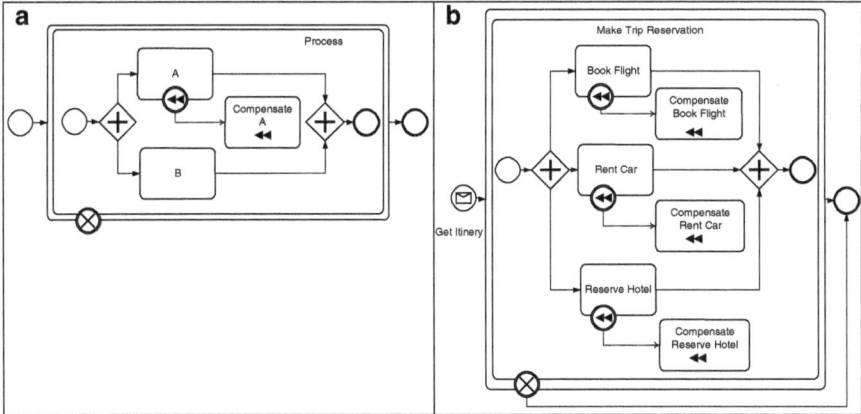

Fig. 6.10 Compensation pattern (Part **a** adopted from [176])

Example 6.14 (Reject). Consider a customer buying digital editions of his favorite magazines via an online platform (cf. Fig. 6.9b). The customer has selected a particular magazine and enters his credit card information to purchase it. Since the selected magazine is not available for the customer's geographic region, the buying process is aborted and the customer is notified. In this example, the rejection is caused by a *semantic activity failure*.

Moreover, it may become necessary to *undo* already completed work (i.e., *compensation pattern*). Figure 6.10a illustrates the *compensation pattern*. If a process has to be canceled, the effects of already completed activities are semantically undone by invoking corresponding compensation activities for each of the completed activities. As a prerequisite for this, corresponding compensation activities need to be implemented (for details see Sect. 6.4).

Example 6.15 (Compensate). Let us assume Wil wants to book a trip to go from San Diego, USA, to Innsbruck, Austria, using an online-trip reservation service. The respective service allows Wil to compose his itinerary with several connecting flights, car rental, and hotel reservations (activities *Book Flight*, *Rent Car*, and *Reserve Hotel* in Fig. 6.10b). If any of these reservations fails, the already completed reservations have to be compensated by the online-trip reservation system (activities *Compensate Book Flight*, *Compensate Rent Car*, and *Compensate Reserve Hotel* in Fig. 6.10b). The reservation process is then aborted.

6.3.1.4   Resource-Related Exception Handler

The exception handling patterns described in Sects. 6.3.1.1–6.3.1.3 are well suited to handle exceptions requiring behavioral changes. In particular, exceptions are addressed by providing alternatives, by inserting additional behavior, or by canceling behavior. In the context of human processes, the handling of many exceptions like resource unavailability or deadline expirations, however, might also involve changes regarding the resource perspective. This includes *delegation, escalation, reallocation,* and *deallocation* of work items [311]. However, only few PAISs provide advanced support for changes of the resource perspective during runtime [311].

Example 6.16 (Resource Unavailability). Assume that work has been assigned to user Boulahrouz. Boulahrouz is on sick leave for several weeks due to a fractured leg. Therefore, the work assigned to him has to be reassigned to his substitute Tasci.

Example 6.17 (Deadline Expiration). Assume that work has been assigned to user Boudewijn. Since the deadline for completing the work has passed, it is reallocated to his superior Maja.

Figure 6.11 illustrates selected *resource patterns*—or more precisely *detour patterns*—that exist to handle work items in exceptional situations [307, 308]. As discussed in Chap. 2, a work item typically passes states Offered, Allocated, and Started before reaching its final state Completed. In addition, there are two variations of this standard work item life cycle. First, a work item may immediately change from its initial state Offered to state Withdrawn. For example, a work item offered to a particular user may be selected by another user. Second, if the execution of a work item fails, its state will change to Failed.

In addition to the states and state transitions constituting the standard way of handling work items (cf. Chap. 2), further options exist to handle work items in exceptional situations and to change resource assignments. These options are illustrated in Fig. 6.11 through additional state transitions represented as dashed lines. *Delegation*, for example, refers to the allocation of a work item to another resource than the one the work item has been previously assigned to. *Escalation*, in turn, refers to the allocation or offering of a stalled work item to another resource.

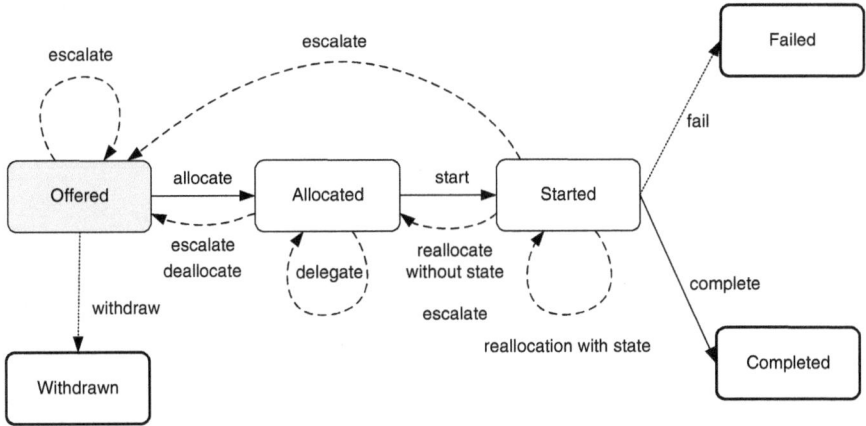

Fig. 6.11 Selected detour patterns

Resource Pattern	Description	Original States	Resulting States
Delegation	A resource allocates a previously allocated work item to another resource (i.e., reallocate).	Allocated	Allocated
Escalation	The system attempts to deal with a stalled work item by offering or allocating it to another resource.	Allocated, Offered, Started	Allocated, Offered
Stateful Reallocation	A resource allocates a work item it has started to another resource and the current state of the work item is retained.	Started	Started
Stateless Reallocation	A resource allocates a work item it has started to another resource, but the current state is not retained (i.e. the work item is restarted).	Started	Allocated
Deallocation	A resource makes a previously allocated work item available, i.e., the work item can be offered to other resources.	Allocated	Offered

6.3.1.5   Flexible Handling of Work Items

Section 6.3 has introduced a set of exception handling patterns frequently used for dealing with exceptions; i.e., trying alternative behavior, adding behavior, canceling behavior, or altering resource assignments. The application of these exception handling patterns often requires changing the life cycle of work items relating to the process instance affected by the exception; e.g., work items may have to be skipped, redone, done ahead of time, canceled, or suspended/resumed [311].

To enable the flexible handling of work items, the standard work item life cycle as introduced in Fig. 2.18 (cf. Chap. 2) is extended with two additional states: Suspended and Skipped (cf. Fig. 6.12). Depending on the PAIS used, different resource patterns for flexible work item handling may be supported [307].

When an exception occurs, it might become necessary to temporarily *suspend* the execution of the affected work item and to *resume* it after having successfully

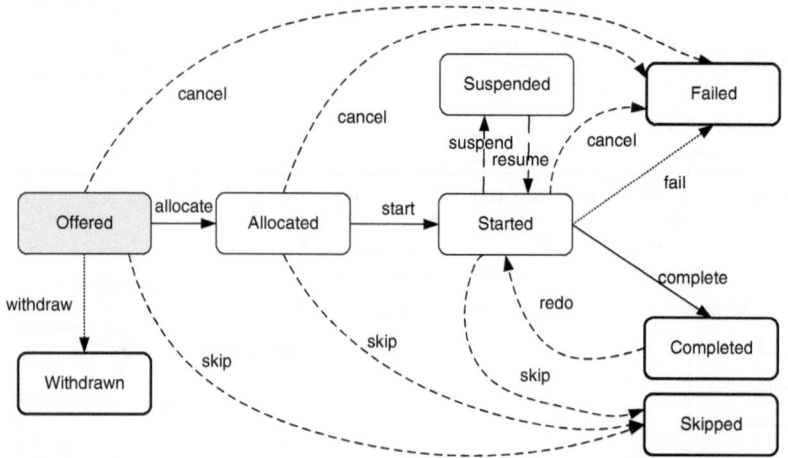

Fig. 6.12 Flexible work item handling

Resource Pattern	Description	Original States	Resulting States
Suspension-Resumption	A resource temporarily suspends the execution of a work item or recommences the execution of a previously suspended work item.	Started Suspended	Suspended Started
Skipping	A resource skips the execution of an offered, allocated, or started work item.	Offered Allocated Started	Skipped
Redo	A resource re-executes a work item already completed earlier.	Completed	Started
Predo	A resource executes an activity not yet enabled (and therefore not yet offered) in the context of a particular process instance; the activity is executed ahead of time.	-	-
Cancel	A work item is aborted and changes to state failed.	Offered Allocated Started	Failed

handled the exception. Certain exceptions, in turn, require the work item to be *canceled*. Skipping, redoing, and predoing work items also constitute frequently needed exceptional actions. Skipping a work item changes its state from Offered, Allocated, or Started to Skipped. *Redo* refers to repeating the execution of a work item already completed earlier. *Predo*, in turn, allows executing an activity ahead of time; i.e., to execute an activity not enabled yet.

In addition to changing the state of a work item, exceptions may require changing the state of the entire process instance, e.g., by suspending, resuming, or terminating the process instance [307]. For example, upon occurrence of an activity failure it might become necessary to suspend the execution of the entire process instance, while compensation activities are executed. Depending on the type of exception, the execution of the process instance may later be resumed or the process instance may have to be terminated.

On one hand, flexible handling of work items and process instances facilitates the definition of exception handlers for coping with anticipated exceptions, since this functionality can be reused in exception handlers. On the other hand, it can also cope with certain kinds of unanticipated exceptions during run-time.

6.4 Compensation Handling

As discussed in Sect. 6.3.1.3, exceptions may require the entire process or parts of it to be canceled. Further, the effects of already completed activities may have to be compensated by semantically undoing them. In this context, Sect. 6.4.1 discusses semantic rollback through compensation, while Sect. 6.4.2 introduces the concept of compensation spheres.

The execution of a prespecified process model in a PAIS may last from days to weeks or even months. Thus, it constitutes a *long-running transaction* [88] or a long-running process respectively. For the latter the ACID transaction properties (Atomicity, Consistency, Isolation, and Durability) as known from database transactions are usually too restrictive and therefore not applicable; e.g., it is usually not possible to hold long-term locks on a process instance sharing resources and data with other process instances. Consequently, advanced techniques are needed to cope with failures of long-running processes which are less restrictive, but still provide some guarantees regarding process execution [88].

6.4.1 Semantic Rollback Through Compensation

This section describes the handling of activity failures and process cancelation in long-running processes and transactions, respectively, based on Sagas [95]. Simply speaking, a long-running transaction is divided into a sequence of sub-transactions (i.e., process activities in our context) called *Sagas*. Assuming that sub-transactions retain their ACID properties (i.e., they show standard transactional behavior), the Saga itself represents the entire long-running transaction and does not possess ACID properties. However, each of the sub-transactions may be associated with a compensation handler comprising a *compensation sub-transaction*. If a running sub-transaction fails, it can be rolled back. However, this does not apply to already committed ones. The latter have to be semantically compensated by invoking their corresponding *compensation handlers* in reverse order of their commitment.

Example 6.18 (Sagas). Consider Fig. 6.13. If activity (i.e., sub-transaction) D fails during its execution, D is rolled back like a standard transaction, and the

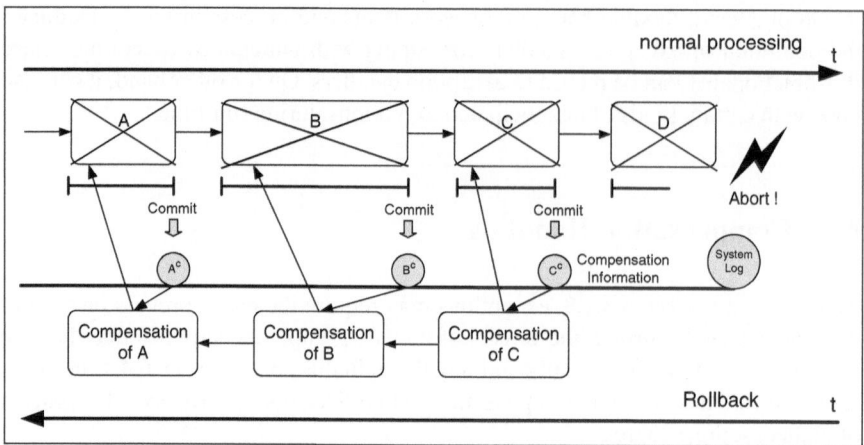

Fig. 6.13 Compensation handling with sagas

Saga invokes the compensation handlers of sub-transactions for activities C, B, and A (i.e., in reverse order of their execution).

One of the first PAISs implementing Sagas was ProMInand [141]. In the context of advanced transaction models [88], numerous refinements and extensions of the Sagas concept were suggested. For example, the original Sagas model, which was restricted to activity sequences (i.e., sequences of saga transactions), was extended toward the nesting of transactions. Respective approaches include Nested Sagas [94], (Open) Nested Transactions [221,362], and Compensation Spheres [177,178]. Another extension was provided by the ConTracts project [280] which additionally applies rollback actions to restore consistency of process data objects when rolling back the process.

6.4.2   Compensation Spheres

Compensation spheres as introduced in [72,177,178] extend the Sagas model, which is restricted to rather simple rollback scenarios. Compensation spheres provide conceptual means to define compensation behavior for a group of activities, e.g., for a process fragment (cf. Fig. 6.14). If one of the activities of the sphere fails, all completed activities of that sphere must be compensated. Moreover, running activities executed in parallel to the failed activity must be aborted and rolled back as well.

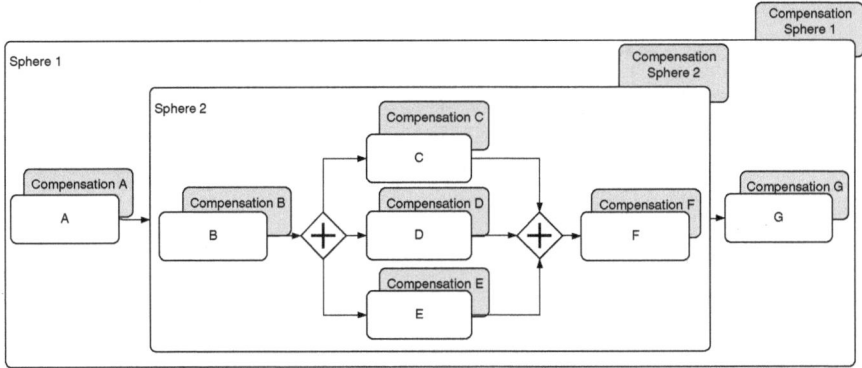

Fig. 6.14 Compensation spheres

For each activity of a compensation sphere a corresponding compensation handler (gray activities in Fig. 6.14) is defined (which might also be a compensation handler without any associated action if no compensation is possible). Moreover, a compensation sphere itself may be associated with a compensation handler. If an activity of a sphere fails, aborting the compensation sphere might become necessary. For this case the PAIS invokes the compensation handlers of already completed activities of the sphere in reverse order. Further, it aborts concurrently running, but not yet completed activities of the sphere.

Example 6.19 (Compensation Spheres). Consider Fig. 6.14 which comprises two compensation spheres (denoted as Sphere 1 and Sphere 2, respectively). Sphere 2, for example, contains activities B, C, D, E, and F. Assume that the execution of F fails, resulting in the compensation handler of Sphere 2 to be invoked. F is then aborted and rolled back. Afterwards, the compensation handlers related to C, D, and E are executed. Finally, B is compensated.

Another scenario assumes that activity G fails; i.e, A and Sphere 2 have already been completed. In this case, G is aborted and rolled back, and the compensation handler associated with Sphere 2 is invoked, which by default invokes compensation handlers of B, C, D, E, and F in reverse order. Finally, A is compensated.

So far, the default behavior of the compensation handler of Sphere 2 has been described. Alternatively, after having completed all activities of Sphere 2, the compensation behavior of Sphere 2 may change; i.e., compensation behavior might be different depending on whether the failure occurred during the execution of Sphere 2 or afterwards. For example, instead of compensating all completed activities in reverse order only selected activities are compensated or an entirely different compensating process is invoked.

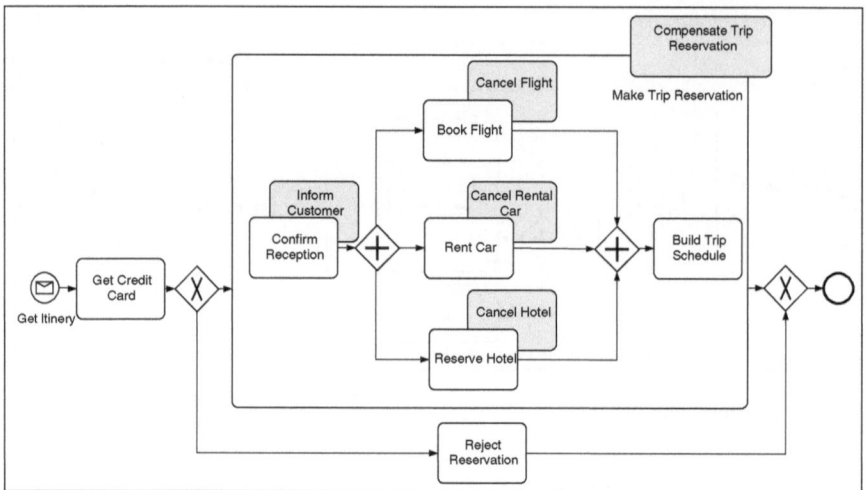

Fig. 6.15 Example of a compensation sphere

Example 6.20 (Compensation Spheres—Concrete Example). Figure 6.15 illustrates the concept of compensation spheres using a trip reservation process as example. Activities *Confirm Reception, Book Flight, Rent Car, Reserve Hotel*, and *Build Trip Schedule* constitute a *compensation sphere*. Activities *Book Flight, Rent Car*, and *Reserve Hotel* all have associated compensation activities to semantically undo them by canceling the bookings. Activity *Confirm Reception*, in turn, can be compensated by informing the customer. Let us assume that during the execution of the trip reservation process one of the reservation activities fails (e.g., *Book Flight*). Then, the respective activity is aborted and the compensation handler of the sphere is invoked, which, in turn, invokes the compensation handlers of already executed activities in reverse order. In this example we assume that *Book Hotel* and *Rent Car* have already been completed. This implies that, first, activities *Book Hotel* and *Rent Car* are compensated by canceling already made reservations. Then activity *Confirm Reception* is compensated by informing the customer about the failed itinerary.

6.5   Exception Handling in Selected Approaches

This section introduces selected and well-known approaches for exception and compensation handling. Common to the described approaches is the separation of exception handling from the "normal" control flow, i.e., exceptions are not modeled

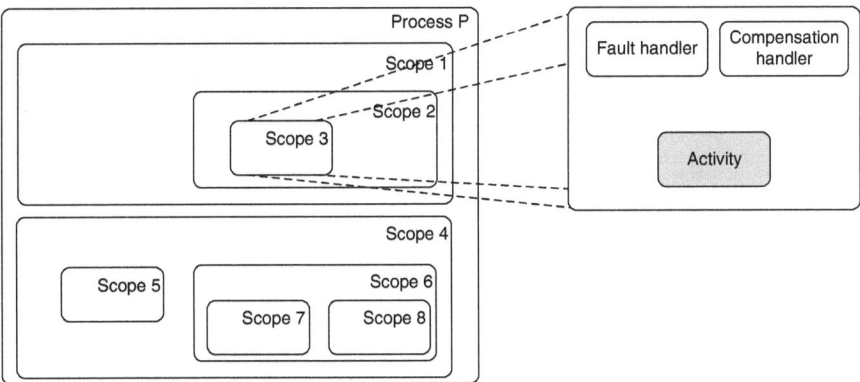

Fig. 6.16 Compensation handling in WS-BPEL

as alternative branches leading to Spaghetti-like process models. Instead, normal flow and exceptional flow are separated. Note that a similar principle is applied in programming languages like Java or Ada as well.

6.5.1   Compensation and Exception Handling in WS-BPEL

Web Service Business Process Execution Language (WS-BPEL) is an industrial standard for specifying executable process models based on XML and for connecting process activities with web services [236]. This section describes how compensation and exception handling are addressed in WS-BPEL.

To enable long-running processes based on WS-BPEL, both exception handlers (called fault handlers in WS-BPEL) and compensation handlers are provided. While *fault handlers* are used to handle the activity failure itself (e.g., to roll back the activity), *compensation handlers* can be optionally specified to compensate already committed activities. Furthermore, activities logically belonging together can be grouped in spheres (called *scopes* in WS-BPEL). Thereby, WS-BPEL supports arbitrary nesting of scopes. Both fault handlers and compensation handlers can be attached to scopes as well (cf. Fig. 6.16).

Example 6.21 (Fault and Compensation Handling WS-BPEL). Figure 6.17 illustrates a process instance being based on WS-BPEL and comprising three activities A, B, and C (with associated services). A and B were already executed (Step 1 in Fig. 6.17), when a fault occurs during the execution of C (Step 2 in Fig. 6.17). This triggers the process-level fault handler (Step 3 in Fig. 6.17). By default, the process-level fault handler invokes the compen-

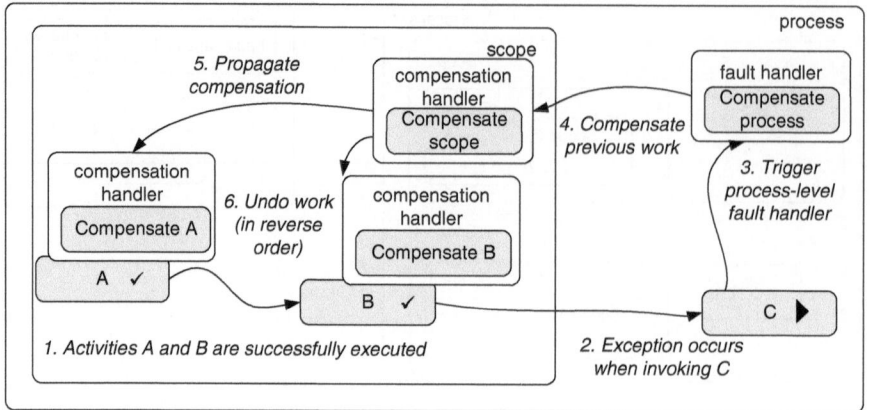

Fig. 6.17   Compensation handling in WS-BPEL

sation handler of its child scopes (Step 4 in Fig. 6.17). This compensation
handler, in turn, invokes the compensation handlers of B and A (in reverse
order) (Step 5 in Fig. 6.17), which then invoke respective compensation
activities (Step 6 in Fig. 6.17). Note that in general, any compensation handler
may be an arbitrary process expressed in terms of WS-BPEL.

Similar to exception and compensation handling in WS-BPEL, in OPERA [122]
process fragments (i.e., activities, groups of activities, and sub-processes) can be
associated with exception handlers allowing process designers to create *spheres of
compensation*.

6.5.2   Exception Handling in the Exlet Approach

The Exlet approach [28, 30] provides advanced capabilities to handle work items
in exceptional situations. To support the handling of exceptions, each activity as
well as the entire process may be associated with a set of exception handling subprocesses (called *Exlets*). The activities of an exception handling subprocess can be
atomic or complex. Thereby, atomic activities are typically related to transitions in
the work item life cycle which allow for the flexible handling of work items (e.g.,
to suspend/resume a work item or cancel a work item) (cf. Sect. 6.3.1.5). Moreover,
the Exlet approach supports the flexible handling of entire process instances (e.g.,
to suspend/resume or terminate process instances). Complex activities, in turn,
refer to subprocesses to realize exception and compensation handling behavior as
described in the context of exception handling patterns (cf. Sect. 6.3.1). If needed,

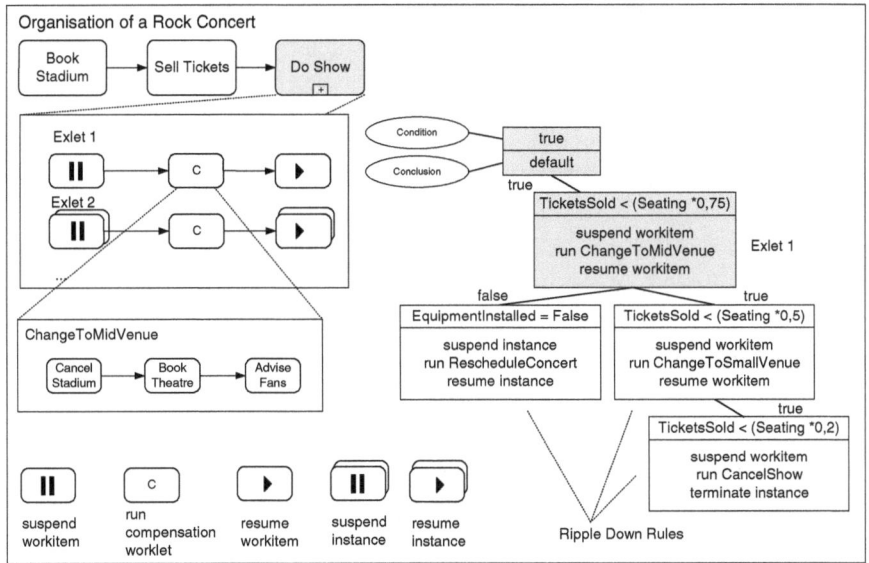

Fig. 6.18   Handling exceptions with Exlets

the set of *Exlets* may be dynamically extended (i.e., additional fragments can be added on the fly) (cf. Fig. 6.18). If an exception occurs during run-time, a suitable exception handling subprocess is dynamically selected using hierarchically organized selection rules–called *ripple down rules*.

Example 6.22 (Handling Exceptions with Exlets).   Figure 6.18 illustrates the Exlet approach using the organization of a rock concert as example (adopted from [28, 30]). The prespecified process model consists of the three activities *Book Stadium*, *Sell Tickets*, and *Do Show*. Activity *Do Show* is linked to a set of exception handling subprocesses, which get invoked during run-time when the preconditions for executing an activity are violated (due to an exception). For this, the ripple down rules are evaluated before activity *Do Show* gets enabled. The evaluation of the rules starts with the root node, which always evaluates to true. As the next step, condition *Tickets Sold < (Seating * 0,75)* is evaluated. If this condition holds condition *Tickets Sold < (Seating * 0,50)* is evaluated next, otherwise condition *EquipmentInstalled = False* is evaluated. In this example we assume that 60% of the available seats have been sold. Hence, *Tickets Sold < (Seating * 0,75)* evaluates to True and *Tickets Sold < (Seating * 0,50)* to False. Consequently, the exception handling subprocess *Exlet 1* is invoked, since it is associated with the last condition evaluating to `True`. When executing *Exlet 1* the work item associated with activity *Do Show* is suspended and a subprocess executing compensation activities is invoked. In this subprocess the stadium is canceled, a smaller medium-size venue is booked, and the fans are informed about the change. Afterwards the execution may continue (i.e., the work item associated with *Do Show* gets resumed).

6.6 Summary

This chapter explored different sources of anticipated exceptions like activity failures and deadline expirations. Moreover, the chapter presented different patterns for handling these exceptions. Exception handling patterns cover typical strategies which can be used when defining exception handlers for a particular process model. However, the automated detection as well as the handling of the exceptions discussed in this chapter is still very limited in many existing PAISs [307]. In addition, the gap between semantic process modeling and technical workflow specification is causing problems in practice. In many cases, exceptions can only be modeled at the technical level, although their handling requires organizational knowledge and thus should be expressed in semantic process models as well.

Even though the handling of anticipated exceptions is fundamental for every PAIS, the latter also needs to be able to deal with unanticipated exceptions. The handling of such unanticipated exceptions through ad hoc changes of single process instances will be discussed in Chap. 7.

Exercises

6.1. Exception Handling Patterns
Consider the check-in process as described in Exercise 3.1. Think about five possible exceptions which might occur in the context of this process and model them using the exception handling patterns introduced in this chapter.

6.2. Exception Handling Patterns
Consider the publication workflow depicted in Fig. 6.19 (adopted from [314]). Several exceptions might arise:

(a) Some authors are unable to view the author kit attachments. Respective authors can download the documents from the publisher's web site.
(b) The author sends the paper, but does not fully comply with the formatting guidelines. In this case, the publisher reformats the paper and charges the author.

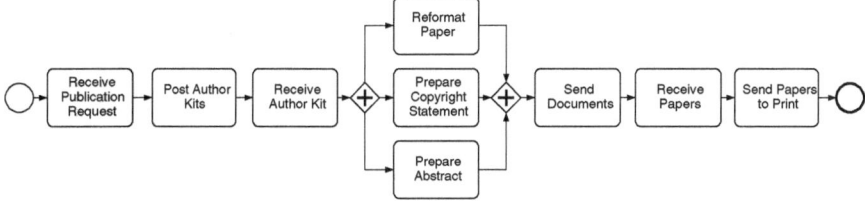

Fig. 6.19 Publication workflow

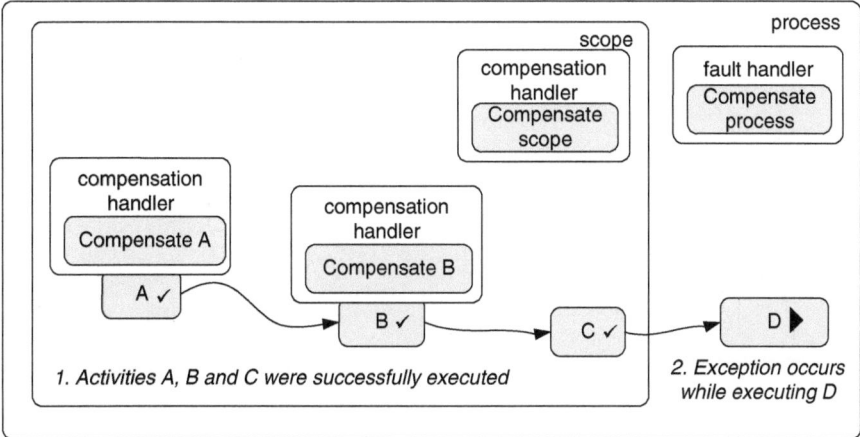

Fig. 6.20 Compensation handling in BPEL

(c) Some authors do not send in their paper, or send it after the deadline has passed. Such papers will not be published.

Model the described exceptions using the exception handling patterns introduced in this chapter.

6.3. Compensation Handling in BPEL
Consider Fig. 6.20. What happens if an exception occurs while invoking Service D?

6.4. Exception Handling with Exlets
To obtain additional information on the Exlets approach first read the article by Adams et al. [28]. Then take the exceptions you modeled in Exercise 6.4. How can the Exlets approach be applied to realize exception handlers for these exceptions?

Chapter 7
Ad hoc Changes of Process Instances

Abstract Generally, it is not possible to anticipate all real-world exceptions and to capture their handling in a prespecified process model at build-time. Hence, authorized users should be allowed to situationally adapt single process instances during run-time to cope with unanticipated exceptions; e.g., by inserting, deleting, or moving activities. Providing PAIS support for such ad hoc deviations from a prespecified process model, however, must not shift the responsibility for ensuring PAIS robustness to end-users. Instead, the PAIS must provide comprehensive support for the correct, secure, and robust handling of run-time exceptions through ad hoc process instance changes. This chapter presents a taxonomy for ad hoc changes, discusses how the behavior of a process instance can be situationally adapted, and presents adaptation patterns that may be applied for this purpose. Moreover, it is shown how PAIS robustness can be ensured when dynamically adapting process instances, and how end-users can be assisted in defining ad hoc changes.

7.1 Motivation

Chapter 6 discussed how to incorporate *exception handlers* into prespecified process models at build-time, which then can be invoked during run-time to cope with emerging *exceptions*. We described typical sources of exceptions as well as patterns for their handling. As a prerequisite for such automated exception handling, however, respective exceptions need to be known a priori, and appropriate exception handlers be added to the process model at build-time.

As illustrated by Fig. 7.1, anticipated exceptions only partially cover practically relevant situations [334]. For many application scenarios, it is unrealistic to assume that all exceptional situations, as well as required exception handlers, can be anticipated at build-time and thus be incorporated into the prespecified process model a priori [71, 87, 169, 194, 222]. As a consequence, situations may emerge during run-time in which a process instance executed in the PAIS no longer reflects

M. Reichert and B. Weber, *Enabling Flexibility in Process-Aware Information Systems*,   153
DOI 10.1007/978-3-642-30409-5_7, © Springer-Verlag Berlin Heidelberg 2012

Fig. 7.1 Classes of
exceptions (adopted from
[314])

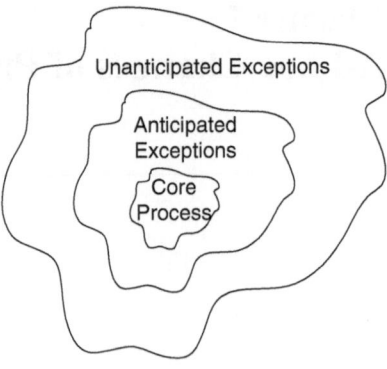

the business case happening in the real world; i.e., there are process instances
for which discrepancies between the computerized and the real-world business
process may occur. In such situations there is no prespecified exception handler to
detect the mismatch and adequately cope with it. Due to this deficiency, authorized
process participants should be allowed to situationally adapt single process instances
running in the PAIS to realign their execution to the real-world business case (e.g.,
by adding, deleting, or moving activities). Moreover, even if all possible exceptions
are known prior to the instantiation and execution of a prespecified process model,
and hence respective exception handlers can be included in the process model
at build-time, this will generally be too costly and time-consuming. Additionally,
predefining all possible exceptions a priori may result in complex and spaghetti-like
process models, which are difficult to comprehend and costly to maintain [118].

   Examples 7.1 and 7.2 describe scenarios from two different domains in which
unforeseen events and high dynamism are common.

*Example 7.1 (Situational Handling of Real-world Exceptions in Health Care
Processes).* Variations in the course of a disease—and hence the patient
treatment process—are to some degree inherent to medicine and unforeseen
events a "normal" phenomenon. Hospital information systems automating
patient treatment processes typically focus on standard procedures [172].
Since physicians and nurses are faced with the need to react to unforeseen
exceptional situations in their daily work, flexible deviations from standard
procedures have to be supported as well [256]. Some examples:

- In an emergency case physicians may collect information about a patient
  by phone and then proceed with the treatment process, i.e., without waiting
  for the arrival of an electronic report.
- A medical procedure may have to be aborted or replaced by another one if
  the patient's health state gets worse or a health care service provider finds
  out that a prerequisite is not met.

- The treatment of a cruciate rupture usually includes the use of magnetic resonance tomography (MRT). However, for a patient with a cardiac pacemaker the MRT may have to be skipped. Assume further that this patient suffers from an effusion in his knee and the physician decides to conduct an additional puncture, i.e., an activity is dynamically added to the case.

Since ad hoc deviations from prespecified processes are frequent in health care [172], any PAIS providing process-oriented assistance to medical staff members should allow them to independently take the initiative whenever needed; i.e., it is not sufficient to only customize a standardized treatment process for the individual patient prior to its instantiation, but it should also be possible to dynamically adapt it to the current situation of a particular patient at any time during process execution (i.e., to apply *ad hoc changes* to the respective process instance).

Another application domain for which it is not possible to completely prespecify the activities and the behavior of a process model a priori is *software engineering*:

Example 7.2 (Dynamically Evolving Processes in Software Engineering). Due to the dynamic nature and high degree of collaboration, communication, and coordination inherent in software engineering projects, a PAIS can assist software engineers by providing process-orientation and guidance [109,110,112,113]. Yet, since there are so many different kinds of issues with ambiguous and subjective delineation (e.g., release management, testing, bug fixing, quality management, and refactoring), it is difficult and burdensome to universally and correctly capture them in a prespecified process model prior to its execution. This would lead to very large process models of high complexity. To alleviate this problem, only a simple process model for each case (i.e., the software project) should be initially created, which utilizing context information can be dynamically extended with activities matching the current situation; i.e., situational and tailored support as well as guidance for software engineers is required [109]. In particular, when allowing for ad hoc extensions during run time (e.g., dynamic insertion of activities), the initial process models can be kept much simpler compared to fully prespecified process models [108].

If a PAIS does not allow authorized users to *deviate* from a prespecified process model or to *extend* it during run-time, it will be bypassed or—even worse—rejected by users. Instead, authorized users should be enabled to change the behavior of a particular process instance in case a mismatch between this computerized process and the corresponding real-world business case occurs.

This chapter is organized as follows: Sect. 7.2 provides an overview of fundamental issues that emerge when changing the behavior of a running process instance. Section 7.3 presents patterns for structurally adapting a prespecified process model. Section 7.4 additionally considers the state of process instances and discusses how soundness can be ensured in the context of ad hoc changes. Following this, Sects. 7.5 and 7.6 deal with the assistance of end-users in defining ad hoc changes at run-time. Section 7.7 extends these considerations by presenting approaches allowing for the automated adaptation of single process instances during run-time. Issues related to the duration, scope, and control of ad hoc changes are discussed in Sects. 7.8–7.10. The chapter concludes with a discussion in Sect. 7.11 and a summary in Sect. 7.12.

7.2   Changing the Behavior of a Running Process Instance

This section provides an overview of the core challenges to be addressed when applying ad hoc changes to running process instances. Further, it presents a basic taxonomy for ad hoc changes, around which the remainder of this chapter is structured.

7.2.1   Core Challenges

Complex behavioral changes require structural process model adaptations. To cope with unanticipated exceptions, a PAIS should allow authorized users to delete activities, to postpone their execution, to bring the execution of activities forward even though their preconditions have not yet been met, or to add activities not considered in the process model so far. Generally, such behavioral changes of a process instance require *structural adaptations* of its corresponding process model. The latter include, among others, the insertion, deletion, or movement of activities and process fragments, respectively. While *movements* change activity positions, and thus the structure of a process model, *insertions* and *deletions* additionally modify the set of activities contained in a process model.

> *Example 7.3 (Structural Adaptations of a Process Model).*   Figure 7.2 depicts a simple example of a structural process model adaptation referring to a highly simplified patient treatment process. As illustrated in Fig. 7.2a, the treatment process typically starts with the admission of the patient to the hospital. After having registered the patient, he is treated by a physician. Finally, an invoice for the treatment provided is created. Assuming that a particular patient is in a

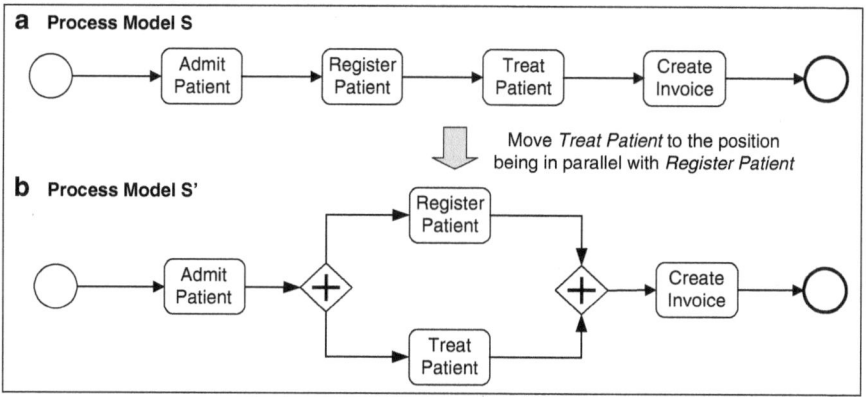

Fig. 7.2 Changing the behavior of a process model through a structural change

critical condition, it might become necessary to deviate from the prespecified process model; the treatment of the patient might have to start right away, performing the necessary steps for his registration at a later stage. To capture this behavior in the model of the respective process instance, activity *Treat Patient* has to be arranged in parallel with activity *Register Patient* (cf. Fig. 7.2b); i.e., the unanticipated exception is handled by restructuring the model of the respective process instance.

Ad hoc changes require adaptations of the process instance state. When adapting the structure of the process model while a particular process instance is running, the state of this instance (i.e., the states of its activities) needs to be adapted as well [5, 260]. Generally, required *state adaptations* depend on the applied process model change as well as on the current state of the process instance. Depending on the position where an activity is inserted, for example, it might become necessary to immediately enable the inserted activity or to disable other ones before continuing with the execution of the process instance. By contrast, when changing a not-yet-entered region of a process instance, state adaptations are not required.

Example 7.4 (Ad hoc Changes and Required State Adaptations). Consider the process instance depicted in Fig. 7.3a. Activity A is completed and its successor B is enabled, i.e., B has not yet been started, but corresponding work items exist. Assume now that the execution order of B and C shall be swapped; i.e., C shall be completed before B becomes enabled. Before continuing with the execution of the process instance on the adapted process

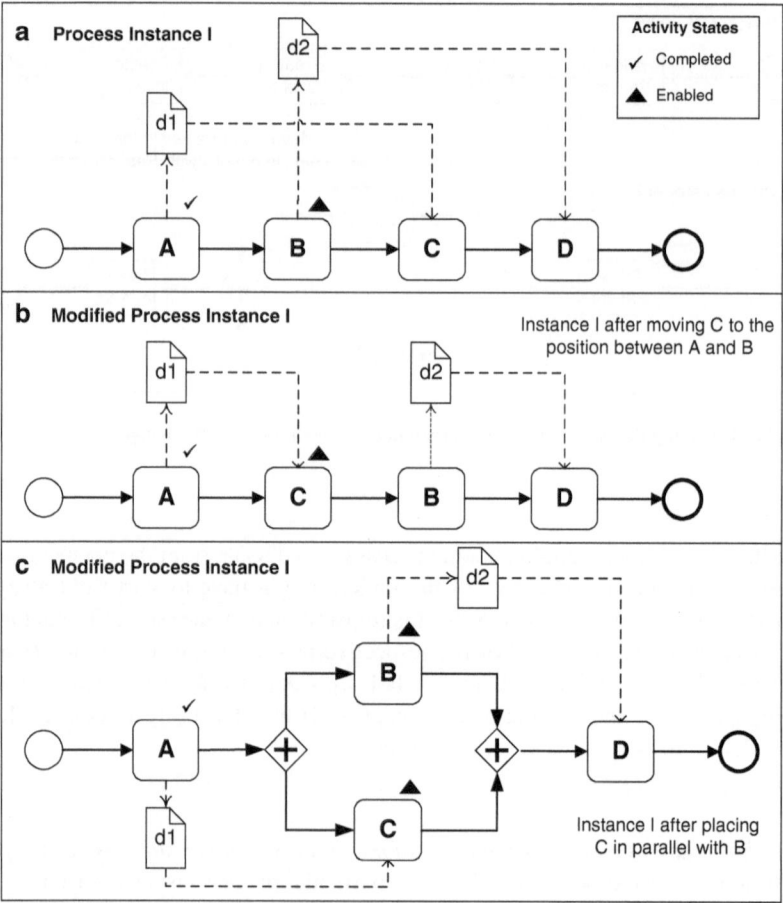

Fig. 7.3 A process instance and two examples of related ad hoc changes

model, concomitant state adaptations are required (cf. Fig. 7.3b): Activity B needs to be disabled (i.e., its work items need to be withdrawn; cf. Chap. 2) and then activity C be enabled (i.e., work items have to be created for C).

Consider another change of process instance *I* from Fig. 7.3a. Assume now that C shall be brought forward due to an exceptional situation and be executed in parallel with B. (Note that this scenario is similar to the one discussed in Example 7.3; cf. Fig. 7.2). In particular, this behavioral change can be realized by ordering C in parallel with B. In addition to this structural adaptation, activity C needs to be enabled (cf. Fig. 7.3c).

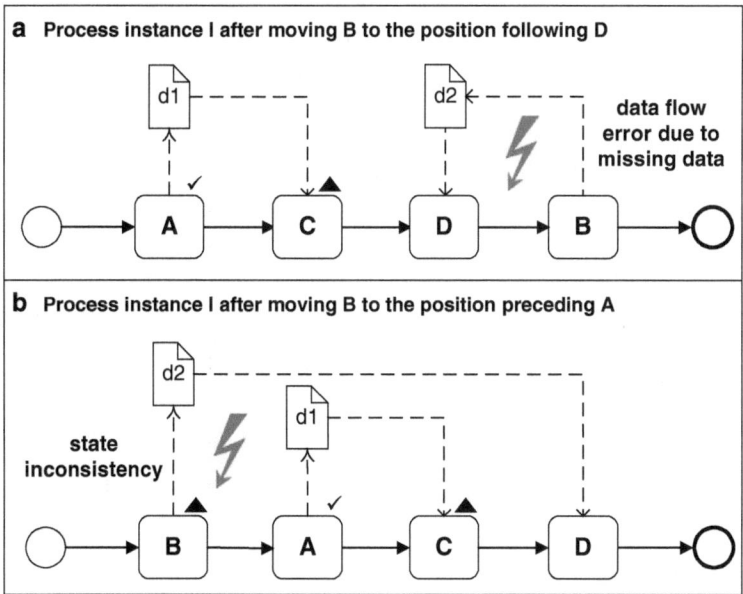

Fig. 7.4 Incorrect ad hoc changes of the process instance from Fig. 7.3a

Ad hoc changes must not violate process model correctness and proper instance execution. On one hand, ad hoc changes provide process participants working on a business case with the autonomy to flexibly deal with unanticipated exceptions. On the other hand, applying structural changes to a long-running process instance—possibly in the midst of its execution—makes the assurance of *PAIS robustness* significantly more challenging [14, 255, 260]; i.e., ad hoc changes of a process instance must not lead to run-time errors.

Example 7.5 (Data Flow Errors Due to Uncontrolled Ad hoc Changes).
Consider again the process instance from Fig. 7.3a. Assume that B shall be moved to the position following D. Obviously, the instance-specific process model resulting from this ad hoc change (cf. Fig. 7.4a) contains a severe flaw due to missing data. D may read data object d2 before it will be written by B; i.e., the instance-specific process model resulting from this uncontrolled ad hoc change contains a data flow error due to missing data (cf. Definition 4.7).

Even though we can detect such flaws by applying respective checks at the process model level, the latter are not sufficient to exclude all potential problems emerging in the context of ad hoc process instance changes (cf. Example 7.6). Hence, when conducting ad hoc changes the state of the process instance to be adapted needs to be considered as well.

Example 7.6 (Inconsistent Instance State Due to Uncontrolled Ad hoc Changes). Consider again the process instance from Fig. 7.3a and assume that activity B shall be moved to the position preceding A. When not considering the current state of the process instance, the resulting process model (cf. Fig. 7.4b) is correct. As depicted in Fig. 7.4b, however, a state inconsistency would result from this ad hoc change. To be more precise, A would be in state `Completed` even though its newly preceding activity B is in state `Enabled`. This *dynamic change bug*, in turn, might lead to severe flaws during run-time (cf. Sect. 7.4 for details). For example, with the completion of activity A all preconditions for enabling activity C are fulfilled. Assuming that C completes before B, a data flow error would occur when starting D since the required data object d2 has not yet been written. Even without this data dependency between B and D, respective state inconsistencies might lead to problems during run-time. Assuming that D completes before B, the process would reach its final state. Since B would still be in state `Enabled` or `Running`, this would constitute a soundness violation not allowing for *proper completion* (cf. Chap. 4).

Allowing for changes at the process instance level must not shift the responsibility for avoiding the described inconsistencies and flaws to end-users or application developers. Instead, well-defined *correctness notions* are required to enable the PAIS to adequately assist end-users in performing ad hoc changes during run-time and to prohibit those changes leading to incorrect process models or inconsistent instance states; i.e., the PAIS must guarantee that process model correctness ensured by formal checks at build-time can be further guaranteed when dynamically adapting a corresponding process instance.

Ad hoc changes of a process instance must not affect the execution of any other instance. Usually, for a particular process model numerous process instances exist whose execution is driven by this model. Adapting the behavior of one of these process instances must not affect the execution of the other instances running on the same process model. To enable such *instance-specific adaptation* at the logical level, the respective process model has to be cloned before applying the desired instance change. At the implementation level, however, it is sufficient to only memorize the difference between original and adapted process model [283, 292].

Example 7.7 (Restricting the Effects of an Ad hoc Change to a Particular Process Instance). The process model S depicted in Fig. 7.5a describes the treatment of ruptures of the cruciate ligament which routinely includes three diagnostic procedures: a magnetic resonance tomography (MRT), an X-ray,

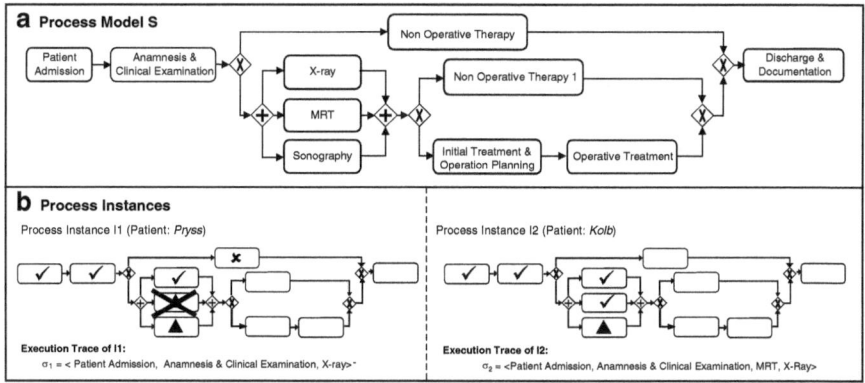

Fig. 7.5 Ad hoc change (i.e., deletion of activity *MRT*) of a process instance

and a sonography. However, for process instance I_1 the MRT is skipped (i.e., activity *MRT* is deleted) as the treated patient has a cardiac pacemaker (cf. Fig. 7.5b). Note that this change has no effect on the execution of process instance I_2 which is also running on S and relates to another patient.

7.2.2 A Basic Taxonomy for Ad hoc Changes

Figure 7.6 depicts a taxonomy describing ad hoc changes of a process instance. The *subject* of an ad hoc change can be both the state of a process instance and the structure of its process model. Further, ad hoc changes may concern different *model perspectives*. In particular, structural adaptations of the control and data flow schema of a process model might become necessary when coping with unanticipated exceptions at the instance level. This chapter focuses on ad hoc changes of the behavior and information perspective of running process instances.

Basically, structural adaptations of a process model can be specified in two different ways: either by defining them at a low level of abstraction through the application of *change primitives* to the process model (i.e., by adding or deleting single nodes and edges) or based on high-level change operations (i.e., *adaptation patterns* like inserting, deleting, or moving activities or entire process fragments). Section 7.3 compares these two alternatives and discusses their pros and cons. When structurally adapting the model of a running process instance, *correctness* and *consistency* as well as *proper continuation of instance execution* on the adapted process model need to be ensured. Further, *state compliance* of the process instance with the adapted process model has to be guaranteed. Section 7.4 discusses respective issues.

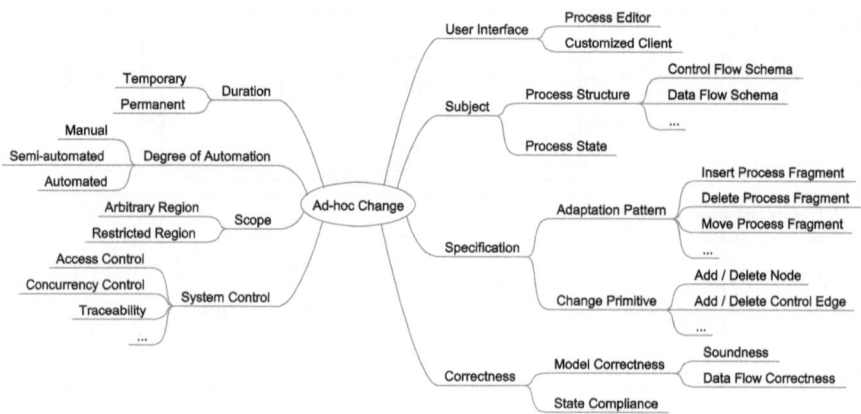

Fig. 7.6 A taxonomy for ad hoc process instance changes

An ad hoc change of a process instance can be specified either by using a *generic process editor* or a *customized user client*. The latter constitutes a software tool that provides an application-specific user interface and can be realized using the application programming interface the adaptive PAIS offers for specifying ad hoc changes [168] (cf. Sect. 7.5). Another dimension concerns the *degree of automation* provided in the context of ad hoc changes. In adaptive PAISs, ad hoc changes of a process instance often need to be manually defined by an experienced user (cf. Sect. 7.5). More advanced PAISs, however, assist end-users in defining ad hoc changes, e.g., by giving recommendations on the reuse of ad hoc changes previously applied in similar problem context (cf. Sect. 7.6). Finally, for certain applications, the models of process instances can be automatically created and adapted during run-time, e.g., based on rules (cf. Sect. 7.7).

In the context of long-running process instances, we further distinguish between *permanent* and *temporary changes* [265]. While the former are valid until completion of the changed process instance (unless the effects of the ad hoc change are compensated by another ad hoc change), the latter are only temporarily valid and will have to be undone if certain conditions are met (e.g., when a loop enters its next iteration). We present related issues in Sect. 7.8. Furthermore, ad hoc changes of a process instance may be applied to *arbitrary regions* of its process model or be restricted to *selected regions* to limit their scope (cf. Sect. 7.9).

Finally, a PAIS should provide mechanisms to control ad hoc changes (cf. Sect. 7.10). First, for security reasons it should be possible to *restrict the access* to change functions *to authorized users*. Second, ad hoc changes have to be logged to ensure *accountability* and *traceability* of changes. Finally, the PAIS should be able to deal with *concurrent changes*, i.e., ad hoc changes applied concurrently to a particular process instance by different users have to be synchronized to preserve PAIS robustness and ensure correct process behavior afterwards.

7.3   Structurally Adapting Prespecified Process Models

This section deals with the definition of structural adaptations of a process model. Run-time adaptations of process instances are then addressed in Sect. 7.4.

7.3.1   Basics

When taking a closer look at existing PAISs or process modeling tools, there are two different approaches for accomplishing structural adaptations of a process model.

Structural model adaptations can be based on a complete set of *change primitives*, which directly operate on single elements of a process model. Examples of such primitives include add node, remove node, add edge, and remove edge. Following this approach, the definition of a particular process model adaptation (e.g., to delete an activity or to add a new one) may require the joint application of several change primitives. Specifying structural model adaptations at this low level of abstraction, however, is both complex and error-prone. When applying a single change primitive, in general, soundness of the resulting process model (e.g., proper completion, no dead activities) as well as data flow correctness cannot be guaranteed by construction. Instead, respective properties have to be explicitly checked after applying the desired set of change primitives.

> **Change Primitives:** Change Primitives denote edit operations like add node, remove node, add edge, and remove edge which can be applied to a process model at both the *type level* and the *instance level* in order to define structural model adaptations.

As an alternative, structural adaptations of a process model can be based on *high-level change operations*, e.g., to move an activity or an entire process fragment within a process model. Usually, respective change operations abstract from the concrete process model transformations to be conducted. Instead of specifying a set of change primitives, the user applies one or more high-level change operations to realize the desired process model adaptation. Existing approaches often associate pre- and post-conditions with the high-level change operations in order to guarantee model correctness after each adaptation, i.e., to ensure correctness by construction [59, 260].[1] This is especially important when ad hoc changes shall be defined by

---

[1]Process editors applying such correctness-by-construction principle usually provide only those change operations to the process designer which allow transforming a sound process model into another one. Deficiencies not prohibited by such an approach (e.g., concerning correctness of the data flow) need to be checked on-the-fly and be continuously reported to the user.

end-users (cf. Sect. 7.5) or—even more challenging—automatically introduced by software agents (cf. Sect. 7.7) during run-time. While change primitives can be applied to numerous process modeling languages relying on different process meta models, the application of high-level change operations often imposes structural restrictions (e.g., block structure as discussed in Sect. 4.4.3) on the process model to be adapted in order to realize the aforementioned correctness guarantees.

High-Level Change Operation: A *high-level change operation* combines a set of change primitives to enable structural adaptations at a more abstract level; e.g., to add, delete, or move an activity. The concrete implementation of a high-level change operation (i.e., the set of change primitives to be applied) usually depends on the properties of the process modeling language used as well as on the change context. For example, in the context of well-structured process models, the correct application of a high-level change operation can be ensured if certain preconditions are met. Finally, high-level change operations can be applied at both the *process type level* (i.e., process designers edit a process model at build-time using the respective change operations in the process editor) and the *process instance level* (i.e., conducting ad hoc changes of single process instances during run-time).

While change primitives operate on single elements of a process model (e.g., activities, control connectors, and control edges), high-level change operations provide a higher level of abstraction. Generally, the number of edit operations needed to transform a process model S into a process model S' significantly differs depending on whether change primitives or high-level change operations are used.

Example 7.8 (High-level Change Operations vs. Change Primitives). Consider Fig. 7.7 and assume that process model S shall be adapted by moving C to the position between A and B. This results in process model S'. Figure 7.7 further depicts the set of change primitives representing the snapshot difference between S and S'. Note that only one high-level change operation (i.e., one move operation) is needed to transform S into S'. By contrast, 13 change primitives are required to define the respective model transformation.

Example 7.8 demonstrates that change primitives require users to conduct changes at a low level of abstraction, whereas high-level change operations partially hide the complexity of low-level model transformations. In particular, high-level change operations can be built upon a set of change primitives which collectively realize the required model transformations. Regarding the change depicted in

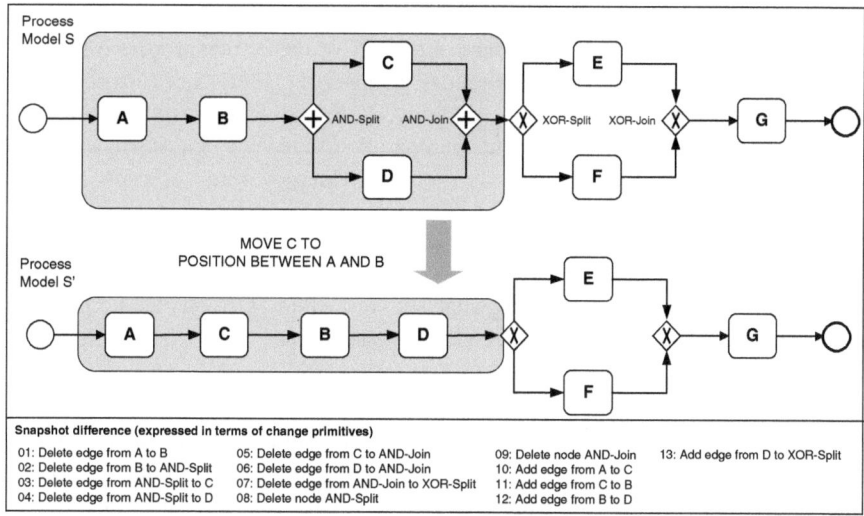

Fig. 7.7 Applying a high-level change operation and resulting snapshot difference

Fig. 7.7, for example, one high-level change operation is sufficient to transform the model from S to S'. Based on the semantics of this operation, required model transformations (e.g., deletion of control connectors) can be accomplished automatically.

For the remainder of this chapter, we will focus on structural process model adaptations based on high-level change operations. As expressed by Definition 7.1, the application of a single change operation or a sequence of change operations to a process model S results in another process model S'.

Definition 7.1 (Structural Model Change). Let $\mathscr{P}$ be the set of all process models and let $S, S' \in \mathscr{P}$. Let further $\Delta = (op) \in \mathscr{C}$ denote a particular change consisting of one change operation op and $\tau = <op_1, \ldots, op_n> \in \mathscr{C}^*$ be a process change that applies change operations $op_i, i = 1, \ldots, n$ sequentially.

1. $S\ [\Delta\rangle$ if Δ is applicable to S.
2. $S\ [\Delta\rangle\ S'$ if Δ is applicable to S (i.e., $S\ [\Delta\rangle$) and S' is the process model resulting from the application of Δ to S (also: $S' = S + \Delta$).
3. $S\ [\tau\rangle\ S'$ if there are process models $S_1, S_2, \ldots S_{n+1} \in \mathscr{P}$ with $S = S_1, S' = S_{n+1}$ and for $1 \leq i \leq$ n: $S_i\ [\Delta_i\rangle\ S_{i+1}$ with $\Delta_i = (op_i)$.

The difference between an original process model (in terms of change operations) and a modified one is denoted as *bias* [181].

Definition 7.2 (Bias and Distance). Let S, $S' \in \mathscr{P}$ be two process models and let $\mathscr{C}^*$ be the set of all potential changes (i.e., sequences of change operations). Then, **Distance** $d_{(S,S')}$ between S and S' corresponds to the minimal number of high-level change operations needed to transform S into S'; i.e., we define

$$d_{(S,S')} = \min\{|\tau| \mid \tau \in \mathscr{C}^* \wedge S[\tau\rangle S'\} \qquad (7.1)$$

Furthermore, a sequence of change operations τ with $S[\tau\rangle S'$ and $|\tau| = d_{(S,S')}$ is denoted as **bias** between S and S' ($B_{S,S'}$ for short).

Given a certain set of high-level change operations, the *distance* between process models S and S' corresponds to the minimum number of concrete change operations needed for transforming S into S'. The corresponding sequence of change operations is denoted as *bias* $B_{S,S'}$. Generally, there may be more than one minimum set of change operations transforming S into S'; i.e., a bias does not have to be unique. Swapping activities A and B, for example, can be realized either by moving A after B or by moving B before A. As another example, consider the scenario from Fig. 7.2: Process model S can be transformed into S' by moving one activity; i.e., either activity *Treat Patient* is moved to position it in parallel with activity *Register Patient* or vice versa. Since this transformation can be performed using one high-level change operation, change distance $d_{(S,S')}$ corresponds to one.

7.3.2   Adaptation Patterns

Process adaptation patterns constitute abstractions of high-level change operations that are independent of concrete implementations and constitute solutions to typical changes [70, 352, 357]. They enable structural changes of process models at a high level of abstraction, e.g., by adding, deleting, or moving activities and process fragments, respectively. Furthermore, adaptation patterns can be applied at both the process type and the process instance level. In the following, we focus on changes of the *control flow schema* of a process model. Table 7.1 shows the catalog of adaptation patterns as identified and presented in [352].

Adaptation patterns AP1 and AP2 allow for the insertion (AP1) and deletion (AP2) of process fragments in a given process model. Moving and replacing fragments are supported by adaptation patterns AP3 (Move Process Fragment), AP4 (Replace Process Fragment), AP5 (Swap Process Fragment), and AP14 (Copy Process Fragment). Adaptation patterns AP6 and AP7 allow for adding or removing levels of hierarchy. The extraction of a subprocess schema from a process model is supported by AP6, whereas the inclusion of a subprocess into a process model is

Table 7.1 Catalog of adaptation patterns (AP)

Pattern category	Pattern	
Adding or deleting	AP1:	Insert process fragment
Process fragments	AP2:	Delete process fragment
Moving or replacing	AP3:	Move process fragment
Process fragments	AP4:	Replace process fragment
	AP5:	Swap process fragment
	AP14:	Copy process fragment
Adding or removing	AP6:	Extract subprocess
Process levels	AP7:	Inline sub-process
Adapting control dependencies	AP8:	Embed process fragment in loop
	AP9:	Parallelize process fragments
	AP10:	Embed process fragment in conditional branch
	AP11:	Add control dependency
	AP12:	Remove control dependency
Change transition conditions	AP13:	Update condition

enabled by AP7. Patterns AP8–AP12 support adaptations of control dependencies: embedding an existing process fragment in a loop (AP8), parallelizing a process fragment (AP9), embedding an existing process fragment in a conditional branch (AP10), and adding or removing control dependencies (AP11, AP12). Finally, AP13 (update condition) enables changes of transition conditions. Note that most of the adaptation patterns change the behavior of a process model in such a way that the change becomes observable by users. By contrast, adaptation patterns AP6 and AP7 only change the structure of the process model, while preserving its behavior.

In the following, selected adaptation patterns are elaborated in more detail, including a pattern description, an example, a description of the problem the respective pattern is addressing, and a corresponding solution (cf. Figs. 7.8–7.11). The complete catalog of patterns is described in [352]. A formalization of the patterns can be found in [300]. The latter is based on a systematic comparison of the trace set producible on the original model and the one producible on the changed model.

7.3.3   Defining Structural Changes with Adaptation Patterns

In the following, a walkthrough scenario for modeling and modifying a business process using both change primitives and process adaptation patterns is provided.

Description	A process fragment X is added to a process model S.
Example	For a particular patient an allergy test has to be added to the model of his treatment process due to a possible drug incompatibility.
Problem	In a real-world process a task has to be accomplished which is not contained in the process model.
Solution	A) X is added between two directly succeeding activities (*serialInsert*)

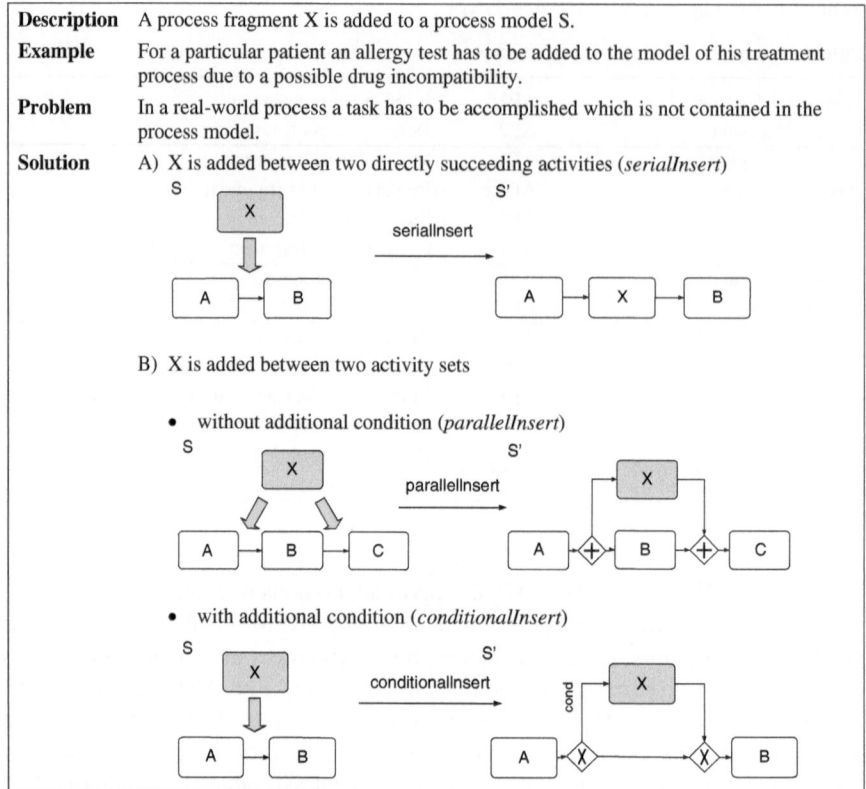

Fig. 7.8 Pattern AP1: insert process fragment

Description	A process fragment is deleted from a process model S.
Example	For a particular patient a planned computer tomography must not be performed in the context of her treatment process as she has a cardiac pacemaker, i.e., the respective activity is deleted from the process model.
Problem	In a real-world process a prespecified activity has to be skipped or deleted.
Solution	The activity (including superfluous control edges and control connectors) is removed from the process model.

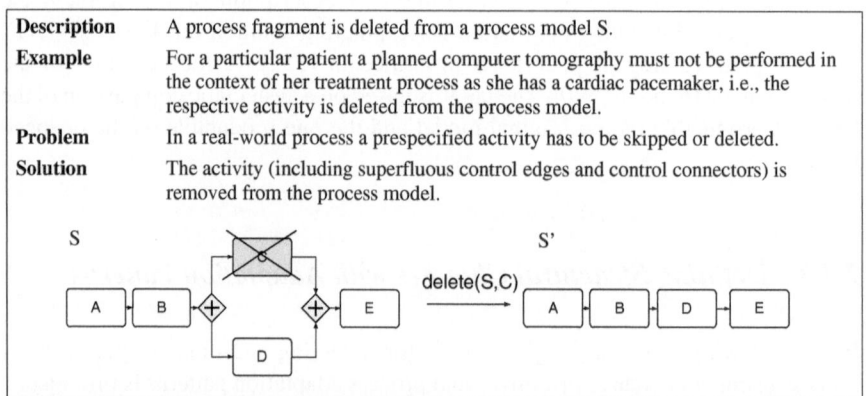

Fig. 7.9 Pattern AP2: delete process fragment

Description	A process fragment is moved from its current position in process model S to another position within the same process model.
Example	Usually, employees may only book a flight after it has been approved by a manager. Exceptionally, for a particular process the booking of a flight shall be done in parallel with the approval activity. Consequently, the *Book Flight* activity has to be moved from its current position in the process model to another one such that it can be executed in parallel with the approval activity afterwards.
Problem	Prespecified ordering constraints cannot be completely satisfied for a set of activities.

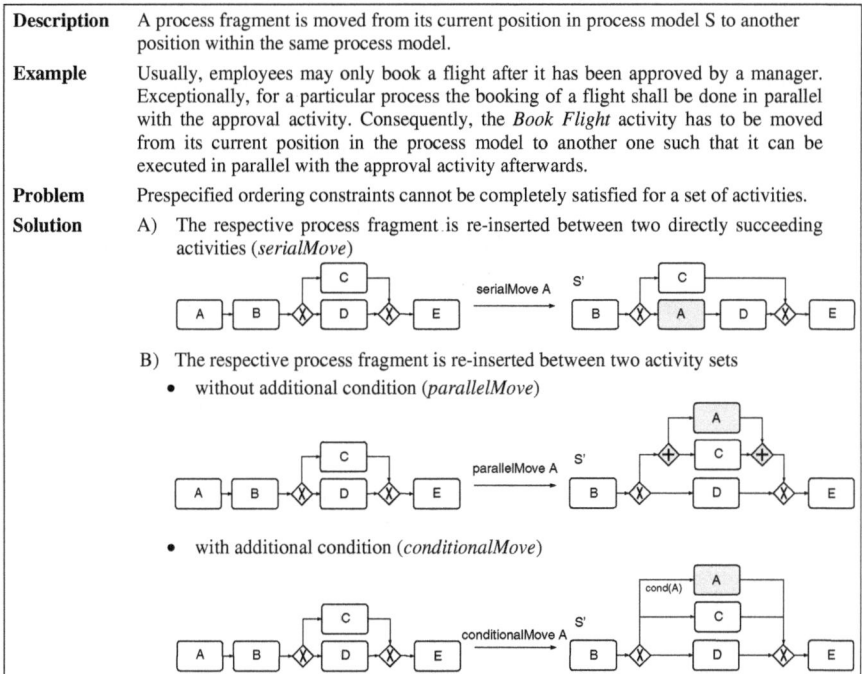

Fig. 7.10 Pattern AP3: move process fragment

Description	An existing process fragment shall be only executed if certain conditions are met.
Example	So far, in company *eTravel* the process for planning and declaring a business trip has required travel applications for both national and international trips. This shall be changed by asking for a respective travel application only when taking an international trip.
Problem	A process fragment shall be only executed if a particular condition is met.
Solution	The respective process fragment is embedded in a conditional branch.

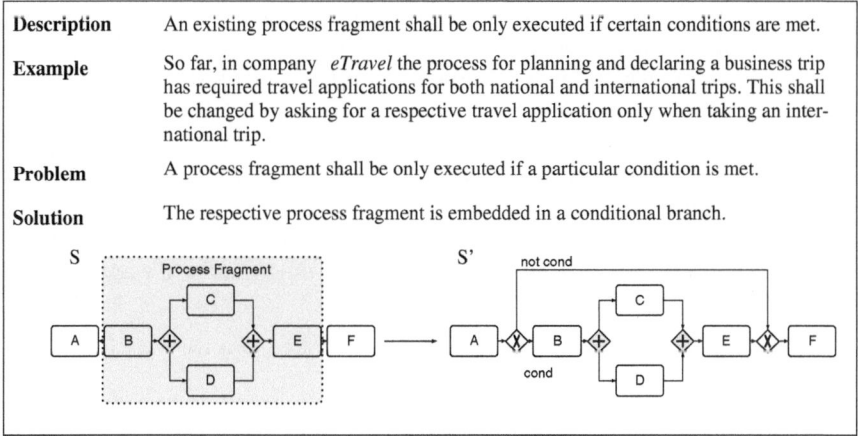

Fig. 7.11 Pattern AP10: embed process fragment in a conditional branch

Example 7.9 (Applying Adaptation Patterns). Figure 7.12 shows a process model from the domain of earthquake response, which is a simplified version of a process run by the "Task Force Earthquakes" of the German Research Center for Geosciences (GFZ). The main purpose of the task force is to coordinate the allocation of an interdisciplinary scientific–technical expert team in the aftermath of a catastrophic earthquake somewhere in the world [89]. The primary goal of a Task Force mission is to deploy a network of seismometers in the disaster area to measure seismic activities, such as earthquake aftershocks. Prior to this main goal, the Task Force members are also responsible for the logistics of their mission like transporting their scientific equipment from Germany to the disaster area. The process model depicted in Fig. 7.12 shows the "Transport of Equipment Process." This process describes how the task force transports its equipment, which can be up to 3 tons, for a mission from Germany to the disaster area. The process begins right after the decision for an in-field mission has been made and must complete before the task force can begin its work in the disaster area.

Modeling Task: *First and foremost, the transport of the equipment to the disaster area is organized by the task force. Once this has been done, all the equipment is presented to German customs. German customs might require the demonstration of equipment devices after the equipment has been presented for inspection. In this case, the demonstration happens right away. Afterwards, the task force flies to the disaster area in the host country. Upon arrival, the members of the task force present themselves at the immigration office in the host country. After passing immigration control, the task force members rent vehicles in the host country. In the meantime, they get road maps for the disaster area and organize accommodations, preferably those with electricity. While this is taking place, all the equipment is presented to the host country's customs. Customs of the host country might also require the demonstration of equipment devices. If so, the demonstration happens right away. Afterward it might be the case that the local car rental companies do not have sufficient transport capabilities. In this case, the task force members will seek vehicles from the partner organizations. Once the equipment has been cleared and sufficient transport capabilities are available, the equipment is transported from customs to a storage location.*

The host country's customs may deny clearance for the equipment after its presentation or the demonstration of its functionality. The process model depicted in Fig. 7.12 should be changed to reflect this situation.

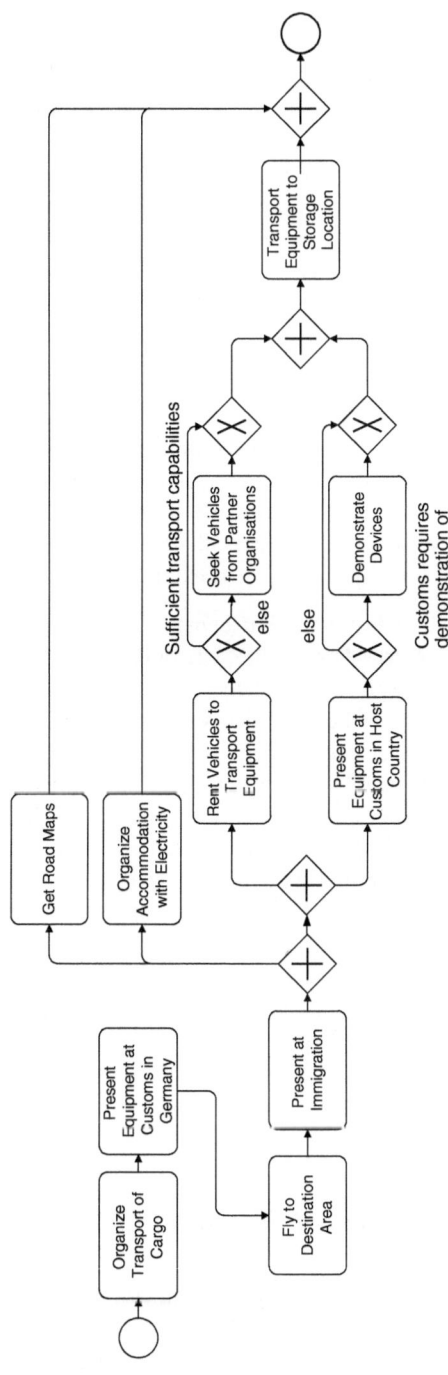

Fig. 7.12 Transport of equipment process—original model

Modification Task: *If the equipment is not cleared by the host country's customs, task force members try to convince customs officials to clear it, even though the related documentation is incomplete. In the meantime, task force members contact their partners to trigger support from higher-ranked authorities of the host country. If customs officials finally clear all the equipment through negotiations and the support of higher-ranked authorities, the equipment is transported to a storage location. In the other case, the equipment is not cleared because some of it is not properly documented. That equipment which has been cleared is transported to the storage location, whereas the missing documents for the remaining equipment are retrieved from the office in Germany. Once the missing documentation is received, the rest of the equipment is transported to the storage location as well.*

Modification Task with Change Primitives: Conducting the respective change with low-level change primitives requires the insertion of 5 activities, 8 control connectors and 20 control edges as well as the deletion of 3 edges (i.e., 36 edit operations in total). Figure 7.13 shows a potential solution for implementing the above-described process change including a list of change primitives required for transforming the original model.

Modification Task with Adaptation Patterns: If the changes are conducted using the adaptation patterns from Table 7.1, only seven high-level change operations are required; i.e., the distance (cf. Definition 7.2) between the original process model and the modified one corresponds to seven. Figure 7.14 illustrates three of these changes (and also depicts the change primitives underlying the applied process adaptations). In a first step, activity *Negotiate with Customs* is serially inserted after activity *Demonstrate Devices* (cf. Fig. 7.14b). Then activity *Trigger Support from Higher-ranked Authorities* is inserted in parallel with activity *Negotiate with Customs* (cf. Fig. 7.14c). Finally, the newly created process fragment is embedded in a conditional branch (cf. Fig. 7.14d). Note that the change primitives marked with an asterisk neutralize themselves and are not considered when counting the number of change primitives needed for conducting a higher-level change.

7.3.4   Ensuring Correctness of Structural Changes

The adaptation patterns described focus on the behavioral perspective of a process model, i.e., changes to its control flow schema. As discussed in Sect. 7.2, the latter cannot be treated independently from other model perspectives. In particular,

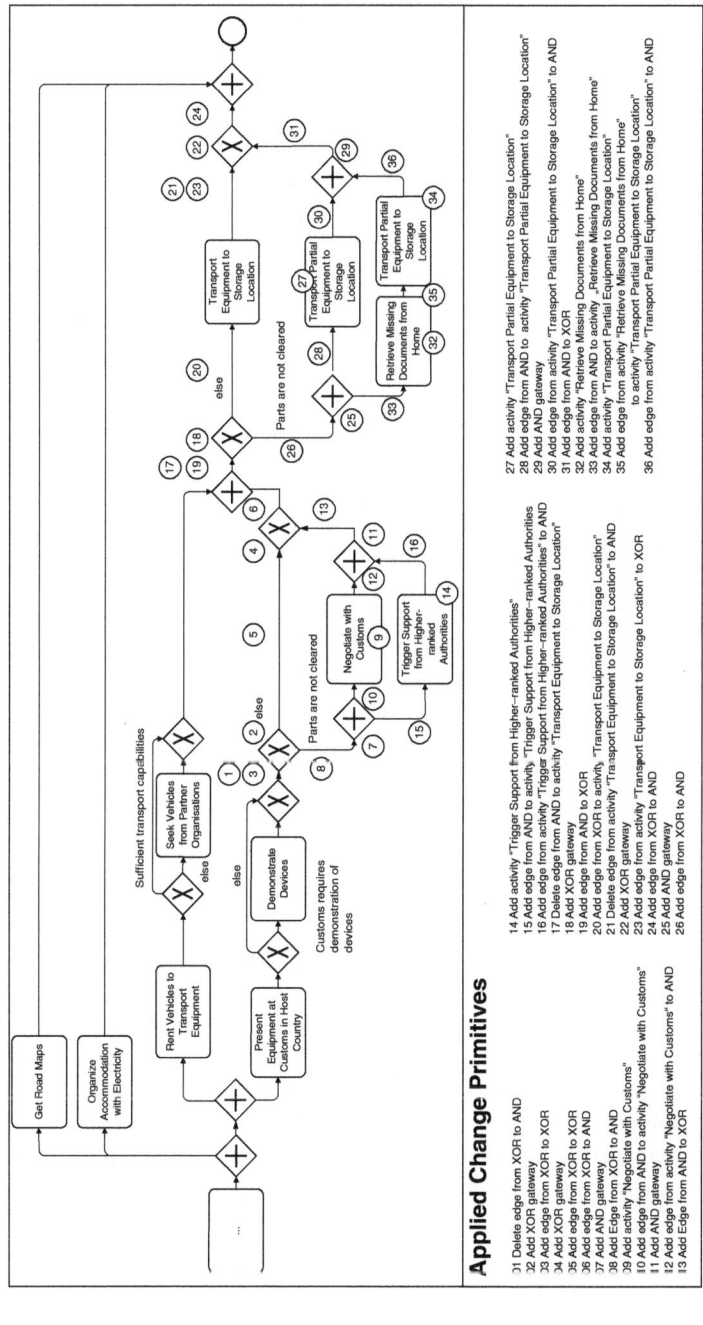

Applied Change Primitives

31 Delete edge from XOR to AND
32 Add XOR gateway
33 Add edge from XOR to XOR
34 Add XOR gateway
35 Add edge from XOR to XOR
36 Add edge from XOR to AND
37 Add AND gateway
38 Add Edge from XOR to AND
39 Add activity "Negotiate with Customs"
10 Add edge from AND to activity "Negotiate with Customs"
11 Add AND gateway
12 Add edge from activity "Negotiate with Customs" to AND
13 Add Edge from AND to XOR

14 Add activity "Trigger Support from Higher--ranked Authorities"
15 Add edge from AND to activity "Trigger Support from Higher--ranked Authorities
16 Add edge from activity "Trigger Support from Higher--ranked Authorities" to AND
17 Delete edge from AND to activity "Transport Equipment to Storage Location"
18 Add XOR gateway
19 Add edge from AND to XOR
20 Add edge from XOR to activity, "Transport Equipment to Storage Location"
21 Delete edge from activity "Transport Equipment to Storage Location" to AND
22 Add XOR gateway
23 Add edge from activity "Transport Equipment to Storage Location" to XOR
24 Add edge from XOR to AND
25 Add AND gateway
26 Add edge from XOR to AND

27 Add activity "Transport Partial Equipment to Storage Location"
28 Add edge from AND to activity "Transport Partial Equipment to Storage Location"
29 Add AND gateway
30 Add edge from activity "Transport Partial Equipment to Storage Location" to AND
31 Add edge from AND to XOR
32 Add activity "Retrieve Missing Documents from Home"
33 Add edge from AND To activity "Retrieve Missing Documents from Home"
34 Add activity "Transport Partial Equipment to Storage Location"
35 Add edge from activity "Retrieve Missing Documents from Home"
    to activity "Transport Partial Equipment to Storage Location"
36 Add edge from activity "Transport Partial Equipment to Storage Location" to AND

Fig. 7.13 Transport of equipment process—changed model

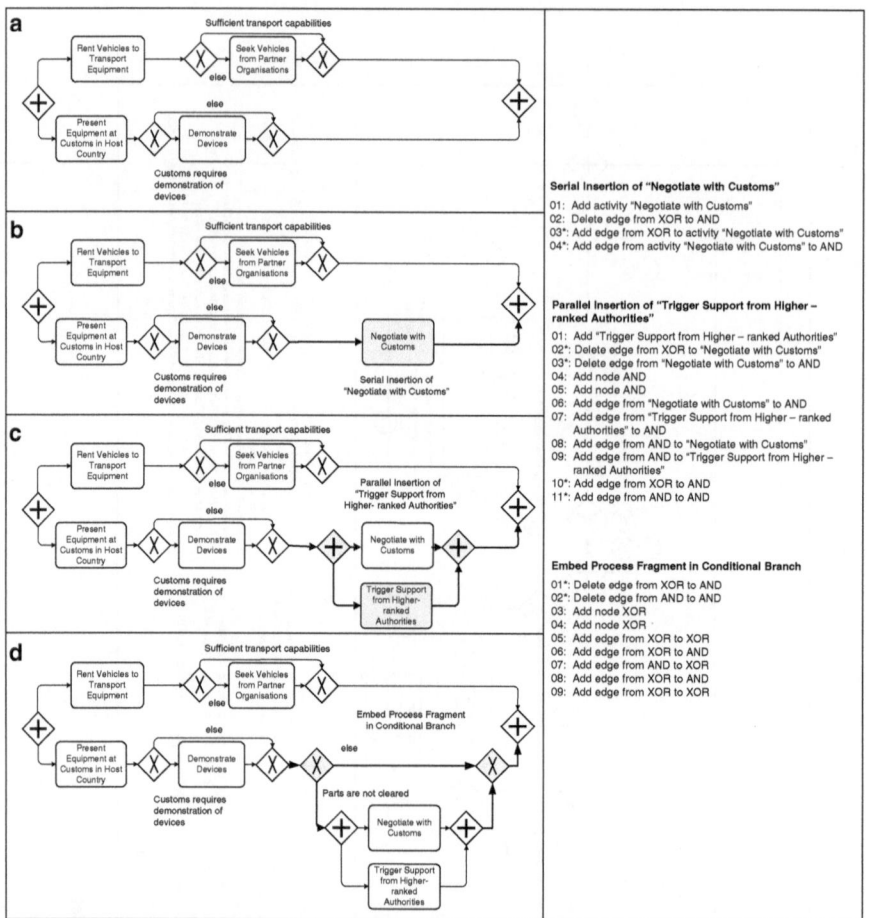

Fig. 7.14 Change task using adaptation patterns

when adapting the control flow schema of a process model the PAIS must ensure data flow correctness (cf. Chap. 4) as well. As illustrated in Fig. 7.4a, for example, the uncontrolled movement of an activity might cause severe data flow errors. Generally, when adapting the control flow schema of a process model, concomitant control and data flow adaptations might become necessary to ensure correctness of the changed process model afterwards (e.g., soundness and data flow correctness). We denote such concomitant adaptations as *secondary changes*.

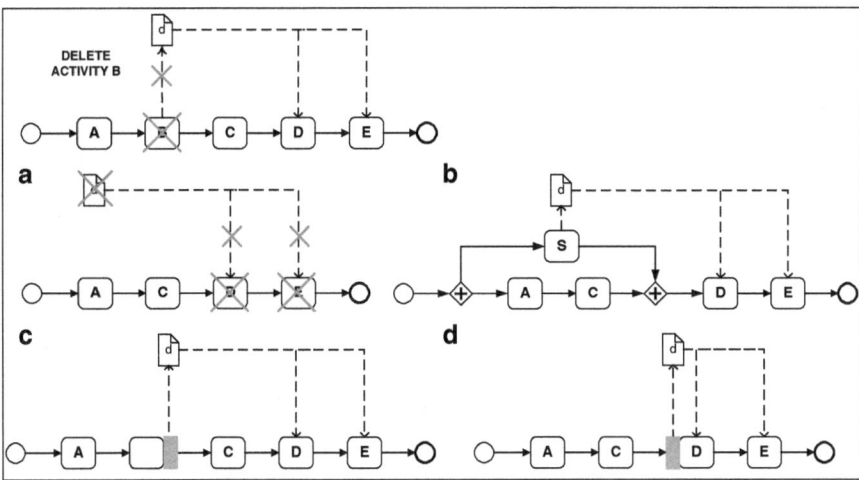

Fig. 7.15 Deletion of an activity and ways for preserving data flow correctness

Example 7.10 (Secondary Changes). We illustrate correctness issues in the context of an activity deletion (i.e., adaptation pattern AP2; cf. Fig. 7.9). Consider the scenario depicted in Fig. 7.15: Activity B, which writes data object d, shall be deleted. This, in turn, will cause data flow errors due to missing data if no concomitant adaptations are made; i.e., activities D and E will access d even though this data object will not have been written before. To avoid such flaws, different strategies are possible (cf. Fig. 7.15a–d): a) cascading deletion of data-dependent activities (i.e., D and E in our example); b) insertion of another activity (i.e., S in our example) writing the respective data object (i.e., d in our example) before any other activity reads it; c) insertion of an auxiliary service (e.g., a user form) which is immediately invoked when deleting activity B, or d), insertion of an auxiliary service which is invoked when starting the first data-dependent activity (D in our example).

Which of these four strategies is most favorable in a given context depends on the respective change scenario as well as on the application semantics of the activity to be deleted. Therefore, an appropriate strategy has to be chosen either by the process designer at build-time or the user requesting the ad hoc deletion at run-time. Note that similar considerations have to be made in the context of the other adaptation patterns.

Example 7.11 (Concomitant Adaptations due to an Activity Deletion).

- In an exceptional situation, a ward physician decides to make the appointment for an X-ray procedure by phone. Therefore she wants to skip process activity *Make Appointment* and manually enter the respective date into the PAIS; i.e., Strategy c, is most favorable.
- A medical examination cannot be carried out as planned. Therefore, activity *Create Report* shall be deleted. Due to this change, it follows that data-dependent activities like *Validate Report* and *Print Report* shall be deleted as well; i.e., Strategy a, is most suitable in this particular situation.

For the remainder of this chapter, we assume that any structural change of a correct process model results in another correct process model; i.e., when factoring out the state of a process instance we presume that the control flow and data flow schemes of the process model resulting from a structural change meet the correctness properties discussed in Chap. 4.

To effectively deal with ad hoc instance changes, support for the correct use of process adaptation patterns is not sufficient. Practical applicability additionally demands a variety of change support features (e.g., correctness of dynamic changes, user assistance, change reuse, access control, concurrency control, accountability, and traceability) as described in the following sections.

7.4   Ensuring State Compliance with a Changed Process Model

As discussed in Sect. 7.2, the uncontrolled change of a process instance might lead to severe run-time errors. Therefore, only those ad hoc changes shall be allowed, which guarantee soundness properties (e.g., option to complete, absence of dead activities) of the resulting process model. However, in the context of ad hoc changes (i.e., dynamic changes) it is not sufficient to only guarantee correctness at the structural level (cf. Sect. 7.3.4). Additionally, the PAIS needs to consider the *state* of a process instance when structurally adapting its process model (cf. Example 7.6). Depending on the current state of a process instance, certain changes should be allowed, while others must be prohibited; e.g., it must not be possible to change the "past" of a process instance (e.g., to delete an already completed activity). Furthermore, activity states might have to be adapted in the context of an ad hoc change in order to enable proper continuation of instance execution afterwards.

We shall characterize these challenges in more detail. For this purpose, let I be a process instance running on a correct process model S. Assume that S is structurally adapted to another correct process model S' by applying change Δ to it. Then two challenging issues emerge:

1. Can Δ be correctly *applied* to I, i.e., without violating soundness of I when running on S'? For this case, I is said to be *state compliant* with S'.
2. Assuming I is state compliant with S', how can we smoothly *relink* I to S' such that its execution can be continued on S' afterwards? Which state adaptations become necessary in this context?

We will show that these two issues are fundamental in order to perform ad hoc changes of single process instances in a correct and consistent way. While the first one concerns *preconditions* regarding the state of I, the second issue is related to *post-conditions* to be satisfied after applying the ad hoc change. In any event, an efficient approach is required enabling automatic state compliance checks as well as correct state adaptations.

Section 7.4.1 gives insights into dynamic change bugs. Following this, Sect. 7.4.2 introduces a universally valid correctness notion considering the two issues mentioned above. Section 7.4.3 then relaxes this correctness notion to be able to cope with changes of loop structures as well. Finally, Sect. 7.4.4 discusses practical aspects regarding the implementation of the described framework in a PAIS.

7.4.1   Ad hoc Changes and Process Instance States

Generally, the applicability of an ad hoc change depends on the state of the respective process instance. We illustrate this by means of Example 7.12.

Example 7.12 (Ad hoc Changes of Process Instances). Consider process model S on the left of Fig. 7.16a. Assume that S is transformed into a correct process model S' by adding two activities (i.e., *Test for Allergies* and *Deliver Drug*) as well as a data dependency between them; i.e., *Test for Allergies* writes data object *Allergy Record* which is then read by *Deliver Drug*. Assume further that this structural model change shall be applied to the process instances depicted in Fig. 7.16b and currently running on S. Regarding instance I_1 the described change can be applied without any problem since its execution has not yet entered the change region (cf. Fig. 7.16c). Changing instance I_2 in an uncontrolled manner, however, would result in an inconsistent process instance state; i.e., activity *Prepare Patient* would be running even though its predecessor, activity *Test for Allergies*, would not have been completed. As a consequence, *Deliver Drug* might be invoked accessing data element *Allergy Record* even though this data element might not have been previously written. Regarding instance I_3, the described change can be applied. However, when relinking the execution of I_3 to S',

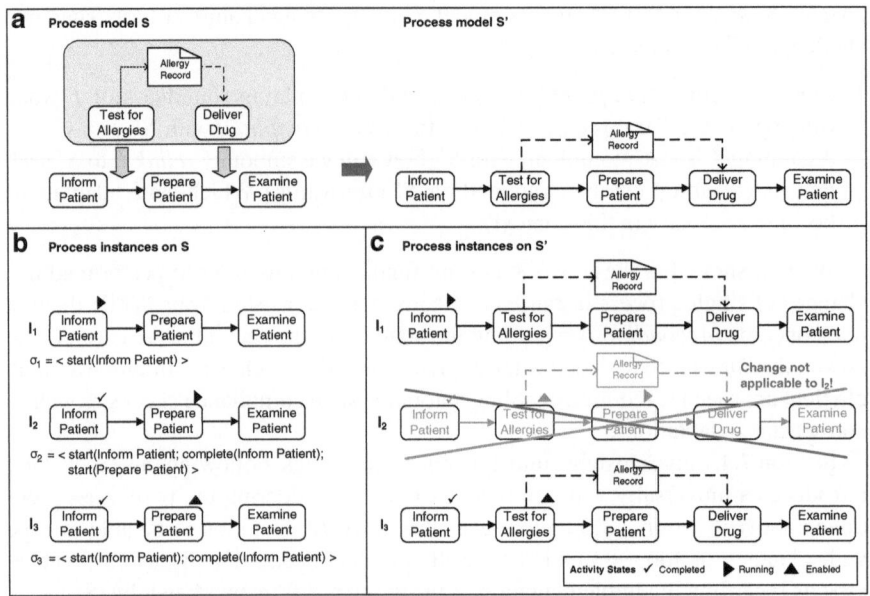

Fig. 7.16 Applying a process model change to process instances

activity *Prepare Patient* needs to be disabled and corresponding work items be withdrawn from worklists. Additionally, the newly inserted activity *Test for Allergies* has to be enabled.

Generally, when applying an ad hoc change to a process instance, the states of its various activities may have to be adapted. Regarding Example 7.12 state adaptations are required for I_3. Note that these adaptations can be easily determined in the given scenario due to the trace-based marking of the activities; i.e., completed activities remain marked when progressing with instance execution. Conversely, Petri nets use simple token-based semantics, i.e., activity markings are usually not preserved when continuing with the flow of control. Hence the marking of a Petri Net only reflects the current state of the respective process instance. In particular, it is not always apparent whether an ad hoc change can be applied to a marked net and—if yes—which state adaptations (e.g., addition of tokens) become necessary to preserve soundness [5,86]. In this context literature reports on so-called *dynamic change bugs* that need to be prevented when applying ad hoc changes [5].

Example 7.13 (Dynamic Change Bug). Consider the Petri Net from Fig. 7.17a for which activity B is enabled. Assume that for the depicted process instance the ordering of B and C shall be changed by rearranging

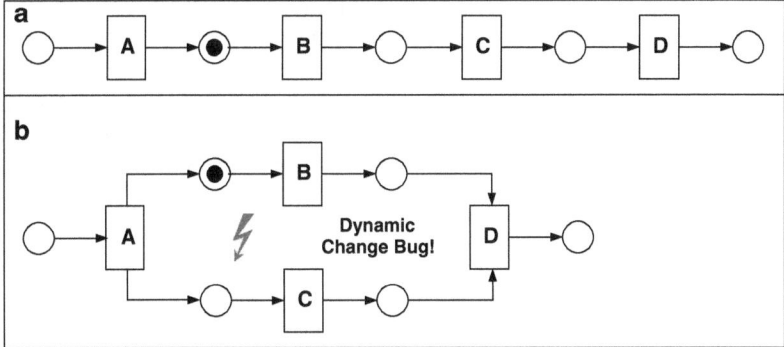

Fig. 7.17 Ad hoc change of a simple Petri Net and resulting dynamic change bug

B and C in parallel with each other. Figure 7.17b shows the Petri Net resulting from this change if it is applied in an uncontrolled manner. Obviously, the control flow schema of the resulting Petri Net contains a deadlock (i.e., it violates the option to complete). After completing B, neither C nor D can be enabled since at least one token is missing in their input places.

7.4.2 A Correctness Notion for Dynamic Instance Changes

To avoid dynamic change bugs in connection with ad hoc changes of a single process instance, adaptive PAISs should rely on appropriate correctness notions [287, 288]. Comparable to serializability known from transaction processing in database systems [114], we need a universal correctness criterion allowing a PAIS to reason about the soundness of a process instance when applying an ad hoc change to it; i.e., we need a correctness notion for deciding about whether or not a particular structural adaptation can be correctly applied to a process instance in its current state.

In the following, fundamental requirements for such a correctness notion are presented. Let S be a sound process model and I be an instance running on S. Further, let Δ be a change applied to S and resulting in model S', i.e., $S[\Delta\rangle S'$. Then:

- *Requirement 1.* Using the criterion it should be decidable whether the correct execution of I on S' (i.e., the proper execution of I after applying change Δ) can be guaranteed; i.e., proper execution and completion of I on S' can be evaluated.
- *Requirement 2.* The criterion should be universally valid; i.e., it should be applicable regardless of the process modeling language used (i.e., the control flow patterns it supports) and the adaptation patterns applied.
- *Requirement 3.* The criterion should be implementable in an efficient way.

A widespread correctness notion which fulfills these requirements and can be applied to decide whether or not a process instance can be correctly relinked from S to S' is *state compliance* [61, 290, 301]. Informally, process instance I on S is *state compliant* with any process model S' derived from S, and therefore its execution can be relinked to S', if the current execution trace σ_I of I is producible on S' as well. Note that this can be always guaranteed if I has not entered the region of S affected by the ad hoc change yet.

Definition 7.3 (State Compliance). Let I be a process instance with execution trace σ_I. Further, let T be a process model. Then, I is state compliant with T if σ_I is producible on T.

Based on the notion of state compliance one can decide whether a particular ad hoc change is correctly applicable to a process instance in its current state. In particular, the latter will be not the case if the process instance has already progressed too far. Consequently, the previously discussed dynamic change bugs can be avoided.

Definition 7.4 (Dynamic Change Correctness). Let $I = (S, \sigma_I)$ be a process instance running on a sound process model S and having execution trace σ_I. Assume further that S is transformed into another sound process model S' by applying change Δ, i.e., $S[\Delta\rangle S'$. Then:

- Δ can be correctly applied to I if I is state compliant with S'.
- Assume I is state compliant with S'. When applying Δ to I correct activity states of I on S' can be obtained by applying σ_I to S'; i.e., by logically replaying the events captured by σ_I on S' in their original order.

Example 7.14 (State Compliance and Dynamic Change Correctness). Consider the change scenario shown in Fig. 7.16a and the process instances I_1 - I_3 depicted in Fig. 7.16b. Obviously, traces $\sigma_1 = $ <start(*Inform Patient*)> and $\sigma_3 = $ <start(*Inform Patient*); complete(*Inform Patient*)> can be produced on the process model resulting from the change as well; i.e., I_1 and I_3 are *state compliant* with the changed process model S'. When replaying execution traces σ_1 and σ_3, respectively, on S', the activity states as depicted in Fig. 7.16c are obtained. Note that for I_3 the newly added activity *Test for Allergies* becomes enabled, while the previously enabled activity *Prepare Patient* is disabled. Finally, the partial execution trace $\sigma_2 = $ <start(*Inform*

Patient); complete(*Inform Patient*); start(*Prepare Patient*)> of I_2 cannot be produced on S'. Hence, the structural change must not be allowed for I_2 in order to further guarantee proper execution of this process instance.

State compliance fulfills Requirement 1 since it forbids changes not compliant with partial instance traces.[2] Furthermore, it presumes no specific process modeling language, but is based on (partial) execution traces instead; i.e., Requirement 2 is met as well. In addition, state compliance can be checked independent of the applied adaptation patterns. Finally, the compliance notion can be implemented in an efficient way, as will be discussed in Sect. 7.4.4 (cf. Requirement 3).

Finally, in the context of Petri Nets other theoretical frameworks exterminating dynamic change bugs for at least certain kinds of structural adaptations have been suggested [9, 86, 87].

7.4.3 A Relaxed Correctness Notion for Coping with Loop Changes

State compliance is too restrictive in certain scenarios [290, 301]. Concerning changes of loop structures, for example, requiring state compliance might prohibit the application of an ad hoc change to a process instance even though the change would not affect proper execution and completion of the instance in the sequel.

Example 7.15 (Unnecessary Prohibition of Ad hoc Instance Changes). Consider the structure and state of process instance I as depicted in Fig. 7.18a. Inspecting the execution trace of I (seen on the left of Fig. 7.18b) reveals that the depicted loop is in its second iteration. Assume now that process model S, on which I has been running so far, shall be dynamically adapted by inserting activity *Perform Test* between *Prepare Patient* and *Deliver Drug*, i.e., the new activity shall be positioned in parallel with activity *Calculate Dose* (cf. Fig. 7.18c). When applying *state compliance* (cf. Definition 7.3) as a correctness notion to decide about the applicability of this ad hoc change to I, the change would be prohibited since the partial trace of the first loop

---

[2]If an instance $I = (S, \sigma_I)$ is not state compliant with a process model S' resulting from a change of S, the change cannot be applied to I. When semantically rolling back I to a previous state (cf. Chap. 6), however, I might become state compliant with S' and hence the change could be applied. More sophisticated strategies for coping with noncompliant instances in the context of dynamic process changes are presented in Chap. 9.

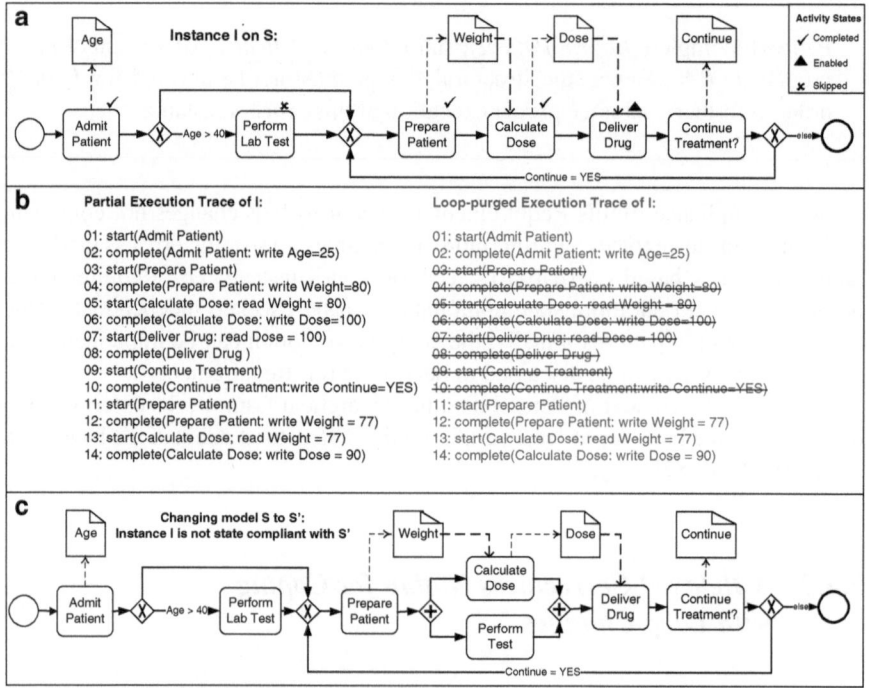

Fig. 7.18 Process instance with a loop and loop-purged execution trace

iteration does not comply with the new process model (cf. Fig. 7.18c); i.e., the execution trace of *I* cannot be produced on the changed process model. However, this ad hoc change would not affect proper instance execution in the sequel since the soundness properties discussed in Chap. 4 (i.e., option to complete, proper completion, and absence of dead activities) would be fulfilled.

Since state compliance is too restrictive in the context of process models containing loop structures, an aligned representation of (partial) execution trace σ is required. By differentiating between completed and future executions of loop iterations, the restrictiveness of the state compliance notion can be overcome [290]. Basically, there are two options: the first one (called *linearization*) is to logically treat loop structures as being equivalent to respective linear sequences (of the loop body). Choosing this option allows for the further use of the state compliance notion (cf. Definition 7.3) based on full trace information. However, a drawback of this approach leads to an explosion of process model size. Adaptive PAISs like ADEPT2 therefore adopt another approach using a *projection* of the given execution trace onto relevant trace information [290]; i.e., the loop construct is maintained, but only a restricted view of the execution trace is considered when checking for the reproducibility of trace information on the changed process model. More precisely, the approach only considers the actual state of a loop body, while excluding all data related to previous loop iterations. Note that this projection of an execution trace onto relevant trace information does not physically delete the information about previous loop iterations, but logically hides it (i.e., traceability of instance execution is not affected).

To realize the desired projection, all entries from the instance execution trace produced by a loop iteration other than the actual one (if the loop is still executed) or the last one (if loop execution has been already completed) are logically discarded. We denote this logical view on traces as a *loop-purged trace* [290]. For the sake of simplicity we presume nested loops here. However, the described projection can be obtained for arbitrary loop structures as well [282].

Definition 7.5 (Loop-purged Trace). Let $I = (S, \sigma_I)$ be a process instance running on S and let σ_I be the corresponding (partial) execution trace. The loop-purged trace σ_I^{lp} can then be obtained from σ_I as follows: If S has no loop structures σ_I^{lp} is identical to σ_I. Otherwise σ_I^{lp} can be derived from σ_I by discarding all entries in σ_I which are related to loop iterations other than the last one (completed loops) or the current one (running loop).

Example 7.16 (Loop-purged Trace). Consider again process instance $I = (S, \sigma_I)$ on S and its partial execution trace σ_I as depicted in Fig. 7.18b (left). The loop-purged trace of I is depicted on the right-hand side of Fig. 7.18b. Since the loop is in its second iteration, all trace entries related to the first loop iteration are logically discarded when determining the loop-purged trace.

Taking the notion of loop-purged trace *relaxed state compliance* can be defined.

Definition 7.6 (Relaxed State Compliance). Let $I = (S, \sigma_I)$ be a process instance on S, and let σ_I be the partial execution trace and σ_I^{lp} be the loop-purged execution trace of I on S. Let further S' denote a process model that can be derived from process model S by structurally adapting S. Then, I is denoted as being *relaxed state compliant* with S' if σ_I^{lp} is producible on S'.

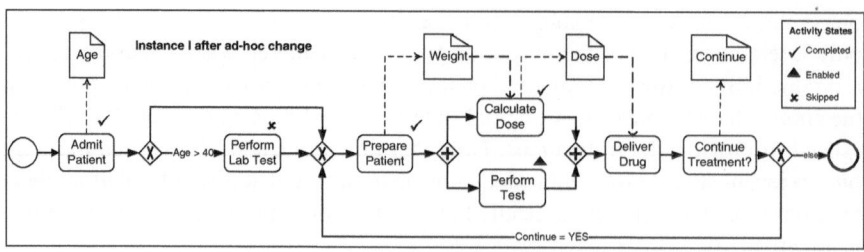

Fig. 7.19   Process instance after applying the change discussed in Example 7.15

Adaptive PAISs supporting process models with loop structures can use relaxed state compliance as a basic correctness notion for deciding whether a particular ad hoc change may be applied to a given process instance. Analogous to Definition 7.4, the latter is possible if the process instance is *relaxed state compliant* with the process model resulting from the change. Furthermore, correct activity states can be obtained afterwards by logically replaying the loop-purged execution trace on the new process model.

Generally, a process instance which is *state compliant* with a process S is also *relaxed state compliant* with S. However, the reverse statement does not always hold as Example 7.17 shows.

Example 7.17 (Relaxed State Compliance).   Consider process instance I on S as depicted in Fig. 7.18a as well as its partial execution trace σ_I and its loop-purged execution trace σ_I^{lp} (cf. Fig. 7.18b). Further consider process model S' from Fig. 7.18c, which can be obtained from S by adding activity *Perform Test* in parallel with activity *Calculate Dose*. As discussed in Example 7.15, I is not *state compliant* with S', since σ_I cannot be replayed on S'. By contrast, σ_I^{lp} can be reproduced on S'. Hence I is *relaxed state compliant* with S' and therefore its execution can be relinked to S' by logically replaying σ_I^{lp} on S'. Finally, this results in the process instance depicted in Fig. 7.19.

As illustrated by Example 7.18, relaxed state compliance can even be ensured in certain cases when moving an already running or completed activity.

Example 7.18 (Moving Running Activities).   Consider Fig. 7.20. Running activity B is moved in order to rearrange it in parallel with C. This movement is possible since I_1 is relaxed state compliant with the resulting process model (see bottom of Fig. 7.20). Generally, moving an already started or completed

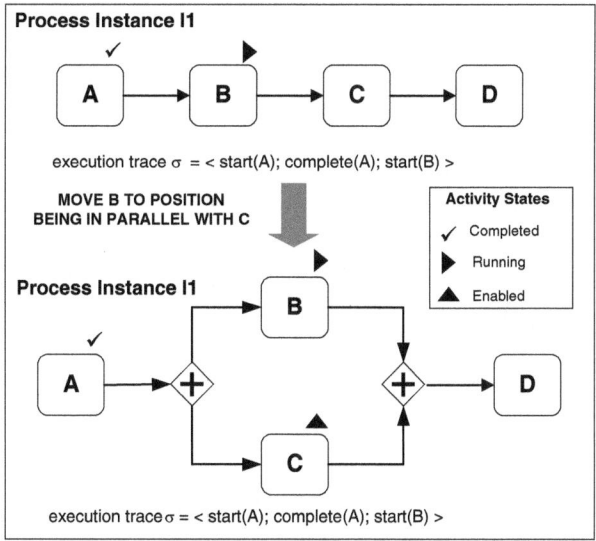

Fig. 7.20 Moving an already running activity

activity is not always possible; e.g., moving B after C and before D would be disallowed due to violation of relaxed state compliance (see [290] for details).

Like *state compliance*, *relaxed state compliance* fulfills the requirements of a correctness notion for dynamic process changes. In the following, we present efficient ways for reasoning about relaxed state compliance.

7.4.4   Efficient Realization of Ad hoc Changes

As discussed in Sect. 7.4.2, an efficient implementation of dynamic process changes is required. This applies to both ad hoc changes of single process instances and process model evolution (cf. Chap. 9) for which (relaxed) state compliance may have to be checked for a large collection of process instances. In particular, it should not be required to access all entries of the execution trace of a process instance in order to check for its (relaxed) state compliance with a changed process model or to adapt its state when relinking it to this model. Note that retrieving such traces from a database and trying to replay their events on the changed process model might cause performance penalties [290].

There exist efficient approaches for realizing dynamic process changes which exploit the operational semantics of the process meta model as well as the formal semantics of the change operations applied [270, 290]. Typically, these approaches presume trace-based instance markings, i.e., it is assumed that each activity has a unique marking representing its current state and that the markings of activities with the final state are preserved (unless a loop back resets them to their initial state). Note that previous examples have already used such trace-based markings.

7.4.4.1   Efficiently Checking State Compliance

For selected adaptation patterns, it is shown how *relaxed state compliance* can be efficiently checked based on simple state conditions by exploiting the semantics of the respective pattern [270, 290, 300]. In this context let $NS(a)$ denote the current state of an activity a.

Pattern AP1: Insert Activity. When *serially inserting* an activity X between the two activities A and B (cf. Fig. 7.8a) relaxed state compliance can be ensured if B has state Enabled or Inactive; i.e., $NS(B) \in \{$Enabled, Inactive$\}$. This means that B has not written any entry to the execution trace of the respective process instance so far. When inserting X in parallel with another activity B (cf. Fig. 7.8a), in turn, relaxed state compliance can be ensured if none of the current successors of B have yet been started; i.e., their state is Inactive or Enabled.

Example 7.19 (Checking Relaxed State Compliance for Activity Insertions). Consider Fig. 7.16 showing two serial insertions. Instance I_1 is relaxed state compliant with S' since $NS(Prepare\,Patient)$ = Inactive and $NS(Examine\,Patient)$ = Inactive hold, i.e., the conditions for serially inserting the two activities *Test for Allergies* and *Deliver Drug* are met. Instance I_2, however, is not state compliant with S' since the state condition for inserting *Test for Allergies* is not satisfied (i.e., $NS(Prepare\,Patient)$ = Running).

Pattern AP2: Delete Activity. Applying the *Delete Activity Pattern* (cf. Fig. 7.9) to an activity X will be allowed (i.e., relaxed state compliance can be ensured) if X has one of the states Enabled, Inactive, or Skipped; i.e., X has not yet written any entry to the execution trace of the respective process instance.

Pattern AP3: Move Activity. The *Move Adaptation Pattern* (cf. Fig. 7.10) can be considered as a combination of the Delete and Insert Adaptation Patterns; i.e., an activity is removed from its current position and reinserted at another one. In case the activity to be moved has not yet been enabled, the conditions for ensuring relaxed state compliance are the same as for the *Insert Adaptation Pattern*; i.e., depending on the position where the activity is reinserted the state condition ensuring relaxed state compliance may be satisfied or not. Furthermore, as shown in Example 7.18, under certain conditions it is possible to move running activities as well (see [290] for details).

Example 7.20 (Ensuring Relaxed State Compliance for Activity Movements). Consider Fig. 7.3a. Assume that B and C shall be swapped by moving C to the position between A and B. For this movement relaxed state compliance can be easily guaranteed since the new successor of C has state Enabled. The resulting process instance is depicted in Fig. 7.3b. Similar considerations hold for the second change depicted in Fig. 7.3. Finally, assume that in Fig. 7.3a activity B shall be moved to the position preceding A; since A has been already completed, relaxed state compliance would be violated for this movement.

Generally, any dynamic change of process instance I on S may involve multiple change operations—realizing the same or different adaptation patterns—to be atomically applied to S [255]; i.e., $S[\phi\rangle S'$ with $\phi = <op_1, \ldots, op_n>$. For applying such a *change transaction*, the state conditions of all change operations op_i need to be satisfied. Otherwise the change transaction has to be aborted due to violation of relaxed state compliance. Altogether, the provided examples demonstrate that relaxed state compliance can be evaluated based on the states of selected activities; i.e., without the need to reproduce (loop-purged) execution traces on the changed process model. In existing implementations like ADEPT2 and AristaFlow (cf. Chap. 15), ad hoc changes leading to a violation of relaxed state compliance are excluded from the start. For example, users must not delete completed activities or insert an activity in an already passed region of a process instance [70]. In this way, compliance conditions are effectively exploited for assisting users in defining ad hoc changes.

7.4.4.2 Efficiently Adapting Instance States

If an instance I on S is (relaxed) state compliant with the model S' resulting from an ad hoc change, I can be relinked to S'. In this context the state of I has to be adapted before continuing with its execution on S' (cf. Sect. 7.4.1). Respective state adaptations should be accomplished automatically to accommodate users. Again access to the entire execution trace of I should be avoided.

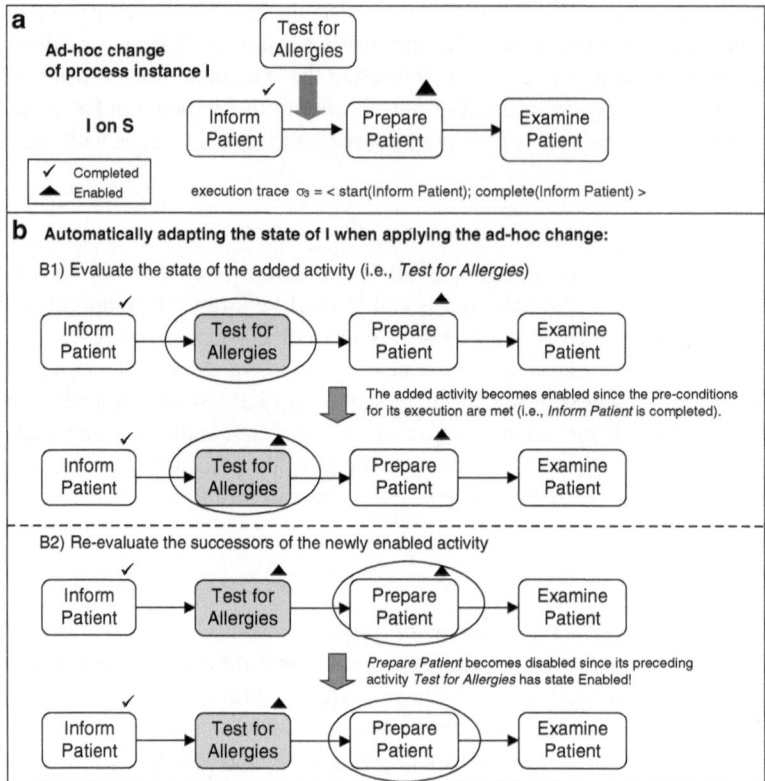

Fig. 7.21 Automatically adapting the process instance state after applying an ad hoc change

In approaches using trace-based markings, usually, only those activities of a process instance are reevaluated in the context of an ad hoc change which belong to the *change region*. What exactly determines a change region depends on the used process meta model and change framework, and is outside the scope of this chapter. Here we only give a simple example (for formal details we refer to [270, 290]).

Example 7.21 (Automatically Adapting Process Instance States). Consider the ad hoc change of instance I as depicted in Fig. 7.21a. First of all, I is (relaxed) state compliant with the process model resulting from this change since $NS(Prepare\ Patient) = \texttt{Enabled}$ holds. Furthermore, when relinking the execution of I to the model resulting from this ad hoc change, state adaptations become necessary. Figure 7.21b shows how the number of state reevaluations can be reduced by only considering activities from the change region; i.e., the newly added activity *Test for Allergies* and its successor *Prepare Patient* in the given context. First, the state of the newly added activity is evaluated and set to `Enabled` since the preconditions for this activity are met. Second, the state of activity *Prepare Patient* which succeeds the new one is reevaluated. Since its preconditions are no longer met, it becomes disabled.

7.5   Manual Definition of Ad hoc Changes

In adaptive PAISs, ad hoc changes often need to be manually defined by authorized users. For this, either the standard process editor of the PAIS or a customized change application offering a user interface tailored toward the specific application context can be used [168]. Typically, respective approaches restrict both the expressiveness of the process modeling language and the adaptation patterns provided to users in order to ease the definition of ad hoc changes.

In many adaptive PAISs (e.g., Breeze [313], WASA [364,365], and SPADE [39]), defining an ad hoc change requires users to suspend the process instance, then load it into the process editor of the PAIS, and manually adjust its structure and state as desired. While this is sufficient for power users, it renders the definition of more complex ad hoc changes by end-users impossible. To enable ad hoc changes by end-users, tailored and application-specific user interfaces are required that hide as much of the complexity of ad hoc changes as possible; e.g., by enabling end-users to define ad hoc changes at a high level of abstraction (e.g., based on abstracted process views and personalized process visualizations [53, 54, 266]), by automatically conducting required model transformations and state adaptations, and by performing required correctness checks transparently. As a prerequisite for realizing such customized change applications, appropriate application programming interfaces (API) are needed [168]. Currently, only a few PAISs provide such APIs. ADEPT [261, 263, 271] and ProMInanD [141], for example, offer an open API not only accessing user worklists and corresponding work items, but also for defining ad hoc changes. Basically, respective APIs provide a powerful means to realize sophisticated process change features in a variety of domains and to build domain-specific user interfaces hiding much of the complexity from end-users. For example, using the ADEPT API customized change user interfaces for domains like health care, software engineering, logistics, transportation, and disaster management have already been realized [168].

Another approach to reduce overall change complexity is to use a simple process modeling language and to only provide restricted support for adaptation patterns. As a consequence respective solutions are only applicable in a very narrow application context. For example, consider process support in the area of office automation.

Example 7.22 (Flexible Office Flows with ProMInanD). An example of an adaptive PAIS providing a specific and simple metaphor to its end-users is ProMInanD [141]. This PAIS was designed for realizing flexible document flows and for enabling office automation. Therefore, a process instance—together with its related process model—is considered as *electronic circulation folder* (ECF) which is sent from end-user to end-user according to a prespecified flow of control. Such ECF comprises a number of documents which may be created, removed, updated, and read by process participants.

In particular, the user who currently has the ECF may change its pre-specified routing, e.g., by dynamically adding an activity (e.g., revising a document) to be performed by a particular user before the ECF can be forwarded to the next process participant. Other change operations include handing back the ECF to the previous user or redirecting it to another user besides the one specified in the ECF model. Basically, sequential flows and related ad hoc changes (e.g., swapping the order of two activities) can be realized. This simplicity, however, significantly limits the applicability of the ECF approach; e.g., parallel and repeated activity executions as well as more complex ad hoc changes are not directly supported. Besides this, the provided change operations only considers behavior (i.e., control flow) while neglecting other model perspectives. In particular, data flow is limited to the exchange of files between activities, i.e., the PAIS has no control over exchanged data. This leaves significant complexity to application programmers and users, who themselves have to ensure data flow correctness when dynamically adapting ECF routing. Note that this is an error-prone task if structured data have to be exchanged through respective files or if concurrent access to certain data is required.

Usually, when ad hoc changes of a process instance have to be defined by end-users without being assisted by the PAIS, significant user experience is required. This is particularly true when ad hoc changes have to be defined from scratch and multiple model adaptations become necessary to handle an exception. As discussed in Sect. 7.3.4, for example, when deleting an activity during run-time, (data-) dependent activities might have to be deleted as well requiring complex user interactions at run-time; or when inserting a new activity its parameters have to be bound to process data objects. The following sections show how end-users can be assisted by a PAIS in accomplishing ad hoc changes in an easy and reliable manner.

7.6   Assisting End-Users Through the Reuse of Ad hoc Changes

As mentioned in Chap. 3, assistance going beyond correctness checks is needed to enable less-experienced end-users to perform ad hoc changes. Instead of defining every ad hoc change from scratch, existing knowledge about previous changes should be exploited, especially when similar exceptional situations have occurred more than once [71, 172, 217]; i.e., an adaptive PAIS should assist end-users in retrieving and reusing knowledge about previously performed ad hoc changes, including the process model adaptations defined by them.

7.6.1   Reusing Knowledge About Similar Ad hoc Changes

Pure syntactical information about the performed model adaptations, as captured in *change logs* (see Chap. 8), is usually not sufficient to adequately support the retrieval and reuse of ad hoc changes. Additionally, information about the *application context*, in which the ad hoc change has become necessary, is required.

> *Example 7.23 (Application Context of an Ad hoc Change).* Regarding a cruciate rupture treatment process (cf. Example 7.7), the context information that the MRT was skipped for a patient with a cardiac pacemaker is also useful for other physicians, particularly when treating patients with similar problems. Consequently, ad hoc changes should be annotated with relevant context information to foster their later retrieval and reuse.

In order to enable end-users to reuse knowledge about ad hoc changes, which are applied in a similar problem context to other process instances, these changes must be annotated with contextual information (e.g., reasons of the ad hoc change) and be memorized by the PAIS. This contextual information is needed to be able to present knowledge only about those previous ad hoc changes to the user that are relevant in the current exceptional situation. For example, an MRT must not be skipped for patients in general, but only for those with a cardiac pacemaker.

In the following, we will present an approach that facilitates ad hoc changes of process instances during run-time by supporting the retention and reuse of previously applied instance changes. In particular, it automates change retrieval by considering structured information about the current application context; e.g., the occurred exception and the current state of the process instance to be adapted. Further, if ad hoc changes applied in a similar context can be retrieved in the given exceptional situations, but cannot be reused directly (e.g., in case the process instance has progressed beyond the point that the ad hoc change can be directly applied), user support for adapting the respective change definition to the situation at hand is provided.

Approaches like ProCycle [293, 355, 358], CBRFlow [359], and CAKE2 [218] use *case-based reasoning (CBR)* for annotating ad hoc changes with contextual information and for memorizing them in the PAIS. Before describing the basic ideas behind these approaches, some background on case-based reasoning is provided.

Case-Based Reasoning. *Case-Based Reasoning (CBR)* is a contemporary approach to problem solving and learning [150]. Problems and their solutions are described as *cases* and are stored in *case–bases*. New problems are dealt with by drawing on past experiences and by adapting respective solutions to the new problem situation. Reasoning based on past experiences is a powerful and frequently applied way to solve problems by humans [26]. A physician, for example, remembers previous cases to correctly diagnose the disease of a newly admitted patient. A banker uses her experiences about previous cases to decide whether or not to grant a loan. Generally, a case is a contextualized piece of knowledge representing an experience [150] that typically consists of a *problem description* and the corresponding *solution*. In particular, CBR uses specific knowledge of past experiences to solve new problems. CBR also contributes to incremental and sustained learning: every time a new problem is solved, information about it and its solution is retained, and therefore immediately made available for solving future problems [26].

The ProCycle approach for annotating and reusing knowledge about ad hoc changes [355], which we will describe in the following sections, relies on an extension of the CBR paradigm—*Conversational CBR (CCBR)*. CCBR actively involves users in the case retrieval process [32]. A CCBR system can be characterized as an interactive system that, via a mixed-initiative dialog, guides users through a question–answering sequence in a case retrieval context. As opposed to traditional CBR, the user is not required to provide a complete a priori problem specification for case retrieval. He does also not need to have a clear picture of what is relevant for problem solving. Instead, CCBR guides users, who might only have a vague idea of what they are searching for, to assess the given situation and to find relevant cases. Users can provide already known information at any time. Therefore, CCBR is especially suited to support inexperienced users in handling unplanned exceptions that cannot be dealt with in a fully automated way.

Section 7.6.2 describes how ad hoc changes and their context can be captured. Section 7.6.3 then shows how knowledge about previous ad hoc changes can be retrieved, adjusted, and reused when similar exceptional situations occur at run-time.

7.6.2 Memorizing Ad hoc Changes

As discussed, when memorizing ad hoc changes of individual process instances, these changes need to be annotated with relevant context information.

7.6.2.1 Representing Ad hoc Changes as Cases

This section describes how ad hoc changes of a single process instance can be represented as *cases* to enable their later retrieval, customization, and reuse. In its simplest form, a *case c* represents an ad hoc change of a process instance consisting of a *textual problem description* and a *solution part*. The textual problem description pd_c briefly describes the exceptional situation that led to the ad hoc change. The solution part sol_c, in turn, comprises the high-level change operations (i.e., adaptation patterns) that were applied to cope with the exception.

Definition 7.7 (Case). A case $c = (pd_c, sol_c)$ is a tuple where

- pd_c is a textual problem description which might be free text or based on a domain-specific ontology.
- $sol_c = <op_1, \ldots, op_k>, k \in \mathbb{N}$ is the solution part of the case comprising a list of high-level change operations, which were sequentially applied to at least one process instance in the given problem context

---

Example 7.24 (Case Representation). Consider the change scenario from Fig. 7.22. It illustrates how an ad hoc change deleting a particular activity (i.e., $Delete(I_1, MRT)$) can be represented as a case and be annotated with contextual information. The problem description pd_{c_1} of this case c_1 briefly describes the reason for skipping the MRT in free text, and the solution part sol_{c_1} contains the change operation needed to delete the MRT activity from the process instance model (i.e., $Delete(S_I, MRT)$). To foster change reuse and allow applying c_1 to other process instances, the parameter representing the modified instance model, is generalized; i.e., parameter I_1 of operation $Delete(I_1, MRT)$ is substituted by a placeholder for an instance-specific process model S_I; i.e., a case description abstracts from a particular process instance.

All instance changes related to a particular process type with model S are stored as cases in the case–base cb_S associated with S.

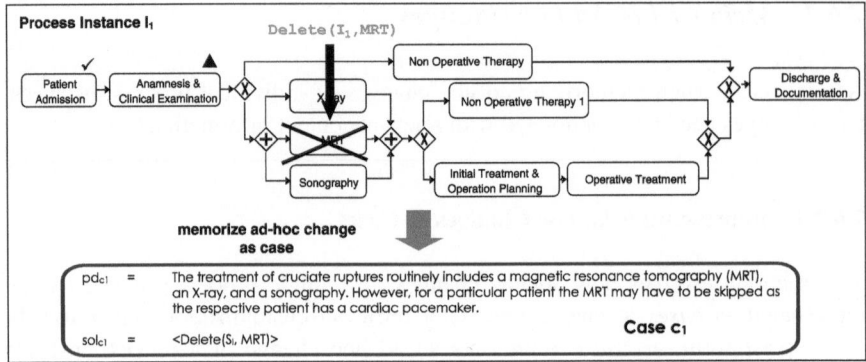

Fig. 7.22   Example of a case representation

Definition 7.8 (Case–Base).   Let $\mathscr{C}$ be the set of all cases representing ad hoc changes of the process instances running in a PAIS. Further, let S be a process model representing a process type. Then, a case–base $\mathrm{cb}_S \subseteq \mathscr{C}$ corresponds to the set of all cases associated with S; i.e., cases which were applied to at least one process instance derived from S.

This simple case representation with an unstructured problem description only allows limited user guidance during case retrieval. It is therefore up to the user to formulate suitable queries. This works well for experienced users having a clear idea of what they are searching for and would therefore know which search terms to use to achieve suitable results. Concerning inexperienced users, however, this lack of guidance might result in either too broadly or too narrowly formulated queries.

7.6.2.2   Capturing the Application Context of Ad hoc Changes

To further facilitate *case retrieval* for end-users, information about the application context of ad hoc changes has to be memorized. This context information can be used during case retrieval to filter out those cases not relevant in a given exceptional situation. Regarding our example (cf. Example 7.24), a case skipping the MRT for a patient should be filtered out for all patients not having a cardiac pacemaker.

When capturing the *application context* of an ad hoc change, one challenge is to adequately represent this context information and to gather it on-the-fly. Usually, the application context cannot be defined in a generic way, but needs to be aligned to a specific domain or application. Consequently, process engineers should be allowed to define application- or domain-specific *context models*. Such a context model

Fig. 7.23 Example of an application context model

Object	Type	Min	Max
⊞ Diagnosis			
⊟ Patient			
age	Integer	1	1
problemList	ProblemList	1	1
weight	Integer	1	1
⊟ ProblemList			
diagnoses	Diagnosis	0	1000
hasPacemaker	Boolean	0	1
therapies	Therapy	0	1000
⊞ Therapy			

defines what context information might be relevant for reusing ad hoc changes and thus should be collected. For example, patient information like age, allergies, and medical history should be part of a context model in the medical domain. By contrast, a context model for the logistics industry might contain information about customers, truck locations, weather, and road conditions.

Definition 7.9 (Application Context Model). An *application context model* $Ctxt = (DataObjSet, AttrSet, Attrs)$ consists of a finite set of data objects $DataObjSet$, a finite set of application context attributes $AttrSet$, and a function $Attrs : DataObjSet \mapsto AttrSet$ which assigns to each data object $d \in DataObjSet$ a set of context attributes $Attrs(d) \subseteq AttrSet$. Each context attribute $attr = (aName, aType, min, max) \in Attrs$ has a name $aName$, a data type $aType$, a minimum occurrence min, and a maximum occurrence max. The data type of a context attribute is either atomic (e.g., *Boolean*, *Integer*, *String*, or *Time*) or complex (i.e., it refers to already defined data objects).

Example 7.25 (Application Context Model). Figure 7.23 shows a simplified example of an application context model in the medical domain. It consists of data objects *Diagnosis*, *Patient*, *ProblemList*, and *Therapy*. Attributes *problemList* and *diagnoses* are examples of context attributes with a complex type, as they are composed of other data objects; in turn, *age*, *weight*, and *hasPaceMaker* constitute attributes of simple type. Attributes with an occurrence greater than 1 constitute collections (e.g., *diagnoses*).

Regarding a particular ad hoc change of a process instance, usually, only a subset of the data objects and attributes from the application context model is relevant to describe the reasons for this ad hoc change. It is therefore not necessary to memorize the full context model in the case–base.

Example 7.26 (Relevant Application Context). The application context model from Fig. 7.23 describes a patient record including the complete patient history. The decision to skip the MRT during the cruciate rupture treatment of a particular patient, however, only became necessary because the respective patient has a cardiac pacemaker.

To effectively support the reuse of similar cases and to avoid storing irrelevant context information, knowledge about the reasons of an ad hoc change is required. Automated discovery of relevant application context data using data mining techniques is not applicable in the given scenario. To statistically identify correlations between ad hoc changes and context attributes, a large set of ad hoc changes would be needed and these deviations would have to occur frequently. As users should be supported from the first ad hoc changes onwards, however, one cannot rely on a long learning process.

To tackle this problem in exceptional situations, users are encouraged to state which parts of the context model are relevant for their decision to deviate from the prespecified process model. Based on this, the reasons for the ad hoc change can be captured. Note that this enables the immediate reuse of ad hoc changes after having added the first case to the case–base of the PAIS. Furthermore, the application context of the ad hoc change can be narrowed to relevant context attributes.

The ProCycle approach [355] enables such memorization of ad hoc changes by adopting and extending conversational case–based reasoning (cf. Sect. 7.6.1). ProCycle allows users to describe the reasons for an ad hoc change in an intuitive manner by way of question–answer pairs $qaSet_c$. Thus, each question–answer pair (q, a) characterizes one particular condition making the ad hoc change necessary. It is especially noteworthy that question–answer pairs are also used during case retrieval to assist users in finding similar cases (cf. Sect. 7.6.3). The question q of such a pair (q, a) corresponds to free text and the answer a is mapped to an answer expression, which can be automatically evaluated by the PAIS. ProCycle uses OCL (*Object Constraint Language*) as the language for representing such answer expressions. Note that end-users are not expected to enter these expressions by hand, but are assisted in describing the reasons for the ad hoc change. For example, consider the medical domain. Instead of requiring physicians to formulate the answer expression, a form can be presented to them with a list of symptoms: they then only need to select those symptoms relevant for the ad hoc change.

Example 7.27 (Question–Answer Pair). Consider Example 7.24, where a physician decides to skip (i.e., to delete) the *MRT* activity for a particular patient, assuming that the decision to perform this ad hoc change is triggered by the fact that the treated patient has a cardiac pacemaker. To record the reasons for this ad hoc change, the physician enters the question *Does the patient have a cardiac pacemaker?* as free text as well as an answer expression which either evaluates to true or false; e.g., *Patient.problem-List.hasPacemaker = 'Yes'* constitutes such an answer expression. It uses the *hasPacemaker* attribute of data object *Patient* from the *application context model* depicted in Fig. 7.23.

To include context information in the representation of a case, Definition 7.7 has to be extended by adding question–answer pairs.

Definition 7.10 (Case-Extended with Question–Answer Pairs). A case $c = (pd_c, sol_c, qaSet_c)$ is a tuple where

- pd_c and sol_c are defined as in Definition 7.7.
- $qaSet_c = \{(q_1, a_1), \dots, (q_n, a_n)\}, n \in \mathbb{N}$ denotes a set of question–answer pairs reflecting the application context of the case ($q_i \in \mathcal{Q}$ and $a_i \in \mathcal{A}$ with $\mathcal{Q}$ and $\mathcal{A}$ respectively denoting the set of all possible questions and answers).

Example 7.28 (Representing an Ad hoc Change as a Case with Application Context). Figure 7.24 shows how case c_1 from Example 7.24 can be enriched with application context information. In addition to the textual problem description pd_c and the solution part sol_c, c_1 contains a question–answer pair defining the application context of the applied ad hoc change.

So far, it has been shown how to annotate ad hoc changes of process instances with application context information and how to make statements about which context attributes are relevant depending on the concrete exceptional situation. In addition to the context attributes specified in the application context model, there might be other criteria not (yet) known to the PAIS, but nevertheless contributes to the decision to deviate from the predefined process. In such a scenario the user should be able to record these criteria as reasons for the deviation.

Example 7.29 (Unforeseen Application Context). Assume that the planned cruciate ligament operation for patient *Sneijders* has to be postponed—an emergency surgery has to be performed for patient *Janssen* and therefore

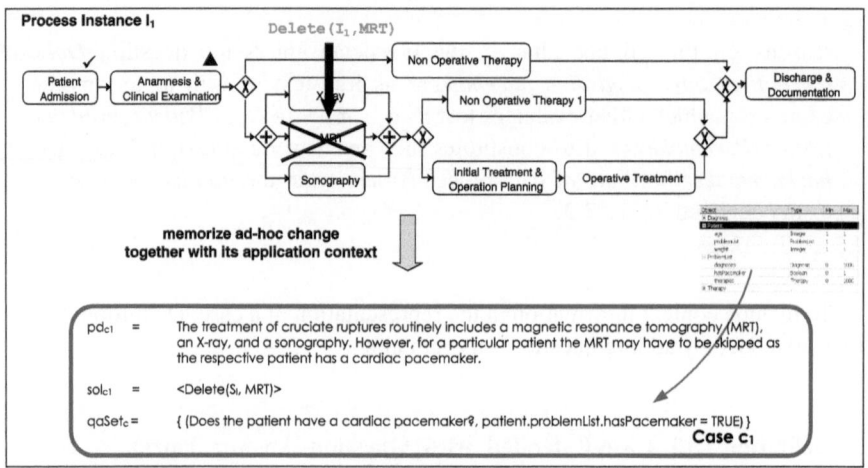

Fig. 7.24   Annotating ad hoc changes with contextual information

Hendricks has to be transferred back to the ward to wait for his intervention. Under such circumstances it is unlikely that the reasons for the ad hoc deviation can be captured automatically. However, reuse of such cases is also desirable and should therefore be supported.

Formal answer expressions are not applicable if the reasons for the ad hoc deviation are outside the scope of the prespecified application context model. Therefore, the answer has to be manually entered by the user. Instead of mapping answers to logical expressions on attributes from the application context model, free text can be used for both the question and answer, thus allowing for the specification of arbitrary reasons even if they have not yet been captured in the PAIS.

7.6.3   Retrieving and Adapting Similar Ad hoc Changes

Once ad hoc changes and their *application context* have been memorized in the PAIS, they can be retrieved, adjusted, and reused when similar exceptional situations occur and thus when similar ad hoc changes become necessary. To effectively support end-users, only such cases should be presented to them which can contribute to their handling of the given exception. For this purpose, those cases that occurred in an application context similar to the exceptional situation at hand will have to be determined. In addition to the application context, the current state of the process instance for which an ad hoc change shall be performed (denoted as a *state context*)

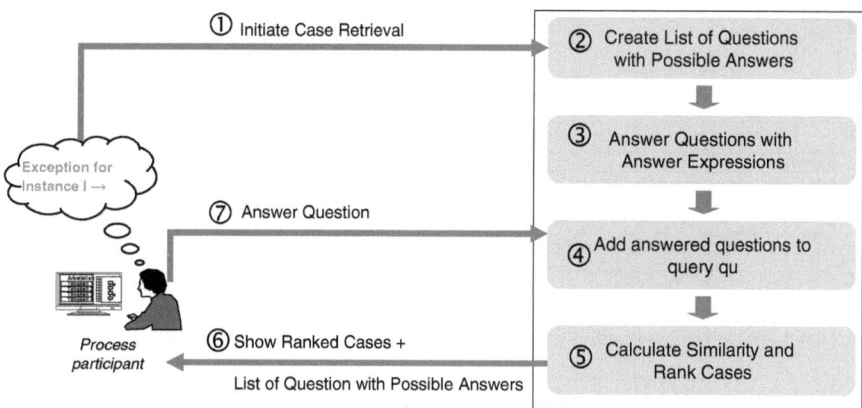

Fig. 7.25 Retrieving similar cases

is taken into account since it restricts the applicability of the adaptations defined by a particular case (cf. Sect. 7.4.1). We will first describe an approach for calculating similarity in respect to an *application context* and then show how the instance state (i.e., *state context*) can be considered when retrieving relevant cases. Finally, we will illustrate how knowledge about previous ad hoc changes of process instances can be reused.

7.6.3.1   Application Context Similarity

Application context similarity measures how well the question–answer pairs of a stored case c (cf. Definition 7.10) match with a query qu representing the application context of the exceptional situation the user is confronted with. For this purpose, conversational CBR (cf. Sect. 7.6.1) can be applied to assist users in formulating this query in an interactive and incremental way. Figure 7.25 gives an idea of a typical case retrieval process as supported in existing approaches like ProCycle and CBRFlow [355, 359]: when an exceptional situation occurs during the execution of a process instance I, case retrieval is initiated (1). Then a list of questions and possible answers is created to guide the user in formulating the query characterizing the exceptional situation (2). As a next step, structured answer expressions are automatically evaluated (3) and the answered questions are added to the query (4). Similarity is then calculated and cases are ranked by decreasing similarity (5). The list of ranked cases as well as the list of questions with possible answers are displayed to the user (6), who then may answer any of the not-yet-answered questions (7). This leads to a query expansion and re-ranking of the cases (5 + 6).

   We describe a case retrieval process using an exemplary case–base $cb_S = \{c_1, c_2\}$ (cf. Fig. 7.26a). After having initiated *case retrieval* an empty query qu is created. To guide the user in incrementally expanding query qu for cb_S, the

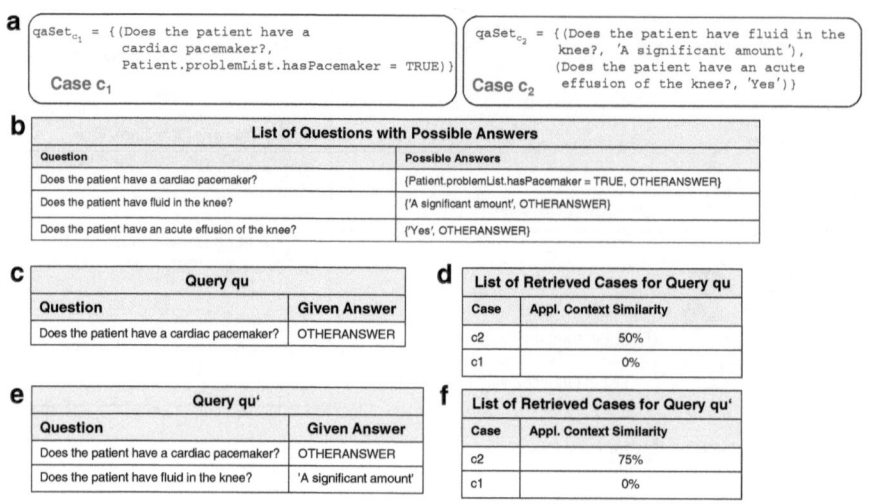

Fig. 7.26 Case retrieval process

set of possible questions $qSet(cb_S)$ is calculated. In addition, for each question q the set of all possible answers $aSet(q)$ is determined. This includes an entry OTHERANSWER, which can be selected if none of the answer options applies. Figure 7.26b shows the (simplified) list of questions with possible answers that can be created for cb_S. In total, this list comprises three questions. For example, question *'Does the patient have fluid in the knee?'* has two possible answers: *'A significant amount'* or OTHERANSWER (if the first answer *'A significant amount'* does not apply).

As a next step, all questions with an associated answer expression are automatically evaluated. Then the derived question–answer pairs (q_i, a_i) are added to query qu. As illustrated in Fig. 7.26c, question $q_1 = $ *Does the patient have a cardiac pacemaker?* evaluates to false (i.e., $a_1 = $ OTHERANSWER) resulting in the intermediate query $qu = \{(q_1, a_1)\}$. After this step, query qu is used to determine cases $c \in cb_S$ whose application context is most similar to the current one represented by qu. To calculate application context similarity between query qu and case c, the question–answer pairs in $qaSet_c$ and qu are matched. For this purpose Definition 7.12 can be used.

Definition 7.11 (Application Context Similarity). Let $c \in cb_S$ be a case and qu be a query representing the present application context. Then, application context similarity $sim(qu, c)$ between qu and c corresponds to the number of questions with the same answers $same(qu, qaSet_c)$, minus the number of questions with different answers $diff(qu, qaSet_c)$, divided by the total number of questions in the case. Finally, to obtain similarity values between 0 and 1, $sim(qu, c))$ needs to be normalized:

$$sim(qu, c) = \frac{1}{2} * \left(\frac{same(qu, qaSet_c) - diff(qu, qaSet_c)}{|qaSet_c|} + 1 \right)$$

Taking query $qu = \{(q_1, a_1)\}$ (cf. Fig. 7.26c), for c_1 we obtain $sim(c_1, qu) = 0$ as the question–answer pair in case c_1 does not match with qu (cf. Fig. 7.26d). Regarding c_2 we obtain $sim(c_2, qu) = 0.5$, because neither of the two questions of c_2 has been answered.

In summary, the described approach displays the list of ranked cases as well as the list of questions with possible answers for users, who can then answer any of the not-yet-answered questions to further refine the query. Whenever an additional question is answered, or an answer is modified similarity is recalculated. Cases are displayed to the user ordered in order of decreasing similarity (cf. Fig. 7.26d+f).

Consider the above example and assume that the user additionally answers question $q_2 = $ *Does the patient have fluid in the knee?* with $a_2 = $ *A significant amount.* This results in the new query $qu' = \{(q_1, a_1), (q_2, a_2)\}$ (cf. Fig. 7.26e). Considering query qu' for c_1, we still obtain $sim(c_1, qu) = 0$. However, for case c_2 similarity $sim(c_2, qu)$ increases to 0.75 (cf. Fig. 7.26f).

7.6.3.2 State Context

In addition to the application context, the state of the process instance needs to be taken into account when retrieving similar cases in an exceptional situation. As discussed in Sect. 7.4, the state of a process instance restricts the applicability of the adaptations defined by the solution part of a particular case. In particular, if this solution part contains change operations that cannot be applied anymore in the current state of the process instance, the respective case should be excluded from the list of offered cases. To determine whether a case c is applicable to a process instance I in its current instance state, we introduce the notion of *case compliance*. It directly builds on *relaxed state compliance* (cf. Definition 7.6).

Definition 7.12 (Case Compliance). Let $c = (pd_c, sol_c, qaSet_c)$ be a case with solution part $sol_c = <op_1, .., op_n>$, $n \in \mathbb{N}$. Then, process instance $I = (S_I, \sigma_I)$ is *case compliant* with c if $S_I[sol_c\rangle S_I'$ (i.e., sol_c can be correctly applied to S_I resulting in S_I') and I is relaxed state compliant with S_I'.

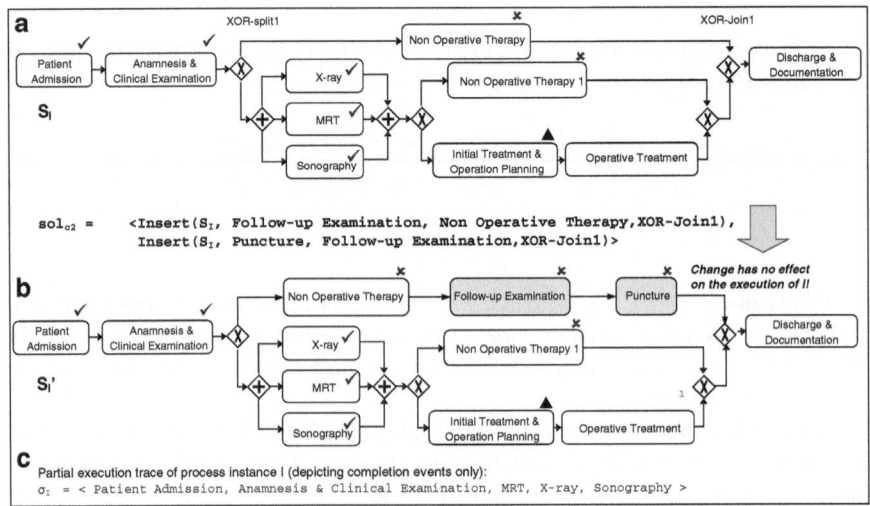

Fig. 7.27 Case compliance and changes without effects

Example 7.30 (Case Compliance). Consider process model S and related process instances I_1 and I_2 from Fig. 7.5. Consider further case c_1 from Fig. 7.24 with solution part $sol_{c_1} = \;<Delete(S_1, MRT)>$. Then, I_1 is case compliant with c_1. This does not apply to I_2 since this instance is not relaxed state compliant with the model resulting from the application of sol_{c_1} to S.

Case compliance is a necessary prerequisite for a case to be directly applicable to the given process instance. It guarantees that no inconsistencies or errors are introduced when applying the case (i.e., the operations of its solution part). As the following example shows, however, it is not sufficient to only consider case compliance when retrieving relevant cases.

Example 7.31 (Effectless Changes). Consider model S_I of process instance I as shown in Fig. 7.27a and assume that the depicted solution part of case c_2 shall be applied to S_I—c_2 inserts activities *Follow-Up Examination* and *Puncture* after activity *Non Operative Therapy* and before node *XOR-Join1*, resulting in instance model $S_I{}'$ (cf. Fig. 7.27b). When considering the execution trace of I (cf. Fig. 7.27c) one can see that I is case compliant with c_2. However, applying c_2 to I does not have any effect on the execution of I as the branch with activity *Non Operative Therapy* was skipped for I

beforehand; i.e., the newly inserted activities will be also skipped due to a
deadpath elimination.

Generally, changes of skipped regions have no effect on a process instance unless
this region is reentered later during run-time; e.g., if a change relates to a loop
entering another iteration later on [355]. During case retrieval cases which would
have no effect on I, or with which I is not case compliant, can be excluded. In
certain scenarios, however, a case belonging to this category might be adjustable
such that it becomes applicable to I. Whether this is possible depends on the
concrete adaptation patterns (i.e., change operations) listed in the solution part of
the case. Regarding adaptation patterns *Delete Process Fragment*, *Replace Process
Fragment*, and *Swap Process Fragment*, for example, no adjustment is possible if
case compliance is not satisfied or the instance change would be without effect.
For adaptation patterns *Insert Process Fragment* and *Move Process Fragment*, the
solution part of the case can be adjusted by changing the parameterization of
the respective operations; e.g., by adjusting the position at which an activity shall be
(re-)inserted.

Example 7.32 (Case Adjustability). Consider process model S_I as depicted
in Fig. 7.27a and assume that the solution part of case c_2 shall be applied
to S_I. As mentioned earlier, inserting activities *Follow-Up Examination*
and *Puncture* after *Non Operative Therapy* and before *XOR-Join1* would have
no effect on I_1 in its current state (cf. Fig. 7.27b). However, in the given
example the parameterization of the change operations can be adjusted in such
a way that c_2 becomes applicable; e.g., activities *Follow-Up Examination* and
Puncture can be inserted after activity *Operative Treatment*.

7.6.3.3   Retrieving Similar Cases

In an exceptional situation, similar cases are retrieved and are ranked with decreasing application context similarity. Before the top n ranked cases are displayed to the
user (cf. Fig. 7.28), this list is filtered by considering additional information about
the state of the given process instance I. Cases that cannot be directly applied to
I (i.e., for which I is not case compliant or whose application to I would have no
effect), but whose solution part can be adjusted, are highlighted together with the
specific change operations to be adapted. By contrast, cases which cannot be applied
directly and also cannot be adjusted are excluded from the list of similar cases.

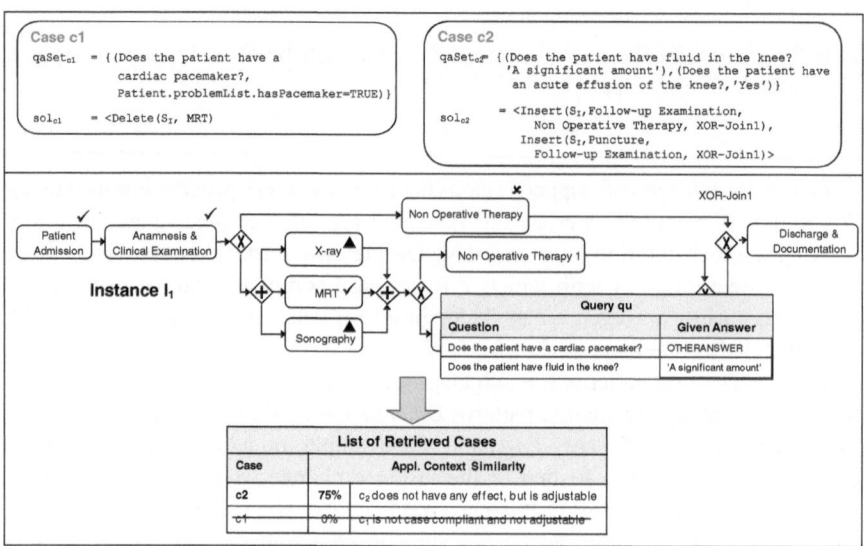

Fig. 7.28 Similar cases displayed to the user

Example 7.33 (Case Retrieval). Consider case–base $cb_S = \{c_1, c_2\}$, process instance I_1, and query qu as depicted in Fig. 7.28. For case c_1 we obtain $sim(c_1, qu) = 0$. Therefore, c_1 is eliminated from the list of similar cases. (Note that I_1 is also not case compliant with c_1.) In turn, for case c_2 we obtain $sim(c_2, qu) = 0.75$. As the application of c_2 (i.e., its solution part) to I would have no effect, the definition of its solution part needs to be adjusted (i.e., the two activities *Follow-Up Examination* and *Puncture* need to be inserted at a position other than the one specified in the solution part of c_2. Thus the respective case is highlighted for the user.

7.6.3.4 Case Reuse

If instance I is case compliant with case c, the user may reuse c directly. The change operations specified in the solution part of this case are then forwarded to the PAIS change component and are carried out by it. For this, in each change operation the placeholder for the instance-specific model S_I needs to be replaced by process instance I. As the reuse of a case necessitates case compliance, correctness and consistency of the process instance after change application can be ensured by the PAIS. Finally, case reuse leads to an increase in the case reuse counter $freq_c$ by 1.

> *Example 7.34 (Case Reuse).* Assume that case c_2 from Fig. 7.26 shall be applied to instance I. As I is case compliant with c_2, no case adjustment is needed and c_2 can be applied directly.

If the instance to be modified is not compliant with c, or this case does not have any effect on I, it can be adjusted prior to its reuse. For this, the case is cloned and then modified. Afterwards the newly created case is added to the case–base.

7.6.4 Concluding Remarks

We have described how ad hoc changes of process instances can be represented, retrieved, and reused. To effectively provide support for reusing cases, however, the quality of the case data maintained in the case–base is crucial. In particular, poor PAIS performance such as long dialogues and inaccurate case data can significantly limit user acceptance. Typically, cases are added by inexperienced end-users and not by process engineers. In addition, case–bases evolve over time. New cases may be added to it when exceptional situations occur, which have never been dealt with before. To ensure accuracy and improve overall performance, regular maintenance becomes increasingly crucial as the case–base grows.

In order to avoid reusing low quality cases, case performance has to be continuously monitored and evaluated. A corresponding approach is described in [353, 355]: To be able to evaluate case performance, for each case c a history $hist_c$ is maintained. Whenever c is applied to a process instance an entry e is added to the case history. Each history entry e refers to the process instance to which the case was applied. In addition, it contains a feedback score $fScore_e$, which either can be highly positive (2), positive (1), neutral (0), negative (-1), or highly negative (-2), reflecting the performance of the respective case. Optionally, a comment may be added to provide feedback on the performance of c. The overall reputation $rScore_c$ of case c corresponds to the average feedback score of the history entries from $hist_c$. While a high reputation score of a case is an indicator for its semantical correctness, negative feedback probably results from problems after performing the respective instance change. Negative feedback leads to immediate notification of the process engineer who may then deactivate the case to prevent its further reuse. The case itself remains in the PAIS to allow for learning from failures and to ensure traceability.

Further quality issues arising in connection with the described approach and related strategies are described in [353, 355, 358].

7.7   Automated Adaptation and Evolution of Process Instances

So far, focus has been on the situational handling of unanticipated exceptions (cf. Example 7.1) by end-users. For specific application scenarios (e.g., engineering processes), it is also required to automatically evolve single process instances during run-time (cf. Example 7.2). Approaches enabling automated process instance changes aim at reducing error-prone and costly manual ad hoc changes, and thus at relieving users from complex adaptations tasks. As a prerequisite for such automated changes, the PAIS must be able to automatically detect exceptional situations, derive the ad hoc change necessary to handle them, identify the process instance to be adapted, correctly apply the ad hoc change to this instance, and notify respective users about the change applied. ARule-based, case-based, and goal-based approaches, among others, exist for enabling such automated instance adaptations.

Rule-Based Approaches. ECA-based (Event-Condition-Action) approaches are suggested for automatically detecting exceptional situations and determining process instance adaptations required to handle these exceptions. In most approaches, adaptations are restricted to currently enabled and running activities, e.g., to abort, redo, or skip activity execution [60, 65] (see also Chap. 6 for basic techniques existing in this context). By contrast, AgentWork [229, 230] enables automated structural adaptations of the not-yet-entered regions of a running process instance (e.g., to add or delete activities) to cope with unplanned situations. Basic to this is a temporal ECA rule model that allows specifying process adaptations at an abstract level and independent from a particular process model. When an ECA rule fires during run-time (e.g., an incoming lab report indicates that a patient has abnormal blood values), temporal estimates are made to determine which parts of a running process instance are affected by the exception identified. These parts are then adapted immediately (predictive change) or—if this is not possible due to temporal uncertainty—at the time they are entered (reactive change). Based on the AgentWork approach, for example, an activity might be automatically added to a process instance when a certain event occurs and specific conditions are met. A similar approach is provided by SmartPM [173].

Case-Based Approaches. Case-based reasoning approaches for automatically adapting process instances to changing situations are suggested by [214, 215]. For this, a case–base representing past process adaptations is maintained, from which cases can be automatically reused in similar situations. For each process adaptation the original model S as well as the modified version S' together with a change request (describing the reasons for the change) are stored. In case an exception occurs, the case–base is searched for suitable past adaptations, which can then be automatically reused. To reuse a past adaptation, the change location is first determined (e.g., it is determined where to insert activities). Once an appropriate change location has been found, the change is automatically applied to the process instance to be changed.

Goal-based approaches, in turn, formalize process goals (e.g., process outputs) and automatically derive the process model (i.e., the activities to be performed as well as their execution order) based on which these goals can be achieved. In addition, if an exception (e.g., activity failure) occurs during run-time violating formal goals, the process instance model is adapted accordingly. In ACT [50], for example, simple instance adaptations are automatically performed if an activity failure leads to a goal violation; e.g., replacing a failed activity by an alternative one. In addition, EPOS [187] allows automatically adapting process instances when process goals change. Both approaches apply planning techniques to automatically derive a process model from goals, and to repair it during run-time if goals change. However, current planning methods do not cover all relevant business process scenarios since important aspects (e.g., treatment of loops, appropriate handling of data flow) are not adequately considered.

7.8 Duration of Ad hoc Changes

When applying an ad hoc change to a process instance, it must be decided whether change effects shall be kept permanently or be only of a temporary nature. This distinction between temporary and permanent changes is important in the context of long-running process instances and ad hoc changes which concern process model regions that may be executed more than once; e.g., when a loop enters its next iteration or a partial roll back (cf. Chap. 6) is performed. While permanent changes are valid until the completion of a process instance, the effects of temporary changes have to be undone in such cases. Generally, the integrated handling of both permanent and temporary ad hoc changes raises a number of challenges. In particular, the definition of a permanent change must not depend on any temporary change to avoid soundness violations in case the effects of the latter are undone during run-time. This requires advanced techniques for defining ad hoc changes as well as for managing them by the PAIS (see [255, 260] for more details).

In the context of loop-related process adaptations, for example, ADEPT differentiates between *loop-permanent* and *loop-temporary* changes [71, 265]. The latter arc only valid for the loop iteration in which the change is applied, but do not affect the behavior of future loop iterations. For example, if an activity is added to a loop body, it must be specified whether the insertion shall be only valid for the current loop iteration or for subsequent iterations as well. In the first case, the added activity is executed at most once and the temporary insertion is semantically undone (i.e., the activity is removed) when the loop enters its next iteration.

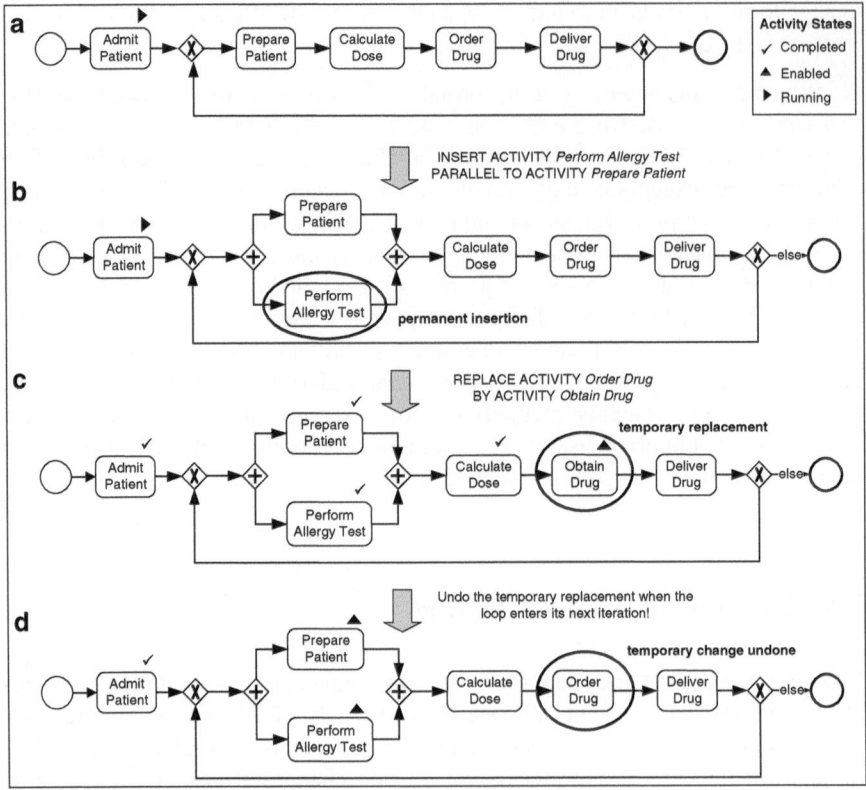

Fig. 7.29 Loop-permanent and loop-temporary ad hoc changes

Example 7.35 (Loop-permanent and Loop-temporary Process Instance Changes). Consider the medication cycle depicted in Fig. 7.29a. Assume that during the execution of activity *Admit Patient* it is decided that at each medication cycle a specific allergy test shall be performed in parallel with the preparation of the patient. To realize this loop-permanent change, activity *Perform Allergy Test* is added to the process instance (cf. Fig. 7.29b). Assume further that during the execution of one particular medication cycle a physician has to obtain the drug on his own since the patient arrived at a late hour after the central pharmacy of the hospital has closed. This exception is handled by temporarily replacing activity *Order Drug* by *Obtain Drug* (cf. Fig. 7.29c). Note that this ad hoc change is only valid for the current treatment cycle and therefore is undone when the next medication cycle takes place (cf. Fig. 7.29d).

7.9   Change Scope

Basically, ad hoc changes of a process instance may be applied to arbitrary regions of its corresponding process model unless model soundness or state compliance are violated. However, in many practical scenarios it is desirable to restrict the applicability of structural ad hoc changes to selected regions of a process model (see also Chap. 11). The following example sketches such an approach and discusses how it appears to the user.

Example 7.36 (Restricting Structural Ad hoc Changes to Predefined Parts of a Process Model). The *Weak Dependencies* approach allows changing predefined parts of a prespecified process model during run-time [152]. For this purpose, it differentiates between strong and weak dependencies. *Strong dependencies* are edges in the process model that must not be altered. *Weak dependencies*, in turn, allow users to insert activities during run-time. Figure 7.30a shows a process model with a weak dependency between A and B. During run-time, as illustrated in Fig. 7.30d, after executing A, the management task M is invoked. The user may then either insert additional activities or decide to complete the management task (if no additional activities are needed). In our example, the user decides to insert C and D in parallel with each other (cf. Fig. 7.30b). After having executed both activities, he adds another activity E to the model (cf. Fig. 7.30c). After its completion no further activities are needed and he completes the management task, which enables B.

7.10   Further Issues

This section discusses further issues which are relevant in the context of ad hoc changes: access control, concurrency control, traceability, and process compliance.

7.10.1   Controlling Access to Process Change Functions

Enabling ad hoc changes of process instances during run-time leads to increased process flexibility. This imposes several security issues as the PAIS becomes more vulnerable to misuse [77, 354]. Therefore, the application of ad hoc changes should be restricted to authorized users. An example of a respective access control framework is SecServ [354]. SecServ constitutes a security service tailored toward

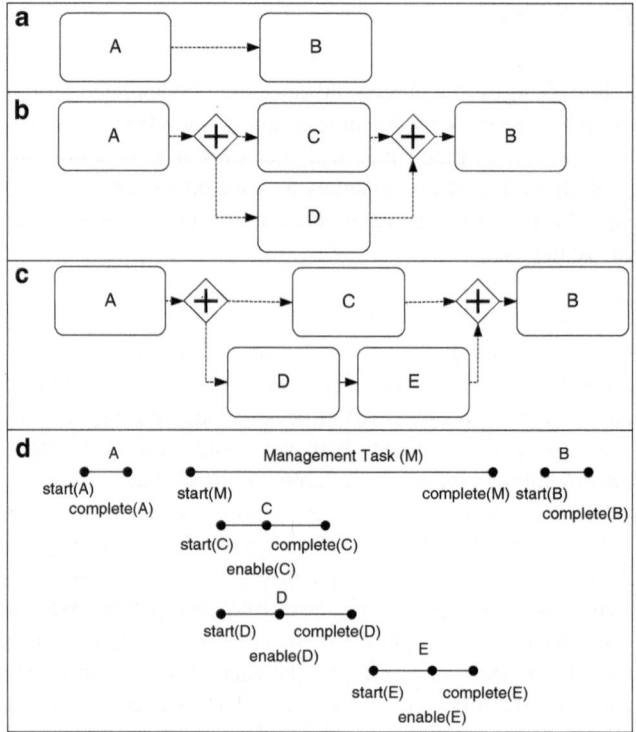

Fig. 7.30 Restricting structural changes to predefined process regions

the specific needs of adaptive PAISs. SecServ allows for both *user dependent* and *process type dependent* access rights. While the former restricts access to authorized users in order to avoid misuse (e.g., only users with role *physician* are authorized to insert the *X-ray* activity at the process instance level), the latter's access rights can be used to restrict certain changes to a particular process context (e.g., activity *Vacation Request* must not be added to a medical treatment process). SevServ supports the specification and validation of static, as well as dynamic constraints (i.e., constraints considering run-time data). For further details we refer to [354].

7.10.2   Controlling Concurrent Ad hoc Changes

A multiuser PAIS must be able to cope with concurrent process changes. For example, two users might want to apply different ad hoc changes to a particular process instance at the same time. If this is done in an uncontrolled manner, errors or inconsistencies (e.g., deadlock-causing cycles) might occur. Another problem is that the state of a process instance might proceed while an ad hoc change is applied concurrently to it. In the latter case any adaptive PAIS has to ensure that the state change does not violate state constraints required for the proper application of the intended ad hoc change (or, at the very least, the ad hoc change has to be prohibited in such a conflicting case).

The easiest way to avoid respective conflicts is to prohibit concurrent changes in general. This can be achieved, for example, by holding exclusive locks on a process instance when changing its structure or state; e.g., a process instance may not be allowed to proceed while applying an ad hoc change to it. WASA2 [364], for example, locks the entire process instance when applying an ad hoc change to it. Although this approach is easy to realize, it is usually too restrictive due to the long-term locks required; e.g., when a change is defined interactively by a user (cf. Sects. 7.5 and 7.6) which might block instance execution for a while. A more flexible approach would allow for concurrent changes of the structure and/or state of a process instance, while ensuring that this does not lead to errors or inconsistencies afterwards. Both, pessimistic and optimistic techniques [114] can be applied in this context to control such concurrent instance changes and to ensure their correctness. Pessimistic locking is an approach where the process instance to be modified is locked until the change is accomplished, while optimistic concurrency control does not hold a lock on the process instance, but checks for conflicts when finally committing changes. While ADEPT2 [261] supports concurrent ad hoc changes of a particular process instance based on optimistic techniques, locking is used in CAKE2 [218]. More precisely, the breakpoint mechanism provided by CAKE2 only suspends those parts of a process instance which have to be changed; i.e., parallel branches not affected by the change may still proceed with their execution.

7.10.3 *Ensuring Traceability of Ad hoc Changes*

As discussed in Chap. 3, traceability and accountability become fundamental issues in the context of ad hoc changes. To ensure traceability of a process instance with a dynamically changing structure, the adaptive PAIS must be able to restore both the model and the state of a process instance at any point in time. Generally, it is therefore not sufficient to merely log normal execution events (e.g., related to the start or completion of activities) in corresponding traces, but it also becomes necessary to store information about applied ad hoc changes in change logs [283, 292]. Further, it should be possible to semantically annotate logged changes (e.g., about the reasons and the context of the instance changes applied) as described in Sect. 7.6.2. The latter is important for analyzing ad hoc changes and to learn from them [293]. We will come back to related issues in Chap. 8 and show how respective log information can be utilized to foster monitoring, traceability, and learning of adaptive processes.

7.10.4   Ensuring Business Process Compliance

When dealing with correctness issues, we have so far focused on syntactical properties and behavioral soundness of a process model. In general, however, any prespecified process model also has to comply with semantic constraints—also denoted as *compliance rules*—stemming from a variety of sources such as standards, regulations, guidelines, corporate policies, and laws. For this purpose, techniques are required to ensure the compliance of a business process with respective constraints. In particular, this does not only constitute a build-time task, but it also has to be ensured that compliance rules are still met when applying ad hoc changes to a process instance. Respective issues and techniques will be discussed in Chap. 10.

7.11   Discussion

In spite of several success stories arising from the increasing use of PAISs [274] and the growing process orientation of enterprises [232], BPM and related technologies have not been adopted on the scale that was expected of them. A major reason for this has been the limited support of dynamic process changes which inhibits the ability of an organization to flexibly respond to an unanticipated exceptional situations. Thus, it has been widely recognized that a PAIS needs to provide run-time flexibility to its users (cf. Chap. 3). In Chap. 6 we have already discussed basic issues related to flexible work item handling; e.g., enabling users to dynamically reallocate a work item assigned to their worklists to other users if required. Furthermore, the exception handling patterns presented in Chap. 6 are well suited for dealing with anticipated exceptions. Opposed to this, the adequate handling of unanticipated exceptions often requires complex behavioral changes of single process instances during run-time. As shown in this chapter, these can be realized through structural ad hoc changes resulting in instance-specific process models to be maintained and executed by the PAIS.

However, any approach allowing for ad hoc changes will be not accepted in practice if PAIS robustness cannot be ensured. Early attempts at providing support for ad hoc changes that did not consider correctness, robustness, and security were not successful. Consequently, the described adaptation patterns as well as correctness notions can be considered as basic ingredients of any adaptive PAIS. As we will see in Chap. 10, however, it is not sufficient to focus only on syntactical issues and behavioral soundness in the context of ad hoc changes. In addition, it has to be ensured that these changes do not violate compliance rules; i.e., semantic integrity constraints have to be taken into account as well as when deciding on the applicability of ad hoc changes.

When designing a PAIS that supports ad hoc changes, there obviously exists a trade-off between the expressiveness of the process modeling language used and the support provided for ad hoc changes. For example, the ADEPT2 process management technology [271] has been designed with the goal enabling the latter.

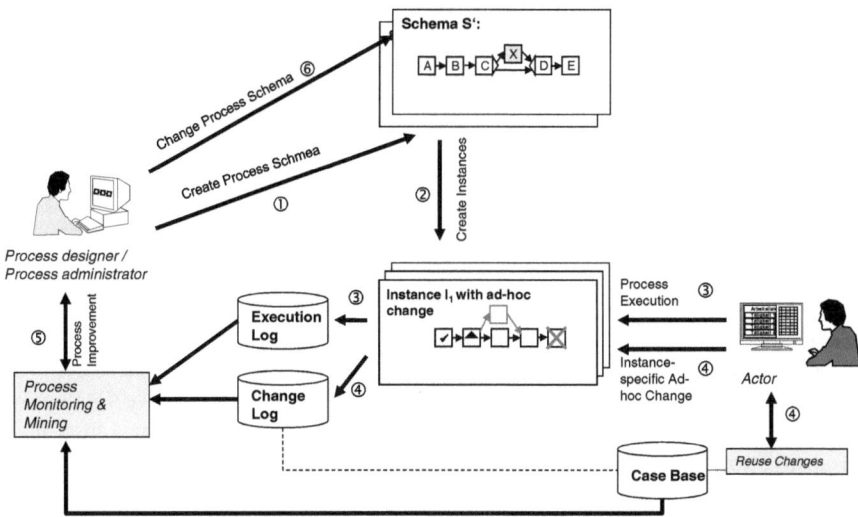

Fig. 7.31   Revised process life cycle

To allow for an efficient implementation of adaptation patterns, well-elaborated restrictions on the process modeling language have been made. Similar restrictions in terms of expressiveness hold for other approaches supporting ad hoc changes (e.g., CAKE2 [218] and WASA2 [364]). On the other hand, YAWL is a reference implementation for workflow patterns and therefore allows for a high degree of expressiveness [135]. Dynamic adaptations as described in this chapter have not yet been addressed in YAWL, and their implementation would be far more difficult due to the high expressiveness of the process modeling language used by YAWL. In this context, it is noteworthy to mention that, in practice, often only a small subset of the workflow patterns supported by YAWL is required [374].

Altogether, the described ability of adaptive PAISs for enabling ad hoc changes in a controlled, correct, and secure way leads to a revised process life cycle (cf. Fig. 7.31) when compared to the one presented in Chap. 2. At build-time an initial representation of a business process is created either by explicitly modeling the process (based on analysis results) or by discovering process models through the mining of execution logs (cf. Chap. 8) (1). New process instances can be derived at run-time from the prespecified process model (2). In general, process instances are executed according to the original process model they were derived from, and (nonautomated) activities are assigned to process participants to perform the respective activities (3). However, when unanticipated exceptional situations occur during run-time, process participants may deviate from the prespecified model by applying ad hoc changes (4). While execution logs record information about the start and completion of activities as well as their ordering (3), process changes are recorded in change logs and may be semantically represented as cases (4). The latter also enables the reuse of ad hoc changes in similar exceptional situations.

The analysis of respective logs by a process engineer and/or process intelligence tools allows the discovery of malfunctions or bottlenecks. This information often results in an evolution of the process model (6). We will show in Chap. 9 how such process model evolution can be effectively accomplished in an adaptive PAIS.

7.12 Summary

This chapter emphasized the need for adapting the control flow schema of single process instances during run-time in order to cope with the unanticipated exceptions of business processes. We discussed fundamental issues that emerge in the context of ad hoc changes and showed how they are addressed by adaptive PAISs. We presented process adaptation patterns for defining ad hoc changes at a high level of abstraction and discussed their advantages in comparison to low-level change primitives. We additionally discussed the importance of considering the state of process instances when applying ad hoc changes to them. In this context we introduced state compliance as a widely used correctness notion for enabling dynamic process changes, and we provided relaxations of it in order to also consider more complex control flow patterns (i.e., loop structures). We further showed how users can be supported in reusing previous ad hoc changes in similar exceptional situations and how process instances may be dynamically adapted during run-time. Finally, we discussed other important features supported by an adaptive PAIS.

Altogether, the ability to support ad hoc changes in a controlled, correct, and secure manner can be considered as a fundamental driver for enabling flexible and dynamic processes in a variety of application domains. Furthermore, by providing support for ad hoc changes, users are no longer forced to bypass the PAIS when unanticipated exceptions occur. Still there is need for more sophisticated interaction support enabling end-users to define ad hoc changes in an intuitive and easy way. Among others, this requires adequate abstractions of process models and process instances, respectively, based on which end-users can easily define ad hoc changes. For example, updatable process views might be used to hide unnecessary process details from end-users, while still enabling them to define ad hoc changes based on abstracted process structures. Furthermore, domain- and application-specific user interfaces are needed to foster the intuitive definition of ad hoc changes in a particular application context in the best possible way. Finally, it has been shown that more work on automated dynamic process changes is needed.

Exercises

7.1. Adaptation Patterns Versus Change Primitives
Discuss the use of adaptation patterns versus change primitives.

7.2. Modifying Business Processes

Cheetah is a tool that provides support for defining and changing BPMN process models based on either change primitives or high-level adaptation patterns. A link for downloading the Cheetah platform can be found at this book's web site.

(a) Perform the modification task described in Sect. 7.3.3 with change primitives using the Cheetah platform.
(b) Perform the modification task described in Sect. 7.3.3 with adaptation patterns using the Cheetah platform.

7.3. Modeling and Modifying Business Processes

In the following the pre-take-off process for a general aviation flight under visual flight rules (VFR) is described. Perform the modeling and modification tasks described in the following with both change primitives and adaptation patterns using Cheetah (cf. Exercise 7.2).

Modeling Task: Before conducting a general aviation flight the pilot first has to perform a weather check. Optionally, she can file the flight plan. This is followed by a preflight inspection of the airplane. For large airports the pilot calls clearance delivery to get the engine start clearance. If an airport has a tower, the pilot has to contact ground to get taxi clearance, otherwise she has to announce taxiing. This is followed by taxiing to the run-up area and then run-up the engine to ensure that the airplane is ready for the flight. If the airport has a tower, it is contacted to get take-off clearance, otherwise take-off intentions have to be announced. Finally, the pre take-off process finishes with the take-off of the airplane.

Modification Task 1: If the weather conditions are below safety limits, no flight can be conducted and the process has to be cancelled.

Modification Task 2: During the preflight inspections the pilot can detect problems with the airplane. If the problems are severe the flight is immediately cancelled. If the airplane can move under its own power it then taxis to the repair station. Alternatively, the airplane is either towed to the repair station or a mechanician comes to the airplane. Depending on how long the repair activities take, the flight is cancelled, or restarted with a second check of the weather conditions, or proceeds with the preflight airplane activity.

Modification Task 3: Problems with the airplane can also be detected during the run-up checks conducted by the pilot. In this case the pilot has to contact ground and ask for taxiing clearance to taxi back to the repair station, assuming that the airplane can still move under its own power. If the latter is not possible, the pilot informs ground about the need for being towed to the repair station. If the airport does not have a tower and the airplane can move under its own power, the pilot announces taxiing back instead. Depending on how long the repair activity takes, the flight is cancelled, or the flight is restarted with a weather check, or the pilot annotates the flightplane before proceeding with the pre-flight airplane activity.

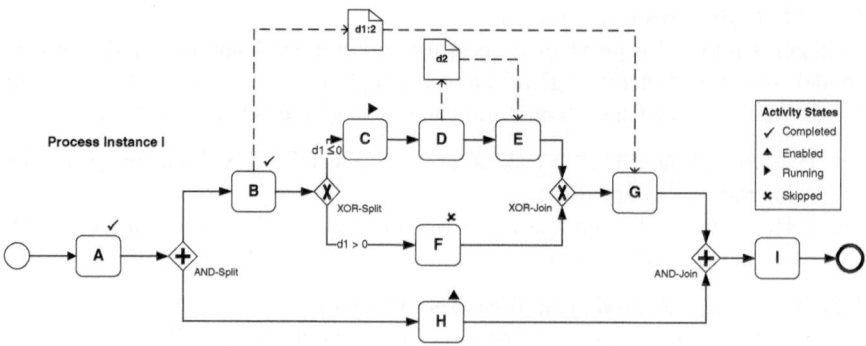

partial execution trace σ_I = < start(A), complete(A), start(B), complete(B) [d1=2], start(C) >

Fig. 7.32 Process instance to be adapted

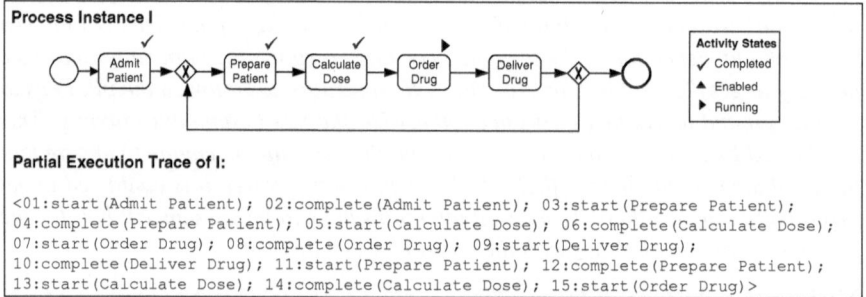

Fig. 7.33 A process instance containing a loop

7.4. Applying Ad hoc Changes to a Process Instance

Consider the process instance depicted in Fig. 7.32. Which of the following ad hoc changes can be applied to *I* and which not? Explain your answer and draw the resulting process instance (i.e., perform the required model transformations and state adaptations) if the ad hoc change is possible!

(a) Serially insert activity X between node AND-Split and activity H.
(b) Delete activity H.
(c) Delete activity B.
(d) Swap activities D and E; i.e., move E to the position between C and D.
(e) Insert activity Y in parallel with activity C.
(f) Move activity G to the position between activities C and D.

7.5. Applying Ad hoc Changes to a Process Instance containing a Loop

Consider process instance *I* and its (partial) execution trace depicted in Fig. 7.33. Assume that an activity *Perform Allergy Test* shall be inserted in parallel with activity *Deliver Drug* in the model of *I*.

(a) Determine the loop-purged execution trace of I.

(b) Is I *(relaxed) state compliant* with the process model resulting from this ad hoc change? Explain your answer.

(c) Explain why the described ad hoc change can be applied to I and draw the process instance resulting from this.

(d) Assume that the conducted ad hoc change is loop-temporary (cf. Sect. 7.8). How does the process instance look like when the depicted loop enters its next iteration during run-time?

7.6. Adaptation Patterns

In this chapter only a subset of the adaptation patterns presented in [352] has been introduced.

(a) To learn more about other adaptation patterns study [352] and visit the book web site.

(b) Have a look at [352]. Which of the evaluated PAISs support adaptation patterns AP1 (Insert Process Fragment) and AP2 (Delete Process Fragment) respectively?

7.7. Change Features

Answer the following questions.

(a) One way to control concurrent changes on a process instance is to hold an exclusive lock on this instance during the definition of the ad hoc change. Why is this approach not applicable in practice?

(b) Give an example of an uncontrolled ad hoc change of a process instance that might affect proper completion of the instance.

(c) Which other process model perspectives might have to be adapted when applying the described adaptation patterns to the control flow schema of a process model?

(d) Consider the process instance from Fig. 7.3a: Determine a bias and the distance (cf. Definition 7.2) between this process instance and the one from Fig. 7.3b (and Fig. 7.3c respectively) assuming that the depicted change is accomplished with the adaptation patterns described.

Chapter 8
Monitoring and Mining Flexible Processes

Abstract Accountability and traceability are important requirements any flexible PAIS needs to fulfill. This chapter describes how execution and change logs can be used to restore the structure and state of a process instance for any given point in time. The information recorded in event and change logs, however, can not only be exploited to ensure accountability and traceability, but used for analysis purposes as well. This chapter discusses different process mining techniques for analyzing flexible business processes. In particular, it presents techniques for the mining of execution logs and change logs. Finally, advanced techniques for analyzing process variant collections in the absence of a change log are introduced.

8.1 Introduction

As discussed in the previous chapters, adaptive PAISs operate on prespecified process models that may have to be adapted at different levels. First, at build-time, a reference process model may have to be configured to fit to a particular business or application context (cf. Chap. 5). Second, to cope with unanticipated exceptions, at run-time, the execution of process instances may spawn ad hoc changes resulting in *instance-specific process variants* (cf. Chap. 7).

Accountability and traceability are fundamental requirements for such flexible processes (cf. Chap. 3). Like traditional PAISs, an adaptive PAIS maintains *execution logs* recording the *sequence of activities* executed for each process instance. In addition, an adaptive PAIS manages *change logs* recording the *sequence of change operations* imposed on the prespecified process model when configuring a process model or changing a particular process instance. Based on this log information, it becomes possible to restore the structure as well as the state of a particular process instance from any given point in time. The information from execution and change logs, however, can be also exploited for enabling process analyses (cf. Fig. 8.1). In particular, integrating process analysis techniques into an adaptive PAIS by way of feedback cycles offers promising perspectives. For example, *process*

M. Reichert and B. Weber, *Enabling Flexibility in Process-Aware Information Systems*, 219
DOI 10.1007/978-3-642-30409-5_8, © Springer-Verlag Berlin Heidelberg 2012

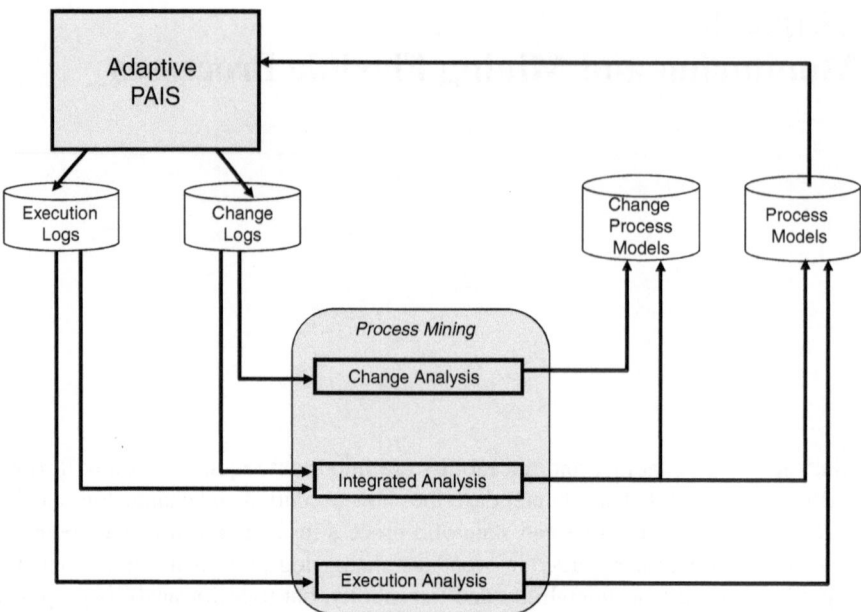

Fig. 8.1 Mining flexible processes

mining techniques that inspect *execution logs* can pinpoint parts of a prespecified process model to be changed, e.g., to discover paths which have never been executed and hence are obsolete. In this way, potential refactoring options for prespecified process models can be identified [75, 351]. Furthermore, mining techniques can also make use of the information from *change logs* or *process variant collections*. For example, respective change analyses allow determining common and popular process variants for each process type, which may then be promoted to replace the original process model (cf. Chap. 9). When utilizing process mining techniques for the consistent design and implementation of feedback cycles in an adaptive PAIS, the latter provides an unprecedented degree of user guidance and autonomous administration.

This chapter deals with the monitoring and mining of flexible processes. Section 8.2 introduces execution and change logs maintained by adaptive PAISs and enabling traceability. Section 8.3 then shows how to analyze the behavior of flexible processes through the mining of execution logs, while Sect. 8.4 deals with the structural analysis of flexible processes through the mining of change logs. More advanced techniques for mining the process variants resulting from either process configurations at build-time or ad hoc changes during run-time are presented in Sect. 8.5. In particular, the latter techniques can be also applied in the absence of change logs. Finally, the chapter closes with a summary in Sect. 8.6.

8.2   Execution and Change Logs

As emphasized in Chap. 3, accountability and traceability are important requirements any flexible PAIS needs to fulfill. For this purpose, executed activities have to
be logged in an *execution log* in order to allow process owners to trace back which
activities were performed in the context of a particular process instance. Moreover,
in connection with ad hoc changes the PAIS has to keep track of conducted changes
by registering them in a *change log*.

Execution logs should at least contain data about (1) the *events* that occurred
during process execution (e.g., start and completion of activities), (2) the *process
instance* an event belongs to, and (3) the *ordering* of these events. The events related
to a particular process instance are also referred to as an *execution trace* as defined
in Chap. 4. Moreover, execution logs may optionally contain additional information
like timestamps, user information (i.e., who performed an activity), and data object
histories (i.e., which data object values were written and read by which activities)
[63]. *Change logs*, in turn, have a structure similar to that of execution logs. Instead
of execution events, however, change logs comprise information about (1) the
applied changes, (2) the corresponding change transaction (which may aggregate
several changes), and (3) the process instance these changes refer to.

Example 8.1 (Execution and Change Log).   Figure 8.2a depicts the process
model of the cruciate rupture treatment process introduced in Chap. 4. In
addition, Fig. 8.2b highlights a particular process instance including its
process model, the ad hoc changes applied to it (i.e., its *bias*), and its
current execution state. Furthermore, Fig. 8.2c shows the execution log of this
particular process instance including information about the activity name, the
event type (i.e., start or complete), the responsible user, and the timestamp
of the event. The last entry of the depicted execution log, for example,
comprises a start event of activity *Puncture* (of the patient's knee joint) by
user `Helen` at `2007/09/12 11:21`. When analyzing the execution log
depicted in Fig. 8.2c, it can also be seen that there is no log entry for activity
MRT, which has been dynamically deleted for the depicted instance (see
Chap. 7 for a discussion of this change scenario). In addition, the execution
log comprises events of activities *Follow-up Examination* and *Puncture*. Both
are not part of process model *S*, but were dynamically inserted during run-
time (cf. Fig. 8.2b).

Additional information about these changes can be obtained from the
change log maintained for this process instance as depicted in Fig. 8.2d.
This change log comprises two change transactions with a total of three
change operations. The first change transaction consists of a single change
operation which deleted activity *MRT*. The second change transaction, in turn,

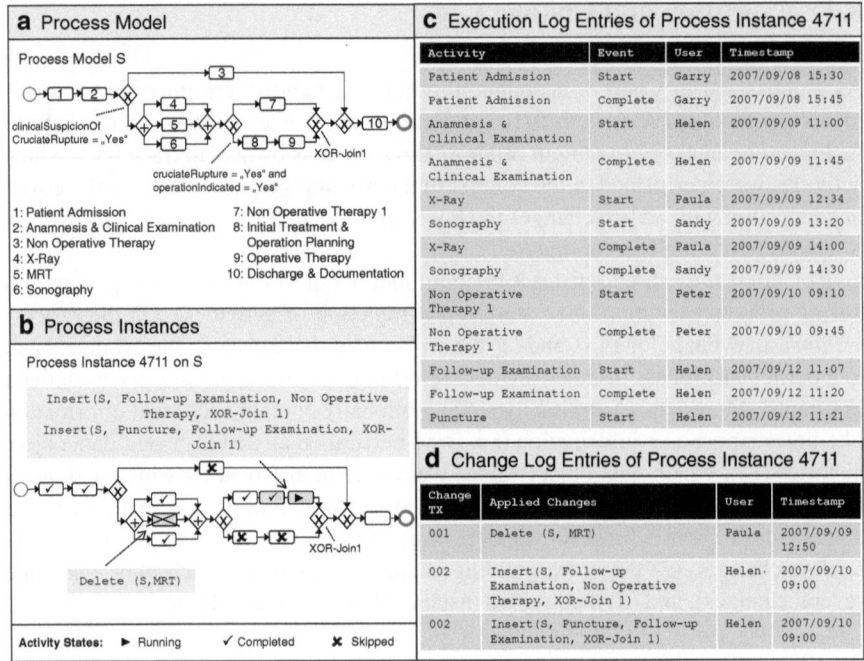

Fig. 8.2 A process instance and selected parts of its execution and change log

comprises two change operations that inserted the two activities *Follow-up Examination* and *Puncture*.

Execution and change logs are complementary to each other and cannot be interchanged [183]. Consider, for example, the missing events of activity *MRT* in the execution log. If only process model *S* and the execution log are given, the applied change operations cannot be completely determined. An option to obtain a respective execution log would be to delete activity *MRT*. Another one is to make activity *MRT* optional. Consequently, in addition to execution logs, change logs are needed to enable full traceability. When being used in combination, execution and change logs allow ensuring traceability and the ability to trace back to find which structure and state a particular process instance had at a given point in time.

Example 8.2 (Traceability based on Execution and Change Logs). Based on the original process model *S* from Fig. 8.2a, as well as the execution and change logs from Fig. 8.2c and Fig. 8.2d, the structure and state of process instance 4711 can be restored from any point in time. Figure 8.3 illustrates this for three different points in time. At 10:30 on 2007/09/09 activity *1:Patient Admission* was completed (see the first two entries of the execution log) resulting in activity *2:Anamnesis & Clinical Examination* being enabled. To restore the structure and state of instance 4711 at 12:51 the same day, the first five entries of the execution log, as well as the first change transaction recorded in the change log, have to be replayed in the order in which they occur in the log. In the resulting instance snapshot, activity *4:X-Ray* is running, activity *6:Sonography* is enabled, and activity *5:MRT* is deleted. At 09:46 on 2007/09/10, in turn, activities *4:X-Ray*, *6:Sonography* and *7:Non Operative Therapy 1* were completed and activities *11:Follow-up Examination* and *12:Puncture* were inserted. In the resulting instance snapshot, activity *11:Follow-up Examination* is enabled.

The execution and change logs of an adaptive PAIS can be used not only for process monitoring and for ensuring traceability, but also for analysis and diagnosis purposes (cf. Fig. 8.1) using process mining techniques [6, 25]. The mining of execution logs in the context of flexible processes (e.g., with the aim of discovering process models) is discussed in Sect. 8.3. Section 8.4 then elaborates on techniques for mining change logs and biased instances to discover change process models and to learn from instance changes.

8.3 Mining Execution Logs

As previously mentioned, information captured in execution logs can be used for analyzing the actual behavior of flexible processes. Analysis techniques provided by contemporary process mining tools (e.g., ProM) can be divided into the following three categories: *discovery*, *conformance*, and *extensions* [6].

- *Discovery* techniques presume the presence of an execution log which is then mined. Most prominent in this context are *control flow mining* algorithms which are able to discover process models by extracting information from such an execution log [6, 11]. Particularly interesting in the context of flexible processes are recently developed techniques for analyzing evolving processes, i.e., processes that change over time [56, 192]. To improve process discovery, these techniques try to identify different versions of the process. Discovery techniques can then be applied to each of the versions separately. Techniques related to the organization perspective, in turn, comprise algorithms for discovering social networks [20, 333], organizational structures [333], or staff assignment rules [197].

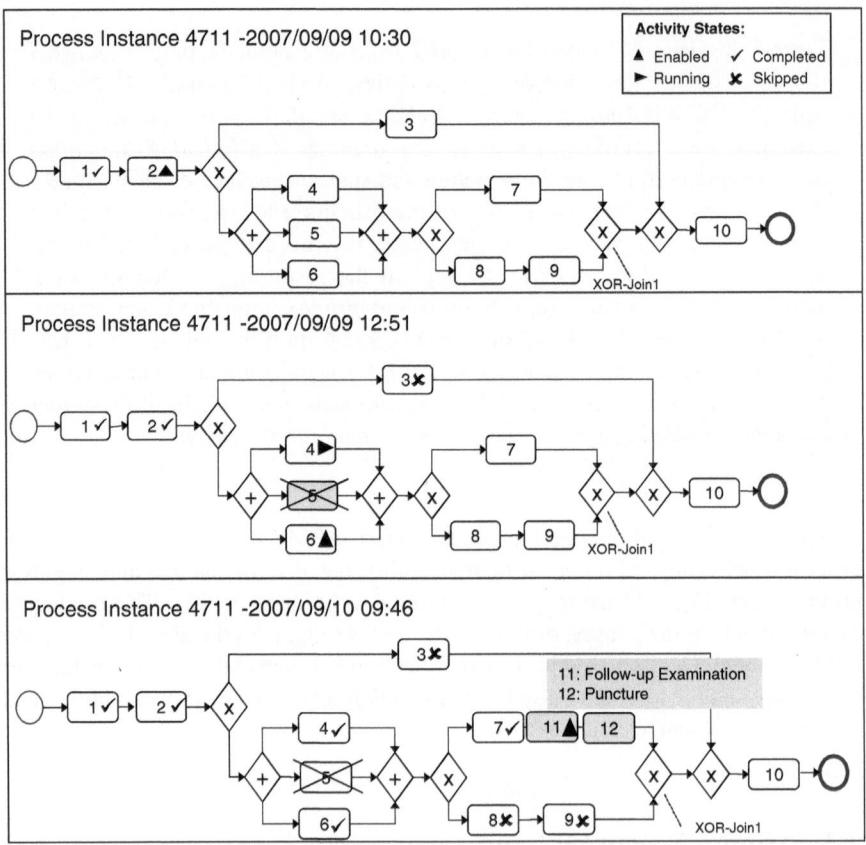

Fig. 8.3 Restoring the structure and state of a process instance

- *Conformance* techniques, in turn, analyze whether or not the process instances captured in the execution log follow prescribed behavior or rules. Using *conformance checking*, for example, it can be assessed in how far an execution log matches a given process model. In particular, discrepancies can be highlighted [305]. Using a model checker, in turn, it can verify whether certain properties hold for a particular log [10].
- *Extension algorithms* enhance an existing process model based on information from an execution log. *Decision mining*, for example, provides a technique for enhancing a (discovered) process model with information about transition conditions [304].

In the following pages, discovery and conformance techniques are applied to adaptive processes, i.e., process instances created from a prespecified process model, while deviating from it through ad hoc changes (cf. Chap. 7). To demonstrate different discovery and conformance techniques the open source process mining toolset ProM[1] is used, which offers support for a wide variety of process mining techniques. Our intention is to give a rather broad overview on available analysis techniques and their characteristics. For algorithmic details we refer interested readers to the respective literature [6].

8.3.1 Process Discovery

In the context of adaptive processes, deviations between the behavior prescribed by a process model and that taking place in reality can occur (cf. Chap. 7). In this context, control flow mining techniques can be used to discover a process model reflecting the actual behavior. Unlike the original process model, the discovered model additionally reflects behavioral changes due to ad hoc deviations from the prespecified process model at run-time. Example 8.3 illustrates the insights one can gain when analyzing execution logs with a heuristic miner.

Example 8.3 (Analyzing Execution Logs using a Heuristic Miner). Figure 8.4a shows the original process model for treating cruciate ruptures, while Fig. 8.4b highlights the results of process discovery using a *heuristic miner* [361] and taking a log with 1,000 process instances as input. Figure 8.4b was generated using ProM V6. Thereby, default settings have been used for most thresholds; for the dependency threshold a value of 85 has been applied. Note that for better readability the figure has been redrawn.

Regarding the 1,000 process instances, in 527 cases the respective patient could be treated with a *Non Operative Therapy*, while in the remaining 473 instances additional medical tests were required. Activities *X-Ray* and *Sonography* were performed for all 473 process instances, while activity *MRT* was apparently only executed for 228 process instances. According to the process model depicted in Fig. 8.4a, activities *X-Ray*, *Sonography*, and *MRT* are part of a parallel branch and should therefore be executed equally as often. Activity *MRT*, however, was executed less frequently compared to the other two activities. This suggests that activity *MRT* was skipped (i.e., deleted) for 245 instances. Furthermore, 227 out of 473 instances required an *Operative Therapy*, while for 246 instances, activity *Non Operative Therapy 1* was performed. From these 246 instances, 132 had some complications and required a *Follow-up Examination* including a *Puncture*; again this constitutes a deviation from the prespecified model. Both activities *Follow-Up Examination* and *Puncture* constitute additional activities when compared

---

[1] www.processmining.org.

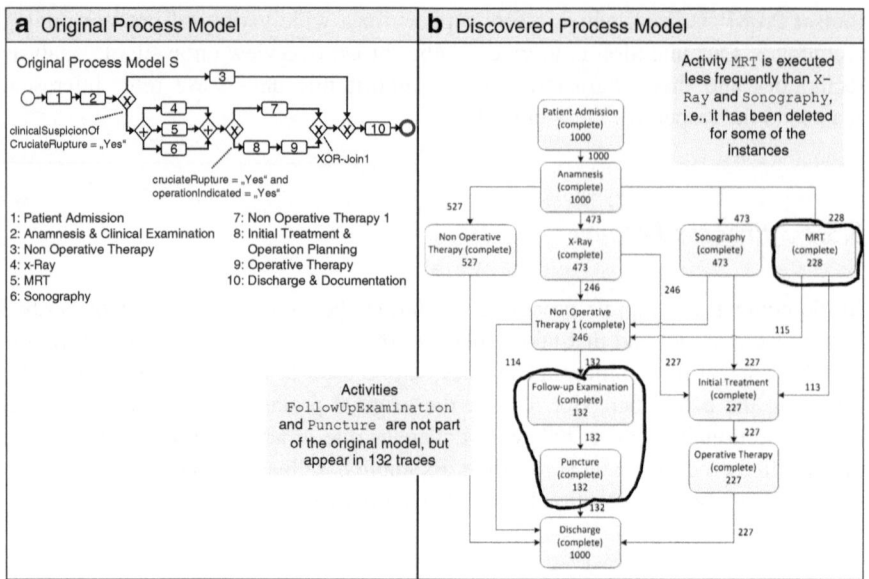

Fig. 8.4 Process discovery analyzing execution logs using heuristic miner

to the original process model from Fig. 8.4b. All 1,000 instances ended with activity *Discharge*.

While the discovered process model provides some insights into how the cruciate rupture treatment process was actually executed, it is not apparent how closely the conducted ad hoc changes are related and what the most frequent paths through the process look like. Using the *Performance Sequence Diagram Analysis* plug-in provided by the ProM process mining toolset, however, these most frequent paths through the model can be determined and visualized (cf. Example 8.4).

Example 8.4 (Performance Sequence Diagram Analysis). Figure 8.5 highlights the seven most frequent paths through the process, which are denoted as *execution patterns* in this example. For better readability, a visualization slightly different from that obtained from ProM is chosen; activities executed in parallel are displayed below each other like activities *MRT*, *X-Ray*, and *Sonography* in Execution Pattern 2.

Execution Pattern 0 is the most frequent path with 527 process instances. It comprises activities *Patient Admission*, *Anamnesis*, *Non Operative Therapy*, and *Discharge*. This pattern and the Execution Pattern 2 (113 instances)

Pattern 0	Patient Adm. → Anamnesis → Non Op. Therapy → Discharge	527
Pattern 1	Patient Adm. → Anamnesis → X-Ray → Initial Treatment → Operative Therapy → Discharge ⬊ Sono. ⬈	114
Pattern 2	Patient Adm. → Anamnesis → X-Ray → Initial Treatment → Operative Therapy → Discharge ⬊ Sono. ⬈ ⬊ MRT ⬈	113
Pattern 3	Patient Adm. → Anamnesis → X-Ray → Non Op. Therapy 1 → Follow-up Ex. → Puncture → Discharge ⬊ Sono. ⬈	71
Pattern 4	Patient Adm. → Anamnesis → X-Ray → Non Op. Therapy 1 → Follow-up Ex. → Puncture → Discharge ⬊ Sono. ⬈ ⬊ MRT ⬈	61
Pattern 5	Patient Adm. → Anamnesis → X-Ray → Non Op. Therapy 1 → Discharge ⬊ Sono. ⬈	60
Pattern 6	Patient Adm. → Anamnesis → X-Ray → Non Op. Therapy 1 → Discharge ⬊ Sono. ⬈ ⬊ MRT ⬈	54

Fig. 8.5   Output of a performance sequence diagram analysis

and Execution Pattern 6 (54 instances) are supported by the original process model. The remaining four execution patterns constitute deviations from the original process model. In Execution Pattern 1 (114 instances), Execution Pattern 3 (71 instances), and Execution Pattern 5 (60 instances) activity *MRT* is missing. Execution Pattern 3 (71 instances) and Execution Pattern 4 (61 instances), in turn, both comprise the additional activities *Follow-up Examination* and *Puncture*. A combination of both changes (i.e., deletion of activity *MRT* and insertion of activities *Follow-up Examination* and *Puncture*) can be found in Execution Pattern 3.

8.3.2   Conformance Checking

Conformance checking is a technique to investigate discrepancies between a process model and an execution log [305]. Example 8.5 illustrates its application.

Example 8.5 (Conformance Checking). Using the *Conformance Checker* plug-in of ProM to analyze the execution log of the cruciate rupture treatment

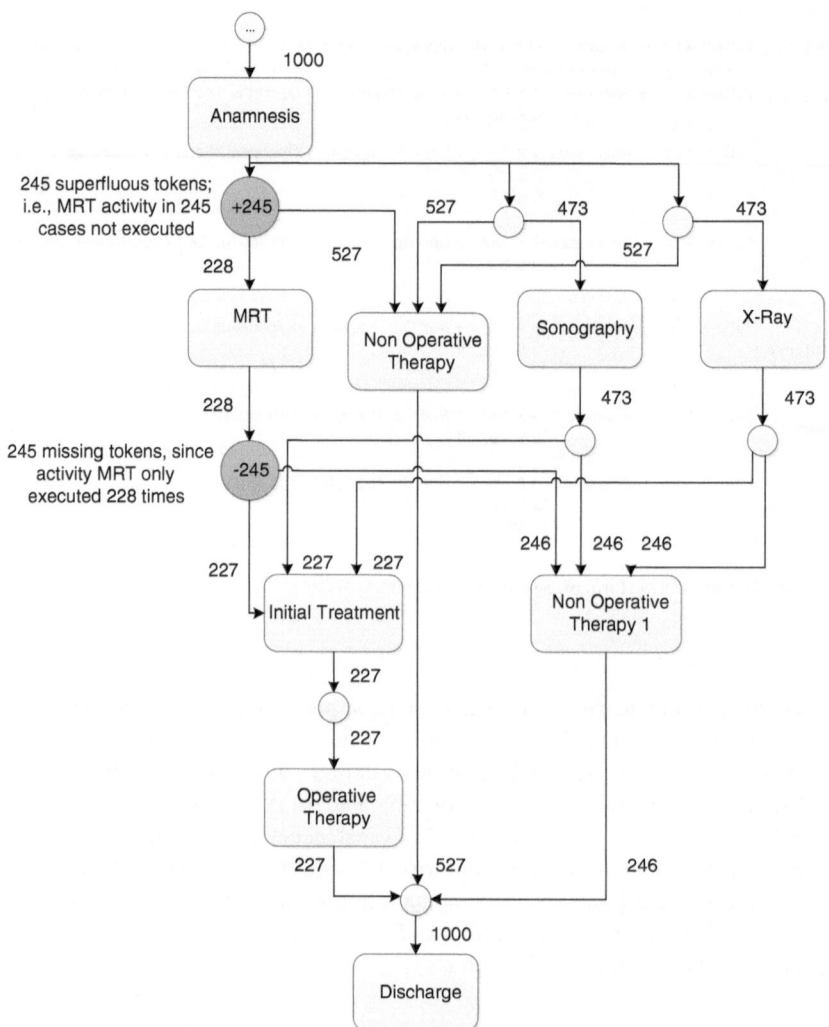

Fig. 8.6 Conformance checking

process (cf. Example 8.3), discrepancies between the original process model and the log can be detected (cf. Fig. 8.6). In particular, it can be seen that 245 process instances (those for which activity *MRT* was deleted) cannot be replayed on the original process model. The insertion of activities *Follow-up Examination* and *Puncture*, however, does not become visible using conformance checking, leading to only a partial picture of the conducted ad hoc changes.

Another option to check for deviations of an execution log from the original model is provided by model checkers like *LTL Checker* [10] or *Sciff Checker* [220], which can be used to check whether certain properties hold for the log. The *Performance Sequence Diagram Analysis* depicted in Fig. 8.5 reveals that the most frequent execution patterns consist of only a single ad hoc change. Using LTL Checker, for example, it can be seen whether there are process instances to which more than one ad hoc change was applied and—if yes—how often the insertion of *Follow-up Examination* and activity *Puncture* as well as the deletion of activity *MRT* co-occurred. Applying LTL Checker to our execution log shows that from the 1,000 process instances in the execution log, 71 instances comprise both ad hoc changes. LTL Checker and Sciff Checker can also be used to check a posteriori whether the conducted changes are compliant with existing business rules and regulations. For example, it can be determined whether the changes have been conducted by authorized persons. Details regarding compliance issues are discussed in Chap. 10.

8.4 Mining Change Logs

As discussed in Chap. 7, adaptive PAISs enable users or software agents to dynamically adapt individual process instances in order to cope with unanticipated exceptions. Section 8.3 has already shown how such dynamically changed process instances can be analyzed through the mining of *execution logs* and what can be discovered from this. In addition, this section presents analysis techniques exploiting the information captured in *change logs*. As will be shown, such change analysis can be also based on existing process mining techniques. Since the latter have not been designed with adaptive processes in mind, and focus instead on the analysis of execution logs, customizations become necessary.

Analyzing ad hoc changes of a process model provides insights in whether or not corresponding process instances were actually executed as planned [56, 120]. In particular, process engineers are interested in understanding when and how users deviated from a prespecified process at the instance level, and what were the reasons for such deviations (e.g., physicians have to document the context and reasons of any deviation from a standard treatment procedure). From this information the process engineers want to learn how to optimize and evolve the process model in the PAIS such that process support better meets users' needs. For this purpose, the changes applied at the instance level have to be aggregated and visualized in an appropriate way; e.g., in terms of a *change (meta) process model*. This section presents mining techniques for discovering such knowledge (i.e., change process models) from change logs [120, 121].

8.4.1   Anatomy of Process Changes

Instance-specific variants of a prespecified process model result from the stepwise application of a *sequence of change operations* to this process model (cf. Chap. 7). In this context, we assume that all changes related to the process instances of a particular process type are recorded in the same *change log*. Section 8.2 has already informally described how the entries of such a change log look like from the perspective of a single process instance (cf. Fig. 8.2). This section additionally provides a formal definition of the notion of change log, but abstracts from details not required by the change analysis techniques presented; e.g., these techniques do not consider the information about the users who applied the changes.

In addition, this section introduces the notion of a *change log instance*. It corresponds to the sequence of change operations applied to the model of a particular process instance in total. Note that a change log instance may comprise several change operations of the same or of different change transactions (e.g., in case changes were applied to the respective process instance by different users or at different points in time). Since the granularity level of change transactions is not required in the presented analysis techniques, Definition 8.1 abstracts from change transactions and considers sequences of change operations instead.

> **Definition 8.1 (Change Log and Change Log Instance).** Let $\mathscr{P}$ be the set of all process models and $\mathscr{C}$ be the set of possible process changes, i.e., any process change Δ is an element of $\mathscr{C}$. Then:
>
> - A *change log instance* cL is a sequence of process changes performed on some initial process model $PS \in \mathscr{P}$, i.e., $cL \in \mathscr{C}^*$ (where $\mathscr{C}^*$ is the set of all possible sequences over $\mathscr{C}$).
> - A *change log* L is a set of change log instances, i.e., $L \subseteq \mathscr{C}^*$.

Note that Definition 8.1 abstracts from whether changes are applied at the type or instance level. In the following pages, we will restrict our considerations to the analysis of instance change logs. Hence, we assume that a change log comprises all change events (i.e., applied change operations) related to the process instances of a particular type; i.e., process instances created from the same prespecified process model.

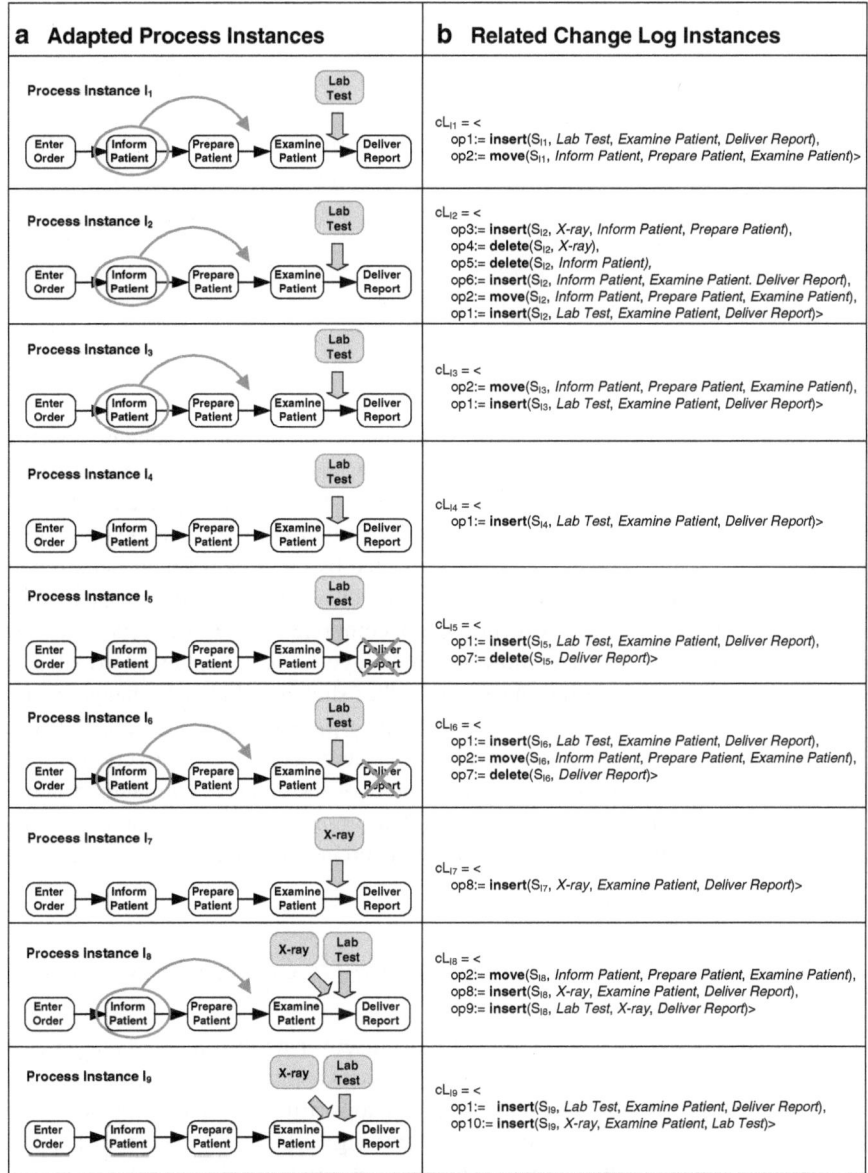

Fig. 8.7 Changed process instances and related change log instances

Example 8.6 (Change Log).   Figure 8.7a shows nine process instances that
were created from the same process model consisting of a sequence of five

activities: *Enter Order*, *Inform Patient*, *Prepare Patient*, *Examine Patient*, and *Deliver Report*. To each of these nine process instances a number of changes have been applied. Figure 8.7b shows the related change log. It comprise nine change log instances cL_{I1}–cL_{I9} of which each reflects the sequence of change operations applied to the respective process instance depicted on the left. The first change log instance (i.e. cL_{I1}), for example, consists of two consecutive change operations $op1$ and $op2$. While $op1$ inserted activity *Lab Test* between activities *Examine Patient* and *Deliver Report*, $op2$ moved activity *Inform Patient* one position to the right, between *Prepare Patient* and *Examine Patient*.

Regarding Example 8.6, the change events recorded in the change log are grouped with respect to the specific process instance they refer to, i.e., applied change operations are subdivided into *change process instances* represented by corresponding change log instances (cf. Fig. 8.7). Furthermore, the change operations applied to a particular process instance are sorted by the order of their occurrence. Note that this structuring of a change log fits well with the common organization of execution logs. While an execution log comprises the events related to the execution of process instances, however, a change log contains events related to structural changes of these instances. As further shown in Fig. 8.7, change events recorded in a change log are characterized by the *type* of change (e.g., insert, delete, and move), the *subject* primarily affected by the change (e.g., the activity to be inserted or deleted), and the *syntactical context* of the change. The latter contains the change operation's *pre- / post-set*, i.e., adjacent process model elements directly preceding/succeeding the change subject in the process model.

8.4.2 Directly Applying Process Mining to Change Logs

Taking a change log as input, the goal is to discover an abstract *change process model* reflecting the sequences of change operations applied to the process instances of a particular type. As shown in [121], change logs structured in the way described in Sect. 8.4.1 can be easily mapped onto existing formats for execution logs. In principle, this enables the direct application of process mining algorithms (cf. Sect. 8.3) not only to execution logs, but to change logs as well.

In simple terms, existing mining algorithms (e.g., α algorithm and heuristic miner) then construct a change process model from the *causality relations* that can be observed in the change log. Basically, these causal relations can be derived as follows: If a change operation op_A is followed by another change operation op_B for at least one process instance (i.e., one change log instance), and no other process instance has a change log instance where op_B is followed by op_A, a causal relation from op_A to op_B is assumed, i.e., "op_A may cause op_B" (cf. Example 8.7). By contrast, when two change operations are found to appear in both orders in the change log, it is assumed that they can be executed in arbitrary order (cf. Example 8.8); i.e., these two change operations are considered as being independent and are therefore ordered in parallel in the discovered change process model.

Example 8.7 (Deriving Causal Relations). In the example change log shown in Fig. 8.7, instance I_2 features a change operation deleting *Inform patient* followed by another change, inserting the same activity again. As no other instance contains these changes in reverse order, a causal relation is established between them. That is, the second change operation depends on the first one, which should be reflected by the discovered change process model.

Example 8.8 (Absence of Causal Relations). Consider again Fig. 8.7. Inserting *X-Ray* and inserting *Lab Test* appear in this order in instance I_8, and in reverse order in instance I_9. Hence, there must be no causal relation, and thus no direct link between these change operations in the mined change process model.

Taking the above into consideration, [346] describes how change logs can be mapped onto MXML—the input format of the ProM process mining tool (cf. Sect. 8.3). Based on this mapping, existing process mining algorithms as supported by ProM (i.e., the α algorithm, multiphase miner, and heuristic miner) are directly applied to change logs. The *change processes* discovered by the different mining algorithms are then compared along different criteria (see [346] for details). The most important one is how reflective a change process is of the actual dependencies between the change operations recorded in the change log. For example, for process instance I_2, change operation op_4 depends on the effects of the preceding change operation op_3 (cf. Fig. 8.7). This dependency should be reflected as a sequence $op_3 \longrightarrow op_4$ in the resulting change process. In contrast, independent change operations should be ordered in parallel.

As shown by [346], when directly applying the mentioned process mining algorithms to a change log, the actual dependencies between the change operations are reflective of simple processes and a restricted set of change operations; i.e., in such scenarios, meaningful and useful change process models are discovered. As further shown in [346], however, this no longer holds when analyzing changes of process instances that were created from large and complex process models. As a fundamental problem, process changes tend to be rather infrequent, i.e., compared to execution logs, there are relatively few cases (i.e., changed process instances) and events to learn from. Hence, the *completeness* of change logs, i.e., their property to record independent (i.e., parallel) change activities (i.e., change operations) in any possible order, cannot be taken for granted. In [346] this is simulated by using an incomplete subset of change logs as can be also expected in a real-life situation. From this, in turn, it can be concluded that constructing a meaningful change process model solely based on the *causality relations*, as observable from the change log, is generally not possible.

8.4.3   Understanding Change Dependencies

This section explores the nature of process changes and change logs in more detail. Based on this, a suitable means for deciding whether a causal relation between two change operations as observed in the change log shall be actually reflected in the discovered change process or whether the two change operations can be considered as independent and hence ordered in parallel.

As opposed to execution logs, change logs do not reflect the enactment of any prespecified (change) process model. This becomes obvious from the fact that if the set of potential changes had been known in advance, these could have been already incorporated in the prespecified process model, and so making obsolete ad hoc changes. Thus, change logs must be interpreted as emerging sequences of *change activities* (i.e., change operations) which are based on a given set of adaptation patterns (cf. Chap. 7).

Each change operation recorded in a change log refers to the original process model through three associations, namely the *subject*, *pre-set*, and *post-set* of the change (cf. Sect. 8.4.1). As each of these associations can be theoretically bound to any subset of the original process model's set of activities, the set of possible change operations grows exponentially with the number of activities in a process model. This situation is different from mining the execution log of a regular process model, where the number of activities is usually rather limited.

Considering these two characteristics, the *meta-process* of changing a process model (i.e., the change process) can be described as a *highly unstructured* process, potentially involving a *large number of distinct activities*. When faced by traditional process mining algorithms, these properties typically lead to overly precise and *Spaghetti-like* models [6]. As discussed, this problem is mainly caused by the rather large number of causal (order) relations in change logs not reflective of the actual dependencies between the change operations. To obtain a more comprehensive and compact representation of change processes, it is therefore beneficial to abstract from some of the causal relations between applied changes.

When mining execution logs (cf. Sect. 8.3), the state of the mined process is treated like a "black box." This is necessary since execution logs only reflect *transitions* in the process, i.e., the execution of activities. By contrast, the information contained in a change log allows tracing the *state of the change process*, which is, in fact, defined by the process model being subject to change. Moreover, the effects of different sequences of change operations can be compared. From that, it becomes possible to explicitly detect whether two consecutive change operations can also be executed in the reverse order without changing the resulting state (i.e., process model); i.e., the concept of *commutativity* allows determining whether there indeed exists a *causal relation* between two consecutive change operations. Thus, the semantic implications of change events can be taken into account.

To compare sequences of change operations and to derive ordering relations between them, an *equivalence relation* for process models is required.

Definition 8.2 (Notation for Equivalent Process Models). Let $\equiv$ be some equivalence relation. For $S_1, S_2 \in \mathscr{P}$ (with $\mathscr{P}$ being the set of all process models): $S_1 \equiv S_2$ if, and only if, S_1 and S_2 are considered to be equivalent.

Note that many notions of process equivalence exist. The weakest one is *trace equivalence*, which considers two process models as being equivalent if the sets of traces they can produce are identical. Since the number of traces a process model can generate may be infinite, such comparison might be complicated. Moreover, since trace equivalence is limited to comparing traces, it fails to correctly capture the moment at which a choice occurs in a process. For example, two process models may generate the same set of traces $\{ABC, ABD\}$. However, the process models may be different with respect to the moment of choice, i.e., the first one may already have a choice after A to execute either BC or BD, while the second one has a choice between C and D just after B. *Branching bisimilarity* is an example of an equivalence notion that can correctly capture this moment of choice. For a comparison of branching bisimilarity and other equivalence notions, the reader is referred to [101,339]. For the remainder of this chapter, we abstract from a concrete notion of equivalence. In particular, the approach described can be combined with different process modeling languages and notions of equivalence.

Taking Definition 8.2, *commutative* process changes can be defined as follows:

Definition 8.3 (Commutativity of Changes). Let $S \in \mathscr{P}$ be a process model, and let Δ_1 and Δ_2 be two process changes. Δ_1 and Δ_2 are commutative in S if, and only if:

- There exist $S_1, S_2 \in \mathscr{P}$ such that $S[\Delta_1\rangle S_1$ and $S_1[\Delta_2\rangle S_2$,
- There exist $S_3, S_4 \in \mathscr{P}$ such that $S[\Delta_2\rangle S_3$ and $S_3[\Delta_1\rangle S_4$,
- $S_2 \equiv S_4$.

Figure 8.8 shows an example of commutative changes. Generally, two change operations are *commutative* if they have exactly the same effects on a given process model regardless of the order in which they are applied. If two change operations

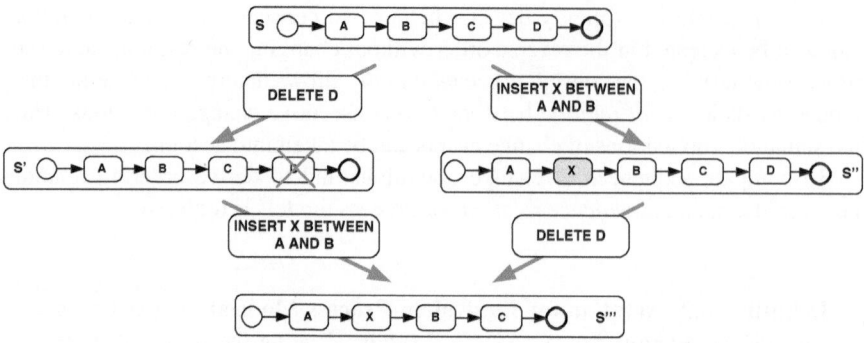

Fig. 8.8 Example of commutative process model changes

are not commutative, they are regarded as *dependent*, i.e., the effects of the second change depends on those of the first one. Note that the concept of commutativity effectively captures the ordering relationship between two consecutive change operations. If two change operations are commutative according to Definition 8.3, they can be applied in any given order. Therefore, no ordering relation between them exists.

8.4.4   Enhancing Multi-phase Mining with Commutativity

To support process engineers in analyzing the changes applied to the process instances of a particular process type, customized mining techniques are required. This section will enhance an existing algorithm originally designed for the mining of execution logs—*multiphase mining* [78]—with the concept of commutativity and applies it to change logs. When discovering a change process model, this approach abstracts from causal (ordering) relations that are irrelevant from a semantical point of view. Although change analysis is illustrated using multiphase mining, it is important to notice that any process mining algorithm based on explicitly detected causalities can be extended in a similar way.

The traditional *multiphase mining* algorithm enables the construction of process models (e.g., Petri nets or Event-driven Process-Chains) from the *causality relations* that can be derived from a given event log (i.e., execution log or change log). In particular, multiphase mining is robust in handling ambiguous branching situations, i.e., it can employ the "OR" semantics to split and join nodes in cases where neither "AND" nor "XOR" are suitable. For an in-depth description of this algorithm the reader is referred to [78].

Taking a change log as input and multiphase mining enhanced with *commutativity-induced concurrence*, a change process model can be discovered in two steps:

- *Phase I (Deriving the change process for each process instance).* For each process instance I, its corresponding change log instance cL_I is analyzed in order to discover an instance-specific change process model. Since the changes of I were applied consecutively, no choices will be added to this instance-specific change process model. Instead, the latter builds on the causal relations that can be derived from the change log instance cL_I. To be more precise, if a change operation op_A precedes a change operation op_B in cL_I and these two change operations are not commutative (cf. Definition 8.3), op_B depends on the effects of op_A. Hence, this causal relation is reflected as sequence $op_A \longrightarrow op_B$ in the resulting change process model. In contrast, commutative change operations are ordered in parallel. Figure 8.9 shows the instance-specific change processes for the nine process instances from Fig. 8.7.
- *Phase II (Aggregating instance-specific change processes to an overall change process).* The instance-specific change process models discovered in Phase I are merged to obtain the change process model reflecting the entire set of change instance logs. Figure 8.10 shows the change process aggregating the instance-specific change processes from Fig. 8.9

Note that in addition to the concurrency directly observable from the change log, the above algorithm applies *commutativity-induced concurrency* as well [120]. The latter is based on the notion of commutativity (cf. Sect. 8.4.3) and allows excluding observed causal relations between commutative change operations, i.e., change operations that are actually independent.

Example 8.9 (Excluding Causal Relations for the Case of Commutativity). Instance I_2 features deleting activity *X-ray* directly followed by deleting activity *Inform Patient* (cf. Fig. 8.7). As no other process instance contains these change operations in reverse order, a regular process mining algorithm would establish a causal relation between them (cf. Sect. 8.4.2). However, it is obvious that it makes no difference in which order the two activities are deleted from a process model. As the resulting process models are equivalent, the two changes are *commutative*. Thus, we can safely discard a causal relation between deleting *X-ray* (i.e., *op4*) and deleting *Inform Patient* (i.e., *op5*), which is why there is no link in the resulting change process shown in Fig. 8.10.

Note that without commutativity-induced concurrency every two change operations would need to be observed in both orders to classify them as concurrent. As previously mentioned, this is problematic in the context of change logs, since changes to a process model typically occur far less frequently than the actual execution of the process model, resulting in less log data.

Example 8.10 illustrates the change process model discovered in Phase II of the enhanced multiphase mining algorithm.

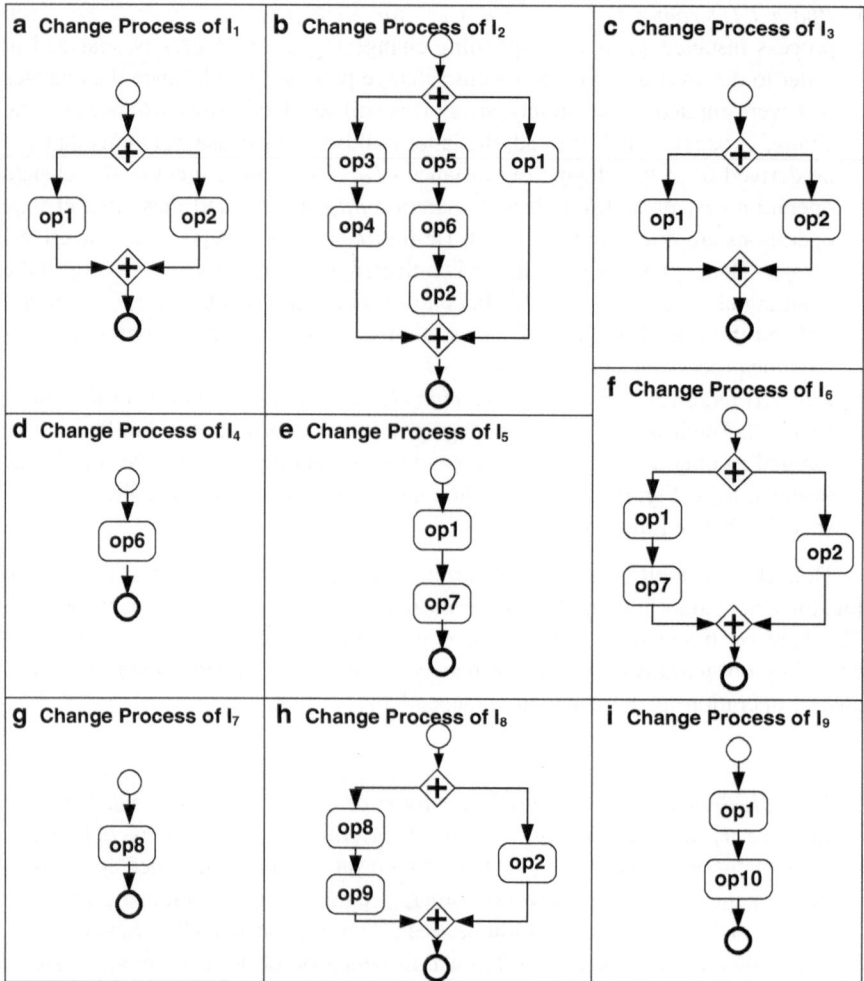

Fig. 8.9 Instance-specific change processes

Example 8.10 (Resulting Change Process). Figure 8.10 shows the change process model discovered from the change log instances depicted in Fig. 8.7. The detected causal relation between deleting and inserting activity *Inform Patient*, for example, is shown as a directed link between these activities. Although the model contains only ten activities, of which each represents a change operation, up to four of them can be executed concurrently. Furthermore, note that the discovered change process allows for some flexibility, i.e. all change activities may be skipped. Considering the very small data

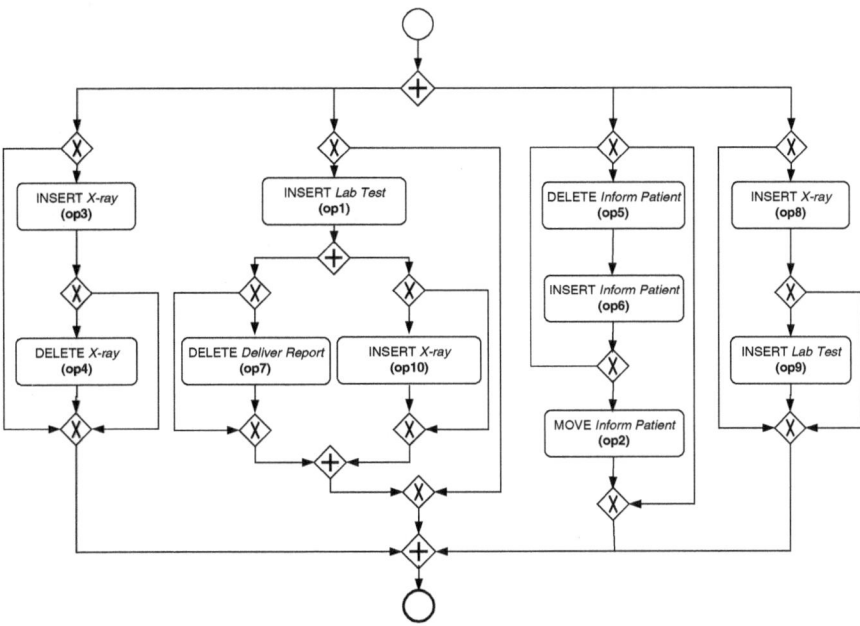

Fig. 8.10 Change process for the given collection of process instances

basis given in Fig. 8.7, where change log instances hardly have common sub-sequences, this model delivers a high degree of abstraction.

In summary, commutativity-induced concurrency removes unnecessary causal relationships, i.e., those causal relations not reflective of actual dependencies between change operations. Enhancing the multiphase mining algorithm with this concept significantly improves both clarity and quality of the discovered change processes.

8.4.5 *Mining Change Processes with Regions*

Another approach for mining change logs is presented in [121]. It is based on the observation that, given the original process model and a sequence of change operations, it is possible to construct the resulting process model. In particular, this can be utilized to derive a *transition system* (cf. Chap. 5), where the states are represented by (intermediate) process models resulting from the application of a (sub-)sequence of change operations. Example 8.11 illustrates this for the change log from Fig. 8.7.

Example 8.11 (Deriving a Transition System from a Change Log).
Figure 8.11 shows the transition system that can be obtained for the change
log from Fig. 8.7b—this change log comprises nine change log instances and
ten different change operations. For the sake of convenience, shorthand terms
are used for activity labels. The change operations from Fig. 8.7 correspond
to the events in the transition system. Moreover, start and end states are
added. Hence, the set of events of the transition system is given by $E =$
$\{start, op1, op2, \ldots, op10, end\}$. The application of a change operation to
some process model (i.e., to a state of the transition system) results in another
process model (i.e., state). Since in this particular example all process models
happen to be sequential, they can be denoted by a sequence, as depicted
on the right in Fig. 8.11. For example, $s1 =< EO, IP, PP, EP, DR >$
corresponds to the original process model before applying any change. When
applying $op1$ from the first change log instance to $s1$, the resulting state is
$s2 =< EO, IP, PP, EP, LT, DR >$ (i.e., the process model with activity
Lab Test being added). When then applying $op2$ from the same change log
instance in $s2$ the resulting state is $s3 =< EO, PP, IP, EP, LT, DR >$ (i.e.,
the process model for which *Inform patient* has been moved). This can be
repeated for all nine instances, resulting in 15 states, plus a start and end state,
i.e., $S = \{s0, s1, \ldots, s15, se\}$.

Using the *theory of regions* [69] the obtained transition model can then be
translated into a Petri Net describing the change process (cf. Example 8.12).

Example 8.12 (Representing a Change Process as a Petri Net). Figure 8.12
shows the Petri Net that can be obtained when applying the theory of regions
to the transition system derived in Example 8.11. In the given example, this
Petri Net is more or less identical to the transition system. However, it should
be noted that the change log from Fig. 8.7 has only nine change log instances;
i.e., compared to the number of change operations, the number of instances is
rather low. Moreover, only few of the possible interleavings seem to be present
in Fig. 8.7. Hence the obtained transition system is the result of a number of
particular examples rather than a description of the full behavior.

Generally, when using the theory of regions, it is possible to significantly reduce
the size of the model if more interleavings are present as in the given example (see
[121] for details). Furthermore, note that the change process model from Fig. 8.12 is
quite different from that depicted in Fig. 8.10. This indicates that the two approaches
for mining change logs produce different results, that is, they provide two different
ways of looking at change processes.

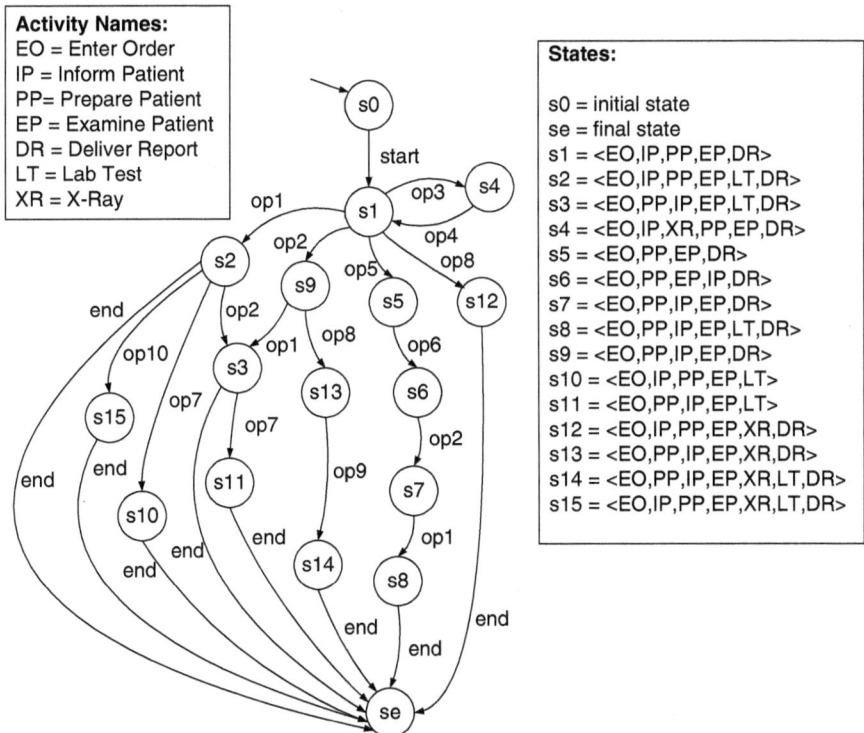

Activity Names:
EO = Enter Order
IP = Inform Patient
PP= Prepare Patient
EP = Examine Patient
DR = Deliver Report
LT = Lab Test
XR = X-Ray

States:

s0 = initial state
se = final state
s1 = <EO,IP,PP,EP,DR>
s2 = <EO,IP,PP,EP,LT,DR>
s3 = <EO,PP,IP,EP,LT,DR>
s4 = <EO,IP,XR,PP,EP,DR>
s5 = <EO,PP,EP,DR>
s6 = <EO,PP,EP,IP,DR>
s7 = <EO,PP,IP,EP,DR>
s8 = <EO,PP,IP,EP,LT,DR>
s9 = <EO,PP,IP,EP,DR>
s10 = <EO,IP,PP,EP,LT>
s11 = <EO,PP,IP,EP,LT>
s12 = <EO,IP,PP,EP,XR,DR>
s13 = <EO,PP,IP,EP,XR,DR>
s14 = <EO,PP,IP,EP,XR,LT,DR>
s15 = <EO,IP,PP,EP,XR,LT,DR>

Fig. 8.11 Transition system derived for the change log from Fig. 8.7

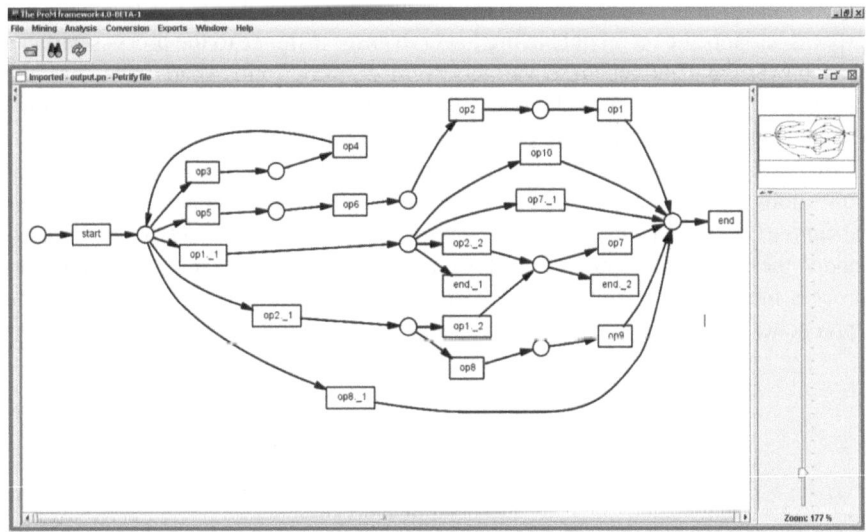

Fig. 8.12 Screenshot of ProM showing the Petri Net obtained for the change log from Fig. 8.7

Aggregating and visualizing changes applied at the process instance level enable process engineers to analyze them and to draw conclusions about potentially optimizing the process model from which the instances were created. Chapter 9 will discuss how respective changes can be introduced at the process type level.

8.5   Mining Process Variants in the Absence of a Change Log

Adaptations of process models are required in different stages of the process lifecycle. At build-time, a reference process model has to be configured to fit to the application context at hand. During run-time, in turn, ad hoc changes of single process instances become necessary to cope with unanticipated exceptions. In both cases, a prespecified process model is structurally adapted, resulting in a collection of process model variants (*process variants* for short) that were derived from the same original process model, but which slightly differ in their structure and behavior (see Fig. 8.14 for an example). Generally, process engineers are interested in learning from respective model adaptations in order to discover an improved (reference) process model that better "fits" the given variant collection than does the original model.

Section 8.4 has shown how existing process mining techniques can be enhanced to analyze change logs capturing all changes that were applied to the process instances of a particular type. Respective techniques consider each change operation as a single "activity" and derive a change process model providing an aggregated visualization of the changes applied and their dependencies. However, the presented algorithms do not discover an "improved" process model that better fits the given process variants, i.e., a model having lower *average distance* to the process variants than the original model these variants were derived from. Apart from this, the presented change analysis techniques presume the existence of a change log, which cannot always be guaranteed in practical settings [161].

To overcome these deficiencies, dedicated algorithms for mining process variant collections were developed [182, 185]. As input, they take a collection of *process variants* (i.e., process models) and—optionally—the original *(reference) process model* these variants were derived from. As output, they create a (reference) process model which is structurally "close" to these variants. As opposed to the approaches described in Sect. 8.4, no change log is required.

8.5.1 Closeness of a Reference Process Model and a Collection of Process Variants

In order to evaluate whether a particular process model constitutes a good reference for a given collection of variants, the closeness between this process model and the variants has to be determined. In the process variant mining framework described in [186], the structural closeness between a (reference) process model and a single process variant is measured in terms of the number of high-level change operations (e.g., to insert, delete, or move activities) needed to transform the (reference) process model into the respective variant model (i.e., the edit distance; see [181] for an approach determining this distance). As reported in [351], the shorter this structural distance is, the less effort (i.e., fewer changes) will be needed for configuring specific process variants from the reference process model. Hence, the goal of *process variant mining* is to discover a reference process model having *minimum average distance* to the given collection of process variants. In this context, process variants may be weighted according to their relevance; e.g., for each process variant, weights may be used reflecting the frequency with which process instances were executed according to this variant.

Definition 8.4 (Average Weighted Distance). Let $S \in \mathscr{P}$ be a (reference) process model. Let further $\mathscr{M}$ be a collection of process variants $S_i \in \mathscr{P}$, $i = 1, \dots, n$, derived from S, with w_i representing the number of process instances that were executed on basis of S_i. The *Average Weighted Distance* $D_{(S,\mathscr{M})}$ between S and $\mathscr{M}$ can be computed as follows ($d_{(S,S_i)}$ describes the edit distance (in terms of high-level change operations) between S and S_i):

$$D_{(S,\mathscr{M})} = \frac{\sum_{i=1}^{n} d_{(S,S_i)} \cdot w_i}{\sum_{i=1}^{n} w_i} \tag{8.1}$$

Note that measuring the distance between two process models in terms of high-level change operations constitutes an NP-hard problem [181]; i.e., computing time is exponential to the size of the process models. Hence, finding a (reference) process model with minimum average weighted distance to the given collection of process variants constitutes an NP-hard problem as well. However, when encountering real-life cases with process variants ranging from the dozens up to hundreds, finding the optimum might be too costly or not feasible at all. Section 8.5.3 introduces a heuristic algorithm for process variant mining tackling this challenge.

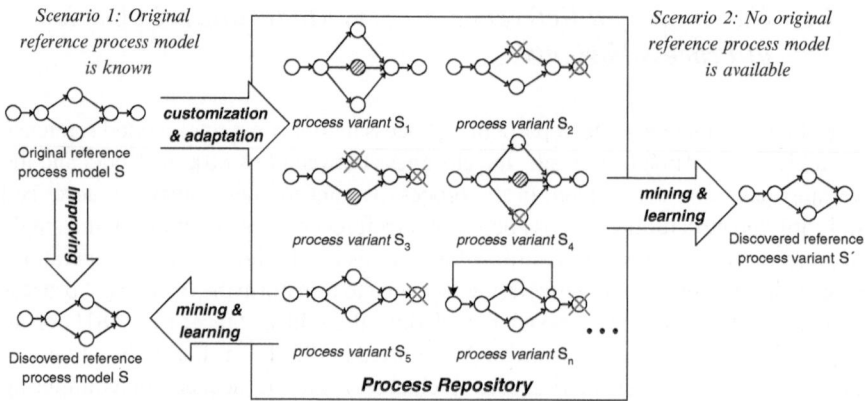

Goal: Discover a (new) reference process model which requires less configuration effort

Fig. 8.13 Scenarios for discovering reference process models

8.5.2 Scenarios for Mining Process Variants

According to [186], two scenarios for process variant mining can be distinguished (cf. Fig. 8.13). In the first scenario, the original (reference) process model is known a priori, while in the second scenario, respective knowledge is not available.

Scenario 1 (Evolving the Original Reference Process Model Through Learning from Past Model Changes). In this scenario, both the original reference process model S and the (weighted) process variants derived from S through structural adaptations are given (see the left-hand side in Fig. 8.13). The goal is to discover a new reference process model S' which is "closer" to the given variant collection than S; i.e., which has lower *average weighted distance* (cf. Definition 8.4) to these process variants than S. Furthermore, process engineers are allowed to control the maximum distance between the original and the newly discovered reference process model. Thus, the effort (i.e., number of changes) required for evolving the original reference process model and for implementing the required process changes can be controlled and Spaghetti-like process models avoided. Note that the closeness between new and old reference process model on one hand and the closeness of the new reference process model to the given variant collection on the other hand act as *counterforces*.

Scenario 2 (Discovering a Reference Process Model Without Having Knowledge About the Original Process Model). Mining techniques addressing this scenario take a collection of process variants as input, but do not presume any knowledge about the original reference process model these variants were derived from (see the right-hand side in Fig. 8.13). The goal is to discover a reference process model with *minimum average distance* to the given variant collection. For this purpose, the process variants need to be "merged" in an appropriate way.

Scenario 1 is illustrated by Example 8.13:

Example 8.13 (Process Variant Mining). Consider the scenario shown in Fig. 8.14. From the original reference process model S, six process variants S_i, i = 1,..., 6, were derived. These differ in their structure as well as their activity sets. For example, activity X appears in 5 of the 6 variants (except S_2), while activity Z only appears in S_5. The 6 process variants are further weighted based on the number of process instances created from them. Furthermore, for each process variant, Fig. 8.14 shows its distance to the original reference process model as well as a related bias (i.e., a minimum sequence of change operations transforming S into S_i). For example, to transform S into S_1, 4 high-level change operations need to be applied. Finally, taking the weight of each process variant into account, an average weighted distance of 4 between S and the process variants is obtained. This means that one needs to perform on average 4 change operations to configure a process variant out of S. Note that this example corresponds to Scenario 1, i.e., the goal is to discover a new reference process model with a lower average weighted distance to the variants than S. Furthermore, it should also be possible to control the maximum distance between the original and the discovered reference process model.

8.5.3 A Heuristic Approach for Process Variant Mining

We describe a *heuristic* approach for process variant mining and the controlled evolution of a (reference) process model, i.e., for addressing Scenario 1 [182]. Generally, a problem requires heuristics if "it may have an exact solution, but the computational cost of finding it may be prohibitive" [193]. Although heuristic algorithms do not aim at finding the real optimum,[2] they are widely applied in practice. In particular, heuristic algorithms provide a nice balance between the quality of the discovered solution and the computation time needed for finding it.

In a simplified schema, the heuristic algorithm for process variant mining as suggested by [182] works as follows[3]:

---

[2]This means, it is neither possible to theoretically prove that the discovered result is the optimum nor can it be stated how close it is to the optimum.

[3]Note that this approach is restricted to block-structured process models (cf. Chap. 4). A discussion of this restriction, as well as a formal description of the algorithm, can be found in [182].

Step 1.	Use the original reference process model S as the starting point.
Step 2.	Search for all *neighboring* process models of the current reference process model S being considered—a neighboring model of S has distance 1 to S; i.e., it can be derived from S by applying one change operation. If a better model S' can be found among these candidate models (i.e., S' is expected to have lower average weighted distance to the given variant collection compared to S), S is replaced by S' (i.e., $S := S'$).
Step 3.	Repeat Step 2 until either no better model can be found or the maximally allowed distance between original and new reference process model is reached. The last S' obtained in the search then corresponds to the discovered reference model.

Informally, the new reference process model is constructed by applying a sequence of high-level change operations to the original reference model. Each change operation within this sequence serves to decrease the average weighted distance between the current candidate process model and the given collection of process variants. Furthermore, those changes significantly contributing to the reduction of the average weighted distance between the discovered reference model and the given variant collection are first considered by the algorithm and then less relevant changes are considered at the end [182]. Finally, in order to avoid the structural difference between the original and the newly discovered reference process model becoming too large, process engineers may limit the number of search steps; i.e., the number of change operations maximally applied to S upon discovering the new reference process model. Note that this allows avoiding Spaghetti-like process models as mining results.

Computing the average weighted distance between each candidate reference process model and the given process variants in Step 2 would be too costly (cf. Sect. 8.5.1). Hence, a quickly computable *fitness function* for measuring a candidate model's quality is used by the sketched algorithm; this fitness function approximately measures the closeness between a candidate reference process model and the given process variants. Basically, it allows evaluating to what degree a candidate model covers the activities occurring in the variant collection and how well its structure fits to these variants (see [182] for details). In particular, the fitness function can be computed in polynomial time.

Example 8.14 (Heuristic Approach for Process Variant Mining). **Consider** the scenario from Fig. 8.14 and Example 8.13 respectively. Figure 8.15 depicts the search result and all intermediate process models we obtain when applying the described algorithm. The search stops after the application of three high-level change operations. When comparing the original reference model S with the intermediate search results R_i (cf. Fig. 8.15), an improvement of the fitness value can be observed in each search step. Since fitness

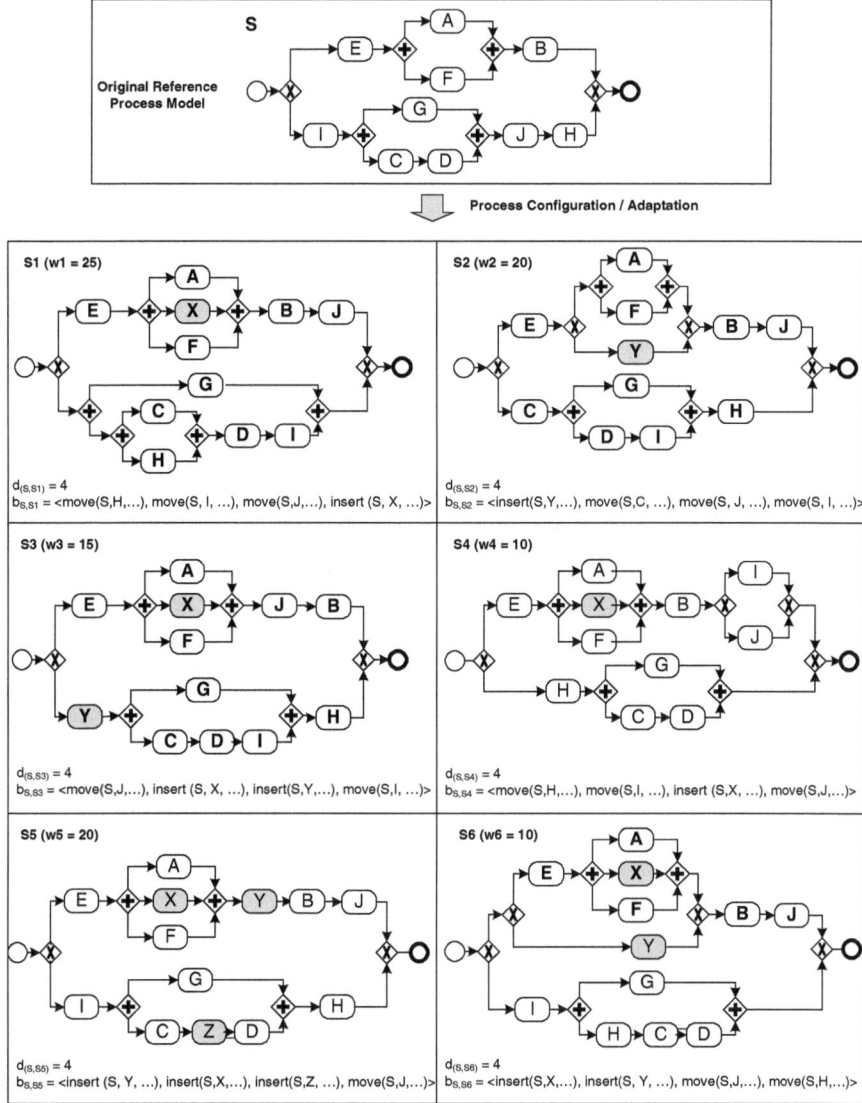

Fig. 8.14   A reference process model and configured process variants

values only constitute a reasonable guessing, Fig. 8.15 also shows the average weighted distance, which is a precise measurement between the respective models and the process variants. Note that in this example the evolution of the fitness value correlates with that of the average weighted distance (i.e., the

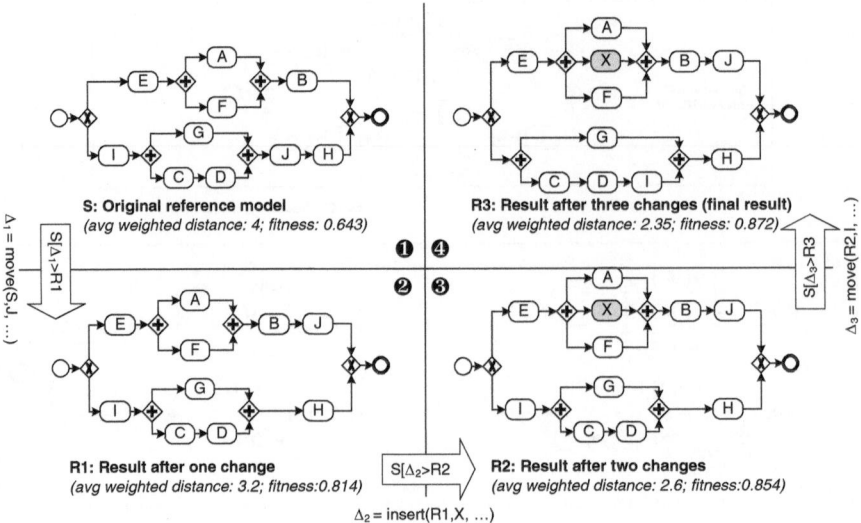

Fig. 8.15 Heuristic search and result after every change

higher the fitness value is, the lower the average weighted distance becomes). Finally, the average weighted distance drops monotonically from 4 (when considering S) to 2.35 (when considering the resulting reference process model R_3); i.e., when replacing the old reference process model S by the discovered one (i.e, R_3) less change operations are required to configure the variants.

The described algorithm for process variant mining has been successfully applied to real-world scenarios. For example, Li et al. [185] describe a case study conducted in the automotive industry, in which the variants of product change management processes were analyzed and an improved reference process model was discovered. Similarly, the practical benefit of the described techniques was proven in another case study conducted in a hospital. Here, more than 90 process variants for handling medical orders (e.g., X-ray inspections, lab tests) were analyzed, and a reference process model was discovered that was significantly closer to the variants than was the old reference model [185].

8.5.4   Other Approaches for Process Variant Mining

In [180, 185] a clustering algorithm for handling Scenario 2 (cf. Sect. 8.5.2) is presented; i.e., for mining a collection of process variants without having knowledge about the original reference process model. This algorithm is restricted to block-structured process models and the new reference process model is constructed by enlarging blocks on a step-by-step basis. Only by requiring a collection of process variant models as input, this clustering algorithm can quickly discover a reference process model in polynomial time and provide additional information on how well each part of the discovered reference process model fits to the given process variants [180, 185]. A qualitative as well as quantitative comparison of this clustering algorithm with the heuristic algorithm presented in the previous section is provided in [186]. Furthermore, Li et al. [186] compare approaches for process variant mining with traditional process mining algorithms.

A technique for ranking activities according to their potential involvement in process changes and process configurations, respectively, is presented in [184]. In particular, this ranking approach allows process engineers to distinguish between more and less critical activities in the context of process changes. However, it cannot provide suggestions on how to involve these activities in the improvement of the original reference process model.

Finally, initial work now exists on mining the context in which structural adaptations of process instances have become necessary [97, 98]. Corresponding techniques will contribute to better understanding the factors leading to process changes and thus also provide better user assistance.

8.6 Summary

This chapter discussed how flexible processes can be monitored and mined. First, the chapter described the information captured in execution and change logs in order to enable accountability and traceability in adaptive PAISs. Based on this information, the structure and state of a particular process instance can be reconstructed from any point in time.

Second, techniques for analyzing the behavior of a collection of process instances through the mining of execution logs were discussed, illustrating how process models can be discovered from execution logs and how discrepancies between the original process model and an execution log can be detected (i.e., conformance checking). Of particular interest in the context of flexible processes are emerging techniques for the analysis of dynamically evolving processes.

Third, process mining techniques originally designed for analyzing execution logs were adjusted and used in the context of change logs. For example, enhanced multiphase mining allows the discovery of an abstract change process model reflecting all changes applied to the instances of a prespecified process model. In order to obtain compact and meaningful change process models, concepts like *commutativity-induced concurrency* or *theory of regions* can be applied. Overall, change processes allow tracing the changes of a prespecified process model. Further, they constitute a good basis for monitoring process changes and can serve as starting point for more sophisticated analyses; e.g., determining the circumstances under which particular classes of change occur, and thus reflecting upon the driving forces behind such changes.

Finally, scenarios and techniques for mining process variants in the absence of change logs were presented. It was shown how an improved reference process model can be discovered from a collection of process variants. Adopting this process model as a new reference process will make future process configurations more efficient, since less effort (i.e., fewer change operations) for configuring the variants will be required. The heuristic algorithm described in this context also takes the original reference model into account, such that process engineers can control to what degree the discovered model differs from the original one. This way, Spaghetti-like process models can be avoided.

Both adaptive processes and techniques for mining execution logs, change logs, or process variants address fundamental issues commonly found in the current practice of business process implementations. Although both approaches are valuable on their own, their full potential can only be harnessed by a tight integration. While process and change mining can deliver reliable information about how process models need to be changed, adaptive PAISs provide the tools to safely and conveniently implement these changes (see Chap. 9 for a detailed discussion). Thus, the described mining techniques can be integrated into adaptive PAISs as a *feedback cycle*.

A next step in the mining of flexible processes will be the development of change analysis techniques utilizing execution as well as change logs in a combined fashion. Both the structural and the behavioral perspective can then be considered in an integrated way in order to cover more general change analyses. Furthermore, context mining and its utilization constitute an important future research path for the mining of flexible processes.

Exercises

8.1. Execution and Change Logs
Discuss why both execution and change logs are needed in adaptive PAISs.

8.2. Mining Flexible Processes
Download the execution log file used in Sect. 8.2 as well as the original process model from the book web site. To work on this exercise you need the process mining tool ProM which can be obtained from processmining.org. To familiarize yourself with ProM check out the tutorial (see the link on the book web site). Having obtained enough insights into ProM try to reproduce the analyses described in Sect. 8.2.

8.3. Commutativity of Process Changes and Change Mining
Give examples of commutative and non-commutative process changes. Why does the utilization of commutativity among change operations contribute to more meaningful and compact change process models?

8.4. Mining Change Logs

Consider the first six process instances depicted in Fig. 8.7 and derive a change process model for them (i.e., ignore the last three process instances in your analysis).

8.5. Process Variant Mining

Discuss potential benefits of process variant mining from the perspective of a process engineer?

8.6. Process Variant vs. Change Mining

Compare process change mining with process variant mining. Discuss commonalities and differences.

Chapter 9
Process Evolution and Instance Migration

Abstract Business processes evolve over time due to changes in their legal, technical, or business context, or as a result of organizational learning. As a consequence, prespecified process models and their technical implementation in a PAIS need to be adapted accordingly. Moreover, prespecified process models often have to be changed to cope with design errors, technical problems, or poor model quality. This chapter presents techniques to tackle these challenges and to change implemented business processes at a technical level. First, it deals with *process model evolution*, i.e., the evolution of prespecified process models over time to accommodate changes of real-world processes. In this context, techniques are introduced for dealing with already running process instances and their on-the-fly migration to the changed process model, without violating any correctness and soundness properties. Second, this chapter introduces *process model refactorings* to foster internal process model quality and to ensure maintainability of the PAIS over time.

9.1 Motivation

As emphasized in Chap. 3, business processes evolve over time due to changes in their legal, technical, or business context, or as a result of business reengineering efforts [131, 202]; i.e., drivers of change are *external* to the PAIS, but require the evolution of the process models prespecified in the PAIS [61, 139, 153, 290]. Moreover, process model evolution is often triggered by design errors, technical problems, or poor model quality [351]; i.e., by drivers *internal* to the PAIS.

This chapter presents concepts and techniques to cope with the evolution of business processes as implemented in a PAIS at a technical level, i.e., to realize respective process changes within the PAIS. The basic assumption is that business processes are represented by prespecified process models in the PAIS, and changes of the real-world process require the corresponding process models to evolve accordingly at the type level. A major challenge in this context concerns the handling of long-running process instances that were created based on the old process model, but are now required to comply with a new specification (i.e., model version) and must therefore be migrated to it. Since thousands of active instances may be affected, the issue of correctness is critical.

This chapter is organized as follows: Sect. 9.2 addresses fundamentals of *process model evolution*, i.e., changes of a process model at the type level. Typically, respective model changes are behavior-altering. It will be shown how to define process model changes and how to dynamically migrate already running process instances to a new process model version in a controlled and correct manner. Sections 9.3 and 9.4 then discuss advanced issues emerging in the context of process model evolution; i.e., how to evolve process instances that were previously subject to ad hoc changes and handle process instances that cannot be migrated in the desired way. Following this, Sect. 9.5 deals with the evolution of PAIS perspectives other than control flow. Finally, Sect. 9.6 addresses behavior-preserving process model changes (i.e., *process model refactorings*) to foster internal process model quality and to ensure maintainability of the PAIS and its process model repository. The chapter concludes with a summary in Sect. 9.7.

9.2   Fundamentals of Process Model Evolution

We first introduce fundamentals related to the evolution of a prespecified process model as well as the dynamic migration of corresponding process instances to a new model version. To limit the scope, we shall first focus on the migration of *unbiased* process instances. That is, a collection of process instances running on the same process model S, and not yet subjected to any ad hoc changes, shall be migrated to a new process model version S'. Section 9.3 then extends these considerations to the migration of biased (i.e., changed) process instances whose model differs from the one the process instance was created from.

9.2.1   Evolving a Process Model at the Process Type Level

To accommodate changes in a real-world process, the model representing this process in the PAIS must be evolved accordingly. Picking up the scenario from Example 3.4 (cf. Chap. 3), Example 9.1 illustrates such a *process model evolution*.

Example 9.1 (Tender Preparation).   Consider Fig. 9.1. In the original process model S, a special offer for gold customers can be made that has to be approved by a supervisor. Since the creation of the special offer turned out to be too expensive, management decides that the special offer should

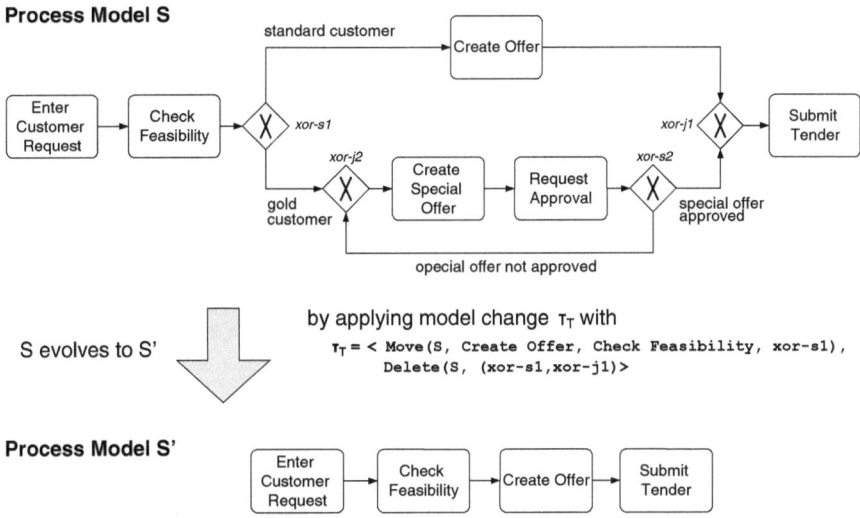

Fig. 9.1 Process model evolution at the type level

no longer be made. To realize this change based on high-level adaptation patterns (cf. Chap. 7), for example, first activity *Create Offer* has to be moved within the model; i.e., it is deleted at its current position and then serially reinserted between activity *Check Feasibility* and gateway *xor-s1*. Following this, the process fragment between the two connector nodes *xor-s1* and *xor-j1* is deleted resulting in a new process model version S'. Thus, the difference between S and S' consists of the high-level adaptations as specified by change τ_T. Note that the concrete adaptation patterns applied in the given context depend on the change framework provided by the respective PAIS.

Like with instance-specific adaptations, structural model changes at the type level can be conducted by either using low-level *change primitives* or high-level *adaptation patterns* (cf. Chap. 7). While change primitives directly operate on single elements of a process model (e.g., to add or remove nodes/edges), adaptation patterns are implemented in terms of *high-level change operations*, e.g., to move an activity or entire process fragment within a process model.

We presume that process model evolution transforms a correct and sound process model S into another correct and sound process model S' by applying a sequence of change operations to S (cf. Definition 9.1). That is, at the type level, process model S' meets the structural properties required by the process modeling language used and it obeys soundness properties like proper completion and absence of dead activities. Furthermore, the data flow defined by S' must meet the correctness properties discussed in Chap. 4, e.g., absence of missing data.

Existing implementations of high-level adaptation patterns usually provide well-defined pre- and post-conditions in order to ensure syntactical correctness and behavioral soundness of a process model when applying the adaptation patterns, i.e., a correctness-by-construction principle is applied [70, 260]. Deficiencies that cannot be prohibited by this approach (e.g., concerning the correctness of the data flow schema) are checked on-the-fly and are continuously reported to the user.

Definition 9.1 (Process Model Evolution). Let $\mathscr{P}$ be the set of all process models and let S, $S' \in \mathscr{P}$. Let further $\Delta = (op) \in \mathscr{C}$ denote a particular change consisting of one change operation op and $\tau= < op_1, \ldots, op_n >$ $\in \mathscr{C}^*$ be a process change that applies change operations op_i, i=1,...,n sequentially.

1. $S\ [\Delta\rangle$ if, and only if, Δ is applicable to S.
2. $S\ [\Delta\rangle\ S'$ if, and only if, Δ is applicable to S (i.e., $S\ [\Delta\rangle$) and S' is the process model resulting from the application of Δ to S (also: $S' = S + \Delta$).
3. $S\ [\tau\rangle\ S'$ if, and only if, there are process models $S_1, S_2, \ldots S_{n+1} \in \mathscr{P}$ with $S = S_1, S' = S_{n+1}$ and for $1 \leq i \leq$ n: $S_i\ [\Delta_i\rangle\ S_{i+1}$ with $\Delta_i = (op_i)$ (also: $S' = S + \tau$).

The *minimum number* of change operations required to transform model S into model S' is denoted as *distance $d_{(S,S')}$*. Furthermore, a *minimum sequence* of change operations transforming S into S' is called *bias* (see Definition 7.2). In Example 9.1, the distance between S and S' is 2 and a bias is given by change sequence τ_T.

9.2.2   Deferred Process Model Evolution

When evolving a process model S to model S' at the type level (cf. Definition 9.1), the PAIS must properly deal with corresponding process instances; i.e., process instances that were started and partially executed on S, but have not yet been completed.

The easiest way to properly complete these running process instances is to continue their execution on the original process model S, whereas new process instances may be created and executed based on the new model version S' [59, 290]. We denote this approach as *deferred process model evolution*. In particular, it requires support for version control as well as for the coexistence of process instances belonging to different model versions of a particular process type (cf. Fig. 9.2).

The coexistence of process instances running on different model versions of a particular process type is illustrated by Example 9.2.

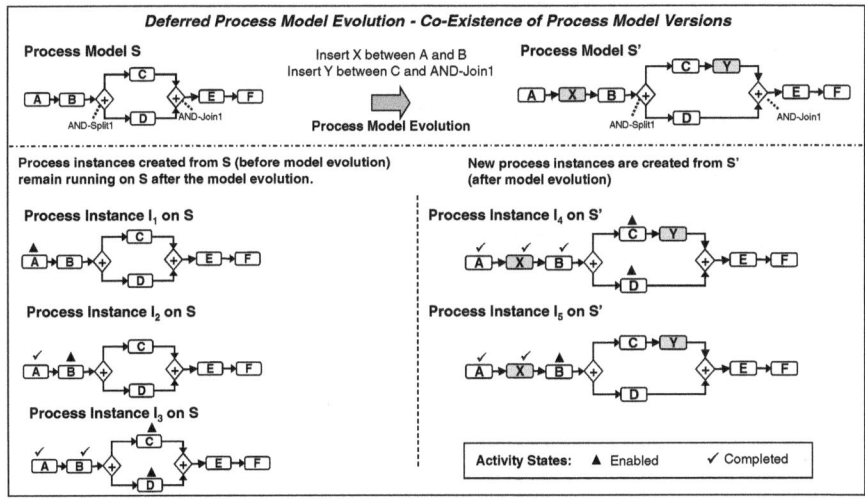

Fig. 9.2 Coexistence of process instances running on different model versions

Example 9.2 (Deferred Process Model Evolution). Consider Fig. 9.2. It shows a process model S evolving to a process model S' by adding two activities X and Y to S. The already running instances I_1, I_2, and I_3 remain associated with the original process model S, whereas instances I_4 and I_5, which are created after evolving the process model, are executed based on S'.

9.2.3 Immediate Process Model Evolution and Instance Migration

While the coexistence of process instances running on different process model versions is sufficient to support deferred evolution, long-running process instances often require *immediate evolution*, i.e., these process instances shall be migrated on-the-fly to the new process model version if possible (cf. Example 9.3).

Example 9.3 (Need for Immediate Process Model Evolution and Process Instance Migration). Consider a patient treatment process and assume that due to newly emerging legal requirements patients have to be informed about certain risks before a specific surgery may take place. Let us further assume that this change is also relevant for patients whose treatment process was already started. If the respective treatment process is supported by a PAIS, stopping all ongoing process instances (i.e., treatments), aborting them, and restarting them does not constitute a viable option. As a large number of treatment processes might be concurrently running, applying this change manually to the instances of ongoing treatment processes in the PAIS is hardly a realistic option. Instead, PAIS support is needed to add this new activity to all patient treatment processes for which this is still feasible (e.g., for which the surgery has not yet been started or completed).

9.2.3.1 Uncontrolled Instance Migration

The immediate migration of a process instance to a new process model version— or, to be more precise, the migration of a collection of process instances—often constitutes a costly manual task since proper migration support is missing in many PAISs. This, in turn, not only causes much manual efforts (e.g., for inspecting process instance states or updating the PAIS run-time database), but is also error-prone.

Even worse, there exist PAISs that allow changing a given process model S and overwriting it with a new model S' in an *uncontrolled manner*. In particular, all running process instances that were created from S are then immediately "relinked" to the new process model version S' regardless of their current state. However, for process instances that have already progressed too far, such uncontrolled migration can lead to severe problems like inconsistent instance states, soundness violations, or data flow run-time errors [288]. Example 9.4 illustrates such an uncontrolled migration using a simple scenario.

Example 9.4 (Uncontrolled Process Instance Migration.). Consider process model S from Fig. 9.3 and the two process instances I_1 and I_2 running on S (see the left-hand side of the figure). Assume that process model S evolves to S' by adding the two activities X and Y, as well as a data dependency between them; i.e., X writes a newly added data element d, which is then read by Y. Assume further that I_1 and I_2 are re-linked to the new process model version S'. Regarding I_1, the described process model change is not critical since the execution of this instance has not yet entered the changed model region; i.e., the migration of process instance I_1 to S' and its further execution based on S' do not cause any problems. By contrast, process instance I_2 will enter an inconsistent state if it is relinked to S' in an uncontrolled manner. In particular, X will then be contained in an already passed region. Depending on

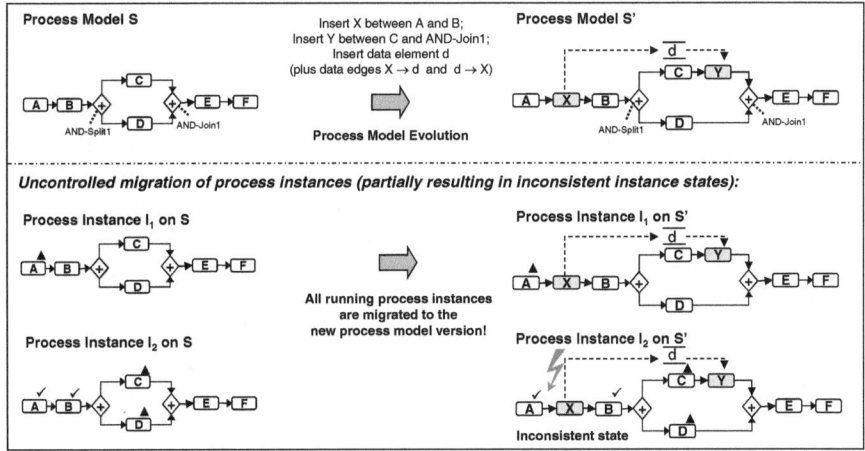

Fig. 9.3 Uncontrolled migration of process instances

the operational semantics of the process execution language used, this might result in a deadlock (i.e, Y might never become enabled due to the missing data element d) or other severe run-time errors (e.g., Y might be invoked even if d has not been written before).

9.2.3.2   Controlled Instance Migration

To avoid run-time problems like those discussed in Example 9.4, immediate instance migrations have to be accomplished in a *controlled manner*, i.e., none of the correctness properties (e.g., soundness and absence of data flow errors) guaranteed through the verification of a process model at build-time must be violated for any of the migrated instances. If this cannot be guaranteed for a particular process instance, it must not be migrated, but remain running on the old process model version.

To meet this goal, it first has to be ensured that the new process model version S' is correct (cf. Sect. 9.2.1); i.e., S' has to satisfy the syntactical and structural properties of the process modeling language used, and it further must constitute a sound process model (cf. Chap. 4). However, as illustrated by Example 9.4, this is not sufficient for ensuring correctness in the context of process instance migrations.

The problem here is the same as when applying an ad hoc change to a single process instance during run-time (cf. Chap. 7); i.e., similar challenges exist as for ad hoc changes. In particular, the state of the process instances to be migrated (i.e., their execution traces) must be taken into account when deciding on whether their execution may be relinked from a process model S to a new model version S' (i.e., whether the instances may migrate to S').

As discussed in Sect. 7.4.2, a widespread correctness notion used for deciding about whether or not a particular process instance may be dynamically migrated to a new process model version S' is *state compliance*—a process instance I is *state compliant* with an updated process model S' and can therefore be migrated to it if the execution trace σ_I of I is producible on S' as well (cf. Definition 7.3). Using this correctness notion in the context of process model evolution, it can be ensured that process instances whose state has progressed too far will not be migrated to the new process model version S', i.e., they will remain running on the original model S. This way, problems like those discussed in Example 9.4 can be avoided.

As further discussed in Chap. 7, when migrating a running process instance to a new process model version its state has to be automatically adapted. For example, an already enabled activity may have to be disabled when inserting an activity directly preceding it or a newly added activity may have to be immediately enabled if the preconditions for its execution are met.

Example 9.5 illustrates a process model evolution together with the controlled migration of related process instances.

Example 9.5 (Controlled Process Instance Migration). Consider the evolution of process model S to S' as depicted at the top of Fig. 9.4. Furthermore, consider the three process instances I_1, I_2, and I_3 now running on S. Only those process instances (i.e., I_1 and I_2) are migrated to the new process model S' that are *state compliant* with it: I_1 can be migrated to S' without need for any state adaptation. Further, I_2 can be migrated to S' as well. However, in this case the newly inserted activity X becomes immediately enabled, whereas the already enabled activity B is disabled. Finally, process instance I_3 cannot be migrated to S', since it is not state compliant with this model. Hence, I_3 remains running on the original process model S.

Note that the controlled evolution of process instances as illustrated in Example 9.5 requires support for the coexistence of process instances running on different model versions of a particular process type, as well as the use of appropriate correctness notions for deciding whether process instances can be correctly executed on the new model version. As with ad hoc changes of single process instances, the notion of state compliance may be further relaxed in order to also cope with loop changes (see Sect. 7.4.3 for a respective discussion).

9.2.3.3 Practical Aspects

In practical settings, there are typically hundreds or thousands of process instances running concurrently on a process model. Therefore, scalability constitutes a particular challenge for enabling process model evolution with immediate process instance migration in a PAIS; i.e., to efficiently migrate a large collection of process

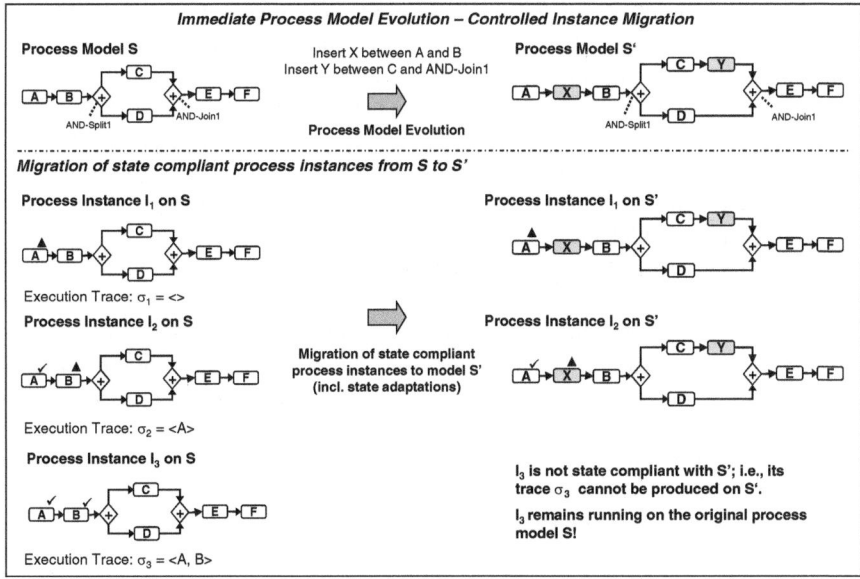

Fig. 9.4 Controlled migration of process instances

instances to the new process model version. In this context, efficient implementations are needed for checking state compliance of each concerned process instance as well as for migrating state compliant process instances to the new process model version (including automated state adaptations as illustrated in Example 9.5).

We have already discussed similar issues in the context of ad hoc changes of single process instances (cf. Sect.7.4.4). Obviously, trying to replay the whole execution trace of each process instance on the new process model version would be too inefficient when dealing with a large number of process instances. For example, this would require costly access to execution logs from secondary storage, as well as significant processing times to replay the complete trace of each process instance on the new process model version. Therefore, existing implementations utilize both the semantics of the adaptation patterns applied and the operational semantics of the process modeling language used. Based on this, they define optimized procedures for both checking state compliance and adapting states when migrating a state compliant process instance to a new process model version [154, 270].

9.2.4 User Perspective

When evolving a process model, the process engineer usually starts the process model editor, loads the respective process model, changes it based on the available adaptation patterns or change primitives, verifies soundness and other correctness properties, and finally stores the resulting process model in the PAIS build-time repository. Following this, the new model version can be deployed to the PAIS run-time environment. In this context, the process engineer also has to specify the date from which on the new process model version becomes effective, i.e., from which it shall be taken as basis for creating new process instances of the respective process type. Finally, PAIS users are informed about the performed changes. To accomplish the latter, for example, a social network can be used in order to figure out who shall be informed about which changes [151].

If the dynamic migration of process instances to a new process model version is not supported by the PAIS, the already running process instances will be completed based on the old process model version (i.e., *deferred process model evolution*). Otherwise (i.e., *immediate process model evolution*), the process engineer may additionally define constraints (i.e., selection predicates based on process attributes) to restrict the set of running process instances that are candidates for being migrated to the new process model version (e.g., all instances started after a certain date or having some other common properties). If no such constraint is specified, all running process instances will be considered as candidates for migration. Finally, for the identified set of migration candidates, the adaptive PAIS checks which of the process instances can actually be migrated to the new process model version and which cannot, taking process instance states and the discussed correctness notions (e.g., state compliance) into account. Following this, all migratable process instances are "relinked" to the new process model version. Among others, this includes the adaptation of process instance states and related data structures (e.g., user worklists). Example 9.6 illustrates this user perspective.

Example 9.6 (User Perspective on Process Model Evolution.). Figures 9.5 and 9.6 show two screenshots illustrating what process model evolution and corresponding process instance migrations look like from the perspective of the process engineer. First of all, Fig. 9.5 depicts version V1 of process model *medical treatment* as loaded in a process model editor. Further, it displays two process instances (i.e., *Instance 1* and *Instance 2*) executed according to this process model (from the overall 2,000 process instances currently running on the depicted process model version *(medical treatment, V1)*. Finally, the execution trace of *Instance 2* is depicted on the right side at the bottom.

Figure 9.6 depicts process model version V2 that results from a simple change to the process model version *(medical treatment, V1)* from Fig. 9.5, namely the serial insertion of activity *Diabetes Test* between activities *Advise* and *Prepare*. Figure 9.6 further shows the two process instances from Fig. 9.5 after relinking the migratable ones to the new process model version. Since *Instance 1* is state compliant with process model version *V2*, it is migrated to *V2*; i.e., its execution is relinked to this new process model version. Opposed to this, *Instance 2* remains running on the old process model version *V1* as it is not state compliant with V2 (cf. Fig. 9.6).

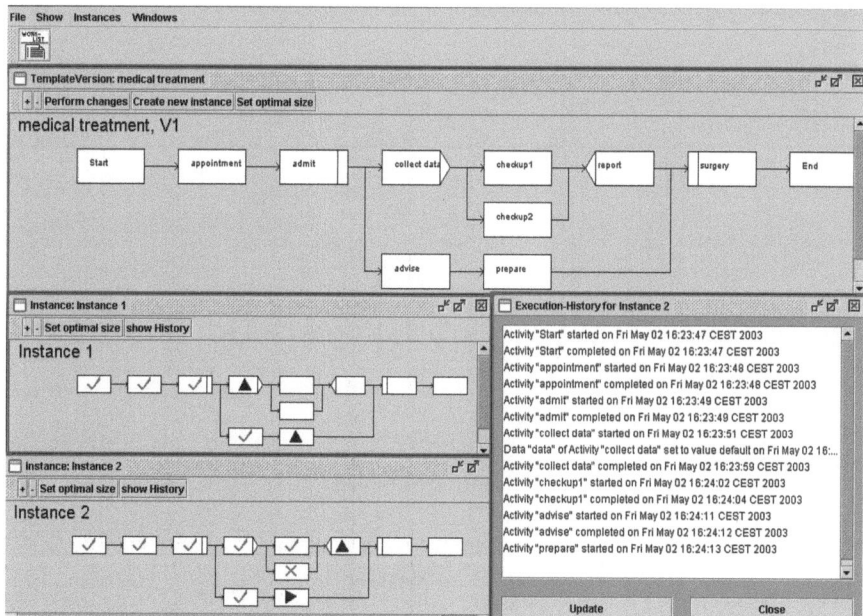

Fig. 9.5 A process model and two related process instances

The results of process model evolution and the corresponding process instance migrations are summarized in a migration report. For example, from the migration report depicted in Fig. 9.6 on the left, the process engineer can see that the checks required to ensure state compliance only took a very small fraction of time. Furthermore, this report states that 667 process instances were migrated to the new process model version, but this was not possible for the remaining 1,334 process instances (e.g., the respective instances may have progressed too far). Finally, the lists comprising migrated and non-migrated process instances are displayed.

9.2.5   Existing Approaches for Migrating Process Instances

At first glance, there are similarities between process model evolution in PAISs [9, 61, 287, 290, 313] and schema evolution in database management systems (DBMS) [35]. Basically, the problems underlying process model evolution are similar to those of schema evolution in DBMS when only considering the mapping

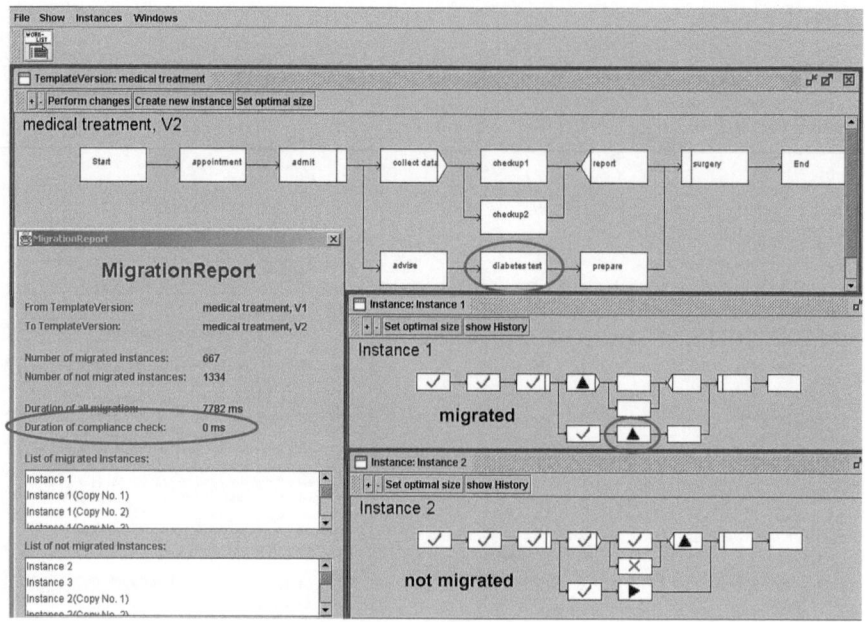

Fig. 9.6 Evolved process model version and migration report

of model elements (e.g., activities, data elements, and control/data flow edges) from the old to the new process model version. As described, however, process model evolution raises additional issues when taking instance states into account. In particular, migratability of a process instance depends on its current execution state.

Existing frameworks enabling process model evolution and process instance migration [9,61,86,90,290,313] can be categorized into *history-* and *snapshot-based* approaches. While the former utilize information from execution traces to ensure state compliance of the process instances with the new process model, the latter only considers the currently enabled activities, but no information about previous instance execution.

History-Based Approaches. For evolving a process model from S to S', WIDE offers a complete and minimal set of elementary change operations [61]. To enable the controlled migration of related process instances from S to S', a restrictive variant of *state compliance* is used; i.e., WIDE applies state compliance as specified in Definition 7.3, but without considering the relaxations discussed in the context of loop changes (cf. Sect. 7.4.3). ADEPT2 picks up state compliance as correctness notion, but additionally provides different kinds of relaxations (e.g., concerning changes of regions contained in a loop body) to increase the number of migratable process instances without affecting PAIS robustness [299, 301]. Besides these relaxations, several optimizations are provided in order to enable both efficient compliance checks and efficient state adaptations of migrated process instances.

Finally, ADEPT2 not only addresses changes of the behavior perspective, but considers the evolution of other model perspectives as well; e.g., the information perspective [282] and the organization perspective [297, 298]. Like ADEPT2, TRAMs defines specific *migration conditions* for each type of change operation [154]. When evolving a process model by applying a set of change operations, the corresponding migration conditions must be met by a process instance to be migratable to the new process model version. Finally, BREEZE provides concepts for rolling noncompliant process instances back to a state, in which they can be safely migrated to the new process model version [313].

Object-oriented approaches are provided by MOKASSIN [139] and WASA$_2$ [363]. MOKASSIN considers generic adaptation patterns and correctness notions (e.g., state compliance) as too inflexible for meeting application-specific needs. Therefore, each process type can be defined as an object type encapsulating specific change operations and implementing specific consistency notions; i.e., process instances correspond to objects that are themselves responsible for ensuring consistency in the context of process model evolution. As opposed to the aforementioned approaches, MOKASSIN neither provides generic techniques nor efficient consistency checks when being confronted with a large collection of process instances. In turn, WASA$_2$ applies a correctness criterion mapping subprocesses of process instances to the changed process model in order to decide about their migratability (see [363] for details).

Snapshot-Based Approaches. In addition to history-based approaches, there exist techniques (e.g., based on Petri Nets) that solely consider the currently enabled (or running) activities when migrating running process instances to a new process model version [5, 9, 86, 87]; i.e., these approaches do not presume the existence of any execution log. For example, [86] captures both the process model and the process instances in the same colored Petri Net in which tokens of different colors correspond to different process instances. Process model evolution is then accomplished by substituting marked sub-nets. However, formal conditions for checking state compliance of process instances with the new model version are missing.

Another serious problem arises from the fact that markings of previously passed regions are not preserved and "skipped" regions are not marked at all. Therefore, the challenge is how to adapt the markings (i.e., states) of a process instance after propagating a process type change to it, with no knowledge of its previous execution. In [87], the process engineer has to manually adapt the markings of each process instance that does not constitute a viable approach in practice. In addition, complex reachability analyses become necessary to check for the consistency of net markings after a change. van der Aalst [5] proposes that process model changes must not be propagated to process instances executed on modified regions. The adaptation of markings is seen as a complex problem—the so-called *dynamic change bug* [9]. To fix this bug, the authors suggest that the process engineer must specify a mapping between the markings of the old and the new net. In particular this mapping has to be applicable to every ongoing process instance [9]. Generally, many approaches based on Petri Nets suffer from the implicit modeling of loops, the mixed modeling of control and data flow, and the missing integration of net markings with trace information.

A survey on the correctness notions applied by these different approaches is provided in [287, 290].

9.3 Common Support of Type and Instance Changes

Adaptive PAISs must be able to support ad hoc changes of single process instances as well as process model changes at the type level and their propagation to related process instances (i.e., process model evolution). So far, these two kinds of dynamic process changes have been treated in an isolated fashion in this book. While Chap. 7 has described how ad hoc changes of single process instances can be realized, Sect. 9.2.1 has shown how a process model is evolved at the type level and how related process instances can be migrated to the new process model version. However, Sect. 9.2.1 has assumed that the process instances to be migrated are *unbiased*, i.e., they had not been previously subjected to any ad hoc changes.

In general, a PAIS hast to ensure the proper interplay between process type and process instance changes. When evolving a process model S to S' by applying change τ_T at the type level (i.e., $S' = S + \tau_T$), the challenge is how to treat a process instance I originally created from S, but adapted afterwards due to an ad hoc change τ_I; i.e., I is *biased* and running on an instance-specific process model $S_I = S + \tau_I$. Preventing *biased* process instances from being migrated to the new process model version would block them from taking benefit of process optimizations or from participating in organizational changes.

However, this would often be too restrictive for practical settings, especially if process instances are long-running and the type and instance changes are neither syntactically nor semantically conflicted with each other (cf. Sect. 9.3.1). In this context, the relation between process type and process instance changes is of particular importance. In certain scenarios, process participants may anticipate later process optimizations (i.e., process model changes at the type level) and apply them to single process instances [293, 355]. For these cases, the process type change might overlap with the previously applied process instance changes. Hence, it must not be propagated to the respective process instances (cf. Sect. 9.3.2).

9.3.1 Migrating Biased Process Instances

When evolving a process model S, we have to distinguish between two classes of related process instances. On one hand, there are process instances created from process model S and still running on it; i.e., *unbiased* process instances not being subject of any ad hoc change. (When evolving S to S' at the type level, these process instances can be treated as described in Sect. 9.2.3.) On the other hand, there may be process instances that had been created from S, but were individually adapted to cope with exceptional situations, i.e., *biased* process instances whose instance-specific model differs from S due to the ad hoc changes applied. Formally:

Definition 9.2 (Biased Process Instance). Let S be a process model. Then:

a) A *biased* process instance $I = (S, \tau_I, \sigma_I)$ on S was created from S, but is now running on an instance-specific process model $S_I = S + \tau_I$ due to the applied ad hoc changes. τ_I corresponds to a bias between S and S_I (cf. Definition 7.2), and σ_I denotes the execution trace of I on S_I.
b) A process instance $I = (S, \tau_I, \sigma_I)$ created from S, and to which no ad hoc change has been applied, is denoted as *unbiased*. Hence, I is executed according to S; i.e., $S_I = S$ and $\tau_I = \emptyset$ (i.e., I has an *empty* bias).

Generally, the uncontrolled propagation of a process type change to a biased process instance might result in critical flaws. In particular, the type and the instance changes might be in conflict with each other as illustrated by Example 9.7.

Example 9.7 (Violating Soundness due to the Uncontrolled Migration of a Biased Process Instance). Consider process model S from Fig. 9.7a. From S, a process instance I was created and later individually changed (cf. Fig. 9.7b). To be more precise, for process instance I, activity X was inserted between E and B, resulting in the instance-specific process model S_I with bias τ_I. Assume further that S evolves to S' at the type level by adding a control dependency between B and E (i.e., by applying type change τ_T); in this context, gateways are added to implement change τ_T in a syntactically correct way. If we now propagate τ_T to the biased process instance I (i.e., to $S_I = S + \tau_I$), this results in the process model depicted in Fig. 9.7c. Obviously, this instance-specific process model contains a deadlock, i.e., a sound execution of I is no longer possible. Basically, this soundness violation is caused by the combined application of the two conflicting changes τ_T and τ_I that were previously applied at the process type and the process instance level in an isolated manner.

Hence, from the correct applicability of different changes at the type and instance level we cannot conclude that these changes can be correctly applied in conjunction with each other as well. As illustrated by Example 9.8, conflicts between process

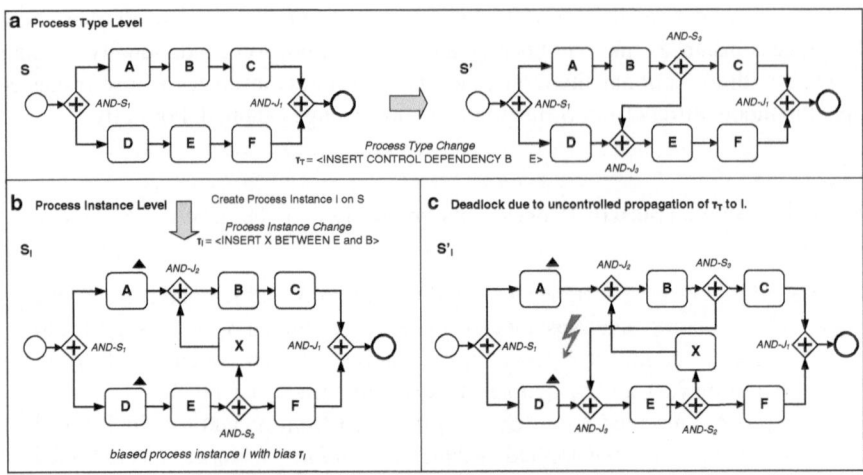

Fig. 9.7 A deadlock caused by the uncontrolled migration of a biased process instance

changes at the type and instance level concern not only the behavioral perspective of a PAIS, but other perspectives as well (e.g., the information perspective).

Example 9.8 (Data Flow Errors due to the Uncontrolled Migration of a Biased Process Instance). Consider the process model S from Fig. 9.8a. Based on S, process instance I was created and then individually adapted. To be more precise, the two activities B and C—together with their data edges— were deleted, resulting in the instance-specific process model S_I with bias τ_I (cf. Fig. 9.8b). Assume further that S evolves to S' at the process type level by adding activity X as well as a read data edge connecting X with data element d (i.e., process type change τ_T). If we propagate τ_T to the biased process instance I (i.e., to $S_I = S + \tau_I$) in an uncontrolled manner, the process model depicted in Fig. 9.7c will result. Obviously, this process model contains a severe data flow error, i.e., there will be missing data when invoking X.

Definition 9.3 provides criteria to avoid such uncontrolled migration of biased process instances in the context of a process type change.

Definition 9.3 (Propagating Process Type Changes to Process Instances). Let T be a process type with current process model version S. Further, let $I = (S, \tau_I, \sigma_I)$ be a biased process instance that was originally created from S, but is now running on the instance-specific process model $S_I = S + \tau_I$.

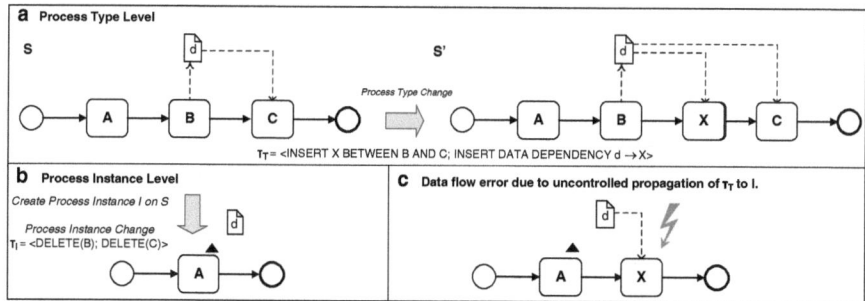

Fig. 9.8 A data flow error caused by the uncontrolled migration of a biased process instance

Finally, assume that S evolves to the correct and sound process model S' by applying type change τ_T to S (i.e., $S' = S + \tau_T$). Then, type change τ_T may be propagated to process instance I (i.e., I may migrate to S'): $\Leftrightarrow$

1. Applying τ_T to S_I (i.e., $S_I[\tau_T]$) results in a *correct* and *sound* process model $S_I^* := (S + \tau_I) + \tau_T$. Note that correctness depends on the syntactical properties of the process modeling language used. Further, it includes correctness of the data flow schema as described in Chap. 4.
2. I is relaxed *state compliant* with S_I^*; i.e., the loop-purged execution trace σ_I^{lp} of I can be reproduced on S_I^*. Remember that execution trace σ_I logs all activity start and activity end events generated during the execution of I. The loop-purged execution trace σ_I^{lp}, in turn, can be determined by logically discarding all entries from σ_I produced by another than the actual loop iteration for each loop contained in S (cf. Definition 7.5).
3. τ_T and τ_I are not semantically in conflict. Concurrent changes must not violate semantic constraints (see below).

According to Definition 9.3, a process type change must not be propagated to a biased process instance if the syntactical correctness, data flow correctness, or soundness of its (instance-specific) process model is violated afterwards. Furthermore, biased process instances must be state compliant with the process model resulting from the application of the type change to the instance-specific process model. Finally, semantically conflicting changes should be excluded. For example, if two activities mutually exclude each other (i.e., they must not co-occur in any execution trace) or a particular activity must not be executed more than once for any process instance, concurrent activity insertions at the type and instance level must not violate these semantical constraints. We exclude semantic issues for the remainder of this chapter and will reconsider them in Chap. 10.

Examples 9.9 and 9.10 illustrate how Definition 9.3 can be used to decide whether a process type change may be propagated to a biased process instance.

Example 9.9 (Forbidden Change Propagation). Reconsider the two change scenarios from Figs. 9.7 and 9.8. In both cases, the biased process instance depicted is state compliant with the process model resulting from the propagation of the type change to the process instance. However, the propagation of the type change to the instance-specific process model would result in an erroneous process model, i.e., either a soundness violation (cf. Fig. 9.7c) or a data flow error (cf. Fig. 9.8c). Hence, according to Definition 9.3, the process type change must not be propagated to the respective process instances.

Example 9.10 (Propagating a Type Change to Biased and Unbiased Instances). Consider the process model evolution depicted in Fig. 9.9a. Process model S evolves to S' by conditionally inserting the activity sequence comprising X and Y. Figure 9.9b and 9.9c show two related process instances that were created from S and shall be relinked (i.e., migrated) to S'. While instance I_1 is still running according to the original process model S (i.e., I_1 is unbiased), instance I_2 was individually adapted during its execution (i.e., I_2 is *biased*). Obviously, I_1 may migrate to S' since it is state compliant with S'. The same applies to I_2: First, the depicted type change τ_T can be correctly applied to the instance-specific process model $S_{I_2} = S + \tau_{I_2}$. Second, I_2 is state compliant with the resulting process model. Hence, according to Definition 9.3, the process type change may be propagated to I_2.

Adaptive PAISs like ADEPT2 provide efficient techniques for ensuring the conditions required by Definition 9.3 [271]. For example, in many cases data flow errors resulting from the concurrent application of type and instance changes can be excluded based on simple and efficient conflict tests; e.g., if the data element sets affected by the type and instance changes are disjoint, no data flow error will occur (see [291] for details).

9.3.2 Overlapping Changes at the Type and Instance Level

Generally, ad hoc changes of single process instances are performed to handle unanticipated exceptions or unplanned situations. However, such instance changes might be also applied if the prespecified process model does not fully reflect reality (e.g., due to bad model design). As discussed in Chap. 8, mining the ad hoc changes

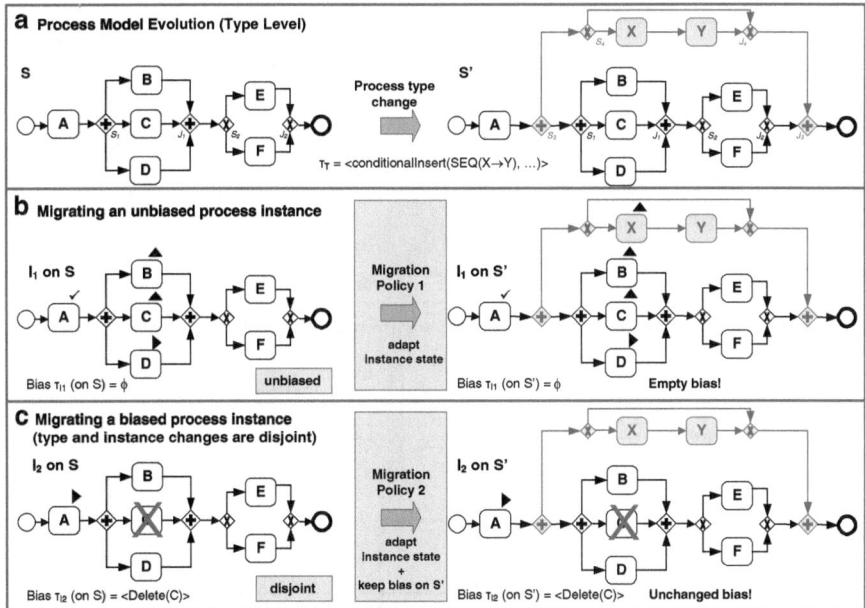

Fig. 9.9 Process model evolution and migration of two process instances

of the process instances created from a particular process model S might reveal potential flaws of process model S and trigger a process model evolution lifting up some of the ad hoc changes to the process type level. Hence, for process instances that have already anticipated the type changes, the latter must not be reapplied in the context of an instance migration.

When propagating the changes of a process type to a biased process instance, therefore, one particular challenge is determining whether the type and instance changes have the same or overlapping effects on the original process model. Information about the *degree of change overlap* is useful in deciding whether a process type change still needs to be (completely) propagated to the biased process instance or has been already anticipated by it. For example, if a certain activity has been already added in the context of an instance-specific ad hoc change, it would normally not be reinserted when propagating a process type change to the respective instance. This section discusses how adaptive PAISs deal with overlapping process type and process instance changes, and it describes advanced migration strategies suggested in this context. Formal details can be found in [282, 289].

Consider again the process model evolution from S to S' as depicted in Fig. 9.9a (cf. Example 9.10). Figures 9.9c and 9.10 show three biased process instances I_2, I_3, and I_4 that were created from S, but are now running on instance-specific process models due to the applied ad hoc changes. Interestingly, the instance-specific changes show specific relations to the process type change from Fig. 9.9a. While the change of I_2 (i.e., bias τ_{I_2}) and the process type change τ_T are *disjoint*,

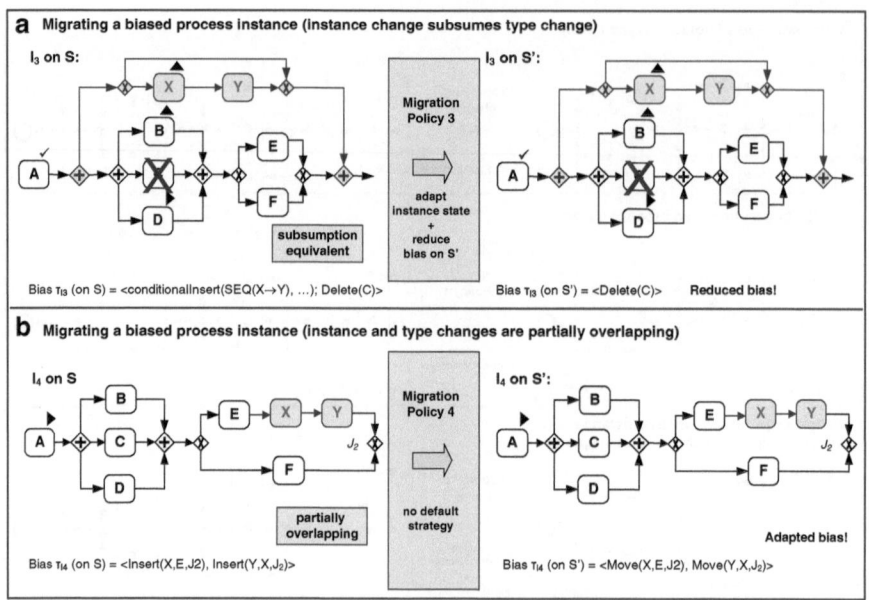

Fig. 9.10   Migrating process instances with overlapping bias and type change (cf. Fig. 9.9)

the instance-specific changes of I_3 and I_4, respectively, *partially overlap* with τ_T. Subsequently, we discuss how this knowledge can be utilized when migrating biased process instances.

Let τ_T denote the process type change (i.e., $S' = S + \tau_T$) and let τ_I describe the bias of a process instance I originally created from S (i.e., $S_I = S + \tau_I$).

Disjoint Type and Instance Changes. Assume that the type change τ_T and the instance-specific change τ_I are *disjoint*, i.e., they have been applied to different regions of S. Then: Process instance I may migrate to the new process model S' if it is state-compliant with S' and τ_T can be correctly applied to the instance-specific model $S_I = S + \tau_I$ (cf. Definition 9.3). In particular, I can keep its current bias (i.e., τ_I) on S' when being migrated to this new model version (cf. Example 9.11).

Example 9.11 (Disjoint Type and Instance Changes). Consider process instance I_2 from Fig. 9.9c. Its bias τ_{I_2} and the process type change τ_T (cf. Fig. 9.9a) are *disjoint*; i.e., they refer to different activities and regions of the original process model S. Furthermore, I_2 is state compliant with S' and τ_T can be correctly applied to $S_{I_2} = S + \tau_{I_2}$. Hence, I_2 can be migrated to the new process model S' by adapting its state and keeping its current bias τ_{I_2} unchanged on S'; i.e., $(S + \tau_{I_2})[\tau_T > (S' + \tau_{I_2})$ (see the right of Fig. 9.9c).

Equivalent Type and Instance Changes. If instance I has anticipated the process type change completely (i.e., $S + \tau_I$ and $S + \tau_T$ are *equivalent*), I can be automatically migrated to the new process model S'. In this case, bias τ_I becomes *empty* after migrating I to S', as the effects of the previous instance change are now entirely covered by S'. Note that there are different equivalence notions for process models, like branching bisimilarity and trace equivalence [339].

Subsumption-Equivalent Type and Instance Changes. If bias τ_I of a process instance I *subsumes* a process type change τ_T (i.e., τ_I covers τ_T, but may comprise additional changes), I can be automatically relinked to S'. When migrating I to S' its bias can be reduced by discarding those changes covered by the type change and already anticipated by I during instance execution (cf. Example 9.12).

Example 9.12 (Subsumption-Equivalent Type and Instance Changes). Consider the process model evolution from Fig. 9.9a and the biased process instance I_3 from Fig. 9.10a. Obviously, bias τ_{I_3} covers all changes defined by τ_T, but also comprises additional ones. More precisely, both τ_I and τ_T conditionally add an activity sequence (comprising X and Y) to process model S. However, τ_I also deletes activity C. Hence, I_3 can be migrated to process model S'. In this context, bias τ_{I_3} needs to be recalculated. In the example given, after migrating I_3 to S', τ_{I_3} only needs to keep those changes not covered by τ_T (i.e., the deletion of C).

Partially Overlapping Type and Instance Changes. In many cases, the changes applied at the type and instance level are similar, but not equivalent. For example, the same activity may be added by the type- and instance-specific changes, but at different positions in the process model. Generally, there is no default strategy to migrate biased process instances in such cases. Instead, interactions with the user become necessary to decide on whether and/or how such a process instance may be relinked to the new process model version S' and how its bias shall look like afterwards. This is illustrated by Example 9.13.

Example 9.13 (Partially Overlapping Type and Instance Changes). Figure 9.10b provides an example of *partially overlapping* changes. Both τ_T and τ_{I_4} insert the same activities (i.e., X and Y), but in different regions of process model S. When migrating process instance I_4 to S', its bias τ_{I_4} needs to be recalculated on S'. In the given case, this can be covered by replacing the insert operations with respective move operations.

In summary, the migration of biased process instances becomes necessary if instances are long-running and the process type change is relevant for them. While such migrations can be easily accomplished if type and instance changes are disjoint, more sophisticated migration policies are required in case these changes overlap. Then, the migration policy to be chosen depends on the concrete relation between these changes [282, 289].

9.3.3 Integrated Change Support in Existing Approaches

Most adaptive PAISs either enable process model evolution at the type level and the propagation of these changes to unbiased process instances, or make ad hoc changes of single process instances during run-time [9, 61, 86, 146, 313, 365]. As discussed in Sect. 9.2.5, most of these approaches focus on correctness notions for deciding whether an instance may be dynamically changed during run-time.

There are few PAISs like WASA2 [365], IntelliGEN [146], and ADEPT2 [271] providing integrated support for process model evolution with immediate instance migrations on one hand and ad hoc changes of single process instances on the other hand. Except for ADEPT2, none of these approaches supports the propagation of process type changes to biased process instances. In WASA2, for example, ad hoc changes are realized by deriving a new process model version with exactly one running instance. In particular, once a process instance has been individually adapted (i.e., it runs on an instance-specific model), it can no longer benefit from process type changes, i.e., from the further evolution of the process model it was originally created from. As discussed, this is not sufficient for long-running processes.

ADEPT2 provides a comprehensive framework for the integrated support of process type and process instance changes [261,271]. Its techniques for dealing with conflicting changes at these two levels are presented in [291]. In particular, ADEPT2 ensures that the propagation of a process type change to a biased instance is always done in a controlled manner and does not lead to deadlocks or data flow errors. Furthermore, ADEPT2 provides advanced techniques for dealing with overlapping type and instance changes as presented in Sect. 9.3.2 [289]. Based on the particular degree of overlap between a type and an instance change, process engineers may choose between different migration policies. In this context, ADEPT2 provides various techniques for deciding on the degree of overlap between process changes (e.g., also coping with noise in change logs [289, 292]). Similarly, the process models resulting from the respective changes can be compared, e.g., using specific inheritance relations expressing the commonalities and differences between two models [8].

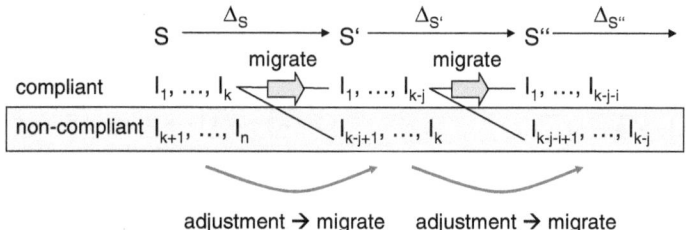

Fig. 9.11 Evolving a process model over time

9.4 Coping with Noncompliant Process Instances

As discussed in Sect. 9.2.3, the migration of process instances to a changed process model version must not affect their further execution; i.e., instance migrations must not result in soundness violations. To ensure this, state compliance was introduced as a basic correctness notion. However, the strict use of this criterion might exclude process instances from future process optimizations, i.e., changes of the new process model and its subsequent versions. This raises the question about how to properly deal with those process instances not being state compliant, i.e., process instances for which their execution has progressed too far.

Consider the scenario from Fig. 9.11: Based on process model S, process instances $I_1, \ldots, I_n$ are created and executed. Then, model S evolves to S' at the type level by applying change Δ_S to it. Assume that instances $I_1, \ldots, I_k$ are state compliant with S' and hence can be correctly migrated to S', whereas I_{k+1}, $\ldots, I_n$ have already progressed too far, i.e., they are not state compliant with S'. As a consequence, $I_{k+1}, \ldots, I_n$ continue running on model S. Later on, process model S' further evolves to S'' by applying change $\Delta_{S'}$ to it. Then, $I_1, \ldots, I_k$ currently running on S' may benefit from this further process change if they are state compliant with S''. By contrast, $I_{k+1}, \ldots, I_n$ are excluded from this migration to S'' since they are still running on S, but not on S'. Such exclusion from process optimizations, in turn, is not always acceptable for long-running processes. For example, think of patients who are excluded from an optimized treatment course because corresponding process instances cannot be migrated to new process model versions.

To increase the number of migratable process instances, advanced migration strategies for coping with noncompliant instances are required. In the context of ad hoc changes of single process instances we have already discussed relaxations of existing correctness notions contributing to this goal (e.g., *relaxed state compliance* as introduced in Chap. 7). In this section, we additionally introduce more advanced migration strategies. On one hand, these should enable the migration of noncompliant process instances, i.e., they should support their relinking to the new process model version. On the other hand, this relinking must not result in any soundness violations. Existing migration strategies handling noncompliant process instances

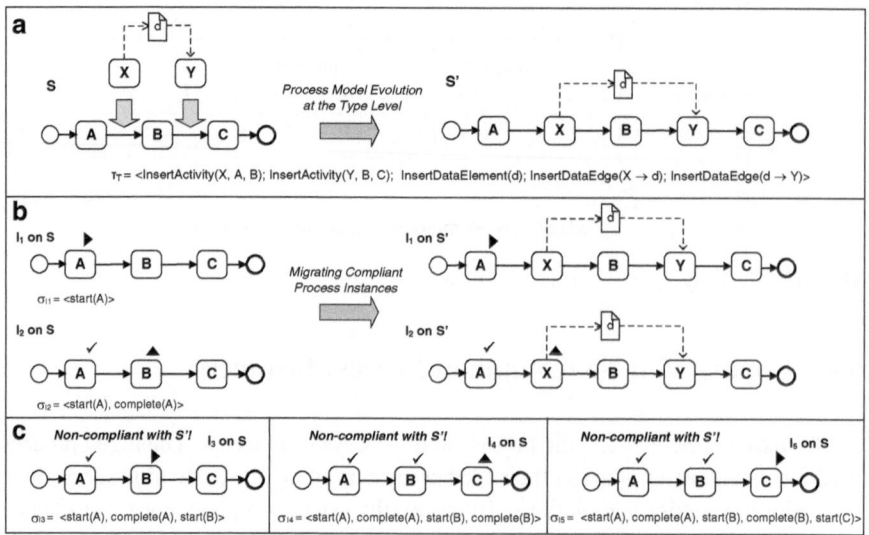

Fig. 9.12 Compliant and noncompliant process instances in a process model evolution

range from the partial rollback of these process instances [262, 313] or their delayed migration [86] to more sophisticated techniques based on adjustments of either the intended type change or the individual process instances. We illustrate the different strategies along an abstract example. Technical details can be found in [299, 301].

9.4.1 Example Scenario

We introduce an example scenario of a process model evolution with both compliant and noncompliant process instances.

> *Example 9.14 (Process Model Evolution with Compliant and Noncompliant Instances).* Consider the process model evolution from S to S' as depicted in Fig. 9.12a: activities X and Y, as well as a data flow between them, are added by type change τ_T. Assume that there are five process instances running on S and being in different states: Instances I_1 and I_2 are state compliant with S' and hence can be migrated to this new process model version (cf. Fig. 9.12b). Opposed to this, I_3, I_4, and I_5 have already progressed too far, i.e., they are not state compliant with S'. Hence, these three instances remain running on S.

Picking up this example, the following section presents different strategies for relinking noncompliant process instances to a new process model version.

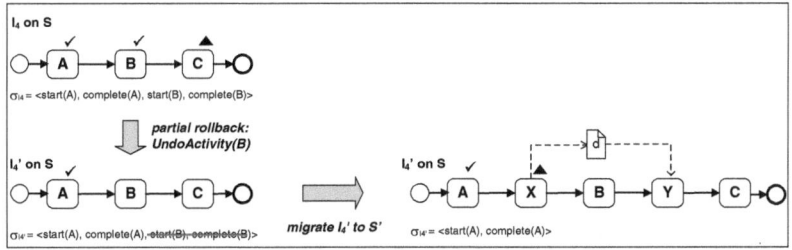

Fig. 9.13   Rolling back a noncompliant process instance to enable proper migration

9.4.2   Bringing Noncompliant Instances into a Compliant State

In certain scenarios, it is sufficient to only migrate state compliant process instances, and to continue with the execution of noncompliant instances on the old process model. For example, assume that the legal requirements for educating a patient about risks before a medical intervention change. While such changes are relevant for all patient treatments that have not yet taken place, already performed treatments are not affected by this change. Thus, no special treatment for noncompliant process instances is required. In general, however, a special treatment of noncompliant process instances is required. First of all, two simple strategies for coping with non-compliant process instances are provided: *partial rollback* and *delayed migration*. Both strategies reset noncompliant process instances to a state in which they become state compliant with the new process model version.

Strategy 1: Partial Rollback. Partial rollback constitutes a widespread strategy for restoring state compliance of noncompliant instances [262, 313]. By (partially) rolling back a process instance, the latter can be reset to a state in which it becomes state compliant with the new process model version. Typically, partial rollback is accompanied with the execution of compensation activities (cf. Chap. 6). For example, assume that an airport is closed down due to an earthquake. Airlines might be required to temporarily change their flight plans due to this disruption. Airplanes that are already approaching this airport might be required to turn around or land at another airstrip.

Example 9.15 (Strategy 1: Partial Rollback of Noncompliant Instances). Consider our example scenario from Fig. 9.12a. For example, I_4 is not state compliant with S'. However, by disabling C and undoing B (i.e., compensating its effects), instance I_4 can be rolled back to a state in which it becomes state compliant with the new process model version S' from Fig. 9.12a. Hence, it can then be migrated to S'. This is illustrated by Fig. 9.13.

Partial rollback of a process instance usually triggers compensating activities (cf. Chap. 6). For example, if a flight is already booked, the compensating activity will cancel the respective booking. It must be noted that the applicability of Strategy 1 is highly situation-dependent, i.e., it might not always be possible to find proper compensating activities. Moreover, even if compensating activities can be defined, such a partial rollback (and loss of work) due to technical reasons will not always be accepted by end-users. Assume, for example, a production process to which a quality inspection step for checking the raw material is added before production. Then all process instances for which the production has already started cannot be made compliant by the described strategy.

Strategy 2: Delayed Migration. An alternative approach for coping with noncompliant process instances is to delay their migration until they become state compliant with the new process model. This strategy can be applied when changing a process model region that is surrounded by a loop construct. For example, if an activity is added to or deleted from a loop body, but the current iteration of the loop has already passed the respective process region for a given process instance, the latter becomes a candidate for migration when the loop enters its next iteration; i.e., relaxed state compliance (cf. Chap. 7) might be satisfied with a delay. As a prerequisite for this approach, respective process instances need to be flagged as "pending to migrate" until the loop enters its next iteration. However, implementation of this migration strategy is not as trivial as it looks like at first glance. First, for process instances with arbitrarily nested loops, several events (i.e., loop backs) might exist which can trigger a delayed migration. Second, it has to be decided how to treat pending instances if another process model evolution takes place (see Fig. 9.11). As with Strategy 1, Strategy 2 is only applicable in specific situations; i.e., changes related to currently executed loop structures.

9.4.3 Advanced Strategies for Treating Noncompliant Instances

This section presents situation-dependent strategies, which either apply type- or instance-specific adjustments; i.e., by adapting the type change or the bias of noncompliant instances, the total number of migratable instances is increased.

Strategy 3: Always-Migrate. In principle, each noncompliant process instance can be migrated to an evolved process model version, i.e., be relinked to it. We denote this strategy as *Always-Migrate*. The basic idea behind it is to adjust the instance-specific bias in such a way that the type change does not become effective for the noncompliant instance; i.e., to neutralize the type change by adding artificial changes to the bias. More precisely, these changes should reverse the effects of the type change τ_T for noncompliant instances.

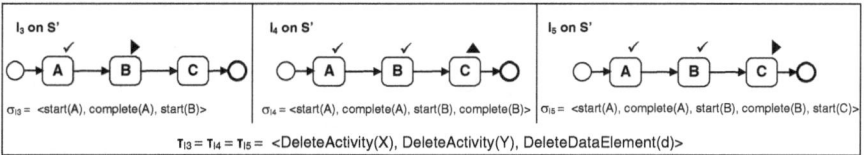

Fig. 9.14 Migrating noncompliant process instances based on bias adaptations

Example 9.16 (Strategy 3: Always-Migrate). Reconsider the scenario from Fig. 9.12 and the three noncompliant instances I_3, I_4, and I_5. The bias of these instances is *empty*. Further, these three process instances have progressed too far and are therefore not state compliant with S'. However, instances I_3, I_4, and I_5 still can be relinked to S' by neutralizing the effects of the process type change τ_T. More precisely, for each of these instances τ_T can be neutralized by deleting the inserted activities and data element (cf. Fig. 9.14). Hence, by creating an instance-specific bias τ_{I_k}, which is logically applied to instance I_k before its start, we obtain valid descriptions of the process instances I_3, I_4, and I_5 now running on S'.

Generally, the challenge is to determine the *inverse* change to be introduced to the biases of migrated, noncompliant instances (see [299] for details).

Strategy 4: Instance-Specific Adjustment. The idea behind this strategy is to apply instance specific adjustments to the changes introduced at the process type level. For example, when adding an activity, the position where to insert it is specified. Obviously, this parameter can be easily adapted, e.g., by inserting the activity at a *later* position in the instance-specific process model than defined by the process type change. On one hand, this makes it possible to relink noncompliant process instances to the new process model version. On the other hand, certain type changes may be applied to the instances, although in a slightly adjusted manner. In general, the semantics of the applied adaptation patterns is exploited when deciding about instance-specific adjustments [299, 301]. For example, activity insertions and movements can be adjusted easily, whereas Strategy 4 is not applicable in the context of activity deletions.

Example 9.17 (Strategy 4: Instance-specific Adjustment). Reconsider the scenario from Fig. 9.12 and the noncompliant instances I_3, I_4, and I_5. By adjusting the positions at which activities X and Y are inserted, for each instance I_k we obtain instance-specific process models being close to S', but with which I_k is state compliant (cf. Fig. 9.15). Obviously, the structural dis-

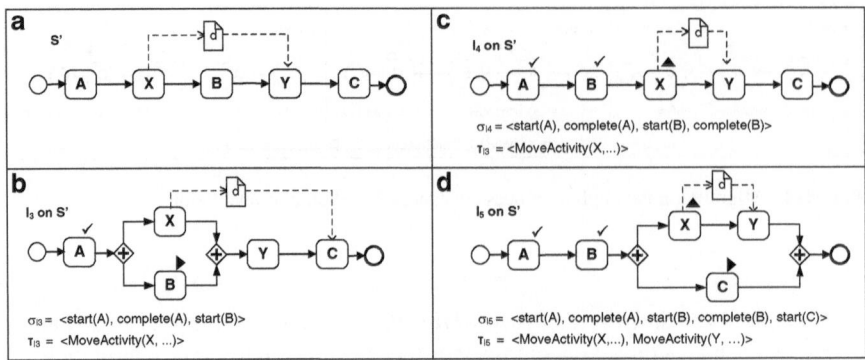

Fig. 9.15   Migrating noncompliant process instances based on instance-specific adjustments

tance between S' and any instance-specific process model S_I should be kept as small as possible. Regarding the given example, the needed adjustments can be realized by applying adaptation pattern *AP3 (Move Process Fragment)* either once (cf. Fig. 9.15b and 9.15c) or twice (cf. Fig. 9.15d).

Generally, for a noncompliant instance I the challenge is determining instance-specific adjustments τ_I in a way that I becomes state compliant with $S_I = S + \tau_I$ and the distance between S_I and S' is minimal (see [181] for a technique measuring such the distance).

Strategy 5: Type-Specific Adjustment. According to this strategy, the type change itself is adjusted to increase the number of migratable process instances. Assume that at the type level process model S shall be transformed into S' by applying change τ_T, but it turns out that the number of noncompliant instances would be too large. Instead of applying multiple instance-specific adjustments, in such case it makes sense to adjust the type change τ_T itself to increase the number of migratable instances. For example, more process instances will become state compliant with a new process model version if new activities are inserted in regions of the process model executed as late as possible during run-time.

Example 9.18 (Migration Strategy: Type-Specific Adjustment). Reconsider the scenario from Fig. 9.12 and the noncompliant instances I_3, I_4, and I_5. By adjusting the type change as shown in Fig. 9.16 (i.e., by inserting X at a later position in model S), the number of state compliant and migratable process instances can be increased from 2 to 4. Generally, it depends on the

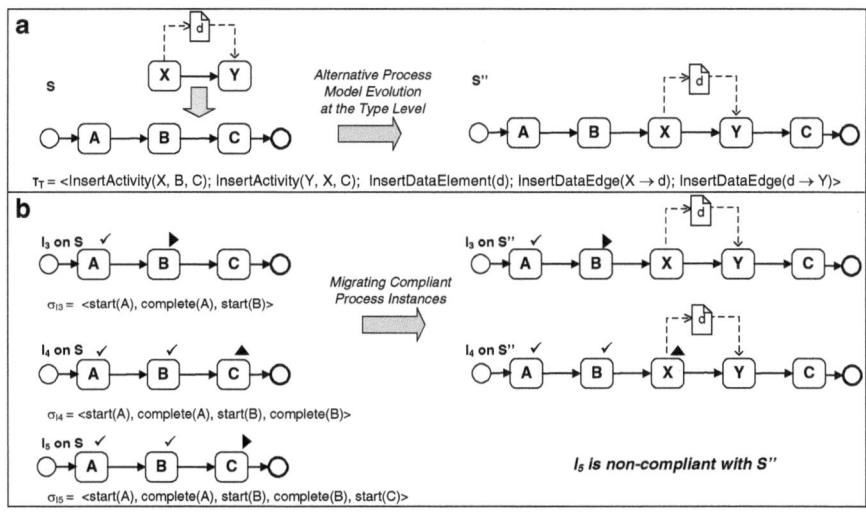

Fig. 9.16   Adjusting a type change to increase the number of migratable instances

application context whether and—if yes—which type-specific adjustments are possible.

9.5   Evolving Other PAIS Perspectives

The previous sections discussed issues related to the evolution of process models. The focus was on the *behavioral perspective* and its evolution over time. In general, however, other PAIS perspectives (cf. Chap. 2) evolve as well.

9.5.1   Changes of the Organization Perspective

In dynamic environments, changes to the organization perspective often become necessary. Usually, the information about organizational entities (e.g., organizational units, roles, actors) and their relationships (e.g., 'user A has role R') is kept in the *organizational model* of the PAIS. The quick and correct adaptation of this model and its related artifacts is therefore fundamental to adequately cope with organization perspective changes, e.g., changing assignments between actors and roles, deleting organizational entities, or merging two organizational units.

Evolving organizational models as a response to real-world changes is not sufficient to guarantee PAIS consistency. Since organizational models provide the basis for defining the access rights of different PAIS components (e.g., actor assignments enabling worklist management [13], access rights for viewing process instances [257], or rights for changing processes [354]), respective information will have to be adapted accordingly; e.g., to avoid orphaned references or non-resolvable actor assignments. Current PAISs often do not adequately address this problem, which leads to security gaps or delays in the implementation of changes. An exception is provided by CEOSIS [298], which is a comprehensive and formal framework for the controlled evolution of organizational models and corresponding access rules. First, CEOSIS provides a set of operators with well-defined semantics for defining and changing organizational models and related access rules. In this context, it defines a correctness notion for access rules. Furthermore, CEOSIS comprises a formal framework for the semi-automated adaptation of access rules when the underlying organizational model is changed. Therefore, the semantics of the applied changes can be exploited toward this end (see [285,297,298] for details).

9.5.2   Changes of the Information Perspective

It is generally a complex task preserving data flow correctness of a prespecified process model when (dynamically) changing it. In this context, a distinction can be made between (1) control flow changes also affecting data flow (e.g., activity deletions) and (2) changes to the data flow schema itself (e.g., inserting new data elements or adding data links between activities and data elements). While for case (1), the already discussed correctness notions (e.g., state compliance) are sufficient to ensure data flow correctness, case (2) necessitates additional techniques. In [296], for example, it is shown how the state compliance criterion can be extended based on augmented execution traces to ensure data consistency in the context of data flow changes. Further, precise conditions to efficiently ensure data flow correctness in the context of dynamic process changes are provided.

9.5.3   Changes of Other Perspectives

In [313], an approach for the integrated management of process changes and the *time perspective* in adaptive PAIS is presented.

Another interesting aspect concerns the transition conditions used for control flow routing in a prespecified process model. In many cases, respective transition conditions are rather complex and change more frequently than the other parts of a prespecified model and PAIS respectively. To avoid being forced to evolve and redeploy a prespecified process model each time a transition condition is changed, the latter are usually outsourced and maintained as separate rules in a *business rule engine* [234]. These rules cover complex business logic and constrain the execution paths a process may take. For example, a business rule must disqualify rental tenants if their credit rating is too low or, to use another example, company agents need to use a list of preferred suppliers and supply schedules. If a business rule evolves, it must, in turn, be adapted accordingly. However, this neither requires process model adaptations nor the redeployment of the respective model if the rule is maintained in a rule engine.

9.6   Process Model Refactoring

While the previous sections have discussed process model evolution to accommodate the evolving needs of business processes, this section introduces process model refactoring. Refactoring refers to *the process of changing a software system in such a way that it does not alter the external behavior of the program code, yet improves its internal structure* [91]. As such, refactoring neither resolves errors nor adds functionality, but improves understandability and maintainability through *behavior-preserving* transformations [239]. Refactorings constitute small changes with little value when applied in isolation, but these become valuable when combined with other refactorings [47]. Thus, process model refactoring constitutes an iterative process which enables designers to improve the quality of a process repository.

Refactoring differs from the model transformations applied when redesigning or adapting processes in the context of process schema evolution, since these transformations are typically not behavior-preserving. Refactoring can be classified as *endogenous* (i.e., transformations between models expressed in same language) and *horizontal* (i.e., source and target model reside at the same level of abstraction) [210].

According to [211] refactoring can be defined by a process consisting of a number of distinct activities (cf. Fig. 9.17).

9.6.1   Identifying Refactoring Opportunities

In the SE domain *code smells* are the most popular method for identifying refactoring opportunities [211]. Picking up on this metaphor, *process model smells* (PMS) serve as indicators for low process model quality (cf. Table 9.1) [351].

In the following we introduce some of the above listed process model smells. For a full catalog we refer to [351].

Non-Intention Revealing Naming of Activity/Process Model. Activities in a process model are normally tagged with textual labels. However, improper labels may not reveal the intended content or purpose to readers, making the model

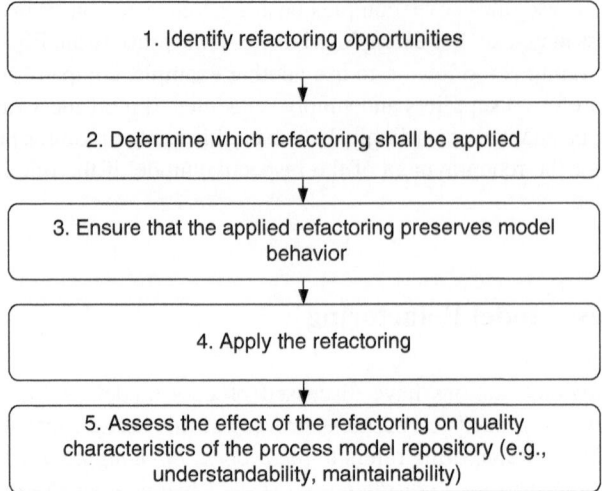

Fig. 9.17 Refactoring process

Table 9.1 Catalog of process model smells

PMS1: Non-intention revealing naming of activity / process model
PMS2: Contrived complexity
PMS3: Redundant process fragments
PMS4: Large process models
PMS5: Lazy process models
PMS6: Unused branches
PMS7: Frequently occurring instance changes
PMS8: Frequently occurring variant changes

more difficult to understand [202, 326, 328]. An analysis of a large collection of industrial process models showed that non-intention revealing labels—in particular, activities with similar intentions, but different labels or labeling styles—constitute a frequently occurring process model smell [351]. Existing empirical evidence suggests that consistently labeling activities following the "verb-object" style fosters process model understandability [206, 208]. Activities not following the "verb-object" style can be automatically detected [175]. Moreover, techniques are available to detect inconsistent labels [75].

Redundant Process Fragments. Redundant process fragments—either within a single process model or across different process models—constitute another frequently occurring process model smell [351]. Whenever it is required to change the control flow logic captured by respective fragments (e.g. due to regulatory changes), the change must be propagated across all these occurrences. When overlooking some of them, or when applying any of the changes incorrectly, inconsistencies arise that make successive maintenance even more problematic. Redundancy in process models should therefore be avoided (e.g., [49, 148]). Techniques for identifying similar process models with overlapping behavior are described in [74,75,81,250].

Large Process Models. With an increasing number of activities, process models become more difficult to understand and to maintain. Overly large process models should therefore be avoided. Existing modeling guidelines suggest keeping the number of activities below 50 at any decomposition level [207]. The authoritative literature already recommends modularizing process models with more than 5–15 [147] or 5–7 activities [326]. Different proposal for the automatic discovery of suitable subprocesses are described in [276].

Frequently Occurring Instance Changes. When executing a particular process instance it may become necessary to deviate from the logic predefined in the process model (cf. Chap. 7). However, a high frequency of such changes can be problematic. It often indicates that the actual process model does not properly reflect the real process, which undermines its role as communication instrument. When exceptions occur frequently, it is desirable to pull similar instance changes up to the process type level [355], since this improves the semantic quality of the process model (i.e., it decreases the gap between the modeled and real-world process) and reduces the need for future instance changes. ProCycle [355], for example, has been explicitly developed to support such discovery of desirable process model changes.

Examples 9.19 and 9.20 illustrate several of the process model smells.

Example 9.19 (Process Model Smells). Consider the following example, which describes (in simplified form) the pre-takeoff process for a general aviation flight under visual flight rules (VFR).

Before conducting a general aviation flight the pilot has to perform a weather check. She then optionally files the flight plan. This is followed by a preflight inspection of the airplane. For large airports, the pilot calls clearance delivery to request the engine start clearance. If an airport has a tower control she has to contact ground to get taxi clearance, otherwise she has to announce taxiing. This is followed by taxiing to the run-up area and performing run-up inspections to ensure that the airplane is ready for flight. If the airport has a tower, it is contacted to get takeoff clearance, otherwise take-off intentions have to be announced. Finally, the pre-takeoff process finishes with the takeoff of the airplane.

During the preflight inspections the pilot can detect problems with the airplane. If the problems are severe, the flight will be immediately canceled. Otherwise, if the airplane can move under its own power, the pilot will taxi it to the repair station. Alternatively, the airplane is either towed to the repair station or a mechanic comes to the airplane in order to deal with the problem. After the repair, the flight is restarted with a weather check.

Figure 9.18 depicts the pre-takeoff process as described above including several process model smells. First, the model does not strictly follow the verb-object style of naming activities, which relates to PMS1 (*Non-Intention Revealing Naming of Activity*). For example, activity *Repair* violates this convention. Second, the process model contains redundant process model fragments (i.e., Fragments 1 and 2), which constitutes an example of PMS3 (*Redundant Process Model*). Third, the depicted model is rather large and complex, constituting an example of PMS4 (*Large Process Model*).

Example 9.20 (Urinary Stone Diagnostics). This example provides an illustration of PMS7 (Frequently Occurring Instance Changes) using a clinical guideline for urinary stone diagnostics as an example (cf. Fig. 9.19a). Physicians deviate from this process quite frequently, for example, in cases where a patient is pregnant or has an increased blood sugar level. In the former case, an additional lab test (*Check Blood Glucose*) is added and activity *Perform Abdominal X-ray* is substituted by activity *Perform MRT*. In the latter case, lab tests are added (i.e., *Test HbA1C* and *Calculate Glycemic Profile*). Figure 9.19b depicts the guideline for taking pregnancy and diabetes into consideration.

Whether the occurrence of a smell really means that a model must be refactored is not a black-or-white decision. The value of a particular refactoring often involves the trade-off between different quality characteristics. For example, extracting (redundant) process fragments from one or several process model(s) decreases the overall model size, but potentially increases the number of process models (with a low number of activities). In the end, process modeling experts have to decide on a case-by-case basis by carefully considering potential trade-offs.

9.6.2 Refactoring Techniques

To address the process model smells introduced in Sect. 9.6.1 and to improve process model quality, techniques for refactoring process models can be applied (cf. Fig. 9.20). Thereby, refactorings constitute structural model changes (cf. Definition 7.1) which are behavior-preserving if certain preconditions are met, i.e., when evolving model S to S' *trace equivalence* is ensured (cf. Definition 9.4).

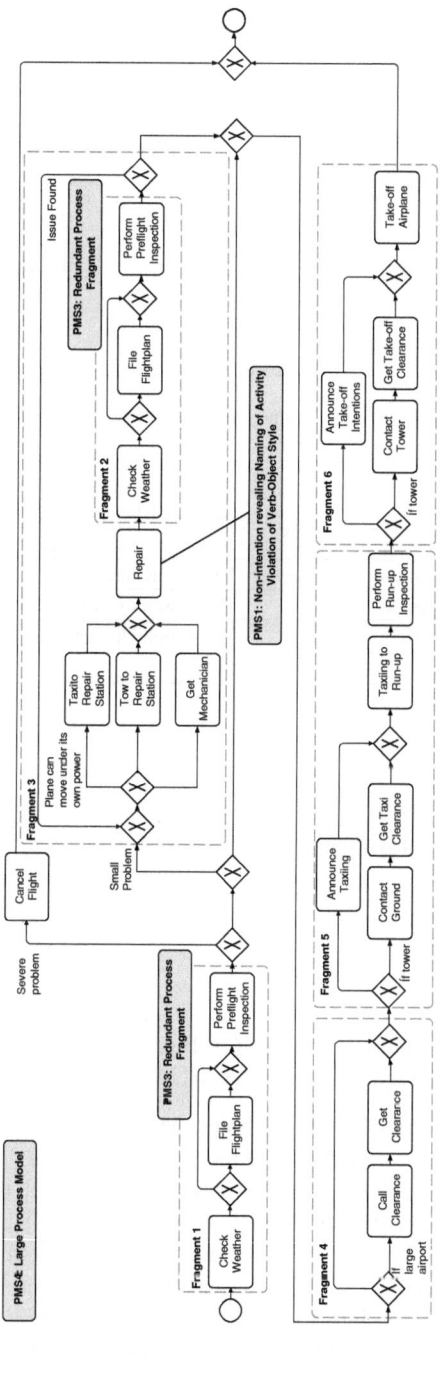

Fig. 9.18 Original model of the pre-takeoff process [351]

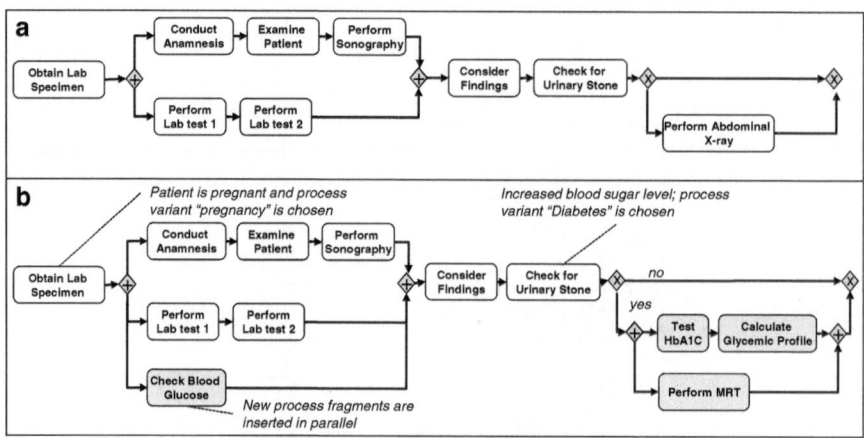

Fig. 9.19 Example of clinical guideline "urinary stone diagnostics" [351]

Refactorings	
RF1: Rename Activity	RF7: Re-label Collection
RF2: Rename Process Schema	RF8: Remove Redundancies
RF3: Substitute Process Fragment	RF9: Generalize Variant Changes
RF4: Extract Process Fragment	RF10: Remove Unused Branches
RF5: Replace Process Fragment by Reference	RF11: Pull Up Instance Change
RF6: Inline Process Fragment	

Fig. 9.20 Refactoring catalog

Definition 9.4 (Trace Equivalence). Let S and S' be two process models. Let further QS_S and QS'_S be the set of completed traces producible on S and S', respectively. Then: S and S' are called trace equivalent if, and only if, $QS_S \equiv QS'_S$.

In the following, selected refactorings (cf. Fig. 9.20) are introduced. For a more detailed description of refactorings we refer to [351].

RF1/RF2 (Rename Activity/Rename Process Model), RF7 (Relabel Collection). With refactoring *Rename Activity* (RF1) the name of an activity can be changed if it is not intention revealing. If an activity occurs several times in a process model, all occurrences of that activity will be renamed. RF1 is comparable to the *Rename Method* refactoring in software engineering (SE) [91]. Similarly, refactoring *Rename Process Model* (RF2) enables designers to rename a process model. A similar refactoring in SE is called *Rename Class* [57]. RF7, in turn, is a composed refactoring for relabeling a particular activity in all models of a model collection. For this, RF1 is applied to all models containing the activities to be relabeled. Altogether these refactorings can be used to address smell *PMS1 (Non-Intention Revealing Naming)*. Labels that do not follow the "verb object" style can be automatically refactored using techniques described in [174].

RF4 (Extract Process Fragment), RF5 (Replace Process Fragment by Reference), RF8 (Remove Redundancies). Refactoring *Extract Process Fragment* (RF4) can be used to extract a single SESE fragment or a sequence of SESE fragments (cf. Chap. 4) from any process model S (e.g., to eliminate redundant fragments or to reduce the size of model S). Applying RF4 results in the creation of a new process model S' implementing the fragment. In addition, in S the original fragment is replaced by a complex activity referring to S'. Refactoring *Replace Process Fragment by Reference* (RF5), in turn, is used to replace a process fragment by a trace-equivalent subprocess model. Finally, refactoring *Remove Redundancies* (RF8) is a composed refactoring based on RF4 and RF5. It can be applied to a collection of models $S_1 \ldots S_n$ to remove redundancies. For this, RF4 is applied to one of these models to extract the redundant fragment. R5 is applied to all other models for replacing the respective fragment by a reference to the (sub)process model created before. Thus, RF4, RF5, and RF8 are potential remedies for model smells *PMS3 (Redundant Process Fragment)* and *PMS4 (Large Process Model)*. The intent of these refactorings is similar to *Extract Method* as known from SE [91]. To guarantee that RF4 does not alter the behavior of the process model, the fragment to be extracted must be a SESE fragment or a sequence of SESE fragments (cf. Sect. 4.2). For applying RF5, the SESE fragment to be replaced, as well as the (sub)process model, need to be trace-equivalent.

RF11 (Pull Up Instance Change). Refactoring *Pull Up Instance Change* (RF11) can be used to generalize frequently occurring instance changes by pulling them up to the process type level. Thus, RF11 serves as a remedy for smell *PMS7—Frequently Occurring Instance Changes*. Trace equivalence cannot be used to exclude errors when applying RF11. By pulling changes from the instance level to the type level, producible behavior is always altered. Instead, state compliance is used as a formal notion.

Example 9.21 (Process Model Refactorings). To address the process model smells highlighted in Example 9.19, the process designer decides to apply several refactorings. To remove PMS1 (*Non-Intention Revealing Naming of Activity*) he selects the respective activity and renames it *Repair Airplane* using RF1 (*Rename Activity*). To deal with PMS4 (*Redundant Process Fragment*), the designer selects Fragment 1 and chooses RF4 (*Extract Process Fragment*) to extract Model *Preflight Process Schema* (RF4 is applicable since the selection constitutes a SESE fragment and thus fulfills the preconditions for RF4). In the next step, he selects Fragment 2 and chooses refactoring

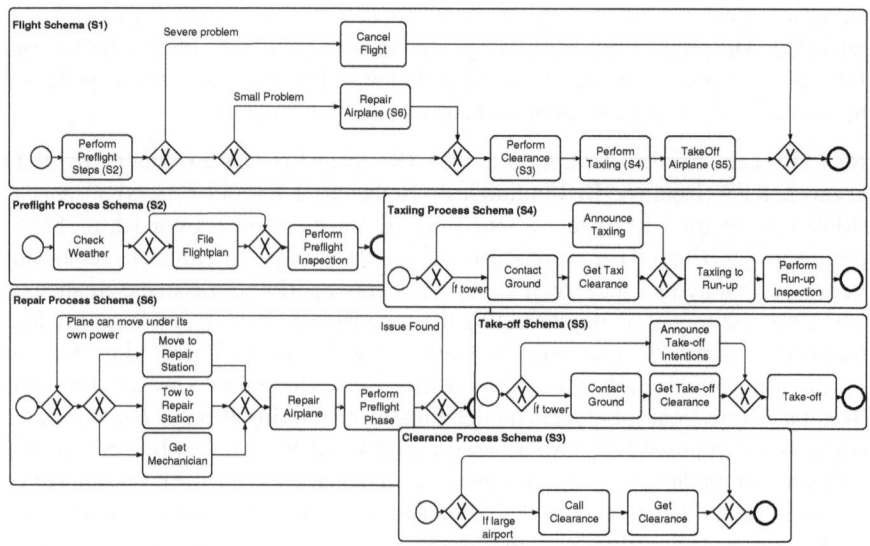

Fig. 9.21 Pre-takeoff process model after refactoring [351]

RF5 (*Replace Process Fragment by Reference*) to replace this fragment with a reference to Model *Preflight Process Schema* (cf. Fig. 9.21).

Although these two changes have already reduced the size of the pre-takeoff process by eight nodes, the process model is still rather large and complex which constitutes an example of PMS 6 (*Large Process Model*). Therefore, the designer decides to also apply refactoring RF4 (*Extract Process Fragment*) to Fragments 3–6, since each of them comprises several activities logically belonging together. For example, Fragment 3 deals with the repair of an airplane if issues are detected during the preflight inspections.

Figure 9.21 illustrates the model after applying all refactorings described above. A summary of the conducted refactorings is depicted in Fig. 9.22.

Example 9.22 (Pulling Instance Changes Up). Since instance adaptations occurred frequently in Example 9.20, it was decided to consider them in a specific variant of the original guideline (cf. Fig. 9.19b).

Before Refactoring	Refactorings	After Refactoring
PMS1 – 1 violation of verb-object style	RF1 (1x)	All activities labeled according to verb-object style
PMS3 – Fragments 1 and 2 are redundant	RF4 (1x) RF5 (1x)	No redundant fragments Reduction of model size by 8
PMS4 – Process model with 42 nodes (22 activities, 18 gateways, 1 start node, 1 end node)	RF4 (4x)	Flight Schema (S1): size 12 Preflight Process Schema (S2): size 7 Clearance Process Schema (S3): size 6 Taxiing Process Schema (S4): size 9 Take-Off Process Schema (S5): size 8 Repair Process Schema (S6): size 11

Fig. 9.22 Overview of conducted refactorings

9.7 Summary

This chapter discussed techniques for supporting the evolution of long-running business processes in a PAIS. In particular, it dealt with *process model evolution*, i.e., the transformation of a process model to a new version. While *deferred model evolution* only requires the versioning of process models, additional challenges are imposed in the context of *immediate model evolution*, since strategies for the controlled and robust migration of running process instances to the new process model version are then needed. This chapter further introduced *process model refactorings*, which are needed to foster internal quality of process models and to ensure maintainability of the PAIS over time. In this context, different process model smells were presented which describe symptoms of bad process model quality. Moreover, different refactoring techniques to address existing process model smells were discussed.

While process model refactorings are behavior-preserving, process model evolution is typically behavior-altering. For behavior-altering changes, it must be ensured that they do not lead to violations of business compliance and related semantical integrity constraints. We will discuss issues related to this challenge in Chap. 10.

Exercises

9.1. Similarities and Differences Between Ad hoc Changes and Propagated Type Changes
Both the ad hoc change of a single process instance, and the propagation of a process type change to corresponding process instances, constitute dynamic process changes. Discuss their commonalities and differences.

9.2. Process Model Evolution and Instance Migration
Figure 9.23 shows the evolution of process model S: Activity I is deleted and activity E is serially inserted between activities B and F, resulting in process model S'. Consider now process instances I_1, I_2, and I_3 running on S as depicted on

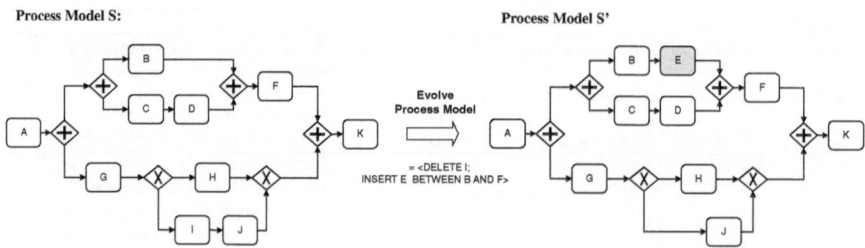

Fig. 9.23 Evolution of a process model

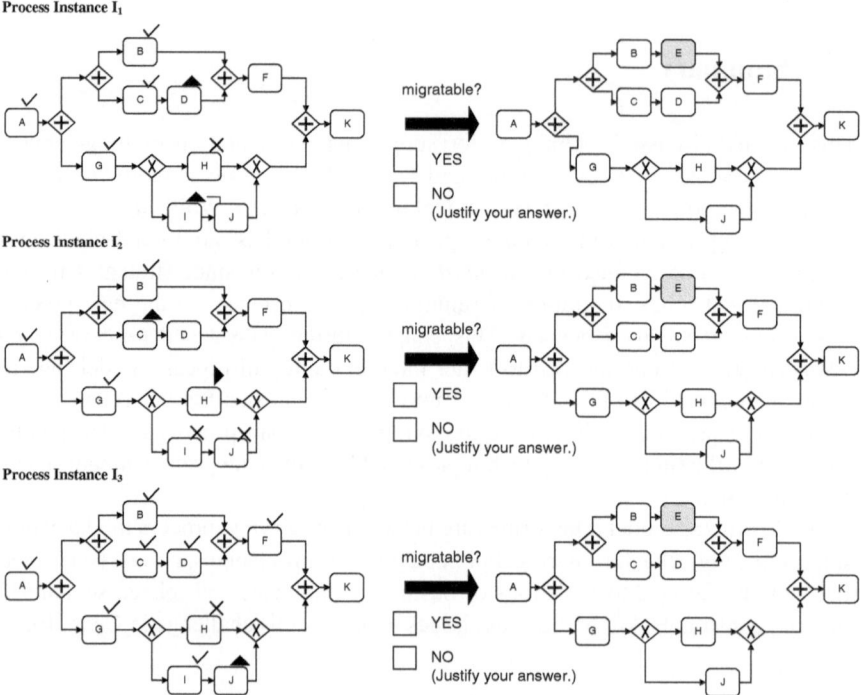

Fig. 9.24 Migration of related process instances

the left-hand side of Fig. 9.24. For each of these instances check whether or not it may migrate to the new process model S' presuming *state compliance* as a basic corrections notion. If I_k migrates to S', draw the process instance and its state resulting from this migration (use the templates on the right-hand side of Fig. 9.24 for this). Otherwise, give a reason why migration is not possible.

9.3. Conflicting Changes at the Process Type and Process Instance Level

Consider the evolution of process model S to S' as depicted in Fig. 9.25a: a control dependency is added indicating that activity D needs to be completed before activity

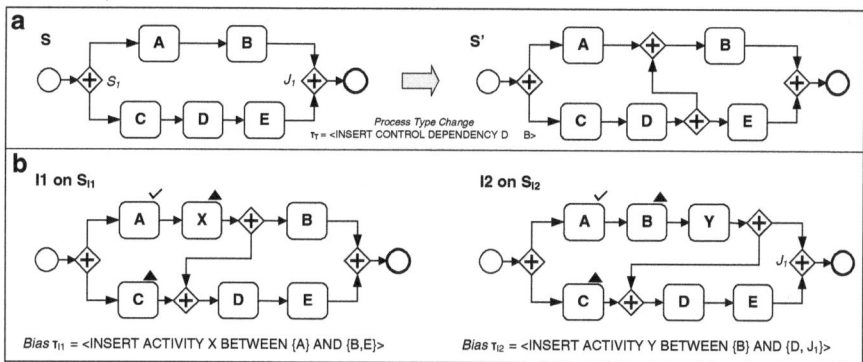

Fig. 9.25 Evolution of a process model and related biased process instances

B may be enabled. Furthermore, consider the two process instances I1 and I2 shown in Fig. 9.25b. Both I1 and I2 were derived from S, but are now running on instance-specific process models S_{I1} and S_{I2}, respectively, due to previous ad hoc changes. For example, S_{I1} was derived from S by adding activity X after activity A and before activities B and D.

To which of the two process instances may the process type change be propagated? Give an explanation referring to Definition 9.3.

9.4. Disjoint and Overlapping Process Type and Process Instance Changes
Consider the evolution of process model S to S' as depicted in Fig. 9.26a: Activity C is deleted (leading to the concomitant deletion of the two gateway nodes) and activities X (between A and B) and Y (between B and D) are added.

(a) Consider the unbiased process instances I_1 and I_2 from Fig. 9.26b that were created from S. For each process instance decide whether it may migrate to S'. Draw the resulting process instance graph if migration is possible.
(b) Consider the biased process instances I_3, I_4, and I_5 from Fig. 9.26c which were created from S. For each of these process instances categorize its instance-specific bias in relation to the process type change τ_T depicted in Fig. 9.26a. Decide whether or not the respective process instance may be migrated to the new process model version. If migration is possible, provide the process instance graph and instance bias resulting afterwards.

9.5. Coping with Noncompliant Process Instances

(a) Discuss the pros and cons of the five migration strategies suggested in the context of noncompliant process instances (cf. Sect. 9.4).
(b) Consider the process model evolution from S to S' as depicted in Fig. 9.4 and the related process instance I_3. In the given scenario, I_3 is noncompliant with S' and is therefore not directly migratable to S'. Which of the five migration strategies can be applied in the given context in order to relink I_3 to S' in the end, i.e., to migrate I_3 to S', while preserving the soundness of I_3? For each applicable migration strategy show the result after the migration of I_3.

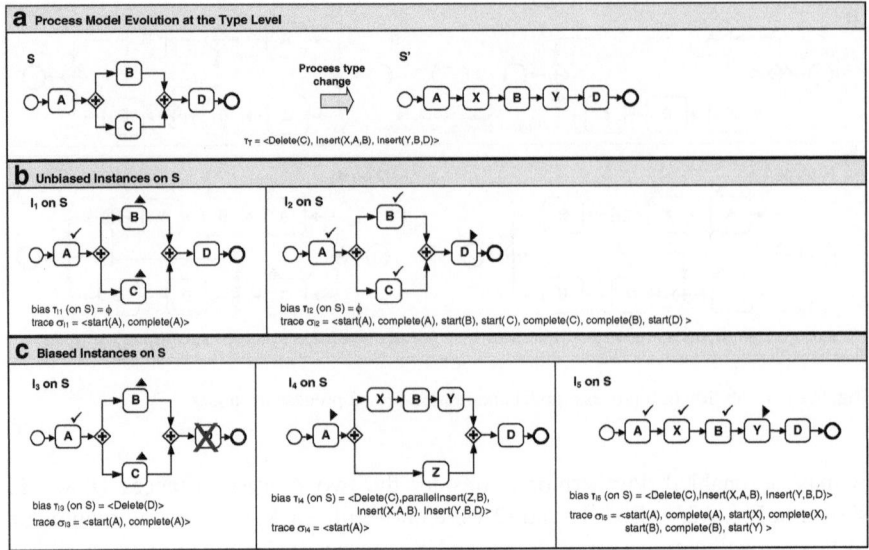

Fig. 9.26 Evolution of a process model and related process instances

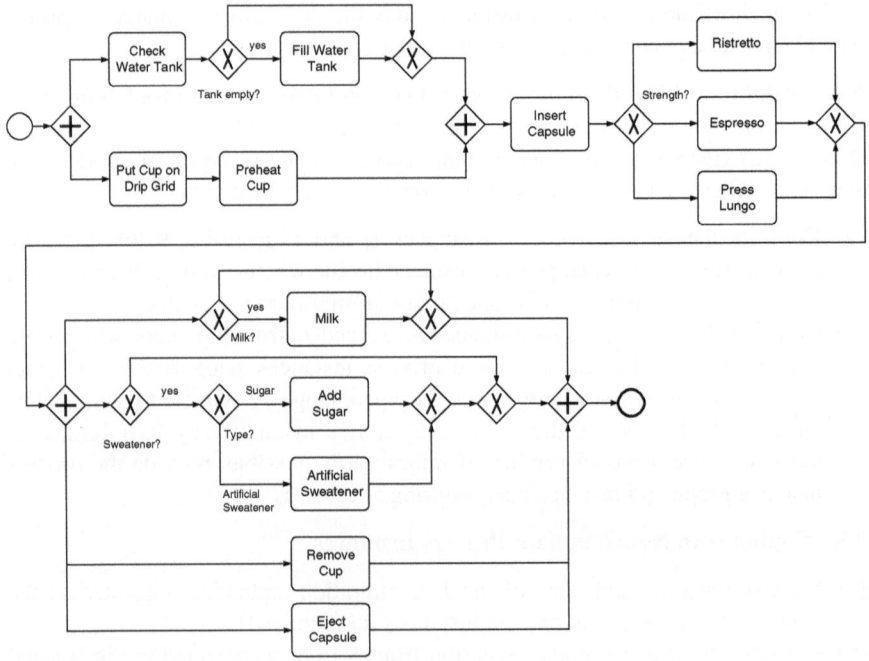

Fig. 9.27 A process model containing process model smells

9.6. Process Model Evolution Versus Process Model Refactorings

Compare process model evolution and process model refactoring. Discuss commonalities and differences.

9.7. Process Model Smells and Process Model Refactorings

Consider the process model depicted in Fig. 9.27. What process model smells can you identify in this model? How would you refactor the process model to improve the quality of the model? Justify your proposal.

Chapter 10
Business Process Compliance

Abstract In the previous chapters, the proper executability of a prespecified process model has been based on syntactical constraints, correctness of its data flow schema, and behavioral soundness. However, business processes are also subject to semantic constraints that stem from regulations, laws, and guidelines—also known as *compliance rules*. Process-aware information systems have to ensure that respective compliance rules are obeyed in order to guarantee semantically correct and error-free execution as well as changes of their business processes. This chapter discusses how such compliance rules can be defined and how they can be ensured in the different phases of the process life cycle.

10.1 Motivation

In Chap. 4, the correctness of a prespecified process model has been related to its syntactical properties, its proper data flow, and its behavioral soundness (e.g., proper completion, absence of dead activities). However, these are not the only constraints a prespecified process model must obey. Typically, prespecified process models and corresponding process instances are also subject to *semantic constraints* stemming from a variety of sources, like standards, regulations, guidelines, corporate policies, and laws (e.g. Basel or Sarbanes-Oxley-Act) [312]. In the following, these semantic constraints are denoted as *compliance rules*. Furthermore, techniques for ensuring the compliance of a business process with these rules are covered under the term *business process compliance*.

When being confronted with large process repositories or a multitude of compliance rules, the demand for techniques automatically ensuring business process compliance raises. In particular, compliance rules may impose constraints on the control flow schema of process models, constrain the data to be managed, require certain types of activities to be present in a process model, or enforce access control policies. To set a focus, this chapter deals with the impact compliance rules have on the control flow schema of a prespecified process model, i.e., we discuss how

M. Reichert and B. Weber, *Enabling Flexibility in Process-Aware Information Systems*,   297
DOI 10.1007/978-3-642-30409-5_10, © Springer-Verlag Berlin Heidelberg 2012

compliance rules restrict the order in which process activities may be executed. Hence, in the context of this chapter, a compliance rule can be defined as a function reflecting whether or not a process instance—represented by its execution trace—complies with the rule (cf. Definition 10.1).

Definition 10.1 (Compliance Rule). Let Σ be the set of all activities and let $\Sigma^\star$ be the set of all possible execution traces of processes based on activities from Σ. Then, a *compliance rule* ϕ defines a function $\phi : \Sigma^\star \to Boolean$ that considers any trace $\sigma = < e_1, \ldots, e_k > \in \Sigma^\star$ either to be true (i.e., to be compliant with ϕ) or false (i.e. to violate ϕ or to be not compliant with it). We further denote $\sigma \models \phi :\Leftrightarrow \phi(\sigma)$ and say trace σ satisfies compliance rule ϕ.

Example 10.1 illustrates the relationship between a prespecified process model and compliance rules.

Example 10.1 (Compliance Rules). Consider process model S_{med} from Fig. 10.1. It shows a variant of the prespecified process model for planning and performing a keyhole surgery in a hospital (cf. Chap. 2). Furthermore, consider the informal compliance rules from Table 10.1, which must be satisfied by all medical processes of the respective hospital. Hence, these compliance rules have to be obeyed by process model S_{med} as well. When analyzing the dynamic behavior of this process model, its soundness (cf. Chap. 4) can be easily verified. However, having a closer look at S_{med} and the compliance rules from Table 10.1, one can recognize that this process model contains semantic errors; i.e., it violates some of the compliance rules given. For example, according to process model S_{med} the *Surgical Ward* may send the patient to the *Surgical Suite* before the patient is prepared; the surgery could be even performed without having prepared the patient at all. Obviously, this violates compliance rule c_1. Furthermore, in the process model given, the patient is either informed about anesthesia or risks, but not about both. However, according to compliance rule c_3 the patient must be always informed about the risks after the examination. Hence, compliance rule c_3 is potentially violated.

Generally, business process compliance concerns the entire process life cycle. Accordingly, the following sections consider business process compliance along the different phases of the process life cycle as suggested in [196, 199] as well. At the modeling phase, *a priori compliance checking* verifies whether or not prespecified process models obey compliance rules [36, 145]. Additionally, compliance must be monitored for process instances during their execution [200, 201]. This is

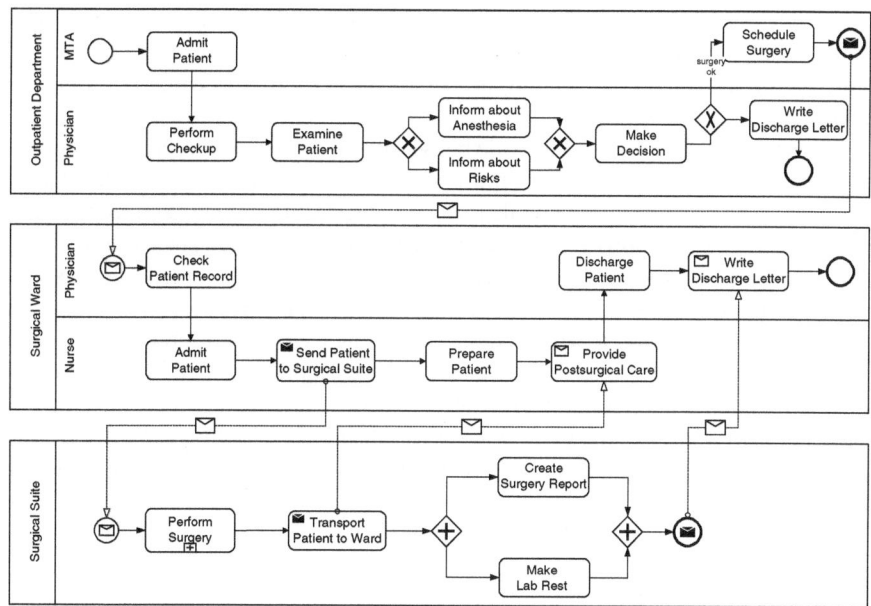

Fig. 10.1 Prespecified process model S_{med}

Table 10.1 Examples of compliance rules for medical processes

c_1	Before a surgery may be performed the patient must be prepared for it and be sent to the surgical suite.
c_2	After examining the patient a decision must be made. However, this must not be done before the examination.
c_3	After the examination, the patient must be informed about the risks of the (planned) surgery.
c_4	Before scheduling the surgery the patient has to be informed about anesthesia.
c_5	If a surgery has not been scheduled it must not be performed.
c_6	After a patient is discharged a discharge letter must be written.
c_7	After performing the surgery and before writing the discharge letter, a surgery report must be created and a lab test be made.

particularly crucial for process instances defined or adapted on-the-fly (cf. Chap. 7), i.e., for which there is no fully prespecified process model. Likewise, *compliance monitoring* at run-time is required if a priori compliance checking is not feasible, e.g., if the process model is too large or the compliance rules are too complex. Regarding completed process instances, in addition, a process-aware information system (PAIS) needs to be able to determine whether these instances were executed in compliance with given regulations, laws, and guidelines. For this purpose, *a*

posteriori compliance checking analyzes execution logs (cf. Chap. 8) accordingly
[10]. Finally, the effects of changes in respect to the compliance of prespecified
process models and corresponding process instances are considered (cf. Chaps. 7
and 9).

Regardless of the process life cycle phase for which business process compliance
must be ensured, compliance rules must be specified in a machine-readable manner.
Hence, this chapter first deals with issues related to the modeling of compliance
rules in Sect. 10.2. Following this, it is shown how compliance can be ensured during
the different phases of the process life cycle. More precisely, Sect. 10.3 addresses a
priori compliance checking in the process modeling phase. Section 10.4 then shows
how compliance rules can be monitored during the execution of process instances,
whereas Sect. 10.5 discusses issues related to the compliance of completed process
instances. Section 10.6 further illustrates how compliance can be ensured in the
context of process model changes. We address the user perspective in Sect. 10.7 and
present existing approaches enabling business process compliance in Sect. 10.8. The
chapter closes with a summary in Sect. 10.9.

10.2 Modeling Compliance Rules

As prerequisite for verifying business process compliance of prespecified process
models, process instances, or process execution logs, corresponding compliance
rules need to be provided in a machine-readable manner. In literature, there exist
different approaches for this [33, 36, 83, 99, 102, 189, 198]. A popular way to define
and represent compliance rules is the usage of *Linear Temporal Logic* (LTL) [93].
LTL is a modal temporal logic with modalities referring to time. It enhances
ordinary propositional logic with additional temporal operators as specified in
Definition 10.2.

Definition 10.2 (Syntax of Linear Temporal Logic). A formula $< LTL >$
is a syntactical correct *LTL formula* if it complies with the following grammar
(expressed in BNF):

$$< LTL >::= \quad \top \mid \perp \mid \neg < LTL > \mid (< LTL >)$$
$$\mid \mathbf{X} < LTL > \mid \mathbf{F} < LTL > \mid \mathbf{G} < LTL >$$
$$\mid < LTL > \wedge < LTL > \mid < LTL > \Rightarrow < LTL >$$
$$\mid < LTL > \vee < LTL > \mid < LTL > \mathbf{U} < LTL >$$
$$\mid < LTL > \mathbf{W} < LTL >$$

In Definition 10.2, $\mathbf{X}$, $\mathbf{F}$, $\mathbf{G}$, $\mathbf{U}$, and $\mathbf{W}$ correspond to *temporal operators*: $\mathbf{X}$ means *next*, $\mathbf{F}$ means *eventually*, $\mathbf{G}$ means *always*, $\mathbf{U}$ means *until*, and $\mathbf{W}$ means *weakly until*. Furthermore, $<LTL>$ may contain propositional variables. In the context given, these variables correspond to the execution of process activities, e.g., $\mathbf{G}$ (*DischargePatient* $\Rightarrow$ $\mathbf{F}$ *Write Discharge Letter*). The temporal operators enable the navigation from point to point on a time line. Definition 10.3 provides the formal semantics of these temporal operators using recursive equitations.

Definition 10.3 (Semantics of Linear Temporal Logic). LTL is defined on infinite traces. Hence, for any execution trace $\sigma = <e_1, e_2, e_3, \ldots, e_n>$ we first define its infinite extension $\overline{\sigma} := <e_1, e_2, e_3, \ldots, e_n, \emptyset, \emptyset, \cdots>$ by adding empty events after event e_n. Further let ϕ and ψ be LTL formulas.

$$\sigma \models \phi :\Leftrightarrow \overline{\sigma} \models \phi$$

$$\overline{\sigma} = <e_1, e_2, e_3, \cdots> \models \mathbf{X}\phi :\Leftrightarrow <e_2, e_3, \cdots> \models \phi$$

1. $\overline{\sigma} \models \mathbf{F}\phi :\Leftrightarrow \overline{\sigma} \models \phi \vee \mathbf{X}\mathbf{F}\phi$
2. $\overline{\sigma} \models \mathbf{G}\phi :\Leftrightarrow \overline{\sigma} \models \phi \wedge \mathbf{X}\mathbf{G}\phi$
3. $\overline{\sigma} \models \phi\,\mathbf{U}\,\psi :\Leftrightarrow \overline{\sigma} \models \psi \vee (\phi \wedge \mathbf{X}(\phi\,\mathbf{U}\,\psi))$
   whereby ψ must occur eventually (i.e., $\mathbf{F}\psi$ holds).
4. $\overline{\sigma} \models \phi\,\mathbf{W}\,\psi :\Leftrightarrow \overline{\sigma} \models \psi \vee (\phi \wedge \mathbf{X}(\phi\,\mathbf{W}\,\psi))$
   whereby ψ does not have to occur eventually (i.e., $\mathbf{G}\neg\psi$ is allowed).

Example 10.2 illustrates how LTL can be used for modeling compliance rules.

Example 10.2 (Modeling Compliance Rules with LTL). Table 10.2 provides examples illustrating the use of LTL. More precisely, the informal compliance rules from Table 10.1 are now formally defined based on LTL.

Obviously, the formal definition of compliance rules based on LTL or other temporal logics (e.g., Table 10.2) requires profound expert knowledge. In particular, LTL expressions will not be understandable to domain experts. Hence, more comprehensible graphical notations like *Compliance Rule Graphs (CRGs)* have been developed [198]. CRGs allow modeling compliance rules on a higher level of abstraction based on graphs. To be more precise, CRGs define a compliance rule by means of an *antecedent pattern* complemented by a *consequence pattern*. Both the antecedent and the consequence pattern consist of *occurrence* and *absence* *nodes*.

Table 10.2 Representing the Compliance Rules from Table 10.1 in LTL

c_1	¬*Perform Surgery* **W** (*Prepare Patient* ∧ (¬*Perform Surgery* **W** *Send Patient to Surgical Suite*))
c_2	(**G** (*Examine Patient* ⇒ **F** *Make Decision*)) ∧ (¬*Make Decision* **U** *Examine Patient*)
c_3	**G** (*Examine Patient* ⇒ **F** *Inform about Risks*)
c_4	¬*Schedule Surgery* **W** *Inform about Anesthesia*
c_5	(**G** ¬*Schedule Surgery*) ⇒ (**G** ¬*Perform Surgery*)
c_6	**G** (*Discharge Patient* ⇒ **F** *Write Discharge Letter*)
c_7	**G** (¬*Perform Surgery* ⇒ (**F** *Write Discharge Letter* ⇒ ((¬*Write Discharge Letter* **U** *Create Surgery Report*) ∧ (¬*Write Discharge Letter* **U** *Make Lab Test*))))

These nodes are connected by directed edges that may also be used to connect antecedent nodes with consequence nodes. While nodes require the existence or absence of activities, the edges connecting them describe respective activity sequences. Note that edges must not connect two absence nodes. Figure 10.2 gives a first impression of how CRGs look like showing two examples (see Examples 10.3 and 10.4 for an explanation).

The semantics of a CRG is as follows: An execution trace (cf. Chap. 4) is compliant with a CRG, if—and only if—for any match of the antecedent pattern to the trace's entries the related consequence pattern has a suitable match as well. Furthermore, if there exists no match of the antecedent pattern, the trace is compliant as well. The latter kind of compliance is denoted as *trivial compliance*.

For an antecedent pattern matching with a trace, each antecedent occurrence node can be mapped to a trace entry referring to the same activity. For sequenced antecedent occurrence nodes, the corresponding trace entries have to obey the same sequence. Furthermore, for each antecedent absence node, no trace entry may exist referring to the same activity and obeying the specified sequence with the trace entries related to antecedent occurrence nodes. A suitable match of a consequence pattern, in turn, allows mapping every consequence occurrence node to a corresponding trace entry. Again, the respective trace entries have to consider the sequence as specified by CRG. In addition, no trace entry may refer to an activity of a consequence absence node and obey the specified sequence.

The following two examples illustrate the semantics of simple CRG-based constraints. While Example 10.3 deals with compliant traces, Example 10.4 presents noncompliant traces.

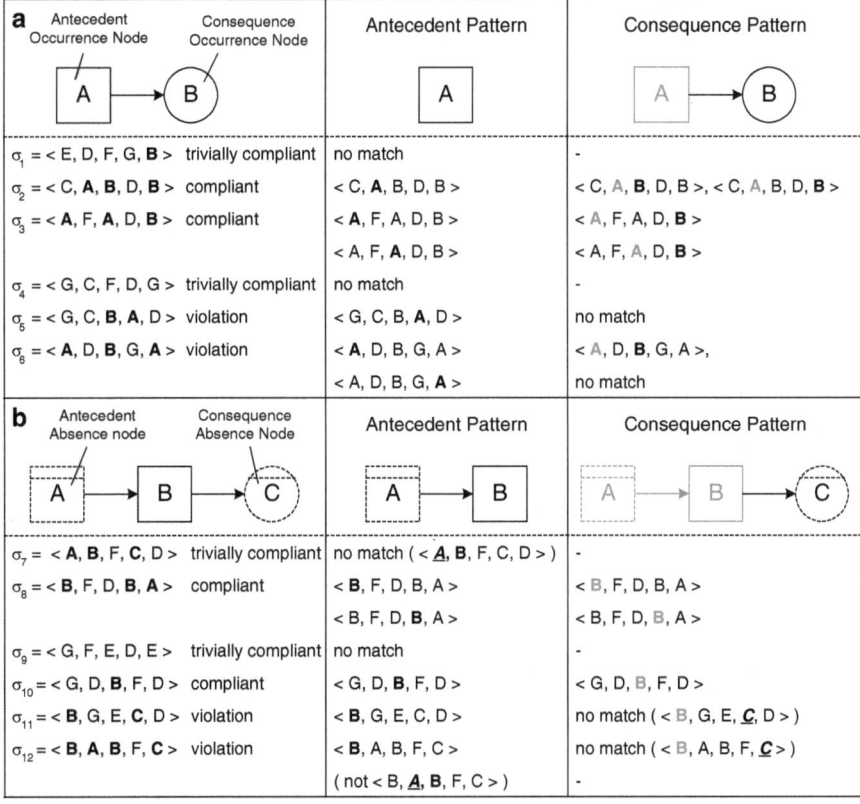

Fig. 10.2 Examples of two simple compliance rule graphs

Example 10.3 (Compliance of Simple CRGs; Compliant Traces).

Consider Fig. 10.2. It depicts two CRGs and related execution traces. For each trace, it is indicated whether or not the corresponding process instance complies with the respective CRG.

Regarding the two CRGs from Fig. 10.2, for example, *trivial compliance* holds for σ_1, σ_4, and σ_9. Obviously, for each of theses traces at least one antecedent occurrence node cannot be mapped to any trace entry; e.g., A does not occur in σ_1. Trace σ_7 corresponds to another example of trivial compliance although the antecedent occurrence node B can be mapped to a trace entry; however, σ_7 contains an entry of activity A (preceding the one of B) corresponding to the antecedent absence node; i.e., this entry prevents the antecedent pattern from matching with σ_7. To achieve a match of the antecedent pattern in the given context, no A may occur that precedes B in σ_7 (which is not the case here).

Consider now nontrivial examples of *compliant traces*: $\sigma_2, \sigma_3, \sigma_8$, and σ_{10}. Concerning σ_2, the antecedent pattern A matches once, and there are two suitable matches of the consequence pattern B. Regarding σ_3, A occurs twice. Since B succeeds both occurrences of A, there exists a suitable mapping of the consequence pattern in both cases. The same applies to σ_8 and the CRG depicted in Fig. 10.2b: There are two mappings of the antecedent pattern in terms of the two occurrences of B not having a preceding A (but a succeeding one). Further, for both mappings there is no C succeeding the B. Hence, trace σ_8 is compliant with the CRG depicted in Fig. 10.2b. Finally, σ_{10} contains exactly one mapping of the antecedent pattern B. Since no C is following, the consequence pattern maps as well.

Example 10.4 (Compliance of Simple CRGs: Noncompliant Traces).
Consider again the CRGs and execution traces from Fig. 10.2. We now have a look at *noncompliant traces*: $\sigma_5, \sigma_6, \sigma_{11}$, and σ_{12}. σ_5 violates the CRG from Fig. 10.2a since the antecedent pattern maps on the A, but no suitable mapping of the consequence pattern with a B following the A can be found (the only occurring B precedes A). Regarding σ_6, the antecedent pattern maps twice. However, while for the first A there exists a suitable mapping of the consequence pattern with the B, the second A is not followed by any B; i.e., trace σ_6 violates the CRG depicted in Fig. 10.2a.

Regarding the CRG from Fig. 10.2b and σ_{11}, the B allows for the antecedent pattern to match, while the succeeding C prevents the consequence pattern from matching. Finally, consider the violation of the CRG from Fig. 10.2b by σ_{12}: Due to the presence of the A, the antecedence pattern cannot map to the second occurrence of B, but only to the first one. Due to the presence of the C as last entry of the trace, however, no suitable match of the consequence pattern is possible.

Example 10.5 presents more complex compliance rule graphs.

Example 10.5 (Compliance of Complex CRGs).
Figure 10.3 shows two complex CRGs and related execution traces. Again, for each trace it is indicated whether the corresponding process instance complies with the respective CRG or violates it.

When considering Fig. 10.3a, for example, *trivial compliance* holds for σ_{13} and σ_{16}. Regarding σ_{13}, the antecedent occurrence node D cannot be mapped to any trace entry. Similarly, for σ_{16} there is no entry to which the antecedent occurrence node A can be mapped. Furthermore, σ_{15}, σ_{21}, and σ_{22} also correspond to examples of trivial compliance although the antecedent occurrence nodes can be mapped to trace entries. However, the traces contain entries of the antecedent absence nodes' activities as well; i.e., these entries prevent the antecedent patterns from being matched. For σ_{15}, there should be no B between A and D allowing for a match of the antecedent pattern from Fig. 10.3a. Regarding σ_{21} and σ_{22}, in turn, no A should occur allowing for a match of the antecedent pattern from Fig. 10.3b.

Consider now the *nontrivial compliant traces* σ_{14}, σ_{19}, and σ_{20}. σ_{14} contains an A succeeded by a D; between these entries there is no B such that the antecedent pattern of the respective CRG matches. Furthermore, the consequence pattern also matches, since σ_{14} contains an entry of the required C between A and D.

With a B and no A the two traces σ_{19} and σ_{20} allow for mappings of the antecedent pattern. Furthermore, both traces contain a D not preceded by a C (while the C in σ_{20} succeeds the D, σ_{19} does not contain any C at all); i.e., both traces allow for a suitable mapping of the consequence pattern, and are thus compliant with the CRG from Fig. 10.3b.

Finally, consider the *noncompliant traces* $\sigma_{17}, \sigma_{18}, \sigma_{23}$, and σ_{24}. Regarding Fig. 10.3a and σ_{17}, the antecedence pattern can be mapped to trace entries A and D, since the B is not in between; however, the consequence pattern cannot match since σ_{17} contains no C. Trace σ_{18}, in turn, enables two matches of the antecedent pattern of the CRG from Fig. 10.3a: the first one consists of the A and the D in the middle, while the second match consists of the same A and the D at the end of the trace. Since the latter D is preceded by C, the second match can be enriched with a suitable mapping of the consequence pattern. Nevertheless, trace σ_{18} violates the CRG from Fig. 10.3a, because there is no C between the A and D of the first mapping. Finally, regarding trace σ_{23}, the antecedent pattern maps to the B, but the D of the consequence pattern is missing (i.e., the C does not matter). Indeed, σ_{24} even contains a D, but this is preceded by a C; i.e., the consequence pattern cannot map while the antecedent pattern maps. Hence, σ_{24} violates the CRG depicted in Fig. 10.3b.

Example 10.6 shows how CRGs can be used for modeling the compliance rules of our application example.

Example 10.6 (Modeling Compliance Rules by the Use of CRGs). In Fig. 10.4, the compliance rules from Tables 10.1 and 10.2 respectively are remodeled by using CRGs.

a

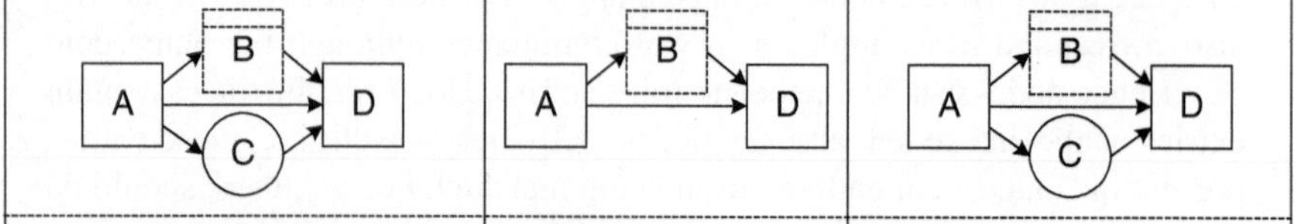

	Antecedent Pattern	Consequence Pattern
σ_{13} = < **A**, C, **B**, G, C > trivially compliant	no match	-
σ_{14} = < E, **A**, E, **C**, **D** > compliant	< E, A, E, C, D >	< E, A, E, **C**, D >
σ_{15} = < E, **A**, E, **B**, **D** > trivially compliant	no match (< E, A, E, **B**, D >)	-
σ_{16} = < G, **B**, E, G, **D**> trivially compliant	no match	-
σ_{17} = < **A**, F, **D**, G, **B** > violation	< A, F, D, G, B >	no match
σ_{18} = < **A**, F, **D**, **C**, **D** > violation	< A, F, D, C, D >	< A, F, D, **C**, D >
	< A, F, D, C, D >	no match

b

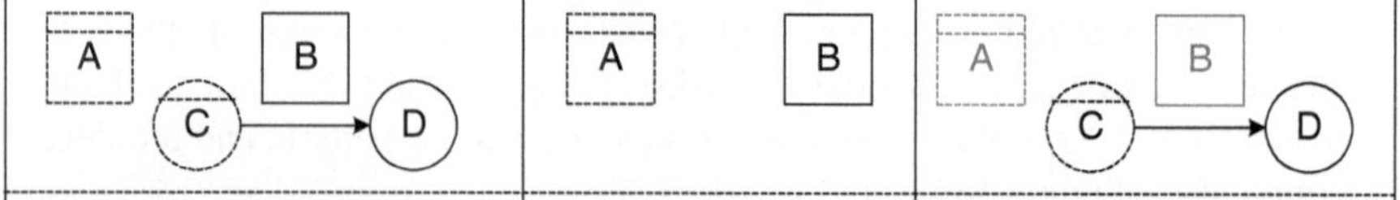

	Antecedent Pattern	Consequence Pattern
σ_{19} = < E, **D**, F, G, **B** > compliant	< E, D, F, G, **B** >	< E, D, F, G, **B** >
σ_{20} = < **D**, F, **C**, E, **B** > compliant	< D, F, C, E, **B** >	< D, F, C, E, **B** >
σ_{21} = < **A**, **B**, **C**, E, **D** > trivially compliant	no match (< **A**, B, C, E, D >)	-
σ_{22} = < G, **C**, **B**, **A**, **D** > trivially compliant	no match (< G, C, **B**, **A**, D >)	-
σ_{23} = < **C**, F, **B**, G, E > violation	< C, F, **B**, G, E >	no match
σ_{24} = < **C**, F, **D**, E, **B** > violation	< C, F, D, E, **B** >	no match (< **C**, F, **D**, E, **B** >)

Fig. 10.3 Examples of more complex compliance rule graphs

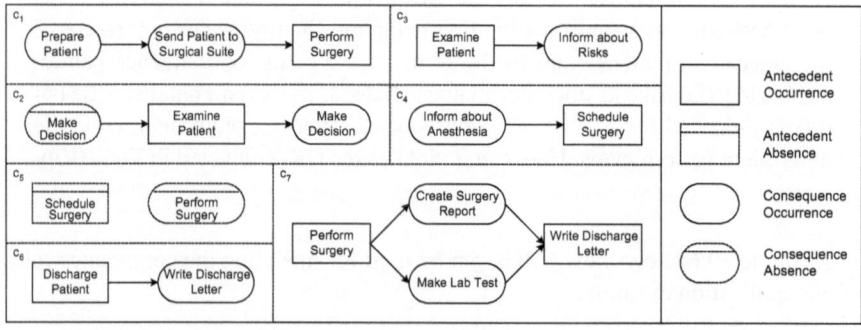

Fig. 10.4 Representing the compliance rules from Tables 10.1 and 10.2 as CRGs

In summary, modeling compliance rules constitutes a prerequisite for enabling business process compliance. In the following, we discuss how to verify compliance of processes with respective rules.

10.3 A Priori Compliance Checking

Once the compliance rules have been modeled (e.g., by using CRGs), compliance of prespecified process models with these rules can be checked. This is denoted as *a priori compliance checking* since the compliance of processes with regulations is checked before deploying their model to the run-time environment of the PAIS, i.e., before any process instance is executed based on the prespecified process model. According to Definition 10.4, a prespecified process model *complies* with a given compliance rule, if—and only if—the model solely allows for traces compliant with the rule. Further, we define the notions of *partial compliance* and *partial violation* as well as *violation*.

Definition 10.4 (Compliance of Prespecified Process Model). Let S be a prespecified process model and let ϕ be a compliance rule (cf. Definition 10.1). Further, let $QS_S \subseteq \Sigma^*$ be the set of all complete traces producible on S; i.e., $\sigma \in QS_S$ represents a completed process instance. Then:

- S *(fully) complies* with ϕ, if, and only if, all complete traces σ producible on S comply with ϕ; i.e., $\forall \sigma \in QS_S : \phi(\sigma)$.
- S *partially complies* with ϕ, if, and only if, there exists a complete trace σ producible on S and complying with ϕ; i.e., $\exists \sigma \in QS_S : \phi(\sigma)$.
- S *partially violates* ϕ, if, and only if, there exists a complete trace σ producible on S and violating ϕ; i.e., $\exists \sigma \in QS_S : \neg\phi(\sigma)$.
- S *only partially complies* with ϕ, if, and only if, S partially complies with ϕ as well as S partially violates ϕ; i.e., $\exists \sigma_1, \sigma_2 \in QS_S : \phi(\sigma_1) \wedge \neg\phi(\sigma_2)$.
- S *(fully) violates* ϕ, if, and only if, all complete traces σ producible on S violate ϕ; i.e., $\forall \sigma \in QS_S : \neg\phi(\sigma)$.

In case S fully complies with ϕ, for brevity we also use the phrase "S complies with ϕ." The same applies if S fully violates ϕ. In this case we also say "S violates ϕ".

Example 10.7 illustrates the different notions.

Example 10.7 (Compliance of a Prespecified Process Model). Reconsider the prespecified process model S_{med} from Fig. 10.1 and the compliance rules from Table 10.1 and Fig. 10.4 respectively. Process model S_{med} *(fully) complies* with compliance rules c_2, c_5, c_6, and c_7. It *only partially complies* with compliance rules c_1, c_3, and c_4.

One common way to perform a priori compliance checking is to use model checking techniques [136]. These allow verifying models and systems against temporal formulas. Generally, one can distinguish between *explicit model checking* and *symbolic model checking*. In the context of LTL, explicit model checking means to first create a state-based automaton that represents the negated formula. This automaton and the state space of the process model are then explored in combination. Symbolic model checking, in turn, transforms both the process model and the compliance rule into propositional logic expressions, and then applies a satisfiability check. When applying model checking to the verification of compliance rules not being modeled in terms of temporal logic (e.g., compliance rules that are modeled based on CRGs), these rules first have to be transformed into temporal logic.

10.4   Compliance Monitoring

Checking business process compliance of a prespecified process model already at build-time is not always feasible (e.g., if the process model is too large, or compliance rules are too complex or depend on run-time data). Besides, loosely specified and dynamically evolving processes require support for ensuring compliance during run-time as well. Hence, *compliance monitoring* is required allowing process engineers to control and monitor compliance rules during the execution of process instances. However, at the process instance level it is not sufficient to only consider one snapshot, i.e. to state whether or not a process instance violates a particular compliance rule at a certain point in time. On one hand, some violations may be cured when the process instance progresses. On the other hand, there are violations for which no adequate continuation exists. Hence, Definition 10.5 distinguishes not only between the process instances that comply and those that violate a compliance rule, but also between curable and incurable violations of process instances regarding an imposed compliance rule.

Definition 10.5 (Compliance and Curability of Process Instances). Let I be a running process instance represented by its partial trace σ_I. Further, the process model based on which I has been executed might not be known. Finally, let ϕ be a compliance rule. Then:

- I *complies* with ϕ, if, and only if, σ_I complies with ϕ; i.e., $\phi(\sigma_I)$.
- I *violates* ϕ, if, and only if, σ_I violates ϕ; i.e., $\neg\phi(\sigma_I)$.
- I *curably violates* ϕ, if, and only if, σ_I violates ϕ, but the execution of I can be continued in such a way that the resulting trace complies with ϕ; i.e., $\neg\phi(\sigma_I) \wedge \exists\tau \in \Sigma^\star : \phi(\sigma_I\tau)$.
- I *incurably violates* ϕ, if, and only if, σ_I violates ϕ, and any continuation of I violates ϕ as well; i.e., $\neg\phi(\sigma_I) \wedge \forall\tau \in \Sigma^\star : \neg\phi(\sigma_I\tau)$.

σ_{I_1}	σ_{I_2}
1 Admit Patient	1 Admit Patient
2 Perform Checkup	2 Perform Checkup
3 Examine Patient	3 Examine Patient
4 Inform about Risks	4 Inform about Risks
	5 Make Decision
	6 Schedule Surgery

Fig. 10.5 Snapshots of instance traces

Example 10.8 illustrates Definition 10.5.

Example 10.8 (Compliance and Curability of Process Instances).
  Consider compliance rules c_2, c_3, and c_4 from Table 10.1 (see also Table 10.2 and Fig. 10.4) as well as traces σ_{I_1} and σ_{I_2} of the running process instances I_1 and I_2 (cf. Fig. 10.5). Obviously, I_1 violates c_2, while it complies with c_3 and c_4. Further, c_2 is curably violated, since σ_{I_1} can be continued by executing activity *Make Decision*. Finally, I_2 complies with c_2 and c_3. However, I_2 incurably violates c_4 since no continuation of σ_{I_2} contains the activity *Inform about Anesthesia* preceding activity *Schedule Surgery*.

In practice, it is not always feasible to only deploy *fully compliant* process models; i.e., there may be prespecified process models that only partially comply with imposed compliance rules. As will be shown in Example 10.9, instances of such prespecified process models need to be monitored at run-time in order to determine whether a compliance violation can be cured in the following. According to this, Definition 10.6 distinguishes between different criticality levels of curable violations.

Definition 10.6 (Temporary and Permanent Compliance Violations). Let $I = (S, \sigma_I)$ be a process instance running on a process model S and having partial trace σ_I. Further, let QS_S be the set of all complete traces producible on S and ϕ be a compliance rule. Then:

- *I temporarily violates* ϕ, if, and only if, I currently violates ϕ, but any continuation on S will comply with ϕ at least at one future point in time:

$$I \text{ curably violates } \phi \wedge \forall \tau \in \Sigma^\star \text{ with } \sigma_I \tau \in QS_S :$$
$$\exists \upsilon, \omega \in \Sigma^\star \text{ with } \upsilon\omega = \tau \wedge \phi(\sigma_I \upsilon).$$

σ_{I_3}	σ_{I_4}
1 Admit Patient	1 Admit Patient
2 Perform Checkup	2 Perform Checkup
3 Examine Patient	3 Examine Patient
	4 Inform about Anesthesia
	5 Make Decision
	6 Schedule Surgery

Fig. 10.6 Additional snapshots of process instance traces

- *I potentially violates ϕ temporarily*, if, and only if, *I* currently violates ϕ, and it holds: On one hand, *I* may be continued in a way such that it will comply with ϕ at least at one future point in time. On the other hand, *I* may be also continued in a way such that it will never comply with ϕ again; i.e.,
  I curably violates $\phi \land \exists \tau_1, \tau_2 \in \Sigma^\star$: for $\sigma_I \tau_1, \sigma_I \tau_2 \in QS_S$ it holds:

$$(\exists \upsilon_1, \omega_1 \in \Sigma^\star \text{ with } \upsilon_1 \omega_1 = \tau_1 : \phi(\sigma_I \upsilon_1)) \land$$
$$(\forall \upsilon_2, \omega_2 \in \Sigma^\star \text{ with } \upsilon_2 \omega_2 = \tau_2 : \neg \phi(\sigma_I \upsilon_2)).$$

- *I permanently violates* ϕ, if, and only if, *I* currently violates ϕ, and any continuation on *S* always violates ϕ; i.e.,

$$I \text{ curably violates } \phi \land \forall \tau \in \Sigma^\star \text{ with } \sigma_I \tau \in QS_S:$$
$$\forall \upsilon, \omega \in \Sigma^\star \text{ with } \upsilon \omega = \tau : \neg \phi(\sigma_I \upsilon).$$

Example 10.9 applies Definition 10.6 to selected process instances.

Example 10.9 (Persistence of Compliance Violations). Reconsider compliance rules c_2, c_3, and c_4 from Table 10.1 (see also Table 10.2 and Fig. 10.4). Further consider traces σ_{I_3} and σ_{I_4} from Fig. 10.6. These traces correspond to the running process instances $I_3 = (S_{med}, \sigma_{I_3})$ and $I_4 = (S_{med}, \sigma_{I_4})$ that are executed on the prespecified process model S_{med} from Fig. 10.1.

- Obviously, I_3 curably violates c_2 and c_3, while it complies with c_4. Further, c_2 is only temporarily violated by I_3, since its continuation on S_{med} will lead to the execution of activity *Make Decision* (e.g., σ_{I_2} and σ_{I_4}). However, c_3 is potentially temporarily violated, since S_{med} allows σ_{I_3} continuing with activity *Inform about Risks* (e.g., σ_{I_1} and σ_{I_2}) or without this activity. (e.g. σ_{I_4}).

σ_{I_5}	σ_{I_6}	σ_{I_7}
1 Admit Patient	1 Admit Patient	1 Admit Patient
2 Perform Checkup	2 Perform Checkup	2 Perform Checkup
3 Examine Patient	3 Examine Patient	3 Examine Patient
4 Inform about Risks	4 Inform about Risks	4 Inform about Anesthesia
5 Make Decision	5 Make Decision	5 Make Decision
6 Schedule Surgery	6 Write Discharge Letter	6 Schedule Surgery
7 Check Patient Recod		7 Check Patient Recod
8 Admit Patient		8 Admit Patient
9 Send Patient to Surgical Suite		9 Send Patient to Surgical Suite
10 Perform Surgery +		10 Prepare Patient
11 Prepare Patient		11 Perform Surgery +
12 Transport Patient to Ward		12 Transport Patient to Ward
13 Create Surgery Report		13 Provide Postsurgical Care
14 Make Lab Test		14 Make Lab Test
15 Provide Postsurgical Care		15 Create Surgery Report
16 Discharge Patient		16 Discharge Patient
17 Write Discharge Letter		17 Write Discharge Letter

Fig. 10.7 Execution traces of completed process instances

- I_4 curably violates c_3, but complies with c_2 and c_4. Further, c_3 is permanently violated by I_4, since no continuation of I_4 on S_{med} will contain the required activity *Inform about Risks*.

10.5 A-posteriori Compliance Checking

Instead of ensuring compliance a priori (i.e., by checking prespecified process models at build-time) or monitoring compliance during processes execution, for completed process instances, compliance may be also checked a posteriori, e.g., determine whether a completed instance complies with regulations that emerged recently. Compliance of completed process instances can be verified based on the definition of compliance rules (cf. Definition 10.1). Example 10.10 illustrates a posteriori compliance checking.

Example 10.10 (Compliance of Process Execution Logs). Consider all compliance rules from Table 10.1 (see also Table 10.2 and Fig. 10.4). Further consider execution traces σ_{I_5}, σ_{I_6}, and σ_{I_7} from Fig. 10.7, which correspond to the completed process instances I_5, I_6, and I_7. Instance I_5 violates c_1 and c_4, and complies with c_2, c_3, c_5, c_6, and c_7. Further, I_6 complies with all compliance rules, and I_7 violates c_1 and c_3, but complies with c_2, c_4, c_5, c_6, and c_7.

Similar to a priori compliance checking, a posteriori compliance checking can be realized based on techniques that build on model checking. The LTL-Checker described in [10] transforms LTL-based compliance rules into a state-based automaton. Taking an execution log as input, this automaton decides whether a completed process instance complies with the original rules or violates them.

10.6 Effects of Process Changes on Compliance

As discussed in Chaps. 7 and 9, prespecified process models as well as the process instances running on them may evolve over time or be subject to dynamic changes. Obviously, such changes might affect compliance of the process models and process instances with the imposed compliance rules. Depending on these effects, we define compliance of changes with a given compliance rule (cf. Definition 10.7).

Definition 10.7 (Compliance of Changes). Let S be a prespecified process model and let $I = (S, \sigma_I)$ be a related process instance. Further, let Δ be a change that correctly transforms the prespecified process model S into another prespecified process model S'. Finally, let $I = (S, \sigma_I)$ be state compliant with S' (cf. Chap. 7), i.e., I can be correctly migrated to S' (with $I = (S', \sigma_I)$). Then:

- The application of Δ to S meets compliance rule ϕ, if, and only if, the application of Δ to S does not weaken the compliance of S with ϕ; i.e.,

  - *if* S complies with ϕ *then* S' must comply with ϕ.
  - *if* S partially complies with ϕ *then* S' must partially comply with ϕ.

- The application of Δ to $I = (S, \sigma_I)$ meets compliance rule ϕ, if, and only if, the application of Δ to process instance I does not weaken the compliance of I with ϕ; i.e.,

  - *if* (S, σ_I) complies with ϕ *then* (S', σ_I) must comply with ϕ.
  - *if* (S, σ_I) temporarily violates ϕ *then* has to hold
    (S', σ_I) temporarily violates $\phi \vee (S', \sigma_I)$ complies with ϕ.
  - *if* (S, σ_I) potentially violates ϕ temporarily *then* has to
    (S', σ_I) potentially violates ϕ temporarily $\vee$
    (S', σ_I) temporarily violates $\phi \vee$
    (S', σ_I) complies with ϕ.

When applying Definition 10.7 in a straightforward manner, one would have to recheck compliance of a process model with all defined compliance rules whenever changing a process. This might become necessary in the context of ad hoc changes

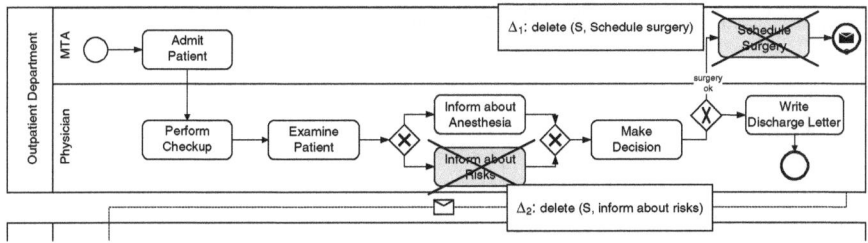

Fig. 10.8 Changes potentially affecting the compliance of process model S_{med}

σ_{I_8}	σ_{I_9}
1 Admit Patient 2 Perform Checkup 3 Examine Patient	1 Admit Patient 2 Perform Checkup 3 Examine Patient 4 Inform about Anesthesia

Fig. 10.9 Further examples for snapshots of process instance traces

of single process instances or changes of a prespecified process model solely at the process type level (i.e., without propagating the type change to already running process instances). However, rechecking business compliance for large collections of running process instances might be too expensive. More precisely, for each process instance, it must be determined whether or not it still meets the imposed compliance rules when migrating it to the new process model version. To cope with this challenge, changes and compliance rules have to be analyzed (e.g., by considering the affected activities) in order to restrict the set of compliance rules to be rechecked.

Example 10.11 (Effects of Changes on Process Model Compliance). Consider compliance rules c_4 and c_5 from Table 10.1 (see also Table 10.2 and Fig. 10.4). Consider further change Δ_1 of the prespecified process model S_{med} as depicted in Fig. 10.8. Obviously, Δ_1 meets c_4. While S only partially complies with c_4, S' fully complies with this rule. By contrast, Δ_1 violates c_5 since S fully complies with c_5, but S' only partially complies with this rule.

Example 10.12 (Effects of Changes on Process Instance Compliance). Consider compliance rule c_3 from Table 10.1 (see also Table 10.2 and Fig. 10.4).

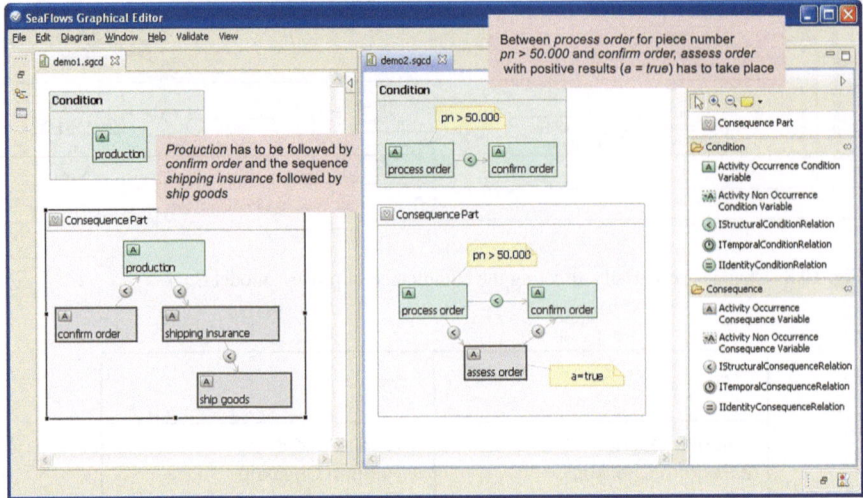

Fig. 10.10 Modeling compliance rules with the SeaFlows graphical editor

Consider further Δ_2 from Fig. 10.8; this change transforms S_{med} into S'_{med}. Finally, consider process instances $I_8 = (S_{med}, \sigma_{I_8})$ and $I_9 = (S_{med}, \sigma_{I_9})$ from Fig. 10.9—both instances run on the prespecified process model S_{med} from Fig. 10.1. Concerning I_8, it turns out that Δ_2 violates c_3: $I_8 = (S_{med}, \sigma_{I_8})$ potentially violates c_3 temporarily, whereas (S'_{med}, σ_{I_8}) permanently violates this rule. Regarding instance I_9, however, Δ_2 meets c_3: $I_9 = (S_{med}, \sigma_{I_9})$ permanently violates c_3, which also applies to (S'_{med}, σ_{I_9}) permanently.

10.7 User Perspective

This section gives an idea how compliance checking looks like from the perspective of the user. Currently, only few tools exist that allow ensuring business process compliance at the process type or process instance level. One notable exception is the SeaFlows Toolset [195] that provides a comprehensive and extensible framework for checking business compliance of prespecified process models. For this purpose, the SeaFlows Toolset provides a user-friendly environment. For modeling compliance rules, SeaFlows uses CRGs as presented in Sect. 10.2 (cf. Fig. 10.10).

The SeaFlows Toolset allows enriching prespecified process models with these rules and checking for compliance with them. Furthermore, compliance checking considers data as well as efficiency issues by applying a number of abstraction techniques. Finally, violations of compliance rules are illustrated by means of a counter example (cf. Fig. 10.11). At the technical level the applied compliance checking approach uses the model checker SAL [51].

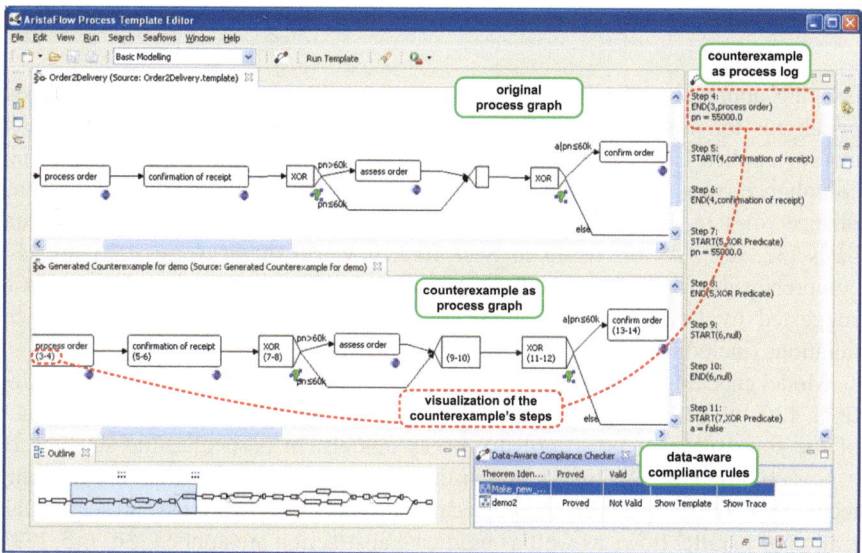

Fig. 10.11   Compliance checking with the SeaFlows Toolset

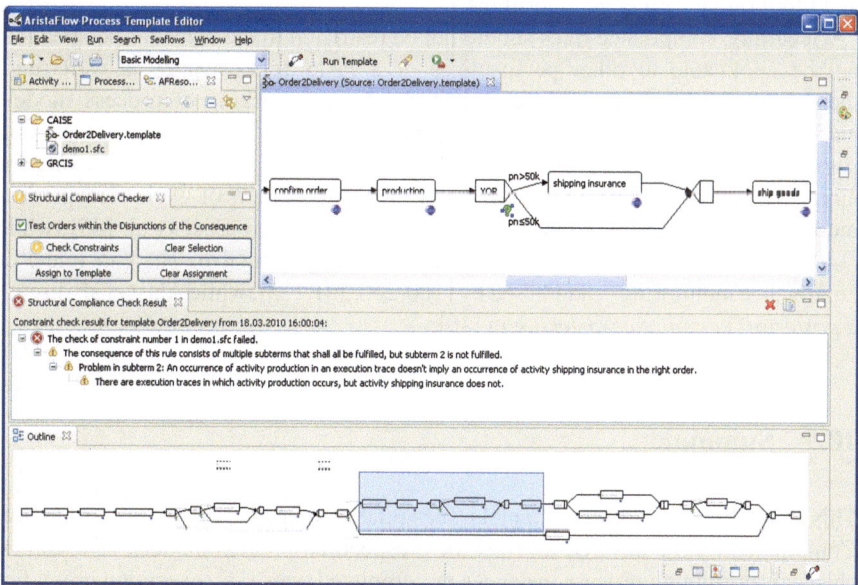

Fig. 10.12   Structural compliance checking with the SeaFlows Toolset

Additionally, a structural compliance checking approach is provided. It first derives structural criteria from compliance rules. Then, it applies these criteria to check business process compliance of cycle-free process models (cf. Fig. 10.12).

10.8 Existing Approaches

Existing approaches dealing with business process compliance suggest different paradigms for modeling compliance rules. For example, the approach presented in [36] applies LTL and the one discussed in [99] relies on CTL for modeling compliance rules. Other logic-based approaches consider the modalities of compliance rules (e.g., obligations or permissions) and use deontic logic as formal basis [33, 102]. As discussed in Sect. 10.2, however, logic expressions are less comprehensible to end-users. To improve usability, a pattern-based notation is suggested by Dwyer et al. in [83]. Finally, several approaches use graphical notations (including CRGs) [36, 189, 198].

Model checking is the most common technique for a priori compliance checking (e.g., [36, 99, 149, 189]). However, model checking depends on the exploration of the state space of prespecified process models. In particular, the state *space explosion problem* constitutes a big obstacle for the practical use of model checking techniques. To tackle this challenge, techniques like graph reduction and sequentialization of parallel flows as well as predicate abstraction are applied [36, 145, 189]. Besides model checking, there exist other techniques ensuring business process compliance a priori. For cycle-free, prespecified process models, for example, [107] and [360] provide efficient algorithms.

Generally, compliance rules should not be restricted to the behavior perspective, but be applicable to other perspectives of a PAIS (cf. Chap. 2) as well (e.g., the information or time perspectives). Compliance checking of process models having state-based data objects (i.e., enumerations), for example, is suggested by Awad et al. [37]. Furthermore, [145] enables *data-aware compliance checking* for larger data types (e.g., integers or reals). The verification of cycle-free process models against temporal compliance rules is addressed by Eder et al. [85], while [149] considers both the information and the time perspective. The enactment of compliance monitoring is addressed by [100,200,201,235], while Aalst et al. discuss *a posteriori compliance checking* in [10].

10.9 Summary

This chapter addressed fundamental issues related to business process compliance. Compliance can be ensured a priori for prespecified process models, or it can be checked for running process instances or completed ones (i.e., execution logs). For each of these artifacts, it can be verified whether or not it complies with compliance rules imposed from regulations, laws, and guidelines. This chapter presented two ways for modeling compliance rules: LTL and CRGs. It first discussed, how to apply a priori compliance checking to prespecified process models, and then gave insights into compliance monitoring and different kinds of compliance violations including compliance checking. Following this, it discussed the potential impact of process changes (at both the type and the instance level) on business process compliance. Finally, the chapter discussed the user perspective as well as recent approaches enabling business process compliance.

Exercises

10.1. Modeling Compliance Rule Graphs
Assume that a manufacturing company is running several *order-to-delivery processes* that are frequently changed. In particular these processes must obey compliance rules c_1, c_2, c_3, and c_4 as depicted in Table 10.3. Assume further that all order-to-delivery process models are built based on the activities from Table 10.4.

Model compliance rules c_1, c_2, c_3, and c_4 based on CRGs and the activities from Table 10.4.

10.2. Understanding Compliance Rules
Consider the following three execution traces σ_1, σ_2, and σ_3:

$$\sigma_1 = < A, \ B, \ C, \ D, \ E, \ F, \ G >$$
$$\sigma_2 = < A, \ B, \ C, \ D, \ A, \ E, \ B, \ D >$$
$$\sigma_3 = < A, \ G, \ C, \ E, \ D, \ B, \ C, \ A, \ G, \ F >$$

(a) *LTL-based Compliance Rules.* Are the execution traces σ_1, σ_2, and σ_3 compliant with the following LTL-based compliance rules c_1, c_2, c_3, and c_4?

Table 10.3 Compliance rules for order-to-delivery processes

c_1	Before goods can be produced, components have to be bought.
c_2	If an order is confirmed, it must have been received and processed before. Furthermore, once confirmed an order must not be declined afterwards. Conversely, for a declined order no confirmation is possible any longer.
c_3	After the production of goods and before shipping them, a shipping insurance must be concluded.
c_4	An invoice must be sent and tracking should be enabled after shipping the goods.

Table 10.4 Activities

Receive order	Conclude shipping insurance
Ship goods	Decline order
Process order	Enable tracking
Send invoice	Buy components
Confirm order	Produce goods

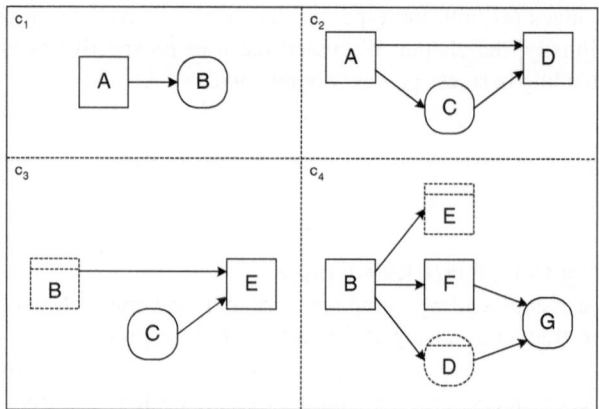

Fig. 10.13 Compliance rule graphs

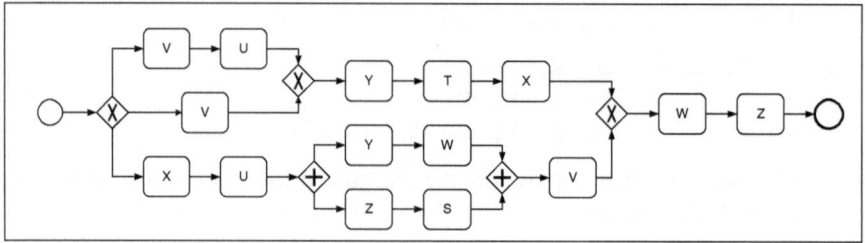

Fig. 10.14 Prespecified process model S_1

$c_1 : \mathbf{G}\,(\text{A} \Rightarrow \mathbf{F}\,\text{B})$
$c_2 : \mathbf{G}\,(\text{A} \Rightarrow ((\neg\text{D})\,\mathbf{U}\,\text{C}))$
$c_3 : ((\neg\text{B})\,\mathbf{U}\,\text{E}) \Rightarrow \mathbf{G}\,(\text{C} \Rightarrow \mathbf{F}\,\text{E})$
$c_4 : \mathbf{G}\,(\text{B} \Rightarrow (((\mathbf{G}\,\neg\text{E}) \wedge (\mathbf{F}\,\text{F})) \Rightarrow ((\neg\text{D})\,\mathbf{U}\,\text{G})))$

(b) *Compliance Rule Graphs.* Are execution traces σ_1, σ_2, and σ_3 compliant with the compliance rules c_1, c_2, c_3, and c_4 from Fig. 10.13?

(c) *Comparing LTL-based compliance rules with Compliance Rule Graphs.* Compare each of the LTL-based compliance rules c_1, c_2, c_3, and c_4 with the corresponding compliance rule from Fig. 10.13. Do both express the same?

10.3. Ensuring Compliance Along the Process Life Cycle
Consider the prespecified process model S_1 from Fig. 10.14 and the related compliance rules from Fig. 10.15.

(a) Classify the compliance of S_1 with the compliance rules c_1, c_2, c_3, and c_4 from Fig. 10.15 based on Definition 10.4.

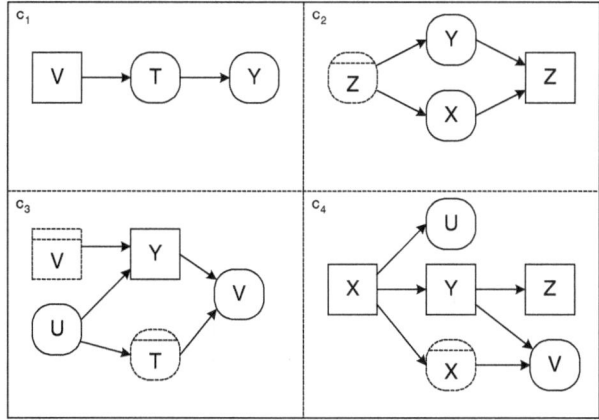

Fig. 10.15 Compliance rules affecting S_1

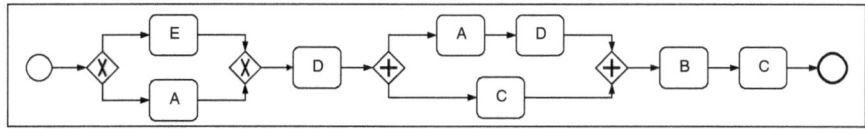

Fig. 10.16 Prespecified process model S_2

(b) Classify the compliance of the following process instances with the given compliance rules from Fig. 10.15 based on Definition 10.8.

$$I_1 = (S_1, \sigma_1) \text{ with } \sigma_1 =< V, Y, T, X >$$
$$I_2 = (S_1, \sigma_2) \text{ with } \sigma_2 =< V, U, Y >$$
$$I_3 = (S_1, \sigma_3) \text{ with } \sigma_3 =< X, U, Z >$$
$$I_4 = (S_1, \sigma_4) \text{ with } \sigma_4 =< X, U, Y, Z, S, W >$$

(c) Classify the persistence of each curable violation based on Definition 10.6.

10.4. Process Change and Process Compliance
Consider the prespecified process model S_2 from Fig. 10.16. Further consider related compliance rules from Fig. 10.17 as well as the two changes of S_2 depicted in Fig. 10.18.

(a) Classify the compliance of process model S_2 with the compliance rules from Fig. 10.17 based on Definition 10.4.
(b) Classify the compliance of process instances I_1, I_2, and I_3 with the compliance rules from Fig. 10.15 based on Definition 10.8.

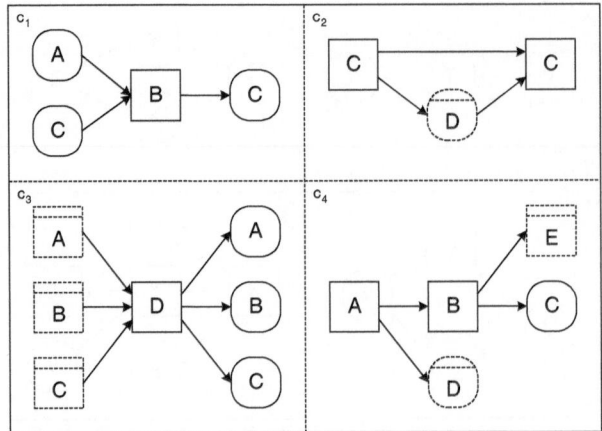

Fig. 10.17 Compliance rules affecting S_2

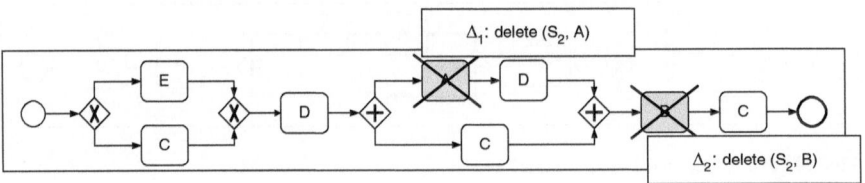

Fig. 10.18 Changes Δ_1 and Δ_2 of the prespecified process model S_2

$$I_1 = (S_2, < A, D, A, D, C, B >)$$
$$I_2 = (S_2, < E, D, A, C >)$$
$$I_3 = (S_2, < E, D, C >)$$

(c) Classify the persistence of each curable violation based on Definition 10.6.

(d) Consider the application of changes Δ_1 and Δ_2 to S_2 separately and in conjunction with each other. Do the three changes meet compliance rules c_1, c_2, c_3, and c_4 according to Definition 10.7?

(e) First, decide for each of the three process instances I_1, I_2, and I_3 whether or not the changes Δ_1 and Δ_2 (cf. Fig. 10.18) may be applied separately or commonly to it. Second, by using Definition 10.7, for each possible application of these changes to the respective instances, decide whether or not it meets the compliance rules c_1, c_2, c_3, and c_4.

Part III
Flexibility Support for Loosely Specified Processes

Chapter 11
Concretizing Loosely Specified Processes

Abstract In many application domains prespecifying the entire process model is not possible. While parts of the process model are known at build-time, others are uncertain and can only be specified during run-time. To better deal with such uncertainty, decisions regarding the exact specification of selected parts of the process have to be deferred to run-time. Since decision deferral can be realized in many different ways, this chapter first introduces a taxonomy for it. It then introduces different decision deferral patterns like Late Selection, Late Modeling and Composition, Iterative Refinement, and Ad hoc Composition. Finally, examples of concrete implementations of the different patterns are presented.

11.1 Motivation

In Part II of the book we have introduced prespecified process models and discussed how variability, adaptability, and evolution can be supported. In many domains, however, this flexibility is not sufficient, since prespecifying the entire process model prior to process execution is not possible (cf. Sect. 3.2.2). While parts of the process model are known at build-time, others are uncertain and can only be specified during run-time, e.g., taking real-world data and events as well as process instance data and resource availability into account.

Example 11.1 (Need for looseness).

- The treatment of a particular patient depends on his actual physical data and the reported list of symptoms, and medical problems.
- In higher education, the courses a student has to take are predefined, while there is some flexibility in the curriculum in deciding their exact ordering sequence.

M. Reichert and B. Weber, *Enabling Flexibility in Process-Aware Information Systems*, 323
DOI 10.1007/978-3-642-30409-5_11, © Springer-Verlag Berlin Heidelberg 2012

To better cope with such uncertainty, decisions regarding the exact specification of the process have to be deferred to run-time. Instead of requiring a process model to be fully prespecified prior to the creation and execution of any process instance, it should be possible that parts of the model remain unspecified at build-time and are defined for each corresponding process instance during run-time. We denote such process models as *loosely specified*.

> **Definition 11.1 (Loosely Specified Process).** A process model which is not fully prespecified, but keeps some parts unspecified at build-time by deferring decisions to run-time is denoted as *loosely specified*.

Generally, decision deferral may affect every process perspective (e.g., behavior perspective or information perspective; cf. Chap. 2).

Decision deferral, which is characteristic of loosely specified processes, can be realized in different ways. Section 11.2 introduces a taxonomy of decision deferral which is used for characterizing existing approaches.

11.2   Taxonomy of Decision Deferral

Decision deferral patterns can be classified according to the *degree of freedom* provided to the user and the *planning approach* employed when concretizing the loosely specified parts of the process model. Moreover, the *scope of decision deferral* (i.e., prespecified parts of the process model or entire process) has to be considered as well as the *process perspective* whose refinement is deferred to run-time. Taken together, these four dimensions determine the provided degree of looseness. To characterize different approaches enabling decision deferral (cf. Sects. 11.4– 11.7), we consider two additional dimensions which are related to the *degree of support*. Variants of the different decision deferral patterns can be further characterized considering the *degree of automation*, and the ways how *decision making* and *decison support* are provided (cf. Fig. 11.1). In the following we explain these dimensions in detail, before introducing different patterns for decision deferral and presenting concrete approaches implementing these patterns.

11.2.1   Degree of Freedom

Decision deferral patterns differ in respect to the degree of freedom they provide. If business processes need to be entirely prespecified in advance, the degree of freedom during run-time will be *none* (cf. Fig. 11.2a). Examples not only include prespecified process models requiring that all decisions regarding the control flow be made during build-time, but also the direct assignment of users (instead of

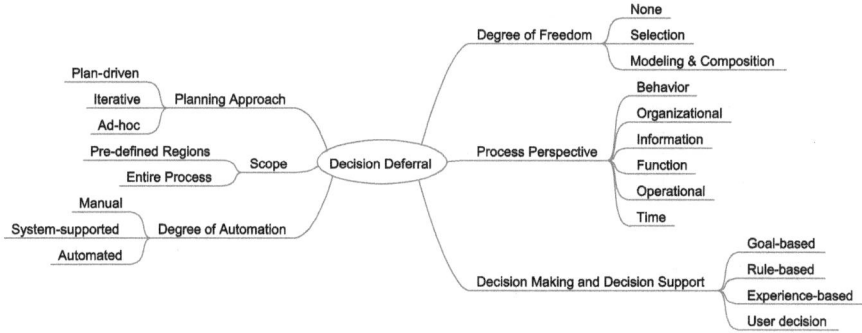

Fig. 11.1 Taxonomy of decision deferral

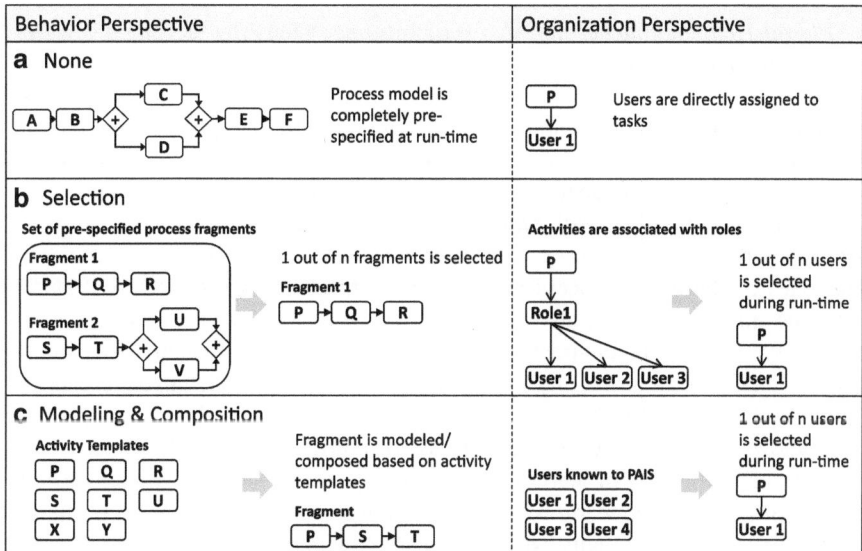

Fig. 11.2 Degree of freedom (illustrated along two process perspectives)

roles) to activities. A slightly higher degree of freedom is provided if parts of
the process can be *selected* from a set of predefined alternatives during run-time
(cf. Fig. 11.2b). Examples include the selection of one out of *n* predefined process
fragments during run-time and the dynamic assignment of users to tasks based on
their roles as captured in an organizational model (cf. Chap. 2). Finally, the largest
degree of freedom is provided, if the *modeling or composition* of (parts of) the
process is enabled during run-time (cf. Fig. 11.2c). This may comprise, for example,
the modeling or composition of a process fragment out of a set of activity templates
and also the dynamic allocation of users to tasks.

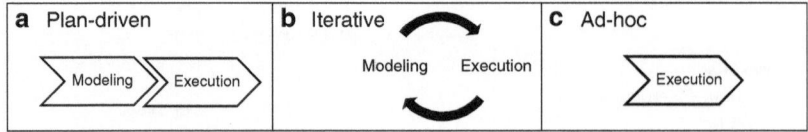

Fig. 11.3 Planning approach

11.2.2   Planning Approach

To cope with uncertainty, different planning approaches may be employed. In particular, it can be differentiated between plan-driven, iterative, and ad hoc approaches.

Plan-driven approaches try to overcome uncertainty by developing a very detailed model up-front, which is then regarded as schema for executing process instances. In the plan-driven approach, modeling and execution are strictly separated (cf. Fig. 11.3a). As models tend to be more imprecise the earlier they are elaborated [55], concentrating all modeling efforts to build-time imposes the risk that process models become useless due to changing conditions and requirements [247].

To mitigate this risk, *iterative and continuous modeling* may be used [47,67,247]. As opposed to the plan-driven approach, no detailed up-front process model is created; i.e., the initial process model remains more coarse-grained [67]. During run-time this model is iteratively refined, allowing for the integration of newly gained knowledge. In contrast to plan-driven approaches, which focus on the process model as an artifact by itself, emphasis is put on modeling as an ongoing activity (cf. Fig. 11.3b). Distributing modeling efforts between build-time and run-time allows deferring decisions to the last responsible moment [247] as well as creating opportunities for learning. The last responsible moment is just before an important option disappears, when no decision is made by then. When this last responsible moment actually will be, largely depends on the characteristics of a business process.

Finally, *ad hoc modeling* copes with uncertainty by evolving a process instance in an ad hoc manner. In contrast to iterative and continuous modeling, ad hoc modeling relinquishes all up-front modeling (cf. Fig. 11.3c).

11.2.3   Scope of Decision Deferral

Decision deferral can be restricted to *predefined regions* of the process model or cover the *entire process*. If the scope is restricted to *predefined regions*, the core process is prespecified as in traditional PAISs, while certain predefined regions remain loosely specified enabling decision deferral [316] (cf. Fig. 11.4a). However, the scope of a decision deferral may also encompass the *entire process*

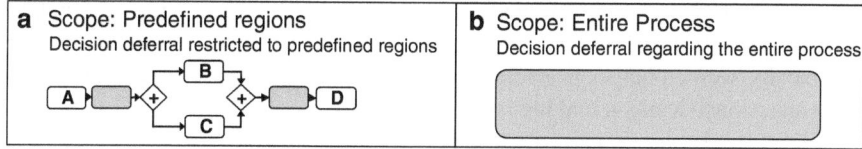

Fig. 11.4 Scope of decision deferral

(cf. Fig. 11.4b). In this case no prespecified process model serving as schema for process execution is created at build-time. Instead process instances unfold during process execution, i.e., their exact course of action only emerges during run-time.

11.2.4 Process Perspective

Generally, decision deferral may affect different process perspectives (cf. Chap. 2). Decision deferral regarding the *behavior* perspective means that only parts of the process are prespecified at build-time, while the exact control flow can be concretized during run-time. Processes, however, may also be loosely specified in respect to the *organization* perspective, i.e., actors executing a particular activity are not predefined, but dynamically assigned during run-time. Further, decision deferral may also concern the *information* perspective, i.e., data objects or data edges might not be fully known during build-time and can be refined during run-time. Decision deferral regarding the *function* perspective means that not all activities executed during run-time have to be predefined. In turn, *operational* decision deferral means that the concrete implementation of an activity does not have to be known in advance. Finally, decision deferral regarding the *time* perspective means, for example, that the concrete start or end times are specified at run-time.

11.2.5 Degree of Automation

The different decision deferral patterns can be automated to a different degree. *Automated* means that process instances are composed in an automated manner during run-time. *Manual*, in turn, means that process instances are created by (end) users without any system support. Finally, *system-supported* means that process instances are created in an interactive manner by (end) users. Thereby, the PAIS assists the user during process execution; e.g., by providing context-specific recommendations or templates which can be adapted.

This dimension is closely related to the question whether the PAIS or the user shall control the ordering and coordination of activities and in how far decisions are made decentrally by users. Typically, if application of decision deferral patterns is automated, the role of the PAIS is rather focused on enabling control and ensuring compliance, i.e., decisions are made automatically by the PAIS; decision making is centralized. If decision deferral patterns are manually applied, in turn, the PAIS is typically seen as helper providing user guidance, i.e., the user is empowered to make decisions; decision making is decentralized.

11.2.6   Decision Making and Decision Support

Decisions on how to concretize a loosely specified process model during run-time (including the decision support provided by the PAIS) can be made in different ways.

Goal-based means that decisions between alternatives (e.g., selection of a particular process fragment, actor, or activity implementation) are made taking the overall goals of the process into account (e.g., to complete the process within 5 days). Following a goal-based approach for decision making, a process instance is considered as being valid if the goal can be reached (e.g., the process instance is completed in 4 1/2 days). By executing activities, a process instance moves from its initial state forward in the state space. Thereby, constraints have to be obeyed which may restrict the set of valid trajectories in the state space. *Rule-based*, in turn, expresses that decisions between different alternatives are made based on a set of rules. *Experience-based* means that decision are made by relying on past experiences made in similar context. For example, decisions can be made by considering the execution logs of the PAIS or user feedback from social networks, by making use of best practices (e.g., templates serving as blueprint), or by querying for similar instances that can be customized and reused. Finally, *user decision* means that decision making is completely left to the human expert.

11.3   Decision Deferral Patterns

This section provides an overview of *decision deferral patterns* focusing on the control flow perspective—traditionally the most dominant perspective. Table 11.1 classifies them accordingly, using the taxonomy from Sect. 11.2. Note that, in principle, each decision deferral pattern is applicable to predefined regions of the process or to the entire process. A detailed description of these patterns and their variants is provided in Sects. 11.4–11.7.

Traditional workflow management systems offer little flexibility to their users and require that the model of a business process be fully prespecify in advance (i.e., Degree of Freedom: None). Thus, they employ a strictly plan-driven approach separating modeling and execution entirely (i.e., Planning Approach: Plan-driven). Process instances are derived in a fully automated manner from the process model that serves as template for both instance creation and execution. Thereby, the

Table 11.1 Decision deferral patterns of the control flow perspective

Pattern	Degree of freedom	Planning approach
Fully prespecified processes	None	Plan-driven
Late selection	Selection	Plan-driven
Late modeling and composition	Modeling and composition	Plan-driven
Iterative refinement	Modeling and composition	Iterative
Ad hoc composition	Modeling and composition	Ad hoc

PAIS acts as a dispatcher [348]; i.e., whenever an activity is completed, the PAIS determines the activities to be enabled next and assigns them to authorized users for their execution.

Late Selection offers slightly more flexibility when compared to traditional PAISs by allowing for placeholder activities within a process model (Scope: Predefined regions). Such a placeholder activity can be substituted by a concrete implementation (i.e., (sub)process model or application service). The selection of the placeholder content may either be conducted upon enablement of the placeholder activity or upon process instance creation. More precisely, at build-time a process model (including its placeholder activities) is created. The placeholder activities are then refined during run-time by choosing a concrete implementation from the available set of alternatives (i.e., Degree of Freedom: Selection). Regarding the implementation replacing the respective placeholder activity, modeling and execution are strictly separated, i.e., modeling of the selected placeholder content needs to be completed before executing it. Thus, this pattern employs a plan-driven approach (i.e., Planning Approach: Plan-driven).

The *Late Modeling and Composition* pattern goes one step beyond *Late Selection*. It additionally allows for the modeling or automatic composition (not only selection) of a (sub)process model during run-time (i.e., Degree of Freedom: Modeling/Composition). Late Modeling and Composition may encompass predefined regions of the process model only or the entire process (i.e., Scope: Entire Process or Predefined Regions). Like with Late Selection, modeling and execution remain strictly separated (i.e., Planning Approach: Plan-driven). Decisions regarding the exact control flow are either made upon instance creation (if the scope of decision deferral is the entire process) or when the placeholder activity gets instantiated (if the scope is restricted to predefined regions).

Iterative Refinement allows users to iteratively compose a process instance or the content of a placeholder activity during run-time by selecting any process fragment from a given pool (i.e., Degree of Freedom: Modeling/Composition). By employing an iterative and continuous modeling approach, the modeling and execution of the process fragments become tightly interwoven (i.e., Planning Approach: Iterative). Like Late Modeling, Iterative Refinement can be restricted to predefined regions of the process model or may concern the entire process (i.e., Scope: Entire Process, Predefined Regions).

Using *Ad hoc Composition*, in contrast to Iterative Refinement, process instances are not iteratively refined, but composed in an ad hoc manner without any planning at all (i.e., Degree of Freedom: Modeling/Composition, Planning Approach: Ad hoc). Ad hoc Composition can be restricted to predefined regions of the process model or may concern the entire process (i.e., Scope: Entire Process, Predefined Regions).

In the following subsections, we discuss the different decision deferral patterns in more detail and provide examples of concrete implementations.

11.4   Late Selection

Figure 11.5 illustrates the *Late Selection* pattern. It allows for the late selection of the concrete implementation of a particular placeholder activity during run-time (i.e., Scope: Placeholder). At build-time the process designer creates a process model which, except for its placeholder activities (e.g., Activity B in Fig. 11.5), is entirely prespecified. In addition, a repository of process fragments or activity implementations is provided from which one alternative can be chosen—either upon instance creation or upon enablement of the placeholder activity—to replace the placeholder activity (e.g., Fragments 1–3 in Fig. 11.5). Compared to purely prespecified process models, this pattern offers the advantage that additional implementation alternatives (i.e., process fragments or activity implementations) may be added on-the-fly, without requiring the process model itself to be structurally adapted. Depending on the chosen pattern variant, the selection of the concrete implementation for the placeholder activity can either be automated, system-supported, or manual (i.e., Degree of Automation: Automated, System Supported and Manual). Again, decision making and decision support depend on the pattern variant and may either be goal-based (i.e., that fragment which best meets the process goals is selected), rule-based (i.e., the fragment is selected based on a set of predefined rules), experience-based (i.e., the fragment is selected based on experience), or based on user decisions. Once a process fragment has been selected, it is bound to the placeholder activity and then treated as ordinary subprocess.

Worklets [29] constitute an approach realizing the *Late Selection* pattern. For this, each activity is associated with a set of subprocess fragments, which may be dynamically extended (i.e., additional fragments can be added on the fly) (cf. Fig. 11.6). Again, the activities of a subprocess may be linked with a set of fragments. During run-time choices are made dynamically out of the set of subprocess fragments when activities become enabled. The selection of a suitable fragment is made using hierarchically organized selection rules—called *ripple down rules* (i.e., Decision Making and Decision Support: Rule-based). Users may adjust the automatic choice by adding selection rules (i.e., Degree of Automation: System Supported). Once a fragment has been chosen, the placeholder activity is replaced by it.

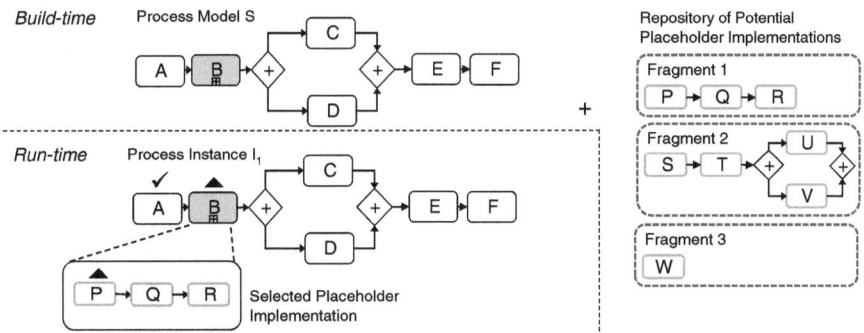

Fig. 11.5 Late selection of process fragments

Example 11.2 (Worklets). Figure 11.6 illustrates the Worklet approach using an example from the health care domain [29]. The prespecified process model consists of the four activities *Admit Patient, Perform Triage, Treat Patient,* and *Discharge Patient.* Activity *Treat Patient* is linked with a set of seven subprocesses. Depending on the actual physical condition of the patient and his list of symptoms, a suitable treatment is chosen during run-time. For this, the ripple down rules are evaluated once activity *Treat Patient* gets enabled. The evaluation of the rules starts with the root node which always evaluates to true. As the next step, condition *"Fever = True"* is evaluated. If this condition holds subprocess *Treat Fever* is selected and *Treat Patient* is replaced by it. Otherwise, evaluation continues with the next rule (i.e., condition "Wound = True").

The approach proposed by Klingemann [144] is an example of fully automated *Late Selection.* During build-time, alternative activities representing different trade-offs in respect to the goal of the process can be specified. Moreover, the process model is enhanced with Quality of Service (QoS) goals (e.g., complete process within 5 days). When processing a damaged motor claim, for example, the processing of the claim should be cost efficient. However, it is also important for the insurance company to handle the claim within 5 days to keep the customer satisfied. Usually, for expensive damages the insurance company contacts an insurance adjuster to perform an independent inspection of the car. If no delays occur, there is enough time for the independent inspection and the claim can be handled within 5 days. If delays occur, the insurance might be willing to drop the car inspection to ensure that the car is repaired in time to maintain customer satisfaction. During run-time one of the predefined alternatives is selected based on the global goals of the process (i.e., Decision Making and Decision Support: Goal-based).

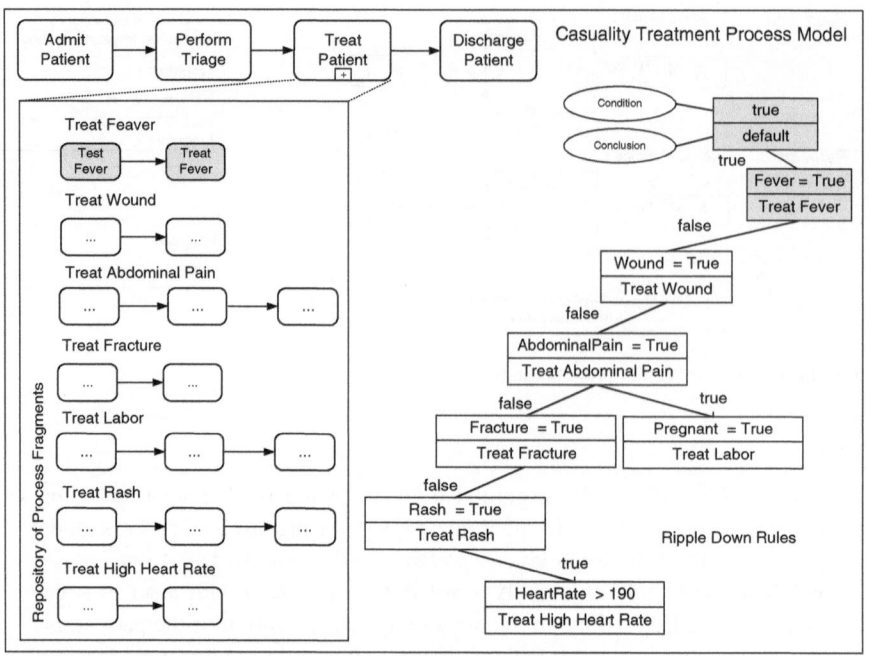

Fig. 11.6 Late selection with Worklets (adopted from [29])

Static process-based composition methods constitute an example of the *Late Selection* of service implementations [31,58,62]. Typically, at build-time an abstract definition of a business process is created, i.e., each activity in the business process corresponds to a service specification and provides a placeholder for services matching the specification. Depending on the concrete approach either upon invocation time or during run-time, services matching the specification are searched using a matchmaking mechanism. In contrast to [144], alternative implementations of a particular activity do not have to be enumerated, but are automatically discovered from a service registry. The decision which service out of several matching ones shall be selected is usually made based on QoS attributes [31,58] or using selection rules [62]. To avoid violations of Service Level Agreement (SLA) when QoS values change, [58] allows QoS-aware rebinding of services at run-time.

Example 11.3 (Automated Late Selection). Figure 11.7 illustrates the basic idea of static process-based composition methods using the process described in [58]. The abstract process definition consists of six activities (i.e., *Collect Data*, *Reserve Restaurant*, *Advertise Award Ceremony*, *Send Invitations*, *Handle Registration*, and *Handle Payment*) serving as placeholders for service implementations. These placeholders are replaced by concrete service

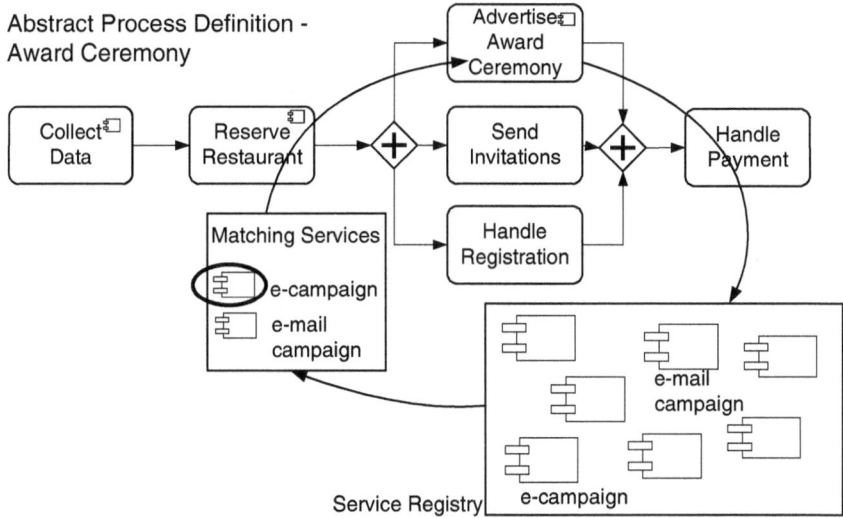

Fig. 11.7 Static process-based composition (adopted from [58])

Table 11.2 Comparison of pattern variants

Approach	Degree of automation	Decision making and decision support
Worklets	System supported	Rule-based
Automated late binding	Automated	Goal-based [31, 58]
		Rule-based [58]

implementations during run-time. For this the *service registry* is searched for matching services. The search for services matching activity *Advertise Award Ceremony*, for example, results in two alternatives: the *e-campaign* service and the *e-mail campaign* service. In our example, the *e-campaign* service is selected and bound to activity *Advertise Award Ceremony*.

Table 11.2 compares the implementations of the *Late Selection* pattern as realized by Worklets and different approaches for automated *Late Selection* [58, 144].

11.5   Late Modeling and Composition

Figure 11.8 illustrates the *Late Modeling and Composition* pattern. It allows modeling or composing a (sub)process model during run-time. Compared to the *Late Selection* pattern described above, the degree of decision deferral is further

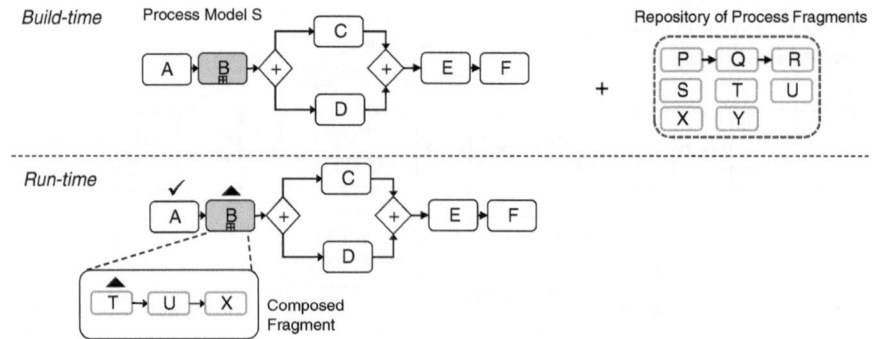

Fig. 11.8 Late modeling (scope: predefined regions)

increased. Instead of just being able to select from a set of predefined process fragments or activity implementations, respective fragments may be modeled or composed dynamically during run-time (Scope: Entire Process or Predefined Regions). Depending on the chosen pattern variant, *Late Modeling and Composition* may take place when creating a process instance or afterwards when the placeholder activity becomes enabled (if the scope is restricted to predefined regions). Before executing the dynamically modeled or composed (sub)process model, its correctness is checked. Having passed this correctness check, the (sub)process model can be executed. Once started, no changes to the (sub)process model may be conducted anymore (unless additional support for ad hoc changes, as discussed in Chap. 7, is available). Depending on the chosen pattern variant process modeling composition may either be automated, system-supported, or manual. Again, decision making and decision support depend on the pattern variant and may either be goal-based, rule-based, experience-based, or user-based decisions.

The *Pockets of Flexibility* approach [317] provides a concrete implementation of the Late Modeling and Composition pattern. To allow for loosely specified processes, placeholder activities may be added to the prespecified process model providing so-called *Pockets of Flexibility*. These activities consist of *process fragments* (i.e., activities or subprocesses) and *constraints* on how these fragments may be composed to an instance-specific process fragment concretizing the Pocket of Flexibility.

Pockets of Flexibility constitute build-activities which can be concretized once they get instantiated. Thereby, users have to obey the constraints imposed by the Pocket of Flexibility. Users are additionally assisted in decision making through a mechanism for querying similar instances that were executed previously [191] (i.e., Decision Making: Goal-based and Experience-based; Degree of Automation: System supported). Before completing the build-activity and binding the dynamically created fragment to it, correctness of this fragment is checked.

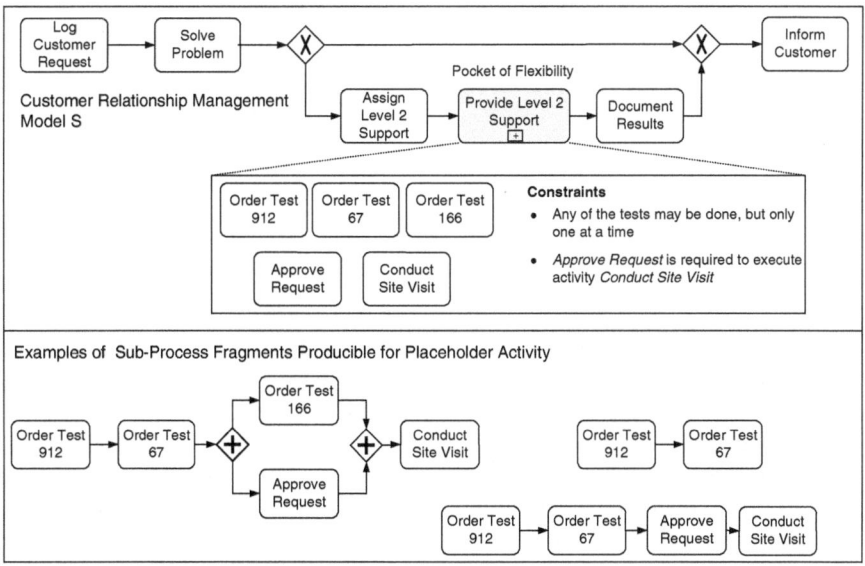

Fig. 11.9 Late modeling using the Pockets of Flexibility approach

Example 11.4 (Pockets of Flexibility Approach). Figure 11.9 illustrates the approach using a process for customer relationship management as described in [317]. When receiving a customer call, the call center agent makes an appropriate request in the system and assigns an engineer (*Log Customer Request*). The engineer then tries to solve the request (*Solve Problem*). In some cases higher level support is needed; i.e., Level 2 support is assigned. The engineer being responsible for Level 2 support may choose from five activities which may be dynamically composed during run-time. Thereby, he has to consider two constraints. First, he may conduct any of the tests, but only one at a time. Second, for conducting a site visit he has to request supervisor approval. Figure 11.9 also shows several valid instances that can be composed using the Pockets of Flexibility approach.

The *Interleaved Routing* pattern [309, 366]—one of the control flow patterns (cf. Sect. 11.4)—can be seen as special implementation of the Late Modeling and Composition pattern (cf. Fig. 4.4e). It allows for the sequential execution of a set of activities, whereby the execution order is decided at run-time and each activity has to be executed exactly once (i.e., Decision Making: Goal-based; Degree of Automation: Manual). Decisions about the exact control flow are deferred to run-time, i.e., the execution ordering of the activities is determined before the first activity of the pattern can get executed.

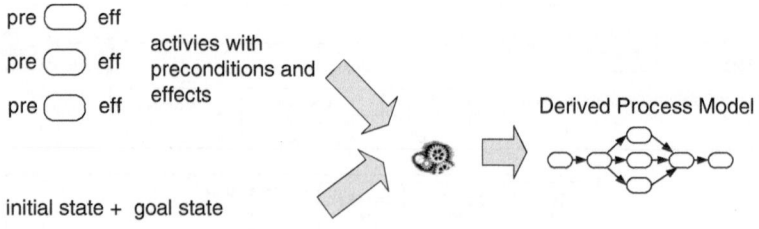

Fig. 11.10 Dynamic process-based composition

Dynamic process-based composition constitutes an example of the automated variant of the *Late Modeling and Composition* pattern. Usually, the scope of decision deferral is the entire process (not just prespecified parts). Instead of starting with an abstract process (cf. Example 11.3), which is then concretized, these approaches completely create the process model dynamically at run-time (e.g., using AI planning techniques) [40, 212, 251, 324, 325, 330, 369]. Typically, respective approaches describe activities (e.g., Web Services) together with their *preconditions* and *effects* (i.e., post-conditions). The planning problem then consists of the *set of activities*, an *initial state*, and a *goal state* (cf. Fig. 11.10). Upon creation of the process instance, a partially ordered set of activities is searched that, when being executed, transforms the process instance from its initial state into a goal state [325]. Note that automated composition only constitutes a technique for decision deferral, when the composition is done upon instance creation (not at build-time). To deal with unanticipated events during run-time replanning may be applied [325, 369].

11.6 Ad hoc Composition

This section illustrates how processes can be dynamically composed during run-time using *Ad hoc Composition*. This enables the on-the fly composition of process fragments from the process repository. Thereby, the process instance evolves incrementally during run-time by executing activities in an ad hoc manner (i.e., activities are not preplanned).

The Declare approach [322] constitutes an example of the *Ad hoc Composition* pattern. At build-time, a loosely specified process model is provided comprising a set of activities as well as constraints that impose restrictions on how these activities may be combined (cf. Fig. 11.11). During run-time, process instances are composed by end-users in an ad hoc manner. Thereby, users may be supported by recommendations on potential next steps [322] (Degree of Automation: Manual, System Supported; Decision Making and Support: Combination of Goal-based and Experience-based). For more details on constraint-based processes, we refer to Chap. 12.

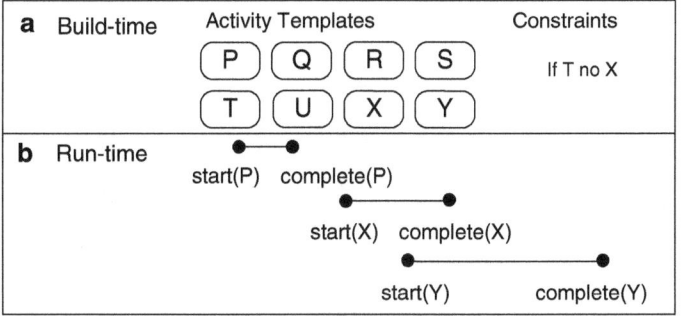

Fig. 11.11 Ad hoc composition of process fragments with declare

Example 11.5 (Declare). Figure 11.11 illustrates the Declare approach using a simple example. After creating a new process instance, the user executes activity P. Afterwards he starts activities X and Y, and executes them. Note that Declare supports *concurrent activity execution*, thus, activity instances may be overlapping (i.e., several activities max be started simultaneously).

Similar to Declare, InConcert [205] and ProMInanD [141] support the ad hoc composition of business processes. While Declare supports overlapping activity instances, InConcert enables sequential activity execution only.

An extended variant of the *Interleaved Routing* pattern [309, 366] (cf. Fig. 4.4e) can be regarded as a special instance of the *Ad hoc Composition* pattern. Thereby, unlike in the above-described example, the execution order of activities can be determined in an ad hoc manner during activity execution and does not have to be specified before starting the first activity.

11.7   Iterative Refinement

The *Iterative Refinement* pattern allows for the iterative refinement of a process instance, i.e., process modeling and process execution are interwoven and may be alternated as needed (cf. Fig. 11.3). Both *Late Modeling and Composition* and *Ad hoc Composition* are special cases of the *Iterative Refinement* pattern covering the two extremes of prespecifying everything and prespecifying nothing. To realize this pattern, it must be possible to preplan the execution of activities without requiring a fully prespecified model that cannot be altered anymore.

The Alaska Simulator (cf. Chap. 16) constitutes an example of a system implementing the *Iterative Refinement* pattern. Iterative Refinement is achieved by extending the *Ad hoc Composition* pattern (as realized by Declare) with a schedule (cf. Fig. 11.12). Regarding the modeling of business processes, Alaska follows

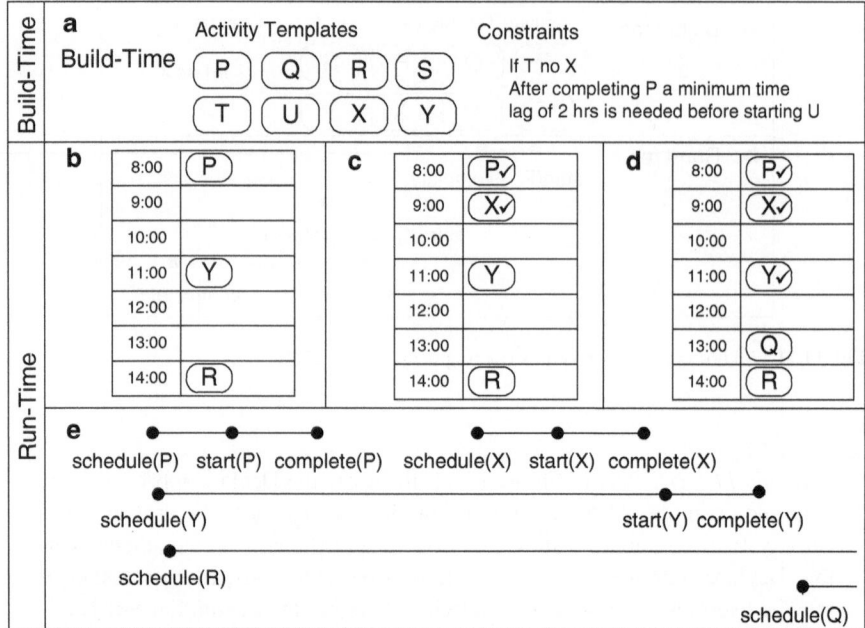

Fig. 11.12 Iterative refinement with Alaska

an approach similar to the one of Declare (cf. Example 11.5). At build-time a set of activities as well as constraints restricting their ordering is defined (cf. Fig. 11.12a). During run-time the process instance may be iteratively modeled and executed. Thereby, the schedule provides a forecast of scheduled, but not yet executed activities (cf. Activities P, Y, and R in Fig. 11.12b). Users are supported during iterative refinement through incremental validation, i.e., users know at every moment whether or not their instance is a valid trajectory in the state space, since potential constraint violations are immediately reported (i.e., Degree of Automation: System-supported; Decision Making and Decision Support: Goal-based). More details on Alaska are provided in Chap. 16.

Example 11.6 (Alaska). After instantiation the user adds activities P, Y, and R to the schedule (cf. Fig. 11.12b). The user executes activity P and decides to extend the schedule with activity X, which he immediately executes (cf. Fig. 11.12c). In a next step the user executes activity Y and adds activity Q to the schedule (cf. Fig. 11.12d). The user may either proceed with executing the next activity (i.e, Q) or continue refining the plan; e.g., by adding activities to the schedule by deleting activities not completed yet, or by moving activities not yet started. When using the *Late Modeling and Composition* pattern

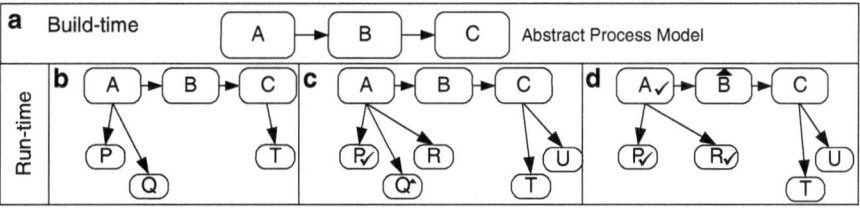

Fig. 11.13 Hierarchical task decomposition

instead of *Iterative Refinement*, once the first activity has started no further refinements are possible, i.e., the user then has to execute the instance exactly as preplanned. Using *Ad hoc Composition*, in turn, the user must not schedule activities Q, R, and U.

Instead of using a schedule, Iterative Refinement can also be achieved using *Hierarchical Task Networks* (e.g., Frodo [27]).

Example 11.7 (Hierarchical Task Networks). Starting from a very coarse-grained process model created at build-time (cf. Fig. 11.13a), the model may be iteratively refined during run-time by adding or deleting activities not yet executed. After instantiation the user adds activities P and Q as subtasks of A to the process model (cf. Fig. 11.13b). The user then executes P, and adds R as subtask of A and T as subtask of C (cf. Fig. 11.13c). The user then decides to delete Q, before executing R (cf. Fig. 11.13d).

11.8 Summary

While Part II has discussed methods and techniques for coping with *variability*, *adaptation*, and *evolution* in the context of prespecified processes, this chapter addressed the need for *looseness* as required by knowledge-intensive processes. More precisely, this chapter introduced different *decision deferral patterns*, which allow keeping parts of the process unspecified at build-time and deferring the decision how to concretize a particular process instance to run-time. For each pattern we presented concrete implementations. Since increasing flexibility also requires an improved user assistance, many approaches discussed in this chapter provide user support. For processes not being entirely (un)predictable, the introduced decision deferral patterns may also be combined with the methods and techniques introduced in Part II, e.g., by using a prespecified process model and allowing for decision deferral in the scope of placeholder activities.

Exercises

11.1. Decision Deferral Patterns
Compare the different decision deferral patterns described in this chapter. Describe their advantages and disadvantages and give examples of their use.

11.2. Addressing Flexibility Needs with Decision Deferral Patterns
Exercise 3.1 describes the check-in and boarding procedures from the perspective of travelers Tom and Tina Traveler. When reading the two scenarios you will see that though the check-in and boarding procedures of both Tom and Tina are similar, there are many differences in the exact course of action.

(a) How could this process be modeled using decision deferral patterns?
(b) Which of the decision deferral patterns do you think are most useful in this context?
(c) Would it make sense to combine a prespecified process model with decision deferral patterns?

Chapter 12
Constraint-Based Process Models

Abstract This chapter introduces constraint-based approaches to process modeling and execution which enable loosely specified processes. While prespecified process models define *how* things have to be done (i.e., in what order and under what conditions activities shall be executed), constraint-based process models focus on *what* should be done by describing the activities that may be performed and the constraints prohibiting undesired execution behavior. In this chapter we address the modeling, verification, and execution of constraint-based process models. Moreover, we discuss how these models can be adapted and evolved over time. We further present techniques for assisting end-users during process execution. Finally, constraint-based process models and prespecified ones are systematically compared, and ways to integrate both approaches are discussed.

12.1 Motivation

Prespecified process models, as discussed in Part II, are the predominant paradigm for modeling and executing business processes in a PAIS (cf. Chap. 4). In Chaps. 5–10 we have discussed how to accommodate the need for variability, adaptation, and evolution of a PAIS relying on prespecified process models. Recently, *constraint-based* approaches have received increased interest [80, 219, 220, 244, 316, 347, 350, 373]. They suggest a fundamentally different way of describing business processes which seems to be promising in respect to the support of highly dynamic processes [244, 347]. As discussed in Chap. 11, the constraint-based approach enables loosely specified process models and allows users to defer modeling decisions to run-time. Advantages commonly attributed to constraint-based processes include the support for "partial workflows" [347], the absence of over-specification [244], and the provision of more maneuvering room for end-users [244].

This chapter deals with the modeling, verification, execution, adaptation, and evolution of constraint-based process models. Section 12.2 discusses how business

M. Reichert and B. Weber, *Enabling Flexibility in Process-Aware Information Systems*,   341
DOI 10.1007/978-3-642-30409-5_12, © Springer-Verlag Berlin Heidelberg 2012

processes can be represented as constraint-based process models. Section 12.3 deals with their interpretation and execution by the PAIS at run-time, and Sect. 12.4 addresses the verification of constraint-based process models. Section 12.5 then discusses issues related to the adaptation and evolution of constraint-based process models. Sections 12.6 and 12.7 present techniques for assisting end-users during process execution. In Sect. 12.8 constraint-based and prespecified process models are systematically compared, and ways to integrate both approaches are discussed. Section 12.9 closes the chapter with a summary.

12.2   Modeling Constraint-Based Processes

While prespecified process models specify exactly *how* things have to be done, constraint-based process models focus on *what* should be done by describing (1) the *activities* that may be performed, and (2) the *constraints* prohibiting undesired process behavior (cf. Fig. 12.1).

Example 12.1 (Fracture Treatment Process). Picking up again Example 2.4 from Chap. 2, the process of treating a fracture comprises activities like *Examine Patient, Perform X-ray, Perform Sling, Prescribe Fixation, Perform Surgery, Apply Cast, Prescribe Rehabilitation*, and *Prescribe Medication*. Moreover, constraints prohibit undesired execution behavior, e.g.:

- Activity *Examine Patient* has to be executed first.
- Each patient gets at least one out of four treatments (i.e., *Perform Sling, Prescribe Fixation, Perform Surgery*, or *Apply Cast*).
- Activity *Apply Cast* and *Prescribe Fixation* are mutually exclusive.
- *Perform X-ray* is a prerequisite for all treatments except *Perform Sling*.
- If activity *Perform Surgery* is performed for a certain patient, the physician will be advised to execute activity *Prescribe Rehabilitation* afterwards.

Definition 12.1 (Constraint-based Process Model). A *constraint-based process model $S = (A, C)$* consists of a finite set of *activities A* and a finite set of *constraints C* prohibiting undesired execution behavior. Further, constraint set $C = C_M \cup C_O$ can be divided into two disjoint subsets. C_M represents mandatory constraints that *must* be obeyed (i.e., obligations and prohibitions), whereas C_O represents optional constraints that *should* be obeyed (i.e., recommendations).

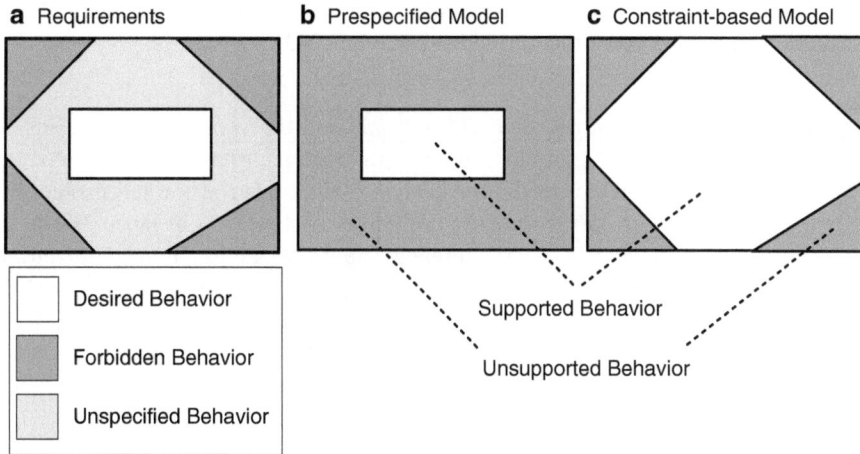

Fig. 12.1 Prespecified vs. constraint-based process models

12.2.1 Constraint-Based Process Models

When formalizing a real-world business process like the fracture treatment process from Example 12.1, prespecified process models and constraint-based ones take a fundamentally different approach as illustrated by Fig. 12.1. Irrespective of the chosen approach, requirements imposed by the real-world business process need to be reflected by the process model. This means that desired behavior (i.e., obligations and recommendations) must be supported by the process model, while forbidden behavior (i.e., prohibitions) must be prohibited [219] (cf. Fig. 12.1a). Therefore, *desired behavior* refers to what has to be done under certain circumstances; i.e., events that must be present in execution traces of corresponding process instances and thus be supported by the process model. *Forbidden behavior*, in turn, refers to what must not be done under certain circumstances, i.e., events that must not occur in execution traces.

Prespecified models follow an "inside-out" approach putting an emphasis on desired behavior, thus avoiding any forbidden one (cf. Fig. 12.1b). Prespecified process models only cover the desired behavior, while behavior which is neither desired nor forbidden remains unsupported (unless the model is changed at the instance level as described in Chap. 7). On one hand, focusing on desired behavior makes prespecified process models well suited for guaranteeing compliance with existing business requirements. On the other hand, this implies rather rigid process models and poses the risk of *over-constraining* as well as *over-specification* [219, 243].

A constraint-based process model, in turn, takes an "outside-in" approach (cf. Fig. 12.1c) and is created by first identifying the set of relevant activities and adding it to the model [243]. At this stage, without the presence of any constraints, activities could be executed arbitrarily often, and in any order. Constraints are then added restricting the behavior of the constraint-based process model by discarding those execution traces that constitute forbidden behavior [243].

Example 12.2 (Desired and Forbidden Behavior). The constraint requiring that for each patient at least one out of several treatments has to be performed (cf. Example 12.1) expresses *desired behavior*. Since this constraint is mandatory, it constitutes an *obligation* to be fulfilled by each process instance. When surgery is performed to treat a fracture, physicians are advised to recommend rehabiliation afterwards. This constraint expresses *desired behavior* as well. However, it is provided in the form of a *recommendation* that should be followed. The constraint stating that cast and fixation are mutually exclusive and thus must not be both executed for the same process instance (i.e., treatment case) expresses *forbidden behavior* in form of a *prohibition*. Finally, the medication is not restricted by any constraint as its execution is neither required, recommended (i.e., *desired behavior*) nor forbidden (i.e., *forbidden behavior*).

By prohibiting forbidden behavior (instead of focusing on desired behavior), constraint-based models also guarantee compliance with business requirements, but typically allow for more flexibility compared to prespecified models. In particular, a constraint-based model allows for all possible behavior as long as it is not forbidden [219].

While prespecified process models only support those execution traces explicitly included in the process model, constraint-based process models implicitly specify the set of supported traces. An execution trace σ is *supported* by a constraint-based process model, if its mandatory constraints are all satisfied.

Definition 12.2 (Supported Traces). Let $S = (A, C)$ be a constraint-based process model with activity set A and constraint set $C = C_M \cup C_O$ where C_M denotes the set of mandatory constraints and C_O the set of optional ones. Further, let $\sigma = < e_1, \ldots, e_k >$ be a completed trace where the order of e_i in σ reflects the temporal order in which events e_i related to the execution of activities from A occurred. Then, σ is supported by S if it complies with all mandatory constraints from set C_M.

12.2.2 Overview of Control Flow Constraints

We explain the operational semantics of typical control flow constraints informally by providing examples for supported and unsupported execution traces. While the former constitute traces that satisfy the respective constraints, the latter are traces

Table 12.1 Categories of control flow constraints

Category	Description
Existence constraints	Specify how often an activity can or must be executed
Choice constraints	Allow specifying n-out-of-m choices
Relation constraints	Restrict the ordering of activities by imposing restrictions on the relation between two activities
Negation constraints	Define negative relations between activities
Branching constraints	Allow specifying relation and negation constraints involving more than two activities

that violate them. For convenience, we use a slightly more compact representation of execution traces compared to Chap. 4. In particular, when describing the different constraints we abstract from start and completion events for activities and only consider a single event representing the execution of a particular activity. To graphically illustrate the constraints the DecSerFlow notation introduced in [18] is used.

Table 12.1 depicts different categories of control flow constraints [243] which will be detailed in the following section.

Existence Constraints. *Existence constraints* (cf. Fig. 12.2) specify how often an activity must be executed for one particular process instance. For example, *existence(a,n)* can be used to express that activity a needs to be executed at least n times. Constraint *at_most(a,n)*, in turn, expresses that activity a can be executed at most n times during process execution. Constraint *exactly(a,n)* specifies that activity a must occur exactly n times in every execution trace. Finally, *init(a)* expresses that activity a needs to appear as the first activity in any trace.

Choice Constraints. *Choice constraints* allow specifying m-out-of-n choices (cf. Fig. 12.3). For example, *choice(m-of-n, {$a_1, \ldots, a_m$})*, $m \leq n$ allows expressing that *at least n* distinct activities from set {$a_1, \ldots, a_n$} have to be executed. Constraint *exact_choice(m-of-n, {$a_1, \ldots, a_n$})*, $m \leq n$, in turn, specifies that *exactly m* distinct activities from set {$a_1, \ldots, a_n$} have to be executed. Note that both constraints constitute deferred choices among activities (see also the *Deferred Choice control flow pattern* described in Chap. 4).

Relation Constraints. *Relation constraints* restrict the ordering of activities by imposing restrictions on the relation between two activities a and b (cf. Fig. 12.4). For example, constraint *response(a,b)* requires that if activity a is executed, activity b has to be executed afterwards (but not necessarily directly afterwards). While, for example, traces <A, B>, <A, A, A, B> and <B> satisfy constraint *response(a,b)*, trace <A> violates it. Constraint *precedence(a,b)* requires activity b to be preceded by activity a (but not necessarily directly preceded). Traces <A, B>, <A, B, B, B> and <A> all satisfy constraint *precedence(a,b)*. By contrast, this does not apply to trace <B>. Constraint *succession(a,b)* is a combination of constraints *response(a,b)*

existence(a, n)	**n..*** a	Activity *a* must occur at least *n* times in every trace
	Example: `existence(A,1)` Supported traces, e.g.: `<A>`, `<A,A,A>` Unsupported trace, e.g.: `<>`	
at_most(a, n)	**0..n** a	Activity *a* must occur at most *n* times in every trace
	Example: `at_most(A,3)` Supported traces, e.g.: `<>`, `<A>`, `<A,A>`, `<A,A,A>` Unsupported trace, e.g.: `<A,A,A,A>`	
exactly(a, n)	**n** a	Activity *a* must occur exactly *n* times in every trace
	Example: `exactly(A,2)` Supported trace, e.g.: `<A,A>` Unsupported traces, e.g.,: `<A>`, `<A,A,A>`	
init(a)	**init** a	Activity *a* must be the first executed activity in every trace
	Example: `init(A)` Supported trace, e.g.: `<A,C,D,B>` Unsupported trace, e.g.: `<D,C,B,A>`	

Fig. 12.2 Existence constraints

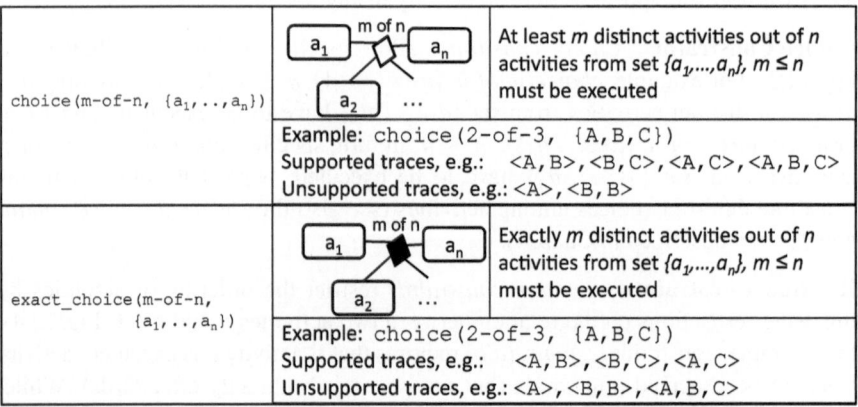

choice(m-of-n, {a₁,..,aₙ})	a_1 *m of n* a_n a_2 ...	At least *m* distinct activities out of *n* activities from set $\{a_1,...,a_n\}$, $m \leq n$ must be executed
	Example: `choice(2-of-3, {A,B,C})` Supported traces, e.g.: `<A,B>`,`<B,C>`,`<A,C>`,`<A,B,C>` Unsupported traces, e.g.: `<A>`, `<B,B>`	
exact_choice(m-of-n, {a₁,..,aₙ})	a_1 *m of n* a_n a_2 ...	Exactly *m* distinct activities out of *n* activities from set $\{a_1,...,a_n\}$, $m \leq n$ must be executed
	Example: `choice(2-of-3, {A,B,C})` Supported traces, e.g.: `<A,B>`,`<B,C>`,`<A,C>` Unsupported traces, e.g.: `<A>`,`<B,B>`,`<A,B,C>`	

Fig. 12.3 Choice constraints

and *precedence(a,b)*. It requires that if activity *a* is executed, *b* has to be executed afterwards (but not necessarily directly afterwards). In addition, the execution of activity *b* has to be preceded by activity *a*. For example, traces `<A,B>`, `<A,A,A,B>` and `<A,B,B,B>` all satisfy constraint *succession(a,b)*, whereas

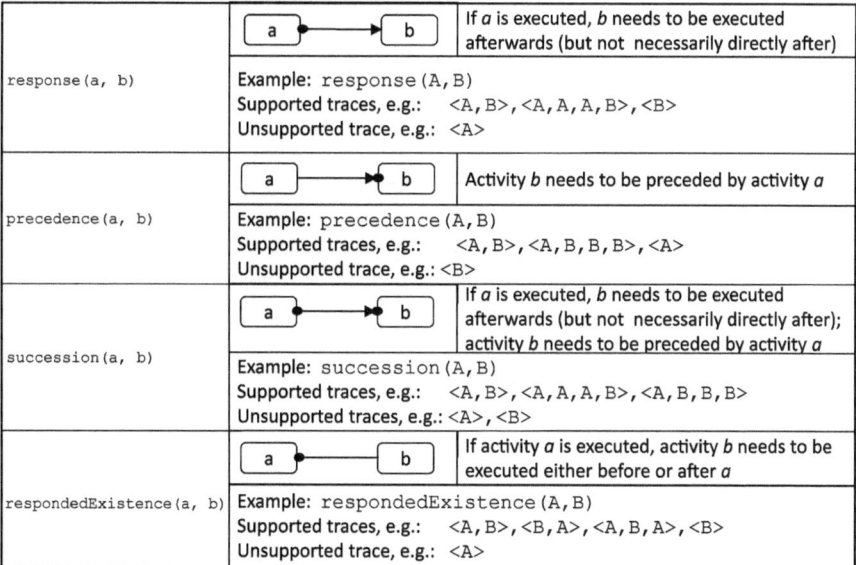

Fig. 12.4 Relation constraints

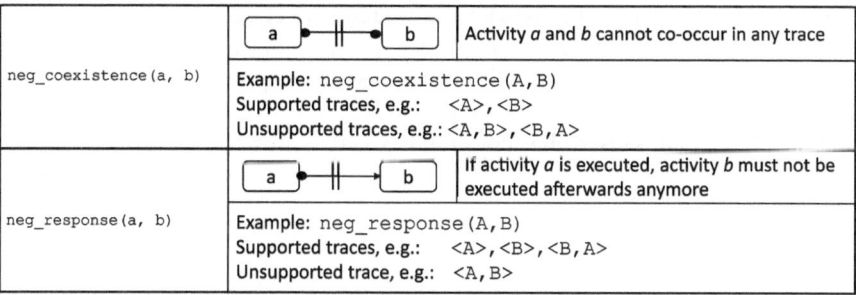

Fig. 12.5 Negation constraints

traces <A> and <B> violate it. Finally, *respondedExistence(a,b)* requires that if activity *a* is executed, activity *b* has to be executed either before or after *a*. For example, traces <A,B>, <B,A>, <A,B,A> and <B> are all valid in respect to constraint *respondedExistence(a,b)*, whereas trace <A> violates it.

Negation Constraints. *Negation constraints* define negative relations between activities (cf. Fig. 12.5). For example, *neg_coexistence(a,b)* prohibits activity *a* and activity *b* from co-occurring in the same trace; i.e., *a* and *b* are mutually exclusive. In turn, *neg_response(a,b)* forbids that *a* is followed by *b* in any trace.

Branching Constraints. Finally, *branching constraints* constitute extensions of both relation and negation constraints. They allow specifying relation and negation constraints involving more than two activities (cf. Fig. 12.6). Constraint

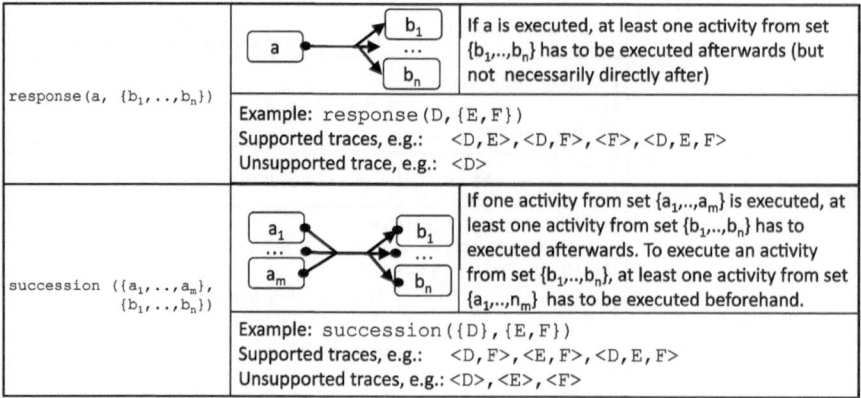

Fig. 12.6 Branching constraints

response(a,{b₁,…,bₙ}) expresses that if *a* is executed at least one activity from set
{$b_1,…, b_n$} has to be executed afterwards. Assume that the execution of activities D,
E, and F is restricted by constraint *response(D,{E,F})*. Traces <D,E>, <D,F>, <F>
and <D,E,F> all satisfy this constraint, whereas trace <D> violates it. Constraint
succession({a₁,…,aₘ}),{b₁,…,bₙ}), in turn, expresses that if one activity from set
{$a_1,…, a_m$} is executed, it needs to be followed by least one activity from set {$b_1,…,$
b_n}. Further, to execute an activity from set {$b_1,…, b_n$} at least one activity from set
{$a_1,…, a_m$} has to be executed beforehand. Assume that the execution of activities
D, E and F is restricted by constraint *succession({D},{E,F})*. Traces <D,F>, <E,F>
and <D,E,F> all satisfy this constraint, whereas traces <D>, <E> and <F>
violate it.

Example 12.3 (Constraint-based Process Model). Figure 12.7 depicts a simple constraint-based process model consisting of six distinct activities A,
B, C, D, E, and F. In addition, it comprises two mandatory constraints.
First, there is a *neg_coexistence* constraint (cf. Fig. 12.5) between A and B
indicating that these two activities are mutually exclusive. In addition, there
is a *response* constraint (cf. Fig. 12.4) between activities C and F requiring
that after the execution of C, F is eventually executed. The *neg_coexistence*
constraint illustrated in Fig. 12.7 (i.e., constraint C1) forbids that activities
A and B co-occur in the same trace. While process instances with traces
σ_1=<A,A,D,E,A>, σ_2=<B,C,F,E,B>, σ_3=<B,E,F>, σ_4=<A,C,E,A>
and σ_5=<B,D,C> satisfy this constraint, σ_6=<A,D,B,F,E> constitutes
an example of a trace violating it. The *response* constraint (i.e., constraint
C2) depicted in Fig. 12.7 requires that every execution of activity C has
to be followed by an execution of activity F before the corresponding
process instance may complete. Instances with traces σ_4=<A,C,E,A>

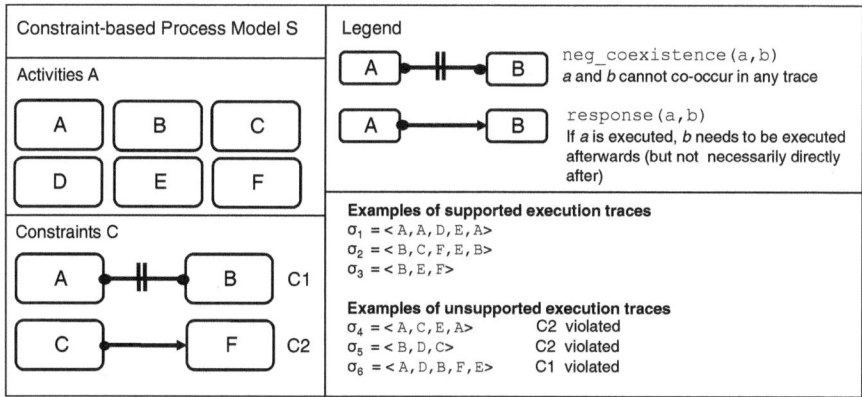

Fig. 12.7 Simple constraint-based process model

and σ_5=<B,D,C> are violating the *response* constraint, while instances with traces σ_1=<A,A,D,E,A>, σ_2=<B,C,F,E,B>, σ_3=<B,E,F> and σ_6=<A,D,B,F,E> satisfy it.

Example 12.4 illustrates the modeling of constraint-based processes in a walk-through scenario using some of the previously described constraints.

Example 12.4 (Writing a Project Proposal). The process of writing a project proposal starts with an idea. Afterwards, it is possible to start working on the project proposal and to refine the idea at any time. If it turns out that the idea is not substantial enough, unfeasible, or that the deadline cannot be met, the work on the proposal will be stopped. Otherwise, as soon as the idea is described sufficiently well, the proposal can be submitted. Note that a proposal can be submitted only once.

As a first step, we derive the activities from this modeling task description and add them to the model: Come up with Initial Idea (I), Write Proposal (W), Refine Idea (R), Cancel Proposal Writing (C), and Submit Proposal (S). When not adding any constraints to the model, these five activities can be executed arbitrarily often and in any order. In a next step we start adding constraints to the model.

Activity *Come up with Initial Idea (I)* is a prerequisite for both activities *Refine Idea (R)* and *Write Proposal (W)*. To reflect this situation two *precedence* constraints need to be added (cf. Fig. 12.4). Activities *Write Proposal (W)* and *Refine Idea (R)* can be executed arbitrarily often and allow iterative improvements to the proposal. Thus, no cardinalities have to be added for these two activities. Activity *Come up with Initial Idea (I)*, in turn, needs some further considerations. On one hand, this activity has to be mandatory, because otherwise none of the other activities can be executed. On the other hand, there should also be an upper bound restricting its occurrence per execution trace to one. To express this restriction, an *exact* constraint with $n = 1$ (cf. Fig. 12.2) needs to be added to activity *Come up with Initial Idea (I)*. Activities *Cancel Proposal Writing (C)* and *Submit Proposal (S)* can never be both executed for the same process instance, i.e., they are mutually exclusive. To express this restriction we have to add a *neg_coexistence* constraint between activities *Cancel Proposal Writing (C)* and *Submit Proposal (S)* to the model (cf. Fig. 12.5). Execution of either *Cancel Proposal Writing (C)* or *Submit Proposal (S)* requires that *Write Proposal (W)* has been executed. In addition, once activity *Write Proposal (W)* has been executed, either *Cancel Proposal Writing (C)* or *Submit Proposal (S)* have to be performed to properly complete the process. Such restrictions can be expressed using a *succession constraint* (cf. Fig. 12.6), where $a = $ *Write Proposal (W)* and $b_1 = $ *Cancel Proposal Writing (C)*, and $b_2 = $ *Submit Proposal (S)*. Finally, both activities *Cancel Proposal Writing (C)* or *Submit Proposal (S)* should be executed not more than once, requiring an *at_most* constraint with $n = 1$ (cf. Fig. 12.2) be added to the model.

Figure 12.8 shows the process of writing a project proposal, including examples for traces which are (not) supported by that particular model.

When looking at trace σ_6 in Fig. 12.8 it is not immediately apparent why activity *Write Proposal (W)* cannot be executed after activity *Submit Proposal (S)*. When closely looking at the interplay of constraints related to these activities, a *hidden dependency* [115, 116] between activities *Write Proposal (W)*, *Submit Proposal (S)*, and *Cancel Proposal Writing (C)* can be observed. If *Write Proposal (W)* is executed after *Cancel Proposal Writing (C)* or *Submit Proposal (S)* the process instance cannot be completed anymore since the succession constraint between *Cancel Proposal Writing (C)* and *Submit Proposal (S)* requires the execution of either *Cancel Proposal Writing (C)* or *Submit Proposal (S)* after *Write Proposal (W)*. This, however, is prohibited by the cardinality constraints of *Cancel Proposal Writing (C)* and *Submit Proposal (S)*.

The above described *hidden dependency* does not affect correct execution of constraint-based process models, since constraint-based PAISs like Declare [19] prohibit the execution of activity *Write Proposal (W)* after activity *Cancel Proposal Writing (C)* or *Submit Proposal (S)* during run-time [243]. However,

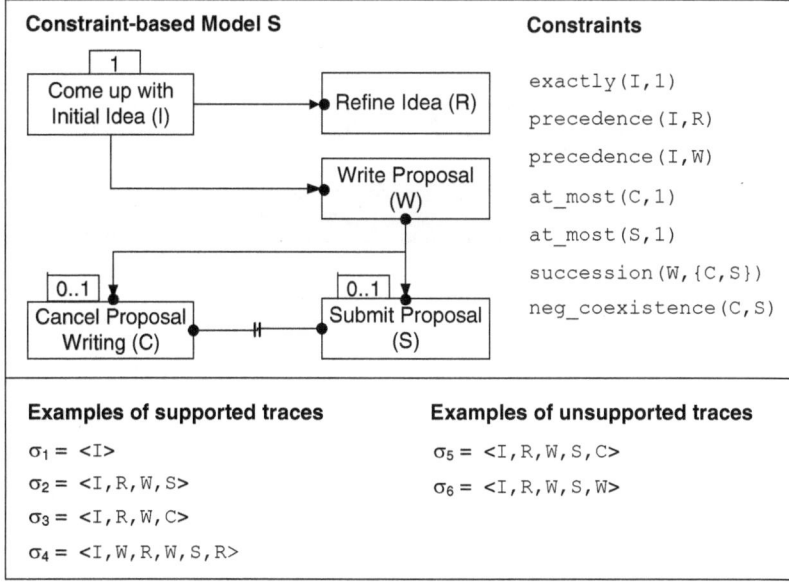

Fig. 12.8   Constraint-based process model for project proposal writing

hidden dependencies hamper understandability, and consequently the main-tainability of constraint-based models and should therefore be avoided as much as possible.

12.3   Executing Constraint-Based Processes

This section discusses how instances of constraint-based process models are executed.

Definition 12.3 (Constraint-based Process Instance). Let $S = (A, C)$ be a constraint-based process model with activity set A and constraint set C. Then, a process instance $I = (S, \sigma_I)$ on S is defined by S and a corresponding trace $\sigma_I = \langle e_1, \ldots, e_k \rangle$ where the order of e_i in σ reflects the temporal order in which events e_i related to the execution of activities from A occurred.

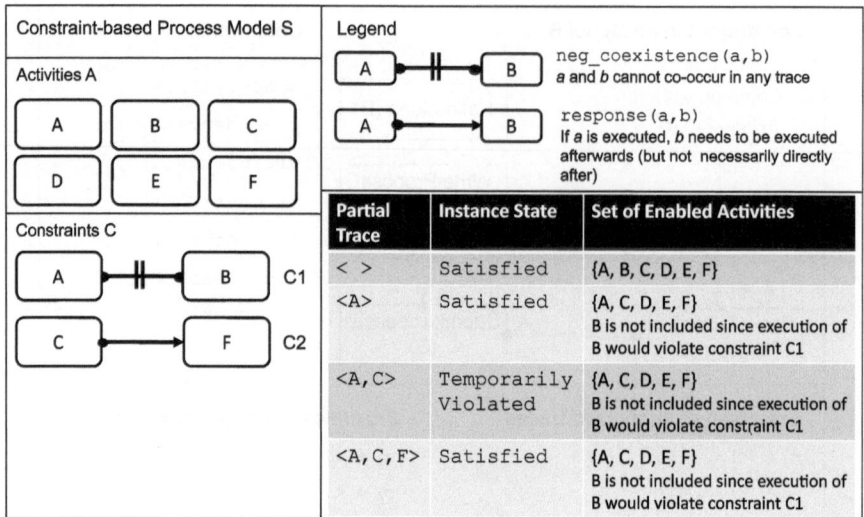

Fig. 12.9 Enabled activities

Complementary to the process instance states introduced in Chap. 2, a constraint-based process instance in state `Running` is in one of the substates `Satisfied`, `Temporarily Violated` or `Violated` [243]. More precisely, a running process instance I is in state `Satisfied` if its current partial trace σ_I satisfies all mandatory constraints of S. Optional constraints, in turn, do not have any impact on the state of I. Instance I is in state `Temporarily Violated`, if its partial trace does not satisfy all mandatory constraints in S, but there is a suffix that could be added to the partial trace such that all mandatory constraints become satisfied (resulting in a supported trace). Finally, an instance is in state `Violated`, if the partial trace violates mandatory constraints in S and there is no suffix that can be added to satisfy them.

Example 12.5 (Instance State). Figure 12.9 shows the state of a process instance I on S for different partial traces. Initially, the partial trace is empty and I is in state `Satisfied`, i.e., both constraints $C1$ and $C2$ are satisfied. After executing activity A instance I still is in state `Satisfied`. Executing activity C afterwards, however, changes the state of I from `Satisfied` to `Temporarily Violated`. This state change is caused by a temporary violation of constraint $C2$, which can be resolved by executing activity F later on. After executing activity F, I reenters state `Satisfied`.

12.3.1   Executing Constraint-Based Models Without Overlapping Activities

Like with prespecified process models, *enabled activities* of a constraint-based process instance are presented to authorized users via their worklists for possible execution. In contrast to prespecified models, for which enabled activities are typically mandatory (except for the deferred choice pattern [309]), activities of constraint-based process models are (if not specified otherwise by constraints) optional. Authorized users are allowed to execute all activities whose execution does not result in instance state `Violated`.

Definition 12.4 (Enabled Activities). Let $S = (A, C)$ be a constraint-based process model with activity set A and constraint set C. Further, let $I = (S, \sigma_I)$ be a corresponding process instance. Then, an activity $a \in A$ of instance I is enabled if a can be executed and the instance state of I is not `Violated` afterwards; i.e., for $\sigma_I = < a_1, \ldots, a_k >$, $a_i \in A$ we obtain $\sigma_{I'} = < a_1, \ldots, a_k, a >$ afterwards and $(S, \sigma_{I'})$ is not in state `Violated`, i.e., there is no suffix which can be added to $\sigma_{I'}$ such that it is satisfied.

Example 12.6 (Enabled Activities). Figure 12.9 shows how the set of enabled activities for a given process model S evolves during the execution of a corresponding process instance I. For the sake of simplicity we chose the example such that activities do not overlap; i.e., activities are sequentially executed only. If the partial trace is empty, the set of enabled activities comprises all activities of schema S (since all constraints are satisfied). Note that activities A, B, C, D, E and F are all optional, i.e., they are presented to authorized users for possible execution, but their execution is not enforced by the PAIS. For partial trace <A> (i.e., activity A was executed for that instance), activity B is not included in the set of enabled activities any longer, since its execution would now violate constraint C1 and consequently change the state of I to `Violated`. Also for partial traces <A, C> and <A, C, F> all activities except B become enabled.

Unlike prespecified process models (cf. Chap. 4), constraint-based process models lack designated end nodes. Since activities (if not forbidden by any constraint) can be executed arbitrarily often, usually constraint-based process models have to be *explicitly completed by the users*. Generally, a process instance can be completed if no activity is in state `Running` and the process instance to be completed is in state `Satisfied` (i.e., all mandatory constraints are satisfied).

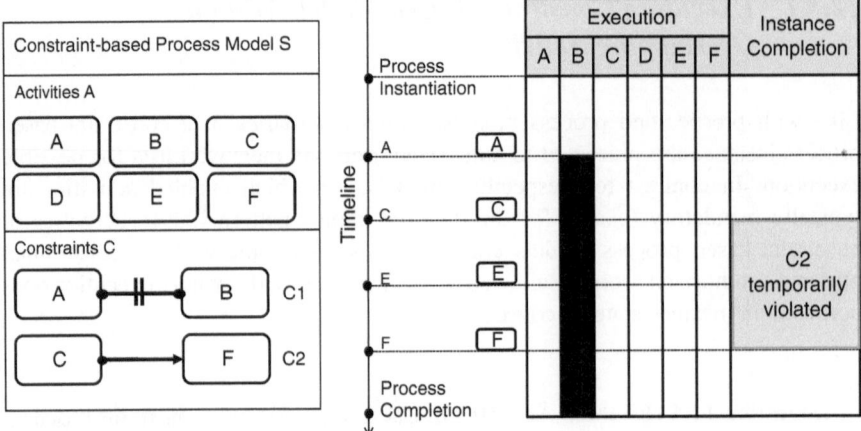

Fig. 12.10 Executing a constraint-based process model

Definition 12.5 (Instance Completion). Let $S = (A, C)$ be a constraint-based process model with activity set A and constraint set $C = C_M \cup C_O$ (where C_M is the set of mandatory constraints and C_O the set of optional constraints). Then, any process instance $I = (S, \sigma_I)$ on S may be completed if it is in state `Satisfied` (i.e., all mandatory constraints $c \in C_M$ are satisfied) and no instance of activity $a \in A$ is in state `Running`.

Example 12.7 (Executing Constraint-based Models). Figure 12.10 illustrates how an instance of a constraint-based process model is executed. The left hand depicts the constraint-based process model, while the right hand illustrates one possible execution of a corresponding process instance. After creating this process instance, all six activities become enabled (reflected by the white bars). After a while, activity A is executed by an authorized user. Due to the mandatory *neg_coexistence* constraint C1 between A and B, activity B then cannot be executed anymore (reflected by the black bar in column B). Execution of A is followed by execution of C, which leads to a temporary violation of the mandatory *response* constraint C2 (i.e., C needs to be followed by F) prohibiting completion of the process instance (gray bar in column "Instance Completion"). Next activity E is executed, which is then followed by activity F. After the execution of activity F the temporary constraint violation is resolved (white bar in column "Instance Completion") and the process instance may be completed.

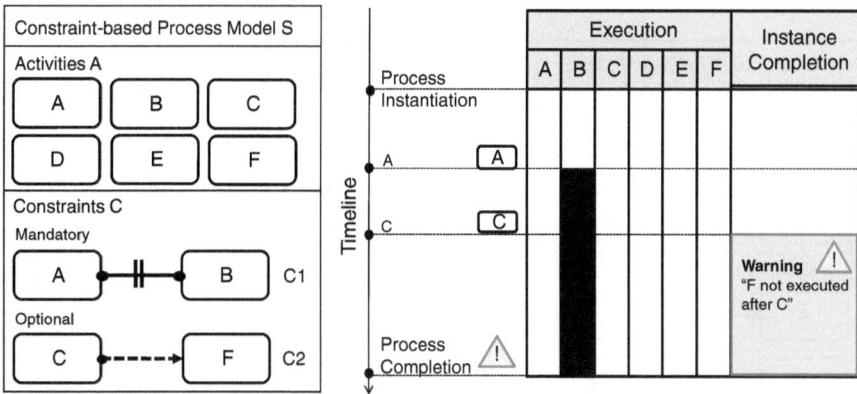

Fig. 12.11 Executing constraint-based process models with an optional constraints

Example 12.8 (Executing Constraint-based Models with Optional Constraints). Figure 12.11 shows a slightly adopted version of the constraint-based process model from Fig. 12.10. While constraints *C*1 and *C*2 in Fig. 12.10 are both mandatory constraints, constraint *C*2 is now marked as *optional* (represented by the dashed line). While the process model in Fig. 12.10 enforces activity F to be executed after activity C, the process model in Fig. 12.11 allows users to ignore constraint *C*2 and to complete the process instance (with a warning) without having executed activity F.

12.3.2 Executing Constraint-Based Models with Overlapping Activities

In our examples so far, we have assumed that activity executions do not overlap, i.e., activities are sequentially executed. In particular, we have abstracted from start and completion events for activities and only considered one single event representing the execution of a particular activity (e.g., ⊏A⊐ meaning that activity A was executed). Example 12.9 illustrates the execution of constraint-based models with overlapping activities. For this, distinct start and completion events of activities have to be considered (e.g., start(A) and complete(A)).

Example 12.9 (Executing Constraint-based Models with Overlapping Activities). Figure 12.12 illustrates the execution of a constraint-based process

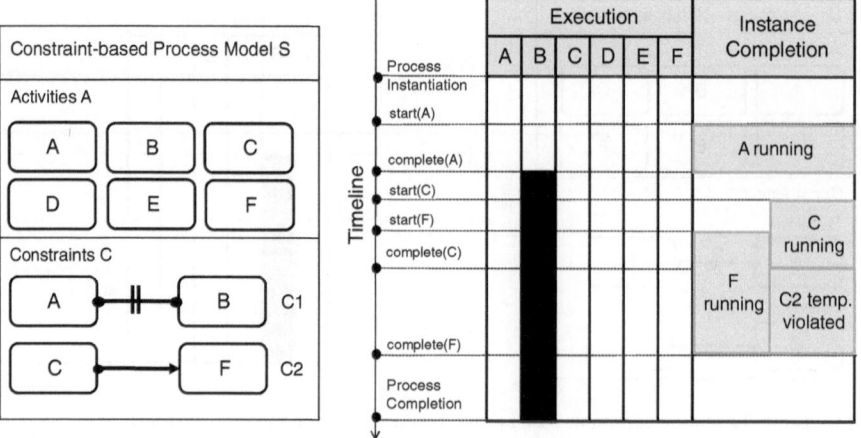

Fig. 12.12 Executing a constraint-based process with overlapping activities

model with overlapping activities of *S* using one particular process instance as an example. Note that depending on the concrete implementation, constraints relate to the completion events of activities (e.g., Declare [19]) or to start events (e.g., Cheetah or Alaska; for details on Alaska see Chap. 16). In the scenario depicted in Fig. 12.12, for example, constraints relate to completion events.

After creating a new process instance, all six activities become enabled (reflected by the white bars in columns A–F). After a while, activity A is started by an authorized user resulting in activity state `Running`. As indicated by the gray bar in column "Instance Completion," it is not possible to complete the respective process instance as long as activity A is in state `Running`, i.e., between events `start(A)` and `complete(A)`. The set of enabled activities, in turn, remains unaffected by the start event of activity A (indicated by the white bars in columns A–F). With the completion of activity A, however, activity B is not enabled anymore (reflected by the black bar in column B), since this would violate constraint C1. This is followed by event `start(C)` resulting in activity instance state `Running`. Since activity C is now in state `Running` the instance cannot be completed in its current state (gray bar in column "Instance Completion"). Next, activity F is started and then activity C is completed. With the completion of activity C, constraint C2 becomes temporarily violated, prohibiting completion of the process instance (gray bar in column "Instance Completion"). After completing activity F the temporary constraint violation is resolved (white bar in column "Instance Completion") and the process instance may be completed.

12.4   Verifying Constraint-Based Process Models

Like with prespecified process models, it has to be ensured that constraint-based process models being deployed to the PAIS run-time environment can be properly executed; i.e., it should be guaranteed at build-time that process instances will always complete in a well-defined state. In Sect. 12.3 we discussed that the state of a constraint-based process instance (i.e., Satisfied, Temporarily Violated or Violated) can change during process execution. To ensure proper completion of a constraint-based process instance, the instance state has to be Satisfied at the end of its execution. For this, errors like *dead activities* or *conflicts* caused by certain combinations of constraints must be prohibited.

Similar to prespecified process models, an activity of a constraint-based process model S is denoted as *dead* if none of the traces supported by S contains that activity.

Definition 12.6 (Dead Activity). Let $S = (A, C)$ be a constraint-based process model with activity set A and constraint set C. Let further QS_S be the set of all traces supported by S. Then, an activity $a \in A$ is called dead if there is no trace $\sigma = <a_1, \ldots, a_n> \in QS_S$ containing activity a. Formally:
$$\exists 1 \leq i < n : a_1 = a$$
$$\nexists \sigma \in QS_S : a \in \sigma.$$

Example 12.10 (Dead Activity). Figure 12.13 provides an example of a constraint-based process model having a dead activity. Since there is a *response* constraint between activities B and C as well as between activities B and D, activity B can only be executed if activities C and D are executed eventually afterwards. However, this is prohibited by the *neg_coexistence* constraint between C and D. Consequently, there is no single trace supported by this process model which includes activity B, i.e., activity B is *dead*.

A *conflict*, in turn, describes a situation in which no single trace is supported by a given process model.

Definition 12.7 (Conflict). Let $S = (A, C)$ be a constraint-based process model with activity set A and constraint set C. Let further QS_S be the set of all supported traces on S. Then, S has a conflict if $QS_S = \emptyset$.

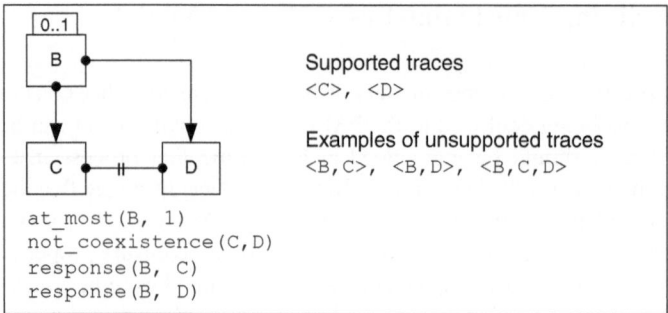

Fig. 12.13   Example of a constraint-based process model having a dead activity

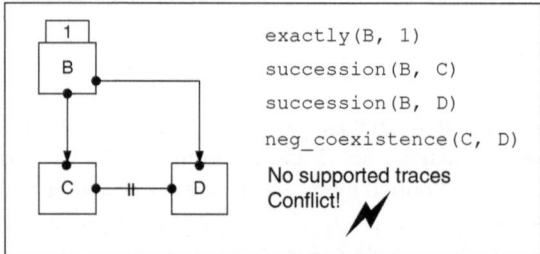

Fig. 12.14   Example of a constraint-based process model with a conflict

Example 12.11 (Conflict). Figure 12.14 shows an example of a constraint-based process model having a conflict. This conflict results from the combination of the *neg_coexistence* constraint and the two *succession* constraints. According to the *neg_coexistence* constraint between activities C and D only one of these two activities may be executed. The two succession constraints, however, require that B is always followed by both C and D and that B is executed before executing these two activities.

To verify constraint-based process models and to detect dead activities and conflicts, existing approaches map constraints onto a logic-based formalism (e.g., linear temporal logic (LTL) [243] or abductive logic [219]).

In Declare, for example, each constraint of a process model is mapped to an LTL formula. The concatenated formulas of all the constraints of a constraint-based process model are then translated into a finite state automaton which can then be exploited for detecting dead activities and conflicts. Moreover, the generated automaton can be used as the basis for process execution (see [243] for details). Since the automaton generated for the concatenated LTL formulas is exponential with respect to the size of the formula, this approach can lead to performance problems when confronted with larger constraint-based process models [220].

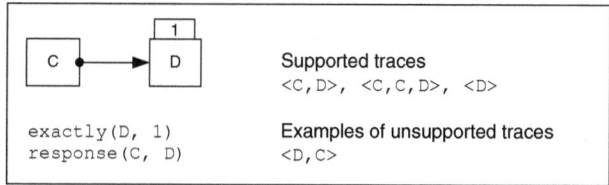

Fig. 12.15 Example of a deadlock

Alternatively, it is proposed to map constraints onto SCIFF [219, 220]—a framework based on Abductive Logic Programming. In contrast to the LTL-based approach employed by Declare, SCIFF does not require the generation of an automaton covering all supported behavior, but does adopt a generative approach.

To ensure that a process instance, once started, can always complete (i.e., the execution of the constraint-based process model is deadlock-free), the automaton generated from the concatenated LTL formulas can be exploited when using LTL. By applying model checking approaches to the generated automaton all paths can be removed that might result in a deadlock during process execution [243]. The adapted version of the automaton then provides a deadlock-free execution mechanism for constraint-based process models *exactly representing all supported execution traces.*

Example 12.12 (Deadlock). Figure 12.15 shows an example of a deadlock which could occur when directly using the automaton generated from the concatenated formulas for executing constraint-based process models. Assuming a partial trace <D>, the execution of activity C would result in a situation where the option to complete does not exist anymore. The *response constraint* between C and D requires that C is followed by D. However, D has already been executed and the *exactly* constraint with $n = 1$ forbids that D is executed more than once. To avoid such deadlock situation, given a partial trace <D>, the constraint-based PAIS must prohibit that C gets enabled; i.e., the automaton used as basis for process execution must not allow activity C to become enabled for partial trace <D>.

12.5   Adapting and Evolving Constraint-Based Process Models

Even though constraint-based process models provide a high degree of flexibility by deferring decisions to run-time, the process model might have to be structurally adapted to deal with unforeseen situations or to react to changing requirements.

Table 12.2 Basic change operations

Change operation	Description
addActivity	Adds an activity to the activity set
removeActivity	Removes an activity from the activity set
addConstraint	Adds a new constraint to the constraint set
removeConstraint	Removes a constraint from the constraint set
updateConstraint	Modifies a constraint in the constraint set

As with prespecified process models, respective changes can be ad hoc and only affect a single process instance (cf. Chap. 7) or *evolutionary*, i.e., they affect all newly created process instances as well as all ongoing process instances which are state-compliant with the changed constraint-based process model (cf. Chap. 9). By applying a sequence of change operations to a constraint-based process model S another constraint-based process model S' results (cf. Definition 7.1). Basic change operations for adapting or evolving a constraint-based process model S to a new version S' are informally depicted in Table 12.2.

> *Example 12.13 (Process Model Evolution).* Assume the following scenario: due to changing requirements the constraint-based process model S depicted in Fig. 12.16a has to be extended with two additional constraints resulting in model S' (cf. Fig. 12.16b). First, an *exactly* constraint C3 with $n = 1$ (cf. Fig. 12.2) is added for activity A, i.e., A should be executed exactly once. In addition, a *respondedExistence* constraint C4 (cf. Fig. 12.4) is added between activities D and E; i.e., if D is executed it should be followed by E.

As detailed above, a particular change may either affect a single process instance or multiple instances. As with prespecified process models, the applicability of a change depends on the state of the process instance(s) to be adapted. To ensure correctness of instance execution afterwards, a structural process change may only be applied to a process instance I, if I is *state compliant* with S. A process instance I is called state compliant with a constraint-based model S if the state of I on S is not Violated.

> **Definition 12.8 (State Compliance).** Let $S = (A, C)$ be a constraint-based process model with activity set A and constraint set C. Let further $I = (S, \sigma_I)$ be a corresponding process instance. Then, I is called *state compliant* with S, if I on S is not in state Violated; i.e., either the state of I is Satisfied or it is Temporarily Violated (i.e., there is a suffix that could be added to trace σ_I such that all constraints are satisfied).

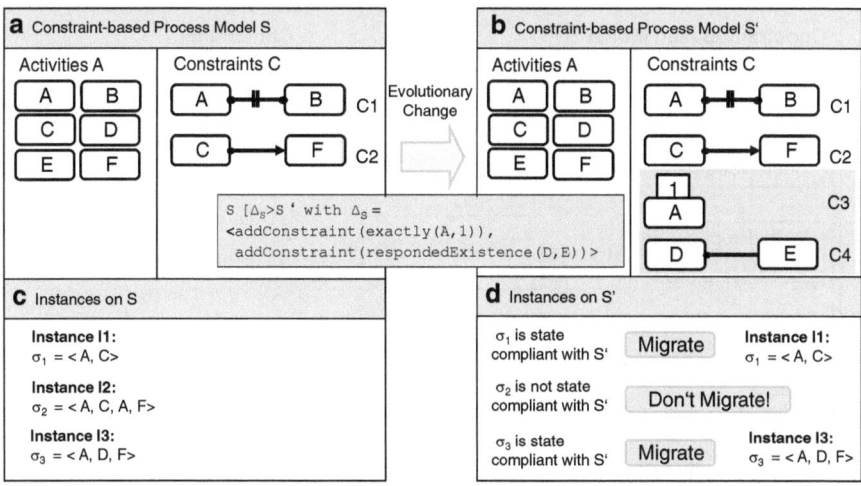

Fig. 12.16 Evolving the constraint set of a constraint-based process model

Example 12.14 (State Compliance). Consider the three process instances I_1, I_2, and I_3 (cf. Fig. 12.16c) running on constraint-based process model S (cf. Fig. 12.16a). When evolving S to S' (cf. Fig. 12.16b) it must be decided which instances on S may be migrated to S' and which must not. Regarding trace σ_1 of instance I_1 (cf. Fig. 12.16c) all constraints are fulfilled, i.e., I_1 is state compliant with S' and therefore may be migrated to it (cf. Fig. 12.16d). Instance I_2, in turn, is not compliant with the change. More precisely, the *exactly* constraint would be violated for I_2 resulting in instance state Violated. Thus, I_2 cannot be migrated to S', but remains running according to the original process model S. Finally, regarding instance I_3 the *responded existence* constraint is temporarily violated resulting in instance state Temporarily Violated. However, this constraint can be still satisfied by executing activity E. Thus, I_3 is state compliant with S' and can be migrated to S' (cf. Fig. 12.16d).

To check state compliance for each process instance all mandatory constraints have to be evaluated. Moreover, for every process instance not being in state Satisfied it has to be determined whether there is a suffix that could be added to the trace such that all constraints become satisfied. For this, existing approaches like Declare [19, 243] map the constraints to a logic-based formalism and create an automaton representing all supported behavior, which can then be analyzed. Checking state compliance for a collection of process instances with an adapted constraint-based process model, however, is a complex and costly task due to the potential state explosion problem resulting from the translation of constraints to

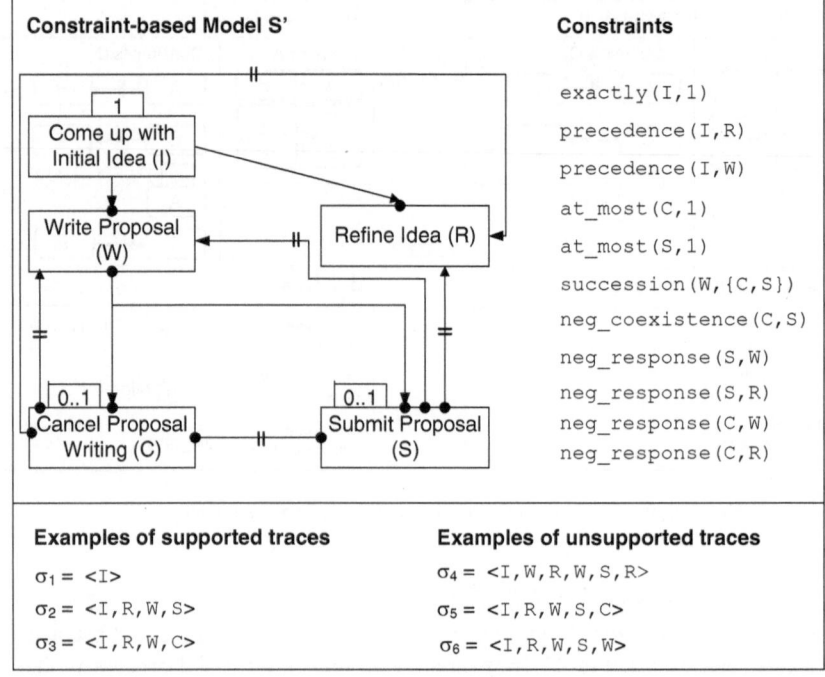

Fig. 12.17 Project proposal writing (after evolution Step 1)

a finite state automaton [220]. In particular, for constraint-based process models there are no such efficient approaches for checking state compliance as presented in Chap. 9 in the context of prespecified process models.

In Example 12.15 a walkthrough scenario for modeling and evolving a simple constraint-based process model is provided (adopted from [373]).

Example 12.15 (Project Proposal Writing-Evolution Step 1). In a first step, the constraint-based process model depicted in Fig. 12.8 will be adapted in such a way that the hidden dependency discussed in Example 12.4 is removed. Moreover, it will be ensured that activity *Refine Idea (R)* cannot be executed after activities *Cancel Proposal Writing (C)* or *Submit Proposal (S)*. In order to address these additional requirements, four *negation response* constraints have to be added to process model S in Fig. 12.5. Figure 12.17 shows the constraint-based process model S' for writing a project proposal resulting from the evolution. Again supported traces as well as unsupported traces by the evolved process model S' are illustrated at the bottom of Fig. 12.17. While traces σ_1, σ_2 and σ_3 can still be "replayed" on the changed model, trace σ_4, as

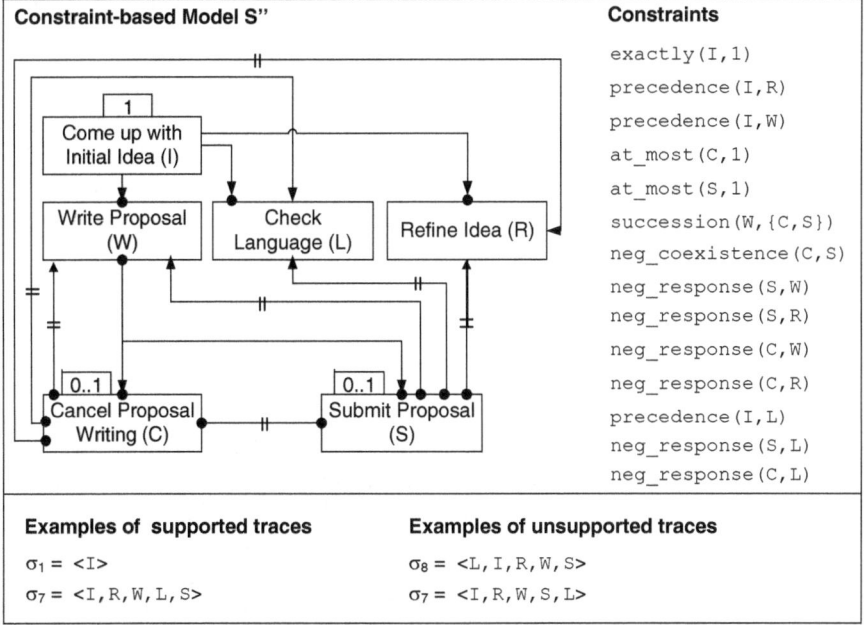

Fig. 12.18 Project proposal writing (after evolution Step 2)

intended, is not supported anymore. Regarding traces σ_5 and σ_6 the change did not have any effect. However, the introduction of the additional *neg_response* constraints helped remove the above discussed hidden dependencies.

Example 12.16 (Project Proposal Writing-Evolution Step 2). In a next step, the constraint-based model S' depicted in Fig. 12.17 is further extended with an activity *Check Language (L)*, which can be performed at any time after activity *Come up with Initial Idea (I)* and before activities *Cancel Proposal Writing (C)* or *Submit Proposal (S)*. To reflect this change a *precedence* constraint between activities *Come up with Initial Idea (I)* and *Check Language (L)* has to be added. Moreover, a *negation response* constraint between activities *Cancel Proposal Writing (C)* and *Check Language (L)* as well as activities *Submit Proposal (S)* and *Check Language (L)* has to be added. The resulting model S'' is depicted in Fig. 12.18.

12.6   Assistance for Modeling and Evolving Constraint-Based Processes

In addition to the hidden dependencies discussed in the context of Example 12.4, constraint-based process models exhibit a number of additional understandability and maintainability issues which will be discussed in Sect. 12.6.1. To overcome these challenges tool support for both modeling and evolving constraint-based processes is presented in Sect. 12.6.2.

12.6.1   Understandability and Maintainability Issues of Constraint-Based Process Models

Example 12.16 points to a major understandability issue related to constraint-based process models. As already pointed out by Pesic [243], "models with many constraints can easily become too complex for humans to cope with." From cognitive research it has been established that the human mind can only hold up to $7 (+/- 2)$ items in short term memory [213]. Constraint-based models with several interrelated constraints (like the model depicted in Fig. 12.18), however, can easily exceed this limit as detailed in the following.

While extracting sequential information (e.g., execution traces) from prespecified models is relatively easy, constraint-based models tend to obstruct sequential information. To determine whether a particular trace is supported by a given process model, for example, the reader of a prespecified model just has to replay the trace; i.e., apply all events $e_i \in \sigma$ in the order of their occurrence to S. For this, the model reader begins with the start node and follows the control flow step-by-step to check whether trace σ leads to the end node—the process model thereby serves as an external memory. The extraction of such sequential information from constraint-based process models, however, can be seen as a *hard mental operation* [115,116], since the required interpretation of constraints has to be performed in the reader's mind. Unlike with prespecified models, the user cannot rely on such an external memory, but has to keep all constraints in mind to determine whether or not a trace is supported.

Another understandability issue relates to the way how constraint-based process models can be read. While graph-based notations inherently propose a way of reading prespecified process models from start to end node(s), this approach does not work for constraint-based models. Since constraint-based models do not have explicit start and end nodes, it is not always obvious where the user should start reading the model. In fact, it is not unlikely for a constraint-based model—due to its inherent parallel nature—to have several potential starting points. Thus, when reading a constraint-based process model, like the one depicted in Fig. 12.22, users have to apply different strategies. One possible strategy could be to rely on *secondary notations* [116] (i.e., visual cues which can help understandability, but are

Fig. 12.19 A simple testcase

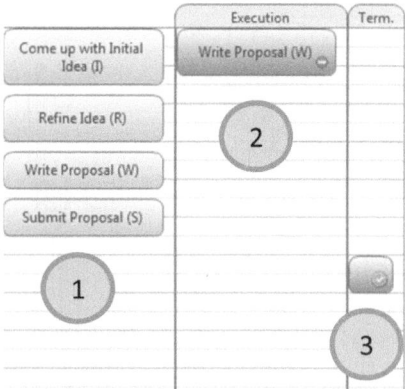

not part of the formal notation, like layout). For example, regarding Fig. 12.22 one might assume that the process starts top left and ends bottom right. Unfortunately, however, it cannot be safely assumed that models are always laid out that way. Another strategy could be to follow precedence and succession constraints between activities.

For an empirical investigation on the understandability of prespecified versus constraint-based models, we refer the reader to [245]).

12.6.2   Test-Driven Modeling of Constraint-Based Process Models

To overcome the aforementioned understandability and maintainability issues and to assist process designers in modeling and evolving constraint-based process models, advanced tool support is needed. In the following, test-driven modeling (TDM) is introduced—a method for improving understandability and maintainability of constraint-based process models (for a detailed discussion we refer to [373]).

A central aspect of TDM is the creation of *testcases* providing a mechanism for validating properties related to control flow. Testcases allow for the specification of the *desired behavior* the process model must exhibit and the *forbidden behavior* the process model must prohibit. First, a testcase consists of a *(partial) trace* reflecting the current instance state. Second, it comprises a set of *assertions*, i.e., conditions that must hold for a process instance being in a certain state. The (partial) execution trace thereby specifies behavior that must be supported by the process model, whereas assertions allow testing for forbidden behavior. A typical example of an assertion would be to check whether or not activity $a \in A$ is executable for a particular process instance $I = (S, \sigma_I)$. Moreover, assertions can be used to check whether or not a given process instance I may complete in its current state. For illustration purpose consider the testcase depicted in Fig. 12.19 (1). It refers to the

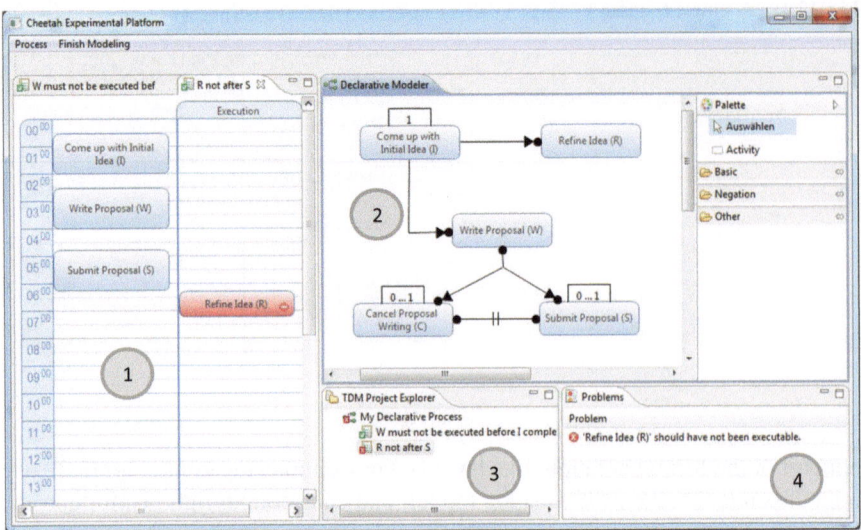

Fig. 12.20 Screenshot of TDMS

constraint-based process model S from Fig. 12.8 and contains the partial trace $<I$, R, W, $S>$ reflecting the current state of process instance I. In addition, Fig. 12.19 (2) shows an assertion specifying that activity W cannot be executed before event complete(I) occurs. Finally, Fig. 12.19 (3) depicts another assertion specifying that I can be completed after event complete(S) has occurred.

As illustrated in Fig. 12.19, testcases provide an additional view on the constraint-based process model. In particular, it allows resolving hidden dependencies by specifying testcases making these dependencies explicit. Furthermore, it supports the interpretation of constraint-based process models. Generally, testcases relieve the process modeler from the need to keep all constraints in mind [373]. However, this additional view is not provided by a single testcase in isolation. Rather, a process model is combined with a set of testcases, each of them focusing on a specific part of the process model.

Concerning maintenance, the close coupling of testcases and constraint-based process models ensures that changes applied to the process model do not violate existing behavior. Similar to regression testing in software engineering, whenever the constraint-based process model evolves, all testcases are validated automatically by replaying the execution trace in a test environment and checking the assertions step-by-step. Testcases thus relieve modelers from checking validity, i.e., to manually test whether the process model appropriately reflects the business requirements, which lowers the cognitive load of modelers and leads to quality improvements [372].

Test-driven Modeling Suite (TDMS) [371, 373] provides an integrated development environment for creating testcases and constraint-based process models. Figure 12.20 shows a screenshot of a constraint-based model S edited in TDMS.

On the left-hand side testcases are visualized (1); for this particular screenshot a testcase with execution trace <I, W, S> and an execution assertion are shown. On the right-hand side TDMS provides a graphical editor for designing the process model (2). Whenever a process model evolves, TDMS immediately validates the testcases against the constraint-based process model and indicates failed testcases in the testcase overview (3)—currently this overview lists two testcases from which one failed. In addition, TDMS provides a detailed problem message about failed testcases (4). In the given example, the process designer defined that given a partial trace <I, W, S>, activity R must not be executed reflecting one of the requirements discussed in Example 12.15. Process model S, however, has not reflected this requirement yet as indicated by the highlighted assertion in Column Execution (1), the testcases marked in (3), and the detailed error message shown in (4). Since TDMS automatically validates all testcases whenever the process model is changed, the modeler is relieved from checking this control flow behavior manually. Instead TDMS will automatically notify the modeler when changes are conducted conflicting with the testcases.

12.7 Assistance for Executing Constraint-Based Process Models

By only excluding forbidden behavior (cf. Sect. 12.2.1), a constraint-based process model provides much flexibility to end-users. To ensure that users can cope with this flexibility, adequate assistance for executing constraint-based process models is required.

In the context of prespecified process models, enabled activities are usually mandatory (except for the deferred choice pattern [309]), thus leaving little maneuvering room to end-users. When executing constraint-based process models, in turn, most of the time end-users have several options on how to proceed with the execution of the current process instance, i.e., to extend its *partial trace*. Considering Fig. 12.10, for example, all six activities get enabled after the creation of a process instance. After executing A, however, B is no longer enabled, whereas all other activities remain enabled. Consequently, numerous options exist for the end-user.

Even though there are many ways to execute a constraint-based process model, some of them might be more preferable in respect to a particular *process performance goal* (e.g., minimizing cycle time or maximizing customer satisfaction). To support end-users during process execution, assistance is needed. Given a partial instance trace and a performance goal, this assistance makes suggestions about what enabled activities should be performed next. In particular, enabled activities should be ranked in such a way that the performance goal can best be met.

To support end-users during process execution and to make recommendations on possible next activities, information from the *execution logs* (cf. Chap. 8)

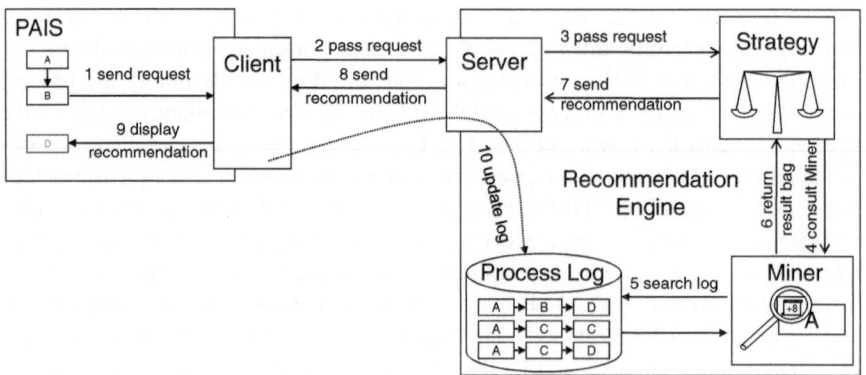

Fig. 12.21 Recommendation service

can be exploited [123, 322]. In the following, the overall architecture of such a *recommendation service* is illustrated. This service mines the log for already completed process instances (i.e., *log traces*) being similar to the current process instance. These log traces are then used for calculating recommendations which, based on the historic information, are expected to best meet a certain performance goal.

Figure 12.21 illustrates how end-users interact with the recommendation service in order to obtain recommendations on possible next activities. At any point during process execution the user of a flexible PAIS may ask the recommendation service for assistance on how to proceed with the execution of a particular process instance (1). The recommendation client then sends the user request containing information about the activities which have already been executed for that particular process instance (i.e., *partial trace*) and all *enabled activities* (i.e., all activities the user may execute in the next step for this particular process instance) to the recommendation engine (2). The recommendation request is then passed to the pre-configured *recommendation strategy* (3), which determines the algorithm to be used for calculating recommendations. Following this, the strategy consults one of the *miners* (4) to search the log for traces similar to the partial trace (5). The miner compares the *partial trace* with the traces existing in the event log (i.e., the *completed traces*) and determines how well they fit the partial trace. In addition, for each completed trace a *weight* (i.e., a number between zero and one) is calculated reflecting the degree of fit with the partial trace. In addition, the miner provides a *result bag* (with the mining results) which is then passed on, together with the weights, to the strategy for further evaluation (6). Based on the obtained results the strategy evaluates each of the *enabled activities* (i.e., possible activities to be executed next) in respect to the *performance goal* and ranks them accordingly. The resulting list of recommendations is then sent to the server (7) and passed on to the client (8), which returns the recommendations to the PAIS for displaying them to the user (9). After the process instance is completed, the PAIS sends the information

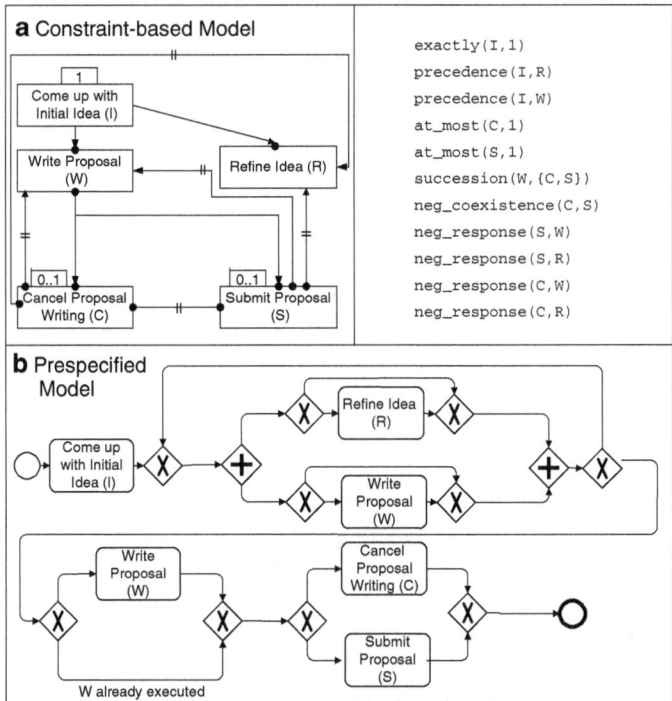

Fig. 12.22 Comparison—constraint-based vs. prespecified models

about the recently executed process instance to the recommendation engine to update the log and to allow for evolved learning (10). A detailed description can be found in [123, 322].

While the described approach base recommendations on historic data obtained from log files, Barba et al. [41] proposes the usage of planning and scheduling techniques for generating recommendations.

12.8   Combining Constraint-Based and Prespecified Models

Figure 12.22 depicts the constraint-based process model from Fig. 12.17 and its prespecified counterpart. When comparing those two models, it is readily apparent that neither variant is optimally suited to capture the paper writing process.

In the constraint-based variant it is comparably difficult to express that either activity *Cancel Proposal Writing (C)* or activity *Submit Proposal (S)* should be the last activity in a trace, i.e., it should be not possible to execute activities *Write Proposal (W)* or *Refine Idea (R)* afterwards. In the prespecified variant, in turn, it is very complicated to state that activities *Write Proposal (W)* and *Refine Idea (R)*

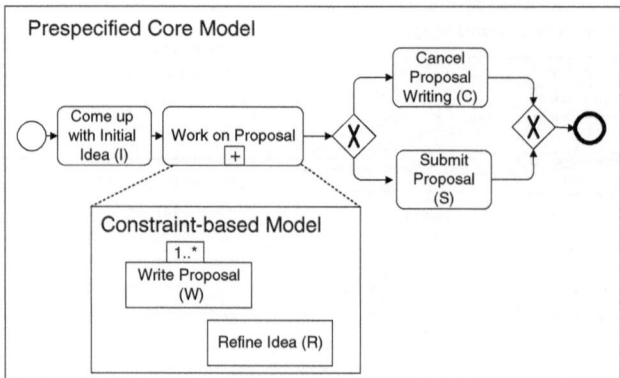

Fig. 12.23 Combining declarative and prespecified models

be executed arbitrarily often between activities *Come up with Initial Idea (W)* and *Cancel Proposal Writing (C)* or *Submit Proposal (S)*. It only has to be guaranteed that activity *Write Proposal (W)* is executed at least once.

When combining language constructs from constraint-based and prespecified models, however, the model can be significantly simplified (cf. Fig. 12.23). The combined process model consists of a prespecified core model with four activities and two XOR gateways. Thereby, activity *Work on Proposal* constitutes a complex activity with reference to a constraint-based subprocess model. The latter only consists of the two activities *Write Proposal (W)* and *Refine Idea (R)* as well as an *existence* constraint requiring that *Write Proposal (W)* is executed at least once.

Several existing approaches allow for the combination of language constructs from constraint-based and prespecified models. For example, the Pockets of Flexibility approach [316] which has been introduced in Example 11.3 relies on a prespecified core process model with placeholder activities. For each placeholder activity, a constraint-based process model (i.e., activities and constraints) can be specified. During process execution placeholder activities are refined; i.e., users define a process fragment that has to satisfy the constraints and which substitutes the placeholder activity. Moreover, constraint-based process models, as described in this chapter, can be combined with prespecified process models in YAWL [368] and be invoked as subprocesses.

12.9 Summary and Discussion

This chapter introduced basic concepts for the modeling, verification, and execution of constraint-based processes. While prespecified processes provide a reliable schema for process execution and are well suited for automating repetitive and rather predictable business processes, constraint-based processes allow for the loose specification of business processes. Compared to prespecified processes more build-in flexibility is provided to end-users making user support indispensable. However, tool support for constraint-based processes is currently much less mature than for prespecified process models and therefore needs further elaboration. In particular, more advanced tool support for constraint-based processes becomes important with increasing size and thus complexity of the process models. Besides this, the integration of prespecified and constraint-based processes also constitutes an emerging area which requires further consideration. In particular, well-established criteria are needed to be able to decide which approach to take in which scenario and how to combine the two paradigms in the best possible way.

Exercises

12.1. Specifying Constraint-Based Process Models
Denali National Park offers visitors a wide range of outdoor opportunities. Table 12.3 depicts the activities which are available for planning your trip to Denali.
    When planning the trip the following constraints need to be considered:

- All activities except for *Visit Visitor Center* can be executed at most once.
- Only one of the following activities can be executed: *White Water Rafting*, *Full Day Rafting* or *4-Hour Scenic Rafting*.
- *Backpacking* requires a permit.
- Only one of the two activities *Denali Natural History Tour* and *Bus Tour Wonderlake (Roundtrip)* may be executed.
- Since activity *Backpacking* starts at Wonderlake you need to take the *Bus to Wonderlake* directly before performing that activity. Directly after the hike you have to take the *Bus from Wonderlake* to get back.

Create a constraint-based process model which correctly reflects the above described constraints. For working on this exercise you can use the DecSerFlow Modeler of the Cheetah platform which you can download from the book web site.

12.2. Understanding Constraint-Based Process Models (1)
Figure 2.3 depicts a constraint-based process model of how to treat fractures,

(a) Trace *<Examine Patient,Prescribe Medication, Perform Sling>* is supported.
(b) If there is activity *Prescribe Fixation* in a trace there must be *Perform X-ray* before.
(c) Trace *<Examine Patient, Prescribe Medication, Perform Sling, Prescribe Medication, Prescribe Fixation>* is supported.
(d) At any point during process execution *Prescribe Medication* can be executed; i.e., for every process instance I in state Running, *Prescribe Medication* is always enabled.
(f) Trace *<Examine Patient, Perform X-ray, Perform Sling, Prescribe Fixation, Perform Surgery>* is supported.

Table 12.3 Activities

Visit visitor center	Short hike
Flightseeing	White water rafting
Full day rafting	4-h scenic rafting
Obtain permit	Backpacking
Take bus from Wonderlake	Take bus to Wonderlake
Bus tour Wonderlake (Roundtrip)	Denali natural history tour

Constraint-based Model S₁   **Constraints**

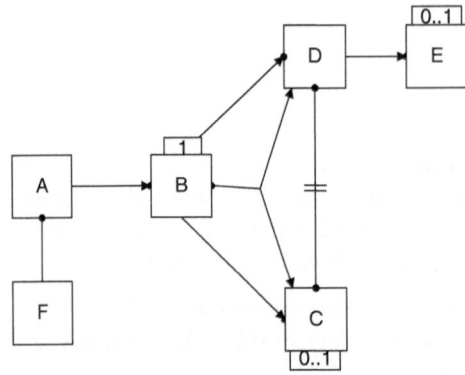

```
exactly(B,1)
at_most(C,1)
at_most(D,1)
precedence(A,B)
precedence(B,D)
precedence(B,C)
precedence(D,E)
response(B,{C,D})
neg_coexistence(C,D)
responded_existence(A,F)
```

Fig. 12.24 Constraint-based process model S_1

12.3. Understanding Constraint-Based Process Models (2)

Figure 12.24 depicts a constraint-based process model consisting of six activities and ten constraints. Which of the following statements are true?

(a) If C occurs in a trace, it must be directly preceded by B.
(b) Trace <F,A,B,C,F> is supported by S_1.
(c) Trace <A,B,D,E,A,A> is supported by S_1.
(d) At any point during process execution A can be executed, i.e., for every process instance I in state Running, A is always enabled.
(e) The number of occurrences for D is greater or equal the number of occurrences for E in every complete trace.
(f) The number of occurrences for A is greater or equal than the number of occurrences for F in every complete trace.
(g) If there is a C, a trace must not contain an E.

12.4. Understanding Constraint-Based Process Models (3)

Figure 12.25 depicts a constraint-based process model consisting of seven activities and twelve constraints. Which of the following statements are true?

(a) Trace <R,D,B> is supported by S_2.
(b) If there is a N there must not be an F afterwards.

Constraint-based Model S₂

Constraints

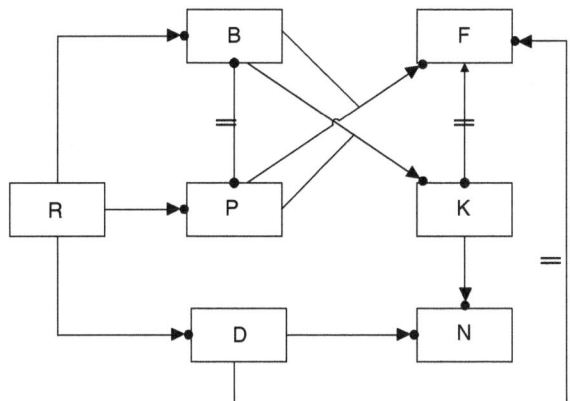

```
precedence(R,B)
precedence(R,P)
precedence(R,D)
precedence(D,N)
precedence(K,N)
neg_coexistence(B,P)
precedence({B,P},F)
precedence({B,P},K)
neg_response(D,F)
neg_precedence(K,F)
```

Fig. 12.25 Constraint-based process model S_2

Constraint-based Model S₃

Constraints

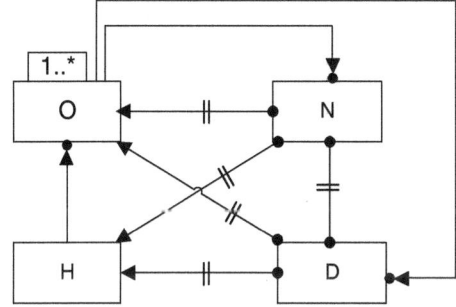

```
existence(O,1)
precedence(O,D)
precedence(H,O)
precedence(O,N)
neg_coexistence(N,D)
neg_response(N,O)
neg_response(N,H)
neg_response(D,H)
neg_response(D,O)
```

Fig. 12.26 Constraint-based process model S_3

(c) Trace <R,P,F,K,F> is supported by S_2.
(d) At any point during process execution R can be executed; i.e., for every process instance I in state Running, R is always enabled.
(f) The number of occurrences of R is greater or equal the number of occurrences of B in every complete trace.
(g) Trace <R,B,K,D,N> is supported by S_2.

12.5. Constraint-Based and Prespecified Process Models (1)

(a) For the constraint-based process model from Fig. 12.26 create a prespecified process model showing the same behavior.

(b) Compare prespecified and constraint-based process models. Describe common-
    alities and differences as well as advantages and disadvantages of the different
    approaches.

**12.6. Evolving Constraint-Based Process Models Supported by Test-Driven
Modeling**
To get some hands-on experience on how to evolve a constraint-based process
model supported by Test-driven Modeling, visit the book web site and follow the
instructions related to this exercise. Given an initial constraint-based process model
and a list of requirements, you will be asked to conduct a list of changes to the
model.

Part IV
User- and Data-Driven Processes

Chapter 13
User- and Data-Driven Processes

Abstract In practice, many business processes are rather unstructured, knowledge-intensive, and driven by user decisions and data. Typically, these processes cannot be straightjacketed into a set of activities with prespecified precedence relations; i.e., the primary driver for the progress of the process is not the event related to activity completion, but the availability of certain values for data objects. When implementing such user- and data-driven processes in a PAIS, a tight integration of processes, data, and users therefore becomes necessary. This chapter presents case handling as an example of such a process support paradigm. Following this, the fundamental characteristics of user- and data-driven processes are elaborated in detail. In particular, it is shown that *object-awareness* is required; i.e., a PAIS should manage data by means of object types that comprise object attributes and relations to other object types. Picking up this metaphor, pioneering work targeting at a tight integration of processes and data is evaluated. Besides case handling, this includes Proclets, business artifacts, data-driven process coordination, and product-based workflows.

13.1 Introduction

The approaches presented in this book so far are *activity-centric*, i.e., they focus on the coordinated execution of a set of business functions, represented by atomic process steps (i.e., activities), as well as the control and data flow between them. Typically, the primary drivers of activity-centric processes are the events related to activity completions. In turn, business data is rather "unknown" to the process engine of an activity-centric PAIS. Remember that the latter only maintains simple data elements needed for control flow routing (i.e., for evaluating transition conditions) and for assigning values to activity input parameters. In particular, business objects and their attributes are usually outside the control of activity-centric PAISs.

M. Reichert and B. Weber, *Enabling Flexibility in Process-Aware Information Systems*,
DOI 10.1007/978-3-642-30409-5_13, © Springer-Verlag Berlin Heidelberg 2012

In actual practice, one can also find business processes that are not activity-centric, but whose execution is driven by user decisions and business data [155, 156, 158, 277, 336]. These processes are usually unstructured or semi-structured, and tend to be knowledge-intensive. In particular, they can not be straight-jacketed into a set of activities with prespecified precedence relations. As a consequence, the activity-centric approaches presented so far do not adequately support these processes [7, 24, 52, 225, 252, 253, 275, 341]. Moreover, the primary driver for the progress of a process is not the event related to activity completion, but the availability of certain values for data objects. When implementing such user- and data-driven processes in a PAIS, a tight integration of processes, data, and users therefore becomes necessary.

There exists pioneering work targeting at user- and data-driven process management and enabling such a tight integration. As a first example, the *case handling* paradigm will be presented. It focuses on the *case* (e.g., a customer request) and its flexible handling, whereby the progress of a case is determined by the values of its data objects. Basic concepts of this user- and data-driven approach are illustrated along an example, and its strengths and weaknesses are discussed. Further on, it is shown how case handling can be integrated with adaptive process management.

While case handling is appropriate for supporting simple process scenarios, it does not provide sufficient abstractions to also deal with more complex and inter-dependent cases. To tackle related challenges, several approaches have emerged that enable *object-aware* or *object-centric* processes; i.e., the PAIS manages data by means of *object types* that comprise *object attributes* and *relations* to other object types. Accordingly, a business process coordinates the processing of several business objects of the same or different type among end-users enabling them to cooperate and communicate with each other.

The chapter elaborates on fundamental characteristics of object-aware processes, which can be related to *object behavior*, *object interactions*, *data-driven execution*, *variable activity granularity*, and *integrated access to processes and data* [159]. Using these characteristics, some of the pioneering approaches for user- and data-driven processes are evaluated and compared with each other. In addition to case handling, we consider Proclets, business artifacts, data-driven process coordination, and product-based workflows. It is shown that each of these approaches focuses on the support of selected characteristics, but does not cover all of them [160]. Chapter 14 will then present PHILharmonicFlows—a comprehensive framework for object-aware process management considering all mentioned characteristics.

Section 13.2 presents case handling as an example of a user- and data-driven process support paradigm. Following this, Sect. 13.3 discusses the role of business objects in PAISs and elaborates on fundamental characteristics of object-aware processes along a running example. Section 13.4 then evaluates existing approaches based on these characteristics. The chapter closes with a summary in Sect. 13.5.

13.2   The Case Handling Paradigm

While prespecified process models (cf. Chap. 4) emphasize the routing between *atomic activities*, the *case handling* paradigm focuses on the *case* itself [24, 233, 336]; i.e., the *case* (e.g., an insurance claim or a customer request) is the primary object of interest. Hence, single activities diminish in importance in favor of the handling of the case. In particular, *activities* are no longer considered as atomic units to be performed in an "all or nothing" manner, but rather correspond to the logical partitions of work between which a transition from one worker to another becomes possible.

13.2.1   Basic Concepts

Like prespecified process models (cf. Chap. 4), a *case type* comprises tasks (i.e., activities), data objects, and a set of precedence relations between the tasks making up a process. However, the primary driver for the progress of a case is not the event related to task (activity) completion, but the availability of values for data objects. While a prespecified process model clearly separates the process from associated data (cf. Chap. 4), *Case Handling* integrates both in a tighter manner, using produced data not only for routing decisions, but also for determining which parts of the process have already been accomplished.

With case handling, each *task* is associated with three sets of *data objects*, each serving a distinct purpose: The first association is between a task and all *data objects that must be accessible while performing this task*. Furthermore, all data objects *mandatory* for a task have to be set (i.e., bound to a value) before the task itself is considered as completed by the case handling system. Finally, every data object can have a random number of tasks to which it is *restricted*, meaning that it can only be updated while performing one of these tasks. Interactive tasks are connected to *forms*, each providing access to a selection of data objects. Note that one form may be associated to multiple tasks. Furthermore, it is possible to associate a form to the case itself, i.e., the case can be accessed at any point in time using this form.

Example 13.1 illustrates the basic principles of the case handling paradigm.

Example 13.1 (Case Handling). Consider Fig. 13.1 showing a simplified example of a *case type*: Three tasks A, B, and C are making up the process, sequentially chained by causal relations (i.e., connecting arrows). Their mandatory relationships to the three data objects x, y and z below are represented by curved arcs, as are their associations with the forms M and N. As can be seen, tasks A and B share the same form M, provid-

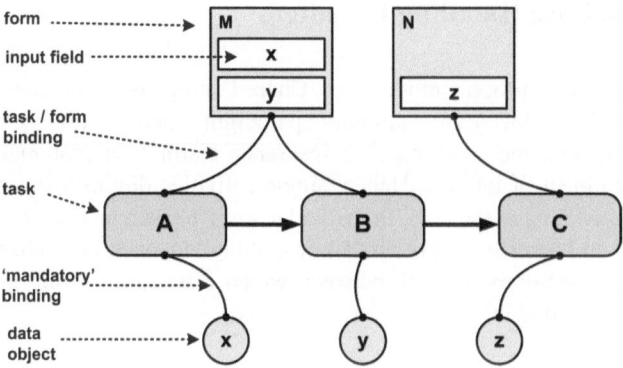

Fig. 13.1   Abstract example of a case type

ing access to data objects x and y. If an authorized worker now starts
handling task A, its associated form M will open and he will start providing values for the presented data objects. In a traditional PAIS with
prespecified process models, activity A would not be finished before form
M is closed. However, the case handling system regards A as finished as
soon as a value for x has been provided (and confirmed appropriately),
automatically enabling task B in the background. If the worker would now
close form M, another employee could pick up the case where he left
it, starting task B, which would provide the same form M with x having
a value filled in (that could now be changed again). Another possibility,
however, is that the first worker keeps on handling the form, providing also
a value for y. The latter triggers the auto-completion of B as all associated
mandatory data elements are provided. Following this, C is immediately
activated.

If a worker closes a form after filling out only parts of the mandatory data fields
of a task, despite the task not considered as finished, data already entered will
remain available to the person who continues working on that task. Such a closely
intertwined relationship between data and process, however, abandons their—often
unnatural—separation as pursued in traditional PAISs. With the status of case data
objects being the primary determinant of the case status, this concept overcomes a
great deal of the problems described in the introduction:

• Work can now be organized by those performing it with a far higher degree
  of freedom. Activities can either be performed only partially, without losing

intermediary results, or multiple related activities can be handled in one go, surpassing the weakened border between tasks.
- Routing is no longer solely determined by the prespecified process model. Case types can be designed in such a manner that multiple activities are enabled concurrently, providing different ways of achieving the same goal.

In addition to the *execute role*, specifying the subset of resources allowed to handle a specific task, case handling introduces two additional roles that are crucial for its operational support:

The *skip role* allows workers to bypass a selected task, which could be interpreted as an *exception*. Exceptions, like skipping a background check for trusted clients, are likely to occur rather frequently. In order to skip a task, however, all preceding tasks that have not yet been completed must be skipped (or completed) beforehand. This becomes necessary to ensure an unambiguous state of the process.

Traditional PAIS use loops for *repeating* parts of the process, e.g., because they have not yielded an expected result. Case handling obsoletes such a construct by introducing a *redo role*, enabling its owner to deliberately roll the cases state back and undo a task. In doing so, the values provided for data objects during this task are not discarded, but merely marked as *unconfirmed*, so that they serve as a template when re-executing the affected task. Before a task can be redone, all subsequent tasks that have already been completed need to be rolled back as well.

Intertwining authorization with distribution of activities has been one major flaw of traditional PAISs. In a case handling system, the *in-tray* (i.e., worklist) known from PAISs, i.e., a list of all activities the user is authorized to perform and that he can choose from, has been replaced by a *query mechanism*. The latter can be used to look for a specific case, based on certain features, e.g. case data or enactment data, like the start date of a case instance. Moreover, it can be used to create predefined *queries* tailored to each worker or group of workers (cf. Example 13.2). Obviously, the query mechanism can also be used to perfectly imitate an in-tray (i.e., worklist), as found in a traditional PAIS (cf. Chap. 2), if required.

Example 13.2 (Querying Cases). A manager is no longer overwhelmed with all possible activities he can perform, but only those are presented to him, which require a certain role or relate to case instances of an order whose value exceeds $1,000.

13.2.2   Strengths and Weaknesses

Adaptive PAISs (cf. Chap. 7) remedy the problem of environmental changes in the real world by enabling ad hoc changes of process instances during their execution.

As opposed to this, case handling addresses the same problem by *anticipating* volatile environments and thus *avoiding* the need for *process changes*.

The fundamental property of case handling supporting this approach is its strong reliance on the *case metaphor*, where the importance of activities is diminished in favor of the global context, and the use of *data dependencies as a primary driver* of the process. These two features are a perfect match for many knowledge-intensive processes as one can find in insurance business, governmental bodies, or call centers. Here the case corresponds to an artifact. Examples are insurance claims or customer requests. Furthermore, handling such cases is mainly performed *from within the system itself*, i.e. the outcome of activities is completely represented in the system by the data produced (as opposed to health care environments, for example, where the main effects are not visible within the PAIS). Using the example of an insurance company, some of the *strengths* of case handling will be illustrated:

- *Case metaphor.* The case (e.g., an insurance claim of a client to be processed) as a metaphor fits naturally to any PAIS. Employees are usually familiar with this metaphor and will need little training to become acquainted with a case handling system.
- *Data as a main driver.* All "products" used or manufactured while handling a case are contained within the case itself as data (e.g., address or claim value). The concept that a certain state in the process is reached when certain data become available (e.g., a letter can be sent once the address is known) also fits the application area naturally. This makes processes easier to design, and easier to understand for workers familiar with the domain.
- *Weak activity boundaries.* Activities are metaphors used to structure complex processes. The way in which a designer perceives a process to be partitioned into activities does not necessarily coincide with the perceptions of all employees. An employee may prefer to handle two activities in one go, or see that he can not finish an activity midway. In a case handling system, this will not affect the correctness of the process, and will be handled transparently to the end-user.
- *Skip and redo roles.* These roles are mostly necessary for responding to exceptions, e.g., when a deadline needs to be met. Thus, it is natural not to model these exceptions explicitly (i.e., using loops and bypass paths), but to use generic skip and redo operations on an as-needed basis instead. These roles can be assigned to superiors, who will need to acknowledge exceptions anyway.
- *Case query.* While a simple change from the classical in-tray of PAISs (cf. Chap. 2), the case query makes a profound difference for end-users. Work is no longer "pushed" to them by the system, but employees can look for specific types of work to perform that better fits their interests, skills, or simply their current mood. Rather than controlling the workforce in a mechanical way, the system becomes a discreet aid in accomplishing one's tasks.

Obviously, these benefits vanish if case handling is used in a context that is neither data-driven, nor has a natural case metaphor. Apart from this more general issue, there exists a number of shortcomings in this approach that may pose limitations. One of these limitations is directly related to the strong role of the case metaphor, where the user handling a case has access to all information at once. Hence, the case then is *exclusively locked*, which makes it impossible to work on it concurrently. Note that this is a strong limitation when facing more complex processes.

Also, while the weak activity boundaries and data-driven nature of case handling largely prevent the need for explicit change, there are situations that require modification of the process definition. In this respect, a case handling system performs like a traditional PAIS—altered *case types* may only be used by newly started cases, while running cases need to follow the old definition. There are ways to work around this problem, e.g., by using global case forms to perform additional actions, or by using the skip role to bypass parts of the process.

13.2.3 Discussion

This section explores how ideas from case handling and adaptive process management may be integrated in order to overcome some of the shortcomings described, and to provide an integrated framework for realizing flexible processes.

As discussed in Chaps. 4–10, the rather rigid nature of prespecified process models does not constitute a problem in adaptive PAISs. On one hand, prespecified process models are well suited for applications for which a large degree of control and accountability is necessary. On the other hand, there exist advanced techniques (i.e., process configuration, exception handling, ad hoc changes, and process evolution) enabling flexible processes. For many scenarios, however, the erosion of activity boundaries as provided by case handling is beneficial, in the sense that it often avoids the need for explicit model changes in the first place. Integrating data as a primary driver to (adaptive) PAISs would introduce this feature, and enable users to work in a more case-based manner in which they are less aware of the single activities handled. In particular, this would also enable exception handling at a higher level of abstraction (see [286] for a respective approach).

In the same way, it would also be rather trivial to introduce skip and redo roles to adaptive process management. Many exceptional situations do not require the process model to be explicitly changed, it is just necessary to deviate on an ad hoc basis by jumping back or forward in the flow of control [262]. By mapping the effects of skip and redo actions onto equivalent changes of the process model, their correctness can be ensured on-the-fly. In an adaptive PAIS, introducing data as a driver and dedicated skip and redo roles could serve as the "poor man's flexibility," as they do not require the end-user to know anything about process design or correctness.

In addition, it would be straightforward to provide case queries instead of, or in addition to, the standard worklist for providing work items. Although technically very similar to a *push model*, the query mechanism is a powerful means for end-users to customize the PAIS and to use it in a flexible manner. On top of this, querying for work instead of having it assigned by the PAIS makes a profound difference on a psychological level, putting the employee back in control.

The biggest problem of the case handling approach is probably its inability to modify case types on-the-fly (i.e., to apply ad hoc changes to cases), and to migrate running cases to an updated case type. If one were to implement such a change manually, it could however be accomplished in a rather simple, although tedious, manner: The new case type is designed, based on the previous version, and a new case is instantiated from it. Subsequently, all data from the (old) case in progress is entered into the new instance. The system will then auto-complete all tasks for which data dependencies have been satisfied, essentially recreating the state of the previous instance. From then on, the old case may be removed from the system, while work continues on the new instance that is based on the updated case type definition. Obviously, this procedure—besides the actual change of the case type—can equally be performed in a (semi-)automatic fashion by the case handling system itself. When problems occur during the replay of the old case (i.e., transferring its data values and auto-completing satisfied tasks), these problems can be resolved manually. Note that this approach can not match the ease of performing the same action in adaptive PAISs, as there are no correctness checks that could assist the user in redesigning the case type. However, it is certainly feasible to implement with comparably little effort, and would bring tremendous advantages when explicit change to the case type is required. A systematic comparison of case handling and (adaptive) activity-centric PAIS can be found in [119, 233, 349].

13.3   Object-Aware Processes

While case handling is suitable for realizing simple process scenarios, it does not provide sufficient means of abstraction to also support large and interdependent cases. Recently, several approaches tackling this challenge have emerged. In particular, *object-awareness* offers promising perspectives to enable user- and data-driven processes for more complex application scenarios. In order to compare existing approaches proposed in this context, this section presents fundamental characteristics of *object-aware processes* (see [159] for a discussion on how these characteristics were derived). For illustrating these characteristics, a process scenario from the area of human resource management will be used (cf. Example 13.3).

Example 13.3 (Object-aware Processes in Recruitment). In the context of recruitment, *applicants* may apply for *job vacancies* via an Internet online form. Once an *application* has been submitted, the responsible *personnel officer* in the human resource department is notified. The overall process goal is to make a decision which *applicant* will get the *job*. If an *application*

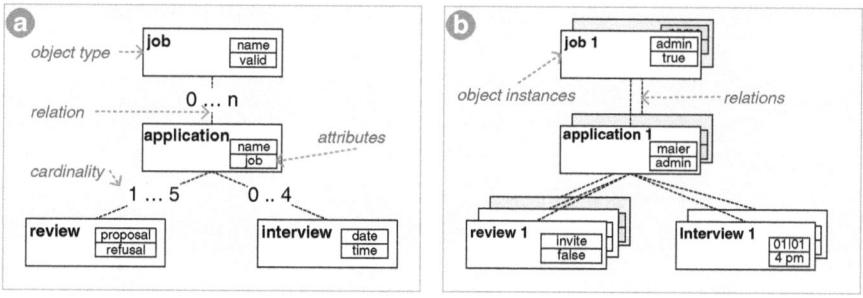

Fig. 13.2 (**a**) Data model (build-time) and (**b**) Corresponding data structure (run-time)

is ineligible, the *applicant* is immediately rejected. Otherwise, *personnel officers* may request internal *reviews* for each *applicant*. In this context, the concrete number of *reviews* may differ from *application* to *application*. Corresponding *review* forms have to be filled by *employees* from functional divisions. They make a *proposal* on how to proceed; i.e., they indicate whether or not to invite the *applicant* for an *interview*. In the former case, an *appraisal* is needed. After the *employee* has filled the *review* form, she submits it back to the *personnel officer*. Meanwhile, additional *applications* might have arrived; i.e., *reviews* related to the same or different *applications* may be requested or submitted at different points in time. The processing of the *application*, however, proceeds while corresponding *reviews* are created; e.g., the *personnel officer* may check the *CV* and study the *cover letter* of the *application*. Based on the incoming *reviews*, he makes his *decision* on the *application* or initiates further steps (e.g., *interviews* or additional *reviews*). Finally, he does not have to wait for the arrival of all *reviews*; e.g., if a particular *employee* suggests hiring the *applicant*, he can immediately follow this recommendation.

Picking up the scenario from Example 13.3, the following sub-sections will discuss fundamental characteristics of *object-aware processes* (see [155, 156, 160] for details).

Basically, data must be manageable in terms of *object types* that comprise *object attributes* and *relations* to other object types (cf. Fig. 13.2a). At run-time, the different object types comprise a varying number of inter-related object instances, whereby the concrete instance number should be restrictable by lower and upper cardinality bounds (cf. Fig. 13.2b). For example, for each *application*, at least one and at most five *reviews* will be initiated. While for a particular *application* two *reviews* might be sufficient, another *application* might require three *reviews* (cf. Fig. 13.3).

In accordance to data modeling, the modeling and execution of processes can be based on two levels of granularity: *object behavior* and *object interactions*.

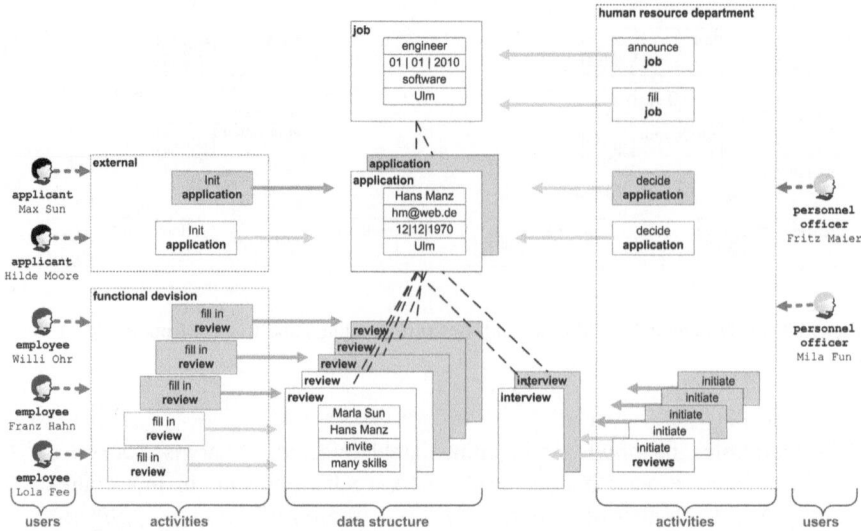

Fig. 13.3 Example of a recruitment process from the human resource domain

13.3.1 Object Behavior

To cover the processing of individual object instances, the first level of process granularity deals with *object behavior*. More precisely, for each object type a separate process definition should be provided (cf. Fig. 13.4a), which then can be used for coordinating the processing of individual object instances among different users. In addition, it should be possible to determine in which order and by whom the attributes of a particular object instance have to be (mandatorily) written, and what valid attribute settings (i.e., attribute values) are. At run-time, the creation of an *object instance* is directly coupled with the creation of its corresponding *process instance* (cf. Fig. 13.4b). In this context, it is important to ensure that mandatory data is provided during process execution. For this reason, object behavior should be defined in terms of *data conditions* rather than based on black-box activities.

> *Example 13.4 (Object Behavior).* In order to request a *review*, the responsible *personnel officer* must provide values for object attributes *return date* and *questionnaire*. Following this, the *employee* responsible for the *review* must assign a value to object attribute *proposal*.

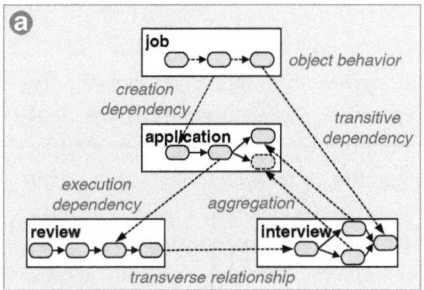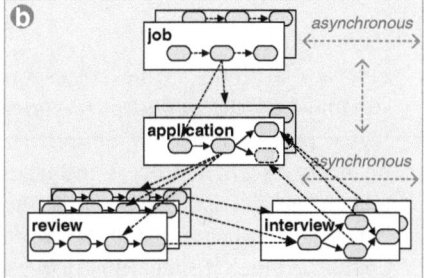

Fig. 13.4 Process structure at (**a**) build-time and (**b**) run-time

13.3.2 Object Interactions

Since related object instances may be created or deleted at arbitrary points in time, a complex data structure emerges that dynamically evolves during run-time, depending on the types and number of created object instances. Furthermore, individual object instances of the same type may be in different processing states at a certain point in time.

Taking the behavior of individual object instances into account, a *complex process structure* corresponding to the given data structure emerges during run-time (cf. Fig. 13.4a). In this context, the second level of process granularity comprises the *interactions* taking place between the different object instances. More precisely, it must be possible to execute individual process instances (of which each corresponds to the processing of a particular object instance) in a loosely coupled manner, i.e., concurrently to each other and synchronizing their execution where needed.

First, it should be possible to make the creation of a particular object instance dependent on the progress of related object instances (i.e., to express *creation dependencies*). Second, several object instances of the same object type may be related to one and the same object instance. Hence, it should be possible to aggregate information; among others, this requires the aggregation of attribute values from related object instances (i.e., *aggregation*). Third, the executions of different process instances may be mutually dependent; i.e., whether or not an object instance can be further processed may depend on the processing progress of other object instances (i.e., *execution dependencies* between the processing of different object instances have to be considered). In this context, interactions must also consider *transitive dependencies* (e.g., reviews depend on the respective job offer) as well as *transverse dependencies* between object instances (e.g., the creation of an interview may depend on the proposal made in a review) (cf. Fig. 13.4).

Example 13.5 (Object Interactions). A *personnel officer* must not initiate a *review* as long as the corresponding *application* has not been finally submitted by the *applicant* (*creation dependency*). Furthermore, individual *review* process instances are executed concurrently to each other as well as to the *application* process instances; e.g., the *personnel officer* may read and change the *application* while the *reviews* are processed. Further, *reviews* belonging to a particular *application* can be initiated and submitted at different points in time. Besides this, a *personnel officer* should be able to access information about submitted *reviews* (*aggregative information*); i.e., if an *employee* submits her *review* recommending to invite the *applicant* for an *interview*, the *personnel officer* needs this information immediately. Opposed to this, when proposing rejection of the *applicant*, the *personnel officer* should only be informed after all initiated *reviews* have been submitted. Finally, if the *personnel officer* makes the decision to hire one of the *applicants*, all others have to be rejected (*execution dependency*). Note that these dependencies do not necessarily coincide with the object relationships. For example, consider *reviews* and *interviews* corresponding to the same *application*; i.e., an *interview* may only be conducted if an *employee* proposes to invite the *applicant* during the execution of a *review* process instance.

13.3.3   Data-Driven Execution

To proceed with the processing of a particular object instance, in a given state, certain attribute values are mandatorily required. Thus, object attribute values reflect the progress of the corresponding process instance. Similar to case handling (cf. Sect. 13.2), the activation of an activity does not directly depend on the completion of other activities, but on the values set for object attributes. More precisely, *mandatory activities* enforce the setting of certain object attribute values in order to progress with the process. If required data is already available, however, mandatory activities can be *automatically skipped* when being activated. In principle, it should be possible to *set respective attributes also up-front*; i.e., before the mandatory activity, which usually writes this attribute, becomes enabled. However, users should be also allowed to *re-execute a particular activity*, even if all mandatory object attributes have been already set. For this purpose, data-driven execution must be combined with *explicit user commitments* (i.e., activity-centered aspects). Finally, the execution of a mandatory activity may depend on attribute values of related object instances. Thus, the coordination of multiple process instances should be also supported in a data-driven way.

Example 13.6 (Data-driven Execution). During the processing of a *review* request, the *personnel officer* must set a *return date.* If a value for this attribute is available, a mandatory activity for filling in the *review* form is assigned to the responsible *employee.* In turn, a value for attribute *proposal* is then mandatory. However, even if the *personnel officer* has not yet completed his *review* request (i.e., no value for attribute *return data* is available), the *employee* may optionally edit certain attributes of the *review* (e.g., *proposal*). If a value of attribute *proposal* is already available when the *personnel officer* finishes the request, the mandatory activity for providing the *review* is automatically skipped. Opposed to this, an *employee* may change his *proposal* arbitrarily often until he explicitly agrees to submit the *review* to the *personnel officer.* Finally, the *personnel officer* makes his decision (i.e., he rejects or accepts the *applicant*) based on the incoming *reviews.*

13.3.4 Variable Activity Granularity

For creating object instances and changing object attribute values, *form-based activities* can be used. Respective user forms comprise *input fields* (e.g., text-fields or check-boxes) for writing, and *data fields* for reading selected attributes of object instances. In this context, however, different users may prefer different work practices. In particular, using *instance-specific activities* (cf. Fig. 13.5a), all input fields and data fields refer to attributes of one particular object instance, whereas *context-sensitive activities* (cf. Fig. 13.5b) comprise fields referring to different, but semantically related object instances (of potentially different type). When initiating a review, for example, it is also possible to edit the attribute values of the corresponding application. Finally, *batch activities* involve several object instances of the same type (cf. Fig. 13.5c); i.e., the values of the different input fields can be assigned to all involved object instances in one go. For example, this enables a *personnel officer* to reject several applications in one go. Depending on their preference, users should be able to freely choose the most suitable activity granularity for achieving a particular goal. In addition to form-based activities, it must be possible to integrate *black-box activities.* The latter enable complex computations as well as the integration of advanced functionalities (e.g., provided by web services).

Moreover, whether or not certain object attributes are mandatory when processing a particular activity might also depend on other object attribute values; i.e., when filling in a form certain attributes might become mandatory on-the-fly. Such form-specific control flows must be also considered.

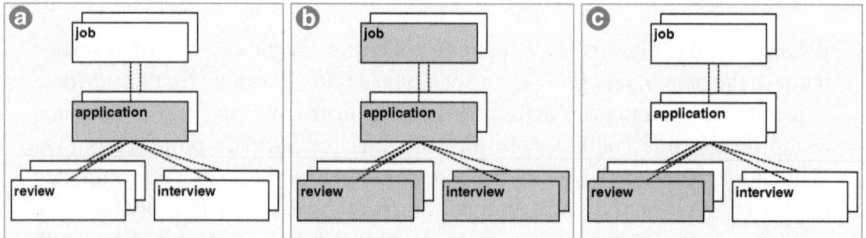

Fig. 13.5 (**a**) Instance-specific activity, (**b**) context-sensitive activity, and (**c**) batch activity

Example 13.7 (Activity Granularities). When an *employee* fills in a *review*, additional information about the corresponding *application* should be provided (i.e. *context-sensitive activity*); i.e., attributes belonging to the *application* for which the *review* is requested. For filling in the *review* form, a value for attribute *proposal* must be assigned. If the *employee* proposes to invite the *applicant*, additional object attributes will become mandatory; e.g., he then must also set attribute *appraisal* (i.e., *form-specific control flow*). This is not required if he assigns value reject to attribute *proposal*. Furthermore, when a *personnel officer* edits an *application*, all corresponding *reviews* should be visible. Finally, as soon as an *applicant* is hired for a *job*, for all other *applications* value reject should be assignable to attribute *decision* by filling one form (i.e. *batch activity*).

13.3.5   Integrated Access to Business Processes and Objects

In order to proceed with the control flow, *mandatory activities* have to be executed by authorized users providing required attribute values. Other attribute values, however, may be *optional*. Moreover, users usually not involved in process execution should be allowed to optionally execute selected activities. In addition to a *process-oriented view* (e.g. worklists), a *data-oriented view* is therefore required enabling users to access and manage data at any point in time. For this purpose, permissions for creating and deleting object instances, as well as for reading and writing their attributes, need to be defined. However, attribute changes contradicting specified object behavior must be prevented. Which attributes may be written or read by a particular form-based activity not only depends on the user invoking this activity, but also on the progress of the corresponding process instance. While certain users must execute an activity mandatorily in the context of a particular object instance, others might be authorized to optionally execute this activity; i.e., a distinction is made between mandatory and optional permissions. Furthermore, for object-aware processes, the selection of actors usually not only depends on the activity to be performed, but also on the object instances processed by this activity. In this context, the relationships between users and object instances must be taken into account.

> *Example 13.8 (Integrated Access).* A *personnel officer* may only make a decision about *applications* for which the name of the *applicants* starts with a letter between 'A' and 'L', while another *officer* may deal with *applicants* whose name starts with a letter between 'M' and 'Z'. An *employee* must mandatorily write attribute *proposal* when filling in a *review*. However, her *manager* may optionally set this attribute as well. The mandatory activity for filling the *review* form, in turn, should be only assigned to the *employee*. After submitting her *review*, the *employee* may still change her *comment*. In this context, it must be ensured that the *employee* may only access *reviews* she submitted before. However, attribute *proposal*, in turn, must not be changed anymore. The *personnel officer* might have already performed the proposed action.

13.4 Existing Approaches

Several research groups have conducted pioneering work with respect to the seamless integration of processes, data, and users in PAISs. Although existing approaches do not cover all phases of the process life cycle and focus on specific characteristics of object-aware processes, they confirm the high need for user- and data-driven processes as well as the flexibility introduced by them. Referring to the fundamental characteristics of object-aware processes (cf. Sect. 13.3), this section evaluates and compares existing approaches.

First, we revisit case handling (cf. Sect. 13.2) and evaluate it regarding its support for enabling object behavior, object interactions, data-driven execution, variable activity granularity, and integrated access to business processes and objects. Following this, further approaches are evaluated, including Proclets, business artifacts, data-driven process coordination, and product-based workflows. It is not our intention, however, to describe these approaches in detail, but to show that each of them at least partially supports the described characteristics [160].[1] Overall, user- and data-driven process management constitutes an active area of research. This confirms the high practical relevance of user- and data-driven processes on the one

---

[1] With PHILharmonicFlows, a comprehensive framework enabling support of all characteristics will be described in Chap. 14.

hand, and indicates that respective techniques have not yet reached the same level of maturity as activity-centric approaches on the other.

13.4.1   Case Handling

Case handling [24,233] is the *data-driven process support paradigm* that has already been presented in Sect. 13.2. As described, activities are explicitly represented through *forms* comprising a number of input fields (i.e., text fields, combo boxes, check boxes). The latter refer to *atomic data elements* that are either defined as *mandatory, restricted*, or *free*. An activity is considered as completed if all mandatory data elements have an assigned value. Besides defining who will perform an activity, case handling allows specifying who may redo or skip this activity.

Object Behavior. Case handling does not provide explicit support for complex objects and the relations between them. However, a "case" can be considered in tight accordance with an "object"; i.e., its data elements can be considered as object attributes. Hence, object behavior can be defined by specifying in which order and by whom object attributes are written. Since it is possible to assign value constraint to each input field, valid attribute settings can be enforced. In addition, data constraints can be assigned to the transitions connecting activities (i.e., user forms). Altogether, processes are defined in terms of data conditions.

Data-Driven Execution. An activity is considered as completed if for all mandatory data elements a corresponding value is available. Since different forms may comprise the same data element, it is possible to provide required attribute values up-front; i.e., before they become mandatory for a particular activity. This way, activities can be automatically skipped (i.e., auto-completed) if mandatory data is already available. Despite the introduction of the redo-role, re-executing activities may be often not possible. In particular, if all data elements mandatory for the current and the subsequent activity are available, both activities are automatically marked as executed. In this case, a user may only re-execute the activity if he also owns the redo-role for both the current and the subsequent activity. In particular, users cannot re-execute a particular activity as long as they have not explicitly confirmed its completion.

Object Interactions. In case handling, it is possible to relate cases based on *sub-plans*. The latter must be instantiated at specific points during the execution of the higher-level case (i.e., creation dependency). Furthermore, these sub-plans can be categorized as dynamic. This enables the creation of a variable number of instances at run-time. In this context, cardinality constraints are considered by defining a minimal and maximal number of instances that must be completed at run-time. However, it is not possible to execute sub-plans asynchronously to the higher-level case. Thus, execution dependencies can not be defined. Aggregations, in turn, are possible. For this purpose, the higher-level case may include an array whose elements are mapped to data elements of the respective sub-plan. Finally, since sub-plans require a strong hierarchical collocation of related cases, the consideration of arbitrary relationships between cases is not supported. It is not possible, for example, to define a dependency between *reviews* and *interviews* (cf. Fig. 13.3); i.e., it is not possible to express that an interview may only be initiated if at least one review proposes to invite the applicant.

Variable Activity Granularity. Using case handling, all forms must be pre-defined at build-time. In particular, it is not possible to automatically generate user forms based on the current processing state of the case and the user performing the activity. However, forms may also refer to data elements corresponding to higher- and lower-level plans. Hence, in addition to instance-specific forms, context-specific forms can be realized. In turn, batch activities are not supported.

Integrated Access. In principle, each involved user may execute the currently activated activity. He then can read all data elements and also write those data elements not categorized as mandatory or restricted. However, it is not possible to assign different permissions for optionally reading and writing data elements to different user roles. Moreover, it is not possible to make these permissions dependable on the process instance state. Opposed to free data elements, mandatory and restricted data elements can only be written by users having the execute-role. This prevents changes of data element values that are contradicting with process execution. However, it is not possible to classify one and the same activity as optional for one user and as mandatory for another user.

13.4.2 Proclets

An activity-centric framework enabling *object-specific process* is provided by Proclets [7, 17]. A Proclet is an *object-specific process* modeled in terms of a Petri net. In particular, the framework enables interactions between different Proclets based on *messages* that are exchanged through *ports* connected by transitions. Each message sent or received is stored in the *knowledge base* of the respective Proclet. Activities have assigned pre- and post-conditions referring to information from the knowledge base. At run-time, an activity becomes enabled if each input place of the corresponding Petri net contains at least one token, its precondition evaluates to true, and all input ports contain a message.

Object Behavior. Although Proclets are object-specific processes, they are defined in an activity-centric manner and not in terms of data conditions. Hence, it is neither possible to determine the order in which object attributes must be written nor to define what valid attribute settings are.

Data-Driven Execution. Since the Proclet framework uses an activity-centric paradigm, a data-driven execution of activities is not possible. However, each activity may be associated with a *pre- and post-condition* based on the information from the knowledge base (i.e., exchanged messages). At run-time, an activity becomes enabled if its incoming transition is activated, the precondition evaluates to true, and required messages are available. This way, data-driven coordination of Proclet instances becomes possible.

Object Interactions. At run-time, for each Proclet type a dynamic number of instances can be handled. In addition, it is possible to send messages to multiple Proclets at the same time; e.g., to all instances of a certain Proclet type. This way, a complex process structure evolves in which the Proclet instances can be executed asynchronously to each other. In this context, for each port a cardinality constraint can be defined determining the number of recipients of a message. Creation and execution dependencies, as well as aggregations, can be defined based on preconditions for activities. However, it is not possible to handle transitive or transverse relationships between Proclet instances; e.g., it is not possible to synchronize a *job offer* instance with the corresponding *reviews* directly. Such dependencies must be specified using (several) intermediate dependencies. More precisely, *reviews* must be synchronized with their corresponding applications and applications with the *job offer* to which they refer. Otherwise, it is not possible to ensure that only the *reviews* required for the *applications* referring to a certain *job offer* are considered; i.e., *reviews* for *applications* referring to other *job offers* are then invoked.

Variable Activity Granularity. All activities are defined in the context of a Proclet type. Hence, instance-specific activities are supported, whereas context-specific activities are not explicitly considered; i.e., it is not possible to access data elements from lower- or higher-level Proclet instances. Regarding the latter, information from other Proclet instances can be transferred using messages. However, there is no interrelationship between activity execution and message contents. Batch activities, in turn, are partially supported by enabling the creation of multiple Proclet instances. The execution of a set of instance-specific activities in one go, however, is not possible. Since activities are treated as black-boxes, internal process logic is not supported.

Integrated Access. Integrated access to process and application data is possible. Each user may access all data of the process.

13.4.3   Business Artifacts

The *business artifacts framework* [52, 188] is a process design methodology focusing on data objects (i.e., *business artifacts*) rather than on activities. A business artifact holds all relevant information of a particular business entity (e.g., a *job application*). This includes *atomic* and *structured attributes*, as well as references to *related artifacts*. In addition, a *life cycle* is defined for each business artifact. This life cycle is specified as a *finite-state machine* that defines the main *processing states* and the *transitions* between them. State transitions may be associated with *conditions* defined in terms of attribute values or relationships to other business artifacts. Attribute values are assigned during the execution of services. In particular, *services* are executed to move business artifacts through their life cycles. Services may be further associated with *pre- and post-conditions* for their execution (i.e., available attribute values, stages). In addition, *associations* specify how services are associated with artifacts; such associations are defined using ECA rules (i.e., event, condition, action). *Events* may comprise currently assigned attribute values, a reached state, a launched or completed service, an incoming message, or a performer request. In turn, conditions are defined using first-order logic (e.g., SQL statements). Finally, *actions* represent service invocations or the activation of a subsequent artifact stage.

Note that artifacts (i.e., life cycle models), services, and ECA rules only constitute a logical representation of business processes and business data. In particular, there exists no well-defined operational semantics for directly executing the defined models. Instead, respective models have to be (manually) mapped to an activity-centric process model in order to implement them in an activity-centric PAIS [66]; i.e., the business artifacts framework focuses on object-centric process modeling, but has not provided specific run-time concepts so far.

Object Behavior. Since state transitions are associated with data-conditions, it is possible to synchronize the states of business processes and business objects. However, it is a challenging task to ensure that the pre- and post-conditions assigned to services are consistent with the defined ECA rules as well as with the conditions defined for the state transitions of an artifact.

Object Interactions. The data structure representing an artifact may also contain related artifacts. Their corresponding life cycles, however, are treated independently based on separate artifact models. Hence, the data structure emerging in the context of a particular artifact and its related artifacts may be distributed over several (overlapping) data models; i.e., an artifact may be defined in the context of several other artifacts making it difficult to comprehend the emerging process structure and to keep it consistent. In addition to the support of object behavior, ECA rules can be used for coordinating artifact life cycles. Hence, there is no clear separation between object behavior and object interactions. Moreover, services may change attribute values of related business artifacts. Finally, aggregations are not possible and transitive and transverse relationships between business artifacts are not considered.

Data-Driven Execution. It is possible to activate a service based on data conditions. However, it is not possible to dynamically skip services even if their post-condition has been already fulfilled.

Variable Activity Granularity. Each service requires its own implementation. Therefore, its granularity is fixed already at build-time; i.e., form-based activities whose granularity is chosen at run-time are not explicitly supported. Furthermore, form-specific control flows coordinating data entry (i.e., certain attribute values may become mandatory on-the-fly depending on other attribute values) are not considered.

Integrated Access. Optional activities for accessing data can be realized using ECA rules without specified event or condition. Since the artifacts framework focuses on process-relevant activities, however, it is not possible for users to distinguish optional from mandatory activities in their worklist. Concerning process authorization (i.e., service execution rights), users are directly assigned to the service they may execute. In this context, it is neither possible to consider the properties of the business artifact nor the relation a user has to the respective artifact. In turn, data authorization (i.e., permissions for creating, deleting, and changing business artifacts) is not explicitly considered. However, services can be annotated with conditional effects (i.e., ensuring that specific attribute values will be set). This way, mandatorily attribute values can be distinguished from optional ones. Finally, attribute values violating a constraint are marked as invalidated. Respective attribute values then have to be changed in a subsequent service invocation.

13.4.4   Data-Driven Process Coordination

The data-driven coordination framework CorePro [225, 226] enables process coordination based on *objects* and *object relations*. Objects are defined in terms of *states* and *(internal) transitions* between them (i.e., *object life cycles*). The latter are associated with processes or services to be executed in order to reach the subsequent state. According to the object inter-relations, so-called *external transitions* connect states belonging to different objects (and object life cycles respectively). This enables the coordination of the individual object life cycles. More precisely, whether a certain state of an object can be activated may depend on the currently activated states of other objects. In addition to correctness constraints (e.g., ensure the proper termination of the dynamically emerging process structure), the approach comprises a well-defined operational semantics for the automatic enactment of object life cycles and process structures. The approach has been applied to release management processes from the automotive domain [223, 228]. In particular, CorePro allows establishing a clear link between product models and data-driven process structures (cf. Fig. 13.6). Finally, a proof-of-concept prototype exists (see [224, 227]).

Object Behavior. Although the behavior of objects is explicitly defined, object attributes and their respective values are not taken into account. For this reason, it is not possible to determine mandatorily required data and to define what valid attribute settings are. Consequently, processes are still defined in terms of black-box activities rather than based on data conditions. Hence, it is not possible to ensure that the actual processing state complies with corresponding attribute values.

Object Interactions. It is possible to asynchronously execute object-related process instances and to synchronize them where required. In particular, creation and

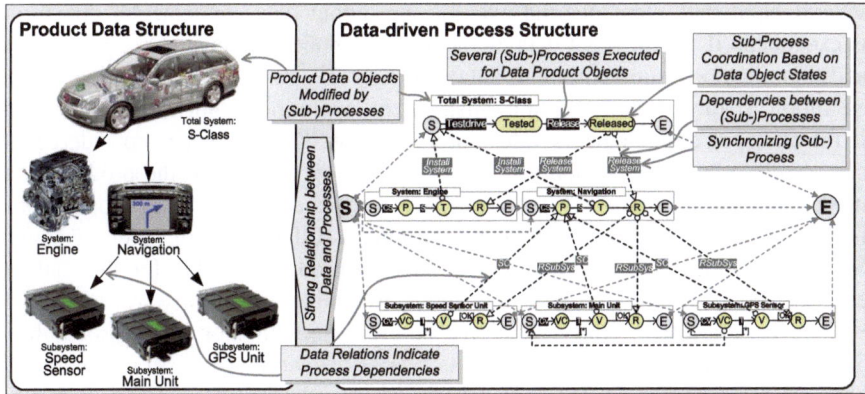

Fig. 13.6 Product data structure and corresponding data-driven process structure

execution dependencies can be defined based on external transitions. The latter, however, need to be specified along direct object inter-relations in the corresponding data structure. In turn, transitive or transverse relations are not supported. Although it is possible to create a variable number of instances at run-time, aggregations are not possible. Nevertheless, CorePro is able to deal with the execution of complex process structures emerging during run-time. In particular, this relieves process engineers from manually keeping track of the inter-dependencies that may exist between instances of object life cycles. Note that this is useful at the occurrence of exceptions whose handling might concern several life cycles (e.g., when rolling back a life cycle, dependent life cycles may have to be rolled back as well).

Data-Driven Execution. Processes are related with object state transitions and are still activity-centric; i.e., the activation of a particular state depends on the completion of a process associated with its incoming state transition. Thus, it is not possible to execute processes or respective activities up-front or to dynamically skip them. Opposed to this, process synchronization follows a data-driven approach.

Finally, since object attributes are out of scope and process execution is based on black-box activities, neither a *variable granularity of activities* nor *integrated access* to processes and application data are considered.

13.4.5 Product-Based Workflow Support

The product-based approach for workflow design and support [340] uses a so-called *product data model* that specifies required data elements to assemble a particular product. A product data model is described in terms of a tree-like structure and consists of *atomic data elements* and *operations* [275]. Nodes of this tree correspond to data elements, whereas operations are represented by arcs having several input data elements and exactly one output data element. An operation is executable if for all input data elements corresponding values are available. In addition, data conditions on input data elements may restrict the execution of the operation. If the condition is not satisfied, the operation is not executable, even if for all input data elements values are available. The product is considered as completely processed as soon as a value for the top element of the product data model (i.e., the root element in the tree structure) is available. Several operations may refer to the same output element, but have a different set of input elements. Such a situation represents alternative ways to produce a value for that output element. For selecting the best execution alternative, operations are associated with different attributes, like execution cost, processing time, or failure probability. This allows considering different execution priorities during process enactment. To obtain a corresponding process model, the product data model may be manually translated [275]. However, since the latter is time-consuming and error-prone, different algorithms are provided to automatically generate a process model based on a given product data model [340].

It is also possible to directly execute a product data model [340, 341]. For this purpose, end-users are supported with recommendations about the operation they must execute next. Such recommendations consider the performance criterion required and determine how alternative executions differ from each other with respect to that criterion.

Object Behavior. Using atomic data elements, it can be specified which data is required during process execution. The order in which data elements have to be written can be determined and valid attribute settings be specified.

Object Interactions. Since the focus is on the processing of single instances, interactions between different instances are not considered.

Integrated Access. Access to data is only possible during the execution of operations specified within the product data model; i.e., users are not allowed to access and manage data at any point in time. It is also not possible to differentiate between optional and mandatory operations.

Data-Driven Execution. When directly interpreting a product data model, data-driven process execution becomes possible. In particular, a subsequent operation can be executed if for all required input data elements a corresponding value is available and the associated data condition evaluates to *true*. Since the activation of activities depends on preconditions, however, it is not possible to automatically skip an activity if the required output data element is already available. Finally, redoing activities is not possible.

Variable Activity Granularity. Each operation requires a specific implementation and therefore constitutes a black-box activity. As a consequence, all operations have a fixed granularity; activity-internal control flows are not considered.

13.4.6 Other Approaches

Similar to the Proclets framework (cf. Sect. 13.4.2), the Object-centric Business Process Modeling framework [252, 253] enables the coordination of object-specific processes along their object relations. However, processes are still defined in an activity-centric manner; i.e., in terms of black-box activities. For process coordination, however, cardinality constraints, as well as creation and execution dependencies, are taken into account. Finally, Sadiq et al. [315] proposes to group and ungroup related activities within user worklists. In particular, an approach enabling batch activities is provided.

13.4.7 Discussion

As illustrated in Fig. 13.7, each characteristics of object-aware processes is addressed by at least one of the presented approaches. Although the latter show limitations (see footnotes in Fig. 13.7), they can be considered as pioneer work towards object-aware process support. However, none of them covers all characteristics in an integrated manner. Note that Fig. 13.7 does not make a distinction between modeling and execution support. Though some approaches (e.g., the business artifacts framework [52]) provide rich capabilities for process modeling, they have not yet covered run-time issues (or at least have not treated them explicitly).

In order to underline the high practical impact of object-aware process support, we contrast the characteristics with the different application scenarios considered by existing approaches (cf. Fig. 13.7). In particular, existing approaches address different characteristics of object-aware processes (see the grey boxes on the bottom of Fig. 13.7). For example, *order processing* was taken as an illustrating scenario by case handling [24], batch activities [315], and business artifacts [52]. Case handling addresses the need for enabling object behavior, data-driven execution, and integrated access. In turn, business artifacts consider data-driven execution, object behavior, and object interactions. Finally, Sadiq et al. [315] describes the need for executing several activities in one go (i.e., the execution of batch activities). Note that this indicates that integrated support of the different characteristics is needed to adequately cope with *order processes*.

Overall, this comparison demonstrates two things: First, the described characteristics of object-aware processes are inter-related. Second, broad support for them is required by a variety of processes from different application domains.

Main Characteristica

E Integrated Access						Domains

E	D	C	B	A	Approach	1	2	3	4	5	6	7	8	9
(X)*1		X*2			Proclets	X	X	X	X					
(X)*3	(X)*4	X			Case Handling		X			X	X	X		
	(X)*6	(X)*5	X		Business Artifacts	X				X		X	X	
	(X)*8	X	(X)*7		Data-driven Coordination				X					
		X*2			Data-centric Process Models							X		X
	(X)*6		X		Product-based Workflow Support			X	X					
X					Batch Activities (Sadiq)						X	X		

D Variable Activity Granularity
C Data-driven Execution
B Object Interactions
A Object Behavior

Human Resources (Hiring People)
Academic(ConferenceManagement)
Insurance (Claim Processing)
Development Processes
Order Processing
Education (Course Management)
Health Care (Patient Treatment)
Hotel Business (Guest Check)
Inspections

*1 no context-sentive activities / limited support of batch activities / activities are treated as black-boxes
*2 no transitive or reverse relationships
*3 optional permissions do not differentiate roles and do not consider process state
*4 no explicit user commitments
*5 indirect support through ECA-rules
*6 no flexible execution (activty acivation is based on pre-conditions rather than on post-conditions)
*7 object attributes are not considered
*8 only for process coordination

1	2	3	4	5	6	7	8	9	
A	A	A	A	A	A	A	A		A Object Behavior
B	B	B	B		B	B	B	B	B Object Interactions
C	C	C	C	C	C	C	C		C Data-driven Execution
D	D	D	D	D	D				D Variable Activity Granularity
E		E	E	E					E Integrated Access

Fig. 13.7 Evaluation of existing approaches

13.5   Summary

This chapter made several contributions. First, it introduced case handling as an example of a pioneering approach enabling user- and data-driven processes. Second, it emphasized the need for object-awareness in PAISs and introduced the major characteristics of object-aware processes. Third, it evaluated existing approaches that have recognized the need for a tight integration of business processes and business objects based on these characteristics. Overall, this evaluation confirms the high relevance of the described characteristics and indicates that their support is fundamental for many application domains. However, as discussed, none of the approaches described so far provides a comprehensive framework for object-aware process management.

For many applications, object-aware process management will support daily work in a more natural manner than this is possible with activity-centric PAISs. In particular, as illustrated in Fig. 13.8, a comprehensive integration of processes and data entails several potential benefits. First, a flexible execution of unstructured, knowledge-intensive business processes becomes possible. Second, an integrated view on business processes, functions, and data is provided to users. Third, generic business functions (e.g., automatically generated form-based activities) can be realized.

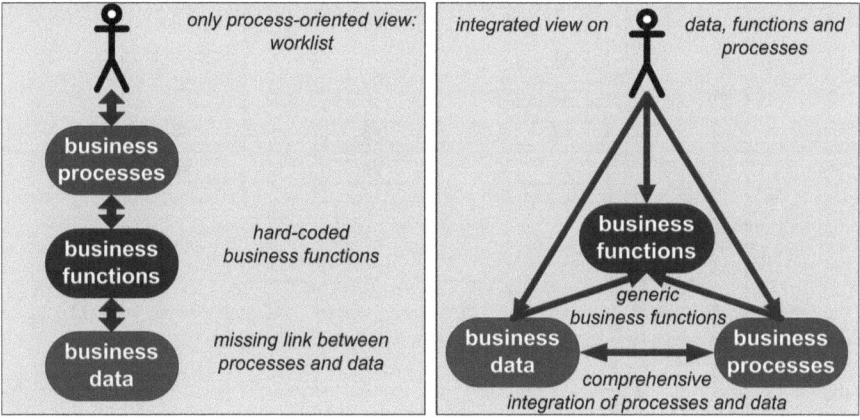

Fig. 13.8 Traditional PAIS (*left*) and object-aware PAIS (*right*)

The PHILharmonicFlows approach presented in Chap. 14 provides a comprehensive framework for object-aware process management. In particular, it enables the major characteristics of object-aware processes as introduced in this chapter. PHILharmonicFlows enforces a *well-defined modeling methodology* governing the definition of processes at different levels of granularity and based on a *well-defined formal semantics*. In particular, the framework differentiates between *micro and macro processes* in order to capture both *object behavior* and *object interactions*.

Exercises

13.1. Activity-Centric Processes

Discuss limitations of activity-centric PAIS in respect to the integration of processes and data.

13.2. Case Handling Concepts

(a) What is the primary driver for the progress of a case during run-time?
(b) Case handling distinguishes between accessible and mandatory data objects of a task. Explain the difference between these two data object sets.
(c) May any data objects be updated by each task of a case type?
(d) A case type comprises a set of tasks (i.e., activities) and precedence relations between them. In which way do these tasks differ from activities known from prespecified process models in activity-centric PAISs (cf. Chap. 4)?
(e) Explain in your own words the meaning of the execute, skip and redo roles.
(f) Discuss weaknesses of the case handling paradigm in respect to concurrent task execution and data access control.

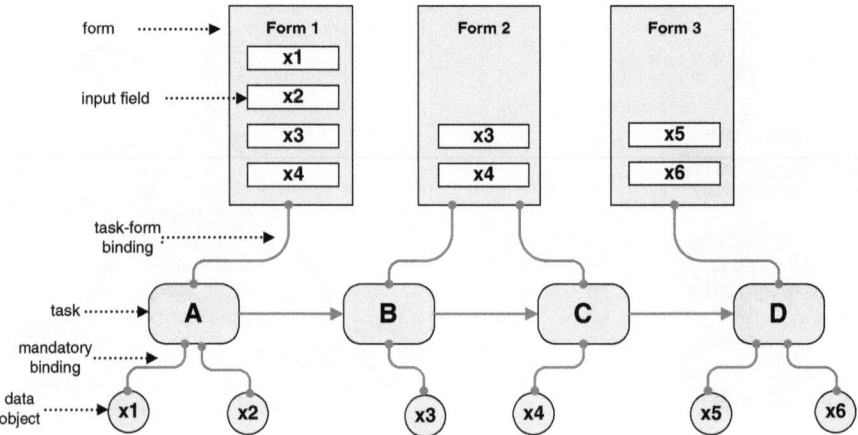

Fig. 13.9 Example of a case type

13.3. Case Type

Consider the case type from Fig. 13.9. It comprises four tasks, six data objects, and three forms. Answer the following questions:

(a) When is task A considered as finished? What does this mean in respect to the succeeding task B?
(b) Assume that the user filling in *Form 1* sets values for data objects x1, x2, and x3, and then closes the form. How will the execution of the case proceed afterwards?
(c) Assume that both B and A are enabled, and that values for data objects x1 and x2 have been set so far. Furthermore, assume that a user holding the skip role for B wants to skip this task. How will the execution of the case proceed afterwards?
(d) Will all data objects have an assigned value when a case of the depicted case type completes?
(e) Assume that tasks A and B are both finished and task C is currently enabled. Furthermore, assume that a user holding the redo role for A wants to redo this task. How is this operation accomplished in the given scenario and how will the execution of the case proceed afterwards?

13.4. Characteristics of Object-Aware Processes

(a) The modeling and execution of object-aware processes is based on two levels of granularity. Describe these two levels and discuss their differences?
(b) How may object behavior be realized using data-driven execution?

(c) Why are *explicit user commitments* useful in the context of data-driven execution?

(d) Explain the differences between instance-specific, context-sensitive, and batch activities. Give examples for their use.

13.5. Object-Aware Processes

Give examples of object-aware business processes other than the ones discussed in this chapter.

13.6. Traditional PAIS vs. Object-Aware PAIS

Consider Fig. 13.8 and explain it in your own words.

Chapter 14
A Framework for Object-Aware Processes

Abstract For large and complex scenarios, the proper coordination of concurrent executions of user- and data-driven processes is crucial. In this context, object-aware processes provide a high degree of abstraction by enabling two levels of process granularity: object behavior and object interactions. Furthermore, object-aware process management supports data-driven process execution, flexible choice of activity granularities, and integrated access to business processes and business data. This chapter introduces the PHILharmonicFlows framework, which enables object-aware process management in the large scale. In particular, the framework allows for a tight integration of processes, functions, data, and users.

14.1 Introduction

As discussed in Chap. 13, there exist business processes not adequately supported by activity-centric PAISs. Typically, these business processes are rather unstructured, knowledge-intensive, and driven by user decisions [329, 336]. In particular, the business functions covered by them cannot be straight-jacketed into atomic activities [24, 315]. Instead, the primary drivers for the progress of respective processes are available business data and explicit user decisions.

The limitations activity-centric PAISs show in respect to user- and data-driven processes can be traced back to the unsatisfactory integration of the different building blocks of an activity-centric PAIS (cf. Fig. 14.1). In particular, business processes and business objects cannot be treated independently from each other, but require a tight integration at the PAIS level. As further emphasized in Chap. 13, *object-awareness* provides the level of abstraction needed in order to enable user- and data-driven process management in the large scale; i.e., to adequately support the *fundamental characteristics of object-aware processes* for large process structures involving multiple dependent object instances and process instances respectively:

M. Reichert and B. Weber, *Enabling Flexibility in Process-Aware Information Systems*, 405
DOI 10.1007/978-3-642-30409-5_14, © Springer-Verlag Berlin Heidelberg 2012

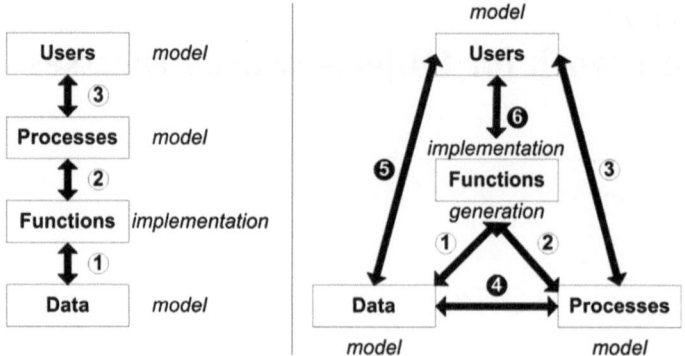

Fig. 14.1 Basic building blocks of activity-centric PAISs (*Left*) and object-aware PAIS (*Right*)

1. *Object behavior.* The behavior of the objects involved in a business process must be considered during process execution.
2. *Object interactions.* The interactions between related objects have to be coordinated in a correct manner taking object relations into account.
3. *Data-driven execution.* Since the progress of a process is determined by the involved object instances and their attribute values, a data-driven process execution is required.
4. *Variable activity granularities.* Different users prefer different work practices. Hence, it must be possible to define activities with different degrees of granularity; e.g., process a number of object instances separately or in one go.
5. *Integrated access to business processes and business objects.* Authorized users should be able to access process-related objects as well as their attribute values at any point in time.

This chapter introduces PHILharmonicFlows—a framework enabling *object-aware process management* [156, 158]. This framework includes components for the modeling, execution and monitoring of object-aware processes. Opposed to the approaches presented in Chap. 13, which focus on selected characteristics or lifecycle phases of object-aware processes, PHILharmonicFlows targets at an integrated and comprehensive framework [160]. In particular, it combines *object behavior* expressed in terms of *object states* and *state transitions* with *data-driven process execution*. Furthermore, it enables *process coordination* in the large scale taking the *behavior* and *semantic relations* of the involved object instances into account. In this context, coordination is not only possible along direct object relations (e.g., a *review* may directly refer to an *application*). Additionally, the processing of object instances and their interactions can be coordinated based on their relationships within the overall data structure (e.g., taking *transitive* relationships between object instances into account). Finally, at run-time, *integrated access* to business processes, business functions, and business data becomes possible. For this purpose, PHILharmonicFlows provides generic services for automatically generating end-user components, like worklists, form-based activities, and overview tables.

Section 14.2 gives an overview of the PHILharmonicFlows framework and its components, which are then described in detail in the following sections. Section 14.3 shows how objects and object relations are modeled. Based on this, Sect. 14.4 deals with the modeling of *object behavior* in terms of *micro processes*. Authorization issues are discussed in Sect. 14.5, while Sect. 14.6 deals with the concurrent processing of multiple object instances and shows how *object interactions* can be coordinated using *macro processes*. The chapter concludes with a discussion of open issues in Sect. 14.7 and a short summary in Sect. 14.8.

14.2 Overview of the Framework

This section gives an overview of the PHILharmonicFlows framework, which comprises build- and run-time components for the integrated support of object-aware processes and their fundamental characteristics as presented in Chap. 13.

Object types and *object relations* are defined in a *data model*, while *object behavior* is expressed in terms of a *process* whose execution is driven by *object attribute changes*. The framework further provides support for coordinating the execution of related processes and the *interactions* of their corresponding objects. In this context, the *object relations* defined by the data model are taken into account. Furthermore, an *authorization component* is provided controlling access to processes and data. In the following sections, these components will be described in detail. The focus will be on their core features and interrelations, whereas a description of their formal semantics driving the execution of processes and the coordination of their interactions will be omitted (see [157]). Finally, basic concepts will be illustrated along the *recruitment* example introduced in Chap. 13.

Figure 14.2 summarizes the components of the PHILharmonicFlows framework. The framework comprises a modeling and a run-time environment that enable lifecycle support for object-aware processes. The *modeling environment* enforces a well-defined methodology that governs process designers in modeling processes at different levels of granularity. More precisely, a distinction is made between *micro* and *macro processes* in order to capture both *object behavior* and *object interactions*. Furthermore, micro and macro processes are modeled in tight integration with business objects. As a prerequisite, object types and their relations have to be explicitly captured in a *data model*.

For each *object type*, a *micro process type* must be specified. The latter defines the behavior of corresponding *object instances* and consists of a set of *states* and the *transitions* between them. Each state, in turn, is associated with a set of *object type attributes*. At run-time, a *micro process instance* in a particular state may only proceed if (specific) values are assigned to the attributes associated with this state; i.e., *data-driven process execution* is enabled. This is usually accomplished with *form-based activities* that must be executed by authorized users.

Process authorization is based on *user roles* assigned to the different *states* of a micro process. When a particular state becomes enabled at run-time, a user holding

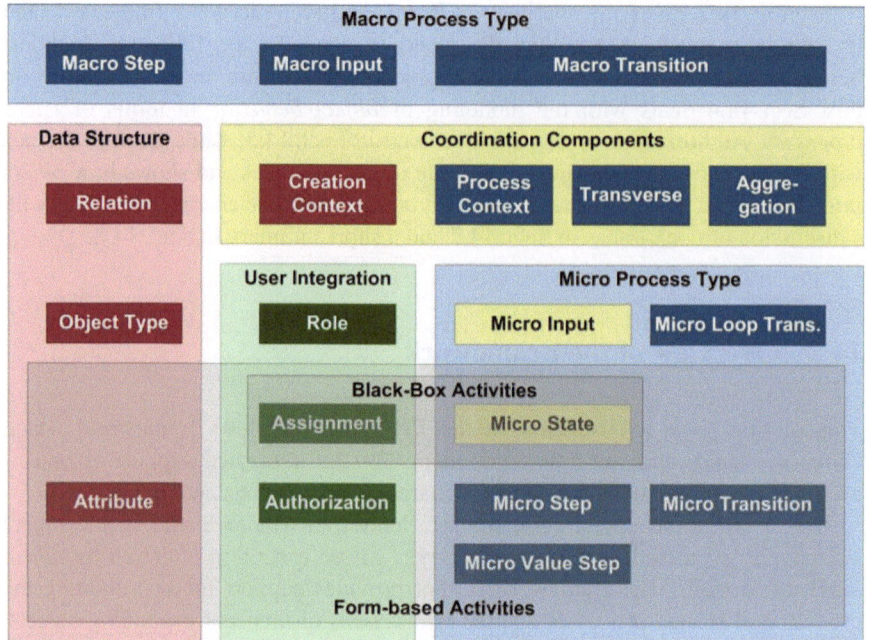

Fig. 14.2 Components of the PHILharmonicFlows framework

the required role must set the values of the object attributes associated with this state. Only then, the flow of the micro process instance may proceed; i.e., users have to perform a number of so-called *micro steps* to set the required attribute values. In turn, *optional access to data* is enabled asynchronously to process execution and based on *permissions* for creating and deleting object instances, as well as for reading and writing their attributes. The latter must also take the current progress of the corresponding micro process instance into account. For this purpose, an *authorization table* is maintained assigning data permissions to user roles depending on the different states of the micro process type.

If an *object instance* is created for a given object type, a corresponding *micro process instance* is automatically created. Taking the relations between the object instances of the overall *data structure* into account, the corresponding micro process instances form a complex *process structure*; i.e., their execution needs to be coordinated according to the given data structure and its (cardinality) constraints. The framework realizes this based on so-called *macro processes*. A macro process refers to parts of the data structure (i.e., object instances of the same and different type) and consists of *macro steps* and *macro transitions* between them. As opposed to micro steps, which refer to single attributes of a particular object type, a macro step refers to a particular object type (and a related state). In particular, a macro process allows hiding the complexity of large process structures from users. In addition, different kinds of synchronization constraints may be defined for coordinating the *interactions* between the object instances of the same or different object types. Finally, in addition to automatically generated *form-based activities*, *black-box activities* can be integrated (e.g., making complex computations, invoking a web service, or sending an e-mail).

The *run-time environment* provides both *data-* and *process-oriented views* to end-users. That is, authorized users may invoke activities for accessing data at any point in time on the one hand, and they may invoke activities needed to proceed with the execution of micro process instances on the other. Furthermore, process execution is based on a well-defined operational semantics [157], which also provides the basis for automatically generating the end-user components of the run-time environment (e.g., overview tables displaying selected object instances, user worklists, or form-based activities). Hence, implementation effort only becomes necessary in the context of black-box activities.

14.3 Data Model

Process and data modeling constitute two sides of the same coin. Hence, the proper integration of the *data model* is crucial for a framework enabling object-aware processes. PHILharmonicFlows uses a *relational data model*, which is based on *object types*, as well as on their *attributes* and *relation types* (cf. Fig. 14.3). Thereby, *attribute types* represent *atomic data elements* describing the properties of the respective object type. Concerning *relation types*, in addition, minimum and maximum *cardinalities* may be specified. Since normalization constitutes an integral part of the relational model, all relations form 1-to-many relationships; i.e., many-to-many-relationships have to be dissolved by using additional 1-to-many-relations. Finally, for each object type, exactly one *key attribute type* exists. Based on its *key attribute value*, an object instance can be uniquely identified at run-time.

Example 14.1 (Data Model). Regarding the recruitment example from Chap. 13 (cf. Example 13.3), relevant object types include *Job Offer*, *Application*, *Review*, *Interview*, and *Participant* (cf. Fig. 14.3). For example, each *Application* corresponds to exactly one *Job Offer*. In turn, for each *Interview*, at minimum two and at maximum five *Participants* must be available. Furthermore, each object type is characterized by a set of attributes. For example, consider attribute *Proposal* of object type *Review*. Using this attribute, the reviewer makes a proposal on how to proceed with the corresponding *Application*.

Fig. 14.3 Example of a data model

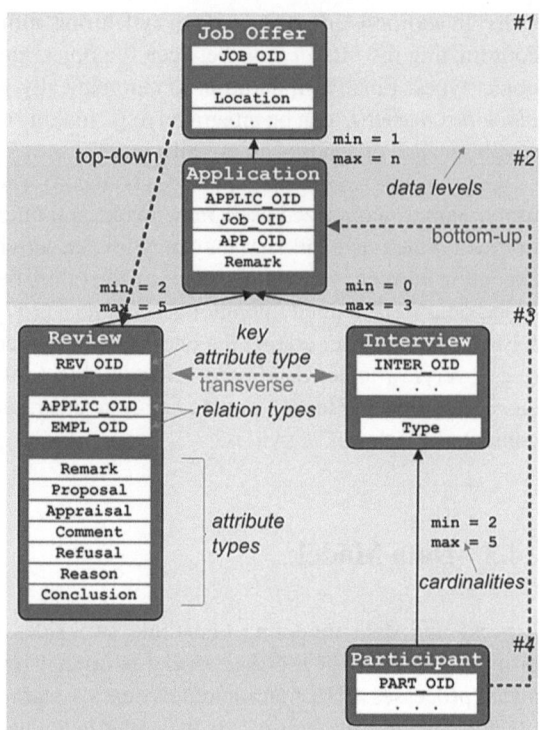

14.3.1   Object Relationships

Direct relations between object instances first need to be captured, e.g., a *Review* object corresponds to a particular *Application* object. In the context of process coordination and user authorization indirect (i.e., *transitive*) relationships also have to be taken into account; e.g., identify and access all *Reviews* related to a particular *Job Offer* object.

PHILharmonicFlows structures a data model into different *data levels*. All object types not referring to any other object types are placed on Level #1. As illustrated in Fig. 14.3, other object types are always assigned to a lower data level as the object types they reference. For the sake of simplicity, self-references and cyclic relationships are not considered in this chapter, although they are covered by the PHILharmonicFlows framework.

Example 14.2 (Data Levels). A *Job Offer* does not reference any other object types. Consequently, this object type is placed on the highest data level. Since object type *Review* contains a relation to object type *Application*, the *Review* object type is placed on a lower data level than object type *Application*.

An object type A directly or indirectly referencing an object type B is denoted as a *lower-level object type* of B. Accordingly, an object type directly or indirectly referenced by other object types is denoted as a *higher-level object type*. As further illustrated in Fig. 14.3, a relationship between object types A and B is categorized as *top-down* (*bottom-up*) if B is a lower-level (higher-level) object type of A. Furthermore, a relation between object types A and B is categorized as *transverse* if there exists another object type C for which both A and B are lower-level object types; i.e., A and B have a higher-level object type in common. Otherwise (i.e., none of the categorizations top-down, bottom-up or transverse applies), the relationship between two object types is categorized as *general*; i.e., there exists no explicit relationship between them. Example 14.3 illustrates the different object relationships from Fig. 14.3.

Example 14.3 (Object Relationship). We take the data model from Fig. 14.3 in order to illustrate the different kinds of relationships between object types:

- *Top-down relationship.* The *Review* object type has a relation to the *Application* object type. In turn, the latter relates to the *Job Offer* object type. Hence, the *Job Offer* object type is transitively referenced by the *Review* object type; i.e., there exists a top-down relationship from the *Job Offer* object type to the *Review* object type.
- *Bottom-up relationship.* A *Participant* object type relates to the *Interview* object type that, in turn, has a relation to the *Application* object type. Consequently, the *Participant* object type transitively references the *Application* object type; i.e., there is a bottom-up relationship from the *Participant* object type to the *Application* object type.
- *Transverse relationship.* Both the *Review* and the *Interview* object type have a relation to the *Application* object type; i.e., there exists a transverse relationship between these two object types.

14.3.2 Integrating Users

Permissions may depend not only on user roles, but also on application data, i.e., on attribute values of object instances. Hence, user roles should not be managed independently from application data. Therefore, PHILharmonicFlows allows for a

Fig. 14.4 User integration
based on user types and
relation roles

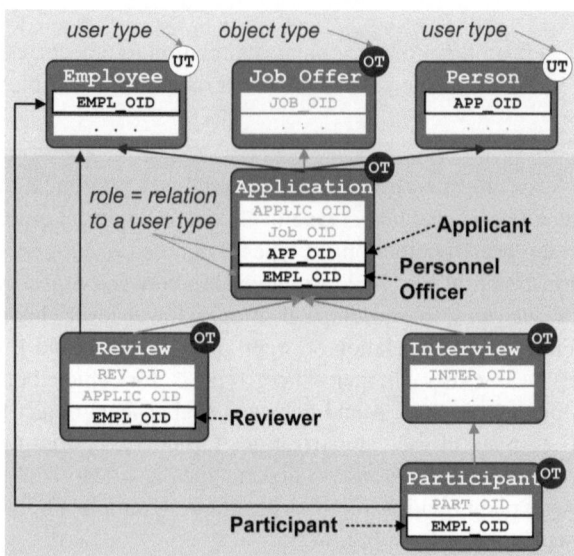

tight integration of users with objects. For this purpose, selected object types may
be flagged as *user types (UT)* (cf. Fig. 14.4). Logically, a user type corresponds to a
user role, whereas each instance of a user type represents a concrete *user*. In order
to authenticate users, each user type has attributes uniquely identifying its instances
(i.e., users) at run-time (e.g., *user name* and *password*). Based on this integration
of application objects and users, it becomes possible to automatically derive further
user roles from the defined user types and their relations to other object types. We
denote such derived user roles as *relation roles*.

> *Example 14.4 (User Types and Relation Roles).* Consider the data model
> from Fig. 14.4. It contains the two user types *Employee* and *Person*. Further-
> more, when considering the relations of object types with these user types,
> one can derive four relation roles: *Applicant, Personnel Officer, Reviewer,*
> and *Participant* (of an interview).

Furthermore, it is possible to restrict data access of a particular user to a subset
of the instances of an object type; e.g., a *reviewer* should only be allowed to access
applications for which she must provide a *review*, but not for other ones. Such a
fine-grained access control is denoted as an *instance-specific role assignment*. While
relation roles can be derived based on relation types (i.e., at build-time), instance-
specific role assignment is based on relations that can be only identified during
run-time. PHILharmonicFlows allows restricting the object instances that may be

accessed by a particular user—this is also denoted as *vertical authorization* [155]. It is also possible to consider the relations between users and object instances in this context, e.g., whether there exists a top-down, bottom-up or transverse relationship between them. This is illustrated by Example 14.5.

Example 14.5 (Instance-specific Role Assignment). Applicants may only access their own *Application*, but not those of other *applicants* (i.e., instance-specific role assignment based on a top-down relationship). Furthermore, *Participants* may access those *Interviews* in which they participated (i.e., instance-specific role assignment based on a bottom-up relationship). Finally, *Reviewers* may only access the *Interviews* belonging to an *Application* they have to evaluate (i.e., instance-specific role assignment based on a transverse relationship).

Based on a data model, a corresponding *data structure* dynamically evolves during run-time. It comprises a collection of object instances and their relations according to the defined data model. In this context, it must be ensured that the data structure meets the cardinality constraints of its corresponding data model at any point in time. For this purpose, a *creation context* is maintained for each higher-level object instance observing whether the minimum number of required lower-level object instances exist; i.e., it is automatically ensured that a sufficient number of lower-level object instances are available. If this is not the case, a respective activity will be automatically assigned to the worklists of authorized users in order to create additional object instances (related to the higher-level object instance). Similarly, this creation context is used to disable the creation of lower-level object instances when the maximum cardinality is reached. The concrete number of lower-level object instances depends on user decisions.

Example 14.6 (Creation Context). If for a particular *Interview* (i.e., object instance) less than two *Participants* are available, a mandatory activity will be generated and assigned to the worklist of the responsible *Personnel Officer* who then may add *Participants*. In turn, after five *Participants* have been specified, it is no longer possible to assign additional ones. Finally, if the number of available *Participants* is between two and four, the *Personnel Officer* may optionally add *Participants*.

Data authorization requires permissions for creating and deleting object instances, as well as for reading or writing corresponding attribute values. In this context, the data model and the permissions defined for each user role provide the basis for dynamically creating *overview tables* (e.g., containing all object instances a particular user may access) and *form-based activities* (e.g., comprising those object attributes that may be read or written by a user in the given context) at run-time. Furthermore, data authorization may be made dependent on the progress of a process. As will be shown in the following sections, data permissions can therefore not only be linked to user roles, but also to process states.

14.4 Micro Processes

The modeling of object-aware processes must consider two levels of granularity—*object behavior* and *object interactions*. While object behavior is described in terms of a specific process model for each object type, object interactions require the definition of processes involving several object types. This section focuses on the specification of object behavior, while object interactions are considered in Sect. 14.6.

For each *object type*, a corresponding *micro process type* is defined representing object behavior. Accordingly, the creation of a *micro process instance* at run-time is directly coupled with the creation of a corresponding object instance. One challenge in this context is coordinating the processing of an individual object instance among different users taking data permissions into account [158]. Another challenge is deriving form-based activities for these users.

At run-time, form-based activities and their internal logic (i.e., the flow between the input fields of the form) are automatically generated. Furthermore, the object behavior represented by a micro process instance depends on available object attribute values; i.e., it becomes transparent which data (i.e., *object attributes*) must be available to proceed with the processing of an object instance in a particular state. For this purpose, *data-driven process execution* is supported, similar to the one described in the context of the case handling paradigm (cf. Chap. 13). Furthermore, the progress of an object instance may depend on explicit user decisions. For this case, even if required object attributes are available, a micro process instance may only proceed after a user has explicitly committed this.

Example 14.7 (Micro Process). Consider the micro process type of a *Review* object type as depicted in Fig. 14.5. Each instance of object type *Review* (see the left-hand side of Fig. 14.5) must be *requested* by a *personnel officer*; then, it is *handed out* to a *reviewer*. The latter may either *refuse* the *review request* (and give a *reason* for the *refusal*) or fill in the corresponding *review* form. In particular, the *reviewer* either suggests *rejecting* or *inviting* the *applicant*. After the *reviewer* has submitted his *review*, the *personnel officer* must evaluate the feedback provided. In order to assist him, the micro process includes two separate states, one for *reviews* proposing to *reject* the *applicant* (i.e., state *rejected*) and one for *reviews* proposing to *invite* him

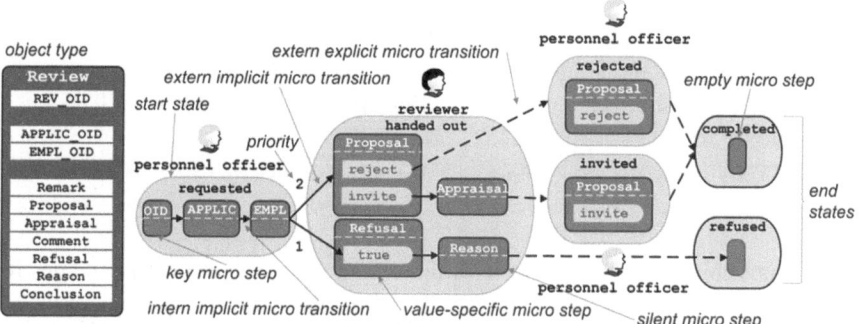

Fig. 14.5 Micro process of a review object

(i.e., state *invited*). Overall, this micro process comprises three activities to be mandatorily executed in order to successfully process an instance of the *Review* object type.

Similar to existing work considering object behavior (cf. Chap. 13), a *state-based approach* is provided, i.e., object behavior is expressed in terms of an *object lifecycle*. As illustrated in Fig. 14.5, abstract process states serve as a basis for coordinating the mandatory activities of a micro process among different users. For this purpose, user roles must be assigned to the different states. As opposed to other approaches, however, PHILharmonicFlows explicitly defines which object attribute values must be set in order to leave a particular micro process state. Hence, abstracted object states and data-driven execution are combined with each other.

14.4.1 Micro Steps

As previously mentioned, micro process states are explicitly defined in relation to object attributes; i.e., it depends on the availability of (specific) attribute values whether a certain micro process state can be entered and left, respectively. For this purpose, each micro process state comprises several *micro steps*. Each of these micro steps represents a mandatory write access on a particular object attribute (or object relation) of the respective object instance. Note that a single micro step does not represent an activity, but refers to an atomic action (i.e., editing an input field within a form). In order to reach a micro step during run-time, a value for the corresponding object attribute (or object relation) is mandatorily required. We denote micro steps, which are completed when setting an arbitrary value for their corresponding attribute, as *atomic micro steps*.

Example 14.8 (Atomic Micro Step). Consider the micro process type from Fig. 14.5. When initiating a *Review* within micro state *requested*, a *personnel officer* must specify a corresponding *Application* object as well as an *Employee* who will be requested to provide the *Review*. For setting these two object relations, two micro steps exist (i.e., micro steps *APPLIC* and *EMPL*).

It is possible to explicitly specify a finite number of values or value ranges for a particular object attribute in the context of a micro step if this is relevant for describing object behavior. Such a micro step is denoted as *value-specific*. In user forms, for example, value-specific micro steps (i.e., the possible values that may be set when executing the micro step) can be displayed using combo boxes or radio buttons. This way, invalid values can be excluded and process control can be based on meaningful object attributes.

Example 14.9 (Value-specific Micro Step). Concerning micro state *handed out* in Fig. 14.5, the *reviewer* must assign a value either to attribute *Proposal* or attribute *Refusal*; i.e., he has two options. As opposed to the micro steps of the preceding state *requested*, for which "arbitrary" values can be set, attributes *Proposal* and *Refusal* require specific values. For example, attribute *Proposal* may either be set to *invite* or *reject*. In turn, regarding object attribute *Refusal*, only value *true* is relevant for the object behavior.

14.4.2 Process States

Each micro process comprises a unique *start state, intermediate micro states*, and one or several *end states*. At any point during micro process execution exactly one state is enabled. More precisely, the start state becomes enabled when a corresponding object instance is created. It is then processed as any other states. As soon as an end state is reached, the micro process instance is completed. Note that end states do not require the setting of any object attributes, and therefore neither comprise atomic nor value-specific micro steps. However, a *silent micro step* (i.e., a micro step not referring to any object attributes; cf. Fig. 14.5) is added to each end state in order to connect it with other micro states. Furthermore, silent micro steps may be added to intermediate micro states as well. This way, it becomes possible to realize activities for reading a particular object instance mandatorily (see Sect. 14.5.2 for details).

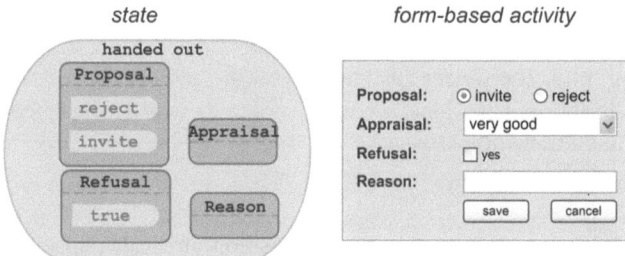

Fig. 14.6 A micro process state and its corresponding form

For each micro state (except end micro states), the attribute values required to leave the state are defined by the corresponding atomic and value-specific micro steps. When a micro state becomes enabled during the processing of an object instance, a form-based activity for entering the required attribute values is automatically generated (cf. Fig. 14.6). As will be shown in Sect. 14.5.2, such forms may also contain attributes that may be read in the given state of the micro process.

Example 14.10 (Micro States). Consider the micro process from Fig. 14.5. If the *personnel officer* requests a new *Review*, a corresponding micro process instance is created and its start state *requested* becomes enabled. Intermediate micro states include the states *handed out*, *rejected*, and *invited*. In state *handed out*, the corresponding *reviewer* must fill in the review form depicted in Fig. 14.6. Furthermore, if state *invited* becomes enabled, the *personnel officer* has to evaluate the *Proposal*. Finally, if the *reviewer* refuses the *Review* request, the *Review* object instance will immediately reach the end state *refused*. Opposed to this, if the *Review* is provided, the end state *completed* will be reached afterwards as soon as the *personnel officer* has evaluated the provided feedback.

14.4.3   Internal Micro Transitions

Ideally, users can be guided in setting the required attribute values when processing a form-based activity; e.g., by highlighting respective input fields in the preferred order. To capture such an *internal logic* for setting a number of object attributes, their corresponding micro steps can be linked using *micro transitions*. Micro transitions linking two micro steps within the same micro state are denoted as *internal micro transitions*. Based on them, the internal logic of a mandatory, form-based activity can be defined; i.e., the default order in which the input fields of the corresponding form will be edited.

Example 14.11 (Internal Micro Transitions). Consider micro state *handed out* in Fig. 14.5. For object attribute *Appraisal*, a value is only required if attribute *Proposal* has value *invite*. In order to express this behavior, an internal micro transition is used.

When considering an outgoing micro transition of a value-specific micro step, the transition may be either associated with a specific value (or value range) of the object attribute corresponding to this micro step, or with the entire micro step. In the former case, the transition is only fired, and hence its target micro step enabled, if the specific value is actually assigned to this object attribute in the micro state given. In turn, for an incoming micro transition of a value-specific micro step, it is possible to connect it to a specific attribute value. This way, it can be expressed that this attribute value is required for the target micro step in the given case.

The internal logic defined for the micro steps of a particular state enables user guidance when filling in corresponding forms. When running a form-based activity, however, users still have the flexibility to decide in which order they actually enter the input fields of the form; i.e., despite the prespecified sequence of micro steps, a user is free to choose the execution order he prefers. Hence, the order in which required values are assigned to object attributes does not necessarily coincide to the one defined for the corresponding micro steps. In particular, at run-time a micro step may be completed as soon as a value is assigned to its object attribute.

Example 14.12 (Internal Logic of a Form-based Activity). Consider start state *requested* of the micro process from Fig. 14.5. When filling in the respective form, a *personnel officer* may first want to set a value for object relation *employee* (i.e., micro step *EMPL*) although he is guided to first enter the input field for relation *application* (i.e., micro step *APPLIC*). Hence, if a value for relation *application* is set afterwards, the subsequent micro step referring to relation *employee* (i.e., micro step *EMPL*) is automatically completed.

Note that the form-based activities described so far constitute *mandatory activities*, required to proceed with the execution of a micro process. By executing *optional activities*, in addition, authorized users may read or write the attributes of an object instance asynchronously to the execution of its corresponding micro process instance. Using optional activities, it therefore becomes possible to set attribute values before they become mandatory during micro process execution. Consequently, if a (specific) value for an attribute is written up-front, the respective micro step will be automatically completed when it becomes enabled (i.e., *autocompletion*).

Even though a micro process instance is always in exactly one micro state, this does not forbid concurrent execution involving multiple users. More precisely, during the execution of a particular activity (i.e., the micro process is in a particular micro state), parallel processing of disjoint sets of mandatory as well as optional object attributes is possible. In addition, different users may concurrently process forms corresponding to the same object instance and the same state of its corresponding micro process instance. In this context, known mechanisms for concurrent data access are applied [114].

14.4.4 External Micro Transitions

As opposed to internal micro transitions, an *external micro transition* connects two micro steps belonging to different micro states of a micro process; i.e., its firing triggers a subsequent micro state. Basically, a micro state is enabled as soon as one of its micro steps is triggered by an incoming external transition. However, to also cover scenarios in which an activity-based paradigm is preferred (i.e., the user wants to explicitly commit the completion of the activity he is working on), a distinction is made between *implicit* and *explicit external micro transitions*.

An *implicit external micro transition* is fired as soon as its source micro step completes. Hence, the data-driven execution paradigm is also applied for enabling subsequent states.

Example 14.13 (Implicit External Micro Transitions). A *reviewer* may fill in the *Review* (i.e., the form associated with micro state *handed out*) as soon as the *personnel officer* has set the values of object relations *application* (i.e., micro step *APPLIC*) and *Employee* (i.e., micro step *EMPL*) (cf. Fig. 14.5).

An *explicit external micro transition* also requires that a user explicitly confirms the completion of its source micro state; i.e., even if the target micro step (and target micro state respectively) can be reached, the progress of the micro process is blocked until an authorized user explicitly confirms that the current micro state may be left (i.e., the activity associated with this micro step can be completed). For example, consider again the micro process from Fig. 14.5 where the dashed lines represent explicit external micro transitions. In order to authorize users to commit the completion of a micro state (i.e., form-based activity), an explicit micro transition must be associated with a user role.

Example 14.14 (Explicit External Micro Transitions). Consider the micro state *handed out* of the micro process depicted in Fig. 14.5. Based on the described semantics, a *reviewer* may re-execute the activity (i.e., form) for filling in her *Review* even if all mandatory object attributes have been already set. This gives her the flexibility to change her *Proposal* if desired. However, after she commits the completion of micro state *handed out*, this is no longer possible and a subsequent micro state will be triggered.

When *re-executing* a mandatory activity associated with a particular micro state, all previously executed micro steps of this micro state have to be reinitialized.

Example 14.15 (Re-initialization). Reconsider the micro process from Fig. 14.5. If the *reviewer* refuses the requested *Review* and gives a *Reason* for this, the next action is to commit the transition of the micro process instance to the subsequent micro state *refused*. However, the *reviewer* may want to re-think her decision and fill in the *Review* once more; i.e., she then re-executes the activity, which requires that already reached micro steps (i.e., the micro steps referring to attributes *Refusal* and *Reason* in our example) are re-initialized.

A particular micro step may have more than one outgoing external micro transition (e.g., micro step *EMPL* in Fig. 14.5). In such a case, it must be ensured that only one of the succeeding micro steps is reached during run-time. This can be accomplished implicitly through respective user decisions; i.e., all micro steps may be first enabled, but as soon as one of them is executed this is no longer possible for the others. However, in certain scenarios (e.g., if object attributes of the subsequent micro state have been set up-front and hence auto-completion is required) such an implicit user choice is not possible. For this reason, for a micro step having several outgoing micro transitions, *priorities* have to be assigned to these transitions (cf. Example 14.16). In conflicting situations, only that target micro step is reached, which is the target of the micro transition with the highest priority.

Example 14.16 (Priorities). Consider the micro process from Fig. 14.5. A *reviewer* may set the values of object attributes *Proposal* and *Refusal* up-front, i.e., while micro state *requested* is still enabled. In this case, the micro steps corresponding to these two attributes will be auto-completed as soon as micro state *handed out* becomes enabled. The *Review* will then be *refused* since the incoming micro transition of micro step *Refusal* has highest priority.

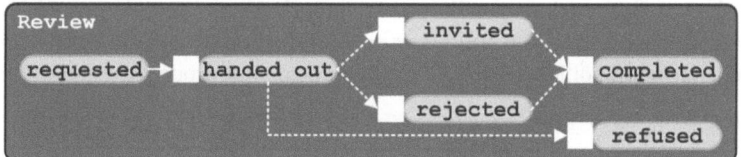

Fig. 14.7 State-based view of a micro process

For each defined micro process, a state-based view is automatically generated (cf. Fig. 14.7). This abstracted view on the micro process is used for process synchronization, process authorization, and process monitoring (see the following sections).

14.4.5   Further Issues

In addition to form-based activities, PHILharmonicFlows allows integrating arbitrary application components (e.g., send an e-mail or invoke an application service). For this purpose, the respective application component must be assigned to a micro process state—in the following sections such components are denoted as *black-box activities*. Thereby, the parameters of a black-box activity may refer to the same object type or to several object types. The latter is useful, for example, when modeling macro processes (see Sect. 14.6).

PHILharmonicFlows allows differentiating between a data- and an activity-driven execution paradigm at run-time. If the latter is chosen, black-box activities are classified as *required*; i.e., the micro state to which such an activity is assigned may only be left after the activity has been executed. To accomplish this, a black-box activity is assigned to the worklists of authorized users (or automatically executed in the case no user role is specified) when the respective state becomes enabled. As opposed to this, for a *non-required* black-box activity, it is allowed leaving the corresponding micro state even if the activity has not yet been executed.

In summary, a particular state of a micro process instance may be associated with different kinds of mandatory activities that may be added to user worklists when this state becomes enabled. This includes form-based activities for setting object attributes, activities for explicitly committing attribute changes before a transition to a subsequent micro state takes place, and (required) black-box activities. Furthermore, the execution of micro process instances is based on a well-defined operational semantics that covers both the data- and the activity-driven paradigm [157]. This operational semantics is required for the proper execution of micro processes and the automatic generation of run-time user interface components (e.g., form-based activities, overview tables of filtered object instances, or worklists).

As already discussed, data and process authorization cannot be treated independently from each other. The following section discusses how the permissions for reading and writing object attributes are integrated with process execution rights.

14.5   Process and Data Authorization

As shown in Chap. 13, there are approaches providing integrated access to business processes and business data. However, these do not consider that (optional) access to process-related data may depend on the current state of the respective process instance; i.e., whether a user may access certain attributes of an object instance often depends on the state of its corresponding micro process instance. Furthermore, approaches like case handling do not consider that optional activities enabling read / write access to object instances may look different from user to user; i.e., depending on the concrete user different sets of attribute values may be read or written in a certain micro process state. Note that such a fine-grained access control is required in many application domains [155]. Finally, another challenge is ensuring that process authorization complies with data authorization and vice versa.

14.5.1   Authorization Table

An activity might be mandatory for a particular user and optional for another one. Consequently, process and data authorization need to be distinguished. In particular, it should be possible that different users (i.e., user roles) may have different access rights on object attributes in a given micro process state.

To ease the proper definition of access rights, PHILharmonicFlows *automatically generates* an initial *authorization table* in accordance with the defined micro process type. For example, consider Fig. 14.8, which depicts the authorization table that was automatically generated from the micro process type shown in Fig. 14.5. As illustrated in Fig. 14.8, this authorization table defines which user role may read or (mandatorily) write which object attributes in the different states of the micro process. To ensure proper authorization, each user (role) who may be assigned to a micro state *automatically* obtains the write permissions required for writing the object attributes corresponding to this micro state. By default, the user (role) also obtains read permissions for all other attributes of the respective object type (note that these permissions may be deleted afterwards; see below); i.e., the automatically generated authorization table reflects the access rights required by the different user roles to execute instances of the respective micro process type.

PO = personnel officer

REV = reviewer

Review	requested		handed out		invited		rejected		refused		completed	
	PO	REV	PO	REV	PO	REV	PO	REV	PO	REV	PO	REV
APPLIC_OID	MW			R	R		R					
EMPL_OID	MW			R	R		R					
Remark	R			R	R		R					
Proposal	R			MW	R		R					
Appraisal	R			MW	R		R					
Comment	R			R	R		R					
Refusal	R			MW	R		R					
Reason	R			MW	R		R					
Conclusion	R			R	R		R					

Fig. 14.8 Automatically generated authorization table for the *review* object type

Example 14.17 (Automatically Assigned Permissions). Since role *reviewer (REV)* is assigned to micro state *handed out* (cf. Fig. 14.8), all users having this role automatically obtain mandatory write permissions for all attributes corresponding to the micro steps of this state (cf. Fig. 14.5). Hence, these users own mandatory write permissions (indicated by *MW* in the respective cell of the table) for attributes *Proposal, Appraisal, Refusal,* and *Reason.* Finally, for all other attributes respective users own read permissions in state *handed out* (indicated by *R* in the respective cells of the authorization table).

In order to enable access control at a fine-grained level, PAIS engineers may adjust the generated authorization table (see Fig. 14.9 for an example); e.g., it may be desired that during the execution of a mandatory activity, users should be also allowed to optionally write certain object attributes although these are not related to micro steps of the current micro state. To realize this feature, PHILharmonicFlows allows customizing automatically created authorization tables in respect to selected object attributes. Even if no mandatory activity is assigned to a user, it must be possible to grant him execution rights for optional activities taking a *data-oriented view.* Note that this allows users, who are not involved in the execution of a micro process instance and its mandatory activities, to read or write selected object attributes. Since permissions can be also restricted to specific micro states, it further becomes possible to make the access to optional activities dependent on the current state of the micro process instance.

Not every user who is allowed to write the attribute values required in a particular micro state should be forced to execute a corresponding mandatory activity. To differentiate between user assignment (i.e., activities a user *must* do) and authorization (i.e., activities a user *may* do), a distinction is made between *mandatory* and *optional* write permissions. Only for users with mandatory permissions, a mandatory activity is assigned to their worklist.

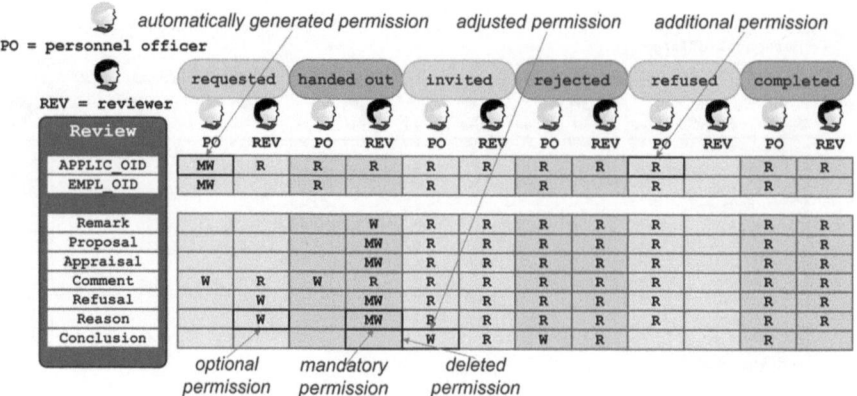

Fig. 14.9 Adjusted authorization table for the *review* object type

Example 14.18 (Adjusting Permissions in an Authorization Table). For user role *reviewer*, a read permission was automatically generated for attribute *Remark* (cf. Fig. 14.8). This permission can be transformed into an optional write permission if desired. Thus, in addition to her mandatory write permissions, the *reviewer* is allowed to optionally write attribute *Remark* (cf. Fig. 14.9). In turn, the user role *personnel officer* may optionally read *reviews* having reached an end state—to enable this, a respective permission is added to the authorization table (cf. Fig. 14.9). Finally, due to the assignment of role *reviewer* to state *handed out*, users with this role automatically obtain read permissions in this state. However, assume that they should not be allowed to read attribute *Conclusion*. In this case, the corresponding read permission must be *deleted* from the initially generated authorization table (cf. Fig. 14.8).

14.5.2 Automatic Generation of Form-Based Activities

On the one hand, a generated authorization table constitutes the basis for controlling access to object-aware processes and related object attributes. On the other hand, it provides the basis for automatically and dynamically generating user-specific activity forms during run-time (cf. Fig. 14.10). Such dynamically generated forms contain (editable) input fields for those object attributes for which the respective user (role) has the permission to write them in the current state of the micro process instance (*form-based activities*). Similarly, a *data-oriented view* is created, e.g., by providing overview tables for each object type listing its corresponding object

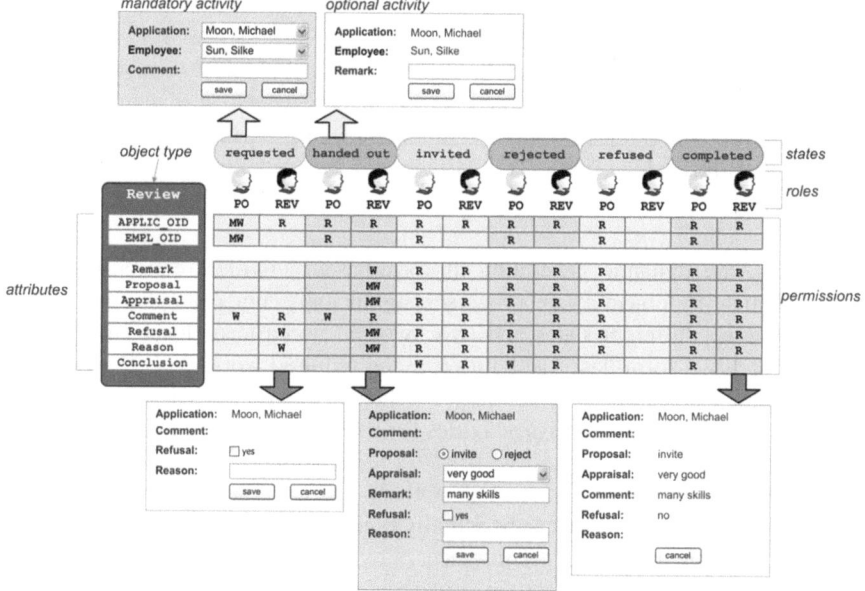

Fig. 14.10 Automatic generation of form-based activities

instances. Based on such overview tables, optional activities—both form-based and black-box activities—may be invoked on a selected object instance (*data-oriented view*).

Since for object type *Review* six different states are defined (cf. Fig. 14.10), in principle, for each involved user role six different form-based activities can be generated. Obviously, doing this manually would be a tedious and error-prone task.

Process instances and activities, in which authorized users are involved, are not strictly linked to each other. In particular, it is possible to execute a particular activity (i.e., a form) in relation to a collection of object instances of the same object type (i.e., *batch activity*). Entered attribute values are then assigned to all selected object instances in one go. Finally, a user may invoke additional object instances of different (i.e., related) types; i.e., he may want to perform a *context-sensitive activity* (cf. Chap. 13). For generating the corresponding activity, the currently enabled micro states of the considered object instances and the permissions assigned to the users in these particular states are considered.

> *Example 14.19 (Batch and Context-sensitive Activities).* An *employee* may want to reject several *Applications* in one go. For this purpose, a *batch activity* is required assigning value *reject* to attribute *Decision* for each selected *Application* object instance. Consider now an activity referring to

an *Application* and a *Job* object instance. Assume that an *employee* wants to hire a certain *applicant* and fill the respective *Job* position at the same time. In particular, it should be possible to assign value *accept* to attribute *Decision* of an *Application* object instance, and value *true* for attribute *Occupied* of a *Job* object instance in one go (i.e., *context-sensitive activity*).

Overall, the dynamic generation of form-based activities reduces the effort for implementing object-aware processes significantly. For example, object type *Review* has six different states and two involved user roles, Hence, in total, 12 instance-specific, form-based activities may be required worst case. Furthermore, an *Application* object instance comprises 5 states. Potentially, there are 120 (= 5 * 2 12) different context-sensitive activities for a *Review* including its corresponding *Application*.

The decision whether a particular state of a micro process instance can be reached (i.e., which activities can be actually executed) also depends on the progress of other (related) micro process instances; i.e., the execution of a micro process instance must be blocked in certain situations until other micro process instances reach certain states. The handling of such interdependencies between micro process instances constitutes a fundamental feature of the PHILharmonicFlows framework as will be discussed in Sect. 14.6.

14.6   Macro Processes

A business process generally involves multiple object instances of the same or different type. In PHILharmonicFlows, such multi-object processes are modeled by means of *macro processes*. As opposed to a *micro process* that defines the behavior of the object instances related to a particular object type, a *macro process* specifies *object interactions*; i.e., the interdependencies that may exist between object instances of the same or different type. Since each object instance is associated with a micro process instance, complex, and large *process structures* covering multiple object instances as well as their interactions emerge during run-time.

Existing approaches enable process coordination either without considering the underlying data structure at all [7], or by only considering direct object relations [225,226,252,253]; i.e., coordination support is solely provided for object instances directly related to each other. In addition to this, the diverse relationships that may exist between object instances of different type must be considered; i.e., the execution of micro process instances may have to be coordinated even if no direct relation between the corresponding object instances exists. For example, micro process instances related to *Interview* objects must be coordinated with those corresponding to *Review* objects. In this context, a particular challenge is enabling

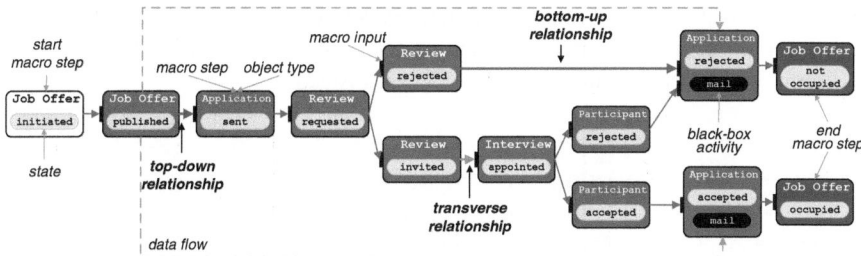

Fig. 14.11 Example of a macro process type

a flexible coordination of micro process instances, although their execution is based on a data-driven paradigm. In particular, the dynamically evolving number of object instances and their asynchronous execution must be taken into account. Note that both micro processes and macro processes are defined and executed based on data; i.e., object types, object attributes, and object states.

14.6.1   Basic Elements

A process structure may comprise dozens or even hundreds of micro process instances together with their numerous interdependencies [223, 226]. To hide this complexity from process engineers and end-users, PHILharmonicFlows allows defining *macro process types* in an aggregated and compact manner. As illustrated in Fig. 14.11, at the type level, a *macro process* consists of *macro steps* and *macro transitions*. A macro step *ot(s)* refers to an object type *ot* and a state *s* of this object type (i.e., a state of its micro process type). As opposed to micro processes whose definition is based on object attributes, the definition of a macro process refers to object types. In this context, the *states* defined by micro process types provide the basis for coordination. At run-time, a particular macro step *ot(s)* represents exactly those object instances of type *ot* whose corresponding micro process instances are in state *s*. Furthermore, to express the dependencies between micro states belonging to micro process instances of different type, macro steps may be connected using *macro transitions* (i.e., these transitions express *object interactions*). For example, consider the macro transition describing a dependency between *job Offers* in state *published* and *applications* in state *sent* (cf. Fig. 14.11).

Both parallel and alternative execution paths can be defined for a macro process. Each *macro step* comprises one or several *macro inputs*. Each *macro transition* then connects a macro step with a macro input of its target macro step. Such a macro input may have more than one incoming macro transition. Whether a particular macro step can be reached during run-time then depends on the activation of its macro inputs. More precisely, a macro step will be only enabled if at least one of its macro inputs becomes activated, i.e., all incoming macro transitions of this macro input are fired. Based on this semantics, alternative and parallel execution paths can be expressed. We omit formal details and present an example instead.

Example 14.20 (Macro Process). Figure 14.11 depicts an example of a macro process. The *Job Offer* must first be *initiated* and *published*. *Applicants* may then send their *Application*. Following this, a *personnel officer* needs to request *Reviews* for each *Application*. If all *reviewers* recommend *rejecting* the *applicant*, the *Application* will be *rejected*. By contrast, if at least one *reviewer* proposes to *invite* the *applicant*, an *Interview* will be arranged. Subsequent activities depend on the proposed actions of the participants.

The semantics of the depicted kinds of relationships (top-down, bottom-up, transverse) is explained below.

As previously mentioned, a macro step will be reached if one of its macro inputs becomes activated; i.e., all incoming macro transitions of this macro input are fired. In turn, whether a particular *macro transition* is fired at run-time, depends on its semantics as well as the object instances related to its source macro step. The semantics of a macro transition is defined by the semantic relationship between the object type of its source macro step and the one of its target macro step (top-down, bottom-up, transverse)—note that this relationship can be directly derived from the given data model (cf. Sect. 14.3). Depending on the present semantics, a particular *coordination component* is chosen to coordinate the execution of the micro process instances related to the object instances of the source and target macro states of the macro transition . More precisely, for each *top-down* relationship, a *process context* must be established, while *bottom-up* relationships require an *aggregation component*. In turn, for relationships of type *transverse*, a *transverse coordination component* must be provided. This will be explained in the following sections.

14.6.2 Process Context Coordination Component

A macro transition for which the object types of its source and target macro steps have a *top-down relationship*, must be associated with a *process context*.

Example 14.21 (Macro Transition Corresponding to a Top-Down Relationship). Consider the macro transition between macro steps *Job Offer(published)* and *Application(sent)* as depicted in Fig. 14.12 (see also Fig. 14.11 for the entire macro process). Since there is a top-down relationship

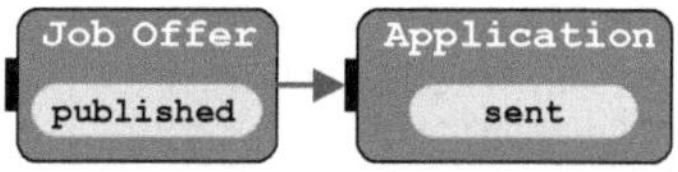

Fig. 14.12 Macro transition
corresponding to a top-down
relationship

Fig. 14.13 Process context

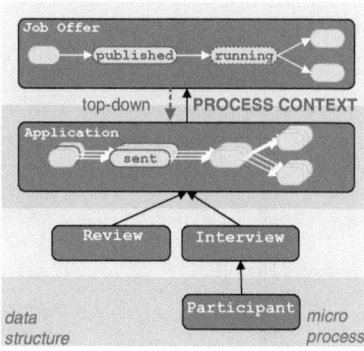

between object types *Job Offer* and *Application* (i.e., *Job Offer* is a higher-level object type compared to *Application*), a *process context* must be defined for this macro transition.

A *process context* refers to one or several states of a higher-level micro process instance. Based on such a process context, the execution of several lower-level micro process instances can be coordinated with the one of the higher-level micro process instance (see Fig. 14.13 for an illustration). More precisely, whether a lower-level micro process instance may reach the state corresponding to the target macro step of the given macro transition depends on the state of the higher-level micro process instance (i.e., the state of the source macro step). In turn, this state is added to the process context of the macro transition. Furthermore, the process context may comprise additional states of the higher-level micro process instance. This way, a more asynchronous execution of different micro process instances becomes possible.

Example 14.22 (Process Context). An *applicant* may only send an *Application* if the respective *Job Offer* is either *published* or *running* (cf. Fig. 14.13). Hence, these two states are added to the process context of the macro transition.

Fig. 14.14 Macro transition
corresponding to a bottom-up
relationship

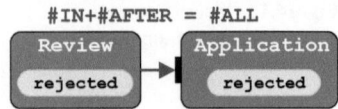

Fig. 14.15 Aggregation

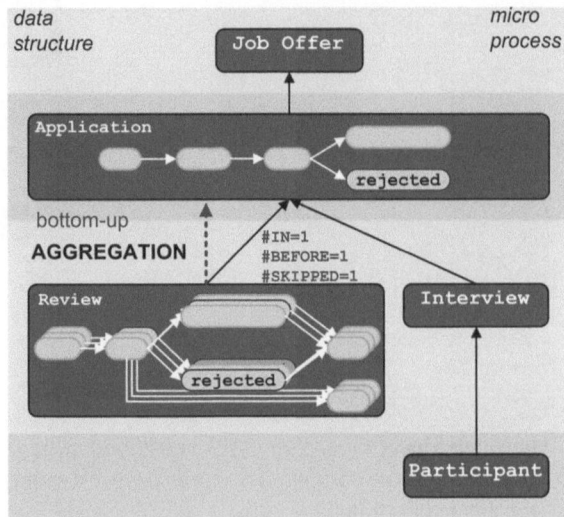

14.6.3   Aggregation Coordination Component

A macro transition for which the object types of its source and target macro steps
have a *bottom-up relationship*, must be associated with an *aggregation coordination
component*.

> *Example 14.23 (Macro Transition Corresponding to a Bottom-Up Relation-
> ship).* Consider the macro transition between macro steps *Review(rejected)*
> and *Application(rejected)* as depicted in Fig. 14.14. Since there is a bottom-
> up relationship between object types *Review* and *Application*, an *aggregation*
> component is required for coordinating the processing of the lower-level
> object instances with the higher-level one.

Aggregations constitute another fundamental concept for coordinating micro process instances. Compared to the previously mentioned process context, aggregations
work the other way around; i.e., the execution of a higher-level micro process
instance is coordinated with the one of related lower-level micro process instances.
As illustrated in Fig. 14.15, whether the higher-level micro process instance may

#ALL	Total number of corresponding lower-level micro process instances.
#BEFORE	Number of corresponding lower-level micro process instances for which the state specified in the source macro step is not enabled. However, it is still possible to enable this state later on.
#IN	Number of corresponding lower-level micro process instances for which the state specified in the source macro step is enabled.
#AFTER	Number of corresponding lower-level micro process instances for which the state specified in the source macro step is not enabled. However, the state was enabled before.
#SKIPPED	Number of corresponding lower-level micro process instances for which the state specified in the source macro step is not enabled. Here, it is not possible to enable the state later on; i.e., an alternative execution path was taken.

Fig. 14.16 Counters of an aggregation

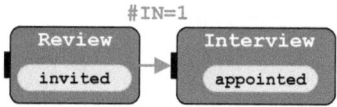

Fig. 14.17 Macro transition corresponding to a transverse relationship

reach the state corresponding to the target macro step (of the macro transition) depends on the states of related lower-level micro processes instances (i.e., micro process instances corresponding to the source macro step of the macro transition; see Example 14.24). For this purpose, an aggregated view on lower-level micro process instances is provided. Finally, to get an overview on how far the lower-lever micro process instances have proceeded in respect to the state belonging to the source macro step, each macro step is associated with the counters depicted in Fig. 14.16.

Example 14.24 (Aggregation). An *Application* may only be *rejected* if all *Reviews* propose to *reject* the *applicant*. In this context, completed *Reviews* corresponding to an *Application* are also considered.

14.6.4 Transverse Coordination Component

A macro transition for which the object types of its source and target macro steps have a *transverse relationship*, must be associated with a *transverse coordination component*.

Example 14.25 (Macro Transition Corresponding to a Transverse Relationship). Consider the macro transition between macro steps *Review(invited)* and *Interview(appointed)* in Fig. 14.17. Since there exists a transverse rela-

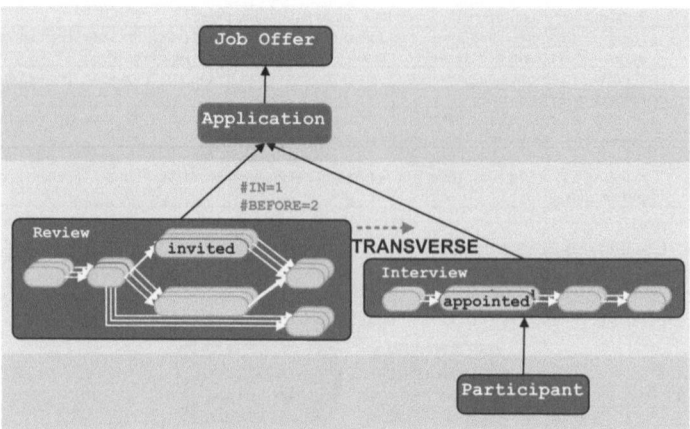

Fig. 14.18 Transverse coordination component

tionship between object types *Review* and *Interview*, a *transverse* coordination component is required for coordinating the corresponding micro process instances.

Transverse coordination components describe a dependency between a micro process instance corresponding to the target macro step, and a number of micro process instances corresponding to the source macro step (cf. Fig. 14.18). In particular, an aggregation is evaluated in respect to a common higher-level micro process instance.

Example 14.26 (Transverse Coordination Component). Consider Fig. 14.17. It is only possible to *appoint* a date for an *Interview* if at least one *Review* proposes to *invite* the *applicant*.

14.6.5 Integrating Black-Box Activities

As illustrated in Fig. 14.11, a black-box activity with multiple object instances as input can be added to a macro process type by assigning it to a corresponding macro step. A black-box activity enables complex computations as well as the integration of application services (e.g., sending e-mails or invoking web services). Furthermore, it is possible to consider semantic data relations between the different input parameters (i.e., object instances) of a black-box activity. For example, consider the data flow dependency illustrated in Fig. 14.11.

> *Example 14.27 (Black-box Activity).* If an *Application* is *rejected* or *accepted*, the corresponding *applicant* receives a notifying *mail*. This *mail* should include information about the corresponding *Job Offer* to which the *applicant* referred (cf. Fig. 14.11).

14.6.6   Further Aspects

During the execution of a large process structure, *deadlock* situations might occur. For example, consider a process context referring to states that belong to a skipped path. Since individual micro process instances are executed asynchronously, aggregation predicates might then never evaluate to *true*. Hence, deadlock situations cannot always be prevented (cf. Example 14.28). The described framework does not exclude such a modeling in all cases since there are real-world scenarios requiring respective coordination constraints. In particular, deadlocks also occur in real-life situations. For this reason, a detection algorithm for identifying deadlocks is provided. These deadlocks are then visualized and users are assisted in dissolving them.

> *Example 14.28 (Deadlock).* If all *reviewers refuse* providing a *Review*, the execution of the micro process instance related to the *Application* is blocked.

If a higher-level micro process instance terminates (i.e., it reaches an end state), all lower-level micro process instances, which have not yet reached an end state, must be determined. We denote these as *bypassed micro process instances*. For dealing with such bypassed instances, different kinds of exception handlers exist; e.g., the respective micro process instances can be skipped or be reassigned to another higher-level micro process instance. This way, correct termination of all micro process instances within a process structure is ensured.

> *Example 14.29 (Bypassed Micro Process Instance).* If an *Application* is *accepted*, the corresponding *Job Offer* is *occupied*. All other *Applications*

referring to the respective *Job Offer* must then be determined and handled in a specific manner (e.g., by assigning them to another *Job Offer* or by skipping them).

Overall, a macro process enables the modeling of large business processes, but abstracts from the complex process structure underlying them. Using the introduced counters and abstraction mechanisms, at run-time, a macro process serves as an advanced monitoring facility that provides an abstracted view of the complex process structure under execution. Finally, whether or not mandatory activities from a particular micro process instance will be actually assigned to user worklists not only depends on the progress of this micro process instance, but also on the coordination components in which this micro process instance is involved. Hence, a coordinated execution of a collection of related micro process instances becomes possible.

14.7   Discussion

PHILharmonicFlows provides a comprehensive framework that covers the characteristics of object-aware processes, i.e., object behavior, object interactions, data-driven process execution, variable granularity of activities, and integrated access to business processes and business data. While object behavior is captured through micro processes, object interactions are modeled by means of macro processes. In turn, a data-driven execution of micro processes is based on micro steps and related object attribute changes. Since states constitute abstractions of micro steps, the execution of macro processes is also data-driven. Furthermore, varying levels of activity granularities may be chosen during run-time, depending on user preferences. Finally, both process- and data-oriented views are provided to end-users, enabling flexible and integrated access to process and data.

A powerful proof-of-concept prototype of both the build-time and the run-time components exists. It implements the basic concepts introduced in this chapter. Example 14.30 illustrates the build-time component using a simple process example.

Example 14.30 (PHILharmonicFlows: Build-time Component). Consider the online shop *Bricolage* that enables business owners to sell their products. The considered process includes several steps, ranging from the selling of products to their delivery to customers. Figure 14.19 depicts the corresponding data model as it can be created with the build-time component of

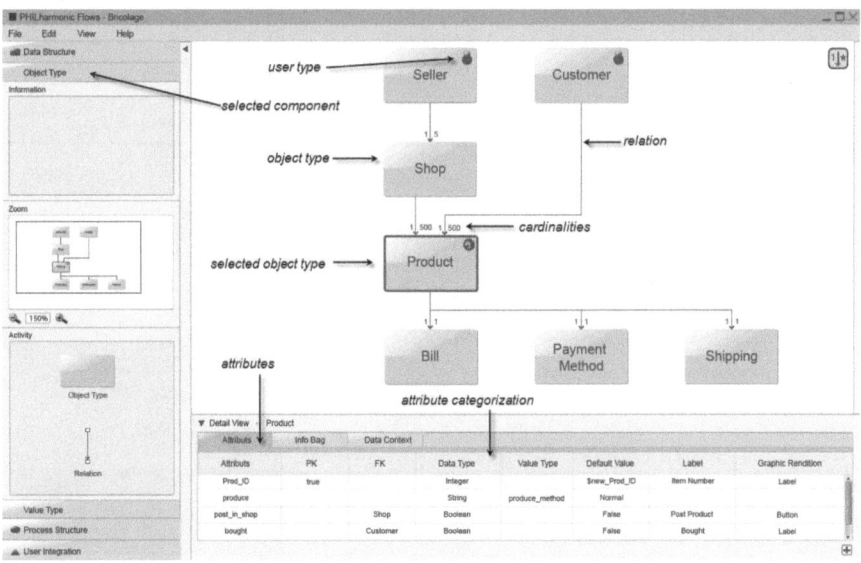

Fig. 14.19 Build-time component: creating a data model

> PHILharmonicFlows. Altogether, this data model consists of seven object types. Furthermore, the micro process corresponding to object type *Product* (cf. Fig. 14.20) comprises a number of states for adding a product to the shop, ordering this product, and shipping it to the customer. Finally, cancelation of an order is also covered by the micro process.

PHILharmonicFlows was applied to processes from different areas, like human resource management, patient treatment, e-commerce, and house building [64, 158]. Overall, respective case studies have proven the benefits of object-aware process management as discussed in Chap. 13. Furthermore, these studies have emphasized the high potential offered by this user- and data-driven paradigm when compared to activity-centric approaches. However, it also has become evident that further developments are required in order to achieve the same level of maturity as for the approaches presented in Part II and Part III of this book.

First, a comprehensive modeling methodology is required, which governs users in designing, implementing, verifying, and testing object-aware processes. In this context, specific modeling and adaptation patterns, correctness notions, compliance rules, and verification techniques for object-aware processes are required. Similar to activity-centric process models, for example, well-defined soundness criteria guaranteeing for the proper and correct execution of micro and macro processes at run-time must be provided. Furthermore, advanced verification techniques must

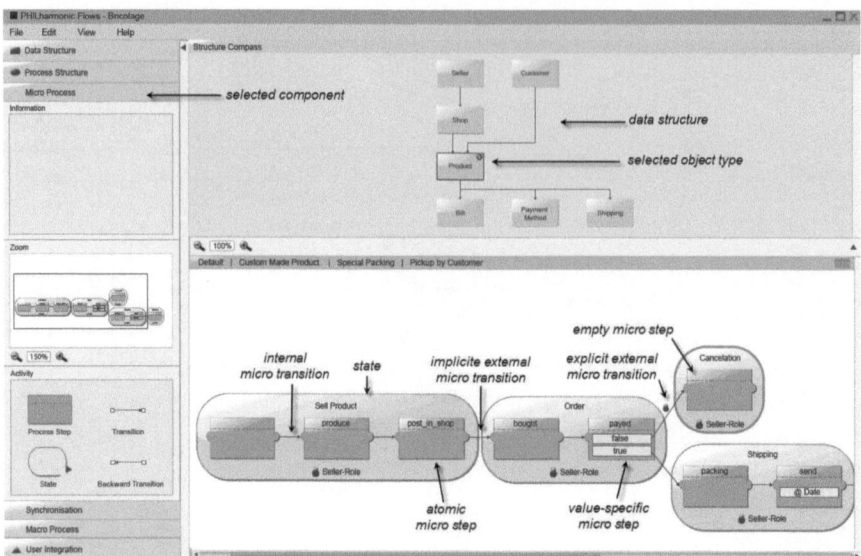

Fig. 14.20 Build-time component: creating a micro process

be developed, taking structural and behavioral soundness (cf. Chap. 4) as well as business process compliance (cf. Chap. 10) into account. Note that the tight integration of processes, data, and users offers promising perspectives in respect to these issues, but also significantly increases complexity compared to activity-centric process models with their strong focus on the behavior perspective. Regarding the run-time support of object-aware processes, in addition, traceability, variability, and flexibility constitute future challenges.

Obviously, the described characteristics of object-aware processes (e.g., variable activity granularities and data-driven process execution) foster process flexibility and reduce the effort for exception handling and ad hoc changes. Still, there might be situations requiring ad hoc changes of object-aware processes during run-time. For example, a low-quality review may have to be replaced by an ad hoc review, an attribute added to one particular object instance, or a micro state deleted for a micro process instance. Furthermore, a PAIS enabling object-aware processes evolves over time, e.g., object types may have to be added, changed, or deleted, object behavior or object interactions changed, and permissions for accessing processes and data adapted. Hence, techniques for evolving the different artifacts (e.g., micro and macro processes, data models, authorization tables) of object-aware processes over time must be provided. As with activity-centric approaches, a particular challenge will be correctly and efficiently migrating running process instances to an updated schema of an object-aware process.

14.8 Summary

PHILharmonicFlows supports the definition of processes, data, and users in separate, but integrated models. Thus, it retains the well-established principle for
separation of concerns. As opposed to existing approaches, it explicitly considers the relationships between processes, functions, data, and users. Furthermore,
PHILharmonicFlows addresses process modeling, execution, and monitoring, and it
provides generic services for the model-driven generation of end user components
(e.g., form-based activities). Opposed to the approaches described in Chap. 13, it
further covers all components of the underlying data structure; i.e., objects, object
relations, and object attributes. For this purpose, the modeling of processes is
based on different levels of granularity. In particular, object behavior is based on
states with data-driven process execution. Finally, advanced support for process
coordination as well as for the integrated access to business processes, functions,
and data is provided.

Exercises

14.1. Properties of Object-Aware Processes

Describe how the major characteristics of object-aware processes (i.e., object
behavior, object interactions, data-driven execution, variable activity granularity,
and integrated access to business processes and business data) have been realized
in the PHILharmonicFlows framework!

14.2. Micro Processes

A micro process type captures the behavior of a specific object type:

(a) Define a micro process type for the object type *Application* depicted in
    Fig. 14.3.
(b) Explain the relationship between micro step and object attribute, and the
    relationship between micro step and micro state?
(c) Discuss the benefits resulting from the introduction of states at the micro
    process level?
(d) Explain the difference between explicit and implicit external micro transitions.
    Why are both kinds of external micro transitions needed?

14.3. Micro Processes vs. Case Handling

What are commonalities and differences between a *micro process type* and a *case
type* (cf. Chap. 13)?

14.4. Process and Data Integration

(a) What kind of information is captured in an authorization table?
(b) Describe how an initial authorization table can be automatically derived?
    Which information is required in this context?

(c) When does an automatically created authorization table have to be adjusted?
(d) Which role do optional activities play in the context of process and data authorization?

14.5. Form-Based Activities

(a) Why is the manual design and implementation of form-based activities a tedious and time-consuming task in the context of object-aware processes?
(b) How is the internal flow logic of a form-based activity captured in a micro process?
(c) Based on which information can form-based activities be automatically generated?

14.6. Macro Processes

(a) How do macro processes ease the monitoring of large process structures?
(b) How is the relation between a macro process and a corresponding data model?
(c) Discuss the different kinds of macro transitions and their semantics?

Part V
Technologies Enabling Flexibility Support in Process-Aware Information Systems

Chapter 15
AristaFlow BPM Suite

Abstract In dynamic environments, it becomes necessary to quickly implement new business processes, to allow for ad hoc deviations from prespecified processes, and to enable controlled process evolution over time. These fundamental features should be provided by any PAISs without affecting the correctness and soundness of the processes it implements. This chapter presents the AristaFlow BPM Suite—an adaptive PAIS that addresses these challenges. It has originated from the ADEPT research projects. Its overall vision is to provide next generation process management technology for the flexible support of dynamic processes along the process lifecycle. Due to its generic services and application programming interfaces, the AristaFlow BPM Suite can be applied to a variety of applications from different domains.

15.1 Introduction

During the last decade, the ADEPT process management technology was developed [70, 255, 269]. Basically, it realizes the concepts and features described in Chaps. 6–10 in an integrated manner. ADEPT provides advanced process modeling concepts for capturing the different perspectives of a business process in a prespecified process model (cf. Chap. 2). Among others, such a process model includes information about process activities, the control and data flow between them, actor assignments of atomic activities, temporal constraints, and required resources. Furthermore, processes can be implemented in a "plug and play" style, ensuring correctness and soundness of the composed process models.

From the beginning, the goal of the ADEPT project was to design a technology being able to flexibly cope with exceptions and to dynamically adapt process instances at run-time. With ADEPT1, a first prototype of this technology was released in 1998 [132, 265, 269]. In particular, ADEPT1 supported the specification, verification, and execution of correct and sound process models (cf. Chap. 4), as well as ad hoc changes of single process instances (cf. Chap. 7). The latter could

M. Reichert and B. Weber, *Enabling Flexibility in Process-Aware Information Systems*, 441
DOI 10.1007/978-3-642-30409-5_15, © Springer-Verlag Berlin Heidelberg 2012

be applied without affecting PAIS robustness [259, 260]; i.e., without violating any of the correctness and soundness properties guaranteed through formal checks at build-time.

Since ADEPT1 provided an open application programming interface, it served as platform for supporting highly dynamic processes in domains like health care, logistics, and e-commerce [43, 44, 230, 231]. In these projects, however, it became obvious that services provided by a PAIS need to be seamlessly integrated into the existing IT infrastructure. To tackle this challenge, the ADEPT2 project was launched in 2004 [70, 261, 271]. Its goal was to develop generic concepts and services of a next generation process management technology that fosters this integration. In particular, ADEPT2 focused on the *ease of use* of its process support features as well as the provision of a high degree of *flexibility* to all user groups involved in the specification, implementation, execution, adaptation, and evolution of processes. One of the most innovative features provided by ADEPT2, in addition to those adopted from ADEPT1, was its ability to migrate running process instances to a new process model version [282, 290] (cf. Chap. 9). Complementary to the these projects, specific aspects were investigated in the research projects MinAdept and SeaFlows. While MinAdept [120, 185, 186] developed advanced techniques for min-ing flexible processes (cf. Chap. 8), SeaFlows [195, 200] investigated how business process compliance can be ensured in the different phases of the process lifecycle (cf. Chap. 10). In both projects, advanced prototypes were built based on ADEPT2.

The great interest in the previously mentioned features triggered the development of the *AristaFlow BPM Suite* in 2008. The goal was to transfer the innova-tive concept developed in the ADEPT projects into an industrial-strength PAIS [168, 169, 264]. In addition, the AristaFlow BPM Suite provides advanced tech-niques for *enterprise application integration* as well as for integrating process support services into existing application suites. This chapter takes a simple process scenario in order to illustrate some of the core features provided by the AristaFlow BPM Suite. Section 15.2 considers the perspective of different user groups regarding the handling of exceptions and errors. For example, it is shown how ad hoc changes may be applied by system supervisors to cope with exceptions and errors. Following this, Sect. 15.3 sketches the architecture of the AristaFlow BPM Suite and Sect. 15.4 reports on its use in different case studies. The chapter closes with a summary in Sect. 15.5.

15.2   Handling Errors and Exceptions in AristaFlow

15.2.1   Illustrating Application Scenario

Example 15.1 presents a scenario that will be used throughout this chapter to illustrate how exceptions and errors can be flexibly handled in the AristaFlow BPM Suite.

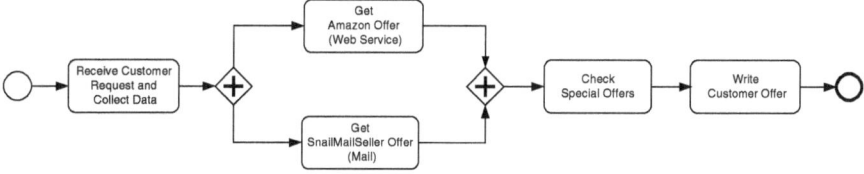

Fig. 15.1 Prespecified process model of an online book store

Example 15.1 (Online Book Store). Consider the prespecified process model
of an online book store as depicted in Fig. 15.1. First, a customer request is
entered and required data is collected (activity *Receive Customer Request and
Collect Data*). Following this, the bookseller requests alternative offers (i.e.,
pricing quotes) from two suppliers. On one hand, he asks for an offer from
Amazon by invoking a corresponding web service (activity *Get Amazon Offer
(Web Service)*). On the other hand, he asks for an offer from a second vendor
(*SnailMailSeller*) by contacting him via e-mail (activity *Get SnailMailSeller
Offer (Mail)*). After having received the offers from the two suppliers, the
bookseller checks whether he can find a better offer for the requested books
in the Internet (activity *Check Special Offers*). Finally, he makes an offer for
the requested books to his customer (activity *Write Customer Offer*).

The scenario described in Example 15.1 contains several sources of potential
errors. While some of these errors can be detected or handled at build-time, this is
not possible for others. Example 15.2 illustrates different kinds of errors:

Example 15.2 (Sources of Error). Consider the scenario from Example 15.1.
Assume that the process implementer has not foreseen a way to enter the offer
from *SnailMailSeller* into the PAIS. In this case, activity *Write Customer
Offer* might fail or produce an invalid output since not all data objects
accessed by its input parameters have been written by preceding activities.
As discussed in Chap. 4, such missing data can be detected already at build-
time by respective data flow checks.
    Another source of error relates to the invocation of the Amazon web ser-
vice. In particular, this service might not be available when making the
request. Hence, activity *Get Amazon Offer* might fail during run-time. As
discussed in Chap. 6, respective errors can be foreseen; i.e., their handling
should be included in the prespecified process model at build-time.
    In the given scenario, unplanned exceptions and errors might occur as well.
For example, activity *Check Special Offers* might fail due to troubles with
the Internet connection, or a user might want to apply an ad hoc change to
deal with an unplanned situation, e.g., by dynamically adding an activity that
requests an offer from a third vendor.

15.2.2   Perspectives on the Handling of Exceptions and Errors

Picking up the scenario from Example 15.1, this section deals with the handling of different kinds of exceptions and errors (cf. Example 15.2) from the perspectives of the *process implementer*, the *system*, the *end-user*, the *system supervisor*, and the *process engineer*. For each of these parties, it is shown how it may be involved in the handling of exceptions and errors. We focus on those user groups dealing with the specification and execution of processes, but exclude other users interested in the analysis of processes at the business level (e.g. business analysts, business process owners).

15.2.2.1   Process Implementer Perspective

The *process implementer* is responsible for creating correct and sound process models. In addition, he must link complex activities with subprocess models and atomic activities with executable application services (e.g., user forms, web services, or Java components). To accomplish this task, appropriate services for implementing, configuring, and managing activities are required.

Process Modeling. Process models can be defined using the *AristaFlow Process Template Editor* (cf. Example 15.3).

> *Example 15.3 (AristaFlow Process Template Editor).* Consider Fig. 15.2 that shows parts of the process model from Fig. 15.1 as it can be defined with the *AristaFlow Process Template Editor*. Additionally, Fig. 15.2 depicts an extract of the data flow schema of this process model; e.g., data element *Customer Name* is read by activity *Write Customer Offer*.

Regarding the implementation of executable processes (i.e., prespecified process models whose activities are linked with executable application services and subprocess models respectively), the *AristaFlow Process Template Editor* pursues the idea of composing processes in a *"plug and play"* style. Furthermore, it realizes a *correctness-by-construction* principle by offering only those high-level change operations to the process implementer that allow transforming a correct and sound process model into another correct and sound model; i.e., change operations are enabled or disabled, depending on the change context (e.g., the reference nodes marked for an insert operation) [70]. Deficiencies not prohibited by this approach (e.g., missing data) are checked on-the-fly and are reported continuously in the problem window of the *Process Template Editor* (cf. Example 15.4). As a prerequisite for this, implicit data flow dependencies among the application services should be made known to the PAIS.

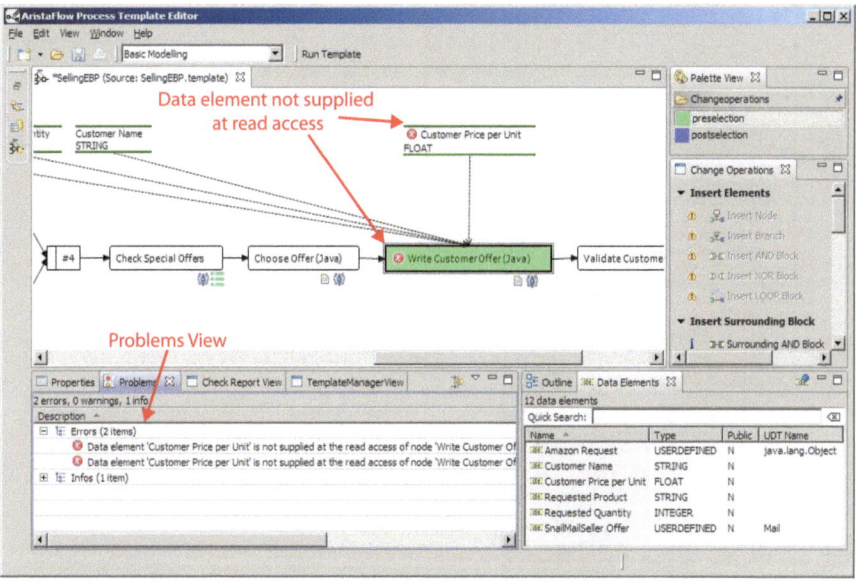

Fig. 15.2   AristaFlow process template editor

Example 15.4 (On-the-fly Correctness Checks). Consider Fig. 15.2. For the depicted process model, AristaFlow has detected that data element *Customer Price per Unit* is read by activity *Write Customer Offer* although this data element is not written by any preceding activities. Such deficiencies are highlighted to the *process implementer* who can then fix the error accordingly.

Activity Implementation and Configuration. Before application services (e.g., user forms, web services, and data access services) may be dragged and dropped to a process model, they have to be encapsulated and registered as *activity templates* in the *Activity Repository* (cf. Fig. 15.3). An activity template provides the information required by the *Process Template Editor* for composing application services in a *"plug and play"* style; e.g., information about input/output parameters of the application service or constraints regarding its execution (e.g., data dependencies on other application services). Furthermore, an activity template defines the execution properties of the corresponding application service; e.g., whether the service can be suspended, aborted, or compensated. An *application developer* who wants to introduce a new application service, therefore, first must create a corresponding activity template and specify its execution properties. He then implements the different operations of the application service, associates them with the activity template, and adds the latter to the *Activity Repository*.

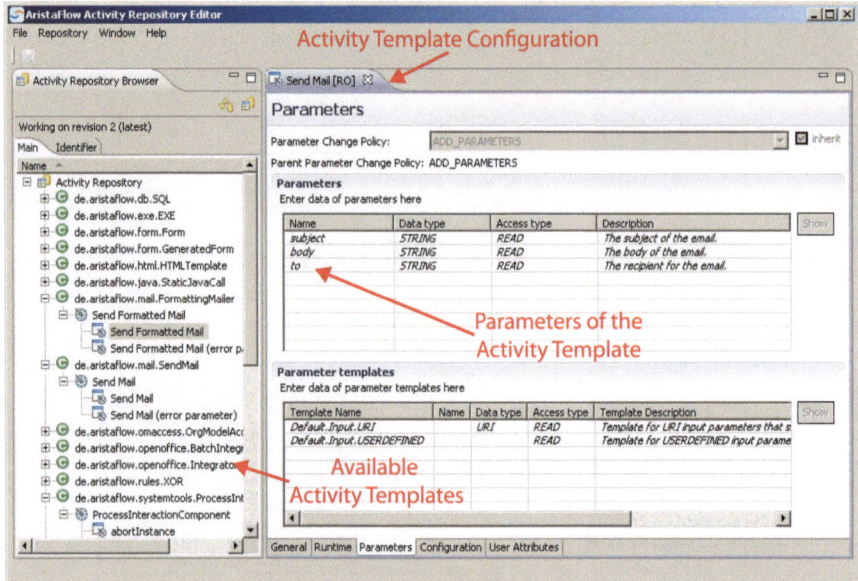

Fig. 15.3 Activity template configuration using the activity repository editor

The implementation of an activity template is usually a non-trivial task, especially if it shall not only be possible to invoke an application service during activity execution, but also to suspend, resume, abort, or undo this execution. To ease this task, AristaFlow provides different levels of abstraction when implementing an activity template. The lowest one is the *execution environment* that allows defining the concrete execution properties of the corresponding application service, as well as the operations one must implement such that it can properly interact with the run-time environment [263] (e.g., initialize, start, suspend, abort, or undo its execution). Usually, this should not be the task of an *application developer* and be accomplished by a *system implementer*. Depending on the intended use of an activity template, the system implementer will design the template in a rather generic or specific manner. Hence, more or less *configuration options* exist for process implementers when using an activity template. Examples 15.5 and 15.6 present two activity templates enabling web service invocation and database access.

Example 15.5 (Web Service Activity Templates). An activity template for invoking a web service may be completely pre-configured; e.g., its input/output parameters as well as its configuration and connection settings may be fully prespecified. When assigning the activity template to a process activity, the only task remaining for the *process implementer* then is to check

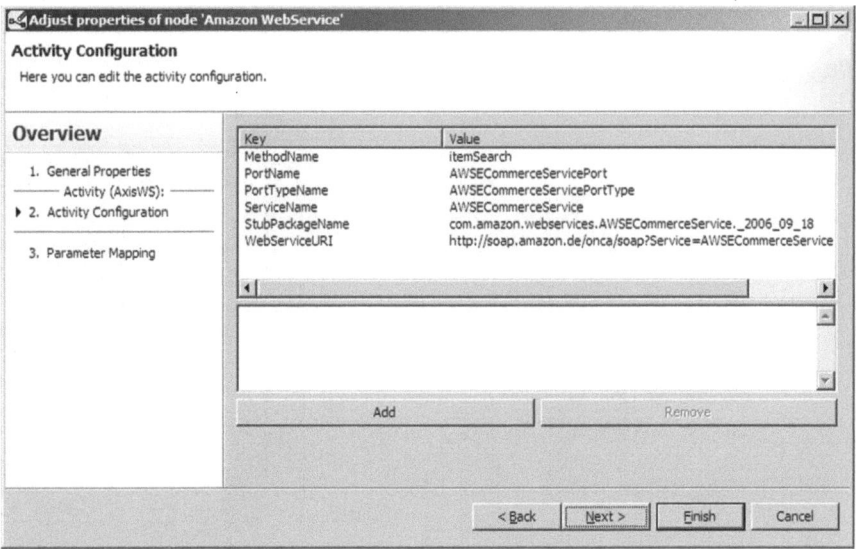

Fig. 15.4 Activity configuration of a generic web service activity template

whether the proposed mapping of activity parameters to process data elements is correct (cf. Chap. 4). A more generic activity template, however, would allow *process implementers* to specify connection and binding details of the web service (cf. Fig. 15.4) or even configure the number and types of its input/output parameters when assigning the activity template to a process model.

Example 15.6 (Database Activity Templates). A specific database activity template, for example, fixes the input/output parameters, the details of the database used, the connection parameters, and the fully prespecified SQL statement. In turn, a more generic database activity template would leave open the SQL statement, the number and types of input/output parameters, or the settings for the database connection (in parts or completely).

Activity templates provide a powerful basis for composing processes in a "plug and play" style. Given the *Process Template Editor* and the *Activity Repository*, the *process implementer* just drags and drops the activity templates from the *Activity Repository Browser* window of the *Process Template Editor* onto the desired location in the process model. Following this, he may set the not yet provided

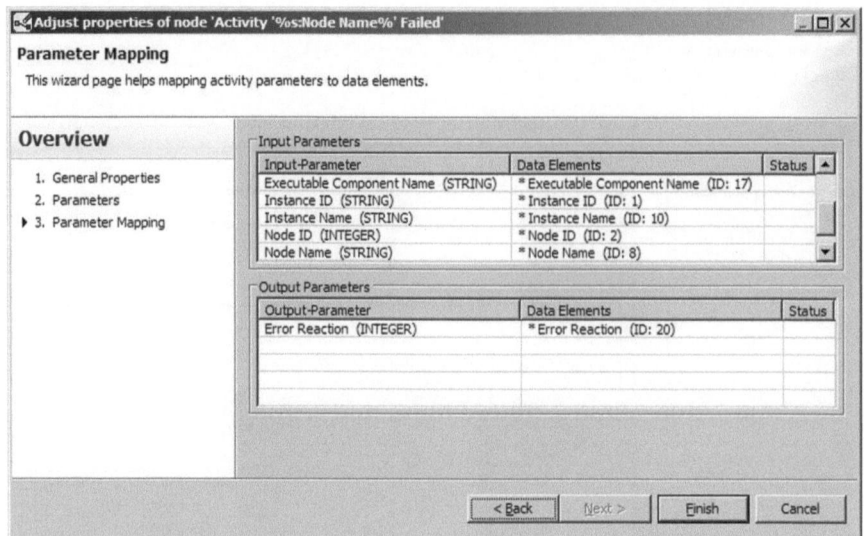

Fig. 15.5 Mapping activity parameters to process data elements

configuration values of the activity template. For this purpose, the configuration wizard of the activity template can be used (cf. Example 15.7).

Example 15.7 (Configuring Activity Templates). Assume that web service activity template will be used to implement a process step (cf. Example 15.5). The first page of the configuration wizard then fixes the required input/output parameters of the web service, the second one the settings of binding information of the web service (e.g., URL of the web service) (cf. Fig. 15.4), and the third one the mapping of activity parameters to process data elements (cf. Fig. 15.5).

As a major advantage of the described approach, common errors in the implementation of processes (e.g., missing data) can be avoided at build-time. Hence, the effort needed for testing and debugging implemented processes can be reduced.

Note that the *correctness-by-construction* principle and the automated checks supported by AristaFlow, allow ensuring structural and behavioral soundness of the process models (cf. Chap. 4). However, semantic errors (e.g., design errors) can not be completely detected through automated checks. Hence, AristaFlow also provides a powerful *Test Environment* that allows *process implementers* to test implemented processes prior to releasing and deploying them to the run-time environment. Using the *AristaFlow Test Client*, it is also possible to run only partially specified processes, i.e., not all activities need to have associated activity templates or staff assignment expressions may still be undefined. In case an activity has no assigned activity template, this test mode supports the process implementer with automatically generated forms that allow him to review the input parameters of the activity and to set its output parameters. In particular, this enables *process implementers* to get rapid feedback from end-users during process implementation.

15.2.2.2   System Perspective

Basically, the approach described in Sect. 15.2.2.1 ensures that released process models can be executed by the PAIS in an error-safe and robust manner. However, during run-time there might be also errors that can not be completely prevented.

> *Example 15.8 (Run-time Error).*   Again, consider the scenario from Fig. 15.1. The web service associated with activity *Get Amazon Offer* might not be available during process execution (e.g., due to network errors or a broken server) leading to an exception that needs to be handled at the process instance level.

Error situations as the one described in Example 15.8 can neither be detected in advance nor be prevented through build-time checks. However, failures of the Amazon web service might be anticipated by the *process implementer* (cf. Chap. 6). Thus, he can assign specific error-handling procedures to the respective activity. Applying a process-centric approach, AristaFlow allows running specific processes to handle errors and exceptions; i.e., it provides a *reflective* approach in which error handling itself can be based on a (normal) process instance whose execution is coordinated by the PAIS. A simple error-handling process is depicted in Fig. 15.6. Depending on whether the failure of the activity was triggered by the user (e.g., through an abort button) either the *system supervisor* is notified about the failure, or the process terminates silently. Generally, error-handling processes may be complex and long-running (e.g., comprising compensation activities and user interactions).

It is noteworthy that AristaFlow treats error-handling processes the same manner as other processes. Thus, an error-handling process may refer to arbitrary activities registered in the activity repository. In particular, this enables error handling at a high level of abstraction as well as the involvement of users if required. Furthermore, it is possible to assign an error-handling process to the activities of another error-handling process; i.e., it becomes possible to implement several layers of error handling that can be based on each other.

If an activity fails, its associated error-handling process is initiated and all data necessary to identify, classify, and handle the error are made available to this process. These data include the identifier of the failed activity and its responsible user, as well as the cause of the error (cf. Fig. 15.6).

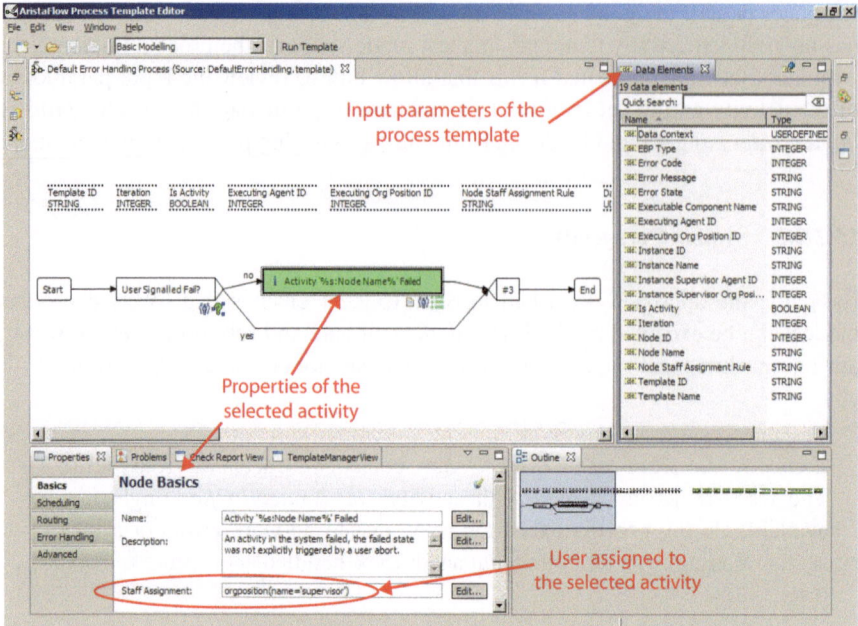

Fig. 15.6 A simple error-handling process

After releasing an error-handling process and deploying it to the PAIS run-time environment, it can be assigned to an activity template. Furthermore, it is not only possible to assign an error-handling process to single activities, but also to entire process models. The latter will be executed if a failed activity has no associated error-handling process (see also Chap. 6). In case neither the failed activity nor the process itself has a predefined error-handling process, a default error-handling process will be applied instead.

Specific error-handling processes can be realized using the described process template editor as well as standard techniques for handling errors (e.g., notification, abortion, and compensation). In particular, *process implementers* do not need to learn any new concepts to realize such error-handling processes. Finally, error-handling can be accomplished at a high level of abstraction, enabling more sophisticated error-handling strategies or ad hoc changes of the process instance being in trouble.

15.2.2.3 End-User Perspective

Simple error-handling processes like the one depicted in Fig. 15.6 are not always appropriate since they increase the workload of the *system supervisor*. In certain cases, activity failures can be also handled in a semi-automatic manner by the user

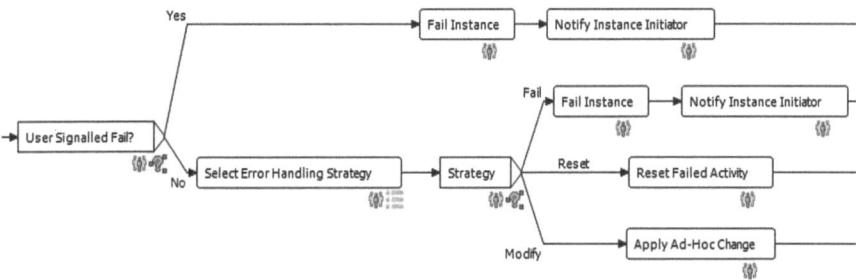

Fig. 15.7 A complex error-handling process involving the user

responsible for the activity. Upon an activity failure, this user is informed about the error-handling strategies he may choose from.

An example of a more complex error-handling process is depicted in Fig. 15.7. Here, the user may choose among several alternatives to handle an error: retrying the failed activity, aborting the entire process instance, or applying predefined changes to fix or compensate the error. Additional error-handling strategies may, for example, include the *escalation* of the respective case to a responsible supervisor or an inquiry involving a more advanced user who is experienced in how to handle the respective error. Finally, the error-handling strategies offered to a particular user may be predicated on his roles and capabilities as defined in the organization model of the PAIS. Hence, error handling can be accomplished in a dynamic and personalized manner.

To flexibly cope with exceptions and errors, end-users may also dynamically change a process instance. In this context, they may retrieve and reuse knowledge about previous ad hoc changes applied in a similar problem context [293, 355]. To express the semantics of ad hoc changes, memorize them, and reuse them in a similar problem context, case-based reasoning techniques are applied (cf. Chap. 7).

In summary, for each process activity a predefined set of possible error-handling strategies can be provided to users. Hence, users do not need to have detailed knowledge about the process to handle exceptions and errors appropriately. Instead, they are guided by the PAIS. This results in reduced waiting times in connection with failed activities since users can handle errors immediately on their own and do not have to wait for their busy help desk to accomplish this task.

15.2.2.4   System Supervisor Perspective

Certain errors and exceptions cannot be handled by the end-user. This applies, for example, to errors not foreseen at build-time, i.e., no prespecified process for error handling exists. In other situations, it might be not possible to handle errors in a standard manner. In such cases, the *system supervisor* should be notified about the error. For example, this can be done either through an automatic notification by

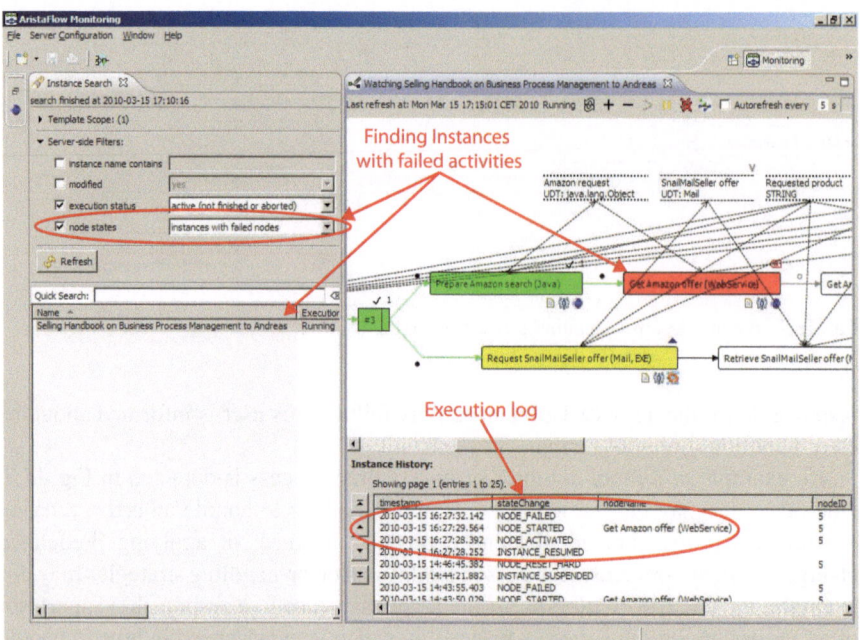

Fig. 15.8   AristaFlow process monitor: monitoring perspective of a system supervisor

the error-handling process or by a user calling the help desk by phone. The *system supervisor* can then use the *AristaFlow Process Monitor* (cf. Fig. 15.8) to identify the process being in trouble. This can be done either by using the process identifier provided by the error process or by applying specific filters to the list of known process instances (cf. Fig. 15.8). For example, relevant process instances can be identified by searching for active process instances with failed activities. Next, the *system supervisor* can take a look at the process instance being in trouble, analyze its execution log, and make a decision about appropriate error-handling measures (cf. Example 15.9). Apart from this, the *system supervisor* can use the *Process Monitor* to keep track of process instances with failed activities. For example, the system supervisor may intervene if a web service becomes unavailable and hence activities of different process instances that refer to this web service can not be invoked for a longer period of time.

Example 15.9 (Error Handling by a System Supervisor).   Consider again the bookseller example from Fig. 15.1. Assume that a process instance wants to issue a request for a book using Amazon's web service facilities, but then fails in doing so. The *system supervisor* detects that the process is in trouble and uses the *Process Monitor* to take a look at this process instance (cf.

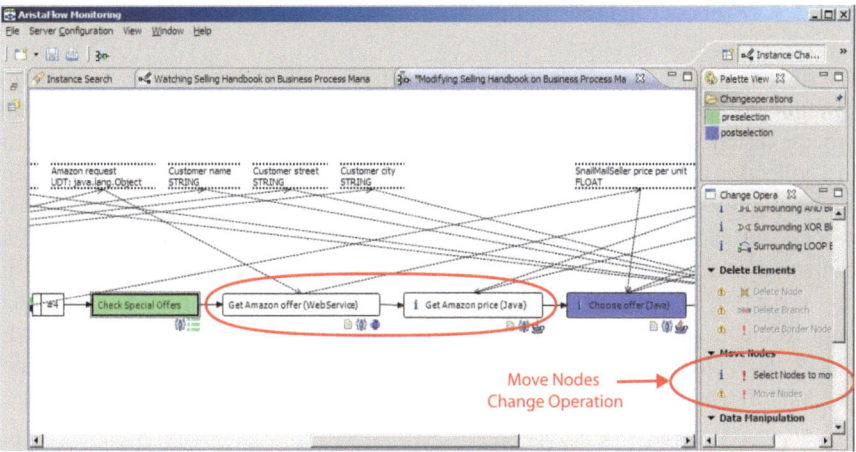

Fig. 15.9   AristaFlow process monitor: instance change perspective

Fig. 15.8). Analyzing its execution log he detects that the execution of an activity failed because the connection to Amazon could not be established. Assume that he considers this as a temporary problem and just resets the activity such that it can be repeated once again. Additionally, he takes a short look at the process instance and its data dependencies, and realizes that the results of the failed activity and its succeeding activity are only needed for executing activity *Choose Offer*. Therefore, he moves these two activities to the position following activity *Check Special Offers* in the process instance; i.e., he performs an ad hoc change of this process instance (cf. Chap. 7). In particular, this allows the user to continue working on this process instance even if the PAIS is unable to immediately reconnect to Amazon (cf. Fig. 15.9).

To accomplish this ad hoc change, the system supervisor switches to the *Instance Change Perspective* of the *Process Monitor*, which provides the same set of change operations as the *Process Template Editor*. In fact, the *Instance Change Perspective* is the *Process Template Editor*, which is aware that a process instance has been loaded and state information must therefore be taken into account when enabling/disabling change operations and applying correctness checks (cf. Chap. 7). The system supervisor then moves the two activities to their new position by applying the respective change operation. The resulting process instance is depicted in Fig. 15.9.

Assume now that the connection problem lasts longer than expected and the user wants to call Amazon by phone to get the price that way. In this case, he would ask the *system supervisor* to delete the activities being in trouble and to replace them with a form-based activity that allows entering the price manually. Note that ad hoc changes provide the means to realize such advanced error-handling processes.

15.2.2.5   Process Engineer Perspective

As shown in Example 15.9, certain exceptions and errors can be handled by dynamically adapting the corresponding process instance. When considering the process instances of a particular type, respective model adaptations typically result in a collection of process instance variants derived from the same process model, but which slightly differ in their structure. AristaFlow fosters learning from respective process instance changes in order to discover an improved process model that can serve as a reference for future process instances. The techniques applied in this context have been described in Chap. 8. Finally, after identifying potential improvements, the process engineer may trigger a process model evolution. In this context, already running instances may be migrated to the new process model version (cf. Chap. 9).

15.3   System Architecture

The design of AristaFlow is based on well-defined principles that realize a modular and extensible system architecture. These principles refer to architectural aspects as well as to conceptual issues concerning the implementation of the features described. The overall goal is to enable ad hoc changes and process model evolution, together with other advanced process support features, in an integrated manner, while ensuring robustness, correctness, performance, and usability at the same time.

To master complexity, a proper and modular system architecture with clear separation of concerns and well-defined interfaces is chosen. This fosters the exchangeability of system components, extensibility of the system architecture, and autonomy of the system components. Furthermore, the system architecture is layered (cf. Fig. 15.10); i.e., components of lower layers offer services to components of upper layers that hide as much complexity as possible from them. In this context, basic components can be combined in a flexible manner to realize higher-level services, like ad hoc changes or process model evolution. Finally, system components can be reused in different context based on advanced configuration options.

To ease its implementation and maintenance, each system component is kept as simple as possible and only has access to the information needed for its proper working. Further, communication details are hidden from component developers and independence from the used middleware (e.g., database management systems) is ensured. Example 15.10 presents two design principles to illustrate this: *avoidance of code redundancies* and *extensibility*.

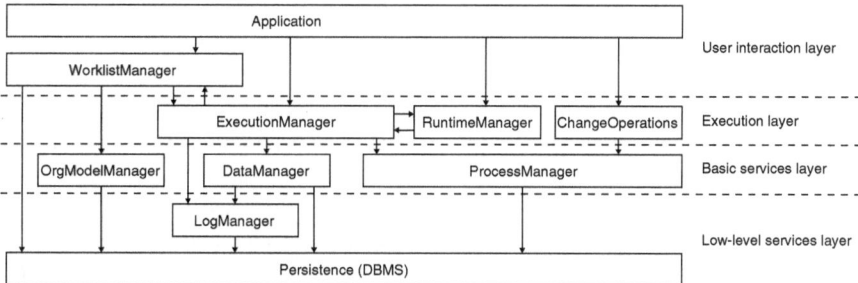

Fig. 15.10 Basic architecture of AristaFlow

Example 15.10 (Design Principles).

Avoidance of code redundancies. In AristaFlow, the components for process modeling, ad hoc process changes, and process model evolution are based on the same set of adaptation patterns. This suggests to implement respective change operations by a separate system component, and to make this component configurable such that it can be applied to all these use cases. Similar considerations are made in respect to components like process visualization, logging, and access control. This way, code redundancies can be reduced and maintainability significantly improved.

Extensibility. It should be possible to add new components to the architecture or to adapt existing ones. Ideally, respective extensions or changes do not affect other components of the architecture; i.e., their implementation should be robust with respect to changes of other components. For example, assume that the set of supported change operations will be extended, e.g., by offering additional adaptation patterns to users. This extension, however, must not affect the components realizing process model evolution or ad hoc changes. This is achieved by internally mapping high-level change operations to a stable set of low-level change primitives (e.g., to add/delete nodes).

Figure 15.10 depicts the simplified architecture of the AristaFlow BPM Suite and its different layers (see [263] for a more detailed description). Each layer comprises a number of components that offer services to upper-layer components. The first layer enables a DBMS-independent implementation of data persistence. The second layer is responsible for storing and locking different entities of the PAIS, e.g., process models and instances. The third layer encapsulates essential process support functions including process execution and change management. Finally, the topmost layer provides different build- and run-time tools to users, e.g., the process template editor and monitoring component described in Sect. 15.2.2. Note that these components may be exchanged by domain-specific ones. The latter can be realized using the application program interface (API) provided by AristaFlow.

The different system components are loosely coupled, enabling the easy exchange of their implementation. Furthermore, basic infrastructure services like storage management or the techniques used for inter-component communication can be easily exchanged. Additional plug-in interfaces are provided that allow extending the core architecture, data models, and user interfaces.

The implementation of the described architecture and features raised many challenges, e.g., with respect to the PAIS-internal representation of process model and process instance data (cf. Example 15.11).

Example 15.11 (Managing Unchanged and Changed Process Instances). Unchanged process instances are stored in a redundant-free manner by referencing their original process model and maintaining instance-specific data (e.g., activity states) separately. For example, consider process instances $I1$, $I3$, $I4$, and $I6$ from Fig. 15.11. For "biased" (i.e., individually changed) instances, however, this approach is not applicable anymore. One alternative is to maintain a complete model copy for each biased instance, another one is to materialize instance-specific models on-the-fly; i.e., by replaying change logs (cf. Chap. 8) on the original process model each time the respective process instance will be accessed. AristaFlow realizes a hybrid approach: For each biased process instance, it maintains a minimum substitution block that covers all changes applied to this instance so far. This block is then used to overlay parts of the original process model when accessing the process instance ($I2$ and $I5$ in our example from Fig. 15.11). A detailed description of techniques storing unbiased and biased process instances in an efficient manner can be found in [283, 284, 292].

AristaFlow provides sophisticated build- and run-time components to the different user groups. This includes tools for modeling, verifying, and testing process models, components for monitoring and adapting process instances, and worklist clients (e.g. Web clients). Several of these components have been already presented in Sect. 15.2. For example, the AristaFlow Test Client provides a fully-fledged test environment for executing and changing process instances. Unlike common test tools, this client runs on a light-weight variant of the AristaFlow BPM Suite. As such, various execution modes, ranging from pure simulation to production mode, become possible.

Many applications require customized user interfaces to integrate process support features into existing information systems and application suites. AristaFlow meets this requirement: the provided user components are configurable in a flexible manner on one hand, and all PAIS services are also made available through an *Open API* on the other. That is, domain-specific applications integrating selected PAIS services can be developed based on the AristaFlow Open API (cf. Sect. 15.4).

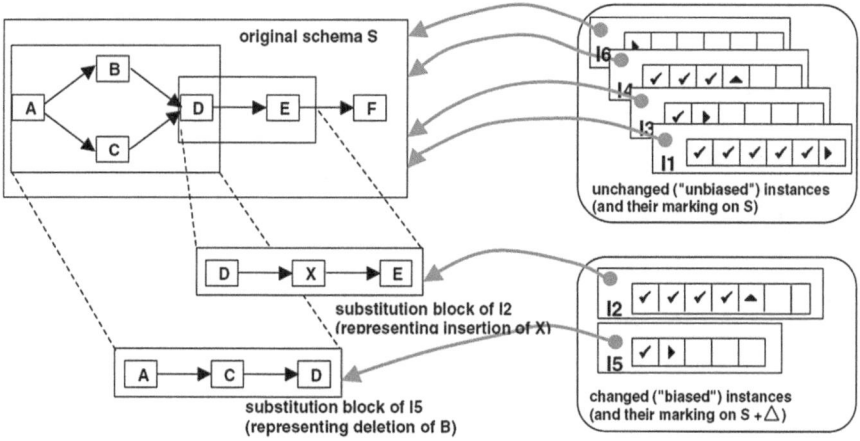

Fig. 15.11 Managing type and instance objects in the process manager (logical view)

Note that the API enables access to high-level services (e.g., worklist management or process model change), as well as to lower-level services of the architecture (e.g., transaction management and logging) (cf. Fig. 15.10). Finally, the Open API allows for the easy integration of different execution platforms and client types (e.g., rich-clients, web-clients, or mobile clients).

15.4   Using the AristaFlow BPM Suite in Actual Practice

Domain experts usually have no or only little IT knowledge. Hence, the standard user interfaces offered by existing PAISs are inappropriate for them. Instead, domain-specific end-user interfaces are required; i.e., the PAIS must be tailored to the specific needs of the respective application domain. Both ADEPT and AristaFlow were applied to challenging applications from different domains [168, 169] of which some will be described in this section.

15.4.1   Case Study 1: Disaster Management

Application Domain. The project on *Process-aware, Cooperative Emergency Management of Water Infrastructures* [345] targets at the support of emergency management processes for flood response. This is a non-trivial task since the collaboration among the involved parties can hardly be trained for these extreme situations. Especially, flood response managers have to flexibly cope with various tasks, while being pressed for time and faced with incomplete information about disaster situations.

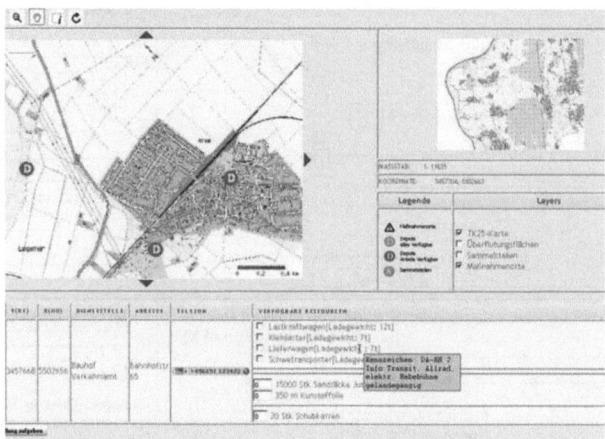

Fig. 15.12 User interface for handling disaster management processes (adopted from [345])

Requirements. The processes identified in the project ought to be mapped to prespecified process models in order to execute and monitor them in a PAIS. This required the modeling of complex information flows as well as the integration of distributed resources. Furthermore, domain-specific user interfaces were required; i.e., process support services had to be integrated into domain-specific user interfaces, providing also geographical information related to disaster situations and activities. Finally, the PAIS ought to support ad hoc changes in the case of unplanned situations.

Applying AristaFlow. AristaFlow was used to model, implement, execute, monitor, and change the processes for managing and controlling the procedures and tasks during flood events, as well as for handling relevant information flows. In particular, AristaFlow supported responders in planning and executing flood response operations. Figure 15.12 shows a domain-specific user interface that was implemented based on the AristaFlow Open API. In particular, end-users may order resources and deploy them to emergency locations in a coordinated and flexible manner.

Discussion. Using AristaFlow, responders could be supported in accomplishing their tasks in a coordinated and flexible manner. One important aspect was to enable the required process flexibility, while still ensuring a correct and robust execution behavior of the supported processes. These requirements and those mentioned above were fully met in the project.

Fig. 15.13 SPOT mobile
client [92]

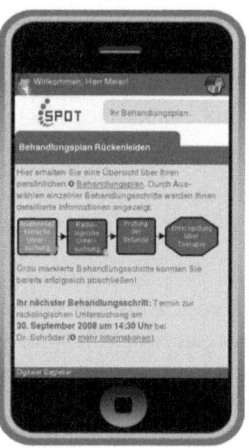

15.4.2   Case Study 2: Health Care Process Management

Application Domain. By supporting domain- and organization-specific views on
patient treatment processes (i.e., clinical pathways), the *SPOT* project [92] (*Service-
based technologies for orchestrating Processes in logistics and health care*) enables
end-users to actively shape the different phases of the process life cycle and to
define, execute, monitor, and adapt patient-specific processes based on prespecified
templates describing clinical pathways.

Requirements. Hospitals crave for IT process support that meets the flexibility
demands of health care environments; e.g., to adequately cope with both anticipated
and unanticipated exceptions [71, 172, 256]. Furthermore, easy to use, domain-
specific end-user interfaces were required in order to enable physicians and nurses
to interact with the PAIS at a high level of abstraction.

Applying AristaFlow. AristaFlow was selected as an implementation platform
for several reasons [281]. Besides its correctness-by-construction principle, which
is fundamental for the IT support of clinical processes, its strict modular design
and service-oriented architecture were basic points in favor of its use in the SPOT
project. In particular, process support features were encapsulated as services, which
simplified their integration into existing application systems. Figure 15.13 shows
an example of a mobile client for patient assistance. For representing clinical
pathways, SPOT uses editable tree structures, which are automatically mapped to
block-structured process models. In particular, user-driven adaptations of a tree
structure are immediately translated into changes of the process model executed
in AristaFlow; the latter are then automatically applied to the considered instance
based on ad hoc changes [281]. This empowered domain experts to adapt process
instances at a high level of abstraction.

Discussion. Again, the AristaFlow Open API facilitated the integration of process support services into the architecture of an existing application system. Additionally, features like robust process execution and user assistance in connection with ad hoc process instance changes were considered as extremely useful.

15.4.3   Case Study 3: Software Engineering Processes

Application Domain. The Q-Advice project targets at the IT support of software engineering (SE) processes. Due to the dynamic nature and high degree of collaboration, communication, and coordination inherent in SE projects, automated processes can assist overburdened software engineers by providing orientation and guidance. Yet, since there are so many different kinds of issues with ambiguous and subjective delineation, it is difficult and burdensome to universally and correctly model all these processes in advance, since this would lead to process models of considerable size and complexity.

Requirements. During the project, it became evident that tailored process support and context-specific guidance for software engineers are needed. However, spaghetti-like process models covering all possible cases were considered as too complex. To alleviate this problem, it should be allowed starting with a basic and simple process model for each case and then, utilizing context information, dynamically extending this model with activities matching the current situation.

Applying AristaFlow. Q-Advice uses the AristaFlow BPM Suite as its process module [108–111, 113]. In particular, it utilizes the AristaFlow Open API for automatically constructing and adapting process models, as well as for developing specialized activity components. For example, based on context information an issue process can be automatically, dynamically, and uniquely constructed for every software engineering issue. The activities of the process are then distributed to the responsible users based on the organization model maintained by AristaFlow. Similarly, [110] discusses how AristaFlow can be used to enable the contextual and dynamic injection of quality measures into SE processes. Figure 15.14 shows an example of a user interface. In the lower section the user can see his current task as well as the next upcoming tasks. In the upper section, additional information is provided.

Discussion. Q-Advice provides situational and tailored support as well as guidance for software engineers. In particular, the executable process models resulting from this approach are much simpler than fully prespecified process models would be. Q-Advice utilizes the dynamic change framework provided by AristaFlow, hiding the complexity coming with process-orientation, dynamic process changes, and flexible task management from software engineers.

Fig. 15.14 Q-advice client [109]

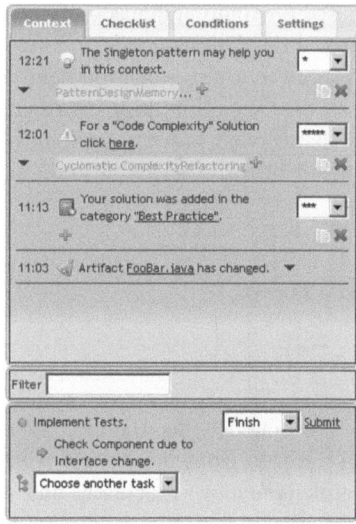

15.4.4 Other Case Studies

Over the last decade, more than 20 other groups from academia and industry applied different versions of the ADEPT technology in the context of research projects. In the E-Commerce domain, for example, CONSENSUS [43] offered flexible and dynamic process support for e-negotiations based on parameters like quality, delivery, warranty, and financial terms. In the MTCT project [44], a PAIS for processing client requests in container transportation, as well as for dynamically handling real-world exceptions, was realized based on ADEPT1. In turn, AgentWork and HematoWork [230,231] developed a rule-based component for automatically adapting IT supported patient treatment processes at the occurrence of exceptions.

15.5 Summary

The AristaFlow BPM Suite realizes the concepts and features described in Chaps. 6–10 in an integrated manner. It enables process composition in a "plug and play" style, ad hoc changes of single process instances, process model evolution and instance migration, and change diagnosis. In particular, all these features also work in interplay. For example, it is possible to propagate process model changes to individually modified process instances or to dynamically compose processes based on configurable activity templates. Other features considered in the research projects and implemented in different prototype versions of ADEPT and AristaFlow, respectively, are exception handling through backward and forward jumps during process execution [262], distributed process execution (including dynamic changes of partitioned process models) [46, 258], mobile process support [248], process model abstraction [53, 54, 266], and end-user assistance [355].

Exercises

15.1. Order Process

To conduct this exercise, first download the screencast *AristaFlowDemo* (cf. Fig. 15.15) from the book's web site. This screencast deals with the modeling, implementation, execution, and change of a simple order process. This process consists of the atomic activity *Fill Out Order Form* succeeded by the complex activity *Send Order*. The former is implemented through a user form, the latter refers to a subprocess that comprises the two activities *Format Message* and *Send Mail*. In detail: First, the screencast demonstrates how the order process and its subprocess can be implemented in a "plug and play" style using the *AristaFlow Process Template Editor* (cf. Fig. 15.15). Second, it shows how the implemented process can be executed using the *AristaFlow Test Client*. Third, it is shown how an ad hoc change is applied to a particular instance of the order process. Play this screencast and answer the following questions in your own words:

(a) Which activity template is used to implement activity *Fill Out Order Form*? How is this activity template configured in the given context?
(b) How is data exchanged between the *Order Process* and the subprocess its activity *Send Order* refers to?
(c) Consider the subprocess implementing activity *Send Order*. Which activity templates are used for implementing activities *Format Message* and *Send Mail*? How are these activity templates assigned to the two activities?
(d) Explain how the described correctness-by-construction principle is applied during the modeling of the *Order Process*.
(e) Consider the execution of activity *Fill Out Order Form* by the *AristaFlow Test Client*. Which run-time artifacts are related to this activity?
(f) Describe the ad hoc change applied to a particular instance of the *Order Process*. Why has this ad hoc change become necessary and on which adaptation pattern (cf. Chap. 7) is it based? Explain how and why activity states and worklists must be also adapted in the given context.
(g) Explain how the ad hoc instance change can be used to evolve the process model at the type level?

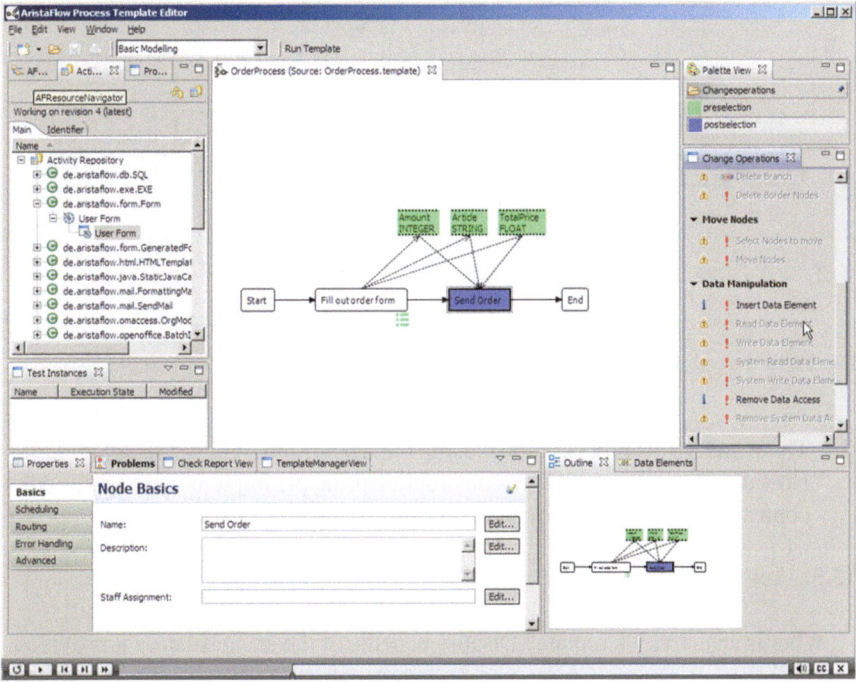

Fig. 15.15   AristaFlow screencast

15.2. AristaFlow Components and Features

Visit the book's web site and download the screencasts demonstrating the different applications, components and features of the *AristaFlow BPM Suite*. Play each of these screencasts to learn more about how these components work.

15.3. Exploring the AristaFlow BPM Suite

The AristaFlow BPM Suite is provided free of charge to universities for research and educational purposes. Please visit the book's web site for more information on this topic and on how to download the software. Furthermore, on the book's web site several exercises related to the use of the AristaFlow BPM Suite are provided.

15.4. Incorrect Process Model

Using the *AristaFlow Process Template Editor*, correct and sound, block-structured process models can be constructed. Obviously, the process model depicted in Fig. 15.16 was not modeled with this editor and contains several flaws.

(a)   Which flaws do the control and data flow schema contain? Explain the different kinds of errors and correct them if possible.

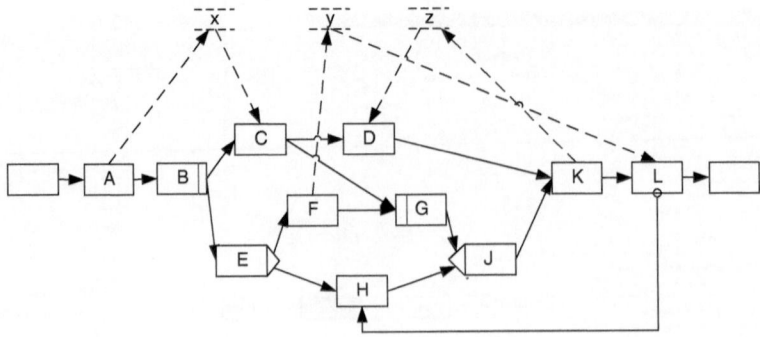

Fig. 15.16 Incorrect process model

(b) Try to create this process model using the *AristaFlow Process Template Editor*. How does the correctness-by-construction principle implemented by this editor contribute to avoid process model flaws?

15.5. Activity Templates

What is an activity template? Discuss benefits of the encapsulation it provides.

Chapter 16
Alaska Simulator Toolset

Abstract This chapter introduces Alaska Simulator Toolset (AST), an open source tool suite for systematically exploring and investigating the decision deferral patterns introduced in Chap. 11. By providing integrated support for Late Binding, Late Modeling and Composition, and Iterative Refinement, AST fosters systematic testing of factors that impact the suitability of these approaches. Thus, AST promotes research in the context of loosely specified processes and hence supports the selection of the right degree of preplanning. The chapter introduces the concepts underlying AST, presents its architecture, and discusses its use.

16.1 Motivation

While the AristaFlow BPM Suite introduced in Chap. 15 has been designed for prespecified processes and provides advanced support for their specification, execution, adaptation, and evolution, this chapter addresses loosely specified processes. In particular, it introduces Alaska Simulator Toolset[1] (AST), a tool suite developed at the University of Innsbruck, which allows exploring and investigating the decision deferral patterns introduced in Chap. 11 in a controlled setting under varying circumstances. By providing integrated support for *Late Selection*, *Late Modeling and Composition*, and *Iterative Refinement*, AST fosters the systematic comparison of different approaches enabling *looseness*.

To support decision deferral patterns, AST provides two modes: *plan-driven* and *agile*. The plan-driven mode enables support for both *Late Selection* and *Late Modeling and Composition* in the context of placeholder activities, and it enables *Late Modeling and Composition* of the entire process. The agile mode, in turn, enables *Iterative Refinement* including two extreme cases: prespecifying everything (i.e., Late Modeling within the scope of the entire process) and prespecifying nothing (i.e., *Ad hoc Composition*).

---

[1]http://www.alaskasimulator.org.

M. Reichert and B. Weber, *Enabling Flexibility in Process-Aware Information Systems*,   465
DOI 10.1007/978-3-642-30409-5_16, © Springer-Verlag Berlin Heidelberg 2012

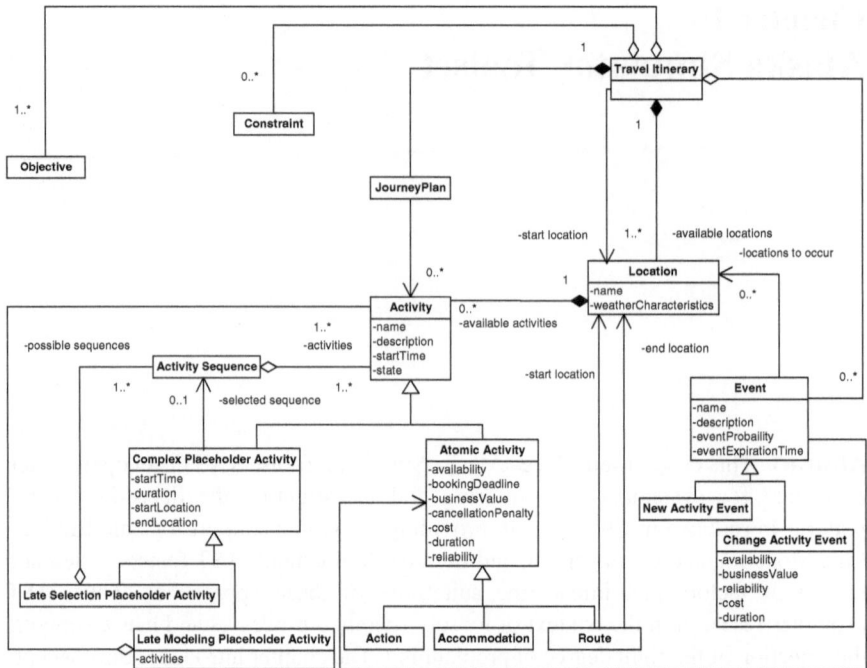

Fig. 16.1 AST meta-model (expressed as UML class diagram)

This chapter explains the concepts underlying AST (cf. Sect. 16.2), discusses how much preplanning is needed in a given scenario (cf. Sect. 16.3), and describes the AST architecture (cf. Sect. 16.4). Moreover, it discusses a case study that was conducted using AST (cf. Sect. 16.5). The chapter concludes with a summary in Sect. 16.6.

16.2   Alaska Simulator Toolset: Meta-Model

AST uses a constraint-based approach for process modeling (cf. Chap. 12) and uses a *travel journey* to represent a *business process*. This scenario has been chosen since the domain of travel planning is well known. In particular, we found that this theme is popular with students in applying the system to both learning and experimental situations. This section describes the main concepts underlying AST (cf. Fig. 16.1) and discusses how these relate to business processes.

Objective. When planning a journey with AST, the objective is to maximize the travel experience of the user (i.e., the overall "business value" of the journey). For optimizing the execution of a journey, information about the benefits (i.e., business value), costs, and duration of actions, and also about their availability and reliability

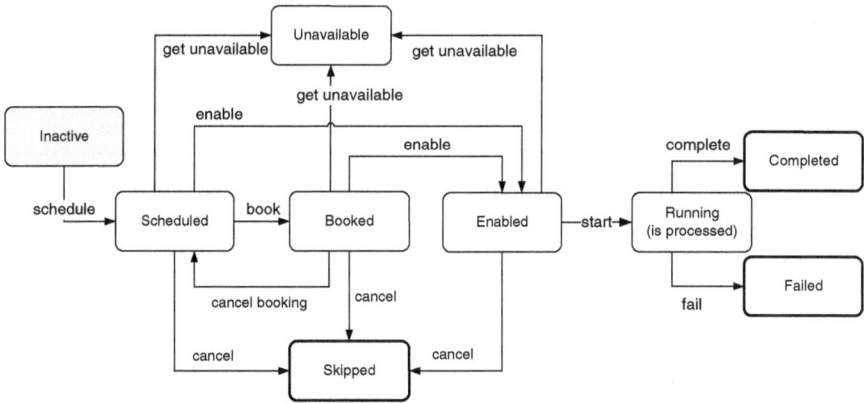

Fig. 16.2 Activity lifecycle and activity states

is essential. While the *objective* of a journey is to maximize the "travel experience," characteristic objectives of business processes are minimizing costs, or reducing cycle times, and optimizing quality or customer satisfaction [273].

Journey, Journey Plan, and Locations. AST assists users in creating travel itineraries—what it calls *journey plan*—based on a prespecified *journey configuration* (i.e., an instance of the meta-model). A journey plan (travel itinerary) is represented by a calendar for scheduling *activities* (i.e., *atomic activities, complex placeholder activities*). During a journey different *locations* can be visited, each providing distinct *activities* to select from (e.g., atomic activity *Visit Denali National Park* is only available at location *Denali*). *Journeys* are composed based on *journey configurations*, likewise *process instances* represent concrete business cases based on a *process schema*. Both journeys and business processes comprise a set of activities. Moreover, in both domains activities are not always available at all *locations*, e.g., for a health care process surgeries may only be performed in an operating room.

Activities. An activity is either *atomic* or *complex*. *Atomic activities* can be subdivided into *actions*, *routes*, and *stays at accommodations*. For each atomic activity, its business value, costs, duration, availability, and reliability are specified. Moreover, a booking deadline as well as cancellation fees are defined. *Complex placeholder activities*, in turn, provide placeholders which can be refined during the execution of a journey.

Late selection placeholder activities represent a set of *activity sequences* from which one may be selected during run-time. *Late modeling placeholder activities*, in turn, allow users to compose an *activity sequence* during run-time from a set of predefined activities satisfying existing constraints. *Activities*, in general, are characterized by their name, description, start time (determined by their position in the journey plan), and current state (e.g., scheduled, booked, started, or executed). Figure 16.2 shows the lifecycle of an activity and its different states.

Duration constraint	Restricts the duration of the overall journey to a certain timeframe. *Example*: The journey must not last more than 5 days.
Execution time constraint	Restricts the time when an activity may be executed to a certain schedule. *Example*: Activity X may be executed every day between 09:00 and 17:00.
Time lag constraint	Requires a minimum/maximum time lag between the execution of two activities. *Example*: Between the completion of activity X and the start of activity Z there must be a minimum time lag of 3 hours.
Fixed date constraint	Specifies the earliest/latest start or completion date of an activity. *Example*: Activity X must not be executed later than 15:00 at Day 3 of the journey.
Time based restrictions constraint	Restricts the number of times a certain activity may be executed per period. *Example*: Activity X may be executed at most once per day.
Budget constraint	Restricts the budget of the overall journey. *Example*: The total expenses for the journey must not exceed 1000 monetary units.
End location constraint	Requires the journey to end at a certain location. *Example*: The journey must be completed at location Z.

Fig. 16.3 Additional constraints supported by Alaska simulator toolset

Both business processes and journeys are composed of *atomic activities* and *complex placeholder activities* allowing for Late Selection as well as for Late Modeling and Composition (cf. Chap. 11).

Users may compose a journey by adding activities from the list of available activities to the journey plan (i.e., by scheduling these activities). This changes the activity's state from `Inactive` to `Scheduled`. Scheduled activities, in turn, may be booked optionally resulting in state `Booked`. Once all preconditions for its execution are met, an activity becomes `Enabled`. An enabled activity may be started by an authorized user resulting in state `Running`. If an activity completes without error this results in state `Completed`, otherwise the activity changes to state `Failed`. Scheduled, booked or enabled activities can be removed from the journey plan resulting in state `Skipped`. Moreover, during journey execution, activities might become unavailable resulting in state `Unavailable`. Finally, users may cancel bookings changing the activity's state from `Booked` to `Scheduled`.

Constraints. When composing a journey different constraints have to be considered. AST provides support for all control flow constraints described in [18] or introduced in Chap. 12. In addition, resource and time related constraints are supported (cf. Fig. 16.3). More precisely, AST supports several of the time constraints described in [170], e.g., a *duration constraint* restricting the duration of a journey, an *execution time constraint* restricting the time when a particular activity may be executed, a *time lag constraint* requiring a minimum/maximum time-lag between the execution of two activities, a *fixed date constraint* specifying the earliest/latest start or completion date of an activity, and a *time-based restriction* *constraint* restricting the number of times a certain activity may be executed per period (i.e., per journey, per day, or per hour). Moreover, AST provides a *budget constraint* restricting the available travel budget, and an *end location constraint* requiring that the journey ends at a particular location.

Constraints are not only relevant when composing journeys, but for representing business processes as well. The support provided by AST is comparable to existing approaches enabling modeling and execution of constraint-based business processes (cf. Chap. 12).

Uncertainty. Journeys are characterized by incomplete information prior to their execution. The outcome of an activity within a journey plan is not predefined and varies with the *weather conditions* encountered. The degree of variation is defined by the activity's *reliability*, e.g., low reliability indicates that the outcome of an activity is highly weather dependent. The overall business value of a journey (e.g., a numeric value representing travel experience) is calculated as the sum of business values of all executed activities. Prior to the journey only the *expected business value* of each activity as well as the activity's reliability are known. The expected business value is calculated based on the activity's reliability and the average weather characteristics of the location where the activity is available. During the journey the activity's *actual business value* is calculated based on the actual weather conditions encountered.

Like journeys, flexible business processes are characterized by incomplete information prior to execution (cf. Chap. 3). In a journey, for example, *uncertainty* is caused by unforeseen weather conditions, while uncertainty in business processes refers to the difficulty to predict the exact activities and resources required to perform a particular process (e.g., due to changing requirements caused by dynamic changes in the business environment) [96].

Resource Scarcity. When planning a journey, the potential for a resource has to be considered. By firmly *booking* an activity, its *availability* can be guaranteed, but its costs must be paid immediately. If the booking is canceled during the journey, a *cancellation penalty* will be applied, thus making too early commitments costly. Furthermore, booking is only possible up to a certain time before executing the activity, as specified by the *booking deadline*.

Resource scarcities also have to be considered in the context of a business process. In health care processes, for example, to deal with the limited availability of surgery rooms, surgeries have to be scheduled in advance [204].

Events. In addition to changing weather conditions, *unforeseen events* (e.g., a traffic jam resulting in a delay) create uncertainty during a journey. On the one hand, a *change activity event* changes values of existing activities during the journey. For example, a particular event might increase or decrease the business value, the availability, the costs or the duration of an activity. On the other hand, a *new activity event* allows introducing new activities at a particular location during the journey. Moreover, events occurring with a predefined probability during run-time, may have

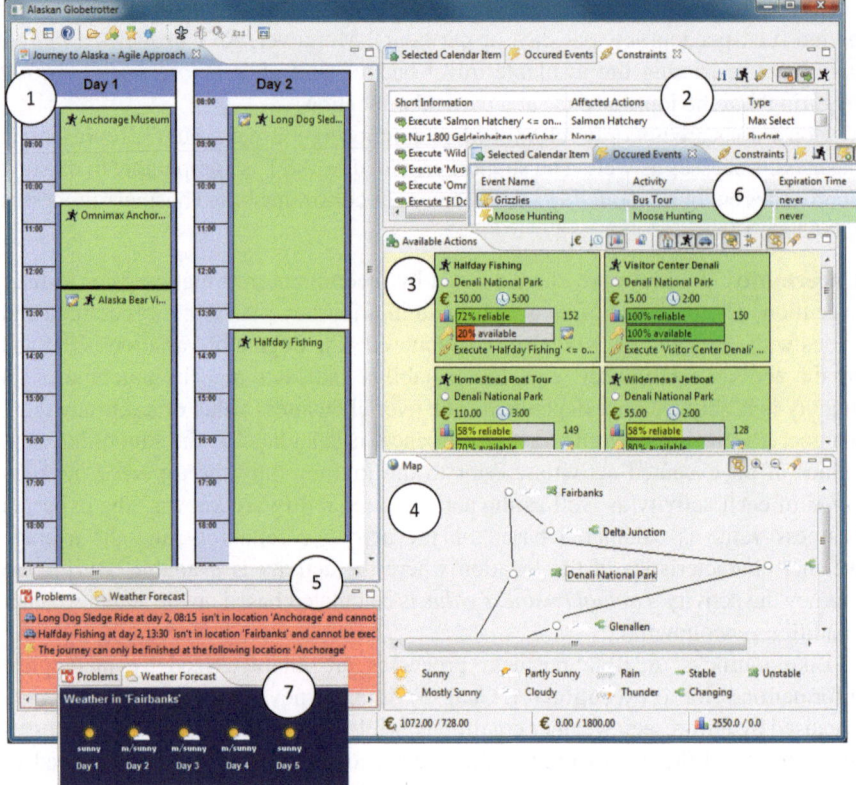

Fig. 16.4 Screenshot of Alaska simulator toolset

an expiration time, and can be attached to a particular location (i.e., the event may only occur when the traveler is at a particular location).

Unforeseen events are not only relevant for conducting a journey, but also when executing a business process (cf. Chap. 6).

Figure 16.4 depicts the graphical user interface of AST. Users may compose their individual journey plan by dragging available activities from the *Available Activities View* (3) onto the travel itinerary (i.e., journey plan) (1). Usually, activities are only available at a particular location on the map (4). Existing constraints are displayed in the *Constraint View* (2) and have to be considered when composing a concrete journey plan. After each user action, the journey plan is validated and the user is informed about occurring constraint violations and plan inconsistencies (5). Unforeseen events are shown in the *Event View* (6). Prior to the journey, users have to rely on weather statistics derived from the weather characteristics of each location, which can be selected on a map (4). A weather forecast is provided during the journey with the current conditions at each location (7).

Fig. 16.5 Deciding at the last responsible moment

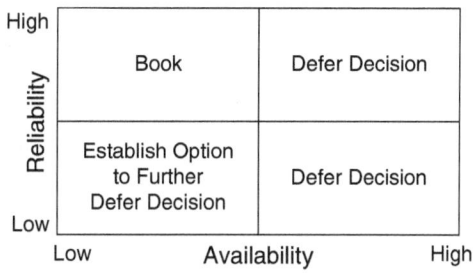

16.3   Deciding at the Last Responsible Moment

As discussed in Chap. 11, decision deferral patterns like *Late Selection*, *Late Modeling and Composition*, *Iterative Refinement*, and *Ad hoc Composition* allow for the deferral of selected modeling decisions to run-time. How much preplanning is "enough" highly depends on the characteristics of the business process—in particular, on its degree of uncertainty and the availability of resources. They determine which parts of a business process can be prespecified and which parts should remain unspecified and be refined during process execution. In the most extreme cases, a fully prespecified process schema like in traditional PAISs or an empty initial schema (as with Ad hoc Composition) might be most appropriate.

Figure 16.5 classifies activities according to their availability and reliability and shows strategies on how to deal best with particular classes of activities.

Figure 16.5 shows that commitments to widely available activities by making a resource reservation should be avoided. Reserving respective activities introduces unnecessary early commitment without any benefit gain. In contrast, activities with high reliability in combination with low availability should be reserved before the reservation deadline to guarantee resource availability, i.e., the last responsible moment is just before the reservation deadline. Activities with low availability and low reliability are most difficult to handle. Depending on the business value that can be gained and the costs of the respective activity, it might be worth to commit to the activity and to schedule a second more reliable one in parallel. Therefore, instead of choosing between one of the activities right away, an option is built. This allows deferring the last responsible moment for deciding between the alternatives.

16.4   Architecture of Alaska Simulator Toolset

This section describes the main components of AST as well as involved roles, and it explains how these roles may interact with, and benefit from, AST.

- *Students* use AST to learn more about constraint-based process models and to get a better understanding of the different constraints. Further, they use AST to study

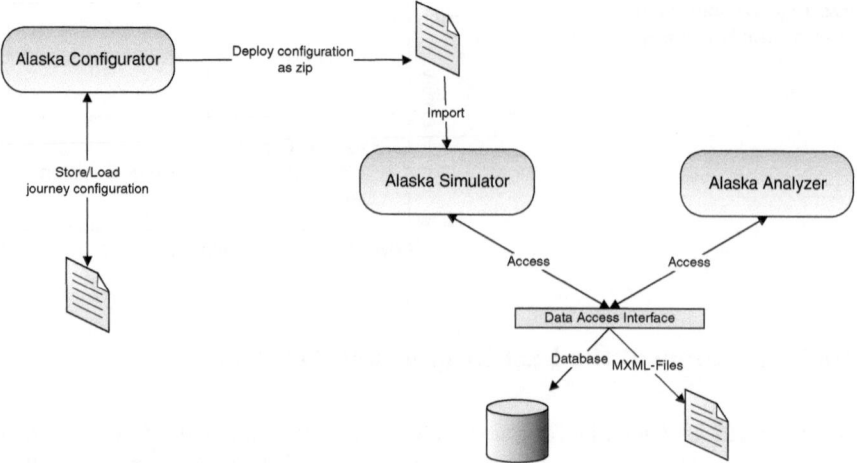

Fig. 16.6 Alaska simulator toolset

existing approaches enabling loosely specified processes. Moreover, they test and analyze their planning behavior with AST and explore how much planning is minimally required under varying circumstances. In particular, they test the suitability of the decision deferral patterns with different levels of uncertainty and different degrees of resource availability (cf. Sect. 11.2).

- *Researchers* investigate the strengths and weaknesses of different approaches enabling process flexibility depending on different factors (e.g., number of constraints and occurring events).
- *Instructors* demonstrate the different flexibility approaches using the journey example and explain the major differences between them.

AST consists of three major components: *Alaska Configurator*, *Alaska Simulator*, and *Alaska Analyzer* (cf. Fig. 16.6).

- *Alaska Configurator* allows both teachers and researchers to design journey configurations executable in Alaska Simulator. Such configurations include locations, activities, events, and constraints, but also information regarding the degree of uncertainty. In addition, Alaska Configurator supports the design of experimental workflows, which guide users through experiments or learning sessions.
- *Alaska Simulator* allows planning and executing journeys by making use of different decision deferral approaches. Thereby, each step performed during the planning and execution of a journey is logged for later analysis, e.g., using the process mining tool ProM (cf. Chap. 8).
- *Alaska Analyzer* allows for a detailed manual analysis of planning behavior by supporting a step-by-step replay of journeys.

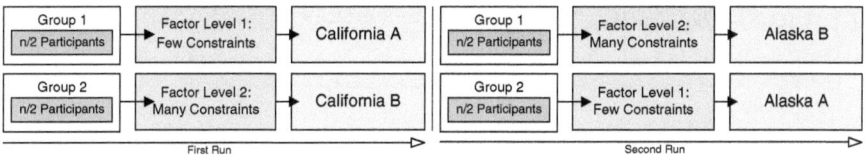

Fig. 16.7 Experiment design

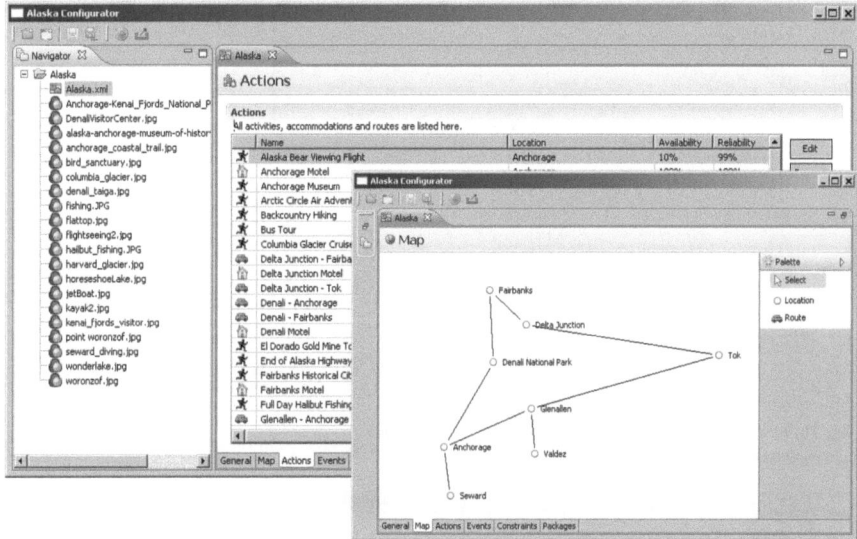

Fig. 16.8 Defining activities and locations with Alaska configurator

AST, including a test configuration, extensive documentation, and screencasts, can be downloaded from the book's web site. For detailed information on the results of controlled experiments conducted with AST we refer to [350, 356].

16.5   Case Studies: Using Alaska Simulator Toolset in Practice

In this section we describe main functionalities of AST and show how it was used for designing and executing the experiment described in [356] (cf. Fig. 16.7 for the experiment design). The experiment investigated how inexperienced process designers can handle constraint-based process models of varying complexity.

Alaska Configurator was used to design two journey configurations (*California* and *Alaska*) including locations, activities, events, and constraints, but also information about weather conditions (cf. Figs. 16.8 and 16.9). For each journey

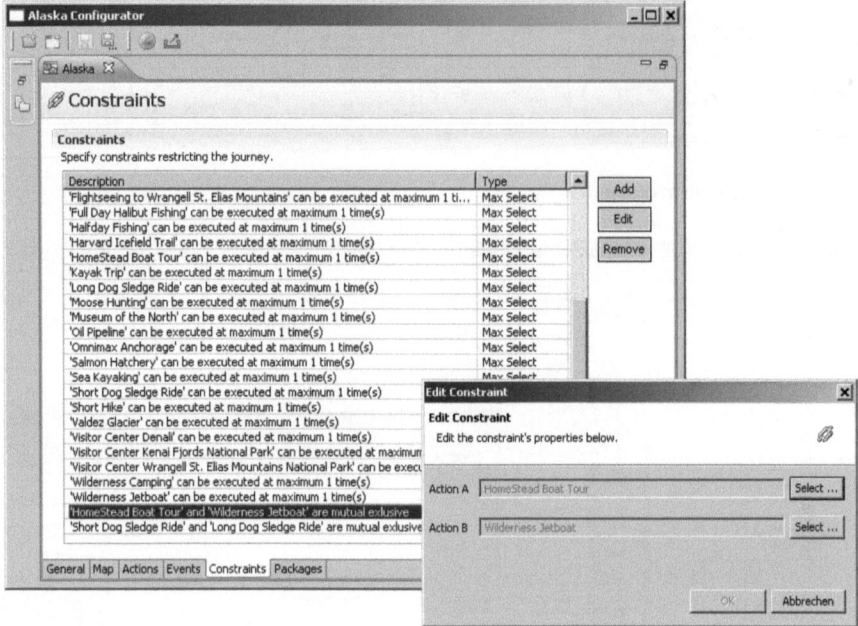

Fig. 16.9 Defining constraints with Alaska configurator

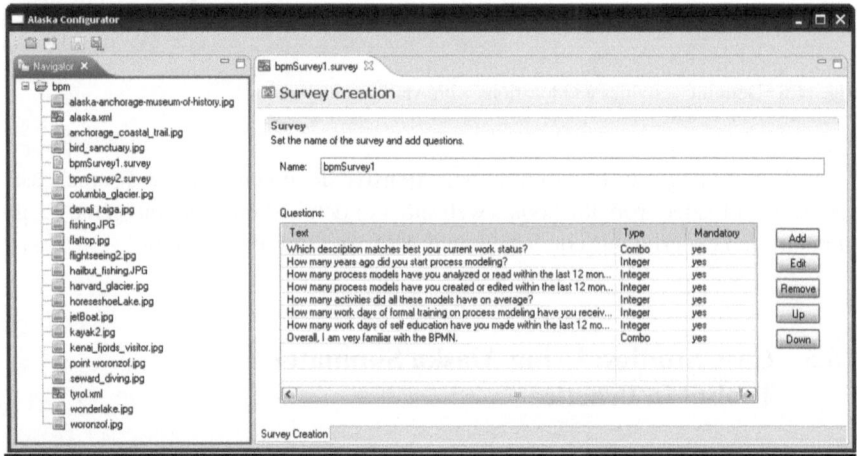

Fig. 16.10 Questionnaire builder

configuration two variants were created, one for each factor level (i.e., few vs. many constraints). To gather the participants' demographic information, a survey was created using Alaska Configurator (cf. Fig. 16.10). The journey configurations and the survey were then assembled in an experimental workflow (cf. Fig. 16.11).

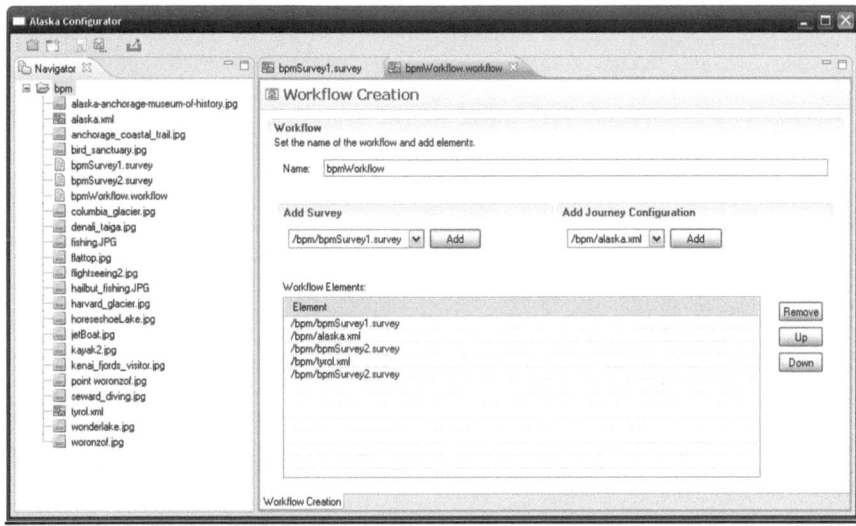

Fig. 16.11 Designer for experimental workflows

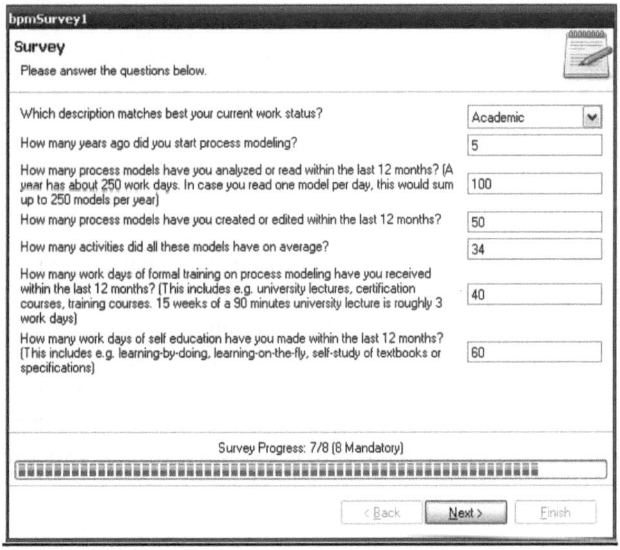

Fig. 16.12 Generated survey using questionnaire builder

During the experiment participants were guided by the experimental workflow.
After the survey (cf. Fig. 16.12), half of the students obtained configuration *California* with few constraints, while the other half obtained the same configuration
with many constraints. The students then planned and executed a journey to

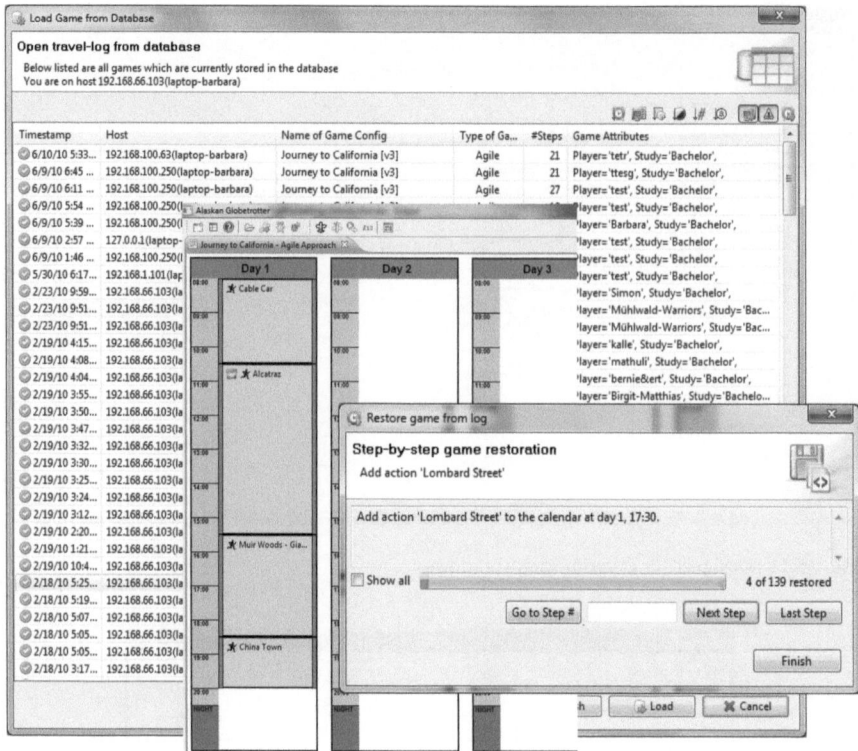

Fig. 16.13 Replaying journeys with Alaska analyzer

California. Each step performed was logged for later analysis. Having completed their *California* journeys, participants planned and executed a journey to *Alaska*.

After the planning session, researchers were supported in analyzing the journeys by enabling a step-by-step replay of the journey, using Alaska Analyzer (cf. Fig. 16.13). This analysis revealed that participants were able to effectively execute constraint-based process models (irrespective of the number of constraints) with the tool support provided. For details regarding the results of this experiment we refer to [356].

16.6   Summary

AST supports users in exploring and systematically comparing different approaches enabling decision deferral in a controlled manner. This chapter described the concepts underlying AST and showed how it supports different decision deferral patterns. In addition, the chapter discussed factors having a potential impact on the suitability of a particular approach for decision deferral. Moreover, we demonstrated how AST can be used in both teaching and experimental settings. In particular, *Alaska Configurator* allows teachers and researchers to design journey configurations executable with Alaska Simulator. It further supports them in designing experimental workflows providing user guidance. *Alaska Simulator* allows planning and executing journeys and makes use of different approaches for decision deferral. Finally, *Alaska Analyzer* supports detailed analysis of data as well as replaying journeys step by step.

Exercises

To conduct the following exercises, download a version of Alaska Simulator from the book's web site and follow the instructions on the web site.

16.1. Agile Versus Plan-Driven: In this exercise you can explore the two different modes of Alaska Simulator (i.e., the plan-driven and the agile mode) using two different configurations (i.e., Alaska and California).

16.2. Dealing with Varying Levels of Constraints: In this exercise you can explore the planning and execution of constraint-based process models with varying levels of constraints.

16.3. Dealing with Varying Unforeseen Events: In this exercise you can explore the planning and execution of constraint-based processes with varying levels of unforeseen events.

Chapter 17
Existing Tool Support for Flexible Processes

Abstract This chapter refers to the tool section on our book web site. The latter provides an evolving source of information on existing tools enabling flexible process support in process-aware information systems. The book's web site covers the tools presented in these chapters as well as others not described here.

17.1 Selected Tools

Most of the concepts and functionalities described in this book—even the advanced features not yet in general use—are supported by existing tools.

For each of the presented paradigms (i.e., prespecified process models, loosely specified process models, and object-aware and data-driven processes), we have already presented one or more selected tools covering large parts of the functionality described in this book. Chapter 15 has described the ADEPT process management technology and its commercial version called BPM AristaFlow Suite. In particular, these tools provide features enabling flexibility throughout the life cycle of prespecified process models. This includes advanced features enabling flexibility-by-design, ad hoc changes of individual process instances and their reuse in similar problem contexts, process change and process variants mining, process schema evolution, and ensurance of business process compliance in connection with process changes.

While the ADEPT system and the Aristaflow Suite respectively focus on prespecified process models and their adaptation and evolution during run-time, Chap. 16 has introduced the Alaska Simulator Toolset, which addresses loosely specified processes. Alaska Simulator Toolset is an open source tool suite for systematically exploring and investigating the decision deferral patterns introduced in Chap. 11 in a controlled setting under varying circumstances. By providing integrated support for *Late Binding*, *Late Modeling*, and *Iterative Refinement*, Alaska Simulator fosters the systematic comparison of different approaches for achieving *looseness*.

Finally, Chap. 14 has introduced the PHILharmonicFlows framework enabling object-aware and data-driven process support.

M. Reichert and B. Weber, *Enabling Flexibility in Process-Aware Information Systems*,   479
DOI 10.1007/978-3-642-30409-5_17, © Springer-Verlag Berlin Heidelberg 2012

17.2   Further Tools

Information on other tools (i.e., commercial systems as well as research prototypes) enabling flexible process support can be found in the tool section of our book's web site.[1] Since our goal is to provide up-to-date information regarding tools for supporting flexible processes, we decided not to include information regarding additional tools in this book itself, but to maintain this information in a special tool section on the accompanying web site. The intention of this tool section is to provide an evolving source of information on existing tools enabling flexible process support. Since the different tools described on the web site have been designed with different goals in mind, we do not aim at providing an in-depth evaluation and comparison of them, but rather focus on demonstrating their core flexibility features.

For each of the tools we provide

- A short tool description.
- Information regarding the vendor and developer respectively.
- A link to the tool web site.
- Information on which flexibility concepts introduced in this book are addressed (including pointers to relevant book chapters).
- Selected references regarding tool applications.
- Teaching material including screencasts and tutorials (if available).

---

[1]http://www.flexible-processes.com.

Part VI
Summary, References, and Appendices

Chapter 18
Epilogue

This chapter concludes this book by summarizing its major contributions and discussing several open research challenges.

When efforts are taken to improve and automate business processes through the introduction of a PAIS, it is of utterly importance that this does not lead to inflexibility and rigidity. Otherwise, the PAIS will not be accepted by its different user groups. Furthermore, variability in business processes is deeply inherent to many domains, and unforeseen events are to some degree a "normal" phenomenon in actual practice. As discussed in Chap. 3, PAISs should therefore enable a high degree of flexibility throughout the entire process life cycle.

To enable the required process flexibility, a number of challenges must be tackled: *First*, variability in business processes, which is known prior to their implementation, should be captured and made known to the PAIS. *Second*, it should be possible to integrate preplanned routines for handling known exceptions during run-time. *Third*, authorized process participants should be free to react in unplanned or exceptional situations by gaining complete initiative and by deviating from the prespecified process whenever required. Note that in many domains the process participants are usually trained to do so, and hence enabling ad hoc deviations from the prespecified process model forms a key part of process flexibility. In all these scenarios, the PAIS should be easy to handle, self-explaining, and— most important—its use should be not more cumbersome and time-consuming than simply handling the unplanned situation or exception by a telephone call to the right person. *Fourth*, process models may evolve over time due to environmental changes (e.g., process redesign or new laws). Consequently, a PAIS should support process model evolution and provide appropriate techniques for dealing with already running process instances in this context. Flexibility features of a PAIS must neither affect its robustness nor the correct execution and compliance of the business processes it implements. *Fifth*, to support knowledge-intensive processes, PAISs should enable the loose-specification of process models during built-time and their refinement during run-time, as well as data- and user-driven processes in cases where activity-centric approaches do not fit at all.

M. Reichert and B. Weber, *Enabling Flexibility in Process-Aware Information Systems*, 483
DOI 10.1007/978-3-642-30409-5_18, © Springer-Verlag Berlin Heidelberg 2012

18.1 Enabling Flexibility in Process-Aware Information Systems

Traditional PAISs have focused on the support of predictable and repetitive business processes whose behavior can be fully described prior to their execution in terms of formal and executable process models.

In the first part of this book, we introduced basic PAIS concepts (cf. Chap. 2) and discussed fundamental flexibility issues that emerge when automating business processes through a PAIS (cf. Chap. 3). We have shown that business processes are rarely fully predictable nor fully unpredictable, but the vast majority of them can be characterized by a combination of predictable and unpredictable elements falling in between these two extremes. Starting from this observation, we have discussed fundamental flexibility needs for supporting dynamic business processes. In the remainder of this book (i.e., Part II to Part V), we then showed how these flexibility needs can be addressed by different paradigms and tools existing for the modeling and execution of business processes (i.e., prespecified, loosely specified, and data-driven).

Part II of this book discussed how support for prespecified process models can be extended such that process flexibility is enabled throughout the different phases of the process life cycle. First, we showed how flexibility-by-design can be achieved based on advanced modeling concepts and patterns for prespecified process models (cf. Chap. 4). We then addressed how variability in business processes, which is a priori known, can be captured and dealt with using configurable process models (cf. Chap. 5). Moreover, we showed how the need to flexibly deal with exceptions can be supported through predefined exception handlers (cf. Chap. 6), but also through ad hoc changes enabling flexible run-time deviations from the prespecified process model (cf. Chap. 7). Regarding the latter, we presented high-level adaptation patterns, correctness issues, and end-user assistance. We further discussed how traceability and accountability of flexible processes can be achieved by recording events related to the execution and change of process instances. Furthermore, we showed how this information can be exploited for analyzing changes (cf. Chap. 8). Chapter 9 elaborated the challenges that arise when business processes evolve over time and hence PAISs need to evolve accordingly. In particular, we showed how process model evolution and process model refactoring address these challenges. Finally, Chap. 10 introduced basic issues related to business process compliance along the process life cycle, particularly when changing and evolving process models.

Part III of this book presented different approaches for dealing with loosely structured business processes that are characterized by their low degree of repetition, knowledge-intensive nature, and emergence. Since loosely structured processes can hardly be entirely prespecified, we presented different techniques for deferring modeling decisions to the run-time (cf. Chap. 11). Moreover, we discussed constraint-based process modeling and execution as one fundamental approach to deal with loosely structured processes (cf. Chap. 12).

Part IV of this book has shown that many of the flexibility limitations known from activity-centric processes can be traced back to the missing integration of business processes and business data. In particular, there are many real-world processes that cannot be straightjacketed into activities, but need to be tightly connected to business objects and their behavior. Respective processes are user- and data-driven. Based on this observation, Chap. 13 introduced case handling as one characteristic paradigm for enabling user- and data-driven processes.

Chapter 13 further emphasized the need for *object-aware processes* and identified characteristic properties for their operational support in a PAIS: object behavior, object interactions, data-driven execution, variable activity granularity, and integrated access to business processes and business data. Using these properties, Chap. 13 evaluated concrete approaches enabling user- and data-driven process support. All of them have recognized the high need for a tight integration of process and data, and have partially realized the above-mentioned properties. Chapter 14 then introduced a comprehensive framework for object-aware processes that addresses the five properties in an integrated way.

Part V of this book gave detailed insights into selected tools enabling flexible process support. Chapter 15 described the AristaFlow BPM Suite, i.e., an adaptive PAIS that implements many of the concepts described in Chaps. 4–10 in an integrated manner. In turn, Chap. 16 introduced the Alaska Simulator Toolset, an open source tool suite for systematically exploring and investigating decision deferral patterns, i.e., Late Binding, Late Modeling & Composition, and Iterative Refinement. Finally, Chap. 17 gave a reference to the book's web site at which information and teaching material about additional tools can be found.

18.2 Open Challenges

Existing approaches for the flexible support of prespecified or loosely specified processes have been already established in actual practice for several years, and hence provide a rather high degree of maturity. By contrast, approaches enabling user- and data-driven processes constitute cutting-edge research, but will become more mature and emerge in practical settings in a few years.

While the conceptual and theoretical foundations of the different paradigms are well understood, there still exist numerous challenges regarding their practical use. Among others, these challenges include better end-user assistance in flexible PAISs, as well as flexible support for mobile processes, real-world aware processes, and cross-organizational processes.

End-User Assistance: Sophisticated and intelligent user interfaces are required to enable domain experts to take full benefit from flexible PAISs. Though we have already discussed selected approaches fostering end-user assistance (e.g., case-based reuse of ad hoc changes, questionnaire-based process model configuration, recommendation support during process execution), additional research is required to introduce flexible PAISs in the large scale. For example, for the different process support paradigms, appropriate model abstractions (e.g., process views, data models) are indispensable [266,331]. These should be comprehensible to end-users and particularly enable them to change a process model (and its process instances respectively) at a high level of abstraction. Moreover, changes of abstracted process models need to be propagated to the underlying process model afterwards, while still ensuring its syntactical and behavioral correctness. Finally, new metaphors for handling dynamic processes from an end-user's perspective as well as their externalization on social media and platforms could be key drivers for next generation user interfaces in PAISs.

Mobile Process Support: Ubiquitous computing and mobile user assistance are considered as key enablers for linking everyday life with information and communication technology. Mobile applications are diverse and encompass domains like health care, logistics, and sales. For example, chronically ill patients may be assisted by mobile devices giving recommendations (e.g., about medications), collecting medical data (e.g., blood pressure or blood sugar), or helping general practitioners in planning encounters with their patients. Recommendations may be made remotely by health care professionals and depend on previously collected patient data. Despite its high potential, so far, no comprehensive process support on mobile devices has been provided. What is needed is a light-weight process engine running on mobile devices, which is able to execute single activities, but also entire process fragments in a flexible manner [248]. One major challenge is deciding which parts of a global process model (i.e., which process fragments) may run on mobile devices (e.g., a patient's smartphone) and which ones shall be controlled by a remote PAIS. In particular, it should be possible to deviate from prespecified process fragments executed on the mobile device if required. Both changes in the local environment (e.g., blood pressure of a patient increases) and changes in the infrastructure or global environment (e.g., a particular sensor is not measuring data) might require such ad hoc changes in mobile processes.

Real-World Aware Processes. A fundamental challenge raised by ad hoc process changes in a PAIS concerns the provision of information about the *business context* and the *real-world situation* in which these dynamic process changes take place. However, contemporary PAISs do not integrate respective information, which often leads to a gap between the business processes orchestrated by them (i.e., the computerized processes), and those actually happening in the physical (i.e., the real) world. Basically, this gap is a direct consequence of the missing alignment between PAISs and information about real-world objects, events, and exceptions. To overcome these limitations, generic techniques for enabling real-world aware business processes are required. On one hand, these need to support the modeling and verification of real-world aware processes; i.e., the alignment of process models with information models capturing real-world objects, events, and exceptions. On the other hand, integrated models need to be seamlessly transferred to flexible PAISs that are able to execute and monitor real-world aware processes, as well as to allow for their dynamic adaptation if required; e.g., to realign a computerized process in case it deviates from the one taking place in the physical world. In this context, another important technology will be an *Event Service Bus*, which should enable processes running in the PAIS to be notified of remote event occurrences and, accordingly, to dynamically adapt to the new circumstances if required. Among others, this necessitates services for capturing, filtering, and consolidating distributed real-time data and to generate business-related events that can be used for business process execution alignment. Note that the realization of this vision is by far not trivial when considering the fact that various sensor technologies and sensor sources need to be integrated and nonrelevant events must be discriminated from those that impact process execution. In the latter case, adequate reactions need to be foreseen in the process engine.

Flexibility Support for Cross-Organizational Processes. Improving the efficiency and quality of their business processes and optimizing their interactions with partners and customers are significant success factors for all businesses. In connection with Web service technology, the benefits of business process automation and optimization from within a single company can be transferred to collaborative (i.e., cross-organizational) business processes. The next step in this evolution will be the emergence of dynamic business networks consisting of multiple business partners being able to rapidly implement new collaborative processes and to quickly adapt existing ones to environmental changes. While flexibility issues of PAISs, which support the internal processes of a company, are well understood, the controlled change of interactions between IT-supported partner processes in a collaborative setting (i.e., process choreographies) has not yet been adequately addressed. If one partner changes its process in an uncontrolled manner, inconsistencies or errors (e.g., deadlocks) regarding these interactions might occur [294, 295]. This is particularly challenging if there are running instances of these process choreographies. As a consequence, adaptations of collaborative business processes turn out to be costly and error-prone. When adapting collaborative processes, consistency and correctness will be crucial as well as the provision of change propagation methods to business partners, without violating autonomy, security, and trust constraints. Additionally, compliance of the changed processes and partner interactions with imposed regulations and laws need to be guaranteed. Here the challenge is to model, integrate, and verify compliance rules imposed on collaborative business processes.

Appendix A
Overview of BPMN Elements

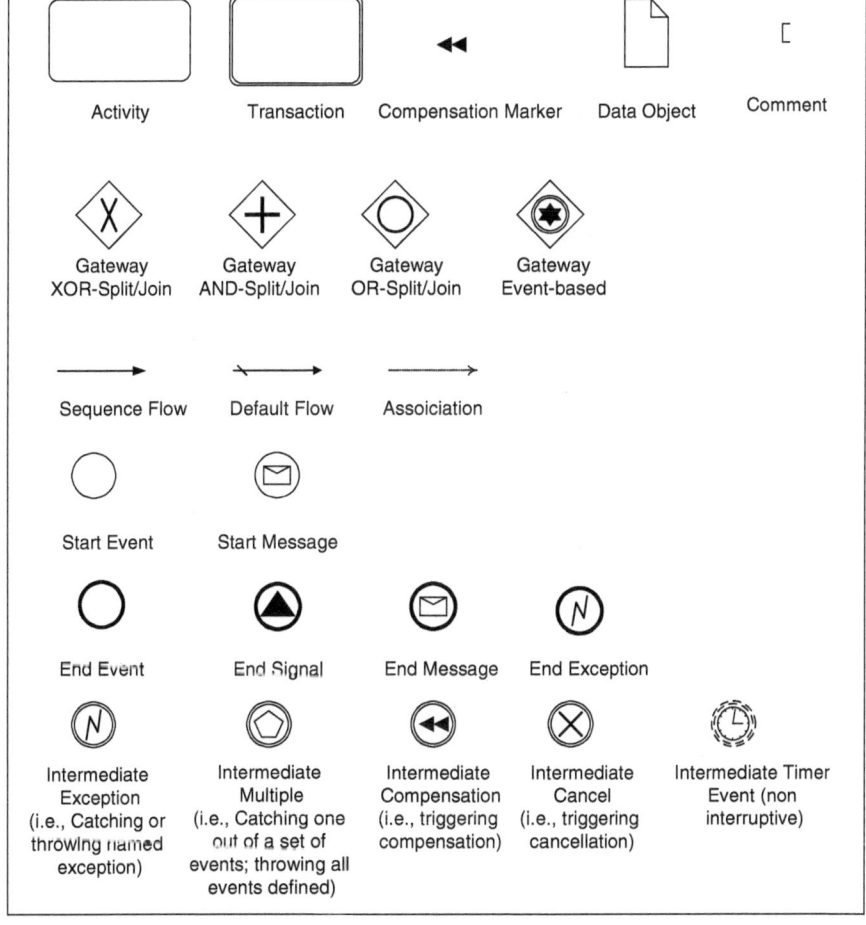

Fig. A.1 Overview of BPMN elements

M. Reichert and B. Weber, *Enabling Flexibility in Process-Aware Information Systems*,   489
DOI 10.1007/978-3-642-30409-5, © Springer-Verlag Berlin Heidelberg 2012

References

1. van der Aalst, W.M.P.: Verification of workflow nets. In: Application and Theory of Petri Nets 1997. Lecture Notes in Computer Science, vol. 1248, pp. 407–426. Springer, Berlin (1997)
2. van der Aalst, W.M.P.: The application of Petri nets to workflow management. J. Circuit. Syst. Comp. **8**(1), 21–66 (1998)
3. van der Aalst, W.M.P.: Formalization and verification of event-driven process chains. Inform. Software Tech. **41**(10), 639–650 (1999)
4. van der Aalst, W.M.P.: Workflow verification: Finding control-flow errors using Petri-net-based techniques. In: van der Aalst, W., Desel, J., Oberweis, A. (eds.) Business Process Management. Lecture Notes in Computer Science, vol. 1806, pp. 161–183. Springer, Berlin (2000)
5. van der Aalst, W.M.P.: Exterminating the dynamic change bug: A concrete approach to support worfklow change. Inform. Syst. Front. **3**(3), 297–317 (2001)
6. van der Aalst, W.M.P.: Process Mining – Discovery, Conformance and Enhancement of Business Processes. Springer, Berlin (2011)
7. van der Aalst, W.M.P., Barthelmess, P., Ellis, C.A., Wainer, J.: Workflow modeling using proclets. In: Scheuermann, P., Etzion, O. (eds.) Proceedings of the 7th International Conference on Cooperative Information Systems (CoopIS'00). Lecture Notes in Computer Science, vol. 1901, pp. 198–209. Springer, Berlin (2000)
8. van der Aalst, W.M.P., Basten, T.: Identifying commonalities and differences in object life cycles using behavorial inheritance. In: Colom, J.M., Koutny, M. (eds.) Proceedings of the International Conference on Application and Theory of Petri Nets (ICATPN'01). Lecture Notes in Computer Science, vol. 2075, pp. 32–52. Springer, Berlin (2001)
9. van der Aalst, W.M.P., Basten, T.: Inheritance of workflows: An approach to tackling problems related to change. Theor. Comput. Sci. **270**(1–2), 125–203 (2002)
10. van der Aalst, W.M.P., de Beer, H.T., van Dongen, B.F.: Process mining and verification of properties: An approach based on temporal logic. In: Proceedings of the 13th International Conference on Cooperative Information (CoopIS'05). Lecture Notes in Computer Science, vol. 3760, pp. 130–147. Springer, Berlin (2005)
11. van der Aalst, W.M.P., van Dongen, B.F., Herbst, J., Maruster, L., Schimm, G., Weijters, A.J.M.M.: Workflow mining: A survey of issues and approaches. Data Knowl. Eng. **27**(2), 237–267 (2003)
12. van der Aalst, W.M.P., Dumas, M., Gottschalk, F., ter Hofstede, A.H.M., La Rosa, M., Mendling, J.: Preserving correctness during business process model configuration. Formal Asp. Comput. **22**(3–4), 459–482 (2010)
13. van der Aalst, W.M.P., van Hee, K.: Workflow Management. MIT, Cambridge (2002)
14. van der Aalst, W.M.P., Jablonski, S.: Dealing with workflow change: Identification of issues an solutions. Int. J. Comput. Syst. Sci. Eng. **15**(5), 267–276 (2000)

M. Reichert and B. Weber, *Enabling Flexibility in Process-Aware Information Systems*, 491
DOI 10.1007/978-3-642-30409-5, © Springer-Verlag Berlin Heidelberg 2012

15. van der Aalst, W.M.P., Lassen, K.B.: Translating unstructured workflow processes to readable BPEL: Theory and implementation. Inform. Software Tech. **50**, 131–159 (2008)
16. van der Aalst, W.M.P., Lohmann, N., La Rosa, M., Xu, J.: Correctness ensuring process configuration: An approach based on partner synthesis. In: BPM. Lecture Notes in Computer Science, vol. 6336, pp. 95–111. Springer, New York (2010)
17. van der Aalst, W.M.P., Mans, R.S., Russell, N.C.: Workflow support using proclets: Divide, interact and conquer. Bull. IEEE Comput. Soc. Tech. Committ. Data Eng. **32**(3), 16–22 (2009)
18. van der Aalst, W.M.P., Pesic, M.: Decserflow: Towards a truly declarative service flow language. Technical report, BPMcenter.org (2006)
19. van der Aalst, W.M.P., Pesic, M., Schonenberg, H.: Declarative workflows: Balancing between flexibility and support. Comput. Sci. Res. Dev. **23**(2), 99–113 (2009)
20. van der Aalst, W.M.P., Reijers, H.A., Song, M.K.: Discovering social networks from event logs. Comput. Support Cooper. Work **14**(6), 549–593 (2005)
21. van der Aalst, W.M.P., Rosemann, M., Dumas, M.: Deadline-based escalation in process-aware information systems. Decis. Support Syst. **43**, 492–511 (2007)
22. van der Aalst, W.M.P., ter Hofstede, A.H.M.: YAWL: Yet another workflow language. Inform. Syst. **30**(4), 245–275 (2005)
23. van der Aalst, W.M.P., ter Hofstede, A.H.M., Kiepuszewski, B., Barros, A.P.: Workflow patterns. Distr. Parallel Database **14**(1), 5–51 (2003)
24. van der Aalst, W.M.P., Weske, M., Grünbauer, D.: Case handling: A new paradigm for business process support. Data Knowl. Eng. **53**(2), 129–162 (2005)
25. van der Aalst, W.M.P., et al.: Process mining manifesto. In: Business Process Management Workshops (1), pp. 169–194 (2011)
26. Aamodt, A., Plaza, E.: Case-based reasoning: Foundational issues, methodological variations and system approaches. AI Comm. **7**(2), 39–59 (1994)
27. Abecker, A., Bernardi, A., van Elst, L., Lauer, A., Maus, H., Schwarz, S., Sintek, M.: Frodo: A framework for distributed organizational memories. Milestone 1: Requirements analysis and system architecture. DFKI document, DFKI (2001)
28. Adams, M., ter Hofstede, A.H.M., van der Aalst, W.M.P., Edmond, D.: Dynamic, extensible and context-aware exception handling for workflows. In: Proceedings of the CoopIS'07. Lecture Notes in Computer Science, vol. 4803, pp. 95–112. Springer, New York (2007)
29. Adams, M., ter Hofstede, A.H.M., Edmond, D., van der Aalst, W.M.P.: A service-oriented implementation of dynamic flexibility in workflows. In: Proceedings of the Coopis'06. Lecture Notes in Computer Science, vol. 4275, pp. 291–308. Springer, New York (2006)
30. Adams, M., ter Hofstede, A.H.M., Edmond, D., van der Aalst, W.M.P.: Dynamic and extensible exception handling for workflows: A service-oriented implementation. Technical Report. BPM Center Report BPM-07-03, BPMcenter.org (2007)
31. Aggarwal, R., Verma, K., Miller, J., Milnor, W.: Constraint driven web service composition in METEOR-S. In: Proceedings of the International Conference on Services Computing (SCC 2004). 2004 IEEE International Conference on Services Computing (SCC 2004), 15–18 September 2004, Shanghai, China. IEEE SCC. IEEE Computer Society, pp. 23–30 (2004)
32. Aha, D.W., Muñoz-Avila, H.: Introduction: Interactive case-based reasoning. Appl. Intell. **14**(1), 7–8 (2001)
33. Alberti, M., Chesani, F., Gavanelli, M., Lamma, E., Mello, P., Montali, M., Torroni, P.: Expressing and verifying business contracts with abductive logic programming. In: Boella, G., van der Torre, L.W.N., Verhagen, H. (eds.) Normative Multi-agent Systems. Dagstuhl Seminar Proceedings, vol. 07122. Internationales Begegnungs- und Forschungszentrum für Informatik (IBFI), Schloss Dagstuhl, Germany (2007)
34. Alonso, G., Casati, F., Kuno, H., Machiraju, V.: Web Services – Concepts, Architectures and Applications. Springer, Berlin (2004)
35. Andany, J., Leonard, M., Palisser, C.: Management of schema evolution in databases. In: Proceedings of the International Conference on Very Large Databases (VLDB'91), Barcelona, pp. 161–170 (1991)

36. Awad, A., Decker, G., Weske, M.: Efficient compliance checking using BPMN-Q and temporal logic. In: Proceedings of the 6th International Conference on Business Process Management (BPM'08), pp. 326–341. Springer, New York (2008)
37. Awad, A., Weidlich, M., Weske, M.: Specification, verification and explanation of violation for data-aware compliance rules. In: Proceedings of the 7th International Conference on Service Oriented Computing (ICSOC'09), pp. 500–515. Springer, New York (2009)
38. Ayora, C., Torres, V., Pelechano, V.: Variability management in business process models. Technical Report 17, PROS - UPV (2012)
39. Bandinelli, S., Fugetta, A., Ghezzi, C.: Software process model evolution in the SPADE environment. IEEE Trans. Software Eng. **19**(12), 1128–1144 (1993)
40. Barba, I., Del Valle, C.: A constraint-based approach for planning and scheduling repeated activities. In: Proceedings of the COPLAS, pp. 55–62 (2011)
41. Barba, I., Weber, B., Del Valle, C.: Supporting the optimized execution of business processes through recommendations. In: Business Process Management Workshops (1), pp. 135–140 (2011)
42. Basel Committee on Banking Supervision: Int'l convergence of capital measurement and capital standards: A revised framework – comprehensive version. Technical Report, Bank for Int'l Settlements (2006)
43. Bassil, S., Benyoucef, M., Keller, R., Kropf, P.: Addressing dynamism in e-negotiations by workflow management systems. In: 13th International Workshop on Database and Expert Systems Applications (DEXA 2002). Proceedings of the Workshop on Negotiations in e-Markets – Beyond Price Discovery (DEXA'02). IEEE Computer Society, Aix-en-Provence, France (2002)
44. Bassil, S., Keller, R., Kropf, P.: A workflow–oriented system architecture for the management of container transportation. In: Desel, J., Pernici, B., Weske, M. (eds.) Proceedings of the BPM'04. Lecture Notes in Computer Science, vol. 3080, pp. 116–131. Potsdam, Germany (2004)
45. Batory, D.S.: Feature models, grammars, and propositional formulas. In: 9th International Conference on Software Product Lines. Lecture Notes in Computer Science, pp. 7–20. Springer, Berlin (2005)
46. Bauer, T., Reichert, M., Dadam, P.: Intra-subnet load balancing in distributed workflow management systems. Int. J. Cooper. Inform. Syst. **12**(3), 295–324 (2003)
47. Beck, K.: Extreme Programming Explained. Addison Wesley, Reading (2000)
48. Becker, J., Delfmann, P., Knackstedt, R.: Adaptive reference modeling: Integrating configurative and generic adaptation techniques for information models. In: Becker, J., Delfmann, P. (eds.) Reference Modeling. Efficient Information Systems Design Through Reuse of Information Models, pp. 23–49. Physica, Heidelberg (2007)
49. Becker, J., Kugeler, M., Rosemann, M.: Process management: A guide for the design of business processes. Springer, Berlin (2003)
50. Beckstein, C., Klausner, J.: A planning framework for workflow management. In: Proceedings of the Workshop Intelligent Workflow and Process Management, Stockholm (1999)
51. Bensalem, S., et al.: An overview of SAL. In: Proceedings of the of the 5th NASA Langley Formal Methods Workshop, pp. 187–196. NASA Langley Research Center (2000)
52. Bhattacharya, K., Hull, R., Su, J.: A Data-Centric Design Methodology for Business Processes, pp. 503–531. IGI Global, Hershey (2009)
53. Bobrik, R., Bauer, T., Reichert, M.: Proviado – personalized and configurable visualizations of business processes. In: Proceedings of the of the 7th International Conference on Electronic Commerce and Web Technologies (EC-WEB'06). Lecture Notes in Computer Science, vol. 4082, pp. 61–71. Springer, Berlin (2006)
54. Bobrik, R., Reichert, M., Bauer, T.: View-based process visualization. In: Proceedings of the BPM'07. Lecture Notes in Computer Science, vol. 4714, pp. 88–95. Springer, Berlin (2007)
55. Boehm, B.W.: Software Engineering Economics. Prentice Hall, Englewood Cliffs (1981)
56. Bose, R.P.J.C., van der Aalst, W.M.P., Zliobaite, I., Pechenizkiy, M.: Handling concept drift in process mining. In: Mouratidis, H., Rolland, C. (eds.) Advanced Information Systems

Engineering - 23rd International Conference, CAiSE 2011, London, UK, June 20-24, 2011. Proceedings. Lecture Notes in Computer Science, vol. 6741, pp. 391405. Springer, New York (2011)

57. Roberts, D., Brant, J., Johnson, R.: A Refactoring tool for Smalltalk. Theor. Pract. Object Syst. 3, 253–263 (1997)

58. Canfora, G., Di Penta, M., Esposito, R., Villani, M.L.: A framework for QoS-aware binding and re-binding of composite web services. J. Syst. Software **81**(10), 1754–1769 (2008)

59. Casati, F.: Models, semantics, and formal methods for the design of workflows and their exceptions. Ph.D. thesis, Milano (1998)

60. Casati, F., Ceri, S., Paraboschi, S., Pozzi, G.: Specification and implementation of exceptions in workflow management systems. ACM TODS **24**(3), 405–451 (1999)

61. Casati, F., Ceri, S., Pernici, B., Pozzi, G.: Workflow evolution. Data Knowl. Eng. **24**(3), 211–238 (1998)

62. Casati, F., Shan, M.C.: Dynamic and adaptive composition of e-services. Inform. Syst. **26**(3), 143–163 (2001)

63. Castellanos, M., Alves de Medeiros, K., Mendling, J., Weber, B., Weitjers, A.J.M.M.: Business process intelligence. In: Handbook of Research on Business Process Modeling, pp. 456–480. Idea Group Inc (2009)

64. Chiao, C.M., Künzle, V., Reichert, M.: Towards object-aware process support in healthcare information systems. In: Proceedings of the 4th International Conference on eHealth, Telemedicine, and Social Medicine (eTELEMED 2012), IARIA (2012)

65. Chiu, D., Li, Q., Karlapalem, K.: Web interface-driven cooperative exception handling in ADOME. Inform. Syst. **26**(2), 93–120 (2001)

66. Cohn, D., Hull, R.: Business artifacts: A data-centric approach to modeling business operations and processes. IEEE Data Eng. Bull. **32**(3), 3–9 (2009)

67. Cohn, M.: Agile Estimating and Planning. Prentice Hall PTR, Upper Saddle River (2006)

68. Combi, C., Gambini, M.: Flaws in the flow: The weakness of unstructured business process modeling languages dealing with data. In: OTM Conferences (1). Lecture Notes in Computer Science, vol. 5870, pp. 42–59. Springer, New York (2009)

69. Cortadella, J., Kishinevsky, M., Lavagno, L., Yakovlev, A.: Deriving petri nets from finite transition systems. IEEE Trans. Comput. **47**(8), 859–882 (1998)

70. Dadam, P., Reichert, M.: The ADEPT project: A decade of research and development for robust and flexible process support. Comput. Sci. Res. Dev. **23**(2), 81–97 (2009)

71. Dadam, P., Reichert, M., Kuhn, K.: Clinical workflows – the killer application for process-oriented information systems? In: Proceedings of the International Conference on Business Information Systems (BIS'00), pp. 36–59. Poznan, Poland (2000)

72. Davies, C.T., Jr.: Data processing spheres of control. IBM Syst. J. **17**(2), 179–198 (1978)

73. Deiters, W., Gruhn, V.: The FUNSOFT net appoach to software process management. Int. J. Software Eng. Knowl. Eng. **4**(2), 229–256 (1994)

74. Dijkman, R., Dumas, M., van Dongen, B., Kaarik, R., Mendling, J.: Similarity of business process models: Metrics and evaluation. Inform. Syst. **36**(2), 498–516 (2011)

75. Dijkman, R., Gfeller, B., Küster, J., Völzer, H.: Identifying refactoring opportunities in process model repositories. Inform. Software Tech. **53**(9), 937–948 (2011). Studying work practices in Global Software Engineering

76. Dijkstra, E.W.: Chapter I: Notes on structured programming. In: Dahl, O.J., Dijkstra, E.W., Hoare, C.A.R. (eds.) Structured programming, pp. 1–82. Academic, San Diego (1972)

77. Domingos, D., Rito-Silva, A., Veiga, P.: Authorization and access control in adaptive workflows. In: ESORICS 2003. Lecture Notes in Computer Science, pp. 23–38. Springer, New York (2003)

78. van Dongen, B.F., van der Aalst, W.M.P.: Multi-phase process mining: Building instance graphs. In: ER'04. Lecture Notes in Computer Science 3288, pp. 362–376. Springer, Berlin (2004)

79. van Dongen, B.F., van der Aalst, W.M.P., Verbeek, H.M.W.: Verification of EPCs: Using reduction rules and Petri nets. In: CAiSE. Lecture Notes in Computer Science, vol. 3520, pp. 372–386. Springer, New York (2005)

80. Dourish, P., Holmes, J., MacLean, A., Marqvardsen, P., Zbyslaw, A.: Freeflow: Mediating between representation and action in workflow systems. In: Proceedings of the ACM Conference on Computer Supported Cooperative Work, CSCW '96, pp. 190–198 (1996)
81. Dumas, M., García-Bañuelos, L., Dijkman, R.M.: Similarity search of business process models. IEEE Data Eng. Bull. **32**(3), 23–28 (2009)
82. Dumas, M., ter Hofstede, A.H.M., van der Aalst, W.M.P. (eds.): Process-Aware Information Systems. Wiley, New York (2005)
83. Dwyer, M.B., Avrunin, G.S., Corbett, J.C.: Property specification patterns for finite-state verification. In: Proceedings of the 2nd Workshop Formal Methods in Software Practice (FMSP'98). ACM, New York (1998)
84. Eder, J., Liebhart, W.: Workflow transactions. In: Lawrence, P. (ed.) Workflow Handbook 1997, pp. 195–202. Wiley, New York (1997)
85. Eder, J., Tahamtan, A.: Temporal conformance of federated choreographies. In: Proceedings of the 19th International Conference Database and Expert Systems Applications (DEXA'08), pp. 668–675. Springer, New York (2008)
86. Ellis, C.A., Keddara, K., Rozenberg, G.: Dynamic change within workflow systems. In: Proceedings of the ACM Conference on Organizational Computing Systems (COOCS'95), Milpitas, pp. 10–21 (1995)
87. Ellis, C.A., Maltzahn, C.: The Chautauqua workflow system. In: Proceedings of the International Conference on System Science. Maui, Hawaii (1997)
88. Elmagarmid, A.K. (ed.): Database Transaction Models for Advanced Applications. Morgan Kaufmann, San Mateo (1992)
89. Fahland, D., Woith, H.: Towards process models for disaster response. In: Dumas, M., Reichert, M., Shan, M.-C. (eds.), Business Process Management, 6th International Conference, BPM 2008, Milan, Italy, September 2–4, 2008. Proceedings. Lecture Notes in Computer Science, vol. 5240, pp. 254–265. Springer, New York (2008)
90. Fent, A., Reiter, H., Freitag, B.: Design for change: Evolving workflow specifications in ULTRAflow. In: Proceedings of the International Conference on Advanced Information Systems Engineering (CAISE'02). Lecture Notes in Computer Science, vol. 2348, pp. 516–534. Springer, New York (2002)
91. Fowler, M., Beck, K., Brant, J., Opdyke, W., Roberts, D.: Refactoring: Improving the design of existing code. Addison-Wesley, Reading (1999)
92. Frauenhofer ISST: SPOT Project. http://www.spot.fraunhofer.de/ (2010). Accessed 13 July 2010
93. Gabbay, D., Pnueli, A., Shelah, S., Stavi, J.: On the temporal analysis of fairness. In: Proceedings of the 7th ACM SIGPLAN-SIGACT Symposium on Principles of Programming Languages, pp. 163–173 (1980)
94. Garcia-Molina, H., Gawlick, D., Klein, J., Kleissner, K., Salem, K.: Modeling long-running activities as nested Sagas. Data Eng. **14**, 14–18 (1991)
95. Garcia-Molina, H., Salem, K.: Sagas. In: Dayal, U., Traiger, I.L. (eds.) Proceedings of the Association for Computing Machinery Special Interest Group on Management of Data 1987 Annual Conference, San Francisco, California, May 27–29, 1987, pp. 249–259. ACM Press (1987)
96. Gebauer, J., Schober, F.: Information system flexibility and the cost efficiency of business processes. J. Assoc. Inform. Syst. **7**(3), 122–147 (2006)
97. Ghattas, J., Peleg, M., Soffer, P., Denekamp, Y.: Learning the context of a clinical process. In: Business Process Management Workshops. Lecture Notes in Business Information Processing, vol. 43, pp. 545–556. Springer, New York (2009)
98. Ghattas, J., Soffer, P., Peleg, M.: A formal model for process context learning. In: Business Process Management Workshops. Lecture Notes in Business Information Processing, vol. 43, pp. 140–157. Springer, New York (2009)
99. Ghose, A., Koliadis, G.: Auditing business process compliance. In: Proceedings of the 5th International Conference on Service-Oriented Computing (ICSOC'07), pp. 169–180. Springer, New York (2007)

100. Giblin, C., Müller, S., Pfitzmann, B.: From regulatory policies to event monitoring rules: Towards model-driven compliance automation. Technical Report, RZ-3662, IBM Research GmbH (2006)

101. van Glabbeek, R., Weijland, W.P.: Branching time and abstraction in bisimulation semantics. J. ACM **43**(3), 555–600 (1996)

102. Goedertier, S., Vanthienen, J.: Designing compliant business processes with obligations and permissions. In: Proceedings of the BPM'06 Workshops, pp. 5–14. Springer, New York (2006)

103. Gottschalk, F.: Configurable process models. Ph.D. thesis, Eindhoven University of Technology, The Netherlands (2009)

104. Gottschalk, F., van der Aalst, W.M.P., Jansen-Vullers, M.H.: Merging event-driven process chains. In: OTM Conferences (1). Lecture Notes in Computer Science, vol. 5331, pp. 418–426. Springer, Berlin (2008)

105. Gottschalk, F., van der Aalst, W.M.P., Jansen-Vullers, M.H., La Rosa, M.: Configurable workflow models. Int. J. Cooper. Inf. Syst. **17**(2), 177–221 (2008)

106. Gottschalk, F., Wagemakers, T.A.C., Jansen-Vullers, M.H., van der Aalst, W.M.P., La Rosa, M.: Configurable process models: Experiences from a municipality case study. In: CAiSE'09. Lecture Notes in Computer Science, vol. 5565, pp. 486–500. Springer, New York (2009)

107. Governatori, G., Milosevic, Z., Sadiq, S.: Compliance checking between business processes and business contracts. In: Proceedings of the 10th International Enterprise Distributed Object Computing Conference (EDOC'06), pp. 221–232. IEEE Computer Society, New York (2006)

108. Grambow, G., Oberhauser, R., Reichert, M.: Employing semantically driven adaptation for amalgamating software quality assurance with process management. In: Second International Conference on Adaptive and Self-adaptive Systems and Applications (ADAPTIVE'10), pp. 58–67. Xpert Publ Services, Wilmington (2010)

109. Grambow, G., Oberhauser, R., Reichert, M.: Semantic workflow adaption in support of workflow diversity. In: 4th International Conference on Advances in Semantic Processing (SEMAPRO'10), pp. 158–165. Xpert Publ Services, Wilmington (2010)

110. Grambow, G., Oberhauser, R., Reichert, M.: Contextual injection of quality measures into software engineering processes. Int. J. Adv. Software **4**(1–2), 76–99 (2011)

111. Grambow, G., Oberhauser, R., Reichert, M.: Semantically-driven workflow generation using declarative modeling for processes in software engineering. In: Workshops Proceedings of the 15th IEEE International Enterprise Distributed Object Computing Conference, EDOCW 2011, Helsinki, Finland, pp. 164–173. IEEE Computer Society (2011)

112. Grambow, G., Oberhauser, R., Reichert, M.: Towards a workflow language for software engineering. In: Proceedings of the 10th IASTED International Confernece on Software Engineering (SE'11), Innsbruck, Austria. IASTED (2011)

113. Grambow, G., Oberhauser, R., Reichert, M.: Towards automatic process-aware coordination in collaborative software engineering. In: ICSOFT'11 (1), Seville, Spain, pp. 5–14. SciTePress (2011)

114. Gray, J., Reuter, A.: Transaction Processing: Concepts and Techniques. Morgan Kaufmann, San Mateo (1993)

115. Green, T.R.: Cognitive dimensions of notations. In: Proceedings of the BCSHCI '89, pp. 443–460. Cambridge University Press, Cambridge (1989)

116. Green, T.R., Petre, M.: Usability analysis of visual programming environments: A 'cognitive dimensions' framework. J. Vis. Lang. Comput. **7**(2), 131–174 (1996)

117. Grosskopf, A., Decker, G., Weske, M.: The Process: Business Process Modeling Using BPMN. Meghan Kiffer Pr, Tampa (2009)

118. Gruhn, V., Laue, R.: Complexity metrics for business process models. In: Proceedings of the 9th International Conference on Business Information Systems (BIS'06), Klagenfurt, Austria. Lecture Notes in Informatics, vol. 85, pp. 1–12. GI (2006)

119. Günther, C.W., Reichert, M., van der Aalst, W.M.P.: Supporting flexible processes with adaptive workflow and case handling. In: Proceedings of the WETICE'08, 3rd IEEE

Workshop on Agile Cooperative Process-aware Information Systems (ProGility'08), pp. 229–234. IEEE Computer Society, New York (2008)

120. Günther, C.W., Rinderle, S., Reichert, M., van der Aalst, W.M.P.: Change mining in adaptive process management systems. In: Proceedings of the CoopIS'06. Lecture Notes in Computer Science, vol. 4275, pp. 309–326. Springer, Berlin (2006)

121. Günther, C.W., Rinderle-Ma, S., Reichert, M., van der Aalst, W.M., Recker, J.: Using process mining to learn from process changes in evolutionary systems. Int. J. Bus. Process. Integrat. Manag. 3(1), 61–78 (2008) (Special Issue on Business Process Flexibility)

122. Hagen, C., Alonso, G.: Exception handling in workflow management systems. IEEE Trans. Software Eng. 26(10), 943–958 (2000)

123. Haisjackl, C., Weber, B.: User assistance during process execution – an experimental evaluation of recommendation strategies. In: Business Process Management Workshops. Lecture Notes in Business Information Processing, vol. 66, pp. 134–145. Springer, New York (2010)

124. Hallerbach, A.: Management von Prozessvarianten. Ph.D. thesis, University of Ulm (2010)

125. Hallerbach, A., Bauer, T., Reichert, M.: Context-based configuration of process variants. In: Proceedings of the TCoB '08, pp. 31–40. Barcelona (2008)

126. Hallerbach, A., Bauer, T., Reichert, M.: Managing process variants in the process life cycle. In: ICEIS 2008 - Proceedings of the Tenth International Conference on Enterprise Information Systems, Barcelona, Spain, June 12–16, 2008, vol. ISAS-2, (3–2), pp. 154–161 (2008)

127. Hallerbach, A., Bauer, T., Reichert, M.: Guaranteeing soundness of configurable process variants in Provop. In: Proceedings of the 11th IEEE Conference on Commerce and Enterprise Computing (CEC'09), pp. 98–105. IEEE Computer Society, New York (2009)

128. Hallerbach, A., Bauer, T., Reichert, M.: Capturing variability in business process models: The Provop approach. J. Software Mainten. Evol. Res. Pract. 22(6/7), 519–546 (2010)

129. Hallerbach, A., Bauer, T., Reichert, M.: Configuration and Management of Process Variants, pp. 237–255. Springer, New York (2010)

130. Hammer, M., Champy, J.: Reengineering the Corporation. Harper Collins, London (1993)

131. Hammer, M., Stanton, S.: The Reengineering Revolution – The Handbook. Harper Collins, London (1995)

132. Hensinger, C., Reichert, M., Bauer, T., Strzeletz, T., Dadam, P.: ADEPT$_{workflow}$ – advanced workflow technology for the efficient support of adaptive, enterprise-wide processes. In: Proceedings of the Software Demonstration Track (EDBT'00), Konstanz (2000)

133. Herbst, J., Karagiannis, D.: Intergrating machine learning and workflow management to support acquisition and adaption of workflow models. In: Proceedings of the Workshop on Database and Expert Systems Applications (DEXA'98), Vienna, pp. 745–752 (1998)

134. Hochstein, A., Zarnekow, R., Brenner, W.: ITIL as common practice reference model for it service management: Formal assessment and implications for practice. In: IEEE International Conference on e-Technology, e-Commerce, and e-Services (EEE'05), pp. 704–710 (2005)

135. ter Hofstede, A.H.M., van der Aalst, W.M.P., Adams, M., Russell, N.: Modern Business Process Automation: YAWL and Its Support Environment. Springer, Berlin (2009)

136. Huth, M., Ryan, M.: Logic in Computer Science: Modelling and Reasoning About Systems. Cambridge University Press, Cambridge (2004)

137. Imai, M.: Kaizen: The Key to Japan's Competitive Success. McGraw-Hill/Irwin, New York (1986)

138. Jablonski, S., Bussler, C.: Workflow Management: Concepts, Architecture and Implementation. Thompson Publishers, London (1996)

139. Joeris, G., Herzog, O.: Managing evolving workflow specifications. In: Proceedings of the International Conference on Cooperative Information Systems (CoopIS'98), New York, pp. 310–321. IEEE Computer Society (1998)

140. Jørgensen, H.D.: Interactive process models. Ph.D. thesis, Trondheim (2004)

141. Karbe, B., Ramsperger, N., Weiss, P.: Support of cooperative work by electronic circulation folders. SIGOIS Bull. 11, 109–117 (1990)

142. Kiepuszewski, B.: Expressiveness and suitability of languages for control flow modelling in workflows. Ph.D. thesis, Queensland University of Technology, Brisbane (2002) (Available via http://www.tm.tue.nl/it/research/patterns)

143. Kiepuszewski, B., ter Hofstede, A., Bussler, C.: On structured workflow modelling. In: Proceedings of the International Conference on Advanced Information Systems Engineering (CAiSE'00). Lecture Notes in Computer Science, vol. 1789, pp. 431–445. Springer, New York (2000)

144. Klingemann, J.: Controlled flexibility in workflow management. In: Proceedings of the CAiSE'00. Lecture Notes in Computer Science, vol. 1789, pp. 126–141. Springer, New York (2000)

145. Knuplesch, D., Ly, L.T., Rinderle-Ma, S., Pfeifer, H., Dadam, P.: On enabling data-aware compliance checking of business process models. In: Proceedings of the 29th International Conference on Conceptual Modeling (ER'2010). Lecture Notes in Computer Science, vol. 6412, Springer, Berlin (2010)

146. Kochut, K., Arnold, J., Sheth, A., Miller, J., Kraemer, E., Arpinar, B., Cardoso, J.: IntelliGEN: A distributed workflow system for discovering protein-protein interactions. Distr. Parallel Databases 13(1), 43–72 (2003)

147. Kock, N.F.: Product flow, breadth and complexity of business processes: An empirical study of 15 business processes in three organizations. Bus. Process Re-eng. Manag. J. 2(2), 8–22 (1996)

148. Koehler, J., Vanhatalo, J.: Process anti-patterns: How to avoid the common traps of business process modeling. Technical Report RZ-3678, IBM Zurich Research Lab (2007)

149. Kokash, N., Krause, C., de Vink, E.: Time and data aware analysis of graphical service models. In: Proceedings of the 8th International Conference on Software Engineering and Formal Methods (SEFM'10). IEEE Computer Society, New York (2010)

150. Kolodner, J.L.: Case-Based Reasoning. Morgan Kaufmann, San Mateo (1993)

151. Koschmider, A., Song, M., Reijers, H.A.: Advanced social features in a recommendation system for process modeling. In: Proceedings of the Business Information Systems (BIS'09). Lecture Notes in Business Information Processing, vol. 21, pp. 109–120. Springer, New York (2009)

152. Kowalkiewicz, M., Lu, R., Baeuerle, S., Kruempelmann, M., Lippe, S.: Weak dependencies in business process models. In: Proceedings of the 11th International Conference on Business Information Systems (BIS'08). Lecture Notes in Business Information Processing, vol. 7, pp. 177–188, Springer, New York (2008)

153. Kradolfer, M., Geppert, A.: Dynamic workflow schema evolution based on workflow type versioning and workflow migration. Technical Report 98.02, University of Zurich, Department of Computer Science (1998)

154. Kradolfer, M., Geppert, A.: Dynamic workflow schema evolution based on workflow type versioning and workflow migration. In: Proceedings of the International Conference in Cooperative Information Systems (CoopIS'99), Edinburgh, pp. 104–114 (1999)

155. Künzle, V., Reichert, M.: Integrating users in object-aware process management systems: Issues and challenges. In: BPM'09 Workshops. Lecture Notes in Business Information Processing, vol. 43, pp. 29–41. Springer, Berlin (2009)

156. Künzle, V., Reichert, M.: Towards object-aware process management systems: Issues, challenges, benefits. In: BPMDS/EMMSAD'09. Lecture Notes in Business Information Processing, vol. 29, pp. 197–210. Springer, Berlin (2009)

157. Künzle, V., Reichert, M.: A Modeling Paradigm for Integrating Processes and Data at the Micro Level. In: Proceedings of the BPMDS'11. Lecture Notes in Business Information Processing, pp. 201–215. Springer, New York (2011)

158. Künzle, V., Reichert, M.: PHILharmonicFlows: Towards a framework for object-aware process management. J. Software Mainten. Evol. Res. Pract. 23(4), 205–244 (2011)

159. Künzle, V., Reichert, M.: Striving for object-aware process support: How existing approaches fit together. In: Aberer, K., Damiani, E., Dillon, T. (eds.) 1st International Symposium on Data-driven Process Discovery and Analysis (SIMPDA'11), Campione d'Italia, Italy (2011)

160. Künzle, V., Weber, B., Reichert, M.: Object-aware business processes: Fundamental requirements and their support in existing approaches. Int. J. Inform. Syst. Model. Des. **2**, 19–46 (2010)

161. Küster, J.M., Gerth, C., Förster, A., Engels, G.: Detecting and resolving process model differences in the absence of a change log. In: BPM'08. Lecture Notes in Computer Science, vol. 5240, pp. 244–260. Springer, New York (2008)

162. La Rosa, M.: Managing variability in process-aware information systems. Ph.D. thesis, Queensland University of Technology, Brisbane, Australia (2009)

163. La Rosa, M., van der Aalst, W.M.P., Dumas, M., ter Hofstede, A.H.M.: Questionnaire-based variability modeling for system configuration. Software Syst. Model. **8**(2), 251–274 (2009)

164. La Rosa, M., Dumas, M., ter Hofstede, A.H.M.: Modelling business process variability for design-time configuration. In: Cardoso, J., van der Aalst, W.M.P. (eds.) Handbook of Research on Business Process Modeling, pp. 204–228. Idea Group Inc (2009)

165. La Rosa, M., Dumas, M., ter Hofstede, A.H.M., Mendling, J.: Configurable multi-perspective business process models. Inf. Syst. **36**(2), 313–340 (2011)

166. La Rosa, M., Dumas, M., ter Hofstede, A.H.M., Mendling, J., Gottschalk, F.: Beyond control-flow: Extending business process configuration to roles and objects. In: Proceedings of the 27th International Conference on Conceptual Modeling (ER'08). Lecture Notes in Computer Science, vol. 5231, pp. 199–215. Springer, New York (2008)

167. La Rosa, M., Dumas, M., Uba, R., Dijkman, R.M.: Merging business process models. In: OTM Conferences (1). Lecture Notes in Computer Science, vol. 6426, pp. 96–113. Springer, New York (2010)

168. Lanz, A., Kreher, U., Reichert, M., Dadam, P.: Enabling process support for advanced applications with the AristaFlow BPM Suite. In: Proceedings of the Business Process Management 2010 Demonstration Track, no. 615 in CEUR Workshop Proceedings (2010)

169. Lanz, A., Reichert, M., Dadam, P.: Robust and flexible error handling in the AristaFlow BPM Suite. In: Proceedings of the CAiSE'10 Forum, Information Systems Evolution. Lecture Notes in Business Information Processing, vol. 72, pp. 174–189. Springer, New York (2010)

170. Lanz, A., Weber, B., Reichert, M.: Workflow time patterns for process-aware information systems. In: Proceedings of the BPMDS and EMMSAD 2010. Lecture Notes in Business Information Processing 50, pp. 94–107. Springer, New York (2010)

171. Laue, R., Mendling, J.: Structuredness and its significance for correctness of process models. Inform. Syst. E-Business Manag. **8**, 287–307 (2010)

172. Lenz, R., Reichert, M.: IT support for healthcare processes – premises, challenges, perspectives. Data Knowl. Eng. **61**(1), 39–58 (2007)

173. de Leoni, M.: Adaptive process management in highly dynamic and pervasive scenarios. In: Proceedings of the Fourth European Young Researchers Workshop on Service Oriented Computing (YR-SOC 2009). Electronic Proceedings in Theoretical Computer Science, vol. 2, pp. 83–97. Open, Publ. Assoc., Australia (2009)

174. Leopold, H., Smirnov, S., Mendling, J.: Refactoring of activity labels in business process models. In: 15th International Conference on Applications of Natural Language to Information Systems (NLDB 2010). Lecture Notes in Computer Science, vol. 6177, pp. 268–276. Springer, New York (2010)

175. Leopold, H., Smirnov, S., Mendling, J.: Recognizing activity labelling styles in business process models. Enterpr. Mod. Inf. Sys. Architect. **6**(1), 16–29 [Int'l Journal (EMISA Journal)] (2011)

176. Lerner, B.S., Christov, S., Osterweil, L.J., Bendraou, R., Kannengiesser, U., Wise, A.E.: Exception handling patterns for process modeling. IEEE Trans. Software Eng. **36**(2), 162–183 (2010)

177. Leymann, F.: Supporting business transactions via partial recovery in workflow management systems. In: Proceedings of the Datenbanksysteme in Büro, Technik und Wissenschaft (BTW'95), Dresden, pp. 51–70 (1995)

178. Leymann, F., Roller, D.: Production Workflow. Prentice Hall, New Jersey (2000)

179. Li, C.: Mining process model variants: Challenges, techniques, examples. Ph.D. thesis, University of Twente, The Netherlands (2009)

180. Li, C., Reichert, M., Wombacher, A.: Discovering reference process models by mining process variants. In: Proceedings of the 6th International Conference on Web Services (ICWS'08), pp. 45–53. IEEE Computer Society, New York (2008)

181. Li, C., Reichert, M., Wombacher, A.: On measuring process model similarity based on high-level change operations. In: Proceedings of the ER'08. Lecture Notes in Computer Science, vol. 5231, pp. 248–264. Springer, Berlin (2008)

182. Li, C., Reichert, M., Wombacher, A.: Discovering reference models by mining process variants using a heuristic approach. In: Proceedings of the 7th International Conference on Business Process Management (BPM'09). Lecture Notes in Computer Science, vol. 5701, pp. 344–362. Springer, New York (2009)

183. Li, C., Reichert, M., Wombacher, A.: Mining based on learning from process change logs. In: Proceedings of the BPM'08 Workshops. Lecture Notes in Business Information Processing, vol. 17, pp. 121–133. Springer, New York (2009)

184. Li, C., Reichert, M., Wombacher, A.: What are the problem makers: Ranking activities according to their relevance for process changes. In: IEEE 7th International Conference on Web Services (ICWS'09), pp. 51–58. IEEE Computer Society, New York (2009)

185. Li, C., Reichert, M., Wombacher, A.: The MinAdept clustering approach for discovering reference process models out of process variants. Int. J. Cooper. Inform. Syst. **19**(3–4), 159–203 (2010)

186. Li, C., Reichert, M., Wombacher, A.: Mining business process variants: Challenges, scenarios, algorithms. Data Knowl. Eng. **70**(5), 409–434 (2011)

187. Liu, C., Conradi, R.: Automatic replanning of task networks for process model evolution. In: Proceedings of the European Software Engineering Conference, pp. 434–450. Garmisch-Partenkirchen, Germany (1993)

188. Liu, R., Bhattacharya, K., Wu, F.Y.: Modeling business contexture and behavior using business artifacts. Adv. Inform. Syst. Eng. **4495**, 324–339 (2007)

189. Liu, Y., Müller, S., Xu, K.: A static compliance-checking framework for business process models. IBM Syst. J. **46**(2), 335–261 (2007)

190. Lohmann, N., Wolf, K.: Compact representations and efficient algorithms for operating guidelines. Fundam. Inform. **108**(1–2), 43–62 (2011)

191. Lu, R., Sadiq, S.W.: Managing process variants as an information resource. In: Proceedings of the BPM'06. Lecture Notes in Computer Science, vol. 4102, pp. 426–431. Springer, New York (2006)

192. Luengo, D., Seplveda, M.: Applying clustering in process mining to find different versions of a business process that changes over time. In: Business Process Management Workshops. Lecture Notes in Business Information Processing, vol. 99. Springer, New York (2011)

193. Luger, G.F.: Artificial Intelligence: Structures and Strategies for Complex Problem Solving. Pearson/Addison Wesley, Boston (2005)

194. Luo, Z., Sheth, A., Kochut, K., Miller, J.: Exception handling in workflow systems. Appl. Intell. **13**(2), 125–147 (2000)

195. Ly, L.T., Knuplesch, D., Rinderle-Ma, S., Göser, K., Pfeifer, H., Reichert, M., Dadam, P.: SeaFlows Toolset – compliance verification made easy for process-aware information systems. In: Proceedings of the CAiSE'10 Forum. Lecture Notes in Business Information Processing, vol. 72, pp. 76–91. Springer, Berlin (2010)

196. Ly, L.T., Rinderle, S., Dadam, P.: Integration and verification of semantic constraints in adaptive process management systems. Data Knowl. Eng. **64**(1), 3–23 (2008)

197. Ly, L.T., Rinderle, S., Dadam, P., Reichert, M.: Mining staff assignment rules from event-based data. In: Proceedings of the BPM'05 Workshops, Lecture Notes in Computer Science, vol. 3812, pp. 177–190. Springer, New York (2005)

198. Ly, L.T., Rinderle-Ma, S., Dadam, P.: Design and verification of instantiable compliance rule graphs in process-aware information systems. In: Proceedings of the 22nd International Conference on Advanced Systems Engineering (CAiSE'10), pp. 9–23. Springer, New York (2010)

199. Ly, L.T., Rinderle-Ma, S., Göser, K., Dadam, P.: On enabling integrated process compliance with semantic constraints in process management systems – requirements, challenges, solutions. Inf. Sys. Front. **14**(2), 195–219 (2012) (Special Issue Governance, Risk and Compliance)

200. Ly, L.T., Rinderle-Ma, S., Knuplesch, D., Dadam, P.: Monitoring business process compliance using compliance rule graphs. In: Proceedings of the 19th International Conference on Cooperative Information Systems (CoopIS'11). Lecture Notes in Computer Science, vol. 7044, pp. 82–99. Springer, New York (2011)

201. Maggi, F., Montali, M., Westergaard, M., van der Aalst, W.M.P.: Monitoring business constraints with linear temporal logic: An approach based on colored automata. In: Proceedings of the BPM 2011. Springer, New York (2011)

202. Malone, T., Crowston, K., Herman, G.: Organizing Business Knowledge: The MIT Process Handbook. MIT, Cambridge (2003)

203. Mann, J.E.: Workflow and EAI. EAI J. **1**(3), 49–53 (1999)

204. Mans, R.S., Russell, N.C., van der Aalst, W.M.P., Moleman, A.J., Bakker., P.J.M.: Schedule-aware workflow management systems. In: T. Petri Nets and Other Models of Concurrency, vol. 4. Lecture Notes in Computer Science, vol. 6550, pp. 121–143. Springer, New York (2010)

205. McCarthy, D., Sarin, S.: Workflow and transactions in inconcert. IEEE Bull. Data Eng. **16**(2), 53–56 (1993)

206. Mendling, J., Reijers, H.A.: How to define activity labels for business process models? In: Proceedings of the AIS SIGSAND'08, pp. 117–127 (2008)

207. Mendling, J., Reijers, H.A., van der Aalst, W.M.P.: Seven process modeling guidelines (7PMG). Inform. Software Tech. **52**(2), 127–136 (2010)

208. Mendling, J., Reijers, H.A., Recker, J.: Activity labeling in process modeling: Empirical insights and recommendations. Inform. Syst. **35**(4), 467–482 (2010)

209. Mendling, J., Verbeek, H.M.W., van Dongen, B.F., van der Aalst, W.M.P., Neumann, G.: Detection and prediction of errors in EPCs of the SAP reference model. Data Know. Eng. **64**(1), 312–329 (2008)

210. Mens, T., Gorp, P.V.: A taxonomy of model transformation. Electr. Notes Theor. Comput. Sci. **152**, 125–142 (2006)

211. Mens, T., Tourwe, T.: A survey of software refactoring. IEEE Trans. Software Eng. **30**(2), 126–139 (2004).

212. Meyer, H., Weske, M.: Automated service composition using heuristic search. In: Proceedings of the 4th International Conference Business Process Management (BPM'06), Vienna, Austria. Lecture Notes in Computer Science, vol. 4102, pp. 81–96. Springer, New York (2006)

213. Miller, G.: The magical number seven, plus or minus two: Some limits on our capacity for processing information. Psychol. Rev. **63**, 81–97 (1956)

214. Minor, M., Bergmann, R., Görg, S., Walter, K.: Towards case-based adaptation of workflows. In: ICCBR'11. Lecture Notes in Computer Science, vol. 6880, pp. 421–435. Springer, New York (2010)

215. Minor, M., Bergmann, R., Görg, S., Walter, K.: Reasoning on business processes to support change reuse. In: CEC'11, pp. 18–25. IEE Computer Press (2011)

216. Minor, M., Schmalen, D., Koldehoff, A., Bergmann, R.: Structural adaptation of workflows supported by a suspension mechanism and by case-based reasoning. In: Proceedings of the WETICE'07, pp. 370–375. IEE Computer Society (2007)

217. Minor, M., Tartakovski, A., Bergmann, R.: Representation and structure-based similarity assessment for agile workflows. In: Proceedings of the ICCBR'07. Lecture Notes in Computer Science, vol. 4626, pp. 224–238. Springer, New York (2007)

218. Minor, M., Tartakovski, A., Schmalen, D., Bergmann, R.: Agile workflow technology and case-based change reuse for long-term processes. Int. J. Intell. Inform. Tech. **4**(1), 80–98 (2008)

219. Montali, M.: Specification and Verification of Declarative Open Interaction Models. Springer, Berlin (2010)

220. Montali, M., Pesic, M., van der Aalst, W.M.P., Chesani, F., Mello, P., Storari, S.: Declarative specification and verification of service choreographiess. TWEB **4**(1) (2010)
221. Moss, E.: Nested Transactions. MIT, Cambridge (1985)
222. Mourao, H., Antunes, P.: Supporting effective unexpected exceptions handling in workflow management systems. In: Proceedings of the ACM symposium on Applied computing (SAC'07), pp. 1242–1249. ACM, New York (2007)
223. Müller, D., Herbst, J., Hammori, M., Reichert, M.: IT support for release management processes in the automotive industry. In: Proceedings of the BPM'06. Lecture Notes in Computer Science, vol. 4102, pp. 368–377. Springer, Vienna (2006)
224. Müller, D., Reichert, M., Herbst, J.: Flexibility of data-driven process structures. In: BPM'06 International Workshops, Workshop on Dynamic Process Management (DPM'06), Lecture Notes in Computer Science, vol. 4103, pp. 181–192. Springer, New York (2006)
225. Müller, D., Reichert, M., Herbst, J.: Data-driven modeling and coordination of large process structures. In: OTM Conferences (1). Lecture Notes in Computer Science, vol. 4803, pp. 131–149. Springer, Berlin (2007)
226. Müller, D., Reichert, M., Herbst, J.: A new paradigm for the enactment and dynamic adaptation of data-driven process structures. In: CAiSE'08. Lecture Notes in Computer Science, vol. 5074, pp. 48–63. Springer, Berlin (2008)
227. Müller, D., Reichert, M., Herbst, J., Köntges, D., Neubert, A.: COREPRO-Sim: A tool for modeling, simulating and adapting data-driven process structures. In: 6th International Conference on Business Process Management (BPM'08 Demonstrations). Lecture Notes in Computer Science, vol. 5240, pp. 394–397. Springer, Berlin (2008)
228. Müller, D., Reichert, M., Herbst, J., Poppa, F.: Data-driven design of engineering processes with COREPRO-modeler. In: 16th IEEE International Workshops on Enabling Technologies: Infrastructure for Collaborative Enterprises (WETICE 2007), pp. 376–378. IEEE Computer Society, New York (2007)
229. Müller, R.: Event-oriented dynamic adaptation of workflows. Ph.D. thesis, University of Leipzig, Germany (2002)
230. Müller, R., Greiner, U., Rahm, E.: AgentWork: A workflow system supporting rule–based workflow adaptation. Data Knowl. Eng. **51**(2), 223–256 (2004)
231. Müller, R., Rahm, E.: Dealing with logical failures for collaborating workflows. In: Proceedings of the International Conference in Cooperative Information Systems (CoopIS'00), Eilat, pp. 210–223 (2000)
232. Mutschler, B., Reichert, M., Bumiller, J.: Unleashing the effectiveness of process-oriented information systems: Problem analysis, critical success factors and implications. IEEE Trans. Syst. Man Cybern. **38**(3), 280–291 (2008)
233. Mutschler, B., Weber, B., Reichert, M.: Workflow management versus case handling - results from a controlled software experiment. In: Proceedings of the SAC'08, pp. 82–89. ACM Press (2008)
234. Nagl, C., Rosenberg, F., Dustdar, S.: Vidre – a distributed service-oriented business rule engine based on ruleml. In: Proceedings of the 10th IEEE International Enterprise Distributed Object Computing Conference (EDOC 2006), pp. 35–44. IEEE Computer Society, New York (2006)
235. Namiri, K., Stojanovic, N.: Pattern-based design and validation of business process compliance. In: Proceedings of the 15th International Conference on Cooperative Information Systems (CoopIS'07), pp. 59–76. Springer, Berlin (2007)
236. OASIS: Web Services Business Process Execution Language Version 2.0 (2007)
237. Oberleitner, J., Rosenberg, F., Dustdar, S.: A lightweight model-driven orchestration engine for e-services. In: TES. Lecture Notes in Computer Science, vol. 3811, pp. 48–57. Springer, New York (2005)
238. Ohno, T.: Toyota Production System. Productivity Press, Cambridge (1988)
239. Opdyke, W.F.: Refactoring: A program restrucuring aid in designing object-oriented application frameworks. Ph.D. thesis, University of Illinois (1992)

240. Ouyang, C., Dumas, M., van der Aalst, W.M.P., ter Hofstede, A.H.M., Mendling, J.: From business process models to process-oriented software systems. ACM Trans. Software Eng. Methodol. **19**(1), 1–37 (2009)
241. Pande, P., Neuman, R., Cavanagh, R.: The Six Sigma Way: How GE, Motorola, and Other Top Companies Are Honing Their Performance. Mc-Graw Hill, New York (2000)
242. Peleg, M., Somekh, J., Dori, D.: A methodology for eliciting and modeling exceptions. J. Biomed. Informat. **42**, 736–747 (2009)
243. Pesic, M.: Constraint-based workflow management systems: Shifting control to users. Ph.D. thesis, Eindhoven University of Technology (2008)
244. Pesic, M., Schonenberg, M.H., Sidorova, N., van der Aalst, W.M.P.: Constraint-based workflow models: Change made easy. In: Proceedings of the CoopIS'07. Lecture Notes in Computer Science, vol. 4803, pp. 77–94. Springer, New York (2007)
245. Pichler, P., Weber, B., Zugal, S., Pinggera, J., Mendling, J., Reijers, H.A.: Imperative versus declarative process modeling languages: An empirical investigation. In: Proceedings of the ER-BPM '11. Business Process Management Workshops (1). Lecture Notes in Business Information Processing, vol. 99, pp. 383–394. Springer, New York (2012)
246. Polyvyanyy, A., García-Bañuelos, L., Dumas, M.: Structuring acyclic process models. In: Proceedings of the 8th International Conference on Business Process Management (BPM'10), Hoboken, NJ, USA. . Lecture Notes in Computer Science, vol. 6336, pp. 276–293. Springer, New York (2010)
247. Poppendieck, M., Poppendieck, T.: Implementing Lean Software Development: From Concept to Cash. Addison-Wesley, Boston (2006)
248. Pryss, R., Tiedeken, J., Kreher, U., Reichert, M.: Towards flexible process support on mobile devices. In: CAiSE Forum. Lecture Notes in Business Information Processing, vol. 72, pp. 150–165. Springer, Berlin (2010)
249. Puhlmann, F.: Soundness verification of business processes specified in the pi-calculus. In: OTM Conferences (1). Lecture Notes in Computer Science, vol. 4803, pp. 6–23. Springer, New York (2007)
250. van Dongen, B.F., Dijkman, R.M., Mendling, J.: Measuring similarity between business process models. In: Proceedings of the CAISE'08 conference. Lecture Notes in Computer Science, vol. 5074, pp. 450–464. Springer, New York (2008)
251. Rao, J., Su, X.: A survey of automated web service composition methods. In: SWSWPC. Lecture Notes in Computer Science, vol. 3387, pp. 43–54. Springer, New York (2004)
252. Redding, G.M., Dumas, M., ter Hofstede, A.H.M., Iordachescu, A.: A flexible, object-centric approach for business process modelling. Service Oriented Comput. Appl. **4**(3), 191–201 (2009)
253. Redding, G.M., Dumas, M., ter Hofstede, A.H.M., Iordachescu, A.: Transforming object-oriented models to process-oriented models. In: Proceedings of the BPM'07 Workshops. Lecture Notes in Computer Science, vol. 4928, pp. 132–143. Springer, New York (2007)
254. Regev, G., Soffer, P., Schmidt, R.: Taxonomy of flexibility in business processes. In: BPMDS. CEUR Workshop Proceedings, vol. 236. CEUR-WS.org (2006)
255. Reichert, M.: Dynamische Ablaufänderungen in Workflow-Management-Systemen. Ph.D. thesis, University of Ulm (2000) (in German)
256. Reichert, M.: What BPM technology can do for healthcare process support. In: 13th Conference on Artificial Intelligence in Medicine (AIME'11). Lecture Notes in Artificial Intelligence, vol. 6747, pp. 2–13. Springer, Belin (2011)
257. Reichert, M., Bassil, S., Bobrik, R., Bauer, T.: The Proviado access control model for business process monitoring components. Enterprise Model. Inform. Syst. Architect. **5**(3), 64–88 (2010)
258. Reichert, M., Bauer, T., Dadam, P.: Enterprise-wide and cross-enterprise workflow-management: Challenges and research issues for adaptive workflows. In: Enterprise-wide and Cross-enterprise Workflow Management. CEUR Workshop Proceedings, vol. 24, pp. 56–64. CEUR-WS.org (1999)

259. Reichert, M., Dadam, P.: A framework for dynamic changes in workflow management systems. In: Proceedings of the 8th International Workshop on Database and Expert Systems Applications, pp. 42–48. IEEE Computer Society Press (1997)

260. Reichert, M., Dadam, P.: ADEPT$_{flex}$ – supporting dynamic changes of workflows without losing control. J. Intell. Inform. Syst. **10**(2), 93–129 (1998)

261. Reichert, M., Dadam, P.: Enabling adaptive process-aware information systems with ADEPT2. In: Cardoso, J., van der Aalst, W.M.P. (eds.) Handbook of Research on Business Process Modeling, pp. 173–203. Information Science Reference, Hershey (2009)

262. Reichert, M., Dadam, P., Bauer, T.: Dealing with forward and backward jumps in workflow management systems. Software Syst. Model. **1**(2), 37–58 (2003)

263. Reichert, M., Dadam, P., Rinderle-Ma, S., Jurisch, M., Kreher, U., Goeser, K.: Architectural principles and components of adaptive process management technology. In: Process Innovation for Enterprise Software. LNI, vol. 151, pp. 81–97. GI, Koellen-Verlag. IEEE Computer Society Press (2009)

264. Reichert, M., Dadam, P., Rinderle-Ma, S., Lanz, A., Pryss, R., Predeschly, M., Kolb, J., Ly, L.T., Jurisch, M., Kreher, U., Göser, K.: Enabling Poka-Yoke workflows with the AristaFlow BPM Suite. In: CEUR Proceedings of the BPM'09 Demonstration Track, Business Process Management Conference 2009 (BPM'09). CEUR Workshop Proceedings, vol. 489. CEUR-WS.org (2009)

265. Reichert, M., Hensinger, C., Dadam, P.: Supporting adaptive workflows in advanced application environments. In: Proceedings of the Workshop on Workflow Management Systems (EDBT'98), Valencia, Spain, pp. 100–109 (1998)

266. Reichert, M., Kolb, J., Bobrik, R., Bauer, T.: Enabling personalized visualization of large business processes through parameterizable views. In: 9th Enterprise Engineering Track at 27th ACM Symposium On Applied Computing (SAC'12), pp. 1653–1660. ACM, New York (2012)

267. Reichert, M., Kuhn, K., Dadam, P.: Prozessreengineering und -automatisierung in klinischen Anwendungsumgebungen. In: Proc. 41. Jahrestagung (GMDS '96), Bonn, pp. 219–223 (1996)

268. Reichert, M., Rechtenbach, S., Hallerbach, A., Bauer, T.: Extending a business process modeling tool with process configuration facilities: The Provop demonstrator. In: BPM Demos. CEUR Workshop Proceedings, vol. 489. CEUR-WS.org (2009)

269. Reichert, M., Rinderle, S., Dadam, P.: ADEPT workflow management system: Flexible support for enterprise-wide business processes. In: Proceedings of the International Conference on Business Process Management (BPM'03). Lecture Notes in Computer Science, vol. 2678, pp. 370–379. Springer, Berlin (2003)

270. Reichert, M., Rinderle, S., Dadam, P.: On the common support of workflow type and instance changes under correctness constraints. In: Proceedings of the International Conference on Cooperative Information Systems (CoopIS'03). Lecture Notes in Computer Science, Catania, Italy, vol. 2888, pp. 407–425 (2003)

271. Reichert, M., Rinderle, S., Kreher, U., Dadam, P.: Adaptive process management with ADEPT2. In: Proceedings of the ICDE'05, pp. 1113–1114. IEEE Computer Society (2005)

272. Reichert, M., Rinderle-Ma, S., Dadam, P.: Flexibility in process-aware information systems. In: Jensen, K., van der Aalst, W.M.P. (eds.) Transactions on Petri Nets and Other Models of Concurrency II. Lecture Notes in Computer Science, vol. 5460, pp. 115–135. Springer, Heidelberg (2009)

273. Reijers, H.A.: Design and Control of Workflow Processes: Business Process Management for the Service Industry. Springer, Heidelberg (2003)

274. Reijers, H.A., van der Aalst, W.M.P.: The effectiveness of workflow management systems: Predictions and lessons learned. Int. J. Inform. Manag. **25**(5), 458–472 (2005)

275. Reijers., H.A., Liman, S., van der Aalst, W.M.P.: Product-based workflow design. Manag. Inform. Syst. **20**(1), 229–262 (2003)

276. Reijers, H.A., Mendling, J., Dijkman, R.M.: Human and automatic modularizations of process models to enhance their comprehension. Inform. Syst. **36**(5), 881–897 (2011)

277. Reijers, H.A., Rigter, J.H.M., van der Aalst, W.M.P.: The case handling case. Int. J. Cooper. Inform. Syst. **12**(3), 365–392 (2003)

278. Reinhartz-Berger, I., Soffer, P., Sturm, A.: Organisational reference models: Supporting an adequate design of local business processes. Int. J. Bus. Process Integrat. Manag. **4**(2), 134–149 (2009)

279. Reinhartz-Berger, I., Soffer, P., Sturm, A.: Extending the adaptability of reference models. IEEE Trans. Syst. Man Cybern. A **40**(5), 1045–1056 (2010)

280. Reuter, A., Schwenkreis, F.: ConTracts – a low-level mechanism for building general-purpose workflow management-systems. IEEE Data Eng. Bull. **18**(1), 4–10 (1995)

281. Reuter, C., Dadam, P., Rudolph, S., Deiters, W., Trillsch, S.: Guarded process spaces (GPS): A navigation system towards creation and dynamic change of healthcare processes from the end-user's perspective. In: Proceedings of the BPM'11 Workshops, 4th International Workshop on Process-oriented Information Systems in Healthcare (ProHealth'11). Lecture Notes in Business Information Processing. Springer, Heidelberg (2011)

282. Rinderle, S.: Schema evolution in process management systems. Ph.D. thesis, University of Ulm (2004)

283. Rinderle, S., Jurisch, M., Reichert, M.: On deriving net change information from change logs – the deltalayer-algorithm. In: Proceedings of the 12th Conference Datenbanksysteme in Business, Technologie und Web (BTW'07). Lecture Notes in Informatics (LNI), vol. P-103, pp. 364–381. GI, Bonn (2007)

284. Rinderle, S., Kreher, U., Lauer, M., Dadam, P., Reichert, M.: On representing instance changes in adaptive process management systems. In: Proceedings of the WETICE'06 Workshops, pp. 297–304. IEEE Computer Society (2006)

285. Rinderle, S., Reichert, M.: On the controlled evolution of access rules in cooperative information systems. In: Proceedings of the 13th International Conference on Cooperative Information Systems (CoopIS'05). Lecture Notes in Computer Science, vol. 3760, pp. 238–255. Springer, Heidelberg (2005)

286. Rinderle, S., Reichert, M.: Data-driven process control and exception handling in process management systems. In: Proceedings of the 18th International Conference on Advanced Information Systems Engineering (CAiSE'06). Lecture Notes in Computer Science, vol. 4001, pp. 273–287. Springer, Heidelberg (2006)

287. Rinderle, S., Reichert, M., Dadam, P.: Evaluation of correctness criteria for dynamic workflow changes. In: Proceedings of the International Conference on Business Process Management (BPM'03). Lecture Notes in Computer Science, vol. 2678, pp. 41–57. Springer, Heidelberg (2003)

288. Rinderle, S., Reichert, M., Dadam, P.: Correctness criteria for dynamic changes in workflow systems – a survey. Data Knowl. Eng. **50**(1), 9–34 (2004)

289. Rinderle, S., Reichert, M., Dadam, P.: Disjoint and overlapping process changes: Challenges, solutions, applications. In: Proceedings of the International Conference on Cooperative Information Systems (CoopIS'04). Lecture Notes in Computer Science, Agia Napa, vol. 3290, pp. 101–120 (2004)

290. Rinderle, S., Reichert, M., Dadam, P.: Flexible support of team processes by adaptive workflow systems. Distr. Parallel Databases **16**(1), 91–116 (2004)

291. Rinderle, S., Reichert, M., Dadam, P.: On dealing with structural conflicts between process type and instance changes. In: Proceedings of the BPM'04. Lecture Notes in Computer Science, vol. 3080, pp. 274–289. Springer, Potsdam (2004)

292. Rinderle, S., Reichert, M., Jurisch, M., Kreher, U.: On representing, purging, and utilizing change logs in process management systems. In: Proceedings of the BPM'06. Lecture Notes in Computer Science, vol. 4102, pp. 241–256. Springer, Heidelberg (2006)

293. Rinderle, S., Weber, B., Reichert, M., Wild, W.: Integrating process learning and process evolution – a semantics based approach. In: Proceedings of the BPM'05. Lecture Notes in Computer Science, vol. 4102, pp. 252–267. Springer, Heidelberg (2005)

294. Rinderle, S., Wombacher, A., Reichert, M.: Evolution of process choreographies in dychor. In: Proceedings of the 14th International Conference on Cooperative Information Systems (CoopIS'06). Lecture Notes in Computer Science, vol. 4275, pp. 273–290. Springer, Heidelberg (2006)

295. Rinderle, S., Wombacher, A., Reichert, M.: On the controlled evolution of process choreographies. In: Proceedings of the 22nd International Conference on Data Engineering (ICDE'06), p. #124. IEEE Computer Society, New York (2006)

296. Rinderle-Ma, S.: Data flow correctness in adaptive workflow systems. EMISA Forum **29**(2), 25–35 (2009)

297. Rinderle-Ma, S., Reichert, M.: A formal framework for adaptive access control models. J. Data Semant. IX. **4601**, 82–112 (2007)

298. Rinderle-Ma, S., Reichert, M.: Comprehensive life cycle support for access rules in information systems: The CEOSIS project. Enterprise Inform. Syst. **3**(3), 219–251 (2009)

299. Rinderle-Ma, S., Reichert, M.: Advanced migration strategies for adaptive process management systems. In: Proceedings of the 12th IEEE Conference on Commerce and Enterprise Computing (CEC' 10), pp. 56–63. IEEE, New York (2010)

300. Rinderle-Ma, S., Reichert, M., Weber, B.: On the formal semantics of change patterns in process-aware information systems. In: Proceedings of the ER'08. Lecture Notes in Computer Science, vol. 5231, pp. 279–293. Springer, Heidelberg (2008)

301. Rinderle-Ma, S., Reichert, M., Weber, B.: Relaxed compliance notions in adaptive process management systems. In: Proceedings of the ER'08. Lecture Notes in Computer Science, vol. 5231, pp. 232–247. Springer, Berlin (2008)

302. Rolland, C.: A comprehensive view of process engineering. In: Proceedings of the CAiSE'98. Lecture Notes in Computer Science, vol. 1413, pp. 1–24. Springer, New York (1998)

303. Rosemann, M., van der Aalst, W.M.P.: A configurable reference modelling language. Inform. Syst. **32**(1), 1–23 (2005)

304. Rozinat, A., van der Aalst, W.M.P.: Decision mining in ProM. In: Business Process Management. Lecture Notes in Computer Science, vol. 4102, pp. 420–425. Springer, New York (2006)

305. Rozinat, A., van der Aalst, W.M.P.: Conformance checking of processes based on monitoring real behavior. Inform. Syst. **33**(1), 64–95 (2008)

306. Rupietta, W.: Workparty – business processes and workflow management. In: Bernus, P., Mertins, K., Schmidt, G. (eds.) Handbook on Architectures of Information Systems, Int'l Handbooks Information System, pp. 569–589. Springer, Heidelberg (2006)

307. Russell, N., van der Aalst, W.M.P., ter Hofstede, A.H.M.: Workflow exception patterns. In: Proceedings of the CAiSE'06. Lecture Notes in Computer Science, vol. 4001, pp. 288–302. Springer, New York (2006)

308. Russell, N., van der Aalst, W.M.P., ter Hofstede, A.H.M.: Exception handling patterns in process-aware information systems. Technical Report BPM Center Report BPM-06-04, BPMcenter.org (2006)

309. Russell, N., ter Hofstede, A.H.M., van der Aalst, W.M.P., Mulyar, N.: Workflow control-flow patterns: A revised view. Technical Report BPM-06-22, BPMcenter.org (2006)

310. Russell, N., ter Hofstede, A.H.M., Edmond, D., van der Aalst, W.M.P.: Workflow data patterns. Technical Report FIT-TR-2004-01, Queensland University of Technology (2004)

311. Russell, N., ter Hofstede, A.H.M., Edmond, D., van der Aalst, W.M.P.: Workflow resource patterns. Technical Report WP 127, Eindhoven University of Technology (2004)

312. Sadiq, S., Governatori, G., Naimiri, K.: Modeling control objectives for business process compliance. In: Proceedings of the 5th International Conference on Business Process Management. Lecture Notes in Computer Science, vol. 4714, pp. 149–164. Springer, Heidelberg (2007)

313. Sadiq, S., Marjanovic, O., Orlowska, M.: Managing change and time in dynamic workflow processes. Int. J Cooper. Inform. Syst. **9**(1–2), 93–116 (2000)

314. Sadiq, S., Orlowska, M.: On capturing exceptions on workflow process models. In: Proceedings of the BIS'2000, pp. 3–19. Springer, New York (2000)

315. Sadiq, S., Orlowska, M., Sadiq, W., Schulz, K.: When workflows will not deliver: The case of contradicting work practice. In: BIS (2005)
316. Sadiq, S., Sadiq, W., Orlowska, M.: Pockets of flexibility in workflow specifications. In: Proceedings of the ER'01. Lecture Notes in Computer Science, vol. 2224, pp. 513–526. Springer, New York (2001)
317. Sadiq, S., Sadiq, W., Orlowska, M.: A framework for constraint specification and validation in flexible workflows. Inform. Syst. **30**(5), 349–378 (2005)
318. Sadiq, S.W., Orlowska, M.E., Sadiq, W., Foulger, C.: Data flow and validation in workflow modelling. In: Proceedings of the ADC'04. CRPIT, vol. 27, pp. 207–214. Australian Computer Society (2004)
319. Scheer, A.W.: ARIS. Vom Geschftsprozess zum Anwendungssystem. Springer, Heidelberg (2002)
320. Schobbens, P.Y., Heymans, P., Trigaux, J.C.: Feature diagrams: A survey and a formal semantics. In: Requirements Engineering, pp. 136–145. IEEE Computer Society (2006)
321. Schonenberg, H., Mans, R., Russell, N., Mulyar, N., van der Aalst, W.M.P.: Process flexibility: A survey of contemporary approaches. In: CIAO!/EOMAS, Lecture Notes in Business Information Processing, vol. 10, pp. 16–30. Springer, New York (2008)
322. Schonenberg, H., Weber, B., van Dongen, B.F., van der Aalst, W.M.P.: Supporting flexible processes through recommendations based on history. In: Proceedings of the BPM'08. Lecture Notes in Computer Science, vol. 5240, pp. 51–66. Springer, New York (2008)
323. Schultheiss, B., Meyer, J., Mangold, R., Zemmler, T., Reichert, M.: Designing the processes for chemotherapy treatment in a women's hospital (in german). Technical report, University of Ulm (1996)
324. Schuschel, H., Weske, M.: Integrated workflow planning and coordination. In: Database and Expert Systems Applications. Lecture Notes in Computer Science, vol. 2736, pp. 771–781. Springer, Berlin (2003)
325. Schuschel, H., Weske, M.: Triggering replanning in an integrated workflow planning and enactment system. In: ADBIS. Lecture Notes in Computer Science, vol. 3255, pp. 322–335. Springer, New York (2004)
326. Sharp, A., McDermott, P.: Workflow modeling: tools for process improvement and application development. Artech House, Norwood (2001)
327. Sidorova, N., Stahl, C., Trcka, N.: Workflow soundness revisited: Checking correctness in the presence of data while staying conceptual. In: Proceedings of the CAiSE'10. Lecture Notes in Computer Science, vol. 6051, pp. 530–544. Springer, New York (2010)
328. Silver, B.: BPMS watch: Ten tips for effective process modeling. Http://www.bpminstitute.org/articles/article/article/bpms-watch-ten-tips-for-effective-process-modeling.html (2009). Accessed 23 July 2012
329. Silver, B.: Case management: Addressing unique BPM requirements. In: Fischer, L. (ed.) Taming the Unpredictable: Real-World Adaptive Case Management, pp. 1–12. Future Strategies, Inc., Lighthouse Point (2011)
330. Sirin, E., Parsia, B., Wu, D., Hendler, J., Nau, D.: Htn planning for web service composition using shop2. Web Semantics: Science, Services and Agents on the World Wide Web **1**(4), 377–396 (2004) (Int'l Semantic Web Conf 2003)
331. Smirnov, S., Reijers, H.A., Weske, M., Nugteren, T.: Business process model abstraction: A definition, catalog, and survey. Distr. Parallel Databases **30**(1), 63–99 (2012)
332. Soffer, P.: Mirror, mirror on the wall, can i count on you at all? Exploring data inaccuracy in business processes. In: BMMDS/EMMSAD, Lecture Notes in Business Information Processing, vol. 50, pp. 14–25. Springer, New York (2010)
333. Song, M., van der Aalst, W.M.P.: Towards comprehensive support for organizational mining. Decis. Support Syst. **46**(1), 300–317 (2008)
334. Strong, D.M., Miller, S.M.: Exceptions and exception handling in computerized information processes. ACM–TOIS **13**(2), 206–233 (1995)
335. Sun, S.X., Zhao, J.L., Nunamaker, J.F., Sheng, O.R.L.: Formulating the data-flow perspective for business process management. Inform. Syst. Res. **17**(4), 374–391 (2006)

336. Swenson, K.D.: Mastering the Unpredictable: How Adaptive Case Management Will Revolutionize the Way That Knowledge Workers Get Things Done. Meghan-Kiffer Press, Tampa, FL (2010)

337. Trcka, N., van der Aalst, W.M.P., Sidorova, N.: Data-flow anti-patterns: Discovering data-flow errors in workflows. In: CAiSE. Lecture Notes in Computer Science, vol. 5565, pp. 425–439. Springer, New York (2009)

338. United States Code: Sarbanes-oxley act of 2002, pl 107–204, 116 stat 745. Codified in Sections 11, 15, 18, 28, and 29 USC (2002)

339. V. Glabbeek, R., Goltz, U.: Refinement of actions and equivalence notions for concurrent systems. Acta Inform **37**(4–5), 229–327 (2001)

340. Vanderfeesten, I.: Product-based design and support of workflow processes. Ph.D. thesis, Eindhoven University of Technology (2009)

341. Vanderfeesten, I., Reijers, H.A., van der Aalst, W.M.P.: Product-based workflow support. Inform. Syst. **36**(2), 517–535 (2011)

342. Vanhatalo, J., Voelzer, H., Koehler, J.: The refined process structure tree. Data Knowl. Eng. **69**(8), 793–818 (2009)

343. Verbeek, E.: Verification of WF–Nets. Ph.D. thesis, Technical University of Eindhoven (2004)

344. Verbeek, H.M.W., Basten, T., van der Aalst, W.M.P.: Diagnosing workflow processes using Woflan. Comput. J. **44**(4), 246–279 (2001)

345. Wagenknecht, A., Rüppel, U.: Improving resource management in flood response with process models and web GIS. In: 16th TIEMS 2009, pp. 141–151 (2009). ISBN 987-7-302-18670-0

346. Waimer, M.: Integration of adaptive process management technology and process mining (in german). Ph.D. thesis, Diploma Thesis, University of Ulm (2006)

347. Wainer, J., Bezerra, F., Barthelmess, P.: Tucupi: A flexible workflow system based on overridable constraints. In: Proceedings of the SAC '04, pp. 498–502. ACM, New York (2004)

348. Wainer, J., de Lima Bezerra, F.: Constraint-based flexible workflows. In: CRIWG. Lecture Notes in Computer Science, vol. 2806, pp. 151–158. Springer, New York (2003)

349. Weber, B., Mutschler, B., Reichert, M.: Investigating the effort of using business process management technology: Results from a controlled experiment. Sci. Comput. Program. **75**(5), 292–310 (2010)

350. Weber, B., Pinggera, J., Zugal, S., Wild, W.: Alaska simulator toolset for conducting controlled experiments on process flexibility. In: Information Systems Evolution. Lecture Notes in Business Information Processing, vol. 72, pp. 205–221. Springer, Heidelberg (2011)

351. Weber, B., Reichert, M., Reijers, H.A., Mendling, J.: Refactoring large process model repositories computers and industry. Comput. Ind. **62**, 467–486 (2011)

352. Weber, B., Reichert, M., Rinderle-Ma, S.: Change patterns and change support features - enhancing flexibility in process-aware information systems. Data Know. Eng. **66**(3), 438–466 (2008)

353. Weber, B., Reichert, M., Wild, W.: Case-base maintenance for CCBR-based process evolution. In: Proceedings of the ECCBR'06. Lecture Notes in Computer Science, vol. 4106, pp. 106–120. Springer, Heidelberg (2006)

354. Weber, B., Reichert, M., Wild, W., Rinderle, S.: Balancing flexibility and security in adaptive process management systems. In: Proceedings of the CoopIS'05. Lecture Notes in Computer Science, vol. 3760, pp. 59–76. Springer, Heidelberg (2005)

355. Weber, B., Reichert, M., Wild, W., Rinderle-Ma, S.: Providing integrated life cycle support in process-aware information systems. Int. J. Cooper. Inform. Syst. **18**(1), 115–165 (2009)

356. Weber, B., Reijers, H.A., Zugal, S., Wild, W.: The declarative approach to business process execution: An empirical test. In: Proceedings of the CAiSE'09. Lecture Notes in Computer Science, vol. 5565, pp. 470–485. Springer, New York (2009)

357. Weber, B., Rinderle, S., Reichert, M.: Change patterns and change support features in process-aware information systems. In: Proceedings of the CAiSE'07. Lecture Notes in Computer Science, vol. 4495, pp. 574–588. Springer, Berlin (2007)

358. Weber, B., Rinderle, S., Wild, W., Reichert, M.: CCBR–driven business process evolution. In: Proceedings of the ICCBR'05. Lecture Notes in Computer Science, vol. 3620, pp. 610–624. Springer, Heidelberg (2005)

359. Weber, B., Wild, W., Breu, R.: CBRFlow: Enabling adaptive workflow management through conversational cbr. In: Proceedings of the ECCBR'04. Lecture Notes in Computer Science, vol. 3155, pp. 434–448. Springer, New York (2004)

360. Weber, I., Hoffmann, J., Mendling, J.: Semantic business process validation. In: Proceedings of the 3rd International Workshop on Semantic Business Process Management (SBPM'08), CEUR-WS Proceedings, vol. 472, RWTH, Aachen, Germany (2008)

361. Weijters, A.J.M.M., van der Aalst, W.M.P.: Rediscovering workflow models from event-based data using little thumb. Integr. Comput. Aided Eng. **10**, 151–162 (2003)

362. Weikum, G., Schek, H.J.: Concepts and applications of multilevel transactions and open nested transactions. In: Database Transaction Models for Advanced Applications. Morgan Kaufmann, San Mateo (1992)

363. Weske, M.: Flexible modeling and execution of workflow activities. In: Proceedings of the 31st Hawaii International Conference on System Sciences (HICSS '98), Hawaii, pp. 713–722. IEEE Computer Society Press, Los Alamitos (1998)

364. Weske, M.: Workflow management systems: Formal foundation, conceptual design, implementation aspects. University of Münster, Germany (2000). Habil Thesis

365. Weske, M.: Formal foundation and conceptual design of dynamic adaptations in a workflow management system. In: Proceedings of the Hawaii International Conference on System Sciences (HICSS-34). IEEE Computer Society Press, Los Alamitos (2001)

366. Weske, M.: Business Process Management: Concepts, Methods, Technology. Springer, Berlin (2007)

367. Workflow Management Coalition: Terminology & glossary. Technical Report WFMC-TC-1011, WfMC (1999)

368. Wynn, M.T., Verbeek, H.M.W., van der Aalst, W.M.P., ter Hofstede, A.H.M., Edmond, D.: Business process verification finally a reality. Bus. Process Manag. J. **15**(1), 74–92 (2009)

369. Zeng, L., Ngu, A., Benatallah, B., Podorozhny, R., Lei, H.: Dynamic composition and optimization of web services. Distr. Parallel Databases **24**, 45–72 (2008)

370. Zhao, W., Hauser, R., Bhattacharya, K., Bryant, B.R., Cao, F.: Compiling business processes: untangling unstructured loops in irreducible flow graphs. Int. J. Web Grid Serv. **2**, 68–91 (2006)

371. Zugal, S., Pinggera, J., Weber, B.: Creating declarative process models using test driven modeling suite. In: CAiSE Forum. Lecture Notes in Business Information Processing, vol. 107, pp. 16–32, pp. 1–8. Springer, Berlin (2011)

372. Zugal, S., Pinggera, J., Weber, B.: The impact of testcases on the maintainability of declarative process models. In: Proceedings of the BPMDS/EMMSAD '11. Lecture Notes in Business Information Processing, vol. 81, pp. 163–177. Springer, Berlin (2011)

373. Zugal, S., Pinggera, J., Weber, B.: Toward enhanced life-cycle support for declarative processes. J. Software Evol. Process **24**(3), 285–302 (2012)

374. zur Muehlen, M., Recker, J.: How much language is enough? Theoretical and practical use of the business process modeling notation. In: CAiSE. Lecture Notes in Computer Science, vol. 5074, pp. 465–479. Springer, Berlin (2008)

Index

M. Reichert and B. Weber, *Enabling Flexibility in Process-Aware Information Systems*,
DOI 10.1007/978-3-642-30409-5, © Springer-Verlag Berlin Heidelberg 2012